AQA AS | A-Level Year 1

Economics

Malcolm Surridge & John Wolinski

We dedicate this book to our grandchildren, who represent the future generation of economists.

To Poppy, Imogen, Archie and Alastair, from Malcolm

To Saskia and Rupert, from John

Published by **Cross Academe Limited**, St John's House, 5 South Parade, Oxford OX2 7JL

Orders
Cross Academe Limited, PO Box 105, Rochester, Kent ME2 4BE
Tel: 01634 729825
Fax: 01634 290175

You can also order through the Cross Academe website: www.crossacademe.co.uk

ISBN 978-1-909592-45-2

Photograph acknowledgements
The cover photograph shows a pair of doors at the Bank of England and is reproduced by permission of Johnny Grieg/Alamy.

Other photographs have been reproduced by permission of david pearson/Alamy (p. 9), DBURKE/Alamy (p. 12), Chris Gomersall/Alamy (p. 22), Mar Photographics/Alamy (p. 28), Foodstock/Alamy (p. 34), Gavin Hellier/Alamy (p. 54), Chris Batson/Alamy (p. 66), David Wootton/Alamy (p. 88), Eye Ubiquitous/Alamy (p. 98), Matthew Chattle/Alamy (p. 112), Mark Boulton/Alamy (p. 113), Action Plus Sports Images/Alamy (p. 125), David Levenson/Alamy (p. 135), Lebrecht Music and Arts Photo Library/Alamy (p. 138), Jeff Gilbert/Alamy (p. 147), Stefan Hofecker/Alamy (p. 158), Alex Segre/Alamy (p. 166), keith morris/Alamy (p. 175), Allan Bell/Alamy (p. 181), UK Stock Images Ltd/Alamy (p. 188), CTK/Alamy (p. 199), Mark Waugh/Alamy (p. 204), Jeff Morgan 15/Alamy (p. 213), Chris Howes/Wild Places Photography/Alamy (p. 216), David J. Green – Lifestyle/Alamy (p. 217), Homer W Sykes/Alamy (p. 220), ian woolcock/Alamy (p. 223), Rosemary Roberts/Alamy (p. 224), Finnbarr Webster/Alamy (p. 225), Rosemary Roberts/Alamy (p. 232), incamerastock/Alamy (p. 238), Roger Bamber/Alamy (p. 244), Network Photographer/Alamy (p. 247), james williamson/Alamy (p. 264), Nigel Roberson/Alamy (top, p. 331), tony french/Alamy (bottom, p. 331), Tommy Trenchard/Alamy (p. 361), Allstar Picture Library/Alamy (p. 363), dpa picture alliance/Alamy (p. 378), Julian Worker/Alamy (p. 385), INTERFOTO/Alamy (p. 403), John Keates/Alamy (p. 421) and Kensplace/Alamy (p. 453).

Design by Ralph Hall

Artwork by Juha Sorsa

Printed by Bell & Bain Limited, Glasgow

The paper on which this title is printed is sourced from managed, sustainable forests.

Contents

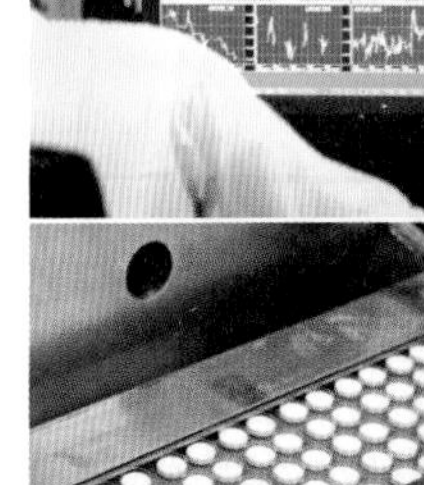

Topic 5 The market mechanism, market failure & government intervention in markets

Section 2 The national economy in a global context

Topic 6 The measure of macroeconomic performance

Topic 7 How the macroeconomy works

Topic 8 Economic performance

Topic 9 Macroeconomic policy

Preface

This textbook has been written to meet the needs of students studying AQA A-level economics during their first year, and provides the content and guidance required for students to sit the AQA AS economics qualification. It offers full coverage of the subject content of the AQA AS specification, topic by topic and chapter by chapter, so that students can be sure that all of the material is relevant to their AS qualification. We have used current examples, the latest data and topical illustrations in order to help you relate your theoretical understanding of economics to the real world and to enable you to appreciate the dynamic and changing nature of economics and its relevance to society.

Special features

AQA AS/A-Level Year 1 Economics includes a number of special features that are incorporated to extend your understanding of the requirements of the AQA AS economics course.

Overviews

Each of the 45 chapters commences with an introduction that describes the content coverage of that chapter. The topics of the book are divided in exact accordance with the topics outlined in the AQA AS economics specification, and the chapters are presented in logical order.

Real World Economics

Each chapter contains one or more Real World Economics feature, relating the theory covered in the chapter to relevant events and examples from the UK and other economies. The feature generally has a number of questions attached to it with mark allocations. Tackling these questions will help you to strengthen your understanding of the relevant economic theory and to develop the skill of applying theories to different situations.

Key terms

Economics has its own vocabulary and it is important for you to understand the key terms to enable you to respond effectively to examination questions and to express your ideas succinctly and accurately. We have defined and highlighted key terms throughout the book, focusing on those that are set out in the AQA specification plus others we think are important.

Number crunching

Handling and interpreting numbers effectively is an important part of studying economics. We have included regular activities to help you to develop relevant skills and understanding. The nature of the subject means that these are much more common in the macroeconomics chapters, which make greater use of numerical data.

Review questions

Each chapter concludes with a set of review questions. These review questions are provided primarily to help you check your understanding of the content of a chapter. The questions are also focused on assisting your revision at the end of the year. Consequently, the marks for some review questions may not be an exact reflection of the exam questions, because the emphasis of the question may be on your knowledge rather than other, exam-focused skills. However, many of these questions do use the exact format of the questions in your AS or A-level papers and so they also offer excellent practice for your examinations. They incorporate each of the style of questions you will face in the AS papers: multiple choice, definitions, data interpretation tasks, calculation questions, the drawing of suitable diagrams, questions requiring application and analysis, and evaluation questions.

Exam-style questions

The AS level is divided into nine topics, five of which cover microeconomics (Section 1) and four of which cover macroeconomics (Section 2). At the end of each topic there is a question paper that is based on the style of the AQA examinations. You are advised to use these questions to check how well you have understood the materials covered in each particular topic. In particular, these exam-style questions will allow you to develop your examination technique. Eight of these nine exam-style end-of-topic question sets are based on AS Paper 1 (microeconomics) and AS Paper 2 (macroeconomics). You should allow 90 minutes to complete each of these papers. For Topic 2 of microeconomics, the exam-style question paper is designed to offer early practice of the A-level examinations that you will sit after two years. You should allow 2 hours for this exam-style question set.

Author tips

We have over 30 years' experience of teaching and have used this to provide advice. This advice will assist you in developing a good understanding of the subject and in preparing for the examinations.

Key notes

There are occassions in the text where we feel a particular point requires emphasis and amplification. The term 'Key note' is used to highlight these instances.

Discussion points

It is important sometimes to reflect on, or talk to fellow students about, aspects or issues arising from the material that comprises AQA AS and A-level (Year 1) economics. In order to help you to do this, we have included discussion points intended to make you think more broadly about the subject.

Malcolm Surridge & John Wolinski

Section 1

Individuals, firms, markets & market failure

Topic 1

Economic methodology & the economic problem

Economic methodology

This chapter seeks to answer the question 'What is economics?' and shows why it is classified as a social science. The methodology of economists is compared to that used by natural and other scientists. The difference between positive and normative statements is outlined and their significance explained, particularly in terms of how value judgements influence economic decision making and policy. The chapter concludes by explaining how people's views relating to choosing between options are influenced by positive factors, and also by moral and political judgements.

What is economics?

A broad definition of economics is based on one provided by the economist, Lionel Robbins: 'Economics is the science which studies human behaviour as a relationship between ends (unlimited wants) and scarce means (resources) which have alternative uses'.

Key term
Economics is the study of scarcity.

This definition recognises that the basic economic problem is that people have unlimited wants, but the world possesses limited resources with which to satisfy those wants. As a consequence, individuals, organisations, countries and the world as a whole all suffer from scarcity. (Scarcity will be examined in Chapter 4.)

The definition notes that economics is a science that studies human behaviour – in other words, it is a social science.

Economics as a social science

The Oxford Dictionary defines a science as: 'The intellectual and practical activity encompassing the systematic study of the structure and behaviour of the physical and natural world through observation and experiment'.

Social scientists try to establish causal relationships between actions, behaviours and events in human existence. This should enable them to anticipate, understand and explain human activity in both the present and future. Examples of social sciences include anthropology, political science, psychology and sociology.

Key term
A **social science** is the scientific study of human society and social relationships.

In the natural world, it is possible to isolate variables so that ideas can be proven beyond doubt. For example, the laboratory chemist can create an environment in which sodium and chlorine mix, in order to prove that sodium chloride (salt) will be formed. Social scientists tend to find it more difficult to create these carefully controlled laboratory conditions, although psychologists regularly use controlled conditions for experiments.

The challenge facing social scientists is that their raw material is people. Unlike in the natural sciences, people do not always behave in the same, predictable manner. In economics, theories are based on people being rational and logical in their thinking, but these theories can be undermined by unpredictable and illogical behaviour.

Similarities to and differences in methodology from natural and other sciences

Natural sciences, such as physics, chemistry, geology and biology, deal with the physical world. With the exception of biology, the sciences study non-living subjects. Biology is classified as a life science.

In terms of methodology, natural sciences have a greater tendency to use experiments and observations. Social sciences rely more on the collection of statistical data and their analysis.

Similarities in methodology

Economics resembles the natural sciences because it uses scientific methodology, including:

- using theories and creating models in order to understand economic forces and events. These models often focus on a particular factor. For example, the theory of comparative advantage indicates that countries will benefit from trade if they specialise in providing products in which they have a relative advantage.
- utilising statistical data in order to prove hypotheses. For example, the Phillips curve uses statistical data to show the relationship between wage inflation and levels of unemployment.
- organising experiments to test theories and hypotheses, although this technique is not as well established as it is in the natural sciences.

Economic theories and models make a number of assumptions about human behaviour and then investigate the outcomes of that behaviour. For example, the law of demand assumes that consumers are rational and think logically and will therefore purchase more (or the same number of) products if the price falls. These simple models can be expanded to gain a broader understanding. For example, the law of demand can be combined with a view on how factors other than price may influence demand, from which economists can begin to understand the relative importance of a range of different factors that influence the demand for a particular product.

REALWORLD ECONOMICS 1.1

Using experiments in economics

According to the Nobel Foundation, American economist Vernon Smith was awarded the Nobel Prize in economics in 2002, 'for having established laboratory experiments as a tool in empirical economic analysis'. Smith used class-based experiments at his university to demonstrate how markets worked. Students acted as buyers and sellers in role-play exercises. The results of these role plays were an excellent match for those predicted by economic theories that had been well established but not tested empirically. Other experiments confirmed the view that paying participants according to their level of success in the marketplace led to high levels of motivation, in accord with economic theory. Smith also found that the greater the rewards, the more quickly participants adopted logical, rational behaviour.

Smith is a member of the ESA (Economic Science Association) that aims to encourage the use of observational science, using controlled experiments to learn about economic behaviour.

Differences in methodology

The methodology of an economist differs from other forms of scientific enquiry. This is because economics:

- does not tend to use experiments to confirm ideas. Natural scientists can formulate hypotheses and then carry out experiments in controlled conditions, in order to discover whether these hypotheses are correct or false. It is difficult to maintain controlled conditions when dealing with people.
- relies predominantly on observations of real-life phenomena in order to confirm hypotheses. Economists may observe results and then develop theories that provide a logical explanation of those observations, *or* may create a theory through logical reasoning and then use real-life observations to test that theory.

In terms of methodology, these factors encourage social scientists to emphasise the use of data collection to create theories, although field observations are also used. They recognise that, if circumstances differ, a similar experiment or analysis of data may lead to different results. For example, the relationship between spending and unemployment changed during the recent recession because, compared to previous recessions, UK firms were reluctant to lay off workers with skills that they would need during the economic recovery. Similarly, the impact of the recession on unemployment varied considerably between different countries.

Although the emphasis is different, it should be recognised that natural sciences and social sciences do share approaches. Natural sciences use statistical analysis, developed mainly through social sciences, to test the effectiveness and suitability of new drugs and medicines. Economists are now using experimental methods, based on natural science methodology, to create and/or verify theories.

A Nobel Prize is offered in economics (economic science) for advancement in research. No other social science is awarded its own Nobel Prize.

The difference between positive and normative statements

Key term
Positive statements can be scientifically proven.

Positive statements include words such as 'will', 'was' or 'is'. They can be proved or disproved because they are based on facts. They may be purely factual, such as the quantity of bananas consumed in the UK in a particular year, or they may describe a relationship that can be tested and thus proved to be correct (or incorrect), such as that banana consumption has increased because consumers' incomes have risen.

Caution is required when dealing with positive statements. 'The UK is the richest country in the world' is a positive statement because it can be proved or disproved. It is clearly a lie, but it is still a positive statement because it can be proved to be false. Similarly, in March 2014 the government forecast that the UK's economy would grow by 2.7%, rather than the 2.4% that had been forecast in the previous December. For 2015, the UK's growth was forecast to be 2.3%. At the end of the year in question, these statements can be proved or disproved.

Key term
Normative statements are matters of opinion and reflect value judgements.

Normative statements tend to include words such as 'should' and 'ought'. They are difficult to prove or disprove because they state an opinion rather than a fact.

Economists may deal with both positive statements and normative statements. Businesses and governments often call upon them to provide evidence to support a strategy. This evidence would be in the form of positive statements. However, others may use this information to make value judgements, such as that 'apple prices should be subsidised in order to encourage a greater consumption of apples'.

One of the aims of economics is to maximise economic welfare (people's happiness) and so economists cannot avoid being involved in value judgements, particularly when they are asked to use their expertise to offer an opinion.

The influence of value judgements

It is generally believed that economists should avoid making value judgements and instead focus on providing positive, objective statements based on economic analysis. Other people, such as business leaders and government advisers, can then use these statements to help inform decisions and policies. For example, an economist might advise a tobacco company about the impact of price changes on factors such as the quantity demanded, projected sales revenue and future profits. However, it will be the executives of the company that decide on the price to be set. Similarly, a government economist might conduct analysis that indicates the likely impact of an advertising ban or packaging redesign on sales of tobacco, but it will be a politician who decides whether to ban advertising or pass laws to enforce changes in packaging design for tobacco.

A further issue relates to the interpretation of data. If Factor A consistently increases at the same time as Factor B, an economist might conclude that the two are closely related. However, is there a causal link? For example, do changes in Factor A *cause* changes in Factor B? This requires logical thinking and may involve a value judgement. It might seem logical to deduce that a reduction in advertising has caused a fall in demand, but the reverse may be the case. A fall in demand leads to lower revenue, perhaps forcing the company to cut its advertising budget. The identification of cause and effect will often involve value judgements and these in turn will affect the final decisions made.

The influence of moral and political judgements

As indicated in the previous section, decisions are often based on value judgements rather than positive statements. In the case of smoking, positive statements from economists and other specialists can provide information to guide the decision, such as the impact of smoking on:

- the health of the smoker;
- the health of 'passive smokers', who suffer from smoke created by other individuals;
- government spending, in terms of costs to the NHS of treating tobacco-related illnesses;
- the level of taxation received, due to the high levels of taxation on tobacco.

Regardless of the evidence provided in the form of positive statements, politicians will want to please the electorate and/or wish for policy to reflect their personal, moral beliefs. Thus the final decision will also be based on:

- the views of the electorate, many of whom believe strongly in a person's right to freedom of choice to make their own decisions;
- the actions of pressure groups such as ASH (Action on Smoking and Health) – this group was established by the Royal Society of Physicians, whose members also provide positive statements relating to smoking;

> **Key terms**
>
> A **moral judgement** is based on what is deemed to be right and good.
>
> A **political judgement** is based on the need to appeal to selected groups of people.

- views of individual politicians, based on their own moral and political beliefs;
- media reports on the impact of smoking, such as comments on the effects on babies of smoking and alcohol during pregnancy;
- personal views on the relative importance of different factors. For example, is the level of taxation paid by smokers enough 'compensation' for any negative effects arising? Should society force people to lead healthier lifestyles? To what extent should individuals be protected from the actions of other people?

Invariably, these value judgements will have a major influence on decisions. However, government action to limit smoking commenced in the 1960s only because medical experts proved that smoking leads to lung cancer.

As economists gain a better understanding of economic factors, their influence will increase. Although it is claimed that 90% of the world's economists failed to predict the financial crisis of 2008, many of their forecasts have proved to be reliable and this makes it harder for decision makers to ignore their advice.

Decisions by individuals and firms will also take into consideration positive consequences alongside moral and political consequences. For example, while location decisions at Starbucks are based on selecting places where their coffee shops can gain sufficient customers to make a profit, the location of subsidiaries in places such as Eire and Luxembourg enables the company to gain tax advantages. However, recent negative publicity on the low amount of tax paid by Starbucks on its profits in the UK has prompted the company to make some voluntary tax payments. This decision may have been made on moral grounds or for political reasons. Alternatively, it may have been made because of positive (objective) consequences – negative publicity led to lower sales and the closure of some Starbucks shops that were no longer profitable.

Google and Amazon were also accused of avoiding tax in the UK. Tax avoidance involves finding loopholes in tax laws. It is therefore legal, but many people believe that it is not moral. These two companies have less direct competition than Starbucks and do not appear to have lost sales. Is the 'morality' of a business linked to the level of competition it faces? Are impersonal organisations such as businesses likely to have lower moral standards than individuals?

REALWORLD ECONOMICS 1.2

UK airport capacity

The capacity of an airport is the maximum number of flights possible in a certain time period. Heathrow is the UK's main 'hub' airport, with many international passengers using it as a place to switch between flights. It operates very close to its maximum capacity and so problems can cause serious delays, when compared to rival European airports that have spare capacity that allows more flights to be rescheduled if necessary.

In May 2010 the coalition government withdrew its support for the previous government's plan to build a third runway at Heathrow Airport. The main reasons given were poor air quality and aircraft noise. Monitoring of these factors indicated that a third runway would increase these forms of pollution. Noise pollution is arguably the most significant factor at Heathrow, as Department for Transport (DFT) data indicate that 725,000 people experience noise that is above 'acceptable levels'. This means that Heathrow is responsible for over a quarter of all aircraft noise sufferers in Europe. Road congestion was also given as a reason, but no specific research had been undertaken into this factor.

The Airports Commission was then established in 2012 in order to advise government on the best way of expanding the capacity of airports in the UK. Headed by an economist, Sir Howard Davies, it concluded that, based on current forecasts of demand for air transport, the UK will need a new runway at a major airport by 2030, with another runway being required by 2050.

Davies stated that a lack of capacity at Heathrow is costing the UK economy £14 billion a year in lost trade, a figure that could rise to £26 billion by 2030, and went on to observe: 'The capacity challenge is not yet critical, but it will become so if no action is taken soon'. In response to this initial finding, the government asked Davies to delay the final report until 2015 because 'the party manifesto had made a promise that Heathrow Airport would not be expanded'.

The commission investigated a number of alternatives, including expansion of Birmingham and Stansted airports. Its interim report was published in December 2013 and indicated that it had shortlisted the following proposals:

- a new 3000 m runway at Gatwick Airport;
- a new 3500 m runway at Heathrow Airport, to the northwest of the existing airport;
- a western extension of Heathrow's existing northern runway, creating a 6000 m runway that could be used for both takeoffs and landings.

The Mayor of London, Boris Johnson, argued that London was not a suitable location for a large airport, stating that putting a new runway at Heathrow would be a 'catastrophe'.

The commission indicated that it would consider a fourth proposal, by the Mayor, to construct a new London Airport on the Isle of Grain in the Thames Estuary in north Kent. A subsequent report in September 2014 rejected this alternative, largely because the commission's calculations revealed that it would cost £112 billion – about five times as much as the other three proposals.

Planes queuing for takeoff at Heathrow Airport

The commission also stated: 'The overall balance of economic impact would be uncertain – particularly as an estuary airport would require the closure of Heathrow for commercial reasons and London City and Southend airports for airspace reasons'.

The estuary proposal has also been criticised because of its location in the middle of a bird and nature reserve – 'the worst possible choice in terms of environmental concerns, political opposition and potential threat to aircraft safety'.

John Cridland, Head of the Confederation of British Industry (CBI), believes that a new runway is vital for UK industry, arguing: 'It is no longer acceptable to bury our heads in the sand on this'.

The favoured option is expected to be the northwest expansion of Heathrow, which is likely to have the lowest costs (£17 billion) and the earliest completion time – 2025. It is expected to create 100,000 new jobs. This option will raise capacity at Heathrow from 70 million to 130 million passengers a year, but will involve the demolition of 950 homes, including two entire villages. This plan is supported by the Back Heathrow campaign that argues that closing Heathrow will mean the immediate loss of 114,000 jobs from the area and possible relocations of many businesses. Two-thirds of the 300 largest international businesses have their headquarters within 25 miles of Heathrow and nearly 70% of the UK's £400 billion of freight exports go through the airport.

One group that supports Boris Johnson's campaign to set up the new hub in the Thames Estuary is Hillingdon Council, the local authority within which Heathrow is located. Council leader, Roy Puddifoot, believes that closing Heathrow offers 'a remarkable opportunity' to create a new community of 250,000 homes. Its transport links make it an ideal location to develop, and Puddifoot believes that it represents a better use of the land than its current use as an airport.

Sources: Adapted from a BBC article on 17.12.13 and an article on 3.3.14 by G. Noakes in *Buying Business Travel*.

Exercises *Total: 50 marks*

1 Identify one positive statement from the article. *(1 mark)*

2 Identify one normative statement from the article. *(1 mark)*

3 What evidence is there to suggest that the coalition's decision to stop the building of Heathrow's third runway was a political decision? *(8 marks)*

4 State five factors that might have been considered when deciding to reject an airport in the Thames Estuary. To what extent do the five factors that you have selected involve normative judgements? *(15 marks)*

5 Evaluate the advantages and disadvantages of a decision to increase the capacity of Heathrow Airport. *(25 marks)*

Review questions

Total: 44 marks

1 Economics is the study of:

A All human behaviour
B Economies
C Production
D Scarcity *(1 mark)*

2 Which one of the following is a normative statement?

A UK consumers bought over 60 million packets of Kellogg's cornflakes last year.
B An increase in people's incomes will lead to an increase in demand for cornflakes.
C An increase in the price of cornflakes will lead to a decrease in demand for cornflakes.
D People should be encouraged to eat more cornflakes. *(1 mark)*

3 Which one of the following is a positive statement?

A Special K is better than cornflakes.
B UK businesses should produce more of their products in the UK.
C Increases in income tax have a negative impact on the demand for products.
D The government ought to promote healthy eating. *(1 mark)*

4 Define the term 'social science'? *(3 marks)*

5 Explain two scientific techniques used by economists. *(8 marks)*

6 Explain one reason why two economists may use similar, scientific approaches but reach different conclusions. *(5 marks)*

7 State one decision that might be taken by an individual (or firm) in which a moral judgement might be more important than objective, positive thinking. Explain why this was mainly a moral decision. *(5 marks)*

8 In 2012 the BBC completed the relocation of its headquarters from London to Salford. Explain, with examples, why this decision would have been based on both positive and normative judgements and been influenced by moral and political judgements. *(20 marks)*

The nature & purpose of economic activity

This chapter explains why economic activity is planned to satisfy needs and wants. It looks at the difficulties in measuring the satisfaction of wants. The second part of the chapter focuses on three economic decisions – what to produce, how to produce, and who is to benefit from the goods and services produced. The ways in which these three decisions are made are demonstrated in the context of a market economy, supported by observations relating to how a mixed economy might impact upon these economic decisions.

The central purpose of economic activity

The central purpose of economic activity is the production of goods and services in order to satisfy needs and wants.

Examples of needs include food, liquid, warmth, shelter and clothing. Some people extend this list to include factors such as social needs and affection. However, there is agreement that needs are finite (limited).

Many examples of wants represent an increase on the basic needs, such as greater quantities of food and clothing. Possessions, such as furniture and household goods, would be classified as wants. Spending on services, such as hairdressing, restaurant meals and entertainment, would also be classified in this way.

People wish to improve their lifestyle and it is human nature to continue to desire more. Once a want is satisfied, humans will typically desire another good or service or an improved version of one that they already have. People's wants are therefore not finite – they are unlimited.

If needs and wants are satisfied, then **economic welfare** is improved. Economic welfare is a measure of the 'happiness' of the population of an economy. However, since happiness is a value judgement, it is impossible to get an objective assessment of economic welfare. Attempts to measure happiness are hampered by the fact that people have different tastes and therefore receive varying levels of happiness from the goods and services they receive. Economic welfare is also difficult to measure not

Author tip

You should recognise that production includes services and not just goods. In fact, in the UK over two-thirds of the working population is employed in the provision of services rather than goods.

Key terms

Goods are tangible items (physical products) that can be seen or touched and that satisfy human needs and wants, such as bread, cars and mobile phones.

Services are intangible items that satisfy human needs and wants, such as bus journeys, television programmes and the provision of telecommunication links.

Production is the provision of goods and services to satisfy needs and wants.

Needs are what people require for basic human survival.

Wants are human desires beyond the basic needs for human survival.

only because some economic activity is unrecorded, such as housework, DIY and gardening, but also because it may be improved by non-activity, such as preserving woodland and natural environments.

In general, measurements of **economic welfare** are undertaken at a national level. The most common method is gross domestic product (GDP), which measures the output of a country in a year. A similar measure, favoured by the United Nations, is gross national income (GNI), which measures the income generated by a country in a year. This figure is different because the income from some output may be sent to other countries, having been earned by foreign residents or multinational businesses.

GNI and GDP are used to measure the level of wants satisfied, because they represent the level of money spent on goods and services in a country or by its population. However, the United Nations likes to use its own Human Development Index (HDI), which is calculated by taking into account the average score achieved in rating the following three factors: GNI per head; life expectancy; years of schooling.

REALWORLD ECONOMICS 2.1

Sex and drugs boost the UK economy

The gathering of statistics to measure GDP and GNI is not an exact science, as many people do not declare all their income to the tax authorities. The government has adopted new accounting methods in order to bring UK statistics into line with European standards. The revised figures, which include income from illegal drugs and prostitution, have increased GDP by about £10 billion a year (0.7% of the UK's GDP). Together, these two 'industries' contribute about the same amount to the UK economy as the level of agricultural production.

Income from prostitution now contributes to GDP

Measuring economic welfare

The United Nations (UN) surveys cover 187 countries, excluding countries such as North Korea. Tables 2.1 and 2.2 show the three highest countries and the three lowest countries in terms of GNI and the HDI as measures of economic welfare and satisfaction of wants. The UK's position is noted for comparison purposes.

Small, oil-rich countries dominate the top of the GNI league table. However, these countries tend to lack the historical infrastructure in healthcare and education. As a consequence, different countries head the HDI league table.

Economists treat these statistics with caution, as they are based on data that are very limited. The UN itself believes that 'income per head' is a very unreliable measure of happiness and the satisfaction of wants because it ignores inequalities. For example, GNI per head figures suggest that residents of Equatorial Guinea have comparable incomes to residents of the UK. However, most of this income is from recent oil extraction and relatively few of the 750,000 people enjoy the benefits of this new-found wealth. The UN does provide a modified HDI that adjusts the results to take into consideration inequalities, but measures of inequality are very subjective and there is no internationally agreed method.

Table 2.1 *Comparisons of gross national income for selected countries, 2013*

Ranking	Country	GNI/head ($)	HDI ranking
1st	Qatar	119,029	31st
2nd	Liechtenstein	87,085	18th
3rd	Kuwait	85,820	46th
26th	UK	35,002	14th
185th	Malawi	715	174th
186th	Central African Republic	588	185th
187th	Congo	444	186th

Table 2.2 *Comparisons of economic welfare, based on the Human Development Index, for selected countries, 2013*

Ranking	Country	HDI score (maximum = 1.0)	GNI/head ranking
1st	Norway	0.944	6th
2nd	Australia	0.933	20th
3rd	Switzerland	0.917	9th
14th	UK	0.892	26th
185th	Central African Republic	0.341	186th
186th	Congo	0.338	187th
187th	Niger	0.337	182nd

In order to measure economic welfare more accurately, the UN has indicated that it would need to take into account the following factors: inequality; poverty; human security; and empowerment. These are not included at present because they are too difficult to measure reliably.

The key economic decisions

Key economic decisions are required on:

- what to produce
- how to produce
- who is to benefit from the goods and services produced

Three types of economy have developed to resolve these issues:

- a **market economy**, in which the market decides. A market is a place where buyers and sellers meet. The market uses demand (representing wants of consumers) and supply (which shows the willingness of producers to supply goods and services);
- a **mixed economy**, in which goods and services are provided through the market system, except where governments choose to intervene (usually to prevent market failure);
- a **planned or command economy**, where the government decides on the production of goods and services.

The key participants in economic activity are individuals (as both consumers and workers), firms and governments. These participants have a variety of objectives:

- **Individuals**, as consumers, aim to maximise satisfaction through purchasing goods and services that give them the greatest level of satisfaction. For most products, such as food and entertainment, the satisfaction gained will be quite immediate. However, consumer durables, such as furniture, kitchen appliances and cars, will be bought because they are expected to bring satisfaction over a long period of time.
- As factors of production, **individuals** seek to gain access to as many resources as possible by selling their labour for the highest possible wage or becoming an entrepreneur and maximising profit. However, other objectives may include supporting charitable causes and having time for leisure. As employees, individuals might want job satisfaction and recognition as well as financial reward. As entrepreneurs, self-esteem and reputation may be important wants.

- **Firms** aim to maximise profit by using factors of production to make goods that can be sold for profit. However, firms also want to grow, guarantee survival or prioritise their workers' or customers' needs. These objectives may conflict with maximising profit.
- **Governments** aim to maximise economic welfare (the happiness of the population). In a mixed economy, such as the UK, this may involve intervention in economic activities (e.g. regulations to restrict tobacco consumption). Governments also want low unemployment and stable prices, and may target greater equality of income and wealth. This latter aim is influenced by value judgements. High rewards to entrepreneurs and highly skilled workers may lead to greater inequality but may encourage greater efforts that lead to higher production from the resources available. However, does society benefit from more production of goods and services if relatively few people reap the rewards? This balance between how much is produced and who receives the products provided is difficult to manage.

The United Kingdom is a mixed economy. Most goods and services are provided through the market mechanism (i.e. through a market economy), but some are provided through government intervention and action. The reasons for government intervention will be covered in Topic 5, which deals with market failure.

What to produce?

In a market economy the decision regarding 'what to produce' is decided by the market, which operates through interaction between buyers and sellers. In this instance the buyers are predominantly individual consumers, who buy goods and services to satisfy their wants. However, buyers may also be firms buying raw materials from other firms. The sellers are firms that provide products in order to achieve their own objectives, such as maximising profits. If a particular product satisfies consumer wants, then consumers will be prepared to pay a price for that product. The greater the level of satisfaction that consumers gain from the product, the higher the price they will be prepared to pay for that product. If the price of a particular product increases, then more firms will try to provide this product as the higher price will mean that they are more likely to make a profit. If a product becomes unpopular, then its price will fall and therefore fewer firms will want to produce and supply that product.

Adam Smith, one of the earliest economists, described this mechanism as the 'invisible hand'. In theory, the invisible hand leads to economic resources being used by firms to provide the products that most satisfy consumer wants at any given time. It automatically adjusts in response to increases and decreases in consumer wants.

A pure market economy can lead to problems. Services such as health and education are usually underprovided because families may not value them sufficiently to pay for private health and private education. It also means that if some individuals are without employment, they have no money and therefore cannot satisfy any of their wants. Although it is a value judgement, most people agree that these situations are undesirable. Market economies can provide socially 'undesirable' goods too, such as tobacco and alcohol.

As a result, governments intervene and so a mixed economy arises, with the government deciding on the production of some goods and services. Action is also taken to limit poverty. Some of the goods and services provided by government may be funded from taxation of undesirable goods.

How to produce?

Firms make the decision regarding 'how to produce'. They buy resources and employ labour in order to make the products that consumers want. Profit is the difference between revenue and costs. Each firm will constantly try to improve its production methods so that they can minimise their costs. This will enable a firm to make more profit because the difference between the price of a product and the cost to make it gets bigger, or the firm can use its lower costs to cut its price, but maintain the profit level from each product. In this way it will make larger profits because the lower price enables it to sell more products.

Firms will constantly strive to increase their profits and so they will benefit from any approaches that cut unit costs (the costs of making one item), such as finding cheaper materials, paying lower wages, introducing capital equipment and training workers so that they produce more products in a given time.

The question of 'how to produce' is answered, in the market economy, by the 'profit motive'. Any improvements in how a product is produced will lead to greater profits for the firm, and so firms are motivated to find the best possible way of making a product. Of course, if customers want quality rather than low prices, then the 'profit motive' will encourage firms to provide high-quality products.

Who is to benefit from the goods and services produced?

In a market economy, goods and services are provided for people who are prepared to pay the market price – in theory, this means the people who value the product most highly. If people have the same or similar incomes, the market mechanism will direct the goods and services towards the people that value them most, ensuring an efficient allocation of resources.

In practice, however, the market mechanism means that resources are directed to those who have the ability to pay. In July 2014, a United Nations report warned that growing inequality was hindering improvements in lifespan, education and income in a world where the 80 richest people have as much wealth as the 3.5 billion poorest. With a world population of 7 billion, this means that the 80 richest people have as much wealth as half of the world's population.

Inequality undermines the working of the market mechanism. People in richer countries are able to satisfy luxury wants at a time when other people are unable to survive because they cannot afford to satisfy their basic needs.

In a mixed economy, the government can intervene to address this issue. Taxes can take more money from the rich and pay benefits or provide services that benefit those with less money.

Review questions

Total: 50 marks

1 Goods and services are provided in order to:

A Create employment
B Prevent scarcity
C Satisfy needs and wants
D Use resources

(1 mark)

2 Which one of the following is unlimited?
   A Needs
   B Production
   C Resources
   D Wants *(1 mark)*

3 Economic welfare is a:
   A Normative measure of happiness
   B Positive measure of happiness
   C Normative measure of output
   D Positive measure of output *(1 mark)*

4 The United Kingdom is an example of a:
   A Command economy
   B Market economy
   C Mixed economy
   D Planned economy *(1 mark)*

5 In a market economy it is assumed that firms try to maximise:
   A Economic welfare
   B Prices
   C Profits
   D Workers' wages *(1 mark)*

6 Define the term 'production'. *(3 marks)*

7 What is the difference between needs and wants? *(4 marks)*

8 Refer to Tables 2.1 and 2.2 (p. 13). Explain two possible reasons why the countries with the highest gross national income (GNI) per head do not feature at the top of the Human Development Index (HDI). *(10 marks)*

9 Explain how the market economy decides 'what to produce'. *(6 marks)*

10 Explain two reasons why the government might intervene in order to influence what is produced in an economy. *(10 marks)*

11 Explain why firms try to ensure that resources are used effectively to produce goods and services. *(6 marks)*

12 Explain how inequality might prevent products being allocated to those who need or want them most. *(6 marks)*

Economic resources

This chapter introduces the concept of economic resources or factors of production. The four factors of production – labour, land, capital and enterprise – are each considered in turn. Specific emphasis is placed on the notion of the environment as a scarce resource. The contrast between renewable and non-renewable resources is examined, particularly with regard to their impact on scarcity.

The classification of economic resources

Economists describe the scarce resources used to produce goods and services as **factors of production**. These are classified into four categories: labour, land, capital and enterprise.

Author tip
On occasions economics uses everyday words but gives them a very particular meaning. Two examples of this are factors of production – land and capital. Ensure that you use the specific meaning that applies to economics when asked to define these terms.

Labour

'Labour' describes those resources that make up the workforce in an economy. It is a heterogeneous factor of production, which means that each individual person (unit of labour) possesses a unique set of skills. Labour can be a very flexible factor of production because its role can range from jobs requiring manual dexterity to those relying mainly on intellectual capability. Although some skills of labour are inherent, constant practice, education and training can improve the efficiency of this factor of production.

However, individuals are often very inflexible, particularly if they have developed a narrow range of skills suited to one particular job. This inflexibility leads to the **immobility of labour**, which describes the inability or reluctance of labour to change.

One type of immobility is **occupational immobility**, where labour is reluctant to change from one job to another job. Occupational immobility may arise because:

- people lack the skills to undertake another role, either because they do not have the basic talent or because they have not gained the experience necessary to achieve a level of skill comparable to other workers;
- people lack training for other roles and may not want to retrain to learn new skills;

Key terms

Labour is the human effort, both physical and mental, used in the production of goods and services.

Land is all natural resources, encompassing not only land but also minerals such as coal and gold, agricultural crops and livestock.

Capital is goods produced solely in order to assist production of other goods. Examples include machinery, office equipment and company vehicles. Capital goods are vital because they enable an economy to increase output in the future.

Enterprise is the combining of the other factors of production in order to produce goods and services. Entrepreneurs undertake this action and are motivated by profit.

- people may enjoy their current role and be reluctant to change;
- commencing a new job may mean that the person has to start at a lower wage level, as they often have less experience in the new role;
- people often prefer to keep to existing patterns of behaviour (inertia), as it involves less risk.

Another type of immobility is **geographical immobility**, where labour is reluctant to move to a different area in order to seek employment. Geographical immobility may arise because:

- friendship groups may be lost if a person relocates;
- relocation may cause disruption to other family members, such as a partner who needs to find a new job in the new location, or children whose education and friendship groups are likely to be affected;
- house prices may make it difficult to move to certain areas, such as the southeast of England;
- finding new houses and organising relocation is likely to be stressful;
- many people are more reluctant to move away from an area that they know than from a job with which they are familiar.

Labour receives 'wages' as a reward for its contribution.

Land

'Land' means the environment and all natural resources. While 'land' in economics includes the common usage of the word – a place on which production can take place – it also includes resources extracted from land, such as oil, gold, gravel and other minerals. Agricultural products are further examples of land, which therefore includes livestock, such as cattle and pigs, and crops and plants, such as wheat, barley, potatoes and flowers. Natural resources from the sea and air, such as fish and wind power, are other examples of land.

'Rent' is the reward paid to land for its contribution to production.

Capital

'Capital' describes those assets used to produce goods and services. Examples include factories and offices, plant, machinery, office furniture, tools, computers involved in business use, and delivery vehicles. Each of the products listed will be purchased or made by a firm because it enables that firm to produce goods and services, rather than because it satisfies a direct want.

Economists distinguish between two types of goods: consumer goods, which are bought because they satisfy the wants of consumers; and capital goods, which are bought by firms in order to produce other goods and services. In some cases it is impossible to classify a product as a capital good or as a consumer good until its exact purpose is known. For example, items such as computers, furniture and vehicles are consumer goods if bought for a household's wants, but are capital goods if a firm uses them in its office or as company cars for its staff.

Governments support business activity and individuals by providing infrastructure for the benefit of society. Production of goods and services is thus helped by capital goods such as roads, bridges and airports. In recent years, many examples of infrastructure that the government has traditionally provided, such as electricity and gas supply, have become the responsibility of private firms.

Ideally, an economy should achieve some balance between capital goods and consumer goods. The latter provide satisfaction to consumers and will therefore impact directly on the lifestyle of the population. However, resources devoted to the production of capital goods, such as machinery, will enable the economy to produce more goods and services in future years. Economists describe this creation of new capital as **fixed capital formation**. The production of capital goods rather than consumer goods is more likely to improve living standards in the future.

Ultimately, the amount of resources devoted to capital will depend on business confidence, as people who create capital goods are relying on people in the future buying the products that the capital goods create.

An important issue is the wearing out of capital over time. This is often known as depreciation, but economists use the term **capital consumption** (or **fixed capital consumption**). Since machinery, transport and other items of capital wear out, each year a large percentage of new spending on capital goods (known as **investment**) is merely matching the loss of value of capital assets elsewhere. In 2013, fixed capital formation in the UK was £226 billion but fixed capital consumption was £189 billion. Overall, the value of the stock of capital held in the UK only increased by £37 billion in 2013. As the value of capital stock in the UK is over £3500 billion, this was an increase in capital stock of just over 1%.

'Interest' is traditionally the reward paid to capital, as the providers of the source of finance used to produce capital are usually paid interest.

Key note

Firms often rely on consumers' savings to finance their production or purchase of capital goods. Rich people are in a better position to save than poor people. Consequently, rich countries are in a better position to enable their economies to grow than poor countries. In the latter countries, people cannot afford to save because their consumer goods are those needed to satisfy basic needs, such as food and shelter.

The distribution of income is also important. The country with the highest percentage of its resources geared towards capital goods is Equatorial Guinea. This is partly because of newly discovered oil reserves that have encouraged investment in oil wells, thus raising business confidence. However, it is also because most of the country's wealth is in the hands of a few people who can afford to direct their wealth into capital goods.

Enterprise

'Enterprise' involves risk taking and decision making. These are known as the entrepreneurial functions. Entrepreneurs provide the finance to establish and run a firm. If the firm fails, it is the entrepreneur's finance that is sacrificed and so the entrepreneur is the person taking the risk.

As the owner of the firm, the entrepreneur also makes the key decisions, such as what to produce, how many products are to be made and where to locate production.

In small businesses, such as sole traders and partnerships, the entrepreneurial functions are carried out by the same person. However, in large public limited companies, such as BP and Sainsbury's, the two entrepreneurial functions are split. The owners are the company's shareholders, who vote at the company's annual general meeting but have little other involvement in the running of the business. They are the risk takers because if the business fails, then they lose money. Decision making is carried out by paid employees – the senior managers of the business. They may own shares but it is likely to be a negligible percentage of the total shareholding. This split between the two entrepreneurial functions is known as the 'divorce of ownership and control'.

Entrepreneurs earn 'profit'. If entrepreneurs make good decisions and the firm achieves a sales revenue that greatly exceeds the cost of the other three factors of production, then the entrepreneurs' reward will be a high level of profit.

The environment – renewable and non-renewable resources

In the context of economics, the environment describes natural resources and their influence on economic activity. Natural resources are often finite: there is a limited amount of land, air and water in the world. At any one time, there is also a finite amount of natural resources that is available for economic activity and so the environment is a scarce resource.

Natural resources can be classified as energy sources, minerals, livestock and plants. When considering these resources, it is important for society to recognise whether they are renewable or non-renewable.

Energy sources

The main sources of energy in the world are fossil fuels, which are non-renewable (Figure 3.1). In 2011, 82% of the world's energy was produced from fossil fuels: coal (44%), oil (24%) and natural gas (14%).

Figure 3.1 *Actual and forecast breakdown of world energy consumption*

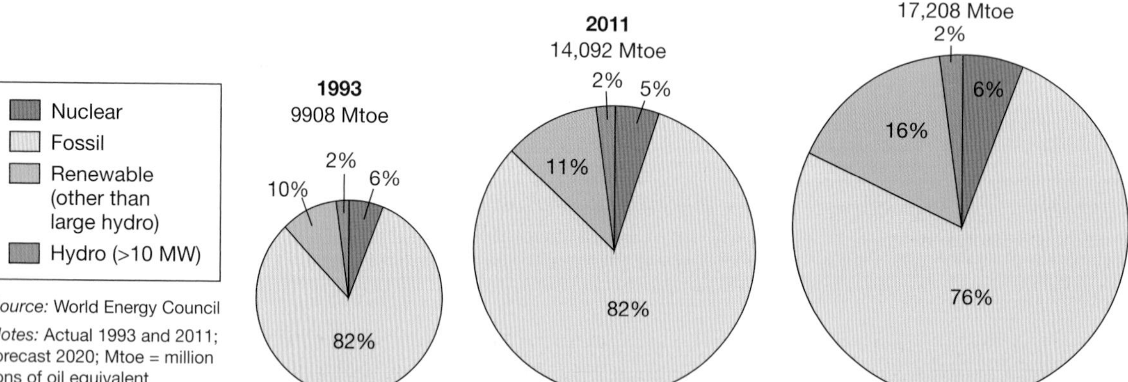

Source: World Energy Council

Notes: Actual 1993 and 2011; forecast 2020; Mtoe = million tons of oil equivalent

Key terms

The **environment** describes the conditions in which a person, animal or plant lives or operates.

A **renewable resource** is one that can replenish itself over time, so that new additions of the resource can match or exceed levels of use of that resource.

A **non-renewable resource** is one that cannot replenish itself over time, so that once it is used it is no longer available in its original form.

Although there have been concerns that these resources will become fully depleted, new discoveries have broadly matched their usage. Since 1945, reserves of oil have been predicted to last for a certain number of years, falling as low as 25 years in some cases. However, as there is a finite supply, there is a definite limit to the amount of oil that can be produced (unless scientists can manage to find a way to manufacture oil).

The other main sources of energy are renewable or long lasting. In 2011, hydro (water), wind and solar power were the main sources. In Figure 3.1, large-scale hydro production is classified separately and accounts for 2% of world energy supply. Nuclear energy accounts for 5% and is expanding after a period of decline. Technically, it is non-renewable but its capability is extremely long lasting. In fact, many people perceive its longevity as a problem because it requires careful disposal of materials.

Minerals

Mineral resources are finite and therefore may become scarce if not managed properly. Most of the world's mineral resources have limited availability, based on current extraction rates. However, unlike fossil fuels, that are lost during processing, many minerals are durable. Consequently, they can be recycled or converted to different uses. However, the current growth rate in the use of mineral resources suggests that a number of the world's mineral resources may become exhausted.

Improvements in technology have impacted on some of the problems of mineral depletion. Synthetic materials can be made from more abundant minerals, and new processes such as miniaturisation in manufacturing have led to fewer minerals being required in certain processes. Synthetic (man-made) diamonds now account for 90% of industrial diamonds.

Livestock

In the UK, 'livestock' refers to animals such as cows, pigs, sheep, chicken and turkeys. It also applies to freshwater and saltwater fish and other sea creatures such as lobsters and crabs.

As animals can reproduce, they are a renewable resource. However, excessive use or misuse can deplete numbers. In the USA, there were tens of millions of bison in 1800. By 1900, hunting had reduced their number to less than 1000. Measures to protect bison have enabled numbers to recover, and bison meat is now considered to be an excellent alternative to beef.

In general, livestock numbers are managed to ensure sustainability because they can be constrained to land owned by individuals who have a financial interest in preserving them. However, fish are an example of a resource that cannot be easily constrained to one specific area owned by certain people. As a consequence, there is an incentive for society to preserve them but less of an incentive for individual fishermen. In 2006, 28,900 tonnes of cod were caught in the North Sea in comparison to annual catches of 300,000 tonnes in the 1970s. It is estimated that cod numbers in the North Sea are now little more than 1% of the numbers in the nineteenth century, mainly as a result of overfishing. Since 2006, numbers have increased as a result of regulations and voluntary actions, but the Marine Stewardship Council still classifies cod as being an 'unsustainable' species at present.

REALWORLD ECONOMICS 3.1

Fish stocks

According to the most recent report by the UN Food and Agriculture Organisation, many fish stocks are depleted or overexploited (see Figure 3.2).

This situation means that the world is in danger of losing a valuable food source. It also means the potential collapse of certain ecosystems.

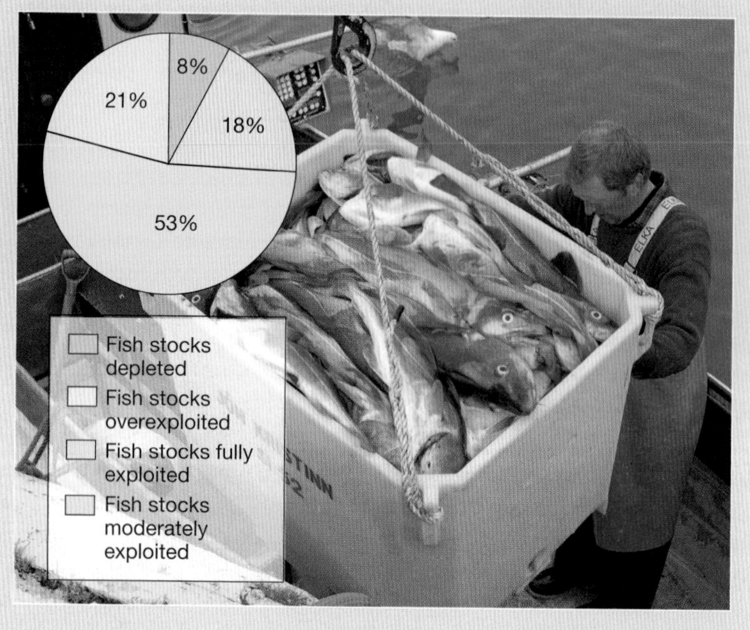

Landing the day's catch – overfishing has resulted in the classification of cod as an 'unsustainable' species

Figure 3.2 *Current levels of fish stocks*

Plants

Activities such as deforestation, and clearance of agricultural land for housing, industrial and commercial purposes, have led to a significant decline in some plant life.

Trees are only sustainable if their use is managed. With hardwood trees it can take over 60 years for a mature forest to be replenished. With agricultural land, a lack of understanding of ecology has led to the loss of tracts of previously fertile land. Furthermore, global warming is impacting on the suitability of some land for growing plants.

With much of the world's population unable to feed itself sufficiently, difficulties in providing food are already severe. Given that the population of the world is expected to increase from over 7 billion in 2014 to more than 10 billion by 2100, it is unlikely that food supplies, and supplies of the other natural resources, will be able to keep pace with growing demand for these scarce resources. (Scarcity will be examined in more detail in Chapter 4.)

REALWORLD ECONOMICS 3.2

Renewable and non-renewable resources

Scarcity of natural resources is a major problem for the world. Tables 3.1 to 3.3 below provide data concerning the relative scarcity of different energy and mineral resources. Figures relating to the number of years before depletion are based on three assumptions:

- existing, known reserves can be accessed cost effectively;
- no new reserves will be discovered;
- annual extraction/supply of these resources will remain at 2011 levels in future years.

Table 3.1 provides a summary of the main sources of non-renewable energy and the known reserves of those sources. Table 3.2 summarises the main sources of 'renewable' or long-lasting energy sources.

Table 3.1 *World production and known reserves of fossil fuels, 2011*

Energy source	Percentage of world's energy	Worldwide production, 2011 (Mtoe[1])	World reserves, 2011 (Mtoe)	Number of years before depletion[2]
Coal	44	7500	892,000	119
Oil	24	4000	223,000	56
Natural gas	14	2450	146,000	60

Notes: (1) Mtoe = million tonnes of oil-equivalent energy. (2) Assuming annual production remains at 2011 levels.
Source: World Energy Council – World Energy Report, 2013

Table 3.2 *World production and maximum annual capacity of other energy sources, 2011*[1]

Energy source	Worldwide production, 2011 (GWh[2])	Worldwide capacity, 2011 (GWh equivalent[3])	Production in 2011 as a percentage of maximum (capacity) production
Uranium and nuclear	2,385,903	3,189,323	75
Hydro	2,767,118	8,288,572	33
Wind	377,613	2,085,309	18
Solar	52,878	603,126	9

Notes: (1) The table excludes bioenergy, as reliable data are not available. (2) GWh = gigawatt hours. (3) Converted from MW to GWh equivalent.
Source: World Energy Council – World Energy Report, 2013

Table 3.3 *Annual use and known reserves of mineral resources*

Mineral	Unit of measure (MT[1] or T[2])	Worldwide production, 2013 (MT)	World reserves, 2013 (MT)	Number of years before depletion[3]
Bauxite (for aluminium)	MT	259	28,000	108
Copper	MT	17.9	690	***Q1(a)***
Gold	T	2770	54,000	19
Iron	MT	2.95	81	27
Lead	MT	5.4	89	16
Manganese	MT	17	570	34
Nickel	MT	***Q1(b)***	74	30
Silver	T	26,000	520,000	20
Tin	MT	0.23	***Q1(c)***	20
Zinc	MT	13.5	250	19

Notes: (1) MT = millions of tonnes. (2) T = tonnes. (3) Assuming annual production remains at 2013 levels.
Sources: Mineral Commodity Summaries 2014, published by the US Department of the Interior; US Geological Survey

Exercises

Total: 66 marks

1 Based on the data in the article, which natural resource will be the first to be depleted?
A Coal
B Oil
C Solar energy
D Lead *(1 mark)*

2 Use the data in Table 3.3 to answer questions (a) to (c).

(a) Calculate the number of years before copper is depleted. *(2 marks)*

(b) Calculate the worldwide production of nickel in 2013. *(2 marks)*

(c) Calculate the world's total reserves of tin in 2013. *(2 marks)*

3 Explain one possible reason why reliable data on biomass energy (e.g. timber and peat) are not available. *(4 marks)*

4 Solar, wind and hydro power are produced at a level well below the maximum possible capacity, whereas nuclear energy production is much closer to its maximum capacity. Analyse possible reasons for these differences. *(15 marks)*

5 Using the data provided, explain why economists are more concerned about 'energy' as a scarce resource than 'minerals'. *(15 marks)*

6 To what extent do you believe that Tables 3.1, 3.2 and 3.3 exaggerate the possible scarcity of the world's natural resources? Justify your view. *(25 marks)*

Review questions

Total: 35 marks

1 In economics, 'labour' describes:
A The factor of production that organises the other factors
B People who are only involved in the manufacturing of goods
C Human effort used in the production of goods and services
D The number of people living in an economy *(1 mark)*

2 In economics, which one of the following is not an example of land?
A Coal B Fish C A gold ring D The sea *(1 mark)*

3 Which one of the following is not a natural resource?
A Energy B Minerals C Livestock D Capital *(1 mark)*

4 Options A to D below describe four possible uses of a table. In which one of these uses is the table an example of capital?
A A table in an economics classroom in a school
B A table for sale in a furniture shop
C A dining table in a house
D A kitchen table used to prepare household meals *(1 mark)*

5 Which one of the following is a reason for occupational immobility of labour?
A The cost of housing
B Lack of awareness of other regions of the UK
C Inappropriate skills
D Reluctance to move children from their school *(1 mark)*

6 Which one of these resources is renewable?
A Silver B Coal C Wind D Natural gas *(1 mark)*

7 Which one of these resources is non-renewable?
A Trees B Livestock C Oil D Solar power *(1 mark)*

8 Options A to D below describe four statements about enterprise. Which *two* of the statements are true?
A The entrepreneur takes a risk
B The entrepreneur's reward is wages
C Entrepreneurs receive all of the revenue of the firm
D The entrepreneur makes decisions *(2 marks)*

9 Define 'capital'. *(3 marks)*

10 What is meant by 'the occupational immobility of labour'? *(3 marks)*

11 Refer to Figure 3.1 (p. 20). Describe two trends in the use of energy shown. *(4 marks)*

12 Refer to Figure 3.2 (p. 22). Describe two possible consequences of the data shown. *(4 marks)*

13 Explain one cause of the geographical immobility of labour. *(4 marks)*

14 Explain the link between savings and the production of capital goods. *(4 marks)*

15 Explain the meaning of 'the divorce of ownership and control'. *(4 marks)*

Scarcity, choice & the allocation of resources

In this chapter we study the fundamental economic problem and the significance of four basic economic ideas, namely that human wants are unlimited, wants vary in importance, means (resources) are limited, and that resources have alternative uses. These characteristics lead to the necessity of choice for consumers, but also choices related to how scarce resources are allocated to different uses. The chapter concludes with an introduction to the concept of opportunity cost.

Scarcity – the fundamental economic problem

In the nineteenth century, historian Thomas Carlyle described economics as the 'dismal science'. The apparent impossibility of resolving the problems of unlimited wants but scarce resources has led to others repeating this description.

In Chapter 1 we introduced the idea that economics is the study of scarcity. Chapter 1 also introduced Lionel Robbins's widely used definition of economics: 'Economics is the science which studies human behaviour as a relationship between ends (unlimited wants) and scarce means (resources) which have alternative uses'. In effect, Robbins's definition is based on four factors:

- human wants are unlimited;
- wants vary in importance;
- means (resources) are limited;
- resources have alternative uses.

Human wants are unlimited

Although human needs are limited, human wants appear to be unlimited. Basic needs, such as food and shelter, have been converted into wants such as luxury food and housing, far in excess of those needed for basic survival. Goods such as televisions and cars were once considered to be a luxury; now they are seen as essential for a normal lifestyle. Advances in technology have led to the introduction of a wide range of new products, such as mobile phones, computers and tablets, which have encouraged humans to find even more wants to desire. As people's affluence increases, they strive to find new ways to benefit from their affluence. Firms are encouraged, by the opportunity for profit, to use the factors of production to find and develop new products to satisfy those wants. Often these new wants arise from a wish to improve a good or service that already exists. One example is mankind's desire for communication. Initially the royal mail enabled people to communicate at a distance. Over time this has evolved into landline telephones and subsequently mobile telephones. In 1922 the BBC began public radio broadcasts. Advances in technology have led to television and the ability to receive radio and TV transmissions through mobile devices.

REALWORLD ECONOMICS 4.1

What wants are people satisfying in the UK?

In the UK, patterns of spending have changed dramatically as the country has become richer and people have been able to satisfy more wants.

Table 4.1 shows how patterns of spending have changed since 1947. In order to measure inflation, the government needs to recognise the types of goods and services that people buy. This process of measurement commenced in 1914, but initially products such as alcohol were excluded from the index as the government made a value judgement that these products should not be consumed. Since 1947, the pattern of spending has been based on what people spend. The government's Expenditure and Food Survey (EFS) examines the choices made by a selection of families in order to gain a breakdown of items purchased. Over 650 goods and services are included in the survey, but for practical reasons results are usually summarised into categories.

The patterns of expenditure show how people's wants have changed in the UK since 1947. Food and drink is the category that most closely reflects basic needs in the table. There has been a dramatic drop in the percentage of a family's income spent on food and drink since 1947. However, as household spending in 2014 was 4.4 times higher than it was in 1947, this still means that people are spending more money on food and drink, particularly as restaurant food is classified elsewhere. The fall in alcohol and drink is largely due to changes in tastes, with many public houses closing (including a number that have become restaurants) in order to cope with changing wants. Of particular significance is the rise in spending on services. Economists generally believe that increasing demand for services, as opposed to goods, is a sign of growing affluence. In 1947, health, education, communication, recreation/culture and restaurants/hotels were classified as 'miscellaneous services'. Their growth since 1947 has seen them classified separately. These five categories of service collectively account for 34.2% of household spending. In 1947, they represented only 5.4% of family expenditure.

Table 4.1 *Patterns of expenditure, 1947 and 2014*

Category of spending	Percentage of household spending in 1947	Percentage of household spending in 2014
Food and drink	34.8	11.2
Alcohol and tobacco	21.7	4.5
Clothing and footwear	9.7	7.2
Housing and utilities	15.3	12.9
Household goods	7.1	6.0
Transport	2.5	15.2
Miscellaneous goods	3.5	8.8
Miscellaneous services	5.4	
Health		2.4
Education		2.2
Communication		3.2
Recreation and culture		14.4
Restaurants and hotels		12.0
TOTAL	**100.0**	**100.0**

Source: Office for National Statistics

Exercises

Total: 26 marks

Based on the above article, answer the following questions:

1 If a typical household spent £3000 a month in 2014, how much is its monthly expenditure on clothing and footwear? *(2 marks)*

2 Using Table 4.1, identify two significant points of comparison between 1947 and 2014. *(4 marks)*

3 Explain the possible reasons for the decline in the relative importance of household spending on food and drink between 1947 and 2014. *(10 marks)*

4 Explain the possible consequences of the increase in spending on services between 1947 and 2014. *(10 marks)*

Wants vary in importance

Individual wants reflect the preferences of the individual. Although our basic needs may be similar, wants are a matter of individual taste. Table 4.1 shows how different wants have changed in importance over time. In 2014, consumers had a much greater desire for recreation and culture and for restaurants and hotels. To some extent, these wants relate to the category of want that has showed the largest increase since 1947 – transport. In 1947, car ownership was rare, and public transport fares were low. Most workers lived close to their workplace and thus did not require transportation. As the UK economy has grown, increased travel opportunities have led to the growth in the leisure and tourism sectors.

Up until this point, 'needs' and 'wants' have been separated. However, many economists refute this distinction, taking the view that every 'desire' is a want but acknowledging that wants vary in importance. Consequently, consumers will place a high priority on food and shelter initially, but once they have acquired sufficient quantities of these items, other wants become more important. The fall in the percentage of spending on food and drink in the UK suggests that people are now looking to satisfy more than just basic requirements.

The level of importance placed on a want can be estimated through the price that a consumer is prepared to pay to satisfy that want. A consumer who expects to gain great happiness from a television set may be prepared to pay £2000 for a set; other consumers may believe a television only provides a value of £500 to them. As these wants are constantly changing (in recent years television sales have been hit by people accessing programmes through other devices), firms must constantly adapt the products that they provide in order to satisfy consumer needs. Where consumers buy a number of items of a product, such as bottles of water, the additional items tend to give less satisfaction than the first item. This is because the first item usually satisfies a greater want than subsequent items. For example, the first bottle of water is needed to overcome a desperate thirst; the second and subsequent bottles help hydration but are not satisfying such a high level of want.

Means (resources) are limited

In Chapter 3 we studied the factors of production – these are the means (resources) that are required in order to produce goods and services to satisfy our wants. Each of the factors of production has limited availability.

- **Land** Many natural resources, such as minerals and fossil fuels, are finite. Even where resources are renewable, such as livestock and plants, they are only sustainable if their use is limited to a particular level. Renewable energy, such as solar power and wind power, is also limited by weather conditions.
- **Labour** At any one time, the potential workforce is limited by population. It is also influenced by factors such as the age distribution of population. The availability of labour to make a particular product is influenced further by geographical and occupational mobility of labour.
- **Capital** The stock of capital goods in an economy has been developed over a number of years and the level of capital goods diminishes over time through capital consumption. Although more of an economy's resources can be devoted to capital goods, there is a limit to the level of capital in an economy at any one time.

- **Enterprise** In theory, enterprise is quite a flexible factor of production. In practice, entrepreneurs will only become active if they have identified potential profit in the production of goods and services. As consumers have limited resources with which to purchase goods and services, there is a finite limit to the level of enterprise in an economy at any particular point in time.

REALWORLD ECONOMICS 4.2

A bug's life

A key question facing society is the use of scarce resources. Do we fully recognise the potential of the resources that we possess, in order to satisfy our wants? Is scarcity, in part, caused by our failure to exploit fully our resources? A recent article in the *Economist* examined the influence of culture on how resources are viewed as suitable. For example, India has an estimated 300 million cows, but for religious reasons they are not consumed by humans. Humans in the west avoid eating bugs, as a rule, but there are many available for consumption.

Around 2 billion people of the world's 7 billion population eat insects regularly. Insects often rival traditional livestock products, such as beef and pork, in terms of nutrition, and yet few westerners see insects as a way of overcoming scarcity.

Figures 4.1 to 4.3 summarise some of the key comparisons between eating insects and eating traditional livestock.

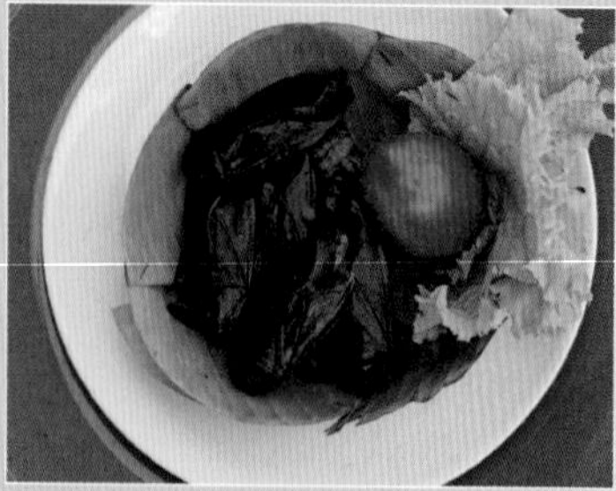

Fried insects sold at a roadside stall in Chiang Mai, Thailand

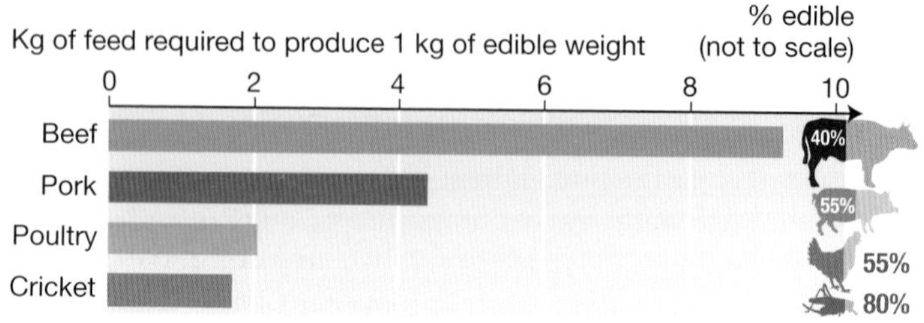

Kg of feed required to produce 1 kg of edible weight

% edible (not to scale)

0 2 4 6 8 10

Beef 40%

Pork 55%

Poultry 55%

Cricket 80%

Figure 4.1

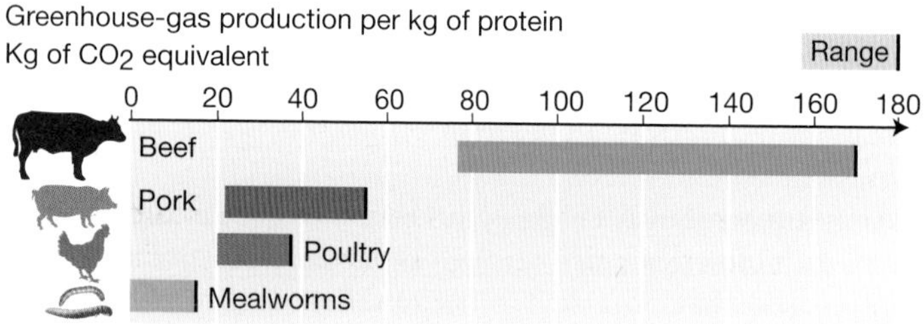

Greenhouse-gas production per kg of protein

Kg of CO_2 equivalent

Range

0 20 40 60 80 100 120 140 160 180

Beef

Pork

Poultry

Mealworms

Figure 4.2

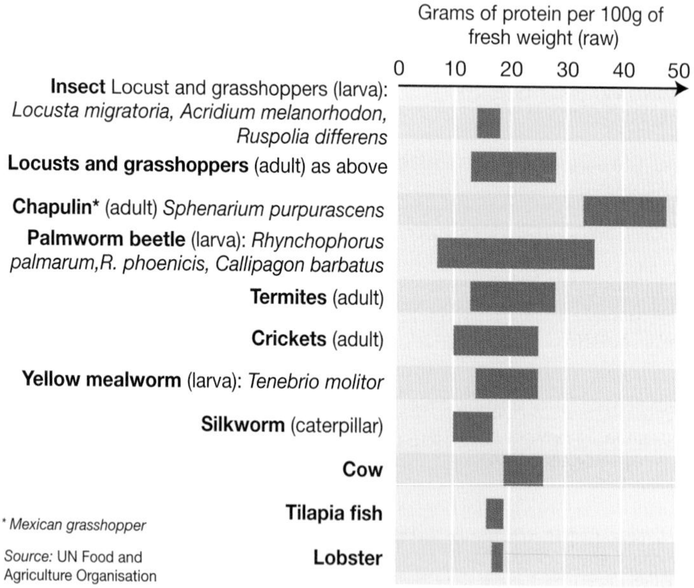

Grams of protein per 100g of fresh weight (raw)

0 10 20 30 40 50

Insect Locust and grasshoppers (larva): *Locusta migratoria, Acridium melanorhodon, Ruspolia differens*

Locusts and grasshoppers (adult) as above

Chapulin* (adult) *Sphenarium purpurascens*

Palmworm beetle (larva): *Rhynchophorus palmarum, R. phoenicis, Callipagon barbatus*

Termites (adult)

Crickets (adult)

Yellow mealworm (larva): *Tenebrio molitor*

Silkworm (caterpillar)

Cow

Tilapia fish

Lobster

** Mexican grasshopper*

Source: UN Food and Agriculture Organisation

Figure 4.3

Source: Economist, Daily Chart on 29.09.14.

Resources have alternative uses

Most resources can be used to satisfy a variety of wants. People can be trained to carry out a wide range of different jobs and thus their labour can be adapted to different purposes according to changes in wants. Entrepreneurs can also adapt their skills, with many business leaders changing jobs to completely different industries in their personal quest to achieve greater rewards. Some capital, such as a light, has no real alternative use, but the components of a light can be used for alternative purposes. Natural resources can also be varied in their use; in fact, land fertility is often improved through regular changes in its usage. Even a basic product, such as a potato, can be adapted so that it can be eaten in many different forms and meals. It is also used in some milkshakes and as a food product for livestock.

How scarce resources are allocated between different uses

Society has to choose between the alternative uses of resources. Which use or uses will satisfy the greatest wants? Which combination of uses is most desirable for society? This may lead to some resources that are well suited to a particular use actually being used for a different purpose. For example, the London area contains some very fertile soil, but the area is not used very much for agricultural purposes because it meets far more wants when used for commercial purposes. Agriculture can be located in other parts of the UK (or the world, as we live in a global economy) that are less suitable for commercial purposes.

In most cases, market forces will make decisions on how scarce resources are allocated – Adam Smith described this as the 'invisible hand' guiding economic activity in order to satisfy people's wants. For example, we have seen how UK wants have moved away from products such as alcohol and tobacco towards leisure and travel services. The sequence of events is shown in Figure 4.4.

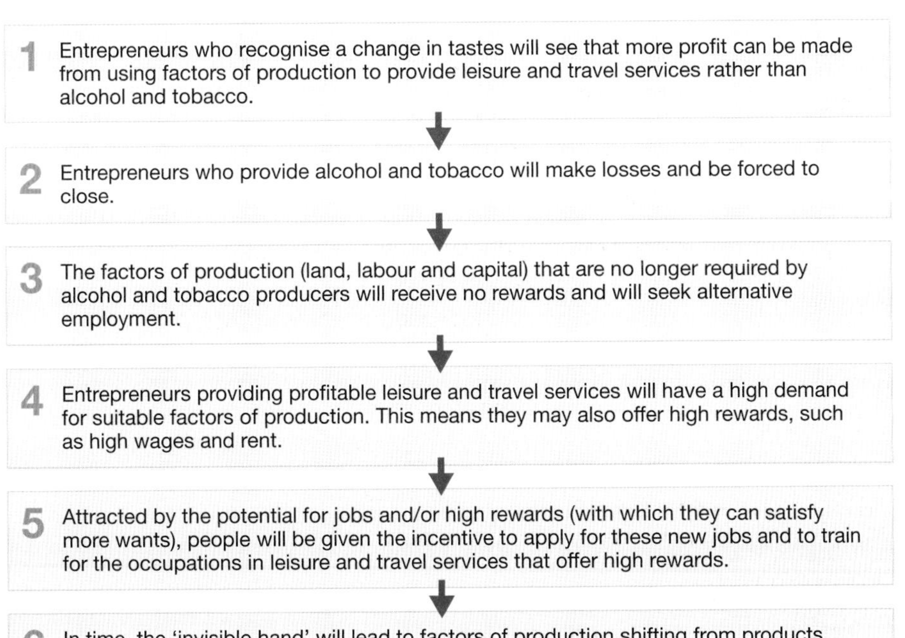

Figure 4.4 *The 'invisible hand' at work: the shift from alcohol and tobacco to leisure and travel services*

Figure 4.4 assumes that all decisions are based on market forces. In the UK we have a mixed economy in which the government intervenes where it feels this is appropriate. In the example given, there has been government influence. The UK government has generated negative publicity, passed laws and imposed high taxes in order to discourage use of tobacco and alcohol, and so the market has been influenced by government action. Furthermore, government has decided to provide certain services that would be underprovided by the market, such as education, health and roads. Less than 5% of 'average household spending' in the UK is on education and health because these services are offered freely by the government. (This figure under-estimates the scale of private health and education because the government's survey of 'average household spending' excludes very high and very low income families.)

Other areas in which government decisions influence the allocation of resources include law and order, defence and the environment.

The market mechanism also tackles the problem of scarcity by encouraging enterprise to find the most efficient way of using the factors of production. Improving efficiency leads to greater profit for enterprise and gives entrepreneurs higher rewards. The other factors of production can improve their rewards too, because if they are more efficient then they are more valuable to entrepreneurs. Increases in efficiency have led to significant increases in the number of goods and services produced in western economies. Table 4.2 shows how UK GDP (a measure of the goods and services produced in the UK) has increased over the last 60 years.

Table 4.2 *UK GDP and GDP per person, 1953–2013 (based on 2010 price levels)*

Year	Value of GDP (£ million), at 2010 price levels	Percentage growth per decade	GDP per head (£), at 2010 price levels	Percentage growth per decade
1953	323,560	n/a	6306	n/a
1963	436,653	35.0	8135	28.5
1973	625,423	43.2	11,125	36.8
1983	705,198	12.8	12,519	12.5
1993	931,452	32.1	16,133	28.9
2003	1,371,948	47.3	21,997	36.3
2013	1,525,955	11.2	23,113	5.1

Source: Guardian and Office for National Statistics

Choices have an opportunity cost

Key term

Opportunity cost is the next best alternative that was given up when making a choice.

People's needs and wants are unlimited – people and organisations always want more than they have. However, the resources available to satisfy those wants (the factors of production) are limited, and so it is not possible to satisfy every want. This means that choice is a key element of economics. Individuals will choose between different products to buy and between different careers to pursue; firms will choose which products to supply and which factors of production to use; and governments will choose when to intervene in the economy in order to improve economic welfare.

Choice involves sacrifice – selecting an option means rejecting an alternative option. Opportunity cost is a very important factor in economics. Opportunity cost applies to any purchasing decision – the choice between an orange and a banana, or between a house extension or a new car, are both examples of opportunity cost. In the former example, if the orange is chosen, the banana is the opportunity cost. Opportunity cost applies to any decisions – whether to get up or stay in bed, to complete homework or chat to friends. Firms decide on which products to make and which ones not to make; the decision to open a new store in London may mean sacrificing the choice to open in Birmingham. Governments must decide on which public services should be expanded and which should be cut (or they may decide that the best alternative is to cut taxes and cut more public services). Owners of factors of production, such as labour, must choose between jobs and also make decisions on the number of hours to work and the number of hours for leisure time.

Goods subject to scarcity are known as economic goods. If there is no scarcity of a good, such as air, it is a free good. In the case of free goods there is no opportunity cost, as society can satisfy wants without giving up an alternative product.

Discussion point
Is air always a free good? Can you think of a situation in which air is an economic good, subject to scarcity?

Review questions

Total: 40 marks

1 Select the statement that is true.
A Human wants are limited
B Resources have a specific use
C Means are unlimited
D Wants vary in importance *(1 mark)*

2 Select the statement that is false. The satisfaction of people's wants:
A Creates happiness
B Is followed by a desire for more wants
C Can be fully achieved
D Uses scarce resources *(1 mark)*

3 Select the statement that is true. A 'free good' is any product that is:
A Used to satisfy basic needs
B Sold at a zero price
C Not subject to scarcity
D Provided by renewable resources *(1 mark)*

4 In a market economy, explain how consumers express their want for a product. *(4 marks)*

5 Explain how capital consumption affects the value of the stock of capital in an economy. *(4 marks)*

6 Explain how the concept of opportunity cost can be applied to:
(a) Consumer wants *(2 marks)*
(b) The allocation of resources *(2 marks)*

7 Explain the process by which the market economy decides on how scarce resources are allocated. *(6 marks)*

8 State three reasons why a government might intervene in a market economy. *(3 marks)*

9 Using the data in Figures 4.1 to 4.3, indicate why insects might be a better source of food than traditional livestock, such as cattle. *(8 marks)*

10 Based on the data in Table 4.2, why might the decade beginning 1963 claim to be more successful in helping the UK population satisfy its wants than the decade beginning 1993? *(8 marks)*

Exam-style essay questions

Total: 25 marks

1 Using the data and information in the chapter, evaluate the view that the more efficient use of resources has been the main factor in solving the basic economic problem of scarcity in the UK since the Second World War. ***(25 marks)***

OR

2 Discuss the extent to which the UK has resolved the problem of scarcity. ***(25 marks)***

Production possibility diagrams

This chapter investigates the concept of production possibility and the use of production possibility diagrams in economic analysis. The logic of the production possibility diagram and the shape of the production possibility boundary are explained. The chapter then examines the main uses of production possibility diagrams, demonstrating how they can be used to show resource allocation, opportunity cost and tradeoffs, unemployment of economic resources and economic growth. The chapter concludes with an introduction to economic efficiency in the form of allocative efficiency and productive efficiency, and shows how the latter can be shown on a production possibility diagram.

Using the production possibility diagram

Figure 5.1 shows the maximum possible combinations of peas and carrots that Langdon's Farm can produce in a year. If the farm focuses wholly on peas, it can produce 90 units of peas per annum. This is shown by Point A on the production possibility diagram. If the farm focuses wholly on carrots, it can produce 120 units of carrots per annum. This is shown by Point E on the production possibility diagram.

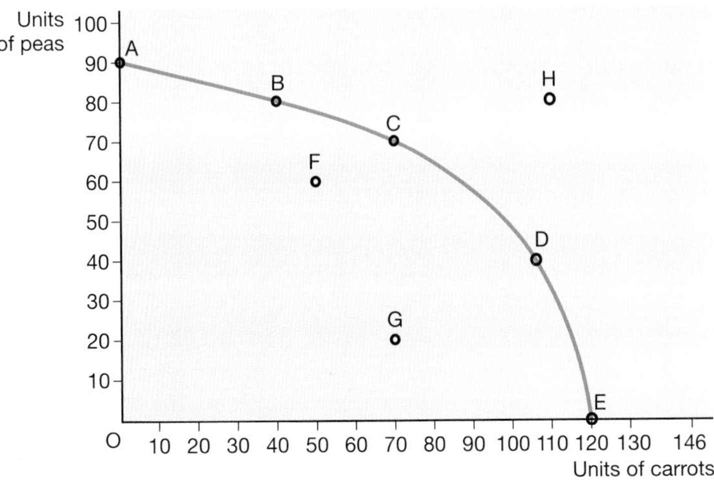

Figure 5.1 *Production possibility diagram of Langdon's Farm*

If the farm chooses to produce both carrots and peas, it can produce a variety of combinations. Examples are shown by points B, C and D. Point B shows the situation where the farm has concentrated mainly on peas but devoted some of its resources to the production of carrots. At Point B, total production is 80 units of peas and 40

Key term

A **production possibility diagram** shows the maximum combination of products (goods and services) that can be provided by an economy or a firm during a given period of time with the resources available.

units of carrots. Point D shows the result of Langdon's Farm concentrating mainly on carrot production. At Point D total production is 106 units of carrots and 40 units of peas. Point C shows a situation where carrots and peas are produced in equal quantities, with 70 units of both peas and carrots being produced.

The line ABCDE is known as the **production possibility boundary (PPB), production possibility frontier (PPF)** or **production possibility curve (PPC)** because it represents all of the possible maximum combinations of production. The farm can choose any position along this line (such as the point where 60 units of peas and 86 units of carrots are produced).

The shape of the production possibility boundary

The production possibility boundary is a curved line because the entrepreneur will want to use scarce resources as effectively as possible. At Point A, all factors of production are devoted to the production of peas. However, the farm may possess some resources that are much more effective in the production of carrots. If the decision is taken to produce 40 units of carrots, the farmer will use those resources that are most suited to carrot production and least-suited to pea production. Point B shows that producing 40 units of carrots still leaves enough resources to produce 80 units of peas. By moving from Point A to Point B, a gain of 40 carrots is made with a loss of only 10 units of peas.

Similar logic applies to the shift from Point E to Point D. At Point E the farm would have been using some unsuitable resources in carrot production. By freeing these resources to make peas, which means shifting from Point E to Point D, a gain of 40 units of peas is made with a loss of only 14 units of carrots.

As the production possibility line moves to the centre, the losses/gains become more even, assuming the firm's overall mix of resources is fairly evenly suited to each of the two products.

> **Key note**
>
> The notion of possibility production can apply to a wide range of alternative products, to show the possible combinations of products provided by a firm or economy. For practical reasons, production possibility is usually shown as a relationship between two different categories or products, so that it can be displayed in the form of a diagram.

Production possibility diagrams and resource allocation

The production possibility diagram shows resource allocation by indicating the possible outcomes from given resources. In Figure 5.1, we saw the alternative outcomes arising from the combination of resources used by Langdon's Farm. But what is the best possible allocation of resources arising from the farm?

Ideally a firm or government will want to maximise the level of production. The boundary or frontier (line ABCDE) shows five different options that represent scarce resources being used to achieve the highest possible combinations of production.

Point H would appear to be ideal because it shows high levels of both peas and carrots. However, since it is beyond the production possibility boundary it represents a combination of peas and carrots that is impossible to reach, using the current level of resources and existing production techniques.

Points F and G are undesirable because they are within the boundary. This may happen because some resources are not being used (such as unemployed labour) or the resources are not being used effectively. It is always possible to find a point on the boundary that is better than any given point inside the boundary. In Figure 5.1, Point C is better than Point F because it represents more peas and more carrots. Similarly, Point D is better than Point G.

Therefore the best position is a point *on* the production possibility boundary. The exact point depends on factors such as the total production level, whether resources are more effective in producing one product than the other, and the relative value of the different products. Total production tends to be maximised towards the middle of the production possibility boundary, but if peas are much more valuable than carrots, then we will want to produce relatively more peas. In Figure 5.1 the diagram shows that resources are more effective at producing a unit of carrots than a unit of peas. If this applies to the whole economy, it might mean that peas are scarcer and therefore have a higher price than carrots.

Key note

The ideal resource allocation depends on both the efficiency with which resources can be used to produce different products and the value that consumers place on different products.

Table 5.1 illustrates the value of different combinations of output at different price levels for peas and carrots.

Table 5.1 *Value of total production at different price levels*

Position on PPB	Value (£) if: peas = £1 per unit carrots = £1 per unit	Value (£) if: peas = £1 per unit carrots = £2 per unit	Value (£) if: peas = £2 per unit carrots = £1 per unit
A	90 (90 + 0)	90 (90 + 0)	180 (180 + 0)
B	120 (80 + 40)	160 (80 + 80)	200 (160 + 40)
C	140 (70 + 70)	210 (70 + 140)	210 (140 + 70)
D	146 (40 + 106)	252 (40 + 212)	186 (80 + 106)
E	120 (0 + 120)	240 (0 + 240)	120 (0 + 120)

- It can be seen that if peas and carrots are both £1 per unit, then D is the best combination of the five shown (C is second best).
- It can be seen that if peas are £1 per unit and carrots are £2 per unit, then D is still the best combination of the five shown (but E is now second best).
- It can be seen that if peas are £2 per unit and carrots are £1 per unit, then C is the best combination of the five shown (but B is now second best).

Production possibility diagrams showing opportunity cost and tradeoffs

Production possibility diagrams can also illustrate opportunity cost. The production possibility boundary traces the sacrifice (or reduction) of carrots, as pea production expands (and vice versa). In the section above, we saw that with peas and carrots both at £1 per unit, D is the best combination of the five shown and C is the next best alternative.

In Figure 5.1, we can see that Point D shows production of 40 units of peas *and* 106 units of carrots. The next best alternative (Point C) is the opportunity cost. This shows production of 70 units of peas *and* 70 units of carrots. If the farmer decides to produce at Point D rather than Point C, we move from Point C to Point D. The movement from C to D leads to an increase of carrots from 70 units to 106 units. However, Point D shows that pea production has fallen from 70 units to 40 units. In order to gain 36 extra units of carrots (106 – 70), the opportunity cost has been the loss of 30 units of peas (70 – 40). This can be calculated as 1.2 units of carrots gained for the loss of every unit of peas (36/30 = 1.2).

These tradeoffs were illustrated in the previous section when prices changed:

- With peas at £1 per unit and carrots at £2 per unit, D is still the best combination of the five shown but E is now the second best alternative. Point E shows zero units of peas and 120 units of carrots, whilst Point D shows 40 units of peas and 106 units of carrots. In order to obtain 40 extra units of peas (40 – 0), we have sacrificed 14 units of carrots (120 – 106). In this case, 40/14 = 2.86 units of peas have been gained for the loss of every unit of carrots.
- With peas at £2 per unit and carrots at £1 per unit, C is the best combination of the five shown but B is now the second best alternative. Point B shows 80 units of peas and 40 units of carrots, while Point C shows 70 units of peas and 70 units of carrots. In order to obtain 30 extra units of carrots (70 – 40), we have sacrificed 10 units of peas (80 – 70). This ratio shows 3 units of carrots gained for every unit of peas that has been sacrificed.

Production possibility diagrams and unemployment of economic resources

Production possibility diagrams can also illustrate unemployment or inefficient use of economic resources. In Figure 5.1, points F and G show that output is not on the production possibility boundary. This means that economic resources are not being fully utilised.

An approximation of the level of unemployment or underuse of resources can be gained from the diagram. Point F shows significant levels of unemployment but is reasonably close to the boundary. Point G is a long way from the boundary and demonstrates a situation in which unemployment is very high and/or resources are very underused.

In a market economy there are financial incentives for resources to be used effectively and so, in theory, production should be on or close to the boundary. In practice, this can be difficult to achieve because factors of production are immobile and do not always easily move between roles. Furthermore, in recent years economists have noted that employment levels have remained higher than expected when spending levels were low or falling. Some economists believe that this is because firms are keeping people in jobs since they know they will need their skills when the economy grows in the future. They are sacrificing short-term profits for future profits.

Production possibility diagrams and economic growth

Figure 5.2 is based on Figure 5.1, with points A to H being identical to those in Figure 5.1. Over time the production possibility boundary shifts. In the case of a firm, this may arise from new production techniques or the firm finding a more efficient way of combining the factors of production available to it. It may also have been caused by an increase in the factors of production at the firm's disposal. For an economy, the same factors apply. If sufficient firms are using better techniques, this will increase the efficiency of the economy as a whole, shifting the production possibility boundary to the right. Population increases, the creation of more capital goods, the use of new natural resources and a desire amongst more people to be entrepreneurs will all contribute to a shift of production possibility to the right.

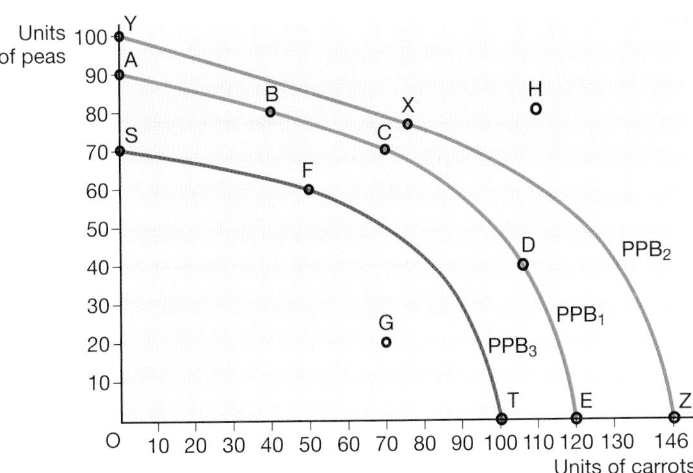

Figure 5.2 *Growth on a production possibility diagram*

The production possibility can also shift to the left. This occurs when demand for products is falling. This leads to falling rewards for factors of production and so owners will offer fewer of them for production purposes. With less enterprise, labour, capital and land, UK output will fall, moving the production possibility boundary to the left.

The line PPB_1 (joining points ABCDE) in Figure 5.2 shows the original production possibility boundary. The line PPB_2 shows growth, with greater levels of output becoming possible. If all of the farm's resources are devoted to pea production (see Point Y), then 100 units of peas are produced (compared to 90 units for PPB_1). Similarly, focusing purely on carrots (see Point Z) will now lead to 146 units of production (compared to 120 units for PPB_1). If production is divided evenly between peas and carrots, then 76 units of both peas and carrots can be produced (compared to 70 units for PPB_1).

'Economic growth' can be negative, when output declines. For the farm, this is shown by line PPB_3. The maximum output of peas is only 70 units (Point S), while the maximum output of carrots is 100 units (Point T).

Economic growth for a country can be caused by factors such as:

- increasing the quantity of factors of production (e.g. new oil discoveries);
- improving the quality of factors of production (e.g. trained workers);
- introducing new technology and techniques that improve business efficiency;
- adopting a long-term growth strategy (e.g. switching some production from consumer goods to capital goods).

Why all points on the boundary are productively efficient but not allocatively efficient

In order to try to resolve the problem of scarcity, an economy must achieve two main goals:

- use its resources to produce the maximum possible output;
- ensure that the goods and services produced are satisfying consumer wants as much as possible.

The achievement of these two goals is a sign of an **efficient** economy. In this context, there are two measures used by economists: **productive efficiency** and **allocative efficiency.**

Key terms

Productive efficiency measures how well an economy or firm uses its resources to produce outputs.

Allocative efficiency means that resources are being used to produce the goods and services that consumers wish to buy.

In order to maximise rewards, all factors of production will be used in the most efficient way possible to produce combinations of goods. This means that individual firms will operate in a manner that achieves **productive efficiency**. In a free market economy, everyone has access to all information and so improvements in manufacturing techniques will be shared by all firms and organisations. The production possibility boundary shows a situation where all resources are fully used.

This means that points on the production possibility boundary show situations in which individual firms use resources in the most productive manner possible *and* it shows situations in which all resources are fully employed. *Any point on the production possibility boundary therefore shows a situation in which productive efficiency is maximised.*

This means that in Figure 5.2, points A, B, C, D and E are all examples of situations in which productive efficiency is achieved when the production possibility boundary is PPB_1. When the production possibility boundary changes to PPB_2, points Y, X and Z represent possible examples of productive efficiency. Any point within the boundary (such as G) shows that there are unemployed resources, and so it is evident that resources are not being used to maximise production levels.

Allocative efficiency means that resources are being used to produce the goods and services that consumers wish to buy. It thus depends on the values placed on different products.

When considering opportunity cost, we saw that the optimum allocation of resources can change. When looking at line PPB_1 in Figure 5.2, we saw that if peas and carrots are valued equally, then Point D is superior to Point C because it provides higher value to consumers overall. Closer investigation suggests that a slight movement to the left of Point D might improve the allocation of resources still further, as the total of goods produced will be higher (and they are all valued at £1).

When values (prices offered) for products change, allocative efficiency changes because the previous allocation of resources may no longer be geared towards satisfying the greatest wants. However, it must be recognised that more resources are being allocated if the firm or economy operates at its production possibility boundary. *There is one single point at which allocative efficiency is maximised, and this can and will change. This point will be on the production possibility boundary but the remaining points on the boundary will not be allocatively efficient.*

Number crunching *Total: 10 marks*

A firm produces two products, X and Y. The table shows five combinations (1 to 5) of X and Y that are on the firm's production possibility boundary.

Combination	Product X	Product Y
1	40	0
2	33	14
3	24	25
4	13	31
5	0	33

1 Calculate the opportunity cost of moving from Combination 1 to Combination 2. *(2 marks)*
2 Calculate the opportunity cost of moving from Combination 5 to Combination 3. *(2 marks)*
3 Which combination would you choose, and why? *(6 marks)*

REALWORLD ECONOMICS 5.1

Consumer goods and capital goods

It is not possible to draw a real-life production possibility boundary because, over a given period of time, the economy only shows one combination of outputs. For economies, as opposed to firms, it is common practice to use diagrams presenting consumer goods and capital goods as the two main categories of products provided.

Table 5.2 shows the various combinations of consumer goods and capital goods produced in the UK in recent years. In order to allow a more objective comparison over time, all of the outputs have been converted to their value at the price level in 2005.

Please note that these figures are not a complete representation of the UK economy, as they exclude elements such as government spending and goods traded between the UK and other countries.

A number of points can be concluded from these data.

- Capital goods are usually between 26% and 28% of consumer spending.
- This ratio peaked in 2007, when capital spending reached its highest level of 29.6%. The ratio recorded its lowest level of 24.9% in 2009.
- Unemployment rose dramatically in the recession of 2009, with an increase of 750,000 people unemployed. Unemployment also rose between 2010 and 2012, even though total spending was increasing slightly.
- The largest change in total spending on these categories of goods was in 2009, when total spending fell by £60 billion.
- The fall in capital goods in 2009 was greater than the fall in consumer spending.
- The highest positive change was a growth in total spending of £37 billion in 2007.
- Although total spending peaked in 2007, consumer spending was at its highest in 2013 and 2008.
- Capital spending in 2013 was still lower than it was in 2007.

Table 5.2 *Annual output of consumer goods and capital goods produced in the UK, 2001–13*[1]

	Consumer goods (£ billion)	Capital goods (£ billion)	Total (£ billion)	Capital goods as a percentage of consumer goods (%)	Mid-year unemployment (millions)
2001	695	186	881	26.8	1.55
2002	720	193	913	26.8	1.47
2003	743	195	938	26.2	1.54
2004	767	205	972	26.7	1.43
2005	784	210	994	26.8	1.43
2006	796	223	1019	28.0	1.70
2007	815	241	1056	29.6	1.64
2008	822	232	1054	28.2	1.72
2009	796	198	994	24.9	2.47
2010	799	209	1008	26.2	2.48
2011	799	214	1013	26.8	2.53
2012	811	216	1027	*See Exercise 1*	2.59
2013	824	223	1047	27.1	2.51

Note: (1) All of the outputs have been converted to their value at the price level in 2005.

Exercises — *Total: 20 marks*

1. Calculate capital goods expenditure as a percentage of consumer goods expenditure in 2012. *(2 marks)*
2. Identify two significant points of comparison in Table 5.2. *(4 marks)*
3. Explain why all the data are based on the price level of one particular year. *(4 marks)*
4. What evidence is there to suggest that the economy in 2013 is not achieving productive efficiency? *(4 marks)*
5. Explain why capital goods as a percentage of consumer goods fell to its lowest level in 2009. *(6 marks)*

Review questions

Total: 30 marks

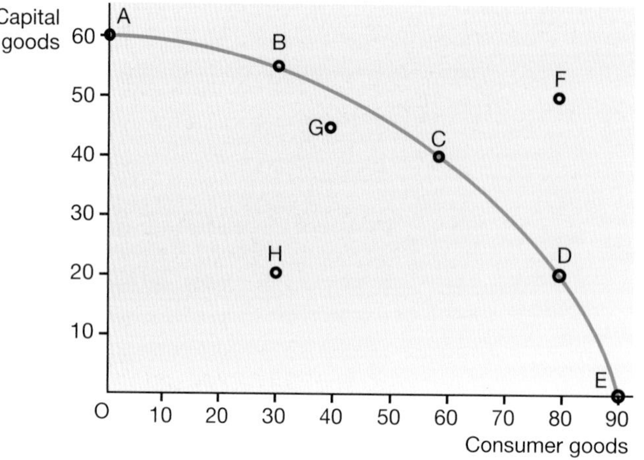

Figure 5.3 *A production possibility diagram*

1 Select the statement that is true. Figure 5.3 shows that:

A Fewer resources are used at A than at B

B Point A shows productive inefficiency because no capital goods are produced

C Moving from C to D shows that 22 units of consumer goods are being sacrificed for 20 units of capital goods

D Point H is both productively and allocatively inefficient ***(1 mark)***

2 As we move along the production possibility curve from Point A to Point E in Figure 5.3, the opportunity cost of additional consumer goods in terms of capital goods:

A Continually decreases

B Continually increases

C Decreases and then increases

D Increases and then decreases ***(1 mark)***

3 With reference to Figure 5.3, which statement is *true*?

A Point G is not possible to reach

B Points F, G and H all show unemployed resources

C Points B, C and D all show allocative efficiency

D Points A and E both show productive efficiency ***(1 mark)***

4 Define the term 'production possibility'. ***(3 marks)***

5 Explain the concept of 'opportunity cost' using Figure 5.3. ***(6 marks)***

6 Explain how 'unemployment' is shown on a production possibility diagram. ***(3 marks)***

7 Explain the difference between 'productive efficiency' and 'allocative efficiency'. ***(6 marks)***

8 Explain, with the help of a diagram, why all points on the production possibility boundary are productively efficient but not all points on the boundary are allocatively efficient. ***(9 marks)***

Topic 1 **Exam-style questions**

AS LEVEL PAPER 1

Total: 50 marks

Context – High-Speed 2 (HS2)

Extract A **Use of different modes of transport in the UK, 1952–2012**

	Billions of passenger miles per annum using:				
Year	Bus/coach	Car/van	Cycle	Rail	Air
1952	92	58	23	38	0
1962	74	171	9	37	0
1972	60	327	4	34	2
1982	48	406	6	31	3
1992	43	583	5	38	5
2002	47	673	4	48	8
2012	42	643	5	70	8

Extract B **High Speed 2 (HS2)**

The government has proposed a high-speed rail link between London and Birmingham, to be opened in 2026. This will be followed by a V-shaped second section to Manchester and Leeds, to be completed by 2033. HS2 is expected to carry 300,000 people a day and cut journey times between some of the UK's major cities. It should also lead to more freight travelling by rail.

HS2 will relieve congestion on roads and other rail networks and improve connection times between some airports. However, the predicted cost has already risen from £32.7 billion to £42.6 billion and many query whether the benefits match this cost. KPMG estimates benefits of £1.40 for every £1 spent on the first section, rising to £1.90 after 2033. However, a government-commissioned report from engineers suggested that 'patching-up' the existing network would be cheaper and bring a return of £6 for every £1 spent. *Argument and opposing view 1*

KPMG concluded that in 2037 this would lead to growth in the West Midlands of about £2.3 billion in output, with significant gains in output in areas close to the improved rail network, such as the East Midlands, Greater Manchester and Leeds. London would increase output by 0.5%. However, the experience of countries such as France and South Korea suggests that the capital city tends to gain most, by widening the distances commuters can travel. All analysts agree that areas such as Wales, Scotland, the Southwest and Northeast will lose in relative terms, leading to more concentration of wealth and income in affluent areas. *Argument and opposing view 2*

One of the major benefits included in the economic case for HS2 is the saving of time and its value. KPMG estimated the value of time saved by using a survey conducted in 2003, at which time business people did little or no work on train journeys. However, since 2003 advances in technology have enabled people to undertake work and leisure activities while travelling, such that travellers now often value time travelled on a train and have less desire for journey times to be cut. Opponents argue that the benefits of HS2 have thus been exaggerated. *Argument and opposing view 3*

HS2 will reduce overcrowding on trains, with four out of the 10 most overcrowded trains using the existing line from Euston to Birmingham. The creation of a completely separate line will enable this overcrowding to be eliminated. However, opponents argue that London terminuses such as Waterloo, Paddington and Liverpool Street are all more overcrowded than Euston. *Argument and opposing view 4*

Extract C **HS2 and the environment**

Extract A shows how patterns of transport have changed since 1952. In a period of 60 years, road transport has increased 11-fold and air transport has risen by 8 billion passenger miles. Rail transport is considered to be much more energy efficient and thus more environmentally friendly. Its growth between 2002 and 2012 is likely to have been a major factor in encouraging the first-ever decline in road transport. It is estimated that HS2 will achieve a significant carbon saving over a 60-year period. However, HS2's 250 mph trains will use 50% more energy than Eurostar, and many critics point out the loss of 600 homes, 250 acres of green belt and areas of natural beauty as the environmental cost.

The overall value of the case depends on its opportunity cost. Could the money be spent more effectively elsewhere? Improvements to roads might yield better benefits, as might money spent on education, health or law enforcement. The final decision may be a value judgement based on political appeal rather than an objective, positive analysis of the economic case.

Questions

Total: 50 marks

1 Define the term 'opportunity cost'. *(3 marks)*

2 KPMG estimated the original cost of the project to be £32.7 billion and estimated benefits of £1.90 per £1 of cost. Calculate the expected total benefit and expected net benefit (total benefit minus cost) of HS2. *(4 marks)*

3 Using Extract A, identify two significant points of comparison in the level of use of different forms of transport since 1952. *(4 marks)*

4 The production possibility boundary in Figure A below shows UK output of goods and services according to geographical areas. Redraw the production possibility boundary to show the impact of the HS2 project. *(4 marks)*

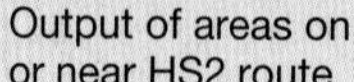

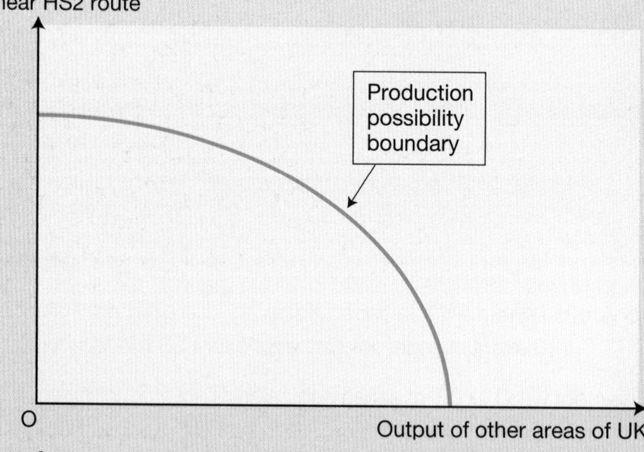

Figure A

5 Explain why the eventual decision on whether to approve the HS2 project is likely to rely on a combination of both positive and normative judgements. *(10 marks)*

6 Using your own knowledge and understanding of economic issues, assess whether the government should go ahead with the HS2 project. *(25 marks)*

Topic 2

Price determination in a competitive market

The determinants of the demand for goods & services

This chapter introduces the concept of demand and investigates the factors that influence the demand for goods and services, focusing on price, income, wealth, the price of substitutes and complements, and individual preferences. The demand curve is introduced and its shape explained. Movements along the demand curve are considered. The chapter concludes by looking at the determinants of demand and the ways in which changes in these determinants lead to changes in demand curves.

Demand

Key term

Demand is the amount of a good or service that consumers in a market are willing and able to buy at any given price over a period of time.

- **Market demand** relates to all consumers in a market and so the key term definition refers to market demand. A market is 'a place where buyers and sellers meet'. This includes street markets and shopping centres, but may be global, such as the market for foreign currency. Markets may not involve a physical place, since in many markets buyers and sellers 'meet' online.
- **Individual demand** is 'the amount of a good or service that an individual consumer is willing and able to buy at any given price over a period of time'.

Features of demand

Demand is:

- a measure of the number of items. Changes in demand are shown by 'x' more or 'y' fewer products being required by consumers.
- based on both willingness and ability to buy. Wishing for a product is *not* demand – demand requires both willingness and the finances needed to purchase a good or service. For this reason, economists often describe 'demand' as **'effective demand'**, to emphasise that consumers must have the ability to pay for the good.
- measured over a period of time. When discussing demand it is important to recognise the time period being considered. For some products, such as bread, demand can be measured daily; for other products, it is more useful to refer to weekly, monthly or annual demand.

The quantity demanded of a particular product may be influenced by a wide range of factors, some of which may be unique to that particular product. However, there are a number of factors that influence the demand for most products. These are considered below.

Key note

Economists often make assumptions when analysing situations, and investigating demand is no exception. Two important assumptions that are made are as follows:

- Consumers are rational. They will make decisions that will maximise their individual welfare. If this logic is applied to the market, then all consumers in the market act logically.
- Other things remain equal (ceteris paribus). 'Ceteris paribus' is a Latin phrase which means that while investigating a specific situation or relationship, all other factors that might influence that relationship remain unchanged. In practical terms, it can be difficult to isolate the impact of a particular factor, but this assumption is needed to enable economists to recognise the impact of each individual factor.

The factors that determine the demand for a good or service

Price and the quantity demanded

The **law of demand** states that 'as the price of a good rises, quantity demanded falls, and as the price of a good falls, the quantity demanded rises'.

Price is a major influence on the quantity demanded. Logically, the more units of a product that a consumer buys, the less satisfaction each additional unit provides for the consumer. For example, if someone is very thirsty, the first glass of water gives a great deal of satisfaction as it is needed to quench the thirst. A second glass may also help, but the main thirst has been quenched and so it gives less satisfaction than the first glass. A third glass is unlikely to provide much satisfaction, but may give some satisfaction as it can help the consumer's hydration. A fourth glass is unlikely to provide any satisfaction to the consumer.

A rational consumer will only buy a product if the amount of satisfaction it gives is equal to or greater than the price charged. In the instance above, the consumer may be prepared to pay £2 for the first glass of water as it provides a great deal of satisfaction. The second glass is worth less than the first glass, say 50 pence, as it helps to quench the remaining thirst. The third glass may be valued at 10 pence, as it provides some satisfaction. If the fourth glass provides no additional satisfaction, then the consumer will value it at zero pence.

This logic applies to the individual's demand. However, as the UK market consists of about 60 million consumers, each making rational decisions, then market demand will follow the same pattern, with rising prices leading to lower demand and falling prices leading to higher demand.

The impact of price on demand will vary with different products and circumstances. For some products, a higher price may lead to a dramatic fall in the quantity demanded. For this type of product, a lower price is likely to result in a dramatic rise in the quantity demanded. For other products, the quantity demanded will stay at similar levels even when price changes are quite large. The exact impact of price on the quantity demanded will be looked at in more detail in Chapter 7.

Income and the quantity demanded

A person's income is usually based on the number of hours worked or in the form of an annual salary. The actual payment is usually made monthly or weekly.

Key term

Income is a flow of earnings paid to labour over a period of time.

Consumer incomes are a major influence on the quantity demanded. Demand is based on willingness, but also on the ability to pay. An individual with a high income will usually have a greater ability to pay than someone on a low income. Economists often focus on household incomes rather than individual incomes. A household of two adults and three children and a total income of £30,000 per annum will have less ability to pay than an individual living alone with the same level of income.

Economists often use 'disposable income' as the most appropriate measure of income. **Disposable income** is the level of income after the deduction of tax and national insurance payments. This is used because it represents the amount of money available for spending more accurately than **gross income** – the individual's income before tax and national insurance payments. This means that consumers' disposable incomes are influenced by government. If the government increases income tax and/or national insurance payments, there will be a decrease in consumers' disposable incomes. This is likely to lead to a fall in market demand for most products. However, if the government decreases income tax and/or national insurance payments, there will be an increase in consumers' disposable incomes, and so market demand for most goods will rise.

The impact of income on the quantity demanded varies according to the product and circumstances:

- Luxury products, such as Rolls-Royce cars and holiday cruises, are expensive and more likely to be purchased by people with high incomes. As a rule, higher incomes lead to significant increases in the quantity demanded of luxury products.
- Standard, mid-range products tend to appeal to people on middle incomes. In general, increases in income lead to similar increases in the quantity demanded.
- Some cheap products mainly appeal to people on low incomes, who are more likely to focus on purchasing cheap alternatives. As their incomes rise, consumers will tend to buy fewer of these items because they can now afford to buy better alternatives. Products where an increase in income leads to a fall in the quantity demanded are known as **inferior goods**.

For the economy as a whole, the distribution of income is also an important influence on market demand. The **distribution of income** is a comparison of the current income levels of inhabitants of a country or community. An unequal distribution leads to inequality and occurs when there are large differences in incomes between inhabitants of a country. In countries with widespread inequality between incomes, there are likely to be large numbers of people demanding the basic needs for survival, such as food and shelter. Those people with the very high incomes will demand expensive luxuries. In countries with greater equality, these two extreme markets are likely to experience lower levels of demand.

Some economists, notably Milton Friedman, take the view that current income is not the major influence on demand. His argument is based on his '**permanent income hypothesis**'. This idea states that spending in any one year is not related to the current income in that year but to the overall permanent income that will be received by that person over their expected lifetime. For example, a university student will spend more than their income and so build up debts. Once their career progresses they spend less than their income, in order to pay off their debts. At the peak of their earning power they will save significant sums, so that they can build up enough savings to enjoy a reasonable pension/income during their retirement. This theory suggests that demand is spread more evenly over a person's lifetime, rather than fluctuating in direct proportion to the income being earned in each year of a person's life.

The impact of income on the quantity demanded will be looked at in more detail in Chapter 7.

Wealth and the quantity demanded

Wealth may take the form of cash, bank deposits and ownership of company shares, or household goods – such as furniture and appliances, cars and property. It may be obtained through inheritance or through the accumulation of assets over a lifetime. As with a person on a high income, a wealthy individual should be able to demand more goods and services. This is because they have access to assets that can be converted into cash (or may already be in the form of cash) in order to buy products. However, the impact of wealth on demand will vary according to the individual's circumstances. An individual with a low income but considerable wealth in the form of property may struggle because the upkeep and maintenance of the property may involve high expenditure.

Key term

Wealth is a stock of assets owned by an individual or organisation.

Illiquid assets are assets that cannot be easily turned into cash without loss or delay. A person whose wealth is in the form of property, or share certificates at a time when share prices are low, may not find it easy or sensible to convert their assets into money. Consequently, their wealth may not be easy to use in order to demand products. In contrast, an individual holding their wealth in the form of **liquid assets** (assets that can be easily turned into cash without loss or delay) will be able to use their wealth to buy products. Thus wealth in the form of cash and bank deposits will have a much bigger influence on demand than wealth held in illiquid assets.

For the economy as a whole, the distribution of wealth is also an important influence on market demand. The **distribution of wealth** is a comparison of the value of the stock of assets held by inhabitants of a country or community. In the UK, as with most countries, the distribution of wealth is more unequal than the distribution of income.

Price of substitutes and the quantity demanded

Examples of substitutes are:

- strawberry jam and raspberry jam;
- orange juice and pineapple juice;
- a Samsung tablet and an Apple iPad;
- a holiday in the countryside or a beach holiday.

Key term

Substitutes are goods or services that can replace each other.

If Product A can be replaced by a substitute (Product B), then products A and B are substitutes. The price of Product B will therefore influence the quantity demanded of Product A. For example, people buying a daily newspaper may see the *Daily Express* and the *Daily Mail* as close substitutes. If the *Daily Mail* reduces its price, more people will want to buy it. As a result, some people will change from the *Daily Express* (which is now relatively expensive in comparison to its close substitute) to the *Daily Mail*. Thus the fall in the price of the *Daily Mail* has led to a decrease in the demand for the *Daily Express*.

Similarly, if the price of the *Daily Mail* rises, fewer people will want to buy it and some or many of these people will start to buy the *Daily Express* instead.

Conclusion: *A rise in the price of a product leads to an increase in the demand for a substitute of that product. A fall in the price of a product leads to a decrease in the demand for a substitute of that product.*

It is important to recognise that there are some products that have many possible substitutes. Newspapers such as the *Daily Telegraph* or the *Sun* might be substitutes for the *Daily Mail*; and some consumers may react to a price change by switching to or from different media, such as radio, online news or TV broadcasting.

Figure 6.1 shows the impact of a change in the price of a substitute on the quantity demanded of a product. Line BB shows the impact of a change in the price of Product B on the quantity demanded of Product A. When the price of Product B is 40 pence, consumers demand 60 units of Product A. A fall in the price of Product B from 40 pence to 20 pence leads to a fall in the quantity demanded of Product A from 60 units to 20 units. Similarly, a rise in the price of Product B to 60 pence leads to a rise in the quantity demanded of Product A to 100 units.

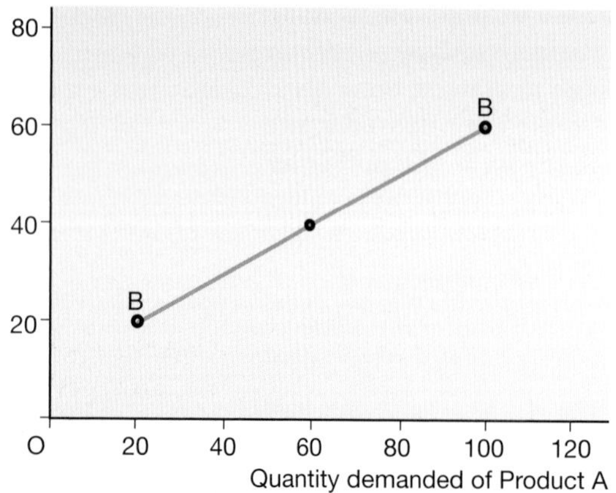

Figure 6.1 *The impact of the price of a substitute (Product B) on the quantity demanded of Product A*

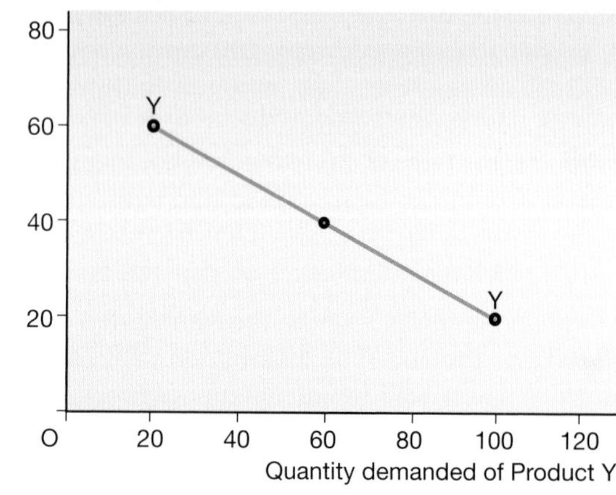

Figure 6.2 *The impact of the price of a complement (Product Z) on the quantity demanded of Product Y*

Where the two products are very close substitutes, the change in quantity demanded is likely to be much greater, for a given change in the price of the substitute, than if the two products are not always seen as substitutes for each other.

Key term

Complements are goods or services that are used alongside each other.

Price of complementary goods and the quantity demanded

Examples of complements are:

- strawberries and cream;
- tea and milk;
- a washing machine and washing powder;
- a cricket bat and cricket ball.

If Product Y is used alongside a complement (Product Z), then Products Y and Z are complements. The price of Product Z will therefore influence the quantity demanded of Product Y. For example, people buying milk will see a breakfast cereal, such as Corn Flakes, as a complement. If the price of Corn Flakes is reduced, more people will want to buy Corn Flakes. As a result, more people will want to buy milk to use with their Corn Flakes. Thus the fall in the price of Corn Flakes has led to an increase in the demand for milk.

Similarly, if the price of Corn Flakes rises, fewer people will want to buy Corn Flakes and so fewer people will buy milk.

Conclusion: *A rise in the price of a product leads to a decrease in the demand for a complement of that product. A fall in the price of a product leads to an increase in the demand for a complement of that product.*

It should be recognised that some products have many possible complements. For example, milk is also used with coffee and as an ingredient in many food dishes.

Figure 6.2 shows the impact of a change in the price of a complement on the quantity demanded of a product.

Line YY shows the impact of a change in the price of a complement (Product Z) on the quantity demanded of Product Y. When the price of Product Z is 40 pence, consumers demand 60 units of Product Y. A fall in the price of Product Z from 40 pence to 20 pence leads to a rise in the quantity demanded of Product Y from 60 units to 100 units. Similarly, a rise in the price of Product Z to 60 pence leads to a fall in the quantity demanded of Product Y to 20 units.

Where the two products are very close complements, the change in quantity demanded is likely to be greater, for a given price change in its complement, than it would be if the two complements are not regularly used together.

Individual preferences and the quantity demanded

Individual preferences are factors, specific to individual consumers, which affect the demand of individuals and thus affect market demand. They are often referred to as **'tastes'**.

Key term

Individual preferences are the range of factors that influence people's desires and consequently their demand for specific products.

Individual preferences may be influenced by:

- *Social and emotional factors* Social influences, such as friends, family and celebrities, can affect 'individual preferences', especially in relation to items such as fashion, music and entertainment preferences. Although economists assume that people act rationally, some demand may be influenced by emotion, such as the desire to support a charity or a wish to be associated with a product or individual associated with that product.
- *Personal likes or dislikes* In some cases 'individual preferences' may be related to individual characteristics, such as the like or dislike of a particular taste, such as Marmite.
- *Medical factors* For example, an allergy or a desire to eat healthily will influence demand for certain products.
- *Quality or value for money* Regardless of their income levels, some people may place a high value on the quality of a good in a particular market, when weighing up whether to buy a product. Other people may be more interested in value for money for goods in that market.
- *Design features* Individual preferences will also vary according to a preference for particular design features or colours.
- *The environment* Factors such as the weather and geographical features of a country will influence the goods that people wish to buy.
- *The population of the market* The UK has a population in excess of 60 million people and so, for products such as water, the market demand is composed of 60 million individual demand curves.

In general, firms will react to 'individual preferences' by offering for sale products that are known to appeal to people's 'tastes'. However, firms can influence individual preferences. Through marketing and advertising, and using celebrity endorsements and social media, firms may be able to influence and change people's individual preferences. Firms such as Apple have been able to build up high levels of brand loyalty, often through a history of meeting people's wishes. Consequently, loyal consumers will decide to purchase their latest product without knowing its full nature because they assume the product will meet their desires. In 'blind' taste tests, where labels are removed from products, UK consumers consistently prefer Pepsi-Cola to Coca-Cola. However, Coca-Cola always outsells Pepsi-Cola in the UK – a fact that is attributed to Coca-Cola's marketing skills. Marketing departments will often draw on consumers' social and emotional needs in order to boost the demand for their goods and services.

A demand curve shows the relationship between price and quantity demanded

Figure 6.3 *The demand curve*

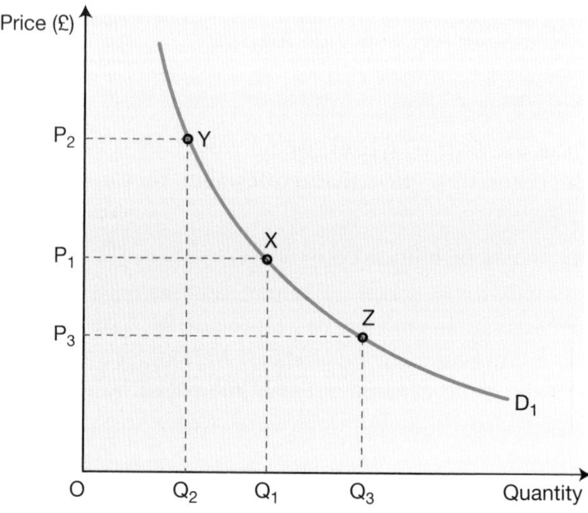

Key term

The **demand curve** shows the relationship between the price of a good and the quantity demanded of that good.

The **law of demand** states that as the price of a good rises, quantity demanded falls. We have seen earlier that this relationship arises because each additional product purchased gives satisfaction and so the second product has less value than the first, the third product has less value than the second, and so on. This relationship is shown in the demand curve D_1 in Figure 6.3.

In a diagram showing a demand curve, price is shown on the 'y' axis and the quantity demanded is shown on the 'x' axis. At price P_1 we read horizontally across the diagram to see the quantity demanded. Point X shows the quantity demanded at price P_1. We then move vertically down from X to read the quantity demanded from the 'x' axis. The quantity demanded at price P_1 is Q_1. If price rises to P_2, some buyers will no longer want to buy the product and so we move from Point X to Y, with demand falling to Q_2. This fall in demand is described as a **contraction in demand** or a **decrease in the quantity demanded.**

If price falls from P_1 to P_3, buyers will want more of the product and so we move from Point X to Z, with demand rising to Q_3. This rise in demand is described as an **extension in demand** or an **increase in the quantity demanded.**

Contractions and extensions in demand mean that we are moving along an existing demand curve, rather than looking at a different demand curve. **The only factor that can cause a contraction or extension in demand is a change in price.**

The market demand curve is the summation of all of the individual demand curves. As the individual demand curves slope downwards from left to right, so will the market demand curve.

Table 6.1 shows the individual demand schedules of three individuals: A, B and C. For the sake of simplicity it is assumed that these are the only individuals in the market.

Table 6.1 *Individual and market demand schedules*

Price (£)	Quantity demanded by A	Quantity demanded by B	Quantity demanded by C	Market demand (units)
6	0	3	2	5
5	1	4	3	8
4	3	5	5	13
3	6	6	8	20
2	10	7	11	28
1	16	9	15	40

It can be seen that at £6 the market demand is 5 units (0 + 3 + 2). At £5, market demand is 8 units (1 + 4 + 3). Completing the table enables us to construct the three individual demand curves *and* the market demand curve. These are shown in Figure 6.4.

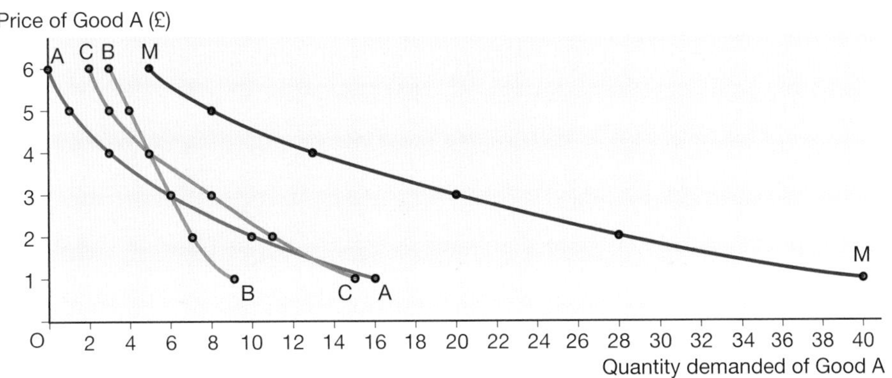

Figure 6.4 *Individual demand curves and the market demand curve*

Note how the shapes of each of the individual demand curves differ, but they all follow the law of demand. As a result, the market demand curve also corresponds to the law of demand. As the population of this market is only three individuals, it is possible to plot the market demand on the same graph as the individual demand curves. For a normal market, individual demand is likely to be measured in units, whereas market demand is possibly measured in millions of units.

Author tip

Remember to explain your diagrams. A diagram is rarely, if ever, self-explanatory. In the examination you will be given some credit for including a *fully labelled* diagram, but to get full credit in most questions it is vitally important that you explain what the diagram and its changes are showing.

Always look closely at the axes on any diagram that you see. The demand curve looks very similar to the diagram showing the impact of the price of a complement on the quantity demanded of a product, but the axes are different and so they show different things. The demand curve considers the impact of the price of a product on the quantity demanded of that product. Economics uses many diagrams, some of which look similar. When constructing your own diagrams, always ensure they are labelled correctly so that their meaning is clear.

The causes of shifts in the demand curve

In the previous section, the demand curve showed us the impact of changes in price on the quantity demanded. What happens if there is a change to one of the other factors that influences demand, such as consumers' incomes or the price of a substitute? Demand curves are not static and will change as circumstances differ.

When one of these factors changes, it leads to a shift in the demand curve. For example, in Table 6.1 we saw that Individual A would demand 3 units when the price was £4, and 6 units when the price was £3. If Individual A receives an increase in income, then they can afford to buy more products at each of these prices. For example, at a price of £4, they may now want to buy 4 units instead of 3, and at a price of £3 their demand may increase from 6 units to 8 units. This means their individual demand curve shifts to the right.

An *increase in demand* shifts the demand curve to the right, showing a greater quantity demanded at each price. A *decrease in demand* shifts the demand curve to the left, showing a lower quantity demanded at each price.

Factors that cause a shift in the demand curve are known as the **determinants of demand.** The major determinants are the factors we have noted earlier, such as income and price of substitutes.

A shift of the demand curve to the right (from D_1 to D_2) in Figure 6.5 shows an *increase in demand.* At price P_1, demand has increased from Q_1 to Q_4. This might

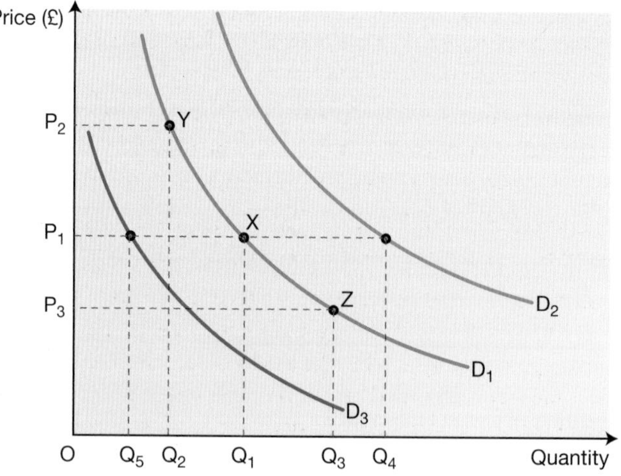

Figure 6.5 *Shifts in the demand curve*

have been caused by a change in individual preferences in favour of the good or a rise in the price of substitutes.

The reverse of these changes, such as individual preferences leading to less desire for a good or a fall in the price of its substitutes, would lead to a *decrease in demand.* This shifts the demand curve to the left (from D_1 to D_3). At price P_1, demand has decreased from Q_1 to Q_5.

Table 6.2 summarises the main factors influencing demand and whether the factor leads to:

- an increase in demand for a good (shifting the demand curve to the right); or
- a decrease in demand for a good (shifting the demand curve to the left).

Factor causing an increase in demand	Factor causing a decrease in demand
An increase in income (for a normal good)	A decrease in income (for a normal good)
A decrease in income (for an inferior good)	An increase in income (for an inferior good)
A decrease in income tax or national insurance contributions (normal good)	An increase in income tax or national insurance contributions (normal good)
An increase in income tax or national insurance contributions (inferior good)	A decrease in income tax or national insurance contributions (inferior good)
An increase in wealth (normal good)	A decrease in wealth (normal good)
An increase in the price of a substitute	A decrease in the price of a substitute
A decrease in the price of a complementary good	An increase in the price of a complementary good
Individual preference moving in favour of the good	A fall in individual preference for the good

Table 6.2 *Factors leading to increases and decreases in demand*

A movement along a demand curve can only be caused by a change in price. It is known as a resultant change in demand.

A rise in price (such as P_1 to P_2 in Figure 6.3) leads to a contraction in demand from Q_1 to Q_2 (also known as a decrease in the quantity demanded).

A fall in price (such as P_1 to P_3 in Figure 6.3) leads to an extension in demand from Q_1 to Q_3 (also known as an increase in the quantity demanded).

A shift to a completely new demand curve is caused by a change in any of the other factors that determine demand (but not price). It is known as a real change in demand because a different quantity is demanded at each price.

An increase in demand (such as the shift from D_1 to D_2 in Figure 6.5) leads to more demand at every price. For example, at price P_1, the quantity demanded has changed from Q_1 to Q_4. This change in demand is described as an increase in demand.

Similarly, a decrease in demand leads to a shift in the demand curve to the left (from D_1 to D_3 in Figure 6.5). Thus at price P_1, the quantity demanded falls from Q_1 to Q_5.

It should be noted that the terms 'increase in demand' or 'decrease in demand' mean a real change in demand (i.e. a shift in the demand curve). For resultant changes in demand (caused by price changes), the phrases 'increase in the quantity demanded' or 'decrease in the quantity demanded' are used. Alternatively, you can use the phrases 'extension in demand' or 'contraction in demand' to describe movements along an existing demand curve.

Author tip

Remember to distinguish between changes that cause a movement along a demand curve and changes that cause a shift to a new demand curve.

REALWORLD ECONOMICS 6.1

Factors influencing touristic demand

Economists often show demand as a mathematical function. For example, Q_d is often used to refer to the quantity demanded, P refers to price and Y_d to disposable incomes. For a normal good the link between income and quantity demanded is a positive one, but the link between price and quantity demanded is an inverse relationship because increases in price lead to decreases in quantity demanded.

Research into domestic tourism in Romania showed that income is the key factor influencing demand.

Romanian tourists visiting medieval Brasov – demand is strongly influenced by income

Tourist numbers were converted into index numbers and compared to index numbers showing changes in income levels, with both sets of index numbers commencing at 100. At first, changes in the number of tourists were linked to changes in disposable income. This relationship was shown by the first equation: $Q_d = -0.07 + 0.88Y_d$. For each 1% increase in disposable income, the demand for tourism increased by 0.88%.

Further investigation discovered that expected future income was even more important than current income. The second equation showed how to calculate the index of quantity demanded based on income (Y_d) and expected future income (Y_f). This second equation was as follows:

$$Q_d = -0.19 + 0.4Y_d + 0.64Y_f$$

Source: Article by Constantin, Mihaela and Corina, published online at www.sciencedirect.com

Exercises *Total: 20 marks*

1. Based on the first equation above, if disposable incomes in Romania fall by 5%, calculate the percentage change in the demand for tourism. *(2 marks)*
2. Based on the second equation above, if disposable incomes in Romania have risen by 10% in a year and are expected to rise by 10% in the following year, calculate the percentage change in the demand for tourism. *(3 marks)*
3. Explain why both income and expectations of future income are likely to be the major influence on the demand for tourist activities in Romania. *(10 marks)*
4. Does the final line of the article provide some proof of Friedman's permanent income hypothesis? *(5 marks)*

Number crunching *Total: 10 marks*

Table 6.3 *Index number of income and sales of vegetables, 2008–13 (Year 2000 = 100)*

Year	Income levels	Beetroot	Celery
2008	130	107	141
2009	132	104	149
2010	131	105	142
2011	129	108	134
2012	129	116	134
2013	132	126	138

1. Identify *two* significant points of comparison between the levels of income and the sales of beetroot and celery in Table 6.3. *(4 marks)*
2. Explain the significance of *one* of these changes for a farmer who grows both beetroot and celery. *(6 marks)*

Review questions

Total: 50 marks

1 In economics, 'a place where buyers and sellers meet' is the definition of:
A An economy
B Demand and supply
C A market
D A shop *(1 mark)*

2 Effective demand means that the desire to buy:
A Leads to a purchase
B Is backed by the ability to pay
C Is reliant on price being very low
D Is measured over a period of time *(1 mark)*

3 A person's monthly disposable income is their gross income *minus*:
A Expenses related to their job, such as travel
B Value added tax
C Monthly bills
D Income tax and national insurance contributions *(1 mark)*

4 A fall in the price of a good usually leads to:
A A contraction in demand
B A decrease in demand
C An extension in demand
D An increase in demand *(1 mark)*

5 Which one of the following changes will lead to an increase in the demand for an inferior good?
A An increase in income
B An increase in price
C A decrease in national insurance contributions
D An increase in income tax *(1 mark)*

6 Figure 6.6 shows the original demand curve for pens (D_1) and the new demand curve for pens (D_2).

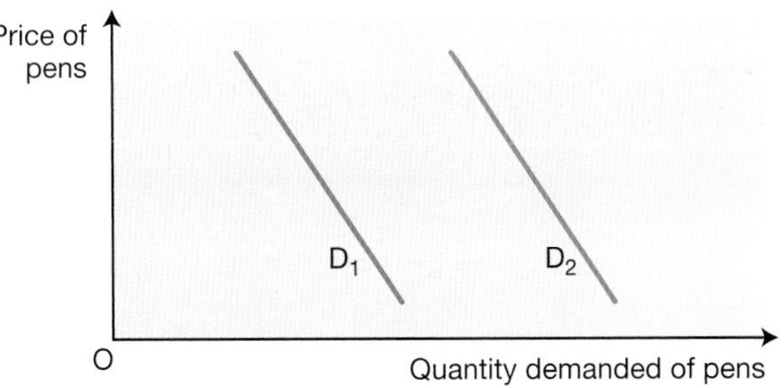

Figure 6.6

Other things being equal, the change in demand curve from D_1 to D_2 might be caused by:
A A decrease in the price of pens
B A decrease in the price of a complement of pens
C A decrease in people's wealth
D A successful advertising campaign by a substitute of pens *(1 mark)*

7 Figure 6.7 shows the original demand curve for umbrellas (D_1) and the new demand curve for umbrellas (D_2).

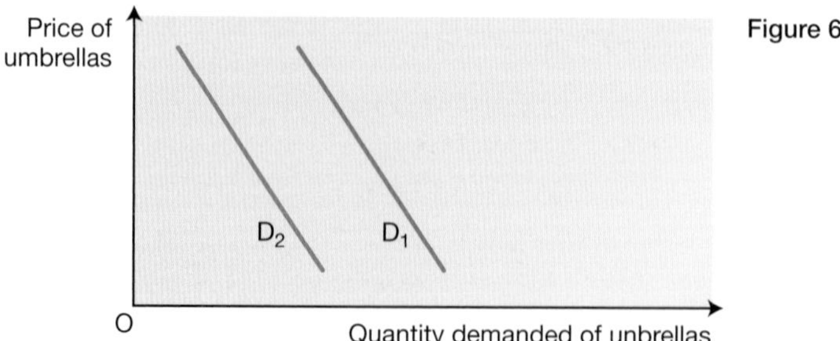

Figure 6.7

Which one of the following factors is most likely to have caused the shift in demand curve from D_1 to D_2?

A An increase in population
B Higher rainfall
C An advertising campaign
D Umbrellas becoming less fashionable *(1 mark)*

8 Consumers' incomes rise and the price of Good B rises. Both of these factors lead to an increase in demand for Good A. This means that:

A Good A is a normal good and a complement of Good B
B Good A is a normal good and a substitute of Good B
C Good A is an inferior good and a complement of Good B
D Good A is an inferior good and a substitute of Good B *(1 mark)*

9 Which one of the following will *not* lead to a shift in the demand curve to the right?

A An increase in consumers' incomes
B A decrease in the good's price
C A decrease in the price of a substitute good
D A change in individual preferences in favour of the product *(1 mark)*

10 Figure 6.8 shows how the price of Good A influences the demand of Good B (Line B) and Good C (Line C).

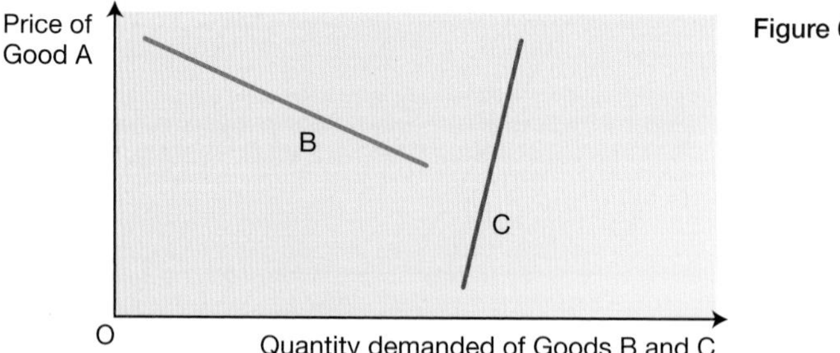

Figure 6.8

From Figure 6.8 it can be concluded that:

A Goods B and C are both substitutes for Good A
B Goods B and C are both complements of Good A
C Good B is a complement of Good A; Good C is a substitute for Good A
D Good B is a substitute for Good A; Good C is a complement of Good A *(1 mark)*

11 Define the term 'demand'. *(3 marks)*

12 What is the ' law of demand'? *(3 marks)*

13 What is the difference between 'income' and 'wealth'? *(4 marks)*

The information below applies to questions 14, 15 and 16.
Table 6.4 shows four individual demand curves (A, B, C and D) that make up the market demand curve for Thingies. All quantities are in kilograms.

Price (£)	Individual A (kilos)	Individual B (kilos)	Individual C (kilos)	Individual D (kilos)	Market demand (kilos)
3	4	0	11	5	
2	8	2	16	14	
1	15	6	31	28	

Table 6.4

14 Complete the table and, on graph paper, plot the market demand curve for Thingies. Label it D_1. Make sure that you label your axes. *(5 marks)*

15 The market demand for Thingies decreases by 25%. Draw the new demand curve on the graph. Label it D_2. *(3 marks)*

16 By how many kilos has demand decreased when the price is £1? *(2 marks)*

17 Explain how a more equal distribution of income might affect the demand for yachts. *(5 marks)*

18 Explain why a wealthy person might have lower demand than a person with high income. *(5 marks)*

19 Analyse two possible factors that have contributed to the increase in demand of coffee shops in the UK in recent years. *(10 marks)*

Chapter 7

Price, income & cross elasticities of demand

This chapter introduces the concepts of price, income and cross elasticities of demand and shows how to calculate each of these elasticities. The relationship between income elasticity of demand and normal and inferior goods is then studied, before moving on to an explanation of the link between cross elasticity of demand and substitute and complementary goods. Price elasticity of demand and its influence on firms' total revenue and consumers' total expenditure is then considered. The chapter concludes with an explanation of the factors that influence each of these elasticities of demand and an interpretation of the meaning of their numerical values.

Price, income and cross elasticities of demand

Elasticity of demand measures the responsiveness of the quantity demanded to a change in one of the factors influencing demand. In all cases, the formula for measuring elasticity divides the percentage change in the quantity demanded by the percentage change in the variable that influences quantity demanded.

In Chapter 6 we examined the main factors that determine demand. These factors are price, income, wealth, price of substitutes and complementary goods, and individual preferences. It is difficult to place a numerical value on 'individual preferences', since they can change quickly as a result of social and emotional factors or changes in fashion and taste. Given that there is no reliable way of measuring 'individual preferences', it is not possible to calculate an elasticity of demand based on them. Although wealth can be measured, we saw in the last chapter that the relationship between wealth and spending is unreliable because it depends on the accessibility of that wealth. Thus a person whose wealth is entirely held in property is unlikely to be able to spend that wealth. In the UK a high percentage of people own their houses in comparison to other European countries, but relatively few people are prepared to sell their property in order to finance spending on goods that they wish to buy.

The remaining factors that influence demand can be measured numerically and so there are three main elasticities of demand:

- price elasticity of demand;

Key terms

Price elasticity of demand (PED) measures the responsiveness of the quantity demanded of a product to a change in the price of that product.

Income elasticity of demand (YED) measures the responsiveness of the quantity demanded of the product to a change in incomes (consumer incomes).

Cross elasticity of demand (XED) measures the responsiveness of the quantity demanded of a product to a change in the price of another product.

- income elasticity of demand;
- cross elasticity of demand. Cross elasticity of demand measures the responsiveness of the quantity demanded to a change in the price of another product and can therefore be used to examine the impact of changes in the price of both substitutes and complements.

All three elasticities are expressed as a number. This calculation divides the percentage (or proportional) change in the quantity demanded by the percentage (or proportional) change in the factor that is influencing the quantity demanded.

Price elasticity of demand

The formula for calculating price elasticity of demand is set out below.

$$\textbf{Price elasticity of demand} = \frac{\text{\% change in quantity demanded of Product X}}{\text{\% change in price of Product X}}$$

The law of demand states that as price falls, quantity demanded increases. This is an 'inverse' relationship and means that the price elasticity of demand will be negative, except in very unusual circumstances.

Price elasticity of demand is **inelastic** if the value lies between 0 and –1 (a large percentage change in price leads to a smaller percentage change in quantity demanded).

Price elasticity of demand is **elastic** if the value lies between –1 and –∞ (a small percentage change in price leads to a larger percentage change in quantity demanded).

In Figure 7.1, D_E shows an elastic demand curve. At a price of £10, we look along the dotted horizontal line to Point A. By tracing the vertical dotted line down from Point A to the 'x' axis, we can see that the quantity demanded is 8 units when the price is £10. Moving along this demand curve to Point B, we can see that at a price of £8, the quantity demanded is 20 units.

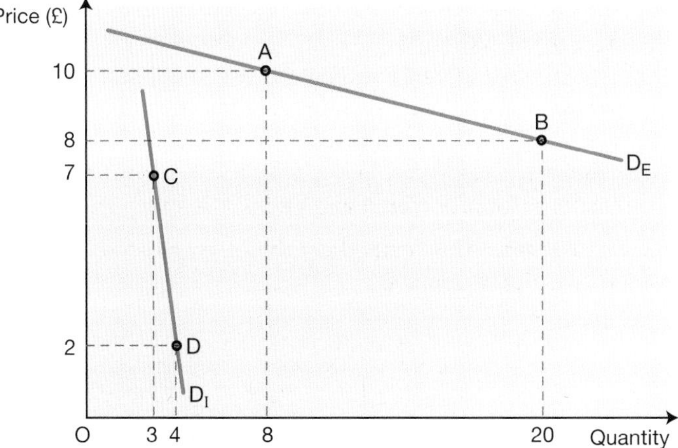

Figure 7.1 *Price elasticity of demand*

Moving from Point A to Point B enables us to calculate the price elasticity of demand. The change in price from £10 to £8 is a 20% fall (–2/10 × 100 = –20%). The change in quantity demanded is an increase of 150%, i.e. (20 – 8)/8 × 100. Therefore price elasticity of demand is 150%/–20% = –7.5.

In Figure 7.1, D_I shows an inelastic demand curve. At a price of £7, we look along the dotted horizontal line to Point C. By tracing the vertical dotted line down from Point C to the 'x' axis, we can see that the quantity demanded is 3 units when the price is £7. Moving along this demand curve to Point D, we can see that at a price of £2, the quantity demanded is 4 units.

Moving from Point C to Point D enables us to calculate the price elasticity of demand. The change in price from £7 to £2 is a 71% fall (–5/7 × 100 = –71%). The change in quantity demanded is an increase of 33%, i.e. (4 – 3)/3 × 100. Therefore price elasticity of demand is 33%/–71% = –0.46.

In a diagram where price elasticity of demand is elastic, the demand curve tends to have a low gradient, giving a fairly flat line, such as D_E in Figure 7.1.

In a diagram where price elasticity of demand is inelastic, the demand curve tends to have a high gradient, giving a fairly steep line, such as D_I in Figure 7.1.

Key note

Price elasticity of demand applies to changes between two prices. It is unlikely to be the same value all the way along a demand curve or even if we move in the opposite direction between two points. For example, moving from Point C to Point D in Figure 7.1 gave a price elasticity of demand of –0.46. If the price had changed from £2 to £7, we would have moved from Point D to Point C instead. In this case the price elasticity of demand would be –25%/250% = –0.1 or –1/10. This is still inelastic but a significantly different result from the elasticity when changing from Point C to D.

Figures 7.2 and 7.3 illustrate rare examples of demand curves, where the price elasticity is the same all the way along the line.

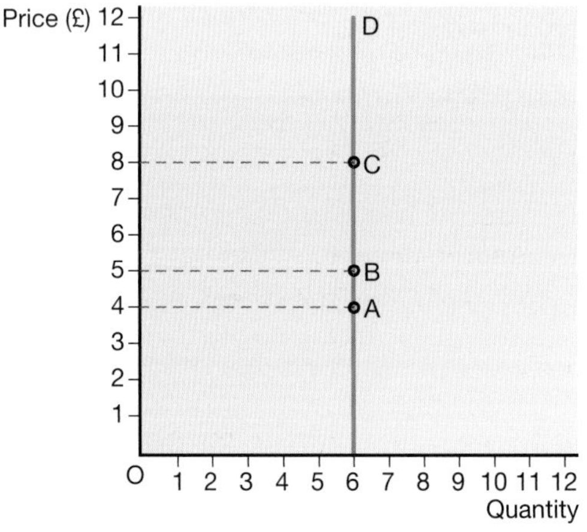

Figure 7.2 *Perfectly inelastic demand or zero elastic demand (PED = zero)*

The demand curve in Figure 7.2 shows zero elasticity of demand. This occurs when there is no change in the quantity demanded when price changes. When price increases from £4 to £5, we move along the demand curve from Point A to Point B. The percentage change in price is:

$$\frac{£5 - £4}{£4} \times 100 = \frac{1}{4} \times 100 = 25\%$$

The quantity demanded remains at 6 units when price rises, so the percentage change in quantity demanded is:

$$\frac{£6 - £6}{£6} \times 100 = \frac{0}{6} \times 100 = 0\%$$

Using the formula for price elasticity of demand, we can see that the price elasticity of demand is 0%/25% = 0 (zero).

Moving from Point B to Point C gives us a 60% increase in price, i.e. +3/5 × 100 = 60%. The change in quantity demanded is still zero. Thus the price elasticity of demand is 0%/60% = 0 (zero).

Zero price elasticity (or perfectly inelastic demand) occurs when people demand the same quantity, regardless of price. This is extremely rare but arguably could be deemed to apply to the demand for air. A certain quantity is demanded in order to stay alive. Fortunately, air is abundant and no price is charged.

The demand curve in Figure 7.3 shows a demand curve whose elasticity of demand is infinity (or minus infinity). This occurs when all consumers are prepared to pay the exact same price for a good.

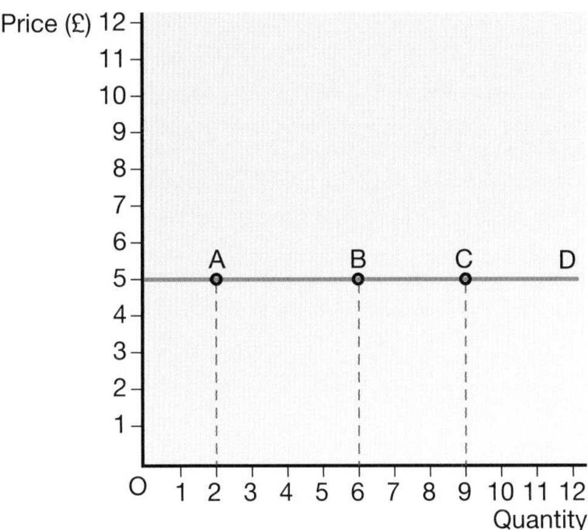

Figure 7.3 *Perfectly elastic demand or infinitely elastic demand (PED = −∞)*

If we start at Point A, price is £5 and quantity demanded is 2 units. If we move along the demand curve from Point A to Point B, the price remains at £5 but the quantity demanded rises from 2 units to 6 units. The percentage change in price is:

$$\frac{£5 - £5}{£5} \times 100 = \frac{0}{5} \times 100 = 0\%$$

The quantity demanded rises from 2 units to 6 units, so the percentage change in quantity demanded is:

$$\frac{6 - 2}{2} \times 100 = \frac{4}{2} \times 100 = 200\%$$

Using the formula for price elasticity of demand, we can see that the price elasticity of demand is 200%/0% = ∞ (or −∞).

Moving from Point B to Point C gives us a 50% increase in quantity demanded +3/6 × 100 = 50%. The change in price is still zero. Thus the price elasticity of demand is 50%/0% = ∞ (or −∞).

Author tip

Always show your working when you are required to make calculations in an exam. Exam boards such as AQA will give credit for the correct elements of an answer even where the final answer is incorrect.

Key note

Price elasticities of demand may also be calculated by proportional changes. The formula is set out below:

$$\textbf{Price elasticity of demand} = \frac{\text{Proportional change in quantity demanded of Product X}}{\text{Proportional change in price of Product X}}$$

Using this formula for the very first calculation in Figure 7.1 gives us the following answer:

$$\frac{(20-8)}{8} \div \frac{(8-10)}{10} = \frac{12}{8} \div \frac{-2}{10} = \frac{12}{8} \times \frac{10}{-2} = \frac{120}{-16} = \mathbf{-7.5}$$

Infinite price elasticity (or perfectly elastic demand) occurs when the market has just one price and so consumers only consider this price when planning their demand. In theory, this occurs in situations where there are so many competitors that firms can only charge the price charged by everyone else in the market. In these situations, an individual firm will find that customers will buy the amount they offer to sell, all at the same price.

Author tip

Remember that elasticity of demand is expressed as a number and *not* a percentage. In the calculation, the percentages on the top and bottom of the fraction cancel each other out, leaving an answer that is a number only, such as –1.5 or –0.4.

Remember too that, because of the law of demand, price elasticity will usually be negative, and so you should always include the negative sign in your answer. (This is particularly important because there are rare instances where it can be positive.)

Price elasticity of demand will change as you move along the demand curve.

Income elasticity of demand

The formula for calculating income elasticity of demand is set out below.

$$\textbf{Income elasticity of demand} = \frac{\text{\% change in quantity demanded of Product X}}{\text{\% change in income}}$$

For example, if a consumer or consumers have a 5% increase in income and this leads to a 3% increase in demand, then the price elasticity of demand is 3%/5% = +0.6.

Table 7.1 *Income and demand for Good X*

Level of income per month (£)	Quantity demanded of Good X
800	40
1000	60
1200	72
1500	81

Table 7.1 shows a consumer's demand for Good X as her income increases. The calculations are as follows:

1 **Income elasticity of demand when income changes from £800 to £1000**

- Between £800 and £1000, the percentage increase in income is:

$$\frac{£1000 - £800}{£800} \times 100 = \frac{£200}{£800} \times 100 = 25\%$$

- The percentage change in quantity demanded is:

$$\frac{60 - 40}{40} \times 100 = \frac{20}{40} \times 100 = 50\%$$

- Income elasticity of demand = 50%/25% = 2.0 (or +2.0).

2 Income elasticity of demand when income changes from £1000 to £1200

- Between £1000 and £1200, the percentage increase in income is:

$$\frac{£1200 - £1000}{£1000} \times 100 = \frac{£200}{£1000} \times 100 = 20\%$$

- The percentage change in quantity demanded is:

$$\frac{72 - 60}{60} \times 100 = \frac{12}{60} \times 100 = 20\%$$

- Income elasticity of demand = 20%/20% = 1.0 (or +1.0).

3 Income elasticity of demand when income changes from £1200 to £1500

- Between £1200 and £1500, the percentage increase in income is:

$$\frac{£1500 - £1200}{£1200} \times 100 = \frac{£300}{£1200} \times 100 = 25\%$$

- The percentage change in quantity demanded is:

$$\frac{81 - 72}{72} \times 100 = \frac{9}{72} \times 100 = 12.5\%$$

- Income elasticity of demand = 12.5%/25% = 0.5 (or +0.5).

As with price elasticity of demand, income elasticity can vary. In this example, its value is falling as income increases.

Author tip

Income elasticity of demand is usually positive, as it is in these three examples, but watch out for instances where the answer is negative.

Cross elasticity of demand

The formula for calculating cross elasticity of demand is set out below.

$$\textbf{Cross elasticity of demand} = \frac{\text{\% change in quantity demanded of Product Y}}{\text{\% change in price of Product X}}$$

For example, if the price of Product X falls by 10% and the quantity demanded of Product Y rises by 7%, then the cross elasticity of demand between the two products is +7%/–10% = –0.7.

Example calculation

- A rise in the price of Product A from 50p to 70p leads to an increase in the quantity demanded of Product B from 160 units to 176 units.
- The percentage change in price of A is:

$$\frac{70 - 50}{50} \times 100 = \frac{20}{50} \times 100 = 40\%$$

- The % change in quantity demanded of B is:

$$\frac{176 - 160}{160} \times 100 = \frac{16}{160} \times 100 = 10\%$$

- The cross elasticity of demand between products A and B is thus 10%/40% = +0.25.

The relationship between income elasticity of demand and normal and inferior goods

Key terms

Normal goods are goods that experience an increase in quantity demanded as incomes increase, other things being equal.

Inferior goods are goods that experience a decrease in quantity demanded as incomes increase, other things being equal.

As demand requires the willingness and ability to pay for goods, increases in consumers' disposable incomes will lead to an increase in their overall level of demand. It can be reasonably expected that a 10% increase in income will lead to a 10% increase in the total spending of a consumer. This would suggest that the average income elasticity of demand is +1.0.

In practice, sometimes extra income will lead to consumers being willing to pay higher prices, rather than buy a greater quantity of products. More significantly, as people's incomes rise, they will save a larger percentage of their income and therefore spending will not increase at quite the same rate as income. As a general rule, the average income elasticity of demand will be positive, but somewhere below 1.0.

For normal goods there is a positive relationship between income and quantity demanded, as higher incomes give more spending power to consumers. Thus **normal goods have a positive income elasticity of demand.** Similarly, if incomes fall, then the quantity demanded of normal goods will also fall.

As incomes rise, people will buy fewer inferior goods (economy products), such as cheap cuts of meat. **Inferior goods have a negative income elasticity of demand.** However, if incomes fall, such as in a recession, then inferior goods will experience an increase in quantity demanded (see Real World Economics 7.1 on p. 66 for an example).

Richer people buy more luxuries and so luxury products tend to have higher (more elastic) income elasticities of demand. **Goods with high, positive income elasticities of demand are sometimes referred to as superior goods.** It should be noted that superior goods are a subset of normal goods, as the latter term applies to all products with a positive elasticity of demand.

Table 7.2 *Incomes and demand for different products*

Level of income (£)	Quantity demanded of Good J	Quantity demanded of Good K	Quantity demanded of Good L
20,000	50	80	30
22,000	53	76	39

Table 7.2 shows the impact of an increase in income from £20,000 to £22,000 on the quantity demanded of three different goods: J, K and L.

The percentage increase in income is thus:

$$\frac{£22{,}000 - £20{,}000}{£20{,}000} \times 100 = \frac{£2000}{£20{,}000} \times 100 = 10\%$$

Their income elasticities of demand are calculated below. Quantity demanded is abbreviated as Q_d and income is abbreviated as Y.

$$\text{Good J: } \frac{\%\text{ change in } Q_d}{\%\text{ change in Y}} = \frac{(53 - 50)/50 \times 100}{10 \text{ (see above)}} = \frac{3/50 \times 100}{10} = \frac{6}{10} = 0.6$$

$$\text{Good K: } \frac{\%\text{ change in } Q_d}{\%\text{ change in Y}} = \frac{(76 - 80)/80 \times 100}{10 \text{ (see above)}} = \frac{-4/80 \times 100}{10} = \frac{-5}{10} = -0.5$$

$$\text{Good L: } \frac{\%\text{ change in } Q_d}{\%\text{ change in Y}} = \frac{(39 - 30)/30 \times 100}{10 \text{ (see above)}} = \frac{9/30 \times 100}{10} = \frac{30}{10} = 3.0$$

From these calculations we can conclude that, for this change in income:

- Good J is a normal good
- Good K is an inferior good
- Good L is a normal good, but also a superior good

Normal goods and inferior goods

Inferior goods are relatively uncommon in comparison to normal goods, but many examples can be found. In general, they are products that people tend to buy because they cannot afford to buy the more expensive alternatives, such as supermarket own-label products or cheap cuts of meat.

Normal goods vary considerably. Some normal goods might be products on which people spend slightly more as their incomes rise, such as many foodstuffs and standard items of clothing such as socks, tights and underwear. However, other normal goods might be luxury products such as yachts and mansions.

Why do firms produce inferior goods, when the growth in people's incomes over the last 100 years suggests that they are likely to decline? There are a few reasons.

- Some inferior goods are popular with certain consumers and so, despite increases in income, these groups of people may continue to buy them as they do not see them as inferior.
- Tastes change over time. In the 1930s, tripe sales were quite high, but these days they are very low (except for pet foods). Buyers of cheap meat have moved on to faggots and then on to mincemeat, which is arguably an inferior good at the present time. Therefore, some firms may find a normal good has become an inferior good over time.
- Incomes are not evenly distributed and so, even when average incomes are rising, some groups may find their disposable income falling and thus they are more likely to buy cheap alternatives.
- The recession of 2009 and further recession and slow recovery meant that average incomes did decline over the four years from 2009. This led to increases in demand for some inferior goods.

It should be noted that classifying a good as superior, normal or inferior is an oversimplification. Each individual reacts differently to products. For example, a Ford Fiesta may be a superior good to a person on a low income, a normal good with income elasticity below 1.0 to those on mid-range incomes, and an inferior good to people on very high incomes.

REALWORLD ECONOMICS 7.1

Pawnbrokers and payday loans

Two services that are generally regarded as 'inferior goods' are pawnbrokers and payday loans. In times of financial difficulty, these types of businesses thrive because people who are short of money will often trade in items such as jewellery to a pawnbroker in return for cash. Alternatively, they may approach a 'payday' loan company such as Payday Express or Quickquid. Table 7.3 shows how the value of one of these short-term loan companies – Wonga – increased during and after the recession.

Companies such as Wonga offer short-term, high-cost loans – an 'inferior good'

	2009	2010	2011	2012	2013
Net worth of Wonga Ltd (£ million)	−0.5	9.9	53.6	112.7	108.9

Table 7.3

In four years, Wonga grew from being a firm that had more debts than assets to one worth over £100 million. As the UK started to emerge from the recession in 2013, the value of Wonga began to fall as the demand for payday loans declined.

Pawnbrokers also experienced growth because they were selling an inferior good/service in this period. The worldwide recession benefited Cash Converters, an Australian-owned pawnbroker, which expanded globally. In 2009 it achieved sales of $94.7 million; by 2014 this had increased to $331.7 million.

The Romans imposed a maximum interest rate of 8% on loans, and in the USA many states have banned these types of loan companies and placed limits on interest rates. In the UK, advertisements must show the annual percentage rate of interest (APR), but the market does not seem to meet with two assumptions made by economists about competitive markets – the assumptions that consumers are rational and that they have perfect information. In 2013, moneysupermarket.com recorded that Wonga charged an APR% of 5853% on some of its short-term loans (and this was not the highest rate charged in the market). The UK's financial watchdog, the Financial Conduct Authority, is clamping down on payday loans, with new rules from January 2015 to ensure that borrowers are never forced to repay more than double the amount of their original loan.

The relationship between cross elasticity of demand and substitute and complementary goods

It can be seen that cross elasticity of demand can be positive or negative. What does this signify?

Substitute goods

If goods A and B are substitutes, then an increase in the price of Good A will lead to a contraction in demand (a resultant change as it is a move along the demand curve for Good A). This means there is a fall in the quantity demanded for Good A. As a result, consumers will seek alternative goods to use instead of Good A. The goods that they will turn to will be substitutes, such as Good B. This means that the quantity demanded of Good B will increase. Note that this is a real change in the quantity demanded of Good B. If the price of Good B stays the same, it will have become more attractive to consumers, some of whom will now see it as better value than Good A. When calculating the cross elasticity of demand, the percentage change in quantity demanded for B will be positive because the quantity demanded has increased. The percentage change in price of Good A is also positive because its price has risen. This gives us a positive number divided by a positive number. Therefore, **if cross elasticity of demand is *positive*, the two goods involved are *substitutes*.**

This can be confirmed by investigating a fall in price. If the price of Good A falls, then consumers will increase the quantity demanded of Good A (an extension, as it is a resultant change along the demand curve for Good A). If consumers are buying more of Good A, they will buy less of the goods that are its substitutes, such as Good B. Therefore the percentage change in quantity demanded of Good B is negative and the percentage change in price of Good A is negative. A negative number divided by a negative number gives a positive number.

Complementary goods

If goods A and B are complementary goods, then an increase in the price of Good A will lead to a contraction in demand (a resultant change as it is a move along the demand curve for Good A). This means there is a fall in the quantity demanded for Good A. As a result, consumers will buy less of the goods that are used with it (its complements). This means that the quantity demanded of Good B will decrease. For example, a fall in demand for tea will lead to a fall in demand for sugar and milk, which are complementary goods used with tea. This is a real change in the quantity demanded of Good B. If the price of Good B stays the same, it will have become less attractive to consumers because they wanted it as a complement to Good A. When calculating the cross elasticity of demand, the percentage change in quantity demanded for B will be negative because the quantity demanded has decreased. The percentage change in price of Good A is positive because its price has risen. This gives us a negative number divided by a positive number. Therefore, **if cross elasticity of demand is *negative*, the two goods involved are *complementary goods*** (or ***complements***).

This can be confirmed by investigating a fall in price. If the price of Good A falls, then consumers will decrease the quantity demanded of Good A (a contraction, as it is a resultant change along the demand curve for Good A). If consumers are buying more of Good A, they will buy more of the goods that are its complements, such as Good B. Therefore the percentage change in quantity demanded of Good B is positive and the percentage change in price of Good A is negative. A positive number divided by a negative number gives a negative number.

As a general rule, the higher the numerical value of cross elasticity of demand, the closer the two products are as either substitutes or complements. However, this rule should be treated with caution. For example, cars and tyres are very close complements, but because tyres are a minor expense in comparison to cars, it is unlikely that a change in tyre prices will affect the quantity of cars demanded (but the price of cars will affect the demand for tyres).

The relationships between price elasticity of demand and firms' total revenue (total expenditure)

Price elasticity and total revenue

Firms like to know the value of price elasticity of demand so that they can assess the impact of price changes on demand and total revenue.

- If demand is **elastic**, then **a fall in price** leads to **increased total revenue.**

- If demand is **inelastic**, then a **fall in price** leads to **decreased total revenue.**

Looking at D_E (elastic demand) in Figure 7.4, when price falls from £10 to £8, total revenue increases from £80 (£10 × 8 units) to £160 (£8 × 20 units).

Looking at D_I (inelastic demand), when price falls from £7 to £2, total revenue decreases from £21 (£7 × 3 units) to £8 (£2 × 4 units).

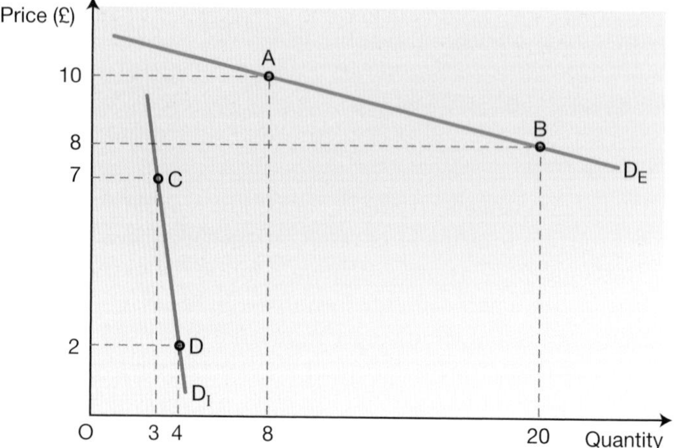

Figure 7.4 *Price elasticity of demand*

- If demand is **elastic**, then a **rise in price** leads to **decreased total revenue.**
- If demand is **inelastic**, then a **rise in price** leads to **increased total revenue.**

If a firm's total revenue is increasing, then this means that total expenditure by consumers is increasing too, as the total revenue received by firms is the same as the total expenditure by the consumers who are buying the goods.

Since a price increase leads to a fall in quantity demanded, the percentage increase in price will be greater than the percentage increase in total revenue (total expenditure). The more inelastic the demand, the larger is the percentage increase in total revenue.

Looking at Figure 7.2 (see p. 60), we saw that the demand curve was vertical. This means that the price elasticity of demand was perfectly inelastic (equal to zero). When we moved from Point A to Point B, there was a 25% increase in price but the quantity demanded stayed the same (6 units). Thus total revenue rose from £4 × 6 = £24 to £5 × 6 = £30. This is a 25% increase in total revenue, which is the same as the price increase. Moving from Point B to Point C showed a 60% increase in price (from 5 × £6 = £30 to 8 × £6 = £48). Thus, **if demand is perfectly inelastic, total revenue will change by the same percentage as the change in *price*.**

Figure 7.3 (see p. 61) showed us a perfectly elastic (horizontal) demand curve. In this case there is nothing to be gained by cutting price because everything that a firm produces can be sold at the same price. In this instance firms should try to increase the quantity that they make available. Moving from Point A to Point B showed that the quantity sold rose from 2 units to 6 units. As the price stayed at £5, this tripling of the quantity led to a tripling of total revenue (from £5 × 2 = £10 to £5 × 6 = £30). Similarly, moving from Point B to Point C represented a 50% increase in quantity (from 6 to 9 units) and led to a 50% rise in total revenue (from £5 × 6 = £30 to £5 × 9 = £45).

Thus, **if demand is perfectly elastic, total revenue will change by the same percentage as the change in *quantity demanded*.** *There is nothing to be gained by changing* *price, because a lower price will not lead to more quantity demanded and a higher price will mean that no consumers will be prepared to buy the good.*

Unit or unitary elastic demand

Figure 7.5 is a special case and represents the border between elastic demand and inelastic demand. It is defined as a demand curve where the price elasticity of demand is –1. Its significance is that the percentage rise/fall in price is the same as the percentage fall/rise in quantity demanded.

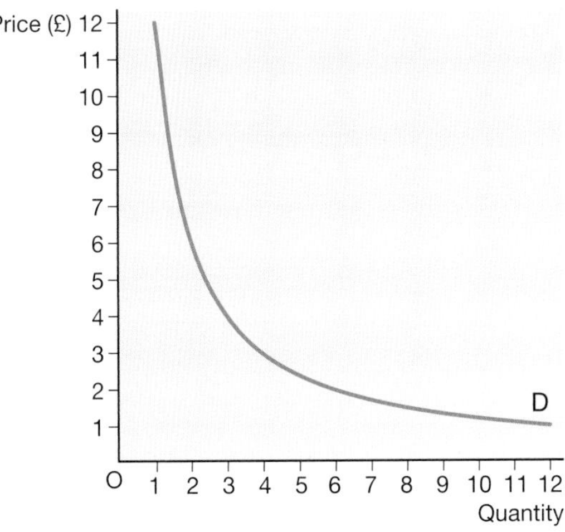

Figure 7.5 *A demand curve with unit elasticity*

It is also defined as a situation where total revenue (TR) remains unchanged when there is a change in price.

In practice, it is highly improbable that a demand curve would have unit elasticity along its whole length; it is much more likely to be a feature of a certain part of a demand curve where demand is neither elastic nor inelastic.

Although it is unlikely that a demand curve will have unit elasticity along its whole length, there is a suggestion that many consumers' demand for holidays may approximate to this shape. This is because consumers often set aside a sum of money for their holiday, when planning their finances. If the price of a preferred holiday increases, this may mean that they select a cheaper alternative or that they take a shorter vacation. Lower prices will mean a longer holiday or a more luxurious alternative. In effect, regardless of price, total expenditure by the consumer remains the same.

The factors that influence these elasticities of demand

Factors influencing price elasticity of demand

The main factors that influence the price elasticity of demand are listed below and shown in Table 7.4.

- *Degree of necessity* Necessary products have inelastic demand as consumers will want to buy them regardless of price. The more necessary a product, the more inelastic is the demand. Using the same logic, luxury products are likely to have a price elastic demand and so price increases are likely to lead to consumers turning to other goods.

- *Habit-forming goods* Products such as tobacco and alcohol tend to have price inelastic demand, as their buyers see them as necessary. In effect, the more a person depends upon a good, the more inelastic their demand becomes. The idea of 'necessity' is, to some extent, subjective and so an addict will see a habit-forming good as a necessity and thus their demand will be price inelastic.
- *Substitutes* Goods with close alternatives have elastic demand. This is because a price rise will encourage consumers to switch to the close alternatives/substitutes available. If a good has a very close substitute and/or a lot of fairly close substitutes, then the price elasticity of demand for that good will be elastic. However, consumers' views on substitutes will vary. For some people, a Samsung mobile phone is a very close substitute for an iPhone, but other consumers do not see them as close alternatives. The price of the substitute will also influence price elasticity of demand. If a close substitute has a price that is very similar to a certain good, then any price change will have a significant impact on the quantity demanded. However, if there is a major difference in price between two substitutes, consumers are much less likely to switch between them.
- *The percentage of income spent on a good* If a good only represents a tiny amount of a person's spending, such as a box of matches or a pencil, it is unlikely that the person will be too concerned if the price rises (or keen to buy more if the price falls). Consequently, price changes will have a minimal effect on the quantity demanded and so demand will be price inelastic.
- *Income of the consumer* As a rule, people on high incomes will be less influenced by price changes. Since they can afford to pay more, they are less likely to react to price rises or cuts. The price elasticity of demand for richer people therefore tends to be more inelastic. Price changes can have a big influence on the spending patterns of people on lower incomes and so their demand is likely to be more price elastic. This factor can 'conflict' with the earlier points concerning necessities and luxuries, as those on lower incomes tend to spend a larger percentage of their income on necessities while richer people buy more luxuries. In practice, many luxury products have price inelastic demand because they are wanted by people who are not too concerned about a rise in price.
- *Generic or branded goods* A generic good is one that covers all versions of a good, such as petrol, water or mobile phones. A branded good is a particular firm's version or brand, such as Shell petrol, Evian bottled water or a Huawei Ascend phone. Most consumers would regard these generic goods as necessities (or habit forming!) and so the demand for petrol or water is price inelastic. However, individual versions of these goods have many close substitutes, such as BP and Esso petrol, or Volvic and Malvern water. Branded goods tend to be more price elastic because they have close substitutes.
- *Time* In the short run, a price increase may mean that consumers are not happy with the new price of a good. However, in the short run consumers may not know which alternatives (substitutes) are available and they will continue to buy the same amount, which means demand remains the same (perfectly inelastic) or changes slightly (inelastic). Over a longer period, consumers find alternative goods and so demand becomes more price elastic in the long run. This factor mainly applies to price rises. A price cut will encourage consumers to buy more of their existing good and there is no need to research alternatives. In the short run, demand therefore tends to be more elastic for price cuts than price rises.

Factor influencing price elasticity of demand	Factor leading to demand being price inelastic	Factor leading to demand being price elastic
Degree of necessity	High degree of necessity	Not a necessity
Habit-forming goods	Very habit forming	Not habit forming
Substitutes	No or few close substitutes	Many close substitutes
The percentage of income spent on a good	Low percentage of income spent on the good	High percentage of income spent on the good
Income of the consumer	High income	Low income
Generic or branded good	Generic good	Branded good
Time	Short-run time period	Long-run time period

Table 7.4 *Summary of main factors that influence price elasticity of demand*

Factors influencing income elasticity of demand

The main factors that influence the income elasticity of demand have been referred to earlier. They are:

- *The nature of the product*
  - A good that is a luxury or superior good will be purchased in much greater quantities as income rises and so it will have a high (>1) positive income elasticity.
  - A good that appeals to consumers with mid-range incomes is likely to have a low but positive (0 to +1) income elasticity of demand.
  - Goods that tend to be purchased because consumers cannot afford a better alternative will have a negative income elasticity of demand – they are inferior goods.
- *Individual preferences* People's views vary and so their spending patterns will change in different ways as their incomes change. As people benefit from increases in their income, they may choose to spend their extra income on holidays, social activities, housing, cars or clothing. In fact, the same person may prioritise all of these items at different times. Thus income elasticity of demand will depend on individual preferences.
- *Income levels and the distribution of income* As incomes rise over time, different goods become the luxuries, the normal goods and the inferior goods and so the income elasticity of demand for individual goods will change over time. The distribution of income also affects income elasticity of demand. If everyone had the same income, there would be no demand for some luxuries and possibly no demand for some inferior goods.
- *Time* As with price elasticity of demand, income elasticity of demand is more income elastic in the long run because it will take people time to discover the new goods available to them within the scope of their new income level.

Factors influencing cross elasticity of demand

The main factors that influence the price elasticity of demand are:

- *Substitutes and how close they are as alternatives* As noted earlier, cross elasticity of demand will be high and positive if a good has close substitutes. A good with substitutes that are not seen as close alternatives will have a low, positive cross elasticity.
- *Complements and how close they are as complementary goods* As noted earlier, cross elasticity of demand will be high and negative if a good has a very close

complement, but is likely to have a low negative value if it is not always used with its complement (such as sugar and tea).

- *Time* As with other elasticities, cross elasticity of demand will tend to have a lower numerical value (positive or negative) until the consumer has had time to discover alternative substitutes (or complements).

Interpreting numerical values of these elasticities of demand

What conclusions can be drawn from the data in Table 7.5?

	Good Y	Good Z
Price elasticity of demand	−2.0	−0.2
Income elasticity of demand	+1.7	−0.2
Cross elasticity of demand with Good X	+1.4	−0.2

Table 7.5 *Data on elasticities of demand for Good Y and Good Z*

Product Y

- Price elasticity of demand for Good Y is −2. This is very price elastic. Good Y could be a good that has close substitutes. It would not be a necessity or a habit-forming good, although it may be a branded rather than generic product and so have lots of alternative goods that could replace it. If the firm increases price by 10%, the quantity demanded will fall by 20% and so total revenue will fall. However, if the price of Good Y were cut by 10%, then the quantity demanded would increase by 20%.
- Income elasticity of demand for Good Y is +1.7. This means that it is a normal good and it appears to be a luxury or superior good. In times of economic growth and rising incomes, total expenditure on Good Y will increase at a faster rate than the rate at which incomes are increasing. If consumers' incomes rise by 10%, then the quantity demanded of Good Y will increase by 17%.
- The cross elasticity of demand between Good Y and Good X is +1.4. This suggests that Good X and Good Y are close substitutes. If the price of Good X rises by 10%, then the quantity demanded of Good Y will increase by 14%. However, a price cut for Good X will have a significant negative effect on the quantity demanded of Good Y.

Product Z

- Price elasticity of demand for Good Z is −0.2. This is very price inelastic. Good Z would appear to have no close substitutes. It may be a generic good rather than a branded good. However, more significantly it appears to be a necessity or a habit-forming good. If the price increases by 10%, the quantity demanded will fall by only 2% and so total revenue will rise by about 8%. However, if the price of Good Z were cut by 10%, then the quantity demanded would increase by only 2% and so total revenue/expenditure would fall by about 8%.
- Income elasticity of demand for Good Z is −0.2. This means that it is an inferior good, although it is not likely to experience a dramatic change in quantity demanded when incomes change. In times of economic growth and rising incomes, quantity demanded of Good Z will decrease. If consumers' incomes rise by 10%, then the quantity demanded of Good Z will decrease by 2%. In a recession, Good Z is the type of good that may experience a rise in demand.

- The cross elasticity of demand between Good Z and Good X is –0.2. This suggests that Good X and Good Z are complementary goods. However, the low numerical value implies that they may not be very close complements, but rather goods that are sometimes used together. If the price of Good X rises by 10%, then the quantity demanded of Good Z will decrease by 2%. However, a price cut for Good X will have a slightly positive effect on the quantity demanded of Good Z.

Number crunching

Table 7.6 shows the changes in quantity demanded for Product A as a result of different changes.

Before		After	
P = £5	Q_d = 100,000	P = £7	Q_d = 90,000
Average Y = £25,000	Q_d = 100,000	Average Y = £26,000	Q_d = 91,000
P of Good B = £15	Q_d = 100,000	P of Good B = £18	Q_d = 92,000
P of Good C = £30	Q_d = 100,000	P of Good C = £27	Q_d = 93,000

Table 7.6

1. Calculate the price elasticity of demand for Good A and indicate whether it is elastic or inelastic.
2. Calculate the change in total revenue as a result of the change in price of Good A.
3. Calculate the income elasticity of demand for Good A. Briefly comment on what your result shows.
4. Calculate the cross elasticity of demand between Good A and Good B. Briefly comment on your result.
5. Calculate the cross elasticity of demand between Good A and Good C. Briefly comment on your result.

REALWORLD ECONOMICS 7.2

The elasticity of alcohol demand

In 2010 the tax authorities in the UK carried out a survey of consumer spending on alcohol in the UK. At this time the UK government generated £9 billion from taxes on alcohol – around 2% of the government's total revenue from taxation. This was fairly evenly split between beer (36%), wine (32%) and spirits (29%). Cider contributed the remaining 3%.

Over the previous 30 years, sales of beer declined, spirits fluctuated at about the same level and wine sales more than tripled. The demand for alcohol is influenced by a greater variety of factors than most other consumption goods. In addition to factors such as price and income, the demand for alcohol is influenced by licensing restrictions, advertising restrictions, age requirements, peer group pressure, social factors, emotional factors, health conditions, location, sex, age, religion and marital status. As a result, it can be difficult to isolate the impact of individual factors on demand. A major factor in determining price elasticity of demand was whether the alcohol was bought 'on trade' (at a licensed premise such as a pub) or 'off trade' (from a shop such as a supermarket).

The government's calculations showed a few key results:

- The demand for alcohol tends to be price inelastic.
- The demand for beer is more price inelastic that the demand for wine and spirit.
- The price elasticity of demand for heavy drinkers is more price inelastic than it is for light users.

- The price elasticity of demand was more price elastic for off-trade purchases than on-trade purchases.
- All types of alcohol have positive income elasticities, although in the late twentieth century surveys indicated that beer had a negative income elasticity of demand.
- Cross elasticities of demand vary considerably, with some being positive and some being negative.

The government also calculated cross elasticities of demand between different types of alcohol. Some example results are as follows:

- The cross elasticity of demand between on-trade beer and on-trade wine was +0.54. This was the highest positive result recorded.
- The cross elasticity of demand between on-trade wine and on-trade alcopops was –0.68.
- The cross elasticity of demand between off-trade beer and off-trade wine was +0.03.
- The cross elasticity of demand between off-trade wine and off-trade cider was –0.91.

Table 7.7 *Price elasticity of demand and income elasticity of demand for certain types of alcohol*

	Price elasticity of demand	Income elasticity of demand
Beer (on trade)	–0.77	+0.31
Beer (off trade)	–1.11	+0.22
Wine (on trade)	–0.46	+0.90
Wine (off trade)	–0.54	+0.42
Spirits (on trade)	–1.15	+0.55
Spirits (off trade)	–0.90	+0.32

Note: This table excludes the data for cider and alcopops, which represent only a small percentage of alcohol demand.
Source: HMRC, 2010 and 2011

Exercises *Total: 45 marks*

1 How would a tax on beer affect total revenue for:
(a) pubs
(b) supermarkets *(5 marks)*

2 Explain why beer has the lowest income elasticity of demand. *(5 marks)*

3 Select *two* of the bullet points on cross elasticity of demand and explain their significance for firms that sell alcohol. *(10 marks)*

4 Evaluate the usefulness of this data to the tax authorities in the UK. *(25 marks)*

Review questions

Total: 70 marks

1 Which one of the following demand schedules would give a demand curve that has a price elasticity of demand of zero?

	Price:	£6	£5	£4	£3	£2	£1
A	Quantity demanded	10	12	15	20	30	60
B	Quantity demanded	1	2	3	4	5	6
C	Quantity demanded	10	10	10	10	10	10
D	Quantity demanded	6	5	4	3	2	1

(1 mark)

2 What measures the responsiveness of the quantity demanded of the product to a change in the price of a different product?

A Demand curve
B Cross elasticity of demand
C Income elasticity of demand
D Price elasticity of demand

(1 mark)

3 In Figure 7.6 the demand curve has shifted from D_1 to D_2.

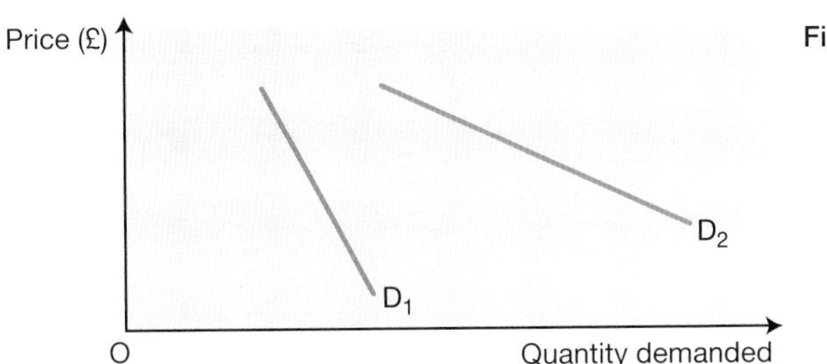

Figure 7.6

The move from D_1 to D_2 shows:

A A decrease in demand and demand becoming more price elastic
B A decrease in demand and demand becoming more price inelastic
C An increase in demand and demand becoming more price elastic
D An increase in demand and demand becoming more price inelastic *(1 mark)*

4 A garden centre lowers the price of packets of daffodil bulbs from £4 to £3.20. As a result, the quantity demanded rises from 400 packets to 600 packets. The price elasticity of demand for daffodil bulbs is:

A −0.4
B −0.75
C −1.33
D −2.5 *(1 mark)*

5 Table 7.8 provides data on the value of income elasticities of demand for four goods – A, B, C and D.

Table 7.8

Good	Income elasticity of demand
A	+2.5
B	+1.0
C	+0.6
D	−1.3

From the data it can be concluded that:

A Good A is the only normal good
B Good B will yield the same total revenue, regardless of income level
C Total revenue from Good C will rise more slowly than income, as income rises
D Good D is a substitute for one of the other goods *(1 mark)*

6 A high negative cross elasticity of demand between two products means that they are:

A Complements
B Luxuries
C Necessities
D Substitutes *(1 mark)*

7 If demand for a good is completely (perfectly) price inelastic, then a decrease in its price by 10% will lead to:

A Total revenue decreasing by more than 10%
B Total revenue decreasing by 10%
C Total revenue decreasing by less than 10%
D Total revenue staying the same *(1 mark)*

8 Write down the formula to calculate income elasticity of demand. *(2 marks)*

9 In Figure 7.7 the demand curve is shown by line D.

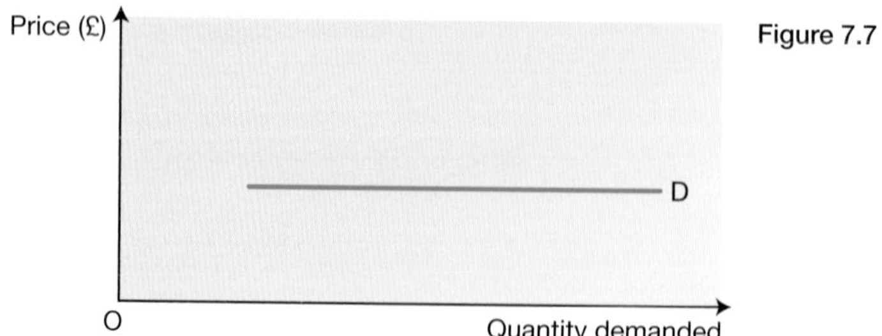

Figure 7.7

For demand curve D:

A Price elasticity of demand = 0

B Price elasticity of demand = –1

C Price elasticity of demand = –∞

D There are different price elasticities of demand along its length *(1 mark)*

10 Define the term 'price elastic demand'. *(3 marks)*

11 Define the term 'inferior good'. *(3 marks)*

12 Price of a good increases from £7 to £9, leading to quantity demanded falling from 60 kilograms to 38 kilograms. Calculate the price elasticity of demand. *(4 marks)*

13 Explain why cross elasticity of demand can be negative or positive. *(6 marks)*

14 Explain the relationship between price and total revenue for a good that has a price inelastic demand curve. *(6 marks)*

15 Read Real World Economics 7.1 (p. 66) and answer the following question: Explain why demand for payday loan companies increased from 2009 to 2013. *(6 marks)*

16 Why do all three types of elasticity of demand become more elastic over time? *(6 marks)*

17 Explain why branded goods tend to be more price elastic than generic goods. *(6 marks)*

18 Evaluate the usefulness of 'elasticity of demand' to a firm that is trying to maximise its total revenue in the long run. *(20 marks)*

The determinants of the supply of goods & services

This chapter introduces the concept of supply and investigates the factors that determine the supply of goods and services, such as price, costs of production and changes in technology. The supply curve is introduced and its shape explained, through recognising that suppliers are motivated by profit and so higher prices provide an incentive to expand production. The chapter concludes by looking at the factors that cause shifts in the supply curve.

Supply

- **Market supply** relates to all firms in a market and so the key term definition refers to market supply.
- **Individual supply** is 'the amount of a good or service that an individual firm intends to offer for sale at any given price over a period of time'.

Key term

Supply is the amount of a good or service that firms intend to offer for sale at any given price over a period of time.

Features of supply

Supply is:

- a measure of the number of items. Changes in supply are shown by 'x' more or 'y' fewer products being offered for sale by firms operating within a certain market.
- based on the desire of suppliers to make a profit. In order to understand supply, a person must put themselves into the position of the firm. If price goes up, the firm will earn more revenue, other things being equal. The actual price arises from the interaction between supply and demand (see Chapter 10) – in a perfect market it is *not* set by the firm. Given this situation, a rational supplier will earn more profit from a high price than a low price and so *if* the price rises, the supplier will offer more for supply. Similarly, *if* the price falls, profit will fall and so the rational supplier will offer fewer goods for sale. The supplier will then look for other, more profitable uses for the resources that are available.
- measured over a period of time. When discussing supply it is important to recognise the time period being considered. For some products, such as beef, it can take a long time to extend the supply if prices rise; for other products, it may be much simpler to extend supply quickly.

The quantity supplied of a particular good may be influenced by a wide range of factors, some of which may be unique to that particular product. However, there are a number of factors that influence the supply of a significant number of products. The main ones are:

- the price of the good itself;
- the price of other goods that the supplier might be able to produce;

- expectations of future prices;
- the costs of labour, such as wages;
- the costs of other factors of production, such as raw material costs and rent;
- technology;
- other factors that influence the efficiency of the factors of production;
- indirect taxes imposed by government, such as VAT;
- government subsidies;
- government legislation and regulation;
- weather and geographical factors.

Each of these factors is considered below.

The factors that determine the supply of a good or service

Price and the quantity supplied

The **law of supply** states that 'as the price of a good rises, quantity supplied rises, and as the price of a good falls, the quantity supplied falls'.

Why is this so? A supplier has factors of production that have alternative uses. For example, a farmer might use the land to plant different crops and may decide to use the farm's labour force to produce different goods. A farm may produce onions and potatoes. The price of a batch of onions or a batch of potatoes may be £16 and both may cost £12 to produce. If factors outside the control of the farmer lead to a rise in the price of onions from £16 to £20, then the potential profit from onions will be greater. This will encourage the farmer to shift more resources into onion production (these resources can be taken from the production of potatoes). Some resources may still be used to produce potatoes as they may not be suitable for onion production, or they may be so inefficient that the cost to the farmer of producing onions would rise too much and cancel out the higher profit.

In exactly the same way, a fall in the price of onions will lead to a fall in the quantity supplied because the expected level of profit has fallen.

The above explanation applies to one supplier. In the market as a whole, entrepreneurs will recognise the greater potential to make profit from supplying onions, and so new suppliers will enter the market, driven by the profit motive. This will lead to a further rise in the supply of onions. Similarly, falling prices will lead to financial losses and firms leaving the market, possibly because the losses have meant that the firm ceases to exist.

As with the law of demand, there are exceptions to the law of supply, but the vast majority of supply curves follow this law.

Author tip

When studying supply, put yourself in the position of the business owner. You are motivated by profit and so higher prices encourage you to offer more products for sale because that will help you to achieve your aim.

Price of other goods and the quantity supplied

The section above shows how the price of onions influences the supply of onions. However, it also shows how changes in the price of onions affect the supply of potatoes. In this example, onions and potatoes are an example of **competitive supply.** Competitive supply means that the two products are competing for the factors of production needed to supply them. As the price of onions increases, onions become more profitable and are able to attract more resources from the rival for those resources – potatoes. Thus an increase in the price of onions will lead to a decrease in the supply of potatoes, other things being equal. This logic also applies when the price of onions falls. This would make onion growing less profitable and so suppliers will switch resources away from onions and towards products in competitive supply with them, such as potatoes.

In some cases two or more goods are in **joint supply.** This means that the production of one good automatically creates the other good, often as a byproduct. An example of joint supply is the supply of beef and hides, with the latter product usually seen as a byproduct when beef is supplied. If the price of beef rises, then suppliers, motivated by the profit incentive, will be eager to supply more beef. As a result, the supply of hides will also rise. Thus an increase in the price of beef will lead to an increase in the supply of hides. By the same logic, a fall in the price of beef will lead to a decrease in the supply of hides. Joint supply will be considered in more detail in Chapter 11.

Expectations of future prices and the quantity supplied

In the two sections above, behaviour was based on changes in price. In the case of retailers, such as supermarkets, supplies of goods can be changed quite quickly to suit sudden rises and falls in price. For many firms, such as farmers and house builders, it takes a long time to produce and supply the good involved. Thus the farmer should not be looking at the current price of onions and potatoes, but should base their supply on what they expect the price to be when the onion or potato is fully grown. Similarly, decisions to build houses are made on the basis of what the price is expected to be once the house has been completed.

This can cause fluctuations in price. If onions are highly priced this year, then many farmers will grow onions for the following year and so the supply of onions may be much higher than the demand. This will force farmers to cut the price of onions in the following year. In the year after that, fewer onions will be supplied, leading to a shortage and high prices.

Labour costs and the quantity supplied

Costs are the key influence on the supply of most goods. Entrepreneurs will not supply a good if they cannot cover their costs. Table 8.1 shows a supply schedule in accordance with the law of supply, with higher prices encouraging entrepreneurs to supply more units of Good X. Entrepreneurs are motivated by profit and so will only supply goods if they can expect to earn a certain level of profit. Economists refer to this level of profit as **normal profit.** Let us assume that the only costs involved in producing Good X are wages of workers. To provide 2 units of Good X requires one hour of labour for each unit produced and workers are paid £6 per hour. Assume also that the entrepreneur's normal profit for Good X is £1 per unit. The entrepreneur

Price (£)	Quantity supplied of Good X
11	15
10	10
9	7
8	4
7	2
6	0

Table 8.1 *Supply schedule for Good X*

will only supply Good X if he can cover his costs and normal profit. This means he will supply two units of Good X if he can sell the good for a price of £7 (£6 + £1), as this covers his 'costs' (wages plus normal profit). At £6 he does not supply because he cannot cover his costs. At higher prices, even though costs rise, he supplies more because there is more scope for profit. Table 8.1 shows that he will supply 15 units if the price is £11. If the price is £12, he will supply 22 units (not shown in the table).

If the hourly wage increases from £6 to £7, then he will no longer supply 2 units of Good X at a price of £7. He now needs £7 + £1 = £8 to cover his costs and normal profit and so he will supply 2 units if the price is £8 (rather than £7). This logic will apply at every level of the supply schedule in Table 8.1. Thus, he will now only supply 4 units at £9 rather than £8 and he will supply 7 units at £10 rather than £9. The new supply schedule is shown in Table 8.2.

Price (£)	Quantity supplied of Good X
12	15
11	10
10	7
9	4
8	2
7	0

Table 8.2 *Supply schedule for Good X, after a wage increase of £1 per hour*

From a comparison of the two supply schedules it can be seen that the increase in the cost of labour has led to a decrease in the supply of Good X. At a price of £7, the quantity supplied has decreased from 2 units to zero units. At a price of £8, the quantity supplied has decreased from 4 units to 2 units. At a price of £9, the quantity supplied has decreased from 7 units to 4 units, and so on.

What happens if wages decrease by £1 per hour to £5 per hour? This means that our original 2 units that were supplied at £7 can now be supplied for £6. The 4 units supplied at £8 are now supplied at £7. Table 8.3 summarises the supply schedules for Good X at three different wage levels.

Table 8.3 *Supply schedules for Good X at different wage levels*

Price (£)	Quantity supplied of Good X at a wage level of:		
Column 1	*Column 2*	*Column 3*	*Column 4*
	£6 per hour	£7 per hour	£5 per hour
11	15	10	22
10	10	7	15
9	7	4	10
8	4	2	7
7	2	0	4
6	0	0	2

The original wage of £6 is shown in the second column. It can be seen that 2 units are supplied at a price of £7. The third column shows that when wages rise to £7 per hour, the quantity supplied decreases to zero units. For every price above £7 there is a fall in the quantity supplied as a result of the wage increase. *This shows that an increase in the cost of labour will lead to a decrease in the supply of Good X.*

The fourth column shows that when wages fall to £5 per hour, the quantity supplied increases, in comparison to the second column. At a price of £7 the quantity supplied increases from 2 units to 4 units. At £8, the quantity supplied increases from 4 units to 7 units. For every price there is a rise in the quantity supplied as a result of the wage decrease. *This shows that a decrease in the cost of labour will lead to an increase in the supply of Good X.*

Other costs and the quantity supplied

Labour is just one of the costs of production. Other factors of production will also be required to provide goods and services and so their costs will also influence the quantity supplied. Costs such as raw materials, rent, capital equipment and interest payments will all contribute towards the total costs of providing a good or service. Their impact on the quantity supplied will vary from product to product – some goods and services, such as energy supply, tend to be very capital intensive and so capital equipment will be a major cost. For production that requires a large area of land, such as agriculture, rent may be a significant cost. These other costs affect the quantity supplied in exactly the same way as labour costs.

An increase in any of these costs will, other things being equal, lead to a decrease in the quantity supplied of the good being produced. A decrease in any of these costs will lead to an increase in the supply of the goods being produced.

Technology and the quantity supplied

Technology is another major influence on the quantity supplied, largely because of its impact on the costs of production. In many industries, new technology has replaced labour. This tends to lead to an increase in costs initially, because of the cost of capital equipment, but significant reductions in costs such as labour thereafter. Technological improvements, such as miniaturisation, have also improved productive efficiency, enabling firms to cut costs of raw materials as finished products require fewer and smaller components.

Technology influences supply through its impact on the efficiency of factors of production. For example, a given area of agricultural land can now yield much greater quantities of crops because of new technology, and labour forces in car manufacturing have become more productive in terms of both the volume of cars produced and the quality (and value) of the individual cars.

By increasing the productive efficiency of factors of production, technology can increase supply. In Table 8.4, the second column shows original quantity supplied

Price (£)	Quantity supplied of Good X	
	Before	After
11	15	22.5
10	10	15
9	7	10.5
8	4	6
7	2	3
6	0	0

Table 8.4 *Supply schedule for Good X, before and after new technology*

(as per Table 8.1). New technology is introduced and improves the output of each worker by 50%. Table 8.1 was based on workers producing one unit per hour. The 50% improvement means that 1.5 units will be produced for every 1 unit produced originally. In Table 8.4, the third column shows the output/supply after the 50% increase in efficiency.

New technology has also enabled new products to be created and has led to the decline or demise of many other, non-technical or technologically inferior products. Consequently, its impact on supply has been much more significant than its influence as a factor that can cut production costs. In this respect technology has also had a major impact on demand, through the creation of new wants.

Other factors that influence productive efficiency and the quantity supplied

Improvements in technology lead to an increase in supply because they improve productive efficiency. Other factors that improve productive efficiency will therefore also increase the quantity supplied. For labour and enterprise, improvements in education and training should improve performance by increasing the efficiency of those two factors of production. This may lead to an increase in supply across the whole economy. In contrast, a lack of education and training is likely to lead to a decrease in the quantity supplied of goods and services in an economy.

For agricultural land, scientific techniques can be applied in order to improve its fertility and therefore increase the efficiency of production. Improvements in management techniques and production methods can also mean that a given volume of factors of production can create an increased level of output.

In Chapter 4 we saw how the UK economy has created greater output per head of population over the last 60 years. Based on 2010 prices, the average production per head in 1953 was £6306; by 2013 this had risen to £23,113 – an increase of 267%. This improvement in output per head has enabled the UK economy to increase its supply of products overall, and it will have largely arisen from improvements in technology, education and training, management techniques and production methods.

Indirect taxes and the quantity supplied

Indirect taxes are taxes on goods and services – for example, VAT and excise duty on products such as tobacco.

In Chapter 6 we saw how changes to income tax affect people's disposable incomes and therefore lead to changes in demand. However, indirect taxes affect supply. In effect, they act like an increase in the cost of making a product. If a firm supplies 24 units at a price of £10 but VAT of 20% is then imposed on that product, then the firm will only wish to supply those 24 units at a price of £12 (£10 + VAT of £2). *Thus an increase in an indirect tax will lead to a decrease in the supply of a good.*

In contrast, a decrease in an indirect tax will lead to an increase in the supply of a good. In 2007, the UK government cut the rate of VAT on products that were supplied in order to help people stop smoking. The rate of VAT fell from 20% to 5%, leading to an increase in supply of these products.

Excise duties are usually set at a fixed level (e.g. £1.50 per litre). In Table 8.3 we saw how an increase in wages by £1 per unit led to a decrease in supply, and how a decrease in wages by £1 per unit led to an increase in supply. The figures in the third column of Table 8.3 would be exactly the same if the government increased excise duty by £1; the figures in the fourth column of Table 8.3 show what would happen to supply if excise duty were reduced by £1 per unit.

Government subsidies and the quantity supplied

Government subsidies are the opposite of taxes. They are a sum of money given to suppliers, usually £x per unit produced. In the UK subsidies are mainly used for agricultural production, to encourage farmers and help the UK/Europe to be self-sufficient in food supply. Their impact on supply is the reverse of an indirect tax.

Subsidies encourage supply and therefore the introduction of a subsidy or an increase in the level of a subsidy leads to an increase in supply. In effect, the subsidy cuts the cost of supplying.

Similarly, *the withdrawal or reduction of a subsidy leads to a decrease in supply* because the cost of supplying now increases.

Again, Table 8.3 can be used to show the effect of subsidies. An increase in a subsidy by £1 will cut costs – its effect is shown by the fourth column of Table 8.3. Column 3 of Table 8.3 shows the effect of a reduction in a subsidy by £1.

Government legislation and regulation and the quantity supplied

For certain products, governments impose laws or regulations that might affect supply. Pharmaceutical products are strictly regulated to ensure their safety, alcohol is regulated and can only be sold in licensed premises and to people of certain ages, and areas of towns and cities are regulated in terms of their use for commercial purposes.

In general, legislation and regulations are intended to restrict supply of goods and services that might have negative effects on users, non-users or both. The removal of restrictions will lead to greater supply.

The use of government legislation and regulations in order to influence supply will be dealt with in more detail in Chapter 29, along with a more detailed study of the impact of indirect taxation and subsidies.

Weather and geographical factors and the quantity supplied

The weather and geographical factors have a limited impact on the supply of many goods and services, but for some products they have a major influence. Service industries, such as the holiday trade and leisure activities, may depend considerably on the suitability of the climate; production of goods, such as crops and fruit, can be helped or hindered by both the weather and the suitability of the terrain. In recent years, it has been claimed that adverse weather conditions have affected supply because people have been unable to get to work.

A supply curve shows the relationship between price and quantity supplied

The **law of supply** states that as the price of a good rises, quantity supplied rises. We have seen earlier that this relationship arises because entrepreneurs are motivated by the profit incentive. As prices increase, there is scope to make more profit and so the

Key term

The **supply curve** shows the relationship between the price of a good and the quantity supplied of that good.

entrepreneur will supply more goods. This relationship is shown in the supply curve S_1 in Figure 8.1.

In a diagram showing a supply curve, price is shown on the 'y' axis and the quantity supplied is shown on the 'x' axis. At price P_1 we read horizontally across the diagram to see the quantity supplied. Point X shows the quantity supplied at price P_1. We then move vertically down from X to read the quantity supplied from the 'x' axis. The quantity supplied at price P_1 is Q_1. If price rises to P_2, more suppliers will want to supply the product and existing suppliers will want to supply more, and so we move from Point X to Y, with supply extending to Q_2. This rise in the quantity supplied is described as an **extension in supply** or an **increase in the quantity supplied.**

Figure 8.1 *The supply curve*

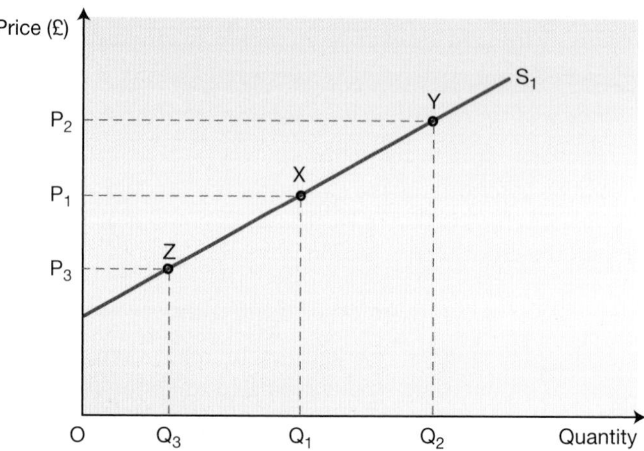

If price falls from P_1 to P_3, sellers will want to supply less, as the scope for profit is reduced. Thus we move from Point X to Z, with supply falling to Q_3. This fall in the quantity supplied is described as a **contraction in supply** or a **decrease in the quantity supplied.**

Contractions and extensions in supply mean that we are moving along an existing supply curve, rather than looking at a different supply curve. **The only factor that can cause a contraction or extension in supply is a change in price.**

The market supply curve is the summation of all of the individual supply curves. As the individual supply curves slope upwards from left to right, so will the market supply curve.

Table 8.5 shows the individual supply schedules of three firms: X, Y and Z. For the sake of simplicity it is assumed that these are the only firms in the market.

Table 8.5 *Individual and market supply schedules*

Price (£)	Quantity supplied by Firm X	Quantity supplied by Firm Y	Quantity supplied by Firm Z	Market supply (units)
6	11	4	20	35
5	10	4	18	32
4	8	3	16	27
3	6	2	12	20
2	4	1	7	12
1	1	0	2	3

It can be seen that at £1 the market supply is 3 units (1 + 0 + 2). At £2, market supply is 12 units (4 + 1 + 7). Completing the table enables us to construct the three individual supply curves *and* the market supply curve. These are shown in Figure 8.2.

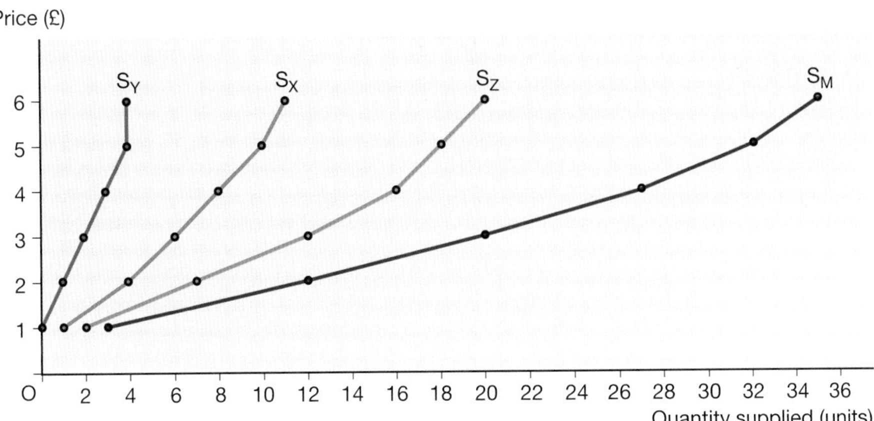

Figure 8.2 *Individual supply curves and the market supply curve*

Note how the shapes of each of the individual supply curves differ, but they all follow the law of supply. As a result, the market supply curve also corresponds to the law of supply. As there are only three firms in this market, it is possible to plot the market supply on the same graph as the individual supply curves. For a normal market, individual supply is likely to be measured in units, whereas market supply is possibly measured in millions of units. However, in markets where there are only a few firms (known as a oligopolists), such as mobile phone networks and energy suppliers, both scales will be the same.

Higher prices imply higher profits and provide the incentive to expand production

It can be seen throughout the two earlier sections that entrepreneurs/firms are motivated by profit. Any increase in price suggests that profit will increase. Increases in price thus provide the incentive to expand production (extend supply). However, this logic also works in reverse. Any decrease in price suggests that profit will decrease. Decreases in price thus provide a disincentive to produce. Firms will cut back on production (contract supply) and even give up production altogether if the price is too low for them to be able to make a profit.

The causes of shifts in the supply curve

The supply curve shows us the impact of changes in price on the quantity supplied. What happens if there is a change to one of the other factors that influences supply, such as labour costs and technology? Supply curves are not static and will change as circumstances differ.

When one of these factors changes, it leads to a shift in the supply curve. For example, in Table 8.5 we can see that Firm X will supply 1 unit when the price is £1 and 6 units when the price is £3. If Firm X cuts the wages of its workforce or improves its productive efficiency by introducing new technology, then it will be able to supply more goods at these prices. For example, at a price of £2 it may now want to supply 5 units instead of 4 and at a price of £3 its supply may increase from 6 units to 8 units.

This means its individual supply curve shifts to the right.

An *increase in supply* shifts the supply curve to the right, showing a greater quantity supplied at each price. A *decrease in supply* shifts the supply curve to the left, showing a lower quantity supplied at each price.

Factors that cause a shift in the supply curve are known as the **determinants of supply**. The major determinants are the factors we have noted earlier, such as the efficiency of factors of production and indirect taxes.

A shift to the right of the supply curve (from S_1 to S_2) in Figure 8.3 shows an *increase in supply*. At price P_1 supply has increased from Q_1 to Q_4. This might have been caused by factors such as a cut in wages or receipt of a government subsidy.

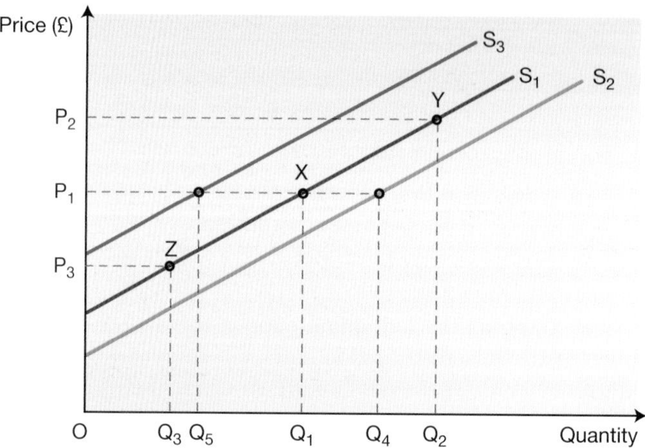

Figure 8.3 *Shifts in the supply curve*

The reverse of these changes, such as higher wages or an indirect tax being imposed, leads to less desire to supply as there is less scope for profit, and so this would lead to a *decrease in supply*. This shifts the supply curve to the left (from S_1 to S_3). At price P_1 supply has decreased from Q_1 to Q_5.

Key note

When shifting supply curves, make sure that you remember that the quantity supplied is measured on the horizontal 'x' axis. This means that quantity is read horizontally and not vertically. Therefore an increase in supply means that the supply curve shifts to the right (rather than upwards). A decrease in supply means that the supply curve shifts to the left (rather than downwards).

An 'upward' move would be caused by factors such as higher costs or lower productive efficiency. These factors will make it more difficult to supply as much as before, at any given price. Similarly, a 'downward' move would be caused by factors such as lower wages or subsidies, both of which make it easier to supply.

This feature often causes difficulties for economics students because supply and demand diagrams are drawn differently from most diagrams. In mathematics, the independent variable is always shown on the 'x' axis and the dependent variable is shown on the 'y' axis. Thus it is usual practice to measure the quantity of the dependent variable (the one being affected by the other factor) vertically, along the 'y' axis. Just remember that in these diagrams the dependent variable (the quantity) is measured along the 'x' axis.

Factor causing an increase in supply	Factor causing a decrease in supply
An increase in the price of a good in joint supply	A decrease in the price of a good in joint supply
A decrease in the price of a good in competitive supply	An increase in the price of a good in competitive supply
Expectations that prices will rise in the future	Expectations that prices will fall in the future
A decrease in labour costs	An increase in labour costs
A decrease in other production costs, such as raw material costs	An increase in other production costs, such as raw material costs
Improvements in technology	Ineffective use of technology
Using other factors that will increase productive efficiency, such as improved production techniques	Changing to new techniques that lower productive efficiency
A decrease in the level of indirect taxation, such as VAT	An increase in the level of indirect taxation, such as VAT
An increase or introduction of a subsidy on the product	A decrease or abolition of a subsidy on the product
The removal of laws or regulations that restrict production of the good	The introduction of laws or regulations that restrict production of the good
Favourable weather or geographical factors relating to production	Adverse weather or geographical factors relating to production

Table 8.6 *Factors leading to increases and decreases in supply*

Table 8.6 summarises the main factors influencing supply and whether the factor leads to:

- an increase in supply for a good (shifting the supply curve to the right); or
- a decrease in supply for a good (shifting the supply curve to the left).

A movement along a supply curve can only be caused by a change in price. It is known as a resultant change in supply.

A rise in price (such as P_1 to P_2 in Figure 8.3) leads to an extension in supply from Q_1 to Q_2 (also known as an increase in the quantity supplied).

A fall in price (such as P_1 to P_3 in Figure 8.3) leads to a contraction in supply from Q_1 to Q_3 (also known as a decrease in the quantity supplied).

A shift to a completely new supply curve is caused by a change in any of the other factors that determine supply (but not price). It is known as a real change in supply because a different quantity is supplied at each price.

An increase in supply (such as the shift from S_1 to S_2 in Figure 8.3) leads to more supply at every price. For example, at price P_1, the quantity supplied has changed from Q_1 to Q_4. This change in supply is described as an increase in supply.

Similarly, a decrease in supply leads to a shift in the supply curve to the left (from D_1 to D_3 in Figure 8.3). Thus at price P_1, the quantity supplied falls from Q_1 to Q_5.

It should be noted that the terms 'increase in supply' or 'decrease in supply' mean a real change in supply (i.e. a shift in the supply curve). For resultant changes in supply (caused by price changes) the phrases 'increase in the quantity supplied' or 'decrease in the quantity supplied' are used. Alternatively, you can use the phrases 'extension in supply' or 'contraction in supply' to describe movements along an existing supply curve.

Author tip

Remember to distinguish between changes that cause a movement along a supply curve and changes that cause a shift to a new supply curve.

REALWORLD
ECONOMICS 8.1

Supply of agricultural produce

In recent years the UK supply of agricultural produce has changed. Competition from abroad has led to a reduction in the number of enterprises from 13,407 in 2008 to 10,955 in 2011. This fall has not led to a fall in overall output – instead it has meant fewer but much larger firms. Large firms are in a better position to introduce new technology in order to improve productive efficiency.

Since 2003, European Union (EU) agricultural subsidies have changed. Prior to 2003 they tended to give much greater support to dairy farming than other types of agriculture. Since then greater emphasis has been given to cereal crops and livestock (beef and sheep) farming. Subsidies are now much lower for horticulture, poultry and pig farming. Subsidies to livestock farmers account for approximately 50% of farm income, with 40% subsidies for some crops. In contrast, horticulture (fruit and vegetables) receives a subsidy of only 15%. One in six horticulture farms made losses in 2011, making horticulture farmers much more likely to leave the industry or change to other forms of agriculture.

Different types of agriculture use varying techniques and so their costs are based on different factors. Table 8.7 gives a breakdown of costs for a typical farm within each category.

New technology has encouraged a move into crop production and horticulture. For example, soil-less production techniques have allowed the strawberry-growing season to be extended to 9 months a year. New production techniques have led to an increase in productivity (efficiency) by 30% in recent years. In most sectors, new technology is considered to be the key to further improvements in productive efficiency.

Source: Migrant Seasonal Workers, published by the Migration Advisory Committee of the Home Office, May 2013

	Percentage of total production costs				
Type of agriculture	**Land**	**Raw materials**	**Labour**	**Machinery**	**Total**
Cereal	10	62	6	22	100
Other crops	10	56	13	21	100
Dairy	8	68	10	14	100
Grazing	9	63	6	22	100
Pig	6	75	11	8	100
Poultry	6	81	8	5	100
Horticulture	4	55	32	9	100
Farming – overall	9	63	11	17	100

Table 8.7 *Contribution of land, raw materials, labour and machinery to total production costs by farm type*

Harvesting in West Norfolk – new technology improves productive efficiency

Exercises *Total: 50 marks*

1 Define the term 'subsidy'. *(3 marks)*

2 Calculate the percentage fall in the number of farms between 2008 and 2011. *(4 marks)*

3 Using Table 8.7, identify two significant points of comparison between the cost of factors of production for different types of agriculture. *(4 marks)*

4 In 2003, the European Union cut its subsidy to dairy farmers. Draw a diagram to show the impact of this change on the supply of milk. *(4 marks)*

5 Explain why poultry farming spends a larger percentage of costs on raw materials than any other industry. *(10 marks)*

6 The information above is extracted from a report that investigated the impact of workers on the supply of agricultural products. Based on the information provided and your own knowledge, to what extent do you believe that the labour supply is the most important influence on the supply of agricultural products? Justify your view. *(25 marks)*

Review questions

Total: 44 marks

1 Entrepreneurs and firms are motivated to supply goods by the:

A Desire to meet people's needs
B Needs of the other factors of production
C Incentive to make profit
D Price of the good *(1 mark)*

2 Which one of the following changes will lead to an increase in the supply of a good?

A An increase in labour costs
B An increase in the price of a good in competitive supply
C An increase in the efficiency of factors of production
D An increase in VAT *(1 mark)*

3 Figure 8.4 shows the original supply curve for beef (S_1) and the new supply curve for beef (S_2).

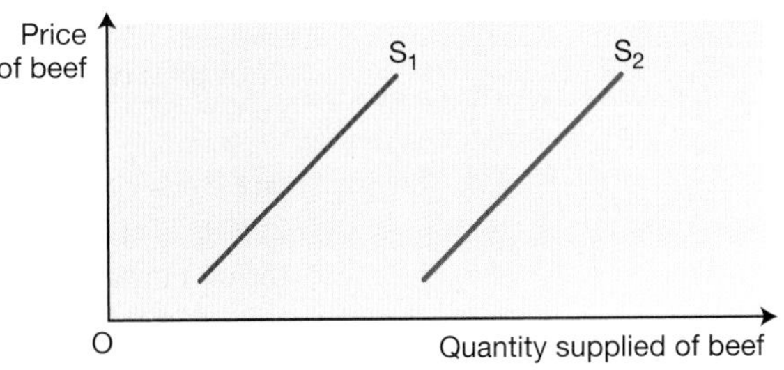

Figure 8.4

Other things being equal, the change in supply curve from S_1 to S_2 might be caused by:

A An increase in the price of horseradish sauce
B A decrease in the price of hides
C A decrease in the price of pork
D Value added tax being imposed on beef *(1 mark)*

4 Figure 8.5 shows the original supply curve for oil (S_1) and the new supply curve for oil (S_2).

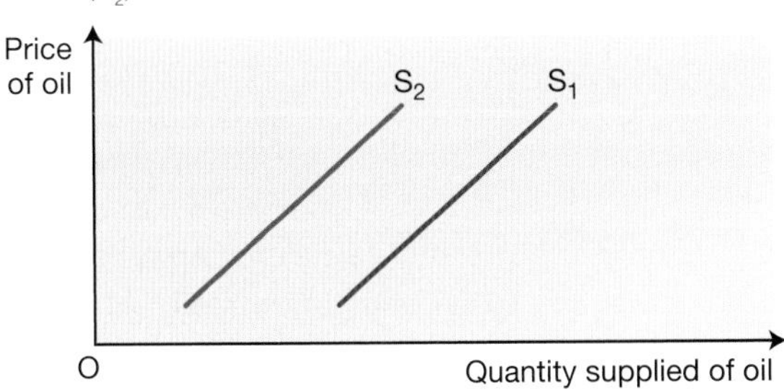

Figure 8.5

Which one of the following factors is most likely to have caused the shift in supply curve from S_1 to S_2?

A A cut in excise duty on oil
B Improvements in technology
C Expectations of a fall in oil prices in the future
D Oil firms achieving higher productive efficiency *(1 mark)*

5 Figure 8.6 shows how the price of Good X influences the supply of Good Y (Line Y) and Good Z (Line Z).

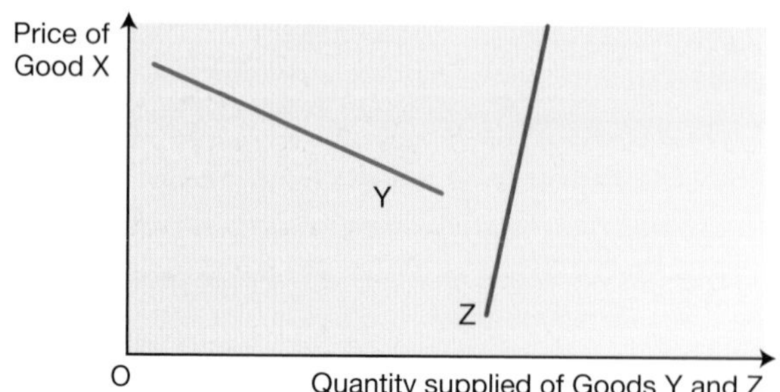

Figure 8.6

From the diagram it can be concluded that:

A Goods Y and Z are both in joint supply with Good X

B Goods Y and Z are both in competitive supply with Good X

C Good Y is in joint supply with Good X; Good Z is in competitive supply with Good X

D Good Y is in competitive supply with Good X; Good Z is in joint supply with Good X *(1 mark)*

6 Choose a particular good or service and state two examples to show how government laws or regulations affect its supply. (The exact names of the laws or regulations are not required.) *(2 marks)*

7 Define the term 'supply'. *(3 marks)*

8 What is the 'law of supply'? *(3 marks)*

9 What is the difference between 'joint supply' and 'competitive supply'? *(5 marks)*

The following information applies to questions 10, 11 and 12. Table 8.8 shows four individual supply curves (A, B, C and D) that make up the market supply curve for Thingies. All quantities are in kilograms.

Price (£)	Firm A (kg)	Firm B (kg)	Firm C (kg)	Firm D (kg)	Market supply (kg)
3	15	10	8	27	
2	11	9	5	21	
1	4	6	0	10	

Table 8.8

10 Complete the table and, on graph paper, plot the market supply curve for Thingies. Label it S_1. Make sure that you label your axes. *(5 marks)*

11 The market supply for Thingies decreases by 50%. Draw the new supply curve on the graph. Label it S_2. *(3 marks)*

12 By how many kilos has supply decreased when the price is £2? *(2 marks)*

13 Explain how the profit motive influences the supply of a good. *(6 marks)*

14 A firm manufactures one product. It gives its workers a 10% pay rise. As a result they work harder and the firm's productive efficiency improves by 5%. Analyse the impact of these changes on the supply curve of the firm's product. *(10 marks)*

Price elasticity of supply

This chapter introduces the concept of price elasticity of supply and shows how to calculate its value. Diagrams are used to show the visual appearance of supply curves with different price elasticities. The chapter concludes with an explanation of the factors that influence price elasticity of supply and an interpretation of the meaning of the numerical values of different price elasticities of supply.

Price elasticity of supply and its calculation

The formula for calculating price elasticity of supply is set out below.

$$\textbf{Price elasticity of supply} = \frac{\%\ \text{change in quantity supplied of Product X}}{\%\ \text{change in price of Product X}}$$

The law of supply states that as price rises, quantity supplied extends (a resultant change). Similarly, as price falls, quantity supplied decreases. This is a 'positive' relationship and means that the price elasticity of supply will be positive, except in very unusual circumstances. Similarly, as price falls, quantity supplied decreases. A negative divided by a negative gives a positive number and so price elasticity of supply is positive for all price changes.

Price elasticity of supply is **inelastic** if the value lies between 0 and +1 (a large percentage change in price leads to a smaller percentage change in quantity supplied).

Price elasticity of supply is **elastic** if the value lies between +1 and +∞ (a small percentage change in price leads to a larger percentage change in quantity supplied).

In Figure 9.1, S_I shows an inelastic supply curve. At a price of £10 we look along the dotted horizontal line to Point A. By tracing the vertical dotted line down from

Key term

Price elasticity of supply (PES) measures the responsiveness of the quantity supplied of a product to a change in the price of that product.

Key note

Price elasticity of supply is the only 'elasticity of supply' that is widely used by economists.

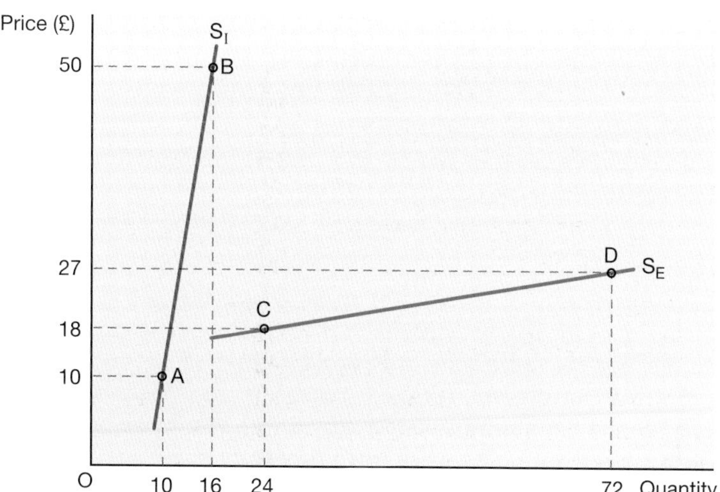

Figure 9.1 *Price elasticity of supply*

Point A to the 'x' axis, we can see that the quantity supplied is 10 units when the price is £10. Moving along this supply curve to Point B, we can see that at a price of £50, the quantity supplied is 16 units.

Moving from Point A to Point B enables us to calculate the price elasticity of supply. The change in price from £10 to £50 is a 400% rise:

$$\frac{50 - 10}{10} \times 100 = \frac{+40}{10} \times 100 = +400\%$$

The change in quantity supplied is a 60% increase:

$$\frac{16 - 10}{10} \times 100 = \frac{+6}{10} \times 100 = +60\%$$

Therefore price elasticity of supply is +60%/+400% = +0.15 or +3/20.

In Figure 9.1, S_E shows an elastic supply curve. At a price of £18 we look along the dotted horizontal line to Point C. By tracing the vertical dotted line down from Point C to the 'x' axis, we can see that the quantity supplied is 24 units when the price is £18. Moving along this supply curve to Point D, we can see that at a price of £27, the quantity supplied is 72 units.

Moving from Point C to Point D enables us to calculate the price elasticity of supply. The change in price from £18 to £27 is a 50% rise:

$$\frac{27 - 18}{100} \times 100 = \frac{+9}{18} \times 100 = +50\%$$

The change in quantity supplied is a 200% increase:

$$\frac{72 - 24}{24} \times 100 = \frac{+48}{24} \times 100 = +200\%$$

Therefore price elasticity of supply is +200%/+50% = +4.

In a diagram where price elasticity of supply is elastic, the supply curve tends to have a low gradient, giving a fairly flat line, such as S_E in Figure 9.1. In a diagram where price elasticity of supply is inelastic, the supply curve tends to have a high gradient, giving a fairly steep line, such as S_I in Figure 9.1.

Key note

Price elasticity of supply applies to changes between two prices. It is unlikely to be the same value all the way along a supply curve or even if we move in the opposite direction between two points. For example, moving from Point A to Point B in Figure 9.1 gave us a price elasticity of supply of +0.15. If we look at a price change in the opposite direction (moving from Point B to Point A), we get a different result. If price had changed from £50 to £10 (moving from Point B to Point A), then the price elasticity of supply would have been −37.5%/−80% = −0.47. This is still inelastic but a significantly different result to the elasticity when changing from Point A to B.

Figures 9.2, 9.3 and 9.4 illustrate supply curves with particular price elasticities of supply. These are rare examples where the price elasticity of supply is the same all the way along the line.

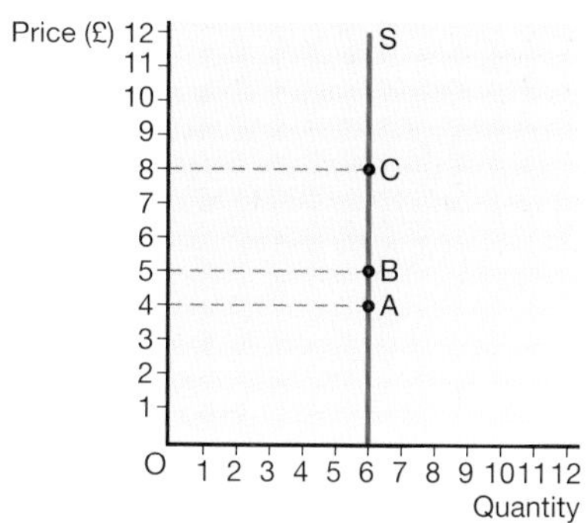

Figure 9.2 *Perfectly inelastic supply or zero elastic supply (PES = zero)*

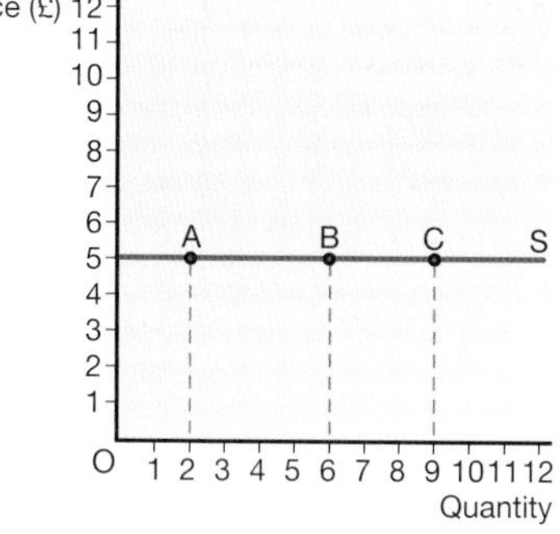

Figure 9.3 *Perfectly elastic supply or infinitely elastic supply (PES = ∞)*

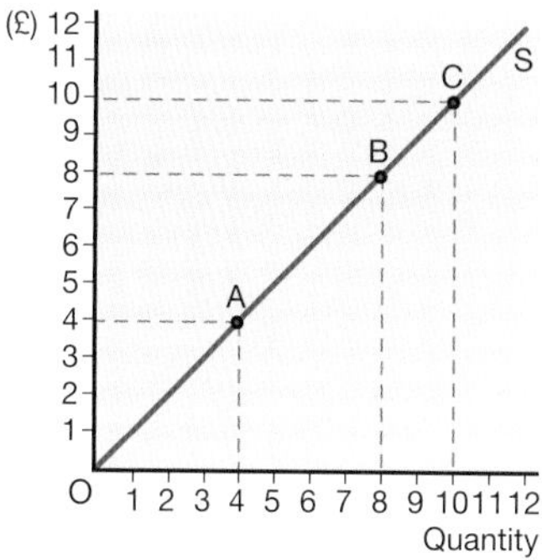

Figure 9.4 *Unit (or unitary) price elasticity of supply (PES = +1)*

The supply curve in Figure 9.2 shows zero elasticity of supply. This occurs when there is no change in the quantity supplied when price changes.

When price increases from £4 to £5, we move along the supply curve from Point A to Point B. The percentage change in price is:

$$\frac{£5 - £4}{£4} \times 100 = \frac{1}{4} \times 100 = 25\%$$

The quantity supplied remains at 6 units when price rises, so the percentage change in quantity supplied is:

$$\frac{£6 - £6}{£6} \times 100 = \frac{0}{6} \times 100 = 0\%$$

Using the formula for price elasticity of supply, we can see that the price elasticity of supply is 0%/25% = 0 (zero).

Moving from Point B to Point C gives us a 60% increase in price: +3/5 × 100 = 60%. The change in quantity supplied is still zero. Thus the price elasticity of supply is 0%/60% = 0 (zero).

Zero price elasticity of supply (or perfectly inelastic supply) occurs when firms supply the same quantity, regardless of price. On occasions economists use a time period known as the 'very short run'. This is the time period in which it is not possible to vary the quantity of factors of production and thus output. In practice it is usually less than a day, but it can be longer. A fully booked hotel in the peak season may not be able to increase supply for a matter of weeks. In agriculture, a firm's supply of crops is limited by the amount of seed that was sowed before the growing period and so perfectly inelastic supply can apply to agriculture too.

The supply curve in Figure 9.3 shows a supply curve whose elasticity of supply is infinity. This occurs when all suppliers are prepared to offer their goods for sale at exactly the same price.

If we start at Point A, price is £5 and quantity supplied is 2 units. If we move along the supply curve from Point A to Point B, the price remains at £5 but the quantity supplied rises from 2 units to 6 units. The percentage change in price is:

$$\frac{£5 - £5}{£5} \times 100 = \frac{0}{5} \times 100 = 0\%$$

The quantity supplied rises from 2 units to 6 units, so the percentage change in quantity supplied is:

$$\frac{6-2}{2} \times 100 = \frac{4}{2} \times 100 = 200\%$$

Using the formula for price elasticity of supply, we can see that the price elasticity of supply is 200%/0% = ∞.

Moving from Point B to Point C gives us a 50% increase in quantity supplied: +3/6 × 100 = 50%. The change in price is still zero. Thus the price elasticity of supply is 50%/0% = ∞.

Infinite price elasticity of supply (or perfectly elastic supply) occurs when the market only has one price. In a perfectly competitive market, which we will cover in Chapter 19, it is assumed that there are so many competitors that firms can only charge the price charged by everyone else in the market (known as the market price). Charging a higher price than the market price will lead to no sales, because consumers will know that they can buy the good at the market price. Charging a lower price than the market price means less revenue, because every good produced could have been sold at the market price. In these situations, an individual firm will find that customers will buy the amount they offer to sell, all at the same price, and so supply is perfectly price elastic.

The supply curve in Figure 9.4 shows unit (unitary) elasticity of supply. This occurs when the percentage change in the quantity supplied moves in lockstep with price change. Unitary price elasticity represents the borderline between supply that is price inelastic and supply that is price elastic.

When price increases from £4 to £8, we move along the supply curve from Point A to Point B. The percentage change in price is:

$$\frac{£8-£4}{£4} \times 100 = \frac{4}{4} \times 100 = 100\%$$

From A to B, the quantity supplied changes from 4 units to 8 units, so the percentage change in quantity supplied is:

$$\frac{8-4}{4} \times 100 = \frac{4}{4} \times 100 = 100\%$$

Using the formula for price elasticity of supply, we can see that the price elasticity of supply is 100%/100% = 1 (unitary).

Moving from Point B to Point C gives us a 25% increase in price: +2/8 × 100 = 25%. The change in quantity supplied is also +2/8 × 100 = 25%. Thus the price elasticity of supply is 25%/25% = 1 (+1).

There is no common real-life situation that creates a supply curve with unit elasticity. In the example given in Figure 9.4, the supply curve is a straight line at an angle of 45° from the origin. In fact, *any supply curve that is a straight line that would go through the origin has unit elasticity of supply.*

Key note

Elasticity of supply may also be calculated by proportional changes. The formula is:

$$\text{Elasticity of supply} = \frac{\text{Proportional change in quantity supplied of Product X}}{\text{Proportional change in price of Product X}}$$

Using this formula for the very first calculation in Figure 9.1 gives us the following answer:

$$\frac{(16-10)}{10} \div \frac{(50-10)}{10} = \frac{6}{10} \div \frac{40}{10} = \frac{6}{10} \times \frac{10}{40} = \frac{60}{400} = +0.15$$

Author tip

Remember that, because of the law of supply, price elasticity will usually be positive. It is not necessary to show the positive sign in your answer. However, in the rare instances where it can be negative it will be vital to show the negative sign.

The factors that influence price elasticity of supply

The main factors that influence the price elasticity of supply are outlined below and summarised in Table 9.1.

Table 9.1 *Summary of the main factors that influence price elasticity of supply*

Factor influencing price elasticity of supply	Factor leading to supply being more price inelastic	Factor leading to supply being more price elastic
Time	Short run	Long run
Spare capacity	Limited or no spare capacity	High level of spare capacity
Ease of acquiring new resources	Difficult to acquire	Easy to acquire
Ease of switching production	Difficult to switch	Easy to switch
Length of the production process	Lengthy production process	Quick production process
Levels of stock held	Low stock levels	High stock levels
Number of firms/ease of entry into the market	Few firms/difficult to enter	Many firms/easy to enter
Direction of price change	Price rise	Price fall

- *Time* Time tends to have a much more significant impact on price elasticity of supply than it has on price elasticity of demand, although it is an important influence on both. As we saw earlier, in the very short run a price increase has no impact on the quantity supplied and so price elasticity of supply is perfectly inelastic (that is, the price elasticity of supply = zero). As time progresses, firms can modify the quantity of factors of production and possibly change their efficiency. The longer the time in which a firm (or market) can adjust to a change in price, the more price elastic its supply becomes. In the long run it is even feasible for price elasticity of supply to be perfectly elastic. In a perfectly competitive market, where everybody has perfect information and so can use the same production techniques, it is assumed that all suppliers supply all of their output at the market price. This gives rise to a horizontal supply curve with infinite price elasticity of supply.
- *Spare capacity* A firm or market has spare capacity if its resources (factors of production) are underused. If a firm is working at 80% capacity, this means that 20% of its resources are not being used. An increase in price will, through the incentive to make profit, lead to a desire to increase production and thus supply more products. In the example above, a firm that is currently supplying 80 units of a good could, if it were profitable, increase production by as much as 20 units. In this case a small increase in price might lead to a significant increase in supply. Thus the higher the level of spare capacity in a firm, the more price elastic its supply would tend to be. In contrast, a firm producing at or close to its maximum

capacity will have no (or little) spare capacity with which to extend its production (supply). In this case, even if there is a very large increase in price, the change in the quantity supplied will be zero or very low. Thus the lower the level of spare capacity in a firm, the more price inelastic its supply would tend to be.

- *Ease of acquiring new resources (factors of production)* If a firm is easily able to acquire (or dispose of) new factors of production, it should be able to adjust its level of supply easily in response to a change in price. Generally this means that it is easier to change the supply of goods that require unskilled labour or readily abundant raw materials and so price elasticity of supply for these goods will be elastic. For goods that require the use of highly skilled labour and/or scarce raw materials, price elasticity of supply will tend be inelastic. This is because skilled workers are harder (and more expensive) to find and it will also take longer to give workers suitable training to carry out skilled jobs.
- *Ease of switching production* In Chapter 8 we saw that firms can switch production between goods in competitive supply if the price of one of those goods changes. Any change in price will affect the possibility of profit and so a rise in the price of a good will encourage the firm to switch production and supply from the other product to the product whose price has risen. However, the extent to which supply can change will depend on the flexibility/mobility of the firm's factors of production. For example, some machinery, raw materials and labour may not be suited to a switch in production to another good. The easier it is to switch production between two goods in competitive supply, the more price elastic supply will be. In contrast, if it is difficult to switch factors of production (and therefore production itself) from one product to another, then the price elasticity of supply will be inelastic.
- *Length of the production process* Some goods, such as loaves of bread, can be produced in less than two hours. As a result, it is much easier to extend supply if the price rises. However, for goods such as cruise liners and passenger airliners, the process can take 18 months or three months respectively (excluding all the preliminary planning stages). For this reason, it is very difficult to extend supply if price rises. This means that the longer the production process, the less it is possible to change supply and so the price elasticity of supply is more inelastic. For goods that can be produced quickly, supply is much more price elastic.
- *Levels of stock held* If firms possess a lot of stocks of raw materials and/or finished products, then it will be much easier for them to react to price rises by extending production. Therefore, high levels of stock will tend to lead to higher elasticity of supply (supply is more price elastic). If firms do not hold many raw materials and/or finished products, then it will be much more difficult for them to react to price rises by extending production. Hence, low levels of stock will tend to lead to lower price elasticity of supply (supply is more price inelastic). For some products, such as perishable goods or goods that require refrigeration when stored, low levels of stock are more likely. Bulky goods can also be expensive to store. These types of goods will have more price inelastic supply. Goods that sell quickly and are cheap to store usually have a more price elastic supply.
- *Number of firms/ease of entry into the market* Some markets are dominated by a single firm (monopolies) or by a few firms (oligopolies). In these cases changes in supply are much more unlikely to occur if price rises, because it can be difficult for new firms to enter into such a market. This is because they cannot produce on

the same scale and at the same level of productive efficiency as the large firms that already dominate the market. In markets with only a few firms, price elasticity of supply tends to be inelastic. If, however, the market is very competitive and it is easy for new firms to enter into the market, then increases in price will lead to higher potential profits and therefore attract many new firms. Thus changes in supply can be much greater when price rises. In markets in which there are many firms and which are easy to enter, the price elasticity of supply tends to be elastic.

- *The direction of change in price* The analysis of price elasticity above has focused on price rises leading to extensions in supply. Similar logic can be applied to price falls leading to contractions in supply. However, in practice it is usually much easier for firms to cut production (supply) than it is to extend production (supply). Therefore, price elasticity of supply is usually more price elastic for a fall in price than it is for an increase in price, particularly in the short run.

Interpreting numerical values of price elasticity of supply

Good Y

- Price elasticity of supply for Good Y in Table 9.2 is +0.1. This is very price inelastic. It means that a 10% increase in price would lead to only a 1% increase in the quantity supplied. A massive 50% rise in price would only lead to 5% more goods being supplied.

	Good Y	Good Z
Price elasticity of supply	+ 0.1	+ 2.1

Table 9.2 *Data on price elasticity of supply for Good Y and Good Z*

- Good Y could be a good that requires skilled and/or inflexible factors of production in its manufacture. Firms are likely to be producing at or close to full capacity and therefore cannot easily extend their supply. Low stock levels are being held, so it may be perishable or expensive to store. New resources are not easy to find and it is unlikely to be a good in competitive supply, because price rises are not leading to a significant extension in supply. The production process may be lengthy, so that it takes a long time to change the quantity supplied. The market is likely to have only a few firms and be difficult for new firms to enter, in order to take advantage of any increase in price.

Good Z

- Price elasticity of supply for Good Z is +2.1 (Table 9.2). This is very price elastic. It means that a 10% increase in price would lead to a larger (21%) increase in the quantity supplied. A 50% rise in price would lead to 105% more goods being supplied – more than double the supply before the price rise.
- Good Z is likely to be a good that requires unskilled and/or flexible factors of production in its manufacture, so that it is easy to change levels of production. Firms may have plenty of spare capacity and therefore can easily extend their supply in response to price changes. High stock levels may be held, so it may be a durable product that is cheap to store. New resources are easy to find and so it may be a good in competitive supply: a price rise will lead to firms quickly switching production from the other goods in competitive supply. The ease with which supply can change suggests that the production process is short, so that it does not take a long time to change the quantity supplied. The market is likely to have many firms and be easy for new firms to enter.

Key note

The price elasticity of supply for Good Y may be short-run price elasticity of supply and based on a price rise. The data for Good Z may be long-run data, based on price cuts.

REALWORLD ECONOMICS 9.1

The elasticity of supply for oil

Research by the Bank of Canada and others suggests that the global price elasticity of supply for oil has become more price inelastic since 1975 (Table 9.3). Easily accessible resources have been extracted in the past and so the oil that is still available is much more difficult and expensive to reach. Unless oil prices are very high, it is not profitable to extract some of this oil. Furthermore, many countries with oil reserves are reluctant to increase supply, because they expect prices to rise significantly when the world's oil reserves become more depleted in the future. Having accumulated wealth from oil in the past, they can afford to leave some reserves in the ground.

Since the accessible reserves have been largely exploited, new reserves are more difficult to reach and so it takes longer for the quantity supplied to increase when prices rise. This feature of oil supply is expected to become more significant in the future. This overall fall in price elasticity of supply for oil can be seen in Figure 9.5.

A key factor leading to the fall in price elasticity of supply has been the level of spare capacity in the oil industry. Between 1985 and 1995 world oil prices stagnated or fell. Anticipating future cuts in price, many firms (and countries) cut back on investment in oil. This meant that the capacity to supply oil has fallen. Although world demand for oil has not grown dramatically since 1985, it has meant that the relatively high levels of spare capacity in the 1980s have been eroded. In 2005 spare capacity in the industry was almost non-existent. Figure 9.5 shows levels of spare capacity since 1975.

Year	Price elasticity of supply for oil
1975	0.33
1980	0.28
1985	0.4
1990	0.12
1995	0.1
2000	0.08
2005	0.02
2010	0.15

Table 9.3 *Estimated price elasticity of supply for oil, 1975–2010*

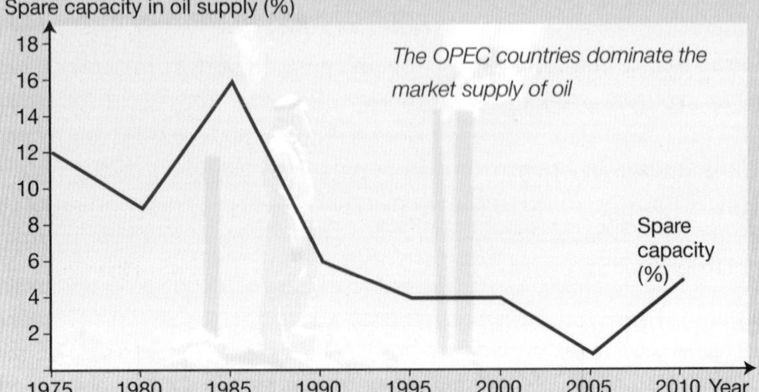

Figure 9.5 *Spare capacity (%) in oil supply, 1975–2010*

Oil supplies are restricted geographically and relatively few firms have the technology and financial resources to be able to supply oil. As a consequence there are major barriers to new firms that might wish to enter the market. Market supply is dominated, to some extent, by the OPEC countries that work together to restrict supply, so that the world price remains high. High prices are also needed to encourage further extraction of known reserves of oil. It is estimated that current production techniques leave two-thirds of oil reserves in the ground because, with the current levels of technology and production techniques, it is too expensive to extract the less accessible oil.

Source: Bank of Canada – Working Paper 2011–28, and other sources

Exercises — *Total: 36 marks*

1. Define the term 'market supply'. *(3 marks)*
2. In 2009 world oil supply was 4000 million tonnes. In 2010 the price of oil rose by 2%. Price elasticity of supply was 0.15. Calculate the amount of oil offered for supply in 2010. *(4 marks)*
3. Identify two significant points of comparison between the level of spare capacity (Figure 9.5) and the price elasticity of supply of oil (Table 9.3). *(4 marks)*
4. Assess the view that changes in the level of spare capacity in the oil industry since 1975 have been the main cause of the changes in the price elasticity of supply for oil in that period. *(25 marks)*

Review questions

Total: 40 marks

1 Which one of the following supply schedules would give a supply curve that has a price elasticity of supply of unit elasticity?

	Price:	£1	£2	£3	£4	£5	£6
A	Quantity supplied	1	1	1	1	1	1
B	Quantity supplied	5	6	7	8	9	10
C	Quantity supplied	2	4	6	8	10	12
D	Quantity supplied	6	5	4	3	2	1

(1 mark)

2 In Figure 9.6 the supply curve has shifted from S_1 to S_2.

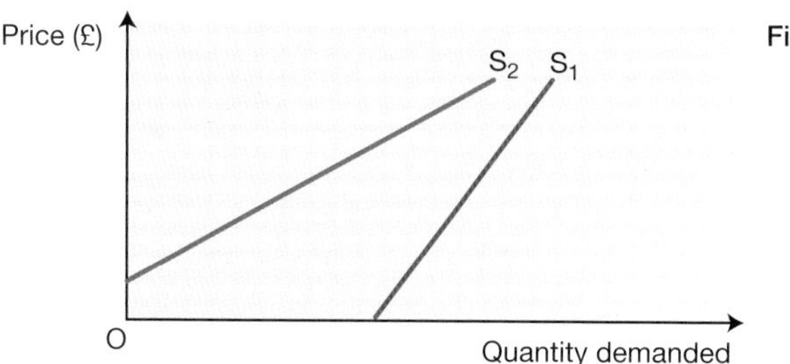

Figure 9.6

The move from S_1 to S_2 shows:

A A decrease in supply and supply becoming more price elastic
B A decrease in supply and supply becoming more price inelastic
C An increase in supply and supply becoming more price elastic
D An increase in supply and supply becoming more price inelastic *(1 mark)*

3 The price of jam falls from £1.50 to £1.20. As a result, the quantity supplied falls from 100 jars to 75 jars. The price elasticity of supply for jam is:

A 0.75 B 0.8 C 1.0 D 1.25 *(1 mark)*

4 The price elasticity of a good is 2. A change in price leads to a 28% increase in the quantity supplied. The change in price was:

A A fall of 56%
B A fall of 14%
C A rise of 14%
D A rise of 56% *(1 mark)*

5 In Figure 9.7 the supply curve is shown by line S.

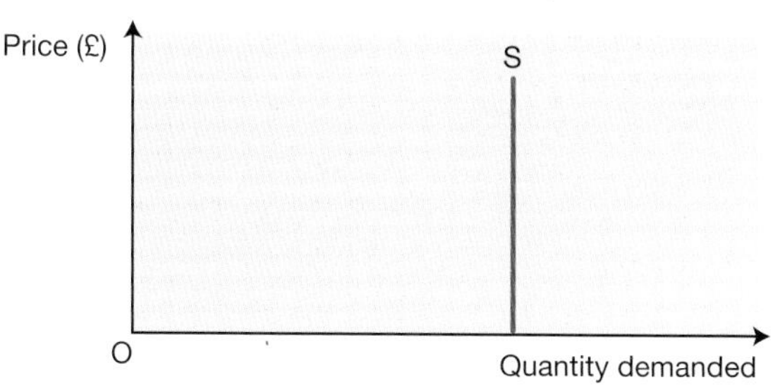

Figure 9.7

Supply curve S has:

A A price elasticity of supply = –1
B A price elasticity of supply = 0
C A price elasticity of supply = +1
D A price elasticity of demand = +∞ *(1 mark)*

6 Price elasticity of supply is likely to be more inelastic when:

A Price falls
B New firms cannot easily enter the industry
C Firms have high stock levels
D The good is in competitive supply *(1 mark)*

7 Price elasticity of supply is likely to be more elastic:

A In the short run
B When firms have high levels of spare capacity
C When firms have low levels of raw materials and components
D When production requires workers with high levels of skill *(1 mark)*

8 The price elasticity of a good is 0.4. A fall in price from £10 to £8 will lead to a fall in the quantity supplied of:

A 5% B 8% C 10% D 50% *(1 mark)*

9 Define the term 'price inelastic supply'. *(3 marks)*

10 Define the term 'spare capacity'. *(3 marks)*

11 Price increases from £11 to £15, leading to quantity supplied rising from 30 boxes to 34 boxes. Calculate the price elasticity of supply. *(4 marks)*

12 Explain why supply becomes more price elastic over time. *(6 marks)*

13 Many firms now train their workers to be 'multi-skilled' (able to do a variety of jobs). Explain the impact of this training on the price elasticity of supply of the products made by that firm. *(6 marks)*

14 Analyse two ways in which a firm might benefit from having supply that has high (elastic) price elasticity of supply. *(10 marks)*

The determination of equilibrium market prices

This chapter looks at how equilibrium prices and quantity/output are determined in competitive markets. The effect of changes in demand and supply are examined and consideration is given to situations in which both supply and demand change simultaneously. The effects of different price elasticities of supply and demand are also considered, when examining shifts in supply or demand. The chapter concludes by studying supply and demand in some real-world markets.

The determination of equilibrium market prices

Buyers and sellers meet in the marketplace to exchange goods and services. Buyers *demand* goods and services, and sellers *supply* goods and services.

The law of demand states that as price rises, the quantity demanded falls and so the demand curve slopes downwards from left to right. This is shown by demand curve D in Figure 10.1.

The law of supply states that as price rises, the quantity supplied rises and so the supply curve slopes upwards from left to right. This is shown by supply curve S in Figure 10.1.

In the diagram it can be seen that, at price P_E, the quantity supplied is the same as quantity demanded. P_E is thus the equilibrium price (or market price or market clearing price). Q_E is the equilibrium quantity.

Key term

Market price is the price at which the market is in equilibrium because the quantity that customers want to buy (demand) is the same as the quantity that firms want to offer for sale (supply).

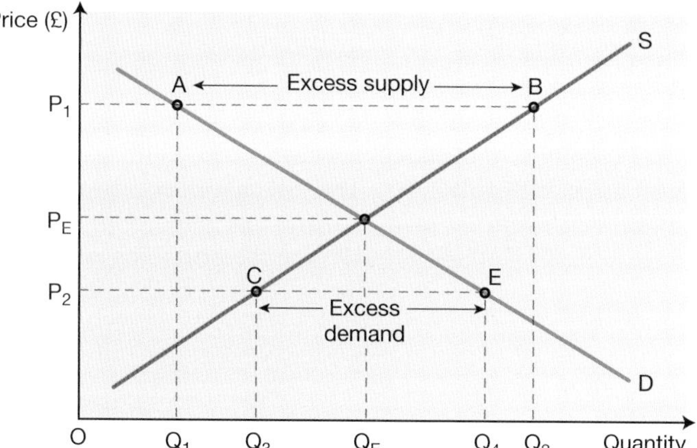

Figure 10.1 *Market equilibrium and disequilibrium*

At price P_E there is no tendency to change since consumers are happy because they are able to purchase the number of goods that they want at this price. Suppliers are also happy because they are able to sell all of the products that they are prepared to supply at this price.

The difference between equilibrium and disequilibrium

In Figure 10.1, we saw that price P_E was the equilibrium price in the market. If the price starts at P_E, there is no tendency to change.

However, what happens if price started at P_1? In this case the quantity demanded is shown by Point A and so Q_1 items would be demanded. However, at price P_1, Point B shows that the quantity offered for supply would be Q_2.This means that only Q_1 items would be bought, leaving suppliers with many items unsold. Suppliers will want to take steps to overcome this problem. Consequently, the market is in disequilibrium at price P_1 because there will be a tendency for the price and the market to change.

There is also a disequilibrium at price P_2. In this case the quantity demanded is shown by Point E and so Q_4 items would be demanded. However, at price P_2, Point C shows that the quantity offered for supply would be Q_3.This means that only Q_3 items would be bought because suppliers are not prepared to supply more at price P_2. Suppliers will want to take steps to overcome this problem too, as there is a lot of demand being left unsatisfied. Since there will be a tendency for the price and the market to change, this is also a market in disequilibrium.

Why excess demand and excess supply lead to changes in price

If, at a certain price, the quantity demanded equals the quantity supplied, then we have an equilibrium. Other things being equal, there is no tendency to change from this equilibrium situation.

If, at a certain price, the quantity demanded does not equal the quantity supplied, then we have a disequilibrium. Other things being equal, there will be a tendency to change from this disequilibrium situation. **Excess demand and excess supply are both examples of market disequilibrium.**

Consider Figure 10.1. If price starts at P_1, Point A shows that quantity demanded will be Q_1. Point B shows that quantity supplied at price P_1 will be Q_2. There is disequilibrium in the market. The difference between points A and B is excess supply (too much supply in comparison to demand). In order to sell unsold products, suppliers cut price until it reaches P_E. At P_E, quantity supplied is the same as quantity demanded and so the market reaches equilibrium. P_E is the equilibrium price and Q_E is the equilibrium quantity.

If price starts at P_2, Point E shows quantity demanded will be Q_4. Point C shows quantity supplied at price P_2 will be Q_3. The difference between points C and E is excess demand (too much demand in comparison to supply). Suppliers see that price is too low and so, to make more profit, will raise the price. The excess demand falls but will persist until price reaches P_E. At price P_E there will be equilibrium and so

Key terms

An **equilibrium** is a position from which there is no tendency to change.

A **disequilibrium** is a position from which there is a tendency to change.

A **market equilibrium** is a situation in which the price is such that the quantity that customers want to buy (demand) is the same as the quantity that firms want to offer for sale (supply).

Excess demand is a situation in which the price is such that the quantity demanded exceeds the quantity offered for supply.

Excess supply is a situation in which the price is such that the quantity offered for supply exceeds the quantity demanded.

price will no longer change.

In summary, then:

- excess supply leads to a fall in price, until the excess supply is eliminated;
- excess demand leads to a rise in price, until the excess demand is eliminated.

The determination of equilibrium market prices when demand and supply are changing

In Figure 10.1 we saw a static situation in which there were no changes to the demand curve (D) and the supply curve (S). Once the equilibrium price (P_E) is reached, there is no tendency to change.

However, it is rare that demand and supply remain unchanged. Consumer demands, in particular, can be very volatile, with people's individual preferences changing because of the weather, emotional responses or access to more money.

What happens if there is a change in demand or supply? There are four possible changes that need to be considered: an increase in demand; a decrease in demand; an increase in supply; and a decrease in supply.

The factors influencing demand were considered in Chapter 6. A summary of the factors that lead to an increase in demand and those factors that lead to a decrease in demand is provided in Table 6.2 on p. 53.

The factors influencing supply were considered in Chapter 8. A summary of the factors that lead to an increase in supply and those factors that lead to a decrease in supply is provided in Table 8.6 on p. 87.

The effect of an increase in demand on market equilibrium

Table 10.1 shows the market supply and demand for Good X. Column 2 shows the quantity supplied of Good X at each of the prices shown in Column 1. Column 3 shows the original quantity demanded of Good X at each of the prices shown in Column 1.

Table 10.1 *Market supply and demand for Good X*

Column 1	Column 2	Column 3	Column 4
Price per kg (£)	Quantity supplied	Original quantity demanded (kg)	New quantity demanded (kg)
9	11	1	5.5
8	10	2.5	7.25
7	9	4	9
6	8	5.5	10.75
5	7	7	12.5
4	6	8.5	14.25
3	5	10	16
2	4	11.5	17.75
1	3	13	19.5

It can be seen that £5 is the equilibrium price, because at £5 the quantity offered for supply is 7 kg and the quantity demanded is 7 kg. At all other prices there is excess demand (for prices below £5) or excess supply (for prices above £5). Other things being equal, £5 will remain as the equilibrium price with 7 kg being the equilibrium quantity.

What happens if there is a change in a factor influencing demand that leads to an increase in demand? There are many factors that might cause such a change. For example, it might result from an increase in consumer incomes (assuming that Good X is a normal good), a decrease in the price of a complement, or individual preferences changing in favour of Good X.

Column 4 shows the increase in quantity demanded of Good X as a result of this change in the factor influencing demand. At price = £9, the quantity demanded has increased from 1 kg to 5.5 kg; at price = £8, the quantity demanded has increased from 2.5 kg to 7.25 kg; and so on.

Looking at Table 10.1, there is now a disequilibrium at a price of £5 because quantity demanded no longer equals quantity supplied. Quantity demanded (Q_d) = 12.5 kg and quantity supplied equals 7 kg. This means that there is an excess demand of (12.5 – 7 =) 5.5 kg.

In order to get rid of this excess demand, the price will rise. At £6, Q_d = 10.75 kg and quantity supplied equals 8 kg. This means that there is still an excess demand, but it has been reduced to 2.75 kg (i.e. 10.75 – 8). If price rises to £7, Q_d = 9 kg and Q_s = 9 kg. The market is now in equilibrium and so the equilibrium price has increased from £5 to £7 and the equilibrium quantity has risen to 9 kg.

Figure 10.2 shows these changes in a diagrammatic form. S_1 is the supply curve shown in Table 10.1, with a price of £1 leading to a supply of 3 kg, a price of £2 leading to a supply of 4 kg and so on. D_1 is the original demand curve. The supply and demand curves meet at Point X – this is known as the equilibrium point. Tracing the line horizontally to the left from X gives us the equilibrium price (£5). Tracing the line vertically down from Point X gives us the equilibrium quantity (7 kg).

Figure 10.2 *Market equilibrium after an increase in demand*

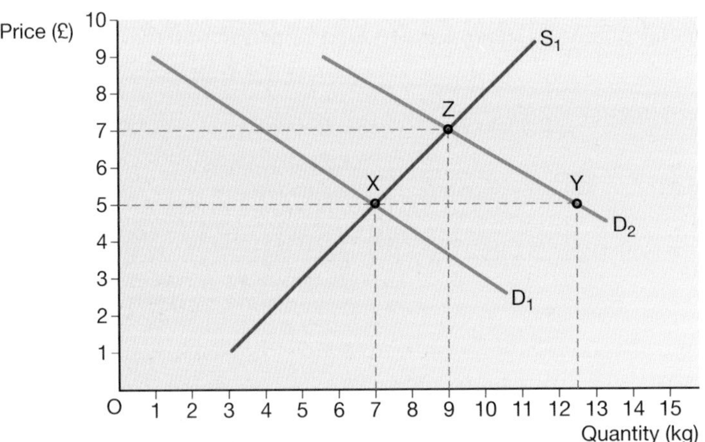

The increase in demand is shown by line D_2. Supply remains unchanged (as shown by line S). At price = £5, the quantity demanded is now shown by Point Y. The quantity supplied at £5 is shown by Point X. There is excess demand shown by the line XY. This excess demand will drive up the price until the excess is eliminated. This occurs when S = D_2, as D_2 is the new demand curve. At £7, the quantity supplied is 9 kg and the new quantity demanded is 9 kg. The disequilibrium in the market is now over.

Point Z shows the new equilibrium point.

In normal circumstances, an increase in demand leads to an increase in price and an increase in quantity.

Author tip

As a rule, supply and demand analysis is used to show the effect of one particular change. In this case it may be a fall in the price of a complement. As the factors affecting demand and supply are very different, any changes that you make are likely to affect *either* demand *or* supply, but not both. Of course, it is possible (but less likely) that you will be expected to analyse two or more simultaneous changes, in which case both lines may change.

The effect of a decrease in demand on market equilibrium

What happens if there is a change that leads to a decrease in demand? This might occur because of any of the factors shown in the final column of Table 6.2. Examples of possible causes of a decrease in demand are an increase in income tax (which lowers disposable income), a decrease in the price of a substitute good or a decrease in consumers' wealth.

In Figure 10.3, S_1 is the original supply curve and D_1 is the original demand curve. The supply and demand curves meet at Point X – the equilibrium point. Tracing the line horizontally to the left from X gives us the equilibrium price (£5). Tracing the line vertically down from Point X gives us the equilibrium quantity (6 kg).

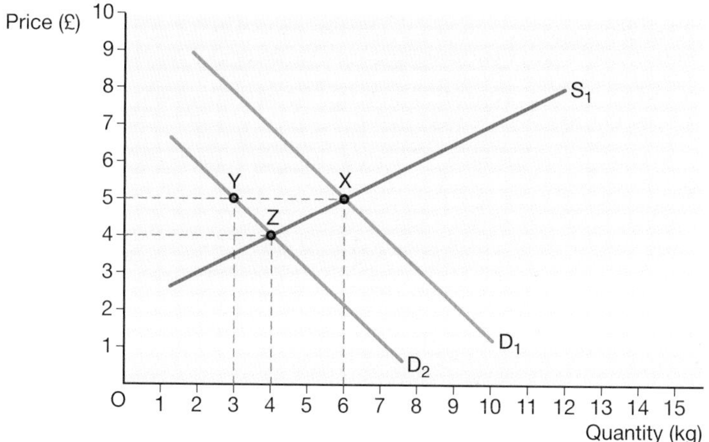

Figure 10.3 *Market equilibrium after a decrease in demand*

The decrease in demand is shown by line D_2. Supply remains unchanged (as shown by line S_1). At price = £5, the quantity demanded is now shown by Point Y. Tracing the line vertically down from Point Y tells us that the quantity demanded is now 3 kg at £5. The quantity supplied at £5 is still shown by Point X (6 kg). There is excess supply shown by the line YX. This excess supply will drive down the price until the excess is eliminated. This occurs when $S_1 = D_2$, as D_2 is the new demand curve. At £4, the quantity supplied is 4 kg and the new quantity demanded is 4 kg. The disequilibrium in the market is now over. Point Z shows the new equilibrium point.

In normal circumstances, a decrease in demand leads to a decrease in price and a decrease in quantity.

The effect of an increase in supply on market equilibrium

In Figure 10.4, S_1 is the original supply curve and D_1 is the original demand curve. The supply and demand curves meet at Point X – the equilibrium point. Tracing the line horizontally to the left from X gives us the equilibrium price (£5). Tracing the line vertically down from Point X gives us the equilibrium quantity (6 kg).

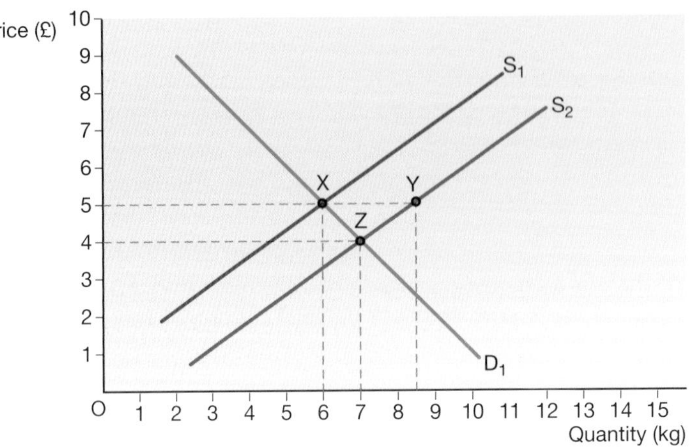

Figure 10.4 *Market equilibrium after an increase in supply*

The increase in supply is shown by line S_2. Demand remains unchanged (as shown by line D_1). At price = £5, the quantity supplied is now shown by Point Y. Tracing the line vertically down from Point Y tells us that the quantity supplied is now 8.5 kg at £5. The quantity demanded at £5 is still shown by Point X (6 kg). There is excess supply shown by the line XY. This excess supply will drive down the price until the excess is eliminated. This occurs when $D_1 = S_2$, as S_2 is the new supply curve. At £4, the quantity demanded is 7 kg and the new quantity supplied is 7 kg. The disequilibrium in the market is now over. Point Z shows the new equilibrium point.

In normal circumstances, an increase in supply leads to a decrease in price and an increase in quantity.

Author tip

Remember – diagrams are *not* self-explanatory. When analysing changes in a market, you should describe the ways in which the market has changed/will change, *using a supply and demand diagram to support your written explanation.*

The effect of a decrease in supply on market equilibrium

In Figure 10.5, S_1 is the original supply curve and D_1 is the original demand curve. The supply and demand curves meet at Point X – the equilibrium point. Tracing the line horizontally to the left from X gives us the equilibrium price (£5). Tracing the line vertically down from Point X gives us the equilibrium quantity (6 kg).

The decrease in supply is shown by line S_2. Demand remains unchanged (as shown by line D_1). At price = £5, the quantity supplied is now shown by Point Y. Tracing the line vertically down from Point Y tells us that the quantity supplied is now 0.5 kg at £5. The quantity demanded at £5 is still shown by Point X (6 kg). There is excess demand shown by the line YX. This excess demand will drive up the price until

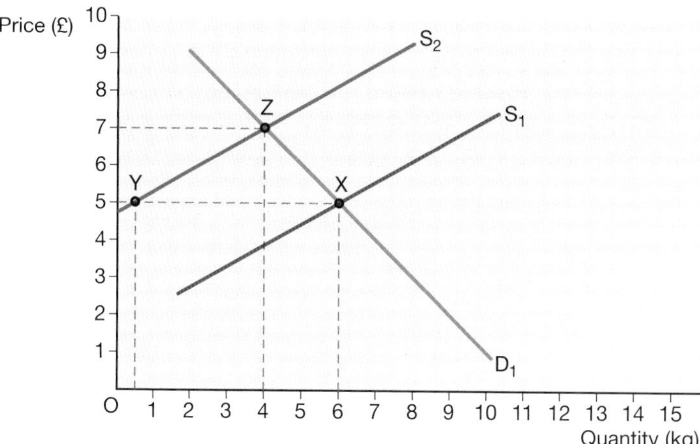

Figure 10.5 *market equilibrium after a decrease in supply*

the excess is eliminated. This occurs when $D_1 = S_2$, as S_2 is the new supply curve. At £7, the quantity demanded is 4 kg and the new quantity supplied is 4 kg. The disequilibrium in the market is now over. Point Z shows the new equilibrium point.

In normal circumstances, a decrease in supply leads to an increase in price and a decrease in quantity.

Figures 10.2 to 10.5 show the four possible shifts in demand *or* supply. Analysing the effects of a single factor will involve only a change to supply *or* a change to demand. For example, an increase in income tax reduces disposable income and so it leads to a decrease in demand. It has no impact on the supply curve. The outcome of this change is shown in Figure 10.3 (a decrease in demand). Note how there is a change in the quantity supplied, but it is a movement along the supply curve. The supply curve is determined by the ability of firms to supply at any given price. An increase in income tax has no impact on firms' ability to supply. However, because it reduces the willingness of buyers to demand the product, it leads to a price fall and so suppliers supply fewer goods. The supply curve S_1 shows that they will supply fewer goods at lower prices.

Similarly, an increase in an excise duty (tax) on a good will *not* affect the demand curve. The effect of an increase in excise duty is shown in Figure 10.5. The tax acts like an extra cost for suppliers and so it decreases supply. This leads to a higher price and so the quantity demanded falls, but it is a movement along the demand curve. The change in VAT has not affected consumers' opinions, as shown by their demand curve – the original demand curve (D_1) showed that consumers would demand fewer goods at a higher price.

The effects of simultaneous changes in demand and supply on market equilibrium

On occasions, it may be necessary to consider two simultaneous changes. There may be situations where both changes affect demand, such as an increase in the price of a substitute at the same time as a decrease in the price of a complement. Both of these factors will lead to an increase in demand and so Figure 10.2 shows the outcome of these changes. Similarly, higher productive efficiency and lower raw material costs will both lead to an increase in supply and so Figure 10.4 shows the outcome of these changes.

What happens if one of the two factors affects supply and the other factor affects demand? This might occur if there is a significant improvement in productive efficiency at the same time as a rise in consumer incomes. Alternatively it might result from changes in the Budget, with the Chancellor of the Exchequer announcing a reduction in income tax and giving a subsidy to producers of this particular good. In the analysis below, we will assume that the shift in the supply curve has been caused by improvements in productive efficiency while the shift in the demand curve has been caused by rising consumer incomes. The outcome is shown in Figure 10.6.

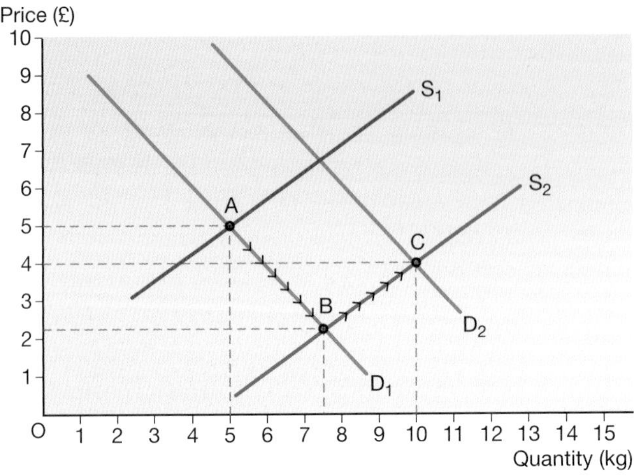

Figure 10.6 *Market equilibrium after an increase in demand and an increase in supply*

In Figure 10.6 we see that the original supply and demand curves are S_1 and D_1 respectively. The original market equilibrium is at Point A, giving an equilibrium price of £5 and an equilibrium quantity of 5 kg.

Taking the two factors in turn, the improvement in productive efficiency leads to an increase in supply (from S_1 to S_2). This change, on its own, would lead to a new equilibrium point at Point B, leading to a fall in the equilibrium price to £2.25 and a rise in equilibrium quantity to 7.5 kg. However, the increase in consumer incomes leads to an increase in demand (from D_1 to D_2). The two new curves (S_2 and D_2) meet at Point C and so this is the new equilibrium point, giving a new equilibrium price of £4 and a new equilibrium quantity of 10 kg. Overall, price has decreased from £5 to £4 and quantity has increased from 5 kg to 10 kg.

The move from A to B and the move from B to C both led to an increase in the quantity because increases in demand and increases in supply have this effect on the equilibrium quantity. However, these two changes have a different impact on price. The increase in supply led to a fall in price (as seen by the move from A to B), but the increase in demand led to a rise in price (as seen by the move from B to C). The final effect depends on factors such as the price elasticities of demand and supply and the degree to which demand and supply have changed. It can be seen in Figure 10.6 that the supply curve change (S_1 to S_2) was greater than the demand curve change (D_1 to D_2) and so the downward pressure on price exceeded the upward pressure.

Author tip
Ensure that you can draw the appropriate diagrams to reach these conclusions.

In conclusion, in normal circumstances, an increase in demand and *an increase in supply will lead to an indeterminate effect on price and an increase in quantity.*

Table 10.2 summarises the effects of the four possible combinations of changes in demand and supply.

Change in demand and supply	Effect on price	Effect on quantity
Increase in demand + increase in supply	Indeterminate	Increase
Increase in demand + decrease in supply	Increase	Indeterminate
Decrease in demand + increase in supply	Decrease	Indeterminate
Decrease in demand + decrease in supply	Indeterminate	Decrease

Table 10.2 *The effects of simultaneous changes in demand and supply*

How price elasticity of demand and supply affect changes in equilibrium

We saw above that the extent to which changes in supply and demand affect price and quantity depends on how much demand and supply increased or decreased.

The eventual outcome also depends on the price elasticity of demand and price elasticity of supply. The effects of elasticity are shown in Figures 10.7 and 10.8: Figure 10.7 shows the effect of price elasticity of supply; Figure 10.8 shows the effect of price elasticity of demand.

> **Author tip**
>
> When analysing changes in demand and supply, using supply and demand diagrams, try to envisage the shape of the demand and supply curves for the good you are analysing. In Chapter 9 we saw that the price elasticity of supply of oil is estimated to be 0.1. This means that analysis of oil should show a supply curve that is almost a vertical line and so quantity supplied will hardly vary as price changes.

In Figure 10.7, the original demand curve is D_1. Demand increases to D_2. (The two demand curves are fairly normal, being neither very elastic nor very inelastic.) *In Figure 10.2 we saw that an increase in demand led to an increase in price and an increase in quantity.*

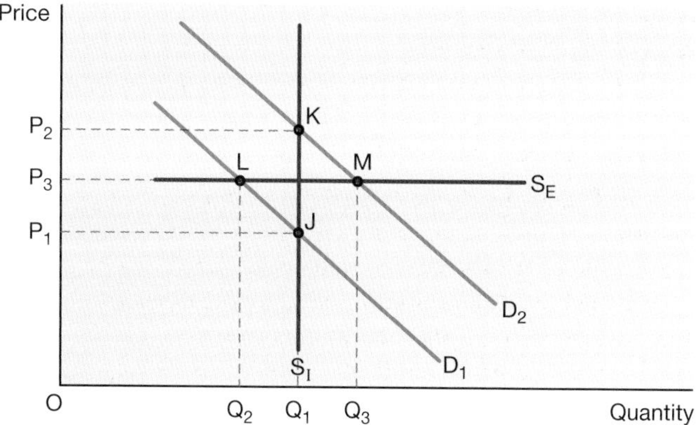

Figure 10.7 *The impact of elasticity of supply on market equilibrium*

What happens if supply is perfectly price inelastic (i.e. PES = 0)? This is shown in Figure 10.7. Line S_I is a vertical supply line, with price elasticity of zero. S_I meets D_1 at Point J and so this is the original equilibrium point. Thus the equilibrium price is P_1 and the equilibrium quantity is Q_1. Demand now increases from D_1 to D_2. The new equilibrium point is K and so the new equilibrium price is P_2. However, the equilibrium quantity is still Q_1.

Conclusion: *If price elasticity of supply is zero, an increase in demand will lead to an increase in price but no change in quantity.* This should not be a surprise because zero price elasticity of supply means that no more items will be supplied if price changes.

What happens if supply is perfectly price elastic (i.e. PES = ∞)? This is also shown on Figure 10.7. Line S_E is a horizontal supply line, with price elasticity of infinity. S_E meets D_1 at Point L and so this is the original equilibrium point. Thus the equilibrium price is P_3 and the equilibrium quantity is Q_2. Demand now increases from D_1 to D_2. The new equilibrium point is M and so the new equilibrium quantity is Q_3. However, the equilibrium price is still P_3.

Conclusion: *If price elasticity of supply is infinity, an increase in demand will lead to an increase in quantity but no change in price.* This should not be a surprise because infinite price elasticity of supply means that all suppliers only offer their items for sale at one particular price (P_3 in this case).

In between these extremes, changes in demand will lead to changes in both price and quantity. However, the logic shown in these diagrams can be extended to cover all situations.

Conclusions:

- *The more price inelastic the supply curve, the greater the change in price when there is an increase or decrease in demand. The more price inelastic the supply curve, the smaller the change in quantity when there is an increase or decrease in demand.*
- *The more price elastic the supply curve, the greater the change in quantity when there is an increase or decrease in demand. The more price elastic the supply curve, the smaller the change in price when there is an increase or decrease in demand.*

In Figure 10.8, the original supply curve is S_1. Supply increases to S_2. (The two supply curves are fairly normal, being neither very elastic nor very inelastic.) *In Figure 10.4 we saw that an increase in supply led to a decrease in price and an increase in quantity.*

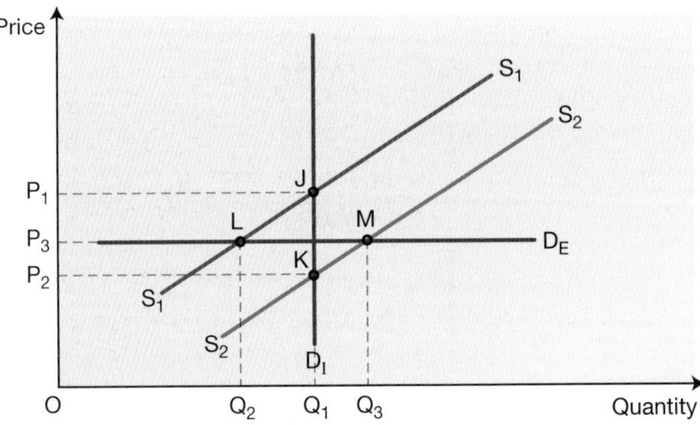

Figure 10.8 *The impact of elasticity of demand on market equilibrium*

What happens if demand is perfectly price inelastic (i.e. PED = 0)? This is shown in Figure 10.8. Line D_I is a vertical demand line, with price elasticity of zero. S_1 meets D_I at Point J and so this is the original equilibrium point. Thus the equilibrium price is P_1 and the equilibrium quantity is Q_1. Supply now increases from S_1 to S_2. The new equilibrium point is K and so the new equilibrium price is P_2. However, the equilibrium quantity is still Q_1.

Conclusion: *If price elasticity of demand is zero, an increase in supply will lead to a decrease in price but no change in quantity.* This should not be a surprise because zero price elasticity of demand means that no more items will be demanded if price changes.

What happens if demand is perfectly price elastic (i.e. PED = $-\infty$)? This is also shown in Figure 10.8. Line D_E is a horizontal demand line, with price elasticity of demand of infinity. S_1 meets D_E at Point L and so this is the original equilibrium point. Thus the equilibrium price is P_3 and the equilibrium quantity is Q_2. Supply now increases from S_1 to S_2. The new equilibrium point is M and so the new equilibrium quantity is Q_3. However, the equilibrium price is still P_3.

Conclusion: *If price elasticity of demand is (minus) infinity, an increase in supply will lead to an increase in quantity but no change in price.* This should not be a surprise because infinite price elasticity of demand means that consumers are only prepared to buy the items for sale at one particular price (P_3 in this case).

In between these extremes, changes in supply will lead to changes in both price and quantity. However, the logic shown in these diagrams can be extended to cover all situations.

Conclusions:

- *The more price inelastic the demand curve, the greater the change in price when there is an increase or decrease in supply. The more price inelastic the demand curve, the smaller the change in quantity when there is an increase or decrease in supply.*
- *The more price elastic the demand curve, the greater the change in quantity when there is an increase or decrease in supply. The more price elastic the demand curve, the smaller the change in price when there is an increase or decrease in supply.*

Author tip

You will need to be able to use demand and supply diagrams to analyse causes of changes in equilibrium market prices. You will also need to be able to predict changes in equilibrium market prices, based on changes in factors that influence supply and demand. When carrying out this analysis you should be able to use demand and supply diagrams to support the logic of your arguments.

Key note

We have looked at the key factors that influence demand and supply and used these factors to explain changes to equilibrium price and quantity. However, most goods and services have their own unique set of factors. It is vital that you consider these factors when applying your analysis to real-world markets. For example, the housing market in the UK is a very important market because it accounts for a significant level of spending. As with most other products, factors such as price and income are key influences on demand. However, interest rates are also very important. Since people tend to use long-term loans (mortgages) to buy houses, the rate of interest on this loan is important to consumers. Currently (January 2015) interest rates on mortgages are at record low levels (below 5%). Low rates increase the demand for mortgages and thus houses. For a period in the 1970s, mortgage interest rates rose to 15%. This meant that a person with a £100,000 mortgage was paying £15,000 a year in interest alone; none of this £15,000 was being used to pay back the loan. As a result, it was effectively much more difficult to demand houses. Other unusual aspects relating to housing are that demand is based on factors such as geographical location and the size of the consumer's family, while the supply of housing is affected by factors such as government regulations (planning permission) and the ability of developers to buy suitable land.

Applying demand and supply to real-world markets

In this chapter we will study two UK markets: the market for coffee and the market for fish.

REALWORLD ECONOMICS 10.1

The demand for and supply of coffee in the UK

Coffee shops have been a major success story in the UK economy since the millennium. Changes to the licensing laws in the late 1990s were introduced in the hope that UK town centres would become more like those in continental Europe, with families and friends able to relax together as they enjoy alcoholic or non-alcoholic drinks. While some public houses and restaurants have adapted successfully, arguably the main beneficiaries have been the coffee shops. In 1995 there were 41 Costa coffee shops in the UK. In mid-2014 there were 1755.

This growth has been assisted by the growth of shopping malls in the UK, enabling customers to relax with better protection from the British climate. According to *Allegra Strategies,* a market research company, coffee shops provide 'an affordable treat' and an opportunity to relax. Even during the recession, demand for coffee grew. Customers continued to visit coffee shops, though they cut their additional spending on items such as cakes.

Location, quality and brand reputation are the key factors influencing demand, according to research. This has led to an increase in the number of outlets – as opposed to the size of individual outlets. The change in individual preferences for coffee has been largely attributed to the growing convenience of outlets and the improvements in the quality and variety of coffee available.

Prior to the millennium, this market was seen to have ease of access for suppliers. The market featured many small suppliers with few national chains. However, promotions and branding have changed the market in the last 20 years. Just three firms – Costa, Starbucks and Caffè Nero – account for two-thirds of UK coffee shop sales. Independent stores have declined in recent years, despite overall growth in the market (Figure 10.9).

Surprisingly, price does not appear to have had a major influence on the quantity sold, with coffee prices rising much faster than inflation since 2005. However, it is possible that price has had little influence because most coffee shops choose to set similar prices in order to remain competitive.

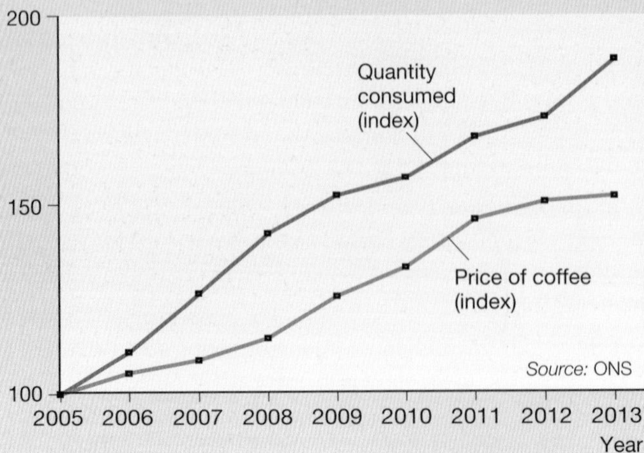

Figure 10.9 *The price and quantity of coffee consumption, 2005–13*

Discussion point

Using supply and demand analysis, explain the changes in coffee prices and the quantity consumed since 2005.

Three national chains account for two-thirds of coffee shop sales in the UK

REALWORLD ECONOMICS 10.2

The demand for and supply of fish in the UK

The level of consumption of fish in the UK in 2013 was the same as in 1975. Overfishing has led to a decline in supplies, particularly of popular species of fish such as cod. In recent years, annual consumption peaked at 519,000 tonnes in 2006, but the quantity consumed has fallen in each year since.

Surveys of consumers suggest that higher prices are the main reason for the decline in demand, with 33% of consumers citing this as the main reason for cutting purchases. Over one-sixth of consumers state that concerns about the sustainability of overfishing have led them to cut consumption.

The most important factor encouraging demand is the increasing awareness of the health properties of fish in people's diets, with over 50% of consumers stating this to be the main reason for consumption. However, only 27% of the people surveyed recognised that 'two-a-week' is the government's guideline for fish consumption. In contrast, 77% were aware of the 'five-a-day' guideline for fruit and vegetables. The average consumption per person in the UK is just under 1.2 fish per week.

Other factors influencing demand are incomes (with those on high incomes 50% more likely to eat fish) and age (with over 55s being the largest buyers of fish).

65% of the fish consumed in the UK belong to five species – cod, tuna, salmon, haddock and prawns. UK consumers have strongly resisted other species but there are signs that consumers are now more prepared to try other species, such as hake, coley and tilapia. In the USA, tilapia is the fifth most popular fish and sales are increasing because it is very adaptable to fish farming.

Many people see fish farming as the solution to supply problems. With EU and government quotas being used to limit the supply of sea fish, onshore fish farming is now growing, particularly as consumers are now more accepting of fish provided in this way. In the UK, fish farming of salmon adds £1 billion per annum to the Scottish economy. In May 2014 the Crown Estate announced plans to use 12 miles of the Cornish coast for sea cages for offshore fish farming of rainbow trout in order to increase supply. A single sea cage can contain up to 90,000 fish.

Salmon farming off the Isle of Mull, Scotland

Year	Price of fish (index)	Quantity consumed (000 tonnes)
2004	101.7	480
2005	102.3	509
2006	108.5	519
2007	115.7	515
2008	124.0	510
2009	130.3	501
2010	138.3	483
2011	151.0	472
2012	157.4	467
2013	163.4	464

Sources: www.thefishsite.com and ONS

Table 10.3 *The price and consumption of fish, 2004–13*

Sources: www.thefishsite.com, ONS and an article by Lewis Smith in the *Independent on Sunday*, 25.5.14.

Exercises

Total: 50 marks

1 Define the term 'supply'. *(3 marks)*

2 Calculate the percentage change in the quantity of fish consumed between 2004 and 2013. *(4 marks)*

3 Identify two significant points of comparison in Table 10.3 between the price of fish and the quantity of fish consumed. *(4 marks)*

4 The survey concluded that 'higher prices are the main reason for the decline in demand'. Draw a demand curve that shows price having a major effect on demand. *(4 marks)*

5 Analyse the probable effects of fish farming of rainbow trout on (a) the price of rainbow trout and (b) the price of other types of fish. *(10 marks)*

6 Evaluate the possible reasons for the change in the price of fish between 2004 and 2013. *(25 marks)*

Number crunching

Table 10.4 gives data on Product A, with some data on products B, C and D (Q_D = quantity demanded; Q_S = quantity supplied).

Price of A (£)	Q_D of A	Q_S of A	Q_D of B	Q_D of C	Q_S of D
2	60	10	20	10	4
3	40	20	10	15	8
4	25	25	6	20	10
5	18	30	3	30	12

Table 10.4

Based on the price of A changing from £4 to £5, calculate:

1 The price elasticity of demand for Product A.
2 The price elasticity of supply for Product A.
3 The cross elasticity of demand between products A and B.
4 The cross elasticity of demand between products A and C.

Based on these data, complete the following sentences:

5 Products A and B are ___________.
6 Products A and C are ___________.
7 Products A and D are ___________.
8 The equilibrium price for Product A is ___.
9 At £2 there is an excess __________ of ___ units for Product A.
10 At £5 there is an excess __________ of ___ units for Product A.

Review questions

Total: 40 marks

1 In Figure 10.10 the equilibrium point has changed from Point A to Point B.

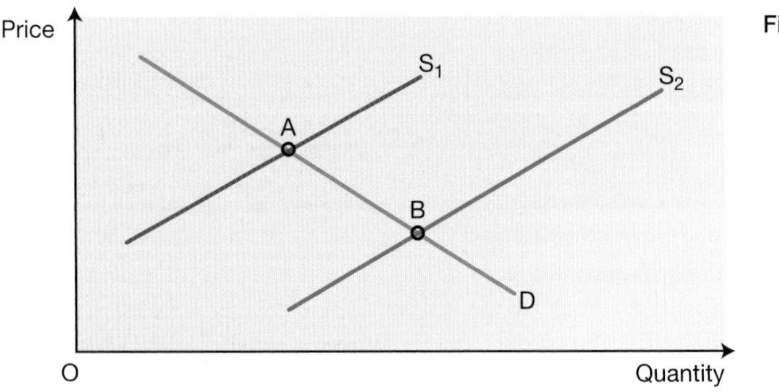

Figure 10.10

This change from A to B might have been caused by:

A An increase in the price of a substitute good
B Higher incomes for consumers
C Greater productive efficiency
D Higher rents for business properties *(1 mark)*

2 In Figure 10.11 the equilibrium point has changed from Point A to Point B.

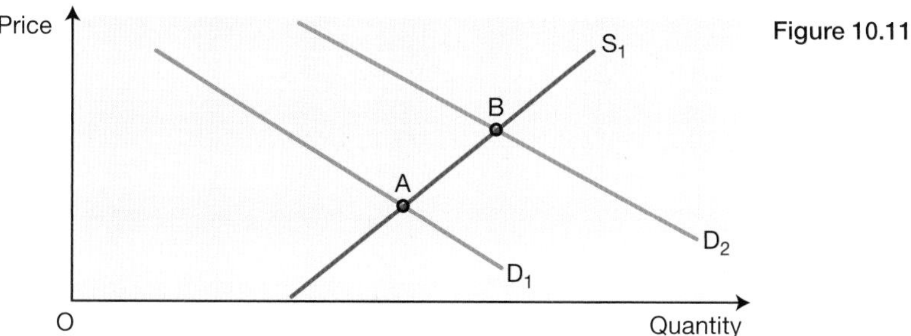

Figure 10.11

This change from A to B might have been caused by:

A A cut in employees' national insurance payments
B An increase in the price of a complementary good
C An increase in raw material costs
D The introduction of a subsidy on the good *(1 mark)*

3 In Figure 10.12 the equilibrium point has changed from Point A to Point B.

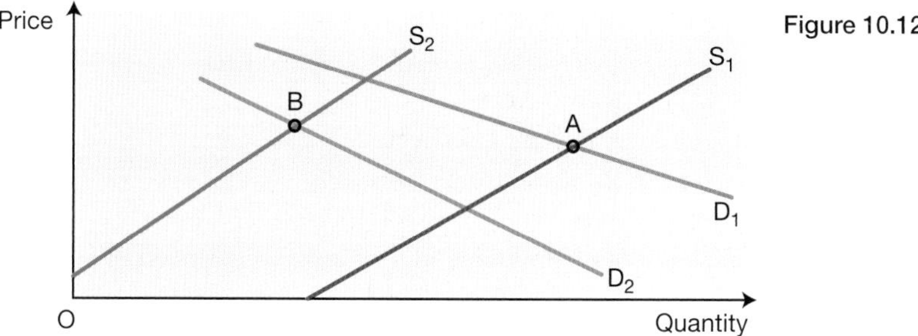

Figure 10.12

This change from A to B shows:

A An increase in demand and an increase in supply
B An increase in demand and a decrease in supply
C A decrease in demand and an increase in supply
D A decrease in demand and a decrease in supply *(1 mark)*

4 In Figure 10.13 the equilibrium point has changed from Point A to Point B.

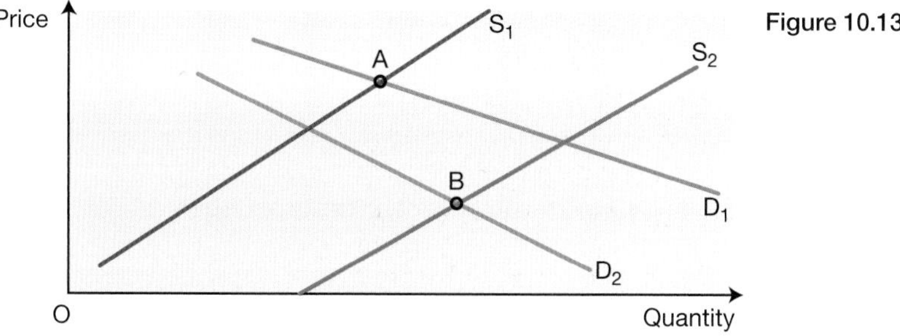

Figure 10.13

This change from A to B would most likely have been caused by:

A An increase in consumers' incomes and a rise in productive efficiency
B An increase in consumers' incomes and a fall in productive efficiency
C A decrease in consumers' incomes and a rise in productive efficiency
D A decrease in consumers' incomes and a fall in productive efficiency *(1 mark)*

The data in Table 10.5 apply to questions 5 and 6.

Table 10.5

Price (£)	Quantity of files demanded	Quantity of files supplied
10	100	20
11	80	40
12	60	60
13	40	80
14	20	100

5 Based on the above data, the equilibrium price is:
A £10 B £11 C £12 D £13 E £14 *(1 mark)*

6 If costs rose and suppliers were only prepared to supply these files if they received £2 more per file, the new equilibrium price would be:
A £10 B £11 C £12 D £13 E £14 *(1 mark)*

7 In a competitive market, what would be the effect on the price and output of games consoles of a successful advertising campaign that leads to a shift in individual preferences towards online games?
A A rise in price and a rise in output
B A rise in price and a fall in output
C A fall in price and a rise in output
D A fall in price and a fall in output *(1 mark)*

8 In a competitive market, what would be the effect on the price and output of strawberries if there were a shortage of raspberries and if the supply of strawberries were perfectly price inelastic?
A A rise in price and a rise in output
B A rise in price and a fall in output
C A rise in price and no change in output
D No change in price and a rise in output *(1 mark)*

9 Own-brand tinned tomatoes are an inferior good. Explain the effect of an increase in income tax on the demand for own-brand tinned tomatoes. *(4 marks)*

10 Good X has a price elasticity of demand of zero and an upward-sloping supply curve. Explain, with the help of a diagram, the effect of the introduction of new technology on the equilibrium price and quantity of Good X. *(9 marks)*

11 Good Y has a supply curve of perfect price elasticity and a downward-sloping demand curve. Explain, with the help of a diagram, the effect of a fall in consumer incomes on the equilibrium price and quantity of Good Y. *(9 marks)*

Question 12 can be used as an alternative to the Discussion Point on p. 112.

12 Read the article on the coffee market on p. 112. Based on the information and data in the article, analyse two possible reasons for the increase in the price of coffee between 2005 and 2013. *(10 marks)*

The interrelationship between markets

This chapter examines situations in which changes to equilibrium price and quantity in a particular market affect equilibrium price and quantity in different but interrelated markets. The interrelationships studied are joint demand, demand for substitute goods, composite demand, derived demand and joint supply.

How changes in a particular market are likely to affect other markets

In Chapter 10 we saw how changes in the factors influencing supply and demand of a particular good might affect the equilibrium price and quantity of that particular good. In this chapter we will look at the interrelationship between different markets and show how changes to the equilibrium price and quantity in one market might change the equilibrium levels of price and quantity in a separate but related market.

In Chapter 10 we studied the coffee shop market. Changes in the coffee shop market have impacted upon public houses, teashops and restaurants, because these types of business are in competition with coffee shops, to varying degrees. In contrast, greater use of coffee shops has tended to lead to longer stays in town centres, and may therefore have a positive impact on spending in town centre shops and car parks. Because coffee shops are taking up increasing amounts of space within town centre shopping areas, they are also in competition for shop sites with other businesses.

The market for fish was also examined. Changes in the quantity of fish demanded will influence the quantity bought of complements, such as chips and mushy peas, substitutes, such as pizzas, curries and meat products, and the quantity demanded of factors of production such as fishermen, fishmongers and trawlers.

In this chapter, five interrelationships will be studied: joint demand, demand for substitute goods, composite demand, derived demand and joint supply.

Key terms

Joint demand is a situation in which two or more goods or services are used together. For example, toothbrushes and toothpaste are jointly demanded.

Demand for a substitute good occurs when a good might be purchased as an alternative to another good. For example, beef and pork are possible substitutes.

Composite demand occurs when a good is demanded for different purposes. For example, milk can be demanded in order to provide milk, yoghurt or cheese.

Derived demand occurs when the demand for a good or service is determined by the demand for another good or service. For example, the demand for tyres derives from the demand for cars, and the demand for train drivers derives from the demand for rail travel.

Joint supply occurs when the supply of one good automatically leads to the production of another good. For example, Marmite is a byproduct of beer breweries and so the supply of beer helps to create Marmite too.

Key note

The next five sections show a variety of causes of different changes in the first market and the subsequent changes in the second, related market. Please bear in mind that the initial changes (increase/decrease in demand or increase/decrease in supply) have been chosen randomly. The key factor to note in the first market is the change in equilibrium quantity. It is the change in quantity (not price) that triggers the change in the second, related market. However, it should be recognised that the change in quantity in the first market will have been influenced by the price in the first market.

Due to the importance of the change in quantity in the first market, it is worth remembering the ways in which changes in demand and supply will affect the equilibrium quantity in a market:

- **an increase in equilibrium quantity** will be caused by *either* an increase in demand *or* an increase in supply;
- **a decrease in equilibrium quantity** will be caused by *either* a decrease in demand *or* a decrease in supply.

The implications of joint demand

Joint demand exists when a change in the quantity demanded for one good leads to a similar change in demand for another good. For example, printers and ink cartridges are complementary products and are thus demanded jointly. Since joint demand applies to complements, it is sometimes referred to as **complementary demand.**

Figure 11.1 *An increase in demand and joint demand*

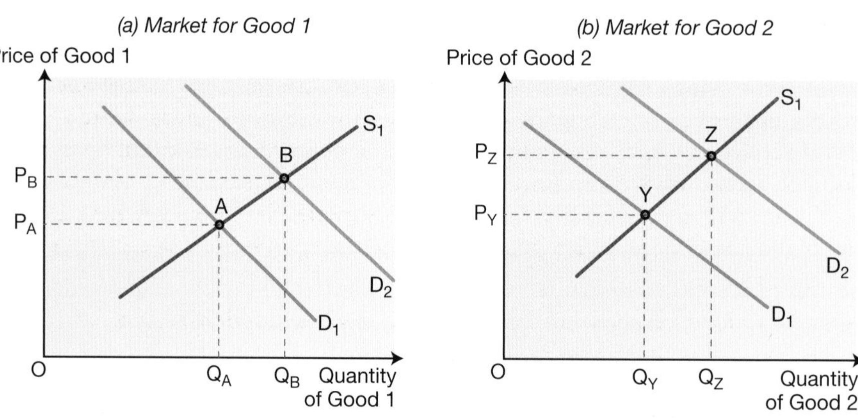

Figure 11.1 shows how an increase in demand for one good (printers) affects the market for a good in joint demand (ink cartridges).

The left-hand diagram – Figure 11.1(a) – shows the effect of an increase in demand for printers on the market for printers. S_1 is the original supply curve and D_1 is the original demand curve. These two lines intersect at Point A, giving an equilibrium price of P_A and an equilibrium quantity of Q_A.

There is then an increase in demand for printers. This would have resulted from a change in any of the factors influencing demand that were described in Chapter 6, such as an increase in consumers' incomes. The demand curve thus shifts to the right, from D_1 to D_2. This changes the equilibrium point from A to B. As a result the equilibrium price changes from the P_A to P_B and the equilibrium quantity changes from Q_A to Q_B. The key consequence shown in this diagram is the increase in the quantity of printers purchased, with quantity rising from Q_A to Q_B.

As more printers are now being purchased, consumers will require more ink cartridges with which to print their documents. Moving to the right-hand diagram – Figure 11.1(b) – we can see the impact on the market for ink cartridges. In this market the demand curve shifts to the right because there is a real increase in demand. Individual preferences for ink cartridges have changed in favour of ink cartridges because more consumers now possess the printers with which to use ink cartridges.

In Figure 11.1(b), we see that the original supply curve was S_1 and the original demand curve was D_1. This gave an equilibrium point of Y. Therefore, the original equilibrium price was P_Y and the original equilibrium quantity was Q_Y.

The increase in demand shifts the demand curve from D_1 to D_2. There is no change in the supply curve, S_1. Thus the new equilibrium point is where S_1 and D_2 intersect – this is Point Z. Therefore, the new equilibrium price is P_Z and the new equilibrium quantity is Q_Z.

Conclusion: *An increase in demand for a good leads to an increase in demand for a good in joint demand with it. This leads to an increase in both the price and quantity purchased of the good that is in joint demand.*

Similar logic can be applied to other changes in demand and supply. For example, a decrease in demand for printers would have led to a decrease in demand for ink cartridges and thus a fall in both the price and quantity purchased of ink cartridges.

The implications of demand for substitute goods

A substitute good is one that might be bought as an alternative to another good. For example, two competing films at the cinema are possible substitutes. Since substitutes compete against each other, demand for substitute goods is often known as **competitive demand.** Competitive demand is common in many markets and is often seen in the form of competition between brands, such as Coca-Cola and Pepsi-Cola in the soft drinks market, or Sony and Samsung in the market for television sets. It is also common in the market for foodstuffs, such as competition between breakfast cereals.

Figure 11.2 shows how an increase in supply for one good (Weetabix) affects the market for a substitute good (Rice Krispies).

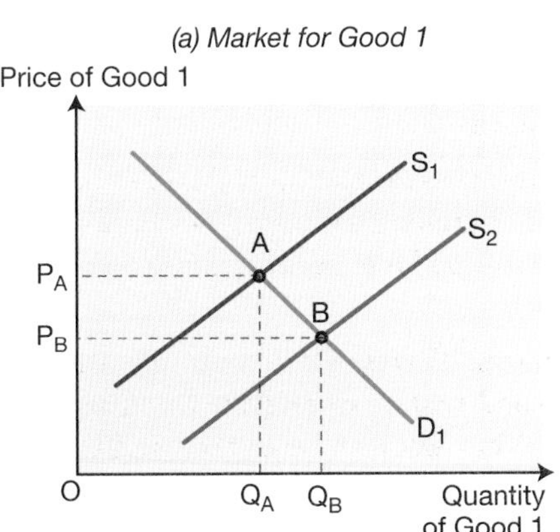

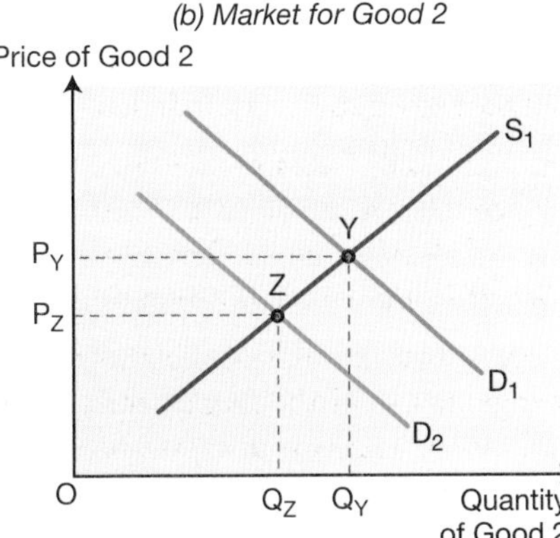

Figure 11.2 *An increase in supply and demand for a substitute good*

Key note

In this example, we consider the impact of a change in supply. This is designed to confirm the fact that the interrelationship between markets relates both to changes in demand and changes in supply. As with joint demand, the demand for substitute goods would be influenced by changes in demand as well as changes in supply.

The left-hand diagram – Figure 11.2(a) – shows the effect of an increase in supply of Weetabix on the market for Weetabix. D_1 is the original demand curve and S_1 is the original supply curve. These two lines intersect at Point A, giving an equilibrium price of P_A and an equilibrium quantity of Q_A.

There is then an increase in the supply of Weetabix. This might have resulted from a change in any of the factors influencing demand that were described in Chapter 8, such as an increase in productive efficiency by the producer or a fall in the price of wheat (the main ingredient). The supply curve thus shifts to the right, from S_1 to S_2. This changes the equilibrium point from A to B. As a result the equilibrium price changes from the P_A to P_B and the equilibrium quantity changes from Q_A to Q_B. The key consequence shown in this diagram is the increase in the quantity of Weetabix purchased, with quantity rising from Q_A to Q_B.

As more Weetabix is now being purchased, consumers will not want to buy so much Rice Krispies because it is a substitute good for Weetabix and consumers are now buying more Weetabix. Moving to the right-hand diagram – Figure 11.2(b) – we can see the impact on the market for Rice Krispies. In this market the demand curve shifts to the left because there is a real decrease in demand. Individual preferences for Rice Krispies have changed against Rice Krispies because more consumers are now buying its close substitute, Weetabix.

In Figure 11.2(b), we see that the original supply curve was S_1 and the original demand curve was D_1. This gave an equilibrium point of Y. Therefore, the original equilibrium price was P_Y and the original equilibrium quantity was Q_Y.

The decrease in demand shifts the demand curve from D_1 to D_2. There is no change in the supply curve, S_1. Thus the new equilibrium point is where S_1 and D_2 intersect – this is Point Z. Therefore, the new equilibrium price is P_Z and the new equilibrium quantity is Q_Z.

Conclusion: *An increase in supply for a good leads to a decrease in demand for a substitute good. This leads to a decrease in both the price and quantity purchased of the good that is a substitute for the original good.*

Similar logic can be applied to other changes in demand and supply. For example, a decrease in demand for Weetabix would have led to an increase in demand for Rice Krispies and thus a rise in both the price and quantity purchased of Rice Krispies.

The implications of composite demand

Composite demand refers to goods that are demanded for different purposes. Potatoes can be used in a variety of different ways (including as an ingredient in milkshakes) and a farmer might need to choose between competing uses for the farm's land. This land could be used to grow crops for human consumption, crops for feed livestock or crops for use as biofuels. In effect, the more alternative uses a good or service has, the greater its overall demand might be. In situations in which composite demand is being applied to the uses of a factor of production, such as farmland (above), it links to the concept of competitive supply.

Figure 11.3 shows how a decrease in demand for one good (cheese) affects the market for a good in composite demand (yoghurts).

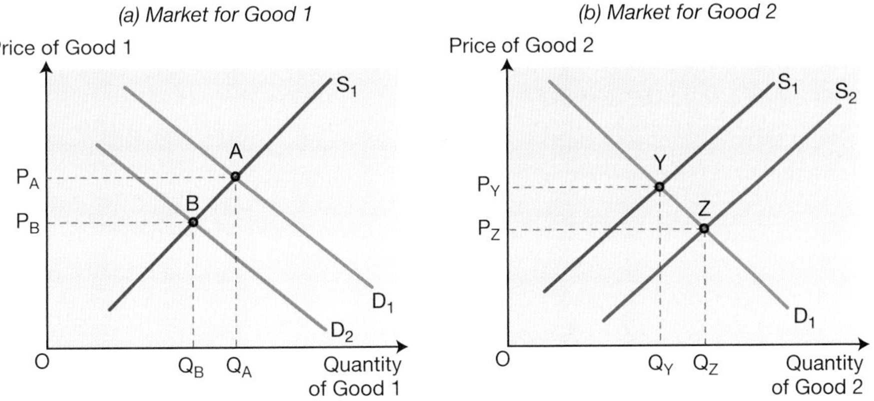

Figure 11.3 *A decrease in demand and composite demand*

The left-hand diagram – Figure 11.3(a) – shows the effect of a decrease in demand for cheese on the market for cheese. S_1 is the original supply curve and D_1 is the original demand curve. These two lines intersect at Point A, giving an equilibrium price of P_A and an equilibrium quantity of Q_A.

There is then a decrease in demand for cheese. This would have resulted from a change in any of the factors influencing demand that were described in Chapter 6, such as a decrease in the price of a substitute good. The demand curve thus shifts to the left, from D_1 to D_2. This changes the equilibrium point from A to B. As a result the equilibrium price changes from P_A to P_B and the equilibrium quantity changes from Q_A to Q_B. The key consequence shown in this diagram is the decrease in the quantity of cheese purchased, with quantity falling from Q_A to Q_B.

As less cheese is now being purchased, suppliers will require less milk for the production of cheese. This means that more milk is now available for the production of yoghurts. (It also means that more milk is available for direct supply as milk for drinking.) Moving to the right-hand diagram – Figure 11.3(b) – we can see the impact on the market for yoghurts. In this market the supply curve shifts to the right because there is more milk available to produce yoghurts: this is a real increase in supply.

In Figure 11.3(b), we see that the original demand curve was D_1 and the original supply curve was S_1. This gave an equilibrium point of Y. Therefore, the original equilibrium price was P_Y and the original equilibrium quantity was Q_Y.

The increase in supply shifts the supply curve from S_1 to S_2. There is no change in the demand curve, D_1. Thus the new equilibrium point is where S_2 and D_1 intersect – this is Point Z. Therefore, the new equilibrium price is P_Z and the new equilibrium quantity is Q_Z.

Conclusion: *A decrease in demand for a good leads to an increase in supply of a good available for a good in composite demand. This leads to a decrease in the price and an increase in the quantity purchased of the good that is in composite demand.*

The implications of derived demand

It is quite commonplace to have derived demand, as demand for many goods automatically leads to the demand for other goods.

It could be argued that many complementary goods are better described as derived demand. For example, the demand for rice (as a complement) could be attributed to the demand for foods such as Chicken Tikka and Beef Curry. Demand for factors of production depend on people wanting the goods and services, so markets for factors of production, such as labour, land, machinery, delivery vehicles and raw materials, are all derived from the demand for the goods that they make.

Figure 11.4 shows how a decrease in demand for one good/service (theatre visits) affects the market for an item in derived demand (actors).

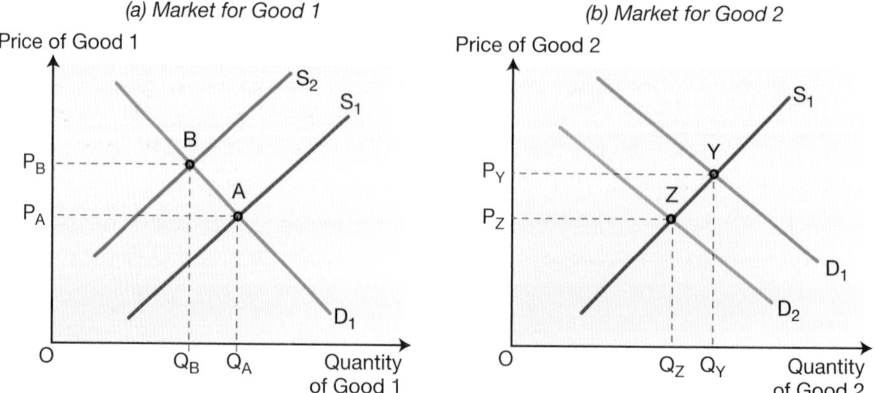

Figure 11.4 *A decrease in supply and derived demand*

The left-hand diagram – Figure 11.4(a) – shows the effect of a decrease in supply for theatre visits on the market for theatre visits. S_1 is the original supply curve and D_1 is the original demand curve. These two lines intersect at Point A, giving an equilibrium price of P_A and an equilibrium quantity of Q_A.

There is then a decrease in supply of theatre visits. This might have resulted from the closure of some theatres or it might have been caused by higher costs, such as an increase in theatre rents. Alternatively, it may have been caused by any of the other factors influencing supply that were described in Chapter 8, such as a tax on theatre visits. The supply curve thus shifts to the left, from S_1 to S_2. This changes the equilibrium point from A to B. As a result the equilibrium price changes from P_A to P_B and the equilibrium quantity changes from Q_A to Q_B. The key consequence shown in this diagram is the decrease in the quantity of theatre visits, with quantity falling from Q_A to Q_B.

As fewer people are visiting theatres, fewer plays will take place and fewer actors will be needed. Moving to the right-hand diagram – Figure 11.4(b) – we can see the impact on the market for actors. In this market the demand curve shifts to the left because there is a real decrease in demand. Individual preferences for actors have changed because the buyers of actors (the theatres) have declined in number and/or they are putting on fewer plays.

In Figure 11.4(b), we see that the original supply curve was S_1 and the original demand curve was D_1. This gave an equilibrium point of Y. Therefore, the original equilibrium price was P_Y and the original equilibrium quantity was Q_Y.

The increase in demand shifts the demand curve from D_1 to D_2. There is no change in the supply curve, S_1. Thus the new equilibrium point is where S_1 and D_2 intersect – this is Point Z. Therefore, the new equilibrium price is P_Z and the new equilibrium quantity is Q_Z. (It should be noted that the prices in this market are the cost of labour – basically the wages paid to actors.)

Conclusion: *A decrease in supply for a good leads to a decrease in demand for a good whose demand is derived from the original good. This leads to a decrease in both the price (wage paid) and the quantity purchased of the good that is in derived demand.*

Similar logic can be applied to other changes in demand and supply. For example, an increase in demand for theatre visits would have led to an increase in demand for actors and thus a rise in both the price and quantity purchased of actors.

The implications of joint supply

If the manufacture of a good leads to the production of another good, then we have joint supply. If consumers want more ham, then more pigs will be slaughtered, leading to a greater supply of bacon and pigs' trotters. When petrol is produced from refining crude oil, a number of byproducts are jointly supplied, such as asphalt, bitumen (tar), paraffin and plastics.

Figure 11.5 shows how an increase in demand for one good (petrol) affects the market for a good in joint supply (tar).

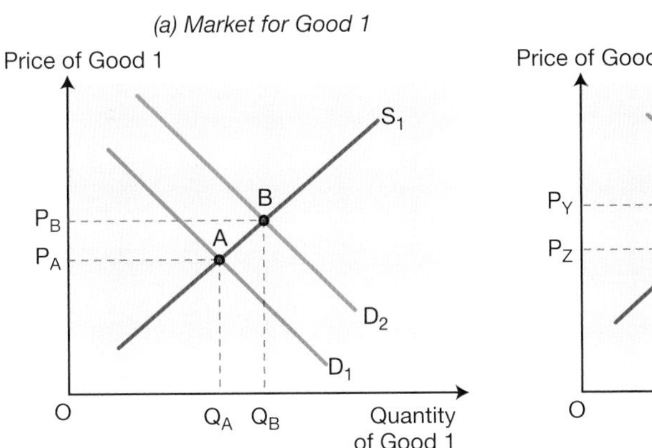

Figure 11.5 *An increase in demand and joint supply*

The left-hand diagram – Figure 11.5(a) – shows the effect of an increase in demand for petrol on the market for petrol. S_1 is the original supply curve and D_1 is the original demand curve. These two lines intersect at Point A, giving an equilibrium price of P_A and an equilibrium quantity of Q_A.

There is then an increase in demand for petrol. This would have resulted from a change in any of the factors influencing demand that were described in Chapter 6, such as an increase in demand for a complement (cars). The demand curve thus shifts to the right, from D_1 to D_2. This changes the equilibrium point from A to B. As a result the equilibrium price changes from the P_A to P_B and the equilibrium quantity changes from Q_A to Q_B. The key consequence shown in this diagram is the increase in the quantity of petrol purchased, with quantity rising from Q_A to Q_B.

As more petrol is now being purchased, suppliers will need to ensure that production rises to meet the change from Q_A to Q_B. Moving to the right-hand diagram –

Figure 11.5(b) – we can see the impact on the market for tar. There is a rise in supply that has come about because more petrol needs to be supplied in order to reach the new equilibrium quantity in the petrol market. Since tar is produced alongside petrol, this means the supply curve for tar shifts to the right because there is a real increase in the supply of tar.

In Figure 11.5(b), we see that the original demand curve was D_1 and the original supply curve was S_1. This gave an equilibrium point of Y. Therefore, the original equilibrium price was P_Y and the original equilibrium quantity was Q_Y.

The increase in supply shifts the supply curve from S_1 to S_2. There is no change in the demand curve, D_1. Thus the new equilibrium point is where D_1 and S_2 intersect – this is Point Z. Therefore, the new equilibrium price is P_Z and the new equilibrium quantity is Q_Z.

Conclusion: *An increase in demand for a good leads to an increase in supply for a good in joint supply with it. This leads to a decrease in the price and an increase in the quantity purchased of the good that is in joint supply.*

Similar logic can be applied to other changes in demand and supply. For example, a decrease in supply for petrol would have led to a decrease in supply for tar and thus a rise in the price and a decrease in the quantity purchased of tar.

REALWORLD ECONOMICS 11.1

Premier League footballers

There is much debate about the level of wages paid to professional footballers, or at least those playing football at the highest levels.

Prior to 1961, the FA imposed a maximum wage on footballers: no footballer could earn more than £20 per week. The abolition of this maximum wage in 1961 led to a steady increase in wages – a trend that has accelerated rapidly in recent years.

The demand for footballers is a derived demand, derived from the demand to watch football matches. In 1961, this meant paying money to watch a game of football. Prices were much lower (12.5 pence for a standing ticket to watch Manchester United) and this affected the ability of some football clubs to pay high wages. At that time only the FA Cup Final was broadcast on television and so football clubs depended on gate money for their revenue. Over the years this situation has changed.

Year	Sources of revenue				Total wages
	Matchday	Broadcasting	Other sources	Total	
1991–92	£78 m 48%	£51 m 31%	£33 m 21%	£162 m 100%	£73 m 45%
2001–02	£396 m 35%	£475 m 42%	£260 m 23%	£1132 m 100%	£706 m 62%
2011–12	£551 m 23%	£1653 m 70%	£156 m 7%	£2360 m 100%	£1652 m 70%
2013–14	£585 m 23%	£1780 m 71%	£160 m 6%	£2525 m 100%	£1793 m 71%

Table 11.1 *Sources of revenue for Premier League football clubs*

In the early 1980s, ITV began to show live football matches, but the revenue represented 2–3% of the income of top-flight football clubs. In 1991, Sky began to pay for exclusive rights to broadcast live football games, putting in a high bid in order to attract subscribers. This led to a significant new source of income for football teams, with Premier League teams finding that broadcasting now provided 31% of their income. Since 1991, this percentage has continued to increase (Table 11.1).

The vast majority of broadcasting money is paid to Premier League teams, and so there is a big incentive to stay in the top league. This has led to a growing demand for top footballers from all over the world. As the fees paid by broadcasters have continued to rise, the benefits to clubs who play in the Premier league have increased too. This has led to a willingness to pay high wages to attract players. This is shown in the final column of Table 11.1. The average wage of a footballer in a Premier League team squad is £22,353 per week.

Premier League footballers – an example of derived demand

In League 2, professional footballers earn an average wage of £38,844 per annum.

Other interrelationships

Football also provides examples of other interrelationships:

- *Joint demand* Items such as football programmes, pies and hot drinks tend to be bought by fans who attend games.
- *Demand for substitute goods* Demand for a football team can be influenced by demand for a nearby rival, such as choosing between Sheffield Wednesday and Sheffield United. Similarly, football is in competition with other leisure activities, and demand to watch a football team such as Leicester City is likely to be affected by demand for the Leicester Tigers rugby team.

Exercises

Total: 16 marks

1 Define the term 'joint demand'. *(3 marks)*

2 Using Table 11.1, identify two significant points of comparison between the different sources of revenue for Premier League football clubs. *(4 marks)*

3 Explain, with the help of a diagram, how TV broadcasting has affected the wages of Premier League footballers. *(9 marks)*

Review questions

Total: 35 marks

1 In Figure 11.6 the equilibrium point for Good X has changed from Point A to Point B.

Figure 11.6

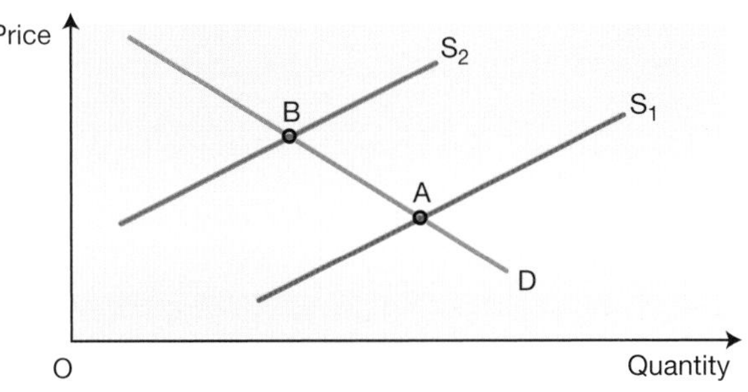

This change from A to B might have been caused by:

A A decrease in the demand for a good in composite demand
B An increase in the demand for a substitute good
C A decrease in the demand for a good in joint demand
D An increase in the demand for a good in joint supply *(1 mark)*

2 If people buy more of Good L, there will be a real increase in the supply of Good M. Goods L and M are examples of:

A Joint demand
B Demand for substitute goods
C Composite demand
D Joint supply *(1 mark)*

3 In Figure 11.7 the equilibrium point for Good Y has changed from Point A to Point B.

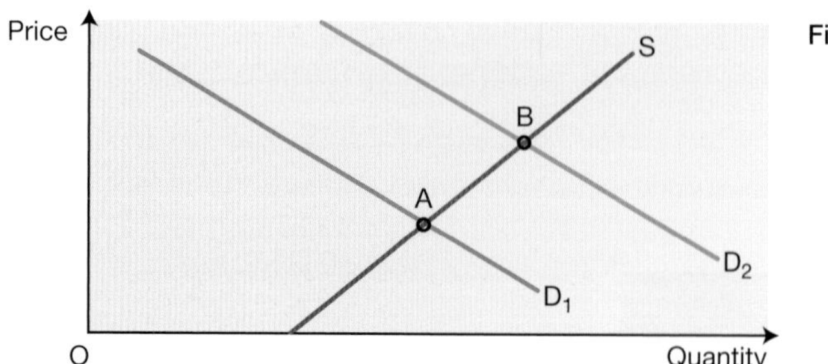

Figure 11.7

This change from A to B might have been caused by:

A An increase in the supply of a good in joint demand
B An increase in the supply of a substitute good
C An increase in the demand for a good in composite demand
D An increase in the demand for a good in joint supply *(1 mark)*

4 Define the term 'composite demand'. *(3 marks)*

5 Explain, using a diagram, the effect of an increase in demand for Coca-Cola on the equilibrium price and quantity of Pepsi-Cola. *(9 marks)*

6 Petrol and tar are examples of joint supply. Explain how a decrease in the demand for petrol will affect the equilibrium price and quantity of tar. *(10 marks)*

7 Explain how a change in individual preferences for milk will affect the price of cheese and the quantity bought. *(10 marks)*

Topic 2 **Exam-style questions**

A-LEVEL PAPER 1

Total: 80 marks

SECTION A Context: The worldwide demand and supply of oil

Read extracts A, B and C and answer all the questions that follow.

Extract A **Data on price and income elasticity of demand for oil and price elasticity of supply**

Table A *Price and income elasticities of crude oil demand in selected countries*

Country	PED (SR)	PED (LR)	YED (SR)	YED (LR)
Sweden	−0.05	−0.12	0.38	0.89
Spain	−0.06	−0.28	0.66	3.26
Italy	−0.05	−0.14	0.60	1.71
Germany	−0.07	−0.10	0.60	0.87
USA	−0.04	−0.07	0.59	1.00
Japan	−0.04	−0.12	0.53	1.71

Notes: PED = Price elasticity of demand; YED = Income elasticity of demand; SR = short run; LR = long run

Source: Article by Christos Tsirimokos on 'Price and income elasticities of crude oil demand', published in 2011 by Swedish University of Agricultural Sciences

Table B *Estimated price elasticity of supply for oil, 1980–2010*

Year	Average price of a barrel of oil ($, 2013 prices)	Price elasticity of supply for oil
1980	80	0.28
1985	55	0.4
1990	38	0.12
1995	30	0.1
2000	35	0.08
2005	60	0.02
2010	95	0.15

Source: Bank of Canada, 2011

Extract B **Oil producers hit by fall in oil prices**

Table B shows how oil prices have fluctuated since 1980. However, these five-yearly figures do not show some more significant variations between those years. For example, in 2008 oil prices reached $145 a barrel but in 2009 they fell below $39 a barrel. In 2014, prices have varied considerably, peaking at $115 dollars in June but falling to $74 in November.

A number of factors have contribute to the volatility of the price of oil, with the wide fluctuations in price attributed to higher output amongst the major oil-exporting countries such as Saudi Arabia, the lack of demand as growth rates fall in countries such as China, the stagnation of demand throughout Europe with most countries experiencing low or zero growth, and increasing self-sufficiency in oil in North America, where 'fracking' has enabled both the USA and Canada to access large deposits of shale oil. These factors have combined to create a situation in which many oil exporters may need to withdraw from the market because of the lack of profit. Table C shows the minimum price per barrel of oil needed for certain countries to be able to supply oil profitably in 2014.

Table C *Minimum oil price per barrel needed for supplying country to make a profit*

Oil price	Iran	Bahrain	Iraq	Saudi Arabia	UAE	Qatar	Kuwait
$ per barrel	130.5	125.4	111.2	97.5	79.3	54.8	54.2

At the November 2014 price of $74 per barrel, only Qatar and Kuwait of the major oil exporters are exporting oil profitably. Even the largest supplier, Saudi Arabia, and major oil-producing countries such as Venezuela and Russia, are unable to make profit at these prices.

Sources: CNBC – articles by Patti Domm, 11.11.14 and 14.11.14; and BBC

Extract C **Views on oil reserves and prices**

In a lecture in December 2013, Dr Richard G. Miller, a former BP geologist, criticised the official industry view that global reserves of oil will last for 53 years at current rates of consumption. He argued that new discoveries of 'unconventional' sources of oil and gas had not prevented a decline in oil production of 4%.

Dr Miller believes that oil prices will rise, in part because 'unconventional' supplies are more costly to access. New discoveries of oil have not matched consumption since 1986, although improved production techniques are enabling more oil to be extracted from existing reserves.

A possible consequence of high oil prices is a recession. The high oil prices in the 1970s are linked strongly to the subsequent worldwide recession, and in the USA there is a strong correlation between high oil prices and recessions, although not all recessions are caused by high oil prices. The argument runs as follows: high oil prices lead to a decline in demand for oil by firms and to high energy costs, forcing down profits. Cuts in jobs lead to lower incomes, and so less demand by consumers. In time, this leads to lower prices for raw materials, such as oil.

Volatility (wide fluctuations) in oil prices are seen as inevitable by many economists.

Questions

Total: 40 marks

1. In November 2014 the price of oil was $74 per barrel. Using the data in Table C, calculate the profit/loss per barrel made by Saudi Arabia. *(2 marks)*
2. Explain how the data in Table C would influence the supply curve of oil. *(4 marks)*
3. Table A shows that the long-run income elasticity of demand for oil in Spain is 3.26. Assuming that the Spanish economy experiences a period of rising consumer incomes in the long run, explain, with the help of a diagram, the likely impact of this growth in consumer incomes on the price and quantity of oil bought in Spain. *(9 marks)*
4. The final line of Extract C states that 'Volatility (wide fluctuations) in oil prices are seen as inevitable by many economists'. Using the data in the extracts and your economic knowledge, assess the view that volatility of oil prices is inevitable. *(25 marks)*

SECTION B Essays

Total: 40 marks

1. Explain how changes in taxation can influence the price of goods and services. *(15 marks)*
2. Between 2009 and 2014, overall income levels remained the same. However, there was a significant change in that people on higher incomes experienced significant increases in income, while those in lower-paid employment experienced a decline in income. Evaluate the impact of this scenario on the supply and demand for restaurant meals. *(25 marks)*

Topic 3

Production, costs & revenue

Production & productivity

This chapter studies the production process – the conversion of inputs into outputs of goods and services. The concept of productivity is introduced, with a specific focus on labour productivity: its meaning, factors that influence it and the benefits of high labour productivity.

Production

Production is measured by the total output of goods and services by a firm or within an economy (Figure 12.1). We saw earlier that the purpose of production is to satisfy human wants, using the scarce resources available. Although production can be measured by volume (e.g. 50 tables), it is usually measured in monetary terms because this type of measurement reflects its value to consumers and thus shows the level of happiness/welfare gained from the act of production. Production is not an end in its own right – it is a means to an end. The end purpose of production is the satisfaction of human wants.

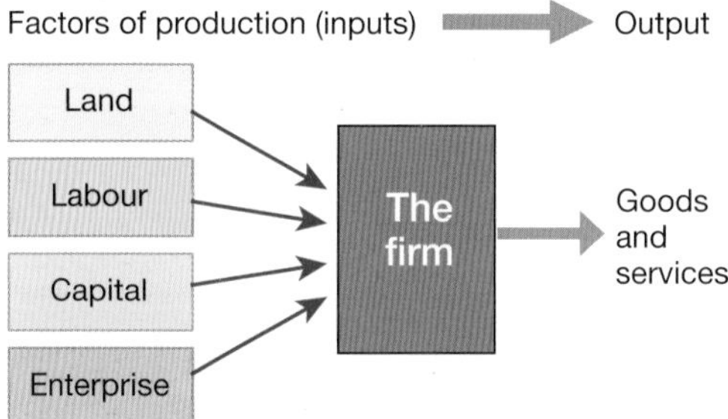

Figure 12.1 *The production process*

> **Key note**
> Production is only complete when the good or service reaches the consumer. It therefore continues beyond the manufacture of a good as it includes activities such as the delivery of the good or service to the consumer. It also includes earlier stages of production, such as discovery and extraction of raw materials.

As resources are scarce, production involves opportunity cost. Owners of factors of production will want to maximise their own rewards and so they will offer their services to the entrepreneurs who are prepared to pay the highest reward. Entrepreneurs are motivated by profit and therefore they will only pay high rewards to a factor of production if the expected value of the output from those factors of production is high enough to enable the entrepreneur to achieve a profit.

In Chapter 5 we saw how the production possibility boundary showed the maximum possible combination of goods and services that an economy could produce over a particular period of time. We now look at how the level of production in an economy can be increased.

Increasing the level of production in an economy

The level of production in an economy will depend on many factors:

- *The quantity of available resources – land, labour, capital and enterprise* In the 1970s, the discovery and exploitation of North Sea oil reserves enabled the UK to increase its level of raw materials (land), which boosted output of goods and services. More recently, net immigration has enabled the UK to increase the quantity of labour and so increase levels of output.
- *The extent to which resources (inputs) are fully utilised* The more fully factors of production are used, the higher the likely level of production in an economy. Productive efficiency relies on the economy operating on its production possibility boundary. During and after the recession, many resources were underutilised. Between mid-2009 and mid-2013, unemployment fluctuated slightly but remained close to 8% of the working population. Between mid-2013 and mid-2014 it fell by 2%, meaning that another half-a-million people were active in the economy. This coincided with an increase in GDP, which measures output of the UK economy.
- *The quality of the factors of production* The quality of labour can be improved by education and training; capital can be improved by new technology leading to more efficient machinery. With people staying in education longer, the UK is developing a more flexible and skilled labour force.
- *The level of specialisation* Different people have different types of skills. By allowing labour (and other factors of production) to specialise, greater production can be achieved. (This will be examined in more detail in Chapter 13.)
- *The scale of production* Firms can help the economy to improve overall production by operating at the most efficient scale of production, in order to gain the benefits of large-scale production without suffering from the problems that it can bring. (This topic will be examined in detail in Chapter 15.)
- *The effectiveness with which the different factors of production are combined* In most countries, greater output has been achieved by focusing on a greater use of capital in comparison to other factors of production, such as labour.

Ultimately, an economy will try to improve the efficiency of its factors of production so that a given level of inputs can generate a greater value of production (output).

Key note

Calculating the value of production

How is the value of production calculated? In general, a good is valued at the price paid. This is not an exact value, but it is the most realistic approach. After all, the equilibrium price in a market is the price that the final (marginal) consumer was prepared to pay.

When government tries to estimate the UK's total production, firms provide a good source of data, as they should record all of their income and expenses. However, government must avoid double counting of production. A Nissan car may sell for £15,000, but it will include components, such as tyres and seats, that were bought from other firms. For this reason, **value added is used to measure production.** If Nissan bought £4000 of components in order to produce a car that it sells for £15,000, then it has added value of (£15,000 – £4000 =) £11,000. Thus Nissan's production is valued at £11,000 and the firms providing components will have production valued at £4000.

Productivity

Key term

Productivity measures the efficiency with which inputs are transformed into outputs.

The key term definition can be applied to a country's use of its factors of production or a firm's use of the resources available to it.

Since there are a variety of inputs (factors of production), the term productivity can apply to all factors of production. There are therefore different measures of productivity. In recent years, multifactor measures of productivity have been introduced, such as capital-labour multi-factor productivity. This measure looks at how output is affected by capital and labour, jointly. Traditionally, however, measures of productivity tended to focus on single-factor productivity measures, such as labour productivity and capital productivity.

An example of single-factor productivity is the productivity of land. This can be measured by comparing output of agricultural crops to the area of land. For cereal crops, such as wheat, rice and barley, the following formula is used to measure the productivity of land:

$$\textbf{Productivity of land} = \frac{\text{Kilograms (kg) of cereal production}}{\text{Hectares (ha) of cultivated land}}$$

(A hectare is equal to 10,000 m^2, or an area of land measuring 100 m by 100 m.)

These data can be used to measure the efficiency with which land is used to produce crops. According to the World Bank, in 2013 the productivity of land in the UK for cereal production was 6630 kg/ha. Excluding countries using artificial production techniques, the UK was the tenth most productive country in the world in terms of cereal production. The most productive countries were:

1st Belgium – 9213 kg/ha
2nd Netherlands – 8653 kg/ha
3rd New Zealand – 8125 kg/ha
4th Ireland – 7803 kg/ha

The productivity of capital tends to be measured by comparing the value of output to the value of capital used. However, the most commonly used measure of productivity is labour productivity.

Key term

Labour productivity is a measure of the efficiency of labour.

Labour productivity is calculated as follows:

$$\textbf{Labour productivity} = \frac{\text{Output (production) over a period of time}}{\text{Number of employees}}$$

Applying the above formula, a firm might produce 800 wardrobes a year with a labour force of 20 people. In this case, annual labour productivity is 800/20 = 40 wardrobes per employee.

Author tip

Do not confuse production and productivity. In the above formula, production is 800 wardrobes. However, productivity is 800/20 = 40 wardrobes per employee.

Labour productivity is often measured in financial terms. If each wardrobe is sold for £500, then output of wardrobes = 800 × £500 = £400,000. In this case, labour productivity is £400,000/20 = £20,000 per employee.

Labour productivity is used to measure the efficiency of individual workers, groups of workers (such as a specific factory), firms or the economy as a whole. In Chapter 4 we saw how output per head of population, based on 2010 prices, had increased from £6306 per head in 1953 to £23,113 per head in 2013. This suggests that the efficiency of labour has grown over time, but it does not identify the causes. This greater efficiency may be due to other factors, such as more efficient capital.

Figure 12.2 shows annual percentage changes in two measures of productivity of manufacturing industry in the UK between 1990 and 2012. The two measures are labour productivity – output per hour in manufacturing (OPHM) – and capital productivity. Levels of capital tend to vary less than employment levels and so capital productivity tends to show greater consistency over time.

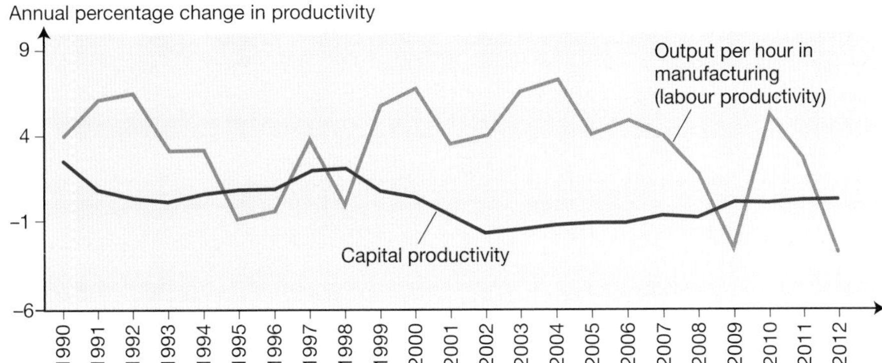

Figure 12.2 *Productivity in UK manufacturing, 1990–2012*

As an economy, the UK has underperformed in terms of its labour productivity when compared to its competitors, such as France, Germany and the USA.

Benefits of improved labour productivity

There are various benefits that arise from improved labour productivity:

- *Better living standards* In Chapter 4 (Table 4.2) we saw how output per head of population, based on 2010 prices, had increased from £6306 per head in 1953 to £23,113 per head in 2013. This means that people in 2013 were able to satisfy considerably more wants because the economy was producing well over three times as much value of products as it was in 1953.
- *Improved international competitiveness* Improved labour productivity leads to more production from the same level of resources. As a result, average costs (cost per item) fall and so UK products are able to compete more effectively with those of other countries.
- *Greater rewards to all factors of production* The first point above shows the benefits to workers. However, greater efficiency means that owners of the other factors of production, such as the landowners and entrepreneurs, will also benefit.
- *Economic growth* Greater output will mean growth in the economy, which should also help people to find jobs more easily. In the macroeconomics section of the course we will see that this is a key objective of any government.

REALWORLD ECONOMICS 12.1

Improving labour productivity

In the section on production we saw how factors such as training and more effective combinations of factors of production can lead to greater output. In general, these measures that will increase production will also increase labour productivity too.

A report by Cranfield University on UK manufacturing productivity identified the key factors influencing labour productivity in the secondary (manufacturing) sector of the UK economy, based on news articles between 1986 and 2014. These factors were those that were the root causes of *either* improved productivity *or* worsening levels of productivity.

It can be seen that over 50% of UK productivity changes resulted from changes in *either* 'skill and education' *or* 'investment'. Of the remaining factors, 'policy' of firms and the quality of 'management' were the most important causes of productivity changes, alongside 'innovation' (new ideas).

The data in Figure 12.3 represent factors over a period of almost 30 years. However, the importance of different factors varies over time.

Figure 12.3 *Root causes of UK productivity, 1986–2014*

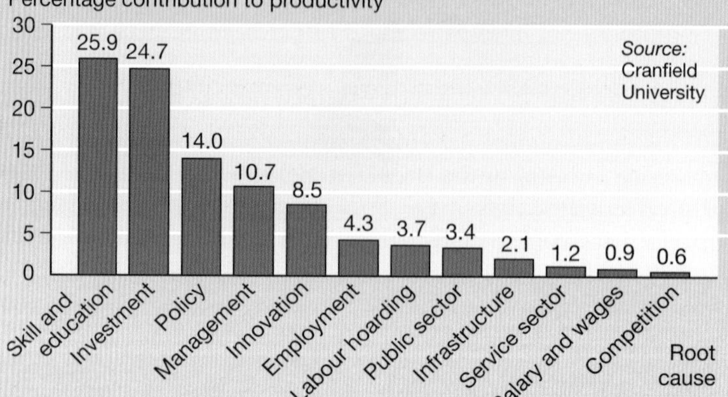

An examination of the most recent period covered by the research indicates that the following three factors were the dominant root causes of productivity in the post-recession period between 2011 and 2014: 'investment' (40%); 'skill and education' (21%); and 'policy' (21%).

The research also showed that 'investment' was the most important factor after the 1991 recession. During the recession, firms cut back on investment in capital equipment; after the recession, this lack of investment prevented productivity from growing.

Unemployment did not rise as quickly as expected during the recent recession because firms wanted to keep their skilled workers (labour hoarding). Although this reduces productivity in the short run, it should help in the long run.

The authors of the research concluded that in order to improve the productivity of UK manufacturing, action needed to be taken by both firms and the UK government. Table 12.1 summarises the five main actions required by firms and the government.

Actions by firms	Actions by government
Investment in training and development	Reduce taxation
Improving manufacturing processes	Attract more direct foreign investment into the UK
Investment in automation	Simplify business regulations
Improving the working environment	Improve general business access to funding
Simplifying products	Help smaller firms to access funding

Table 12.1 *Actions required to improve labour productivity of UK manufacturing firms in 2014*

Exercises *Total: 20 marks*

1. Explain how 'investment' by firms leads to higher labour productivity. (4 marks)
2. Analyse why 'skills and education' is such an important influence on labour productivity. (10 marks)
3. Select any *one* of the 'actions by government' listed in Table 12.1 and explain how it will help to improve labour productivity. (6 marks)

- *Impact on resources* Although growth of an economy can deplete resources, improved productivity means that a given level of resources produces more output. As a result, improved productivity means that resources may not be depleted so quickly. Current levels of technology are now enabling firms to use resources that were previously considered to be waste and successfully to extract levels of minerals that were considered to be uneconomic by previous generations.

How useful is labour productivity as a measure of efficiency?

Labour productivity is useful as a measure of efficiency for a number of reasons:

- It is easy to calculate and interpret. Dividing output (production) by the amount of labour is a straightforward calculation and the result is clear – the average worker is responsible for producing 'x' units of output.
- The data to calculate labour productivity are readily available. Most firms in most countries are required to keep information about their labour force and the volume and value of their production.
- Labour productivity is thus the most reliable way of comparing different firms and different economies historically, over a long period of time.
- It is an objective and reliable way of comparing different firms or factories.
- It can be measured in different ways and can be adapted to different purposes. For example, output per worker is the best measure to use when looking at the impact of labour productivity on living standards. However, to compare the efficiency of UK workers to those in other countries, output per hour per worker might be more useful.

There are a number of drawbacks, though, in using labour productivity as a measure of efficiency:

- Output can be measured in different ways and some may not be easy to use for comparisons. For example, labour productivity in the car industry is usually measured by cars per worker, but this approach ignores the value of the car and so it undervalues productivity in factories that are producing high-value cars, such as the Rolls-Royce.
- Labour productivity only focuses on a single factor – labour – and thus ignores the impact of other inputs, such as capital. In recent years, multifactor measures have become more important.
- It is often misinterpreted as a causal link. Labour productivity shows the statistical relationship between labour and output. However, the reason for the higher labour productivity may be the introduction of new capital or better management techniques introduced by entrepreneurs.
- It can be difficult to use to compare firms and economies. In the UK, many firms subcontract a lot of work to other firms and so they have few employees. This means that dividing output by employees gives a higher level of labour productivity when compared to a firm that uses its own labour force for all activities.
- Labour productivity ignores the cost of factors of production. In manufacturing, UK industries often have much higher labour productivity than developing countries but also much higher wages. Labour productivity can therefore be unreliable when examining the costs of making a product.

The production line at Rolls-Royce's factory in Goodwood, West Sussex – measuring labour productivity by cars per worker fails to take into account the value of the cars produced

- Labour productivity assumes that growth is the main objective of firms and governments. Consequently, improving labour productivity may conflict with other aims, such as improving the welfare of the workforce or protecting the environment.

Review questions

Total: 45 marks

1 Production is the:
A Conversion of inputs into outputs
B Level of output per person
C Manufacturing of goods
D Reward to entrepreneurs *(1 mark)*

2 Which one of the following is not an input into the production process?
A Capital goods
B Consumer goods
C Enterprise
D Land *(1 mark)*

3 Production of a good is completed when the:
A Manufacturing process is completed
B Consumer agrees to buy the good
C Consumer receives the good
D Consumer consumes the good *(1 mark)*

4 Other things being equal, which one of the following would usually increase the level of production in an economy?
A Net emigration of population
B Mineral resources becoming exhausted
C Unemployment increasing
D Labour becoming more specialised *(1 mark)*

5 A firm sells a good for £20,000. It pays £6000 to suppliers for components and pays £5000 to its labour force. Calculate the level of value added by the firm. *(3 marks)*

6 Define the term 'productivity'. *(3 marks)*

7 What is the difference between multifactor productivity and single-factor productivity? *(4 marks)*

8 A farm produces 20,000 kg of wheat, using 4 ha of land and 20 hours of labour from its workforce. Calculate its:
(a) land productivity; *(2 marks)*
(b) labour productivity. *(2 marks)*

9 Refer to Figure 12.2 on p. 133. Identify two significant points of comparison between capital productivity and labour productivity in the graph. *(4 marks)*

10 Explain two benefits of improved labour productivity. *(8 marks)*

11 Assess the advantages and disadvantages of using labour productivity as a measure of efficiency. *(15 marks)*

Specialisation, division of labour & exchange

In this chapter we introduce the concepts of specialisation and division of labour and examine the extent to which they are beneficial to individuals, firms and countries. The chapter concludes by looking at why specialisation requires exchange to take place and the necessity of money as a means of exchange.

The benefits of specialisation and division of labour

Specialisation

Specialisation means that an economic unit, such as an individual or region, focuses on producing a specific product or a limited range of products. Specialisation applies to countries, regions, firms and individuals.

Key term
Specialisation occurs when an individual, firm, region or country concentrates on producing a limited range of products.

Countries Some countries focus on a narrow range of products because they possess particular natural resources or because their population has developed particular skills. Although the UK economy is quite diversified (non-specialised) by international standards, the UK has a reputation for the provision of financial services, such as banking and insurance. Service industries provide 78% of the UK's production, with London being the world's largest banking centre. The UK also specialises in insurance (providing 7% of the world's total insurance) and has the second largest Aerospace industry in the world. Mauritania is considered to be the most specialised country in the world, with 50% of its production consisting of agriculture and 40% of its exports being iron ore. However, the most specialised countries tend to be poorer economies that are still predominantly agricultural.

- *Regions* Historically, UK regions often specialised in certain industries, mainly because their locations were influenced by the location of raw materials. For example, the West Midlands was the focus of metal manufacturing, South Wales specialised in coal and iron, Yorkshire was the base of the wool trade, and Lancashire was the centre of cotton production. Individual cities were often associated with particular products, such as Belfast and Newcastle for shipbuilding, Sheffield for steel and Stoke for pottery. As these industries declined and service industries expanded, the UK became more diversified. However, some regional specialisations have developed, with the M4/M3 region known as a centre for ICT-based industries, and call centres often choosing locations in Northern Ireland and Scotland. Many services, such as entertainment and catering, are designed for local use and so they tend to be spread more evenly geographically. However, a recent survey by the Office of National Statistics (ONS) indicated that specialisation on the Isles of Scilly is greater than any other area of the UK, with 85% of income coming from tourism. Of the larger regions, London is the most specialised. While financial services account for 9.4% of the UK's output, they are a remarkable 22% of London's output of goods and services. London's other specialism is the information and communication industry. According to the ONS, three cities that were originally very specialised – Leeds, Birmingham and Bristol – are now the most diversified in the UK, providing a broad range of goods and services that most closely reflects the UK economy as a whole.

- *Firms* Businesses will usually focus on a specific product or range of products in order to benefit from specialisation. In the 1960s and 1970s many large firms diversified, to spread their risks, but since then there has been a return to the idea that firms should focus on their core specialisation.
- *Individuals* Specialisation by individuals is referred to as 'division of labour'. This means that a worker focuses on a particular job – often a job that is just one aspect of the production process. In recent years, firms have tried to become more flexible, aiming to provide goods and services at the time and place that is most suitable for customers. This has led to firms moving away from encouraging narrow specialisation amongst their workforce. Workers are now encouraged to become 'multiskilled', so that they can move between different jobs to suit the firm's most urgent need.

Division of labour

Key term

Division of labour refers to specialisation by individual workers. It involves breaking down production into many different tasks, with each worker specialising in one task.

Division of labour means breaking the production process down into many tasks, allowing factors of production (mainly capital and labour) to focus on one small part of the production process. In 1776, Adam Smith wrote *An Enquiry into the Nature and Causes of the Wealth of Nations*. In this book he described how the manufacture of a simple product – the pin – could be divided up into many stages, with each worker specialising in one particular task. This division of labour would lead to more efficient production:

- Workers specialise in jobs that suit their skills. By playing to their strengths, they improve both the quantity and the quality of the items that they produce. This means that an economy can produce more goods and services.
- Constantly doing the same task improves workers' skills still further, based on the assumption that 'practice makes perfect'. Constant repetition enables workers to produce more quickly, thus improving production and productivity.
- Production lines can be used, so that workers remain in one place, usually with the partly assembled product being sent along a conveyer belt system. This saves time because workers need not move from their workplace. On production lines, the product moves along the line and workers carry out their respective roles as the product passes.
- As workers stay in a particular place, each worker can have one machine, thus saving costs as the production line only needs one machine for each task.

However, there are disadvantages that arise from this type of division of labour, mainly because the repetitive nature of the job can lead to boredom and as a result:

- low output, as workers are unable to sustain their concentration because their jobs lack variety;
- high absenteeism, because workers might dislike their work and pretend to be ill;
- poor quality, as a lack of focus caused by boredom can result in mistakes which lead to lower quality.

Adam Smith, 1723–90

Mass production, using division of labour, can also lead to difficulties in the production process. If one part of the process is not working, or is providing faulty parts, then either the whole production line ceases to function or the finished products will be faulty.

Excessive specialisation can also impact on consumers. As people's incomes and wealth increase, they tend to place a higher value on choice, variety and individuality. Thus firms need to avoid excessive specialisation because they will need to provide variety rather than high volumes of identical products.

Summary

The ability to specialise enables firms and economies to increase both production and productivity, thus enabling more goods and services to be produced with the scarce resources available. However, there are limits to the benefits of specialisation. Some resources may not be suited to certain specialisation. Some diversification into other products is therefore necessary if a country is to maximise its output. Similarly, individual workers have different skills and capabilities, and so an economy should ensure that it maximises the potential of its labour force.

A key point to consider is the fact that an economy's strengths may change over time. The UK is generally considered to have been the first country to industrialise, during the industrial revolution. A major cause of this process was the discovery and exploitation of mineral resources such as coal and iron. These resources gave the UK a competitive advantage over other countries and led to the UK specialising in the manufacture of products such as steel. However, as these mineral resources have depleted, the UK no longer has a competitive advantage in these products. The UK has needed to adapt to new goods and services, such as information and communications technology. Countries such as the UAE and Saudi Arabia are using their oil revenue to diversify into new industries, so that their economies will survive when the oil is used up.

Overspecialisation can be a high risk because there is no guarantee that an economy will maintain its strengths, or that the goods in which it specialises will continue to be popular. The decline of the UK coal industry is partly due to a loss in the UK's specialist skills but also due to a decline in the popularity of coal as a source of energy.

Specialisation and exchange of goods and services

If there is no specialisation, individuals provide for their own needs. This requires them to grow food and provide their own shelter and clothing. Even in the most primitive of economies, mankind learned to specialise, with different individuals providing different goods or services for the family or tribe.

Specialisation means that individuals and organisations must trade/exchange the limited range of goods that they produce to acquire the other resources they need to satisfy their wants. By definition, specialisation means that an individual/firm/economy will produce a surplus of the good in which they are specialising (that is, they will produce more than is necessary to satisfy their own wants). In primitive economies this would involve barter, where basically one good would be exchanged for another. The use of barter, however, depends on a *double coincidence of wants*. If an individual specialises in providing meat, but wants clothing, they would exchange meat for clothing. However, this system only works if there is a *double coincidence of wants*. In this instance it only works if the person who specialises in providing clothing wants meat at the same time as the meat provider wants clothing.

Over time, a **means of exchange** has evolved. Originally this would have been a product such as salt, which would be needed by all individuals and which could be stored for future use (either as an item to consume or one to use to barter for other goods). In modern society, **money** provides this function. Anything that is widely accepted in return for goods and services can act as money.

Key term

Money is anything that is widely accepted in exchange for goods and services.

In the UK, banknotes and coins are clear examples of money. However, an alternative definition of money is: 'money is what money does'. Anything that carries out the functions of money (below) can be classified as money.

Functions of money

Money has four main functions, each of which assist the exchange process that is necessary if specialisation is to take place.

1 **A means of exchange** Money can be exchanged for goods and services.

2 **A store of value** If an individual wishes to postpone consumption, and 'save' for the future, money must be something that can be stored for future use.

3 **A measure of value** Money must have a precise measure, so that its value can be known and maintained.

4 **A standard of deferred payments** On occasions, exchange is agreed whereby a good or service is received with a promise to pay for it in the future. Money must be something that can be used for this type of transaction. (In effect, this is the opposite of money as a store of value.) If money keeps a consistent value, it will fulfil this function.

In modern society, bank accounts/bank cards can be seen as money because they can be used to carry out each of these functions. Societies often used livestock, such as sheep and goats. Why might goats not be a good form of money?

In order to be widely acceptable in exchange for goods and services, money needs to be:

- widely acceptable;
- stable in value;
- portable or easy to transfer;
- storable/durable;
- divisible into both large and small values;
- recognisable (if it is homogeneous – all the same – it is likely to be recognisable).

The UK currency (sterling) meets all of these requirements. However, electronic transfers of money have become more important as a means of exchange, particularly for international transactions, as they are more secure and easier to transfer.

Key term

Exchange is the trading of goods and services between sellers and buyers.

Exchange

In order to benefit from specialisation, trade is needed. We saw earlier how the meat producer and clothing provider traded their products. From the viewpoint of an economy, specialisation will only yield benefits if the surplus of the good(s) in which the economy specialises can be exchanged for goods that it does not produce (or produces in insufficient quantities). Trade or exchange is needed in order to ensure that economies can benefit. These benefits will be easier to obtain if:

- there are markets in which international buyers and sellers can meet;
- an internationally accepted exchange of money is possible (international currency markets);
- firms in different countries can communicate easily;
- transport costs do not erode the financial gains from specialisation. For example, if specialisation cuts costs by £2 per item, there will be no benefit if the transport costs exceed £2 per item.

Political and economic stability can also play a big part in encouraging trade and exchange.

REALWORLD ECONOMICS 13.1

Is specialisation best for countries?

Although specialisation seems to work well for individuals and firms, there is evidence to suggest that specialisation is not necessarily best for economies as a whole.

Research published by the United Nations Industrial Development Organisation (UNIDO) suggests that the gains from specialisation depend on the level of development of a country. As countries develop, they tend to go through five stages (as shown in Figure 13.1):

- **Stage 1: Slow-growing low-income countries** These countries have the highest levels of specialisation, focusing on less sophisticated products such as foodstuffs and raw materials. These low-income countries benefit from trade because it allows them to gain the benefits of their specialisation. The income earned from exports may be used for essential items that the country cannot produce or in order to acquire more sophisticated products through importing.
- **Stage 2: Fast-growing low-income countries** These countries are still largely reliant on less sophisticated products but are moving towards sophisticated products, such as manufactured goods and personal or commercial services. In doing so they have become less specialised and are diversifying into a wider range of goods and services.
- **Stage 3: Slow-growing middle-income countries** These countries have high levels of diversification of goods and services and tend not to specialise.
- **Stage 4: Fast-growing middle-income countries** These countries are moving towards highly sophisticated products. A wide range of products are made, but these countries are beginning to focus more on

Table 13.1 *The most specialised and the most diversified countries*

Most specialised countries			Most diversified countries		
Rank	Country	Rank GDP per head	Rank	Country	Rank GDP per head
1	Mauritania	159	1	USA	14
2	Burundi	193	2	Germany	23
3	Mali	172	3	UK	27
4	Central African Republic	186	4	Italy	29
5	Sudan	150	5	France	26
6	Ethiopia	191	6	Spain	31
7	Benin	168	7	Netherlands	17
8	Gabon	50	8	China	92
9	Algeria	98	9	Belgium	20
10	The Gambia	183	10	Austria	16

Notes: Research based on 116 countries; ranking of GDP per head based on UN ranking of 193 countries. *Source:* 'Diversification vs specialisation as alternative strategies for economic development', by F. Kaulich, UNIDO specialised goods and services.

- **Stage 5: High-income countries** These countries focus on highly sophisticated products and thus tend to have higher levels of specialisation than middle-income countries. Trade is used to reap fully the benefits of their specialisms.

Conclusion: *High-income countries tend to reap the greatest benefits from specialisation because they tend to specialise in sophisticated products that generate higher income.*

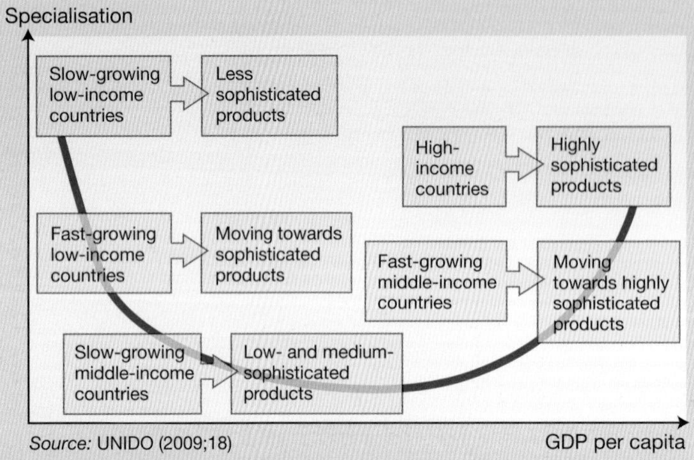

Specialisation

Slow-growing low-income countries	→ Less sophisticated products		
Fast-growing low-income countries	→ Moving towards sophisticated products	High-income countries	→ Highly sophisticated products
Slow-growing middle-income countries	→ Low- and medium-sophisticated products	Fast-growing middle-income countries	→ Moving towards highly sophisticated products

GDP per capita

Source: UNIDO (2009;18)

Figure 13.1 *Specialisation and development*

Table 13.1 confirms that there is a strong link between low income and high degrees of specialisation. However, most of the highly diversified economies tend to be high-income countries (although not those with the highest GDP per head, which tend to be more specialised). In general, these are long-established European countries with a long history of trading and exchange.

Exercise ***Total: 15 marks***

1 Using the data in Table 13.1, compare and explain the link between the level of specialisation and the level of income (GDP per head) of the countries shown. ***(15 marks)***

Review questions

Total: 35 marks

1 Which one of these statements is *false*? Division of labour may lead to lower productivity because constant practice and repetition can lead to:
   - A Mistakes and therefore low-quality products
   - B Workers losing their natural skills and so producing less
   - C Boredom and high absenteeism by workers
   - D Lower output because of lower concentration ***(1 mark)***

2 Many people regard credit cards as money. Which function of money is *not* carried out by credit cards?
   - A Means of exchange
   - B Measure of value
   - C Store of value
   - D Standard of deferred payments ***(1 mark)***

3 Define the term 'specialisation'. ***(3 marks)***

4 Define the term 'money'. ***(3 marks)***

5 Explain why specialisation requires an efficient means of exchange. ***(4 marks)***

6 Explain why overspecialisation can cause problems for a country. ***(5 marks)***

7 Explain two reasons why regions might specialise. ***(8 marks)***

8 Analyse the benefits of division of labour. ***(10 marks)***

Costs of production

In this chapter we focus on the costs of production. Costs are influenced by time and so the chapter explains the distinction between the short run and the long run. The concepts of fixed costs and variable costs are introduced and explained in the context of both the time period and the level of output of the firm. The chapter concludes by explaining the difference between average and total costs and demonstrating how they are calculated.

The difference between the short and long run

Different production costs behave in different ways over time. For this reason it is vital to define time periods before examining the nature of production costs.

The quantity of some factors of production cannot easily be changed. For example, if a firm expects demand to increase, it will take a long time to build or acquire a new factory in which to produce the extra products that it will need to make. Even if a building can be acquired, there may be a long time lapse before capital equipment can be made and installed. This can make it very difficult (and thus very costly) to increase the level of output in a firm.

However, some factors of production can be changed much more quickly when the firm wants to increase production. For many firms, raw materials or stocks can easily be increased. Supermarkets often place orders for products and expect the quantity ordered to be delivered within 24 hours. Labour can also be very flexible, as workers may work late if necessary in order to help increase production. However, if specialist skills are needed, such as the skills of a brain surgeon, the amount of labour available may not be very flexible.

Economists use the factors of production to define time periods: the **short run** is the time period in which the amount of *variable factors of production* can vary, but in which *fixed factors of production* are fixed. Based on this logic, the **long run** is the time period in which the amount of both *variable factors of production* and *fixed factors of production* can vary. These time periods are not rigid; a firm such as a shipbuilder can take years to adjust output, whereas for a window-cleaning firm the long run might be only a matter of a few weeks.

Some economists use the term 'the very short run' to describe a time when *all factors*

Key terms

The **short run** is the time period in which it is only possible to change the level of input of variable factors of production.

The **long run** is the time period in which it is possible to change the level of input of all of the factors of production.

Fixed costs are costs that do *not* vary directly with output in the short run.

Variable costs are costs that do vary directly with output in the short run.

of production are fixed. In practice, this time period is likely to be a matter of hours for most firms.

The difference between fixed and variable costs

Definitions of time periods and costs are interlinked. In effect, fixed costs are the costs of the fixed factors of production, while variable costs are the costs of the variable factors of production.

Table 14.1 shows examples of the main types of costs the firm is likely to incur. It is an oversimplification. Jobs of office staff are assumed to be unrelated to how much is produced, whereas higher production levels are assumed to mean additional hours of work for production line workers. Vehicle costs are assumed to be fixed, even if output increases. In reality, these assumptions can be challenged: greater output may mean that more office staff are needed and it will mean more maintenance costs for vehicles. However, it is possible that some increases in output do not need additional working hours. Having said that, on the whole the classification in Table 14.1 provides a useful summary.

Table 14.1 *Classification of fixed and variable costs*

Fixed costs	Variable costs
Rent for land	Raw materials/components
Capital	Wages of production line workers
Salaries and office costs	Power to run machinery
Vehicles	Fuel costs for delivery
Marketing	
Entrepreneur's normal profit	

What happens to fixed and variable costs in the short run as output rises?

In the short run, fixed costs remain the same. However, the fixed factors of production will impose a limit on the amount that a firm can produce. If the amount of land and equipment only enables production of 110 units per day, then even with additional variable factors of production, output cannot exceed 110 units per day.

At low levels of output, variable factors of production are unlikely to work efficiently. For example, if there is only one worker, then that worker has to carry out every job. There is no specialisation or division of labour and so the worker produces a very low level of output. The fixed costs per unit are high. As a consequence, the cost of making each item tends to be very high when few units are produced.

As more workers are employed, division of labour can improve labour productivity. This means that the level of efficiency improves and so the costs of each unit should fall.

If output continues to rise, efficiency will fall when output gets close to the maximum capacity of the firm. This is because there is very little flexibility because all of the fixed factors of production are being used fully and so additional variable factors are not able to increase output by very many units. At this level of output the cost of making additional items rises considerably.

Table 14.2 on p. 146 shows how fixed and variable costs will change in the short run as more variable factors of production are added to increase output.

What happens to fixed and variable costs in the long run as output rises?

In the long run, the introduction of additional fixed factors of production, such as more capital equipment, can solve the problem of overused fixed factors of production. Larger-scale production allows the firm to benefit from division of labour and specialisation. The firm will also benefit from internal economies of scale. (These will be discussed in Chapter 15.) Capital equipment will no longer be overused and so production becomes more efficient because firms can plan the optimum (best) mix of the different factors of production. In the short run, firms may face situations in which they have insufficient fixed assets, such as a factory that is too small.

In the long run, firms can prevent sudden rises in costs because they can plan their fixed capital more carefully. As a firm approaches its maximum capacity, it can introduce additional machinery to prevent the sudden rises in costs that can occur as a firm approaches its maximum capacity. If output is expected to increase significantly, then the firm may build a new factory so it can meet demand.

The difference between average and total costs

Firms aim to make profit. Profit can be improved by earning more revenue or by reducing costs. *It is therefore vital that firms understand their costs so that they can try to limit them.* Rational consumers will buy goods at the lowest possible price and so lowering costs will help firms to be competitive. Lower costs will increase supply and thus help firms to increase the quantity sold.

Since fixed costs and variable costs behave differently, it is important to distinguish between them when calculating costs. The following definitions and calculations are important to understand costs of production:

- **Fixed costs (FC) or total fixed costs (TFC)** are the costs that remain the same (in the short run) regardless of the amount of output.
- **Total variable costs (TVC)** are the costs which vary/change (in the short run) as the amount of output changes.
- **Total costs (TC)** are the overall costs of producing a certain amount of output.

It can be seen that:

- Total costs = Fixed costs + Total variable costs

  TC = FC + TVC
- Average costs (AC) or average total costs (ATC) = Total costs/Output

  ATC = TC/q where q = quantity produced (output)
- Average fixed costs (AFC) = Fixed costs/Output

  AFC = FC/q
- Average variable costs (AVC) = Total variable costs/Output

  AVC = TVC/q

Example calculations

A firm produces 50 units of output. Fixed costs are £80 and total variable costs are £120.

TC = FC + VC = £80 + £120 = £200

ATC = £200/50 = £4.00

Key terms

Total costs (TC) are the sum of fixed costs and variable costs.

Average costs (AC) or **average total costs (ATC)** are the total costs divided by the number of units produced.

AFC = £80/50 = £1.60

AVC = £120/50 = £2.40

It can be seen that as TC = FC + TVC, then ATC = AFC + AVC

The short-run average cost curve

Key term

Short-run average costs (SRAC) show how the average costs of production change as output changes in the short run (the time period in which only variable factors can change).

In the previous section we saw how costs changed in the short run as the level of output increased. Table 14.2 provides an illustration of the link between the number of units of production, total costs and average costs.

In Table 14.2 it can be seen that fixed costs are the same (£30), regardless of output. This does not change because the capacity of the firm is fixed – it cannot be changed (in the short run).

As expected, total variable costs increase as output increases because more variable factors of production are needed. However, due to the lack of opportunity for division of labour, these costs are relatively high at low levels of output. The AVC of the first unit of output is high, at £20, but as output increases the AVC falls because there is more opportunity for division of labour that increases labour productivity and efficiency. As production gets closer to capacity, the lack of fixed factors of production leads to a rise in AVC – this occurs because the variable factors of production (such as labour) become less productive if there are not enough fixed factors (such as machinery) to help them to produce. In Table 14.2, this occurs after 6 units of output.

Table 14.2 *Total costs and average costs in the short run*

Production (units)	Fixed costs (FC) (£)	Total variable costs (TVC) (£)	Total costs TC (£)	Average fixed costs (AFC) (£)	Average variable costs (AVC) (£)	Average total costs (ATC) (£)
0	30	0	30	na	na	na
1	30	20	50	30.00	20.00	50.00
2	30	30	60	15.00	15.00	30.00
3	30	36	66	10.00	12.00	22.00
4	30	38	68	7.50	9.50	17.00
5	30	40	70	6.00	8.00	14.00
6	30	45	75	5.00	7.50	12.50
7	30	54	84	4.29	7.71	12.00
8	30	68	98	3.75	8.50	12.25
9	30	87	117	3.33	9.67	13.00
10	30	110	140	3.00	11.00	14.00
11	30	146	176	2.73	13.27	16.00
12	30	198	228	2.50	16.50	19.00

Table 14.2 shows how total costs are quite high at low levels of output because fixed costs have to be paid. Since division of labour helps to improve productive efficiency, total costs then rise quite slowly. As capacity is approached, total costs then start to rise quite steeply.

Figure 14.1 shows the link between output and average costs in the short run. ATC and AVC curves tend to be U-shaped. ATC and AVC fall as more division of labour is possible, but eventually rise again as capacity is approached. The AFC line curves downwards, continuously, because the fixed costs are spread over more output.

The short-run average cost (SRAC) curve shows average costs when the capacity of the firm cannot be altered.

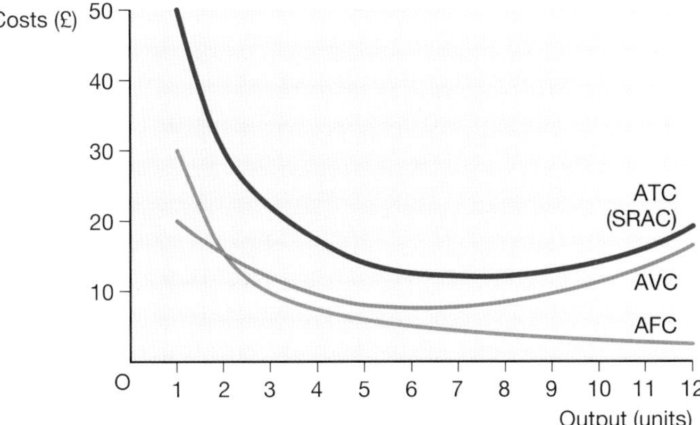

Figure 14.1 *Average costs in the short run*

The long-run average cost curve

The long-run average cost (LRAC) curve shows average costs when the capacity of the firm can be altered and expanded. In the long run, both variable and fixed factors of production can vary and so the firm can, for example, build a new factory. This means that there will not be a steep rise in average costs as the firm's capacity is approached because in the long run the firm can plan ahead and introduce more capital equipment (if a small increase in output is expected) or build new factories (if a large increase in output is expected).

The shape of the long-run average cost curve is determined by economies and diseconomies of scale. As these two topics are covered in Chapter 15, the nature and shape of the average cost curve in the long run will be shown in Chapter 15.

Key term

Long-run average costs (LRAC) show how the average costs of production change as output changes in the long run (the time period in which both the fixed and variable factors can change).

REALWORLD ECONOMICS

The link between labour productivity and average costs

Can the relative fall in UK manufacturing be explained by worsening labour productivity?

In manufacturing industries, labour costs represent about 70% of the total costs of manufacturing. In the UK there has been a steady increase in the output of services provided in comparison to the output of goods. In 1986, manufacturing accounted for 23% of the UK's national output. By 2011 it had fallen to 10%. This fall has been more significant for the UK than for its main competitors, as

Table 14.3 *Percentage of GDP provided by manufacturing, 1986 and 2011 (%)*

Year	UK	France	Germany	USA
1986	23	20	29	19
2011	10	10	23	13

Source: World Bank

Table 14.4 *Changes in labour productivity and average labour costs, 1986–2011*

Year	UK Index of:		France Index of:		Germany Index of:		USA Index of:	
	Labour productivity	Average labour costs	Labour productivity	Average labour costs	Labour productivity	Average labour costs	Labour productivity	Average labour costs
1986	58.6	66.8	57.7	89.5	62.7	73.9	50.9	104.2
2011	133.9	111.6	125.8	108.4	133.4	92.3	147.7	88.4

Note: Base year = 2002. *Source:* World Bank

shown in Table 14.3.

Some observers blame this relative fall in manufacturing industry on high average costs, and state that this is the result of worsening labour productivity. Most UK manufacturing companies tend to have labour-intensive production and so relatively low labour productivity will cause high labour costs for each good produced, leading to high average costs of production for manufactured goods.

Table 14.4 shows how labour productivity and average labour costs have changed since 1986 in four selected countries.

Discussion point

The article states that 'Some observers blame this relative fall in manufacturing industry on high average costs, and state that this is the result of worsening labour productivity'. Do you agree with this statement? Justify your view.

Review questions

Total: 25 marks

1 Which one of the following items would usually be classified as a fixed cost?

A Power to run machinery
B Raw materials
C Rent for land
D Wages of production workers *(1 mark)*

2 Which one of the following items would usually be classified as a variable cost?

A Capital equipment
B Fuel costs for deliveries
C Marketing costs
D Office costs *(1 mark)*

3 Which one of the following statements is correct?

A Average fixed costs = Average total costs *minus* Average variable costs
B Average fixed costs fall as output falls
C Average fixed costs rise as output approaches capacity
D Average fixed costs will increase if raw material costs rise *(1 mark)*

4 In a U-shaped ATC curve, the output at which ATC starts to increase is one at which:

A AFC is falling and AVC is falling
B AFC is falling and AVC is rising
C AFC is rising and AVC is falling
D AFC is rising and AVC is rising *(1 mark)*

5 Define 'the long-run'. *(3 marks)*

6 Define 'variable costs'. *(3 marks)*

7 Table 14.5 provides the data required to answer questions (a) to (e).

Table 14.5

Output (units)	Fixed costs (£)	Total variable costs (£)	Total costs (£)
0	40	0	40
1	40	25	65
2	40	40	80
3	40	(b)	90
4	40	64	104

(a) Calculate TVC at 3 units of output. *(1 mark)*
(b) Calculate AFC at 3 units of output. *(2 marks)*
(c) Calculate AVC at 4 units of output. *(2 marks)*
(d) Calculate ATC at 2 units of output. *(2 marks)*
(e) At what level of output is ATC at its lowest? What is the ATC at this level of output? *(3 marks)*

8 Explain why the average cost line will usually be U-shaped in the short run. *(5 marks)*

Economies & diseconomies of scale

This chapter introduces the concept of economies of scale and examines the difference between internal economies of scale and external economies of scale. Diseconomies of scale and their reasons are explained. The chapter concludes by studying the relationship between economies of scale and diseconomies of scale and their impact on the shape of the long-run average cost curve.

The difference between internal and external economies of scale

> **Key note**
> In order to understand economies of scale, you need to distinguish between the firm and the industry. A firm is a single business, such as Nissan; the industry is the collection of all firms providing that good or service – in this case, the car or motor industry.

Key terms

Internal economies of scale are the advantages that an organisation gains due to an increase in its size. These advantages cause an increase in productive efficiency and thus a decrease in the average (total) cost of production.

External economies of scale are the advantages that an organisation gains due to growth in the size of the industry within which it operates.

Internal economies of scale mean that larger firms can benefit from lower average costs, which will improve their ability to compete in their marketplace.

External economies of scale mean that larger firms can benefit from lower average costs too, but these benefits should also be available to competitors that operate within the same industry. External economies of scale apply specifically to situations in which industries are localised, with many firms in the same area. For example, London's reputation for finance means that many support industries and services, such as consultancies and training providers, are located within easy access.

> **Author tip**
> Remember that both small and large firms benefit from external economies of scale – it is the scale of the industry as a whole that creates the external economies. However, for internal economies of scale it is the scale of the firm that matters.

Internal economies of scale

The main examples of internal economies of scale are:

- **Technical economies of scale**
  These focus on equipment and resources. Larger firms can benefit from:
  - *expensive capital equipment*, which can lead to more efficient production, thus reducing average costs, and higher quality products, which should lead to an increase in demand.
  - *economies of increased dimension*. Larger firms can use large-scale equipment

more effectively. For example, doubling the size of containers (for transportation) and doubling the size of warehouses and factories will not lead to a doubling of costs, and so average costs will fall. Smaller firms cannot reap these benefits because they are not producing and transporting enough goods to use these large-scale items efficiently.

- *specialisation and division of labour.* Larger firms can more fully exploit specialisation because they produce enough products for it to be cost effective to divide production into many specialised tasks.
- *efficient use of capital.* Specialisation ensures that each item of capital equipment is used throughout the day, rather than only being used when a worker reaches a certain stage of the production process.
- *research and development.* Large firms can afford the high costs of R&D and are thus more likely to introduce new products or processes. If these are patented, this can restrict competition and thus help firms to increase demand and benefit from high prices.
- *economies of indivisibility.* Many goods need to be produced on a large scale in order to maximise efficiency. Smaller firms may be forced to underuse machines (or use a smaller scale of production that is less efficient) and so small firms will have higher average costs than larger firms.

- **Financial economies of scale**
  It is cheaper for larger firms to access finance because they present a lower risk than small firms. For this reason they will find it easier to get loans and overdrafts from banks. Furthermore, the terms of the loan, such as the interest rate to be paid and the length of time allowed before repayment, will be more favourable. In effect, the cost of borrowing will be cheaper for larger firms. In addition, larger firms tend to find it easier to sell shares, which are the main form of finance when a limited company is set up. Usually, the most important source of finance is retained profits. Shareholders are entitled to the profits made by limited companies but usually agree that the company can retain a significant percentage of its profits in order to buy items such as buildings and new ICT systems and machinery. Shareholders agree to this because the firm can use the retained profit to make more money in the future and so it helps to boost the share price. This allows shareholders to make money when they decide to sell their shares. In effect, retained profits are a zero cost to firms because there is no interest to be paid (although there is the opportunity cost of what they might have received if they had saved it in a bank instead of using it to buy new capital).

- **Purchasing economies of scale**
  Greater output means that materials can be bought in bulk at lower cost. Thus large firms can buy materials much more cheaply than small firms. Large firms can also use their size to bargain with suppliers, since many of these suppliers will rely on these large firms continuing to buy the items that they make. Large firms, such as supermarkets, have been able to use this bargaining power to keep down prices of products such as milk.

- **Marketing economies of scale**
  Costs such as advertising can be spread over more units of output if a firm produces on a large scale and so advertising campaigns tend to be more cost effective for large firms. Smaller firms cannot afford to use expensive forms of media, such as

television advertising, and therefore are less likely to be successful. The internet and online advertising has reduced many costs of advertising and so this economy is less prominent than it was when TV advertising dominated advertising and promotions. However, sophisticated databases still enable larger firms to be able to target their marketing more effectively than most small firms.

- **Risk-bearing economies of scale**
  Large firms often diversify into different products and different markets. They can also ensure that they have a choice of suppliers when ordering supplies. These actions help to protect such firms from sudden changes such as a fall in demand, a decline in a particular market or the liquidation of a supplier. The firm is less at risk from the detrimental effects of these changes because it has alternative products to sell or suppliers from which to buy materials. It should be noted that risk-bearing economies may protect a firm from the risk of overspecialisation, but this can mean that the firm is operating in so many markets that it may not fully exploit the other internal economies of scale.

- **Managerial economies of scale**
  Large firms can employ specialist managers, thus benefiting from division of labour amongst their management staff as well as their production line employees. Large firms can also afford to employ the most successful senior managers. Good decision making by the chief executive, for example, can mean huge increases in profits, and so large firms can usually offer much higher salaries in order to attract the best managers.

Author tip

The classification of different internal economies of scale varies between sources. This classification is often a matter of personal preference. However, categorising internal and external economies precisely is important because internal economies result from the firm's scale, whereas external economies of scale result from the scale and localisation of the industry.

External economies of scale

If a firm operates within a large industry, this can help it to reduce its average costs regardless of its size, especially if it is located in a place where that particular industry is concentrated.

Examples of external economies of scale are:

- **Specialist firms and infrastructure**
  In areas where an industry is located, specialist firms tend to locate too. These firms may be suppliers, such as suppliers of parts for car manufacturers in the area around Sunderland or close to Oxford and Swindon. Alternatively, they may specialise in distribution, such as refrigerated transport of agricultural products in Lincolnshire. Firms of all sizes will benefit from having easy access to these specialist firms. The local infrastructure, such as the transport system and facilities provided by the local council, might be adapted to suit the needs of firms within industries that dominate that locality. This concentration of firms can also greatly reduce transport costs and so cut average costs.

- **Training and education**
  Local colleges and universities will offer courses suited to the local community, thus helping all firms involved in the main industries in that area. Training firms will also provide facilities and courses geared towards the needs of the local community. In the UK, many business parks have developed in university cities in order to take advantage of the skilled graduates available.
- **Reputation**
  Sometimes a city or area gains an excellent reputation for the provision of a certain good or service. This can greatly assist firms that are located in that city or area, as they can use its reputation to boost sales of their goods. For example, any financial firm operating in the City of London will benefit from its reputation for financial services. Similarly, Milan has a reputation for fashion items.

Key note

Both internal and external economies help to cut costs. For internal economies of scale, these benefits apply mainly to large firms; for external economies of scale, they apply to all sizes of firms, but only if they are located close to other firms in the industry.

Developments in ICT have tended to reduce some of the benefits of large-scale production because small firms can often match the ICT resources of larger firms. Similarly, physical locations have become less important in many service industries. As a consequence, ICT has reduced the effect of both internal and external economies of scale.

Reasons for diseconomies of scale

Diseconomies of scale occur because as the firm (or industry) gets larger, problems begin to appear. These problems lead to higher average costs of production.

Internal diseconomies of scale

As output increases, some firms find that their average costs of production start to increase rather than decrease. In most instances this tends to occur at the highest levels of output, when the benefits of internal economies of scale seem to have been exhausted or negated.

Key term

Internal diseconomies of scale are the disadvantages that an organisation experiences due to an increase in size. These cause a decrease in productive efficiency and therefore an increase in the average (total) costs of production.

The main examples of diseconomies of scale are as follows:

- **Coordination difficulties**
  - There may be a loss of control by management as a firm grows, particularly if the firm has expanded internationally. Growth may also lead to increasing workloads for managers, who thus lose some degree of control of their subordinates.
  - Individuals are less likely to follow organisational policies if the level of control is reduced. This may mean that individuals do not follow the company approach and may make poor decisions without senior managers being aware of the problems this might cause.
  - In order to help senior managers keep control, large firms often have rigid and inflexible policies, which are imposed to limit the loss of control described above. Greater control can improve efficiency, but by limiting the power given to subordinates, who are likely to be the people dealing directly with customers,

a firm will reduce its ability to respond to customer needs. This is likely to lead to the alienation of customers.

- **Communication problems**
  - In large firms, the effectiveness of communication is reduced. Messages can be distorted and it is possible that communications do not reach everyone. Sometimes the time taken for a message to reach an individual can cause problems for the firm.
  - In very large firms, managers may find it more difficult to meet their subordinates and so there may be a lack of understanding of particular issues.
  - In large firms, large-scale approaches to communication, such as the circulation of standard emails, are more common. Employees may feel unvalued and demotivated.
- **Technical diseconomies**
  These occur where production on a very large scale becomes extremely difficult to organise as efficiently as smaller-scale production, and so average costs start to increase.
- **Excessive bureaucracy**
  As firms get larger, the number of levels of management increases and this may slow down decision making and add to the costs of production.
- **Industrial relations problems**
  The poor quality of communication within the firms may lead to more staff leaving and higher absences. In extreme cases it may cause industrial disputes, such as a strike. There is a strong correlation between the size of a firm and the number of industrial disputes occurring.
- **Less flexibility**
  In a time of rapid change, flexibility is vital because customer needs are constantly changing. The structure of many large firms makes it difficult for them to adapt to change as quickly as smaller firms.

External diseconomies of scale

Key term

External diseconomies of scale are the disadvantages that an organisation experiences due to growth in the size of the industry within which it operates.

When an industry becomes very large, this can cause difficulties, especially within the geographical area in which firms in that industry are concentrated. These difficulties can lead to an increase in average costs of production for firms.

- **Pollution and traffic congestion**
  Pollution and traffic congestion are common external diseconomies of scale because facilities often lag behind the growth of an area. Pollution can add costs or lower quality of output, whereas transport problems affect the speed and reliability of transport and thus increase average costs of production.
- **Competition**
  Competition can be fierce because many competitors will be located nearby in order to gain the external economies of the area. This may hinder a firm's ability to attract customers and may lead to lower prices and lower profits.
- **Higher costs of factors of production**
  Due to the high numbers of firms operating in the area, there may be shortages of factors of production, especially land. As a result, average costs may rise.

Internal economies and diseconomies of scale and the shape of the long-run average cost curve

Figure 15.1 shows a typical long-run average cost curve and its relationship to short-run average costs. $SRAC_1$ shows the short-run cost curve of the firm when it is operating one factory, $SRAC_2$ shows the short-run cost curve of the firm when it is operating two factories, and so on, up to $SRAC_7$, which shows the short-run cost curve of the firm when it is operating seven factories.

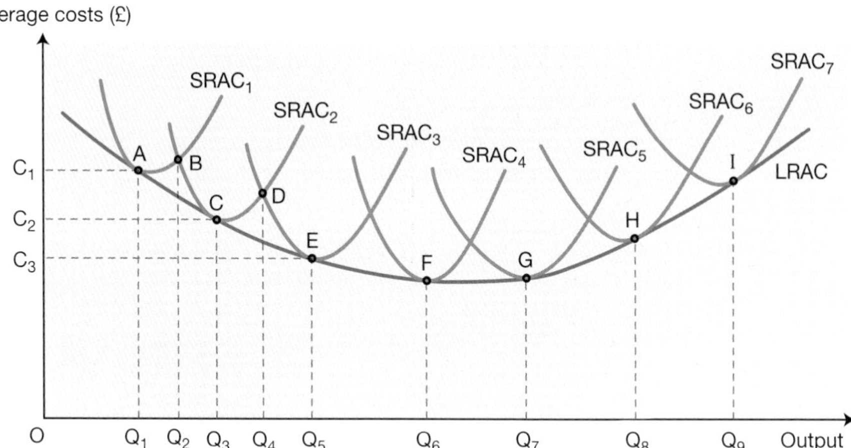

Figure 15.1 *The long-run average cost curve*

In the short run the firm cannot change its capacity, represented in this diagram by the number of factories it uses. When the firm's demand is low, it will therefore only have a low output of goods. If its output is low, it will only require one factory and so its short-run average cost curve is the line $SRAC_1$. If its output is OQ_1, then its average cost is shown by Point A. Point A shows a high level of productive efficiency as it is close to the lowest point of $SRAC_1$. If output increases beyond Q_1, average cost starts to rise (as shown by the move from A to B).

In the long run a firm can change its capacity. The firm can see that if output is below OQ_2, it is cheaper to produce using one factory. However, Point B shows the output (OQ_2) at which average costs of production are the same for both one factory or two factories. In the case of one factory, it is approaching maximum capacity and so average costs are rising (as shown by the move from A to B). In the case of two factories, Point B is where average costs are falling, but they are still quite high because fixed costs are much higher if there are two factories.

If output increases beyond OQ_2, the firm will find its average costs are lower if it operates two factories. In the long-run, firms can add new factories and so, if the firm has anticipated the increasing demand for its goods, it will have planned to have completed a second factory by the time demand (and thus output) reaches OQ_2 units.

The same logic applies when Point C is reached. It is worth keeping the second factory until Point D is reached (at output OQ_4). Beyond this level of output it becomes cheaper to operate with a third factory.

Based on the assumption that the firm can only increase its output by building new factories, its long-run average cost curve would follow the sequence shown above and therefore be a line joining points A, B, C, D and E.

In practice, firms can increase output without the need for a new factory. The existing factory may be extended or additional capital equipment introduced, so that small increases in capacity can be planned. However, once output reaches OQ_3 it would be cheaper to use a second factory rather than use additional capital in a single factory. For this reason, firms can avoid the rise in average costs shown by the move from A to B. The introduction of new capital allows average costs to keep falling so that the long-run average costs line falls along the line from A to C.

Similarly, once the firm is operating with two factories, new capital equipment can be introduced into the second factory as output rises from OQ_3 to OQ_4 to prevent average costs rising from C to D. The introduction of new capital into the second factory allows average costs to keep falling so that the long-run average costs line falls along the line from C to E.

The long-run average cost curve is often described as an 'envelope' curve because it envelops the SRAC curves. In Figure 15.1 it is shown by the line ACEFGHI. Why is it shaped like a shallow 'U'?

The explanation is provided by internal economies and diseconomies of scale. Up until Point F, the LRAC curve slopes downwards, showing a steady fall in average costs of production. This fall in LRAC continues until output reaches OQ_6. This fall in LRAC is caused by internal economies of scale, which are improving productive efficiency and thus lowering average costs.

Between points A and F there are **internal economies of scale because LRAC is falling.**

Between points F and G the LRAC line is horizontal. This means that average costs are staying at the same level because any internal economies of scale are being cancelled out by internal diseconomies of scale.

Between points F and G there are **constant returns to scale** because LRAC remains the same. Between OQ_6 and OQ_7 units of output, average costs are at their lowest level. This lowest level is first reached at Point F (output level OQ_6). This output level (OQ_6) is referred to as the **minimum efficient scale (MES)**. If output is lower than the MES, then LRAC is higher. If output is higher than the MES, then LRAC is either equal to or higher than it is at the MES.

From Point G onwards, the diseconomies of scale outweigh the economies of scale and so LRAC slopes upwards.

Between points G and H, and H and I, there are **internal diseconomies of scale because LRAC is rising.**

Key note

The LRAC line shown in Figure 15.1 is a very common LRAC curve. However, it is feasible for a firm never to reach an output at which the internal diseconomies of scale outweigh the internal economies of scale. In this case the LRAC line will continue to fall. (In effect it is the LRAC between points A and F in Figure 15.1.)

It is also possible (but less likely) for a firm always to experience rising costs as output increases because the diseconomies outweigh the economies at low levels of output. In this case the LRAC line will continue to rise. (In effect it is the LRAC between points G and I in Figure 15.1.)

It is possible, but very unlikely, that constant returns to scale may occur. In this case the LRAC line will be horizontal. (In effect it is the LRAC between points F and G in Figure 15.1.)

External economies and diseconomies of scale and the shape of the long-run average cost curve

Figure 15.1 shows the impact of **internal** economies and diseconomies of scale on the LRAC. This diagram relates averages costs of production to the level of output and so the LRAC shows how internal economies reduce LRAC as output rises, but when output is very high the diseconomies are more likely to have an impact.

External economies and diseconomies of scale are *not* related to the size/output of the firm; instead they relate to the size of the industry. For this reason their impact is different, as shown in Figure 15.2.

In Figure 15.2, $LRAC_1$ is the original long-run average cost curve of the firm. External factors, such as improvements in the local infrastructure or local training courses being provided for employees, lead to greater efficiency. This lowers the average cost curve for the firm as, regardless of its level of output, these improvements enable it to produce goods at a lower average costs. As a result of these external economies of scale, the long-run average cost curve falls from $LRAC_1$ to $LRAC_2$.

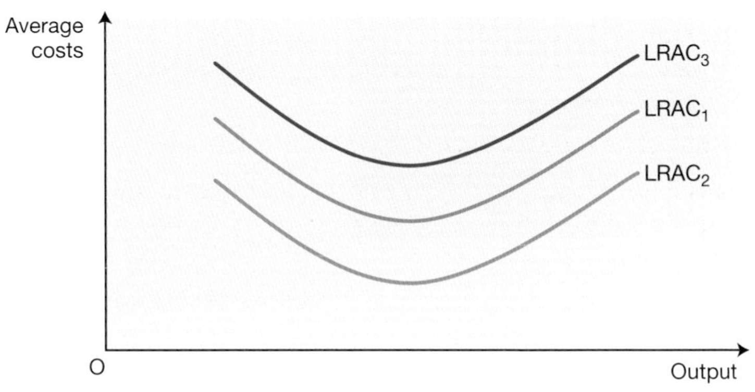

Figure 15.2 *The impact of external economies and diseconomies of scale on the LRAC curve*

If the firm experiences external diseconomies of scale, perhaps through traffic congestion or more expensive raw materials in the local area, then its average costs will rise. As a result of these external diseconomies of scale, the long-run average cost curve rises from $LRAC_1$ to $LRAC_3$.

REALWORLD
ECONOMICS 15.1

Economies of scale in shipping

In the 1950s, the 'container' was introduced into trade between nations. These standardised metal storage units are based on a standard size (known as a TEU) of 20 feet by 8 feet (or 2 TEUs – 40 feet by 8 feet). These dimensions allow them to fit neatly into rail, road and sea transportation systems.

For long-haul trade, the 1950s container ships could carry between 500 and 800 TEUs. In 2013, shipping giant Maersk launched its latest container ship – able to carry 18,000 TEUs.

Larger ships lead to three main internal economies of scale. The capital costs of these massive ships (over 400 metres in length) are high, but not in relation to the amount of cargo that they can carry. The design of these vessels means that a crew of only 13 people is needed per journey, instead of the 23 people needed on much smaller ships. Fuel costs are also lower. The combination of these factors has meant that the cost of transporting a container from China to Europe is $218 for an 18,000 TEU container ship compared to $333 for a 13,000 TEU container ship. Other ship operating costs, such as insurance and administration, are also lower. The efficiency of these ships is so great that the cost of transporting T-shirts from China to Europe amounts to less than 1.5 pence per T-shirt.

However, to date only the world's largest shipping line – the Danish firm, Maersk – has been able to justify the expenditure needed to order these new ships from their South Korean shipyards. Many countries, such as New Zealand, do not have ports that can cope with such large ships, and some trade routes, such as those using the Panama Canal, are unsuitable for these ships.

There is also the question of capacity. On average, Maersk's ships operate at 85% capacity between Asia and Europe, but they are only 55% full on journeys from Europe to Asia. The slowing growth rate in China and the recession and its after-effects have led to a situation in which there is too much capacity in the shipping industry. Maersk is relying on economies of scale to push smaller competitors out of the market, since they are unable to afford these huge container ships.

The latest container ship – Maersk exploits economies of scale to gain competitive advantage

Discussion point

Identify the main internal and external economies and diseconomies of scale featured in the article. Do you think Maersk is taking too big a risk?

Review questions

Total: 25 marks

1 A firm is able to reduce its average costs because it is located in close proximity to other firms within the industry in which it operates. This is an example of an:

A External economy of scale
B External diseconomy of scale
C Internal economy of scale
D Internal diseconomy of scale *(1 mark)*

2 Internal economies of scale must exist when:

A Average cost rises as the firm's output rises
B Total cost rises as the firm's output rises
C Average cost falls as the industry's output grows
D Average cost falls as the firm's output rises *(1 mark)*

3 Which *one* of the following is most likely to be an internal economy of scale?

A Bulk buying
B Industrial disputes
C Reputation of an area
D Specialised transport firms in the region *(1 mark)*

4 Which *one* of the following is most likely to be an external economy of scale?
A Ease of acquiring finance
B Good transportation networks
C Research and development skills
D Indivisibility of production *(1 mark)*

Figure 15.3 applies to questions 5, 6 and 7.

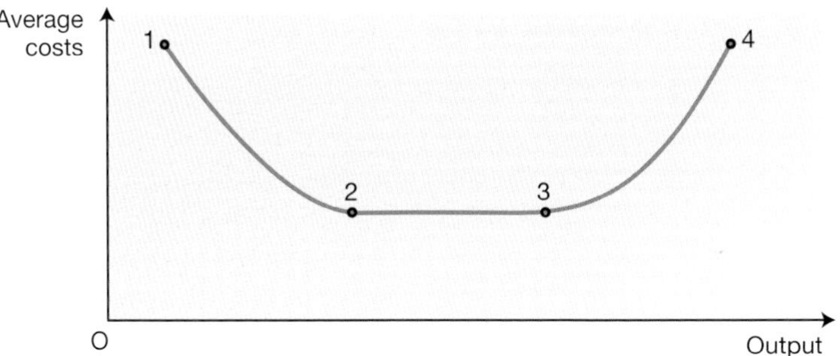

Figure 15.3

5 Diseconomies of scale occur between points:
A 1 and 2
B 2 and 3
C 2 and 4
D 3 and 4 *(1 mark)*

6 The minimum efficient scale (MES) is at point:
A 1
B 2
C 3
D 4 *(1 mark)*

7 Productive efficiency is at its greatest between points:
A 1 and 2
B 1 and 3
C 2 and 3
D 3 and 4 *(1 mark)*

8 Explain one possible cause of external economies of scale. *(4 marks)*

9 Distinguish between internal economies of scale and external diseconomies of scale. *(6 marks)*

10 Explain two possible causes of internal economies of scale. *(8 marks)*

Average revenue, total revenue & profit

This chapter introduces the concepts of total revenue and average revenue and shows how they are calculated. The reason why the average revenue curve is the firm's demand curve is then analysed. The notion of profit is introduced and its calculation shown.

Total revenue and average revenue

Key terms

Total revenue (or **sales revenue**) is the total money received from the sale of a firm's goods and services. Total revenue can also refer to the total money received from the sale of a particular good or service.

Average revenue is the average receipt of money for each good or service that is sold.

A firm's revenue is a measure of the money received from the sale of its goods and services. However, when studying total revenue and average revenue, economists usually focus on the revenue from a particular good. Total revenue and average revenue are calculated as follows:

Total revenue (TR) = Price per unit (p) × Quantity of units sold (q)

For example, if a firm sells 500 goods at a price per unit of £5, then its total revenue is £5 x 500 = £2500.

Average revenue (AR) = Total revenue (TR)/Quantity of goods sold (q)

For example, if a firm receives total revenue of £8000 and sells 400 goods, then its average revenue is £8000/400 = £20.

The nature of total revenue and average revenue depends on the market structure in which the firm operates. (The different market structures will be dealt with in Topic 4.)

In Topic 2 we saw that the equilibrium price is determined by the interaction of demand and supply. This analysis was based on the assumption that the market is perfectly competitive and so all firms are producing the same good – there is nothing to distinguish one firm's version of the good from another firm's version of it. Every firm charges the market price because if a firm were to try to set a higher price, nobody would buy that firm's goods. However, charging a price below the market price would not be sensible either because each firm will be able to sell everything it produces at the market price. Thus charging a price below the market price would not increase the amount sold but would reduce the amount received from selling each good.

Conclusion: *In a perfectly competitive market, all firms charge the same price.*

Table 16.1 shows average revenue and total revenue in a perfectly competitive market in which the equilibrium market price is £6.

Figure 16.1 plots AR and TR on a graph, with output (quantity) on the 'x' axis.

It can be seen that the total revenue line is a straight line, sloping upwards from left to right. The gradient of this line is determined by the price. As the price is £6, the gradient of the TR line shows a £6 increase in total revenue (TR) for every 1 unit increase in the quantity.

Table 16.1 *Total revenue and average revenue for a particular good*

Quantity	Price (£)	Total revenue (£)	Average revenue (£)
1	6	6	6
2	6	12	6
3	6	18	6
4	6	24	6
5	6	30	6
6	6	36	6
7	6	42	6
8	6	48	6

Note: TR = p x q; AR = TR/q

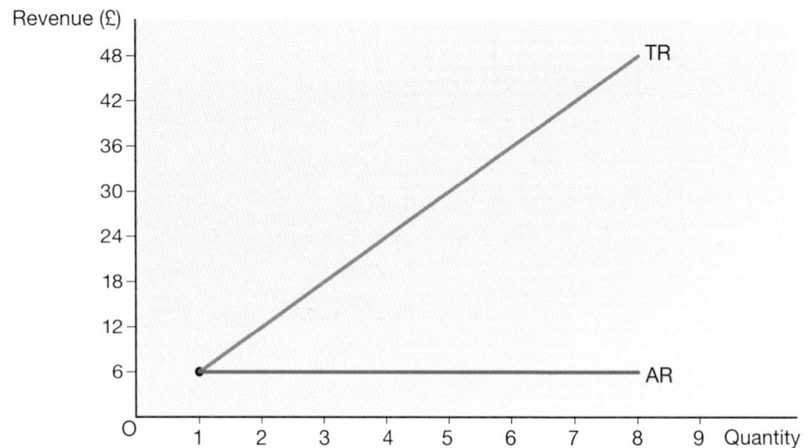

Figure 16.1 *TR and AR when price is fixed (constant)*

Why the average revenue curve is the firm's demand curve

In the previous section we saw how TR and AR are determined in a perfectly competitive market. What happens in the case of a monopoly, where only one firm provides the good or service? And how will TR and AR be determined in a market where goods are *not* homogeneous (all the same), such as the cosmetics market? In this market, individual firms each make different goods and may have customers who are brand loyal (willing to pay more for one firm's cosmetics than those of another firm) because they believe that the goods are different (differentiated).

In the two situations described above, the demand for the good provided by the monopolist or the particular brand of cosmetic will be downward sloping. Thus the firm will find that in order to sell a higher quantity of the good, it must reduce the price of the good. Table 16.2 presents data for a downward-sloping demand curve for a monopolist or a firm with a good that is differentiated from similar goods in some way.

As with Table 16.1, average revenue is identical to price. When 2 units are sold, they are both sold for £6 (so AR= £6); when 3 units are sold they are all sold for £5 (so AR = £5); and so on.

Table 16.2 *Total revenue and average revenue for a particular good*

Quantity	Price (£)	Total revenue (£)	Average revenue (£)
0	8	0	8
1	7	7	7
2	6	12	6
3	5	15	5
4	4	16	4
5	3	15	3
6	2	12	2
7	1	7	1

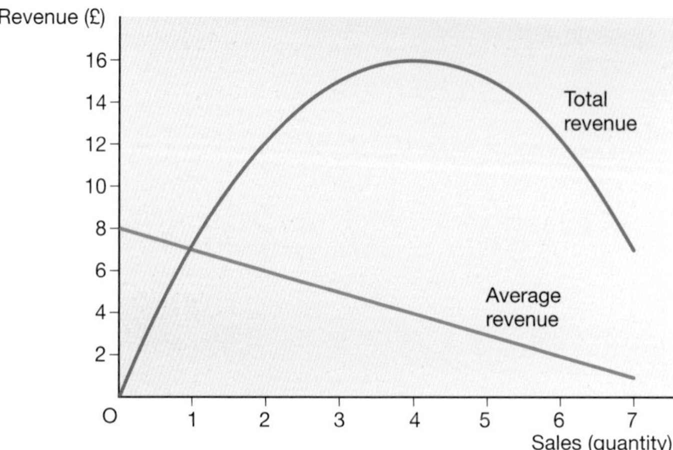

Figure 16.2 *TR and AR when the demand curve is downward sloping*

Figure 16.2 shows total revenue and average revenue for a firm faced with a downward-sloping demand curve. For this particular demand curve, **total revenue** follows the pattern described below.

TR increases as quantity rises from zero to 4 units, but peaks at that point. Up to this quantity the amount of revenue gained from selling an additional unit outweighs the loss of revenue from having to charge a lower price for each unit sold. However, as quantity moves from 4 units to 7 units, total revenue falls because the revenue from the extra unit sold does not outweigh the revenue lost from having to charge a lower price. For example, moving from selling 5 units to 6 units means having to cut the price from £3 to £2. The sixth unit brings in an extra £2, but the 5 units have each been sold for £1 less (£2 instead of £3), meaning that £1 x 5 = £5 has been sacrificed. Overall, the £2 gained from the sixth unit has been outweighed by the £5 lost from the first 5 units. This gives an overall fall in total revenue of £3 (£5 – £2). This can be confirmed by looking at Table 16.2, which shows that TR has fallen from £15 (from selling 5 units) to £12 (from selling 6 units).

For this particular demand curve, **average revenue** follows the pattern described below. AR falls by £1 for every 1 unit increase in output. **The AR line is identical to the demand curve.** This rule applies to every demand curve. **The average revenue curve is the firm's demand curve.**

This rule can also be seen in Table 16.1. A firm in a perfectly competitive market can sell all of its goods at the equilibrium price (£6 in this case). For a single firm this means that any quantity it can produce will be sold for the market price and so the demand for its goods can be shown by a horizontal line at that price. In Table 16.1, the demand curve represents a horizontal line at £6; in Figure 16.1 the resulting AR line is exactly the same – a horizontal line at £6.

Profit, total revenue and total costs

A firm's profit is calculated as follows:

Profit = Total revenue (TR) – Total costs (TC)

There are two ways of improving profit: total (sales) revenue can be increased or total costs can be decreased. A combination of both ways would be the ideal method by which the highest possible profit is achieved, which is a key objective of most firms. We will study other objectives in Chapter 18. However, much of economic theory is based on the idea of profit maximisation, where firms try to make as much profit as possible.

Key terms

Profit is the difference between the total (sales) revenue of a firm and its total costs.

Profit maximisation means making the highest possible level of profit.

The measurement of profit by economists

Total revenue minus total costs is the method of calculating profit used by economists and students of other disciplines, such as accounting and business. However, there is one significant difference in approach to total costs. Since economists are concerned with scarcity, they acknowledge the alternative use of the resources being deployed by a firm. What is the 'opportunity cost' of those resources? If the entrepreneur could have earned a profit of £1000 from the next best alternative use of the resources, then the entrepreneur will only use those resources if the profit (TR – TC) exceeds £1000. This £1000 is known as **normal profit.** It is the minimum profit necessary to persuade the entrepreneur to keep operating the firm in its present use. If profit falls below the normal profit, the entrepreneur will no longer wish to continue operating the firm.

Since normal profit is necessary for the firm to keep operating, economists classify it as a cost – in effect, it is the cost of the entrepreneur. Hence total costs to an entrepreneur will include normal profit.

Any profit made over and above normal profit is described as **abnormal profit** or **supernormal profit.** Thus any profit shown in Table 16.3 is abnormal profit because the normal profit is included in the total costs.

Showing profit in a table and graph

Table 16.3 shows how total revenue and total costs change as output increases. Total revenue is based on the assumption that the firm is operating in a competitive market in which the equilibrium price is £15. Thus selling one unit gives TR of £15, selling 2 units gives TR of £30, and so on.

The total cost line is identical to the TC line in Table 14.2. (If you wish to remind yourself of why total costs change in the way shown, please revisit Chapter 14.)

Column 5 shows the profit at each level of output. It is calculated by subtracting total costs (Column 4) from total revenue (Column 3). At zero units of output there is a loss because fixed costs have to be paid, even if there is no output. This loss increases slightly when output is 1 unit because there is little scope for specialisation and division of labour and so production is very inefficient. As output increases, more specialisation and division of labour lead to greater efficiency and so total costs rise more slowly. The fourth and fifth units of output only add £2 to total costs. After the fifth unit, total costs begin to rise more noticeably as output increases. This rise in TC becomes particularly noticeable at the highest levels of output (11 and 12 units) when production is close to the firm's maximum capacity.

Table 16.3 *Total revenue, total costs and profit for a firm in a perfectly competitive market*

Output (units) q	Price p (£)	Total revenue TR (£)	Total costs TC (£)	Profit π (£)	Average revenue AR (£)	Average costs AC (£)
0	15	0	30	–30	na	na
1	15	15	50	–35	15	50
2	15	30	60	–30	15	30
3	15	45	66	–21	15	22
4	15	60	68	–8	15	17
5	15	75	70	5	15	14
6	15	90	75	15	15	12.5
7	15	105	84	21	15	12
8	15	120	98	22	15	12.25
9	15	135	117	18	15	13
10	15	150	140	10	15	14
11	15	165	176	–11	15	16
12	15	180	228	–48	15	19

It can be seen in Column 5 that profit is negative (a loss is made) if output is between 0 and 4 units, because TR < TC. From 5 units to 10 units, a profit is made because TR > TC. For 11 and 12 units, a loss is made. A profit-maximising firm will choose to produce 8 units of output and earn £22 profit (abnormal profit). This data can also be shown on a graph.

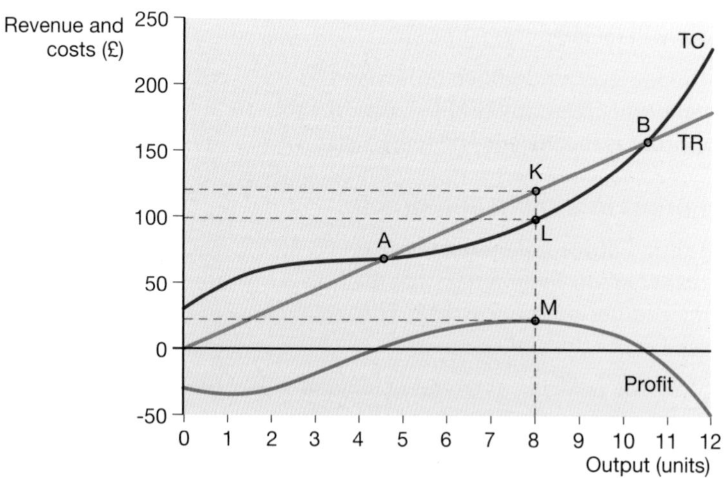

Figure 16.3 *Total revenue, total costs and profit*

Figure 16.3 shows how profit changes as output increases. A loss is made when output is low because TC > TR. At Point A the two lines intersect and so TR = TC and profit is zero. TR > TC between points A and B, at which point TR = TC again. When output increases beyond Point B, TC > TR again, and so a loss is made. The highest level of profit is made when the vertical gap between TR and TC is at its greatest. Measured in whole units, this occurs at 8 units of output. Point K shows that TR = £120 and Point L shows that TC = £98. Profit at 8 units is £120 – £98 = £22 (shown by Point M).

Figure 16.4 shows how AR and AC (ATC) change as output increases. A loss is made when output is low because AC > AR. At Point A the two lines intersect and so AR = AC and profit is zero. AR > AC between points A and B, at which point AR = AC again. When output increases beyond Point B, AC > AR again, and so a loss is made.

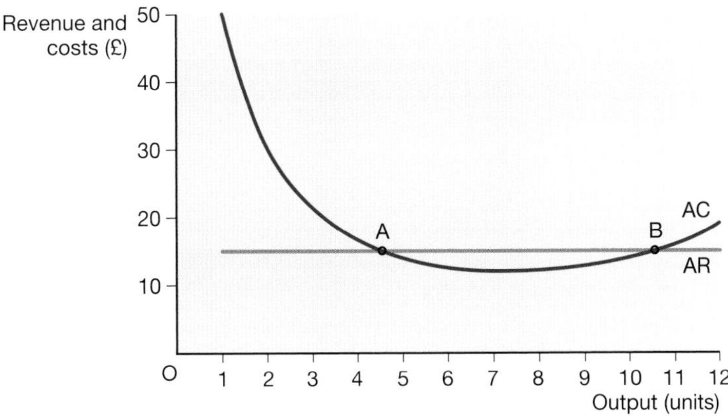

Figure 16.4 *Average revenue, average costs and average profit*

Author tip

Figure 16.4 is included because the use of AR and ATC lines is very important in Year 2 of the A-level course. In its current form it shows where profits or losses are made in the same way as Figure 16.3, but it only shows where average profit (not profit as a whole) is at its highest.

REALWORLD ECONOMICS 16.1

How rail operators increase total revenue

The UK's railways are reputed to be the most expensive in Europe (Table 16.4).

It is argued that the UK has a higher density of population than countries with comparable populations and so land costs are higher and congestion more likely for competing forms of transport. Despite these high prices, the use of rail transport has increased by over 125% in the last 30 years. How do rail companies try to maximise the revenue they receive?

Rail operators have identified two distinct submarkets of customers – commuters and casual users. Commuters need to travel at peak times (during the morning and

Table 16.4 *The cost of a sample of comparable rail journeys in five selected European countries (£)*

Country	Length of journey:		
	1–10 miles	100–150 miles	200+ miles
UK	17	96.50	125
Belgium	7	16	n/a
Italy	4.79	16	35
France	9.60	29	54
Poland	2.87	9	11

Source: Article in the *Daily* Telegraph – 'Rail fare hike: Britain vs rest of Europe', by Helena Kealey, 19.8.2014

evening rush hours). Since their employment income is reliant on their travel, they are prepared to pay a higher price. Commuter transport has two key elements that lead to price inelastic demand – it is a necessity (to the commuter) and it has no realistic close substitute (particularly if the commuter is travelling into a congested city, such as London). This means that increases in prices have little impact on the quantity demanded.

Rush hour at Paddington Station – an expensive time to travel

In contrast, casual users travel away from the congested times of the day. The journeys are not so important to the user, as competing leisure activities can be found in many places, and the other forms of transport are less likely to be congested. These factors lead to lower and more price elastic demand for rail travel at off-peak times. As a result, lower prices are charged. For leisure users who may be on low incomes, such as students, further reductions are possible through railcards.

Total revenue is thus maximised by charging high prices to commuters and much lower prices to attract casual users.

The following prices of a daily return ticket between Reading and London show the differences in fares:

- Peak-time travel: £43.30
- Off-peak travel: £17.70
- Off-peak, with Railcard: £11.70

Discussion points

Why are UK fares so much higher than those in other European countries?

Why is it better for rail companies to more than halve their prices for off-peak trains?

Review questions

Total: 20 marks

Study Table 16.5 and use the data to answer each part of Question 1.

Table 16.5

Output	TR (£)	TC (£)	Profit (£)	AR (£)	AC (£)
1	22	35	–13	22	35
2	44	59	1(b)	22	29.50
3	66	1(a)	–4	22	23.33
4	88	77	11	22	19.25
5	110	97	13	22	1(c)
6	132	133	–1	22	22.17

1 (a) Calculate total costs at 3 units of output. *(1 mark)*

(b) Calculate profit at 2 units of output. *(1 mark)*

(c) Calculate average costs at 5 units of output. *(2 marks)*

(d) At what output is profit maximised? *(1 mark)*

(e) What is the equilibrium price in this market? *(1 mark)*

(f) Explain why this table applies to a perfectly competitive market, rather than a monopoly market with only one firm. *(5 marks)*

2 Define the term 'profit'. *(3 marks)*

3 Explain why the AR curve is the firm's demand curve. *(6 marks)*

Topic 3 **Exam-style questions**

AS LEVEL PAPER 1

Total: 50 marks

Context – The Apple iPad

Extract A **Price and costs of manufacturing a 16 GB iPad**

Components/elements	2010 ($)[b]	2014 ($)
Retail price	**685**	**499**
Cost of components:		
Display and touchscreen	87.10	115
Electromechanical and mechanical	38.45	44
Battery	19.05	15
Wireless	26.70	33
Processor	18.50	22
Box contents	8.15	5
Other components	70.40	36
Cost of manufacturing/assembly	12.20	5
Total manufacturing cost (components + assembly)	**280.55**	**275**
Surplus[a] (retail price – manufacturing cost)	**404.45**	**224**

Notes: (a) Surplus = profit, excluding costs such as research and development, marketing and administration. These three categories of costs represent 8.5% of Apple's total revenue and so most of this 'surplus' is profit for the company. (b) 2010 figures adjusted to 2014 price levels to allow for effects of inflation.

Sources: *www.cnet.com* and IHS Technology

Extract B **Factors influencing total revenue from the iPad**

Between 2010 and 2014 global sales of tablets have increased each year. In 2010 the iPad was introduced into a market with little direct competition, but the high levels of profit available have encouraged new firms to enter the industry. iPad sales grew rapidly, but, as the graph shows, they appear to have peaked. Forecasts for tablet sales suggest that the market as a whole is also reaching its peak, with customers moving from tablets to '2 in 1' devices that also act as phones.

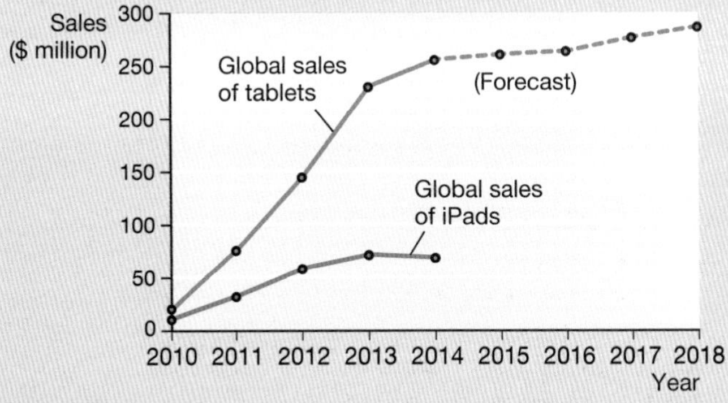

Figure A *Actual and forecast worldwide sales of tablets, 2010–18*

Although the iPad's price has fallen for a 16 GB tablet, customers have tended to move on to devices with more memory and so, whereas 16 GB was common in 2010, most customers in 2014 were paying higher prices for additional memory. An iPad with 64 GB memory retails for $599 (or $729 if it has mobile phone capability).

Apple has an attractive brand name and consumers eagerly await its new releases of products. In fact, Apple's rapid growth has led to problems in obtaining sufficient components, particularly the screen which Apple has found difficult to obtain from its suppliers. Some industry analysts suggest that Apple has kept the price of the iPad high in order to limit demand, so that there would not be a shortage of finished iPads in the market.

Retailers like to stock tablets, and the iPad in particular, as they attract consumers into stores and help sales of products such as apps and accessories. For this reason, manufacturers of tablets can get high prices from retailers, with discounts between 5% and 15% of the retail price. For iPads, the discount is as low as 3% and so a £500 iPad would cost the retailer £485. This helps Apple to ensure that its own Apple Stores, which provide half of the retail sales of iPads, are unlikely to be undercut by other retailers.

Sources: www.techrepublic.com, www.statista.com and investor.apple.com

Extract C **Factors influencing total costs of the iPad**

Apple's rapid growth has enabled it to benefit from internal economies of scale, particularly in areas such as the bulk buying of components. However, as it has continued to expand, it has become more difficult to manage this growth and some diseconomies of scale have emerged, leading to higher average costs for some components. There have also been issues with technical difficulties because some manufacturing processes have not kept pace with other advances in technology.

Apple makes its own software and designs its own chips. It also uses its bargaining power and sheer scale to persuade suppliers to offer its components at low cost, as the component suppliers can achieve high labour productivity in their manufacturing processes and also sell so many items when supplying Apple.

For most components, Apple relies on firms that specialise in the production of specific goods, such as computer screens and batteries.

Sources: www.techrepublic.com, investor.apple.com and *http://wallstreetpit.com*

Questions

Total: 50 marks

1 Define the term 'labour productivity'. *(3 marks)*

2 In Extract A, costs for research and development, marketing and administration costs are excluded. If these are 8.5% of the retail price, calculate the average profit (in dollars) made on an iPad in 2014? *(4 marks)*

3 Using Extract A, identify two significant points of comparison in the iPad's level of price or costs between 2010 and 2014. *(4 marks)*

4 The demand curve D_1 shows the demand for iPads. Draw a new demand curve to show the effect of competitors introducing new tablets into the market. Label it D_2. *(4 marks)*

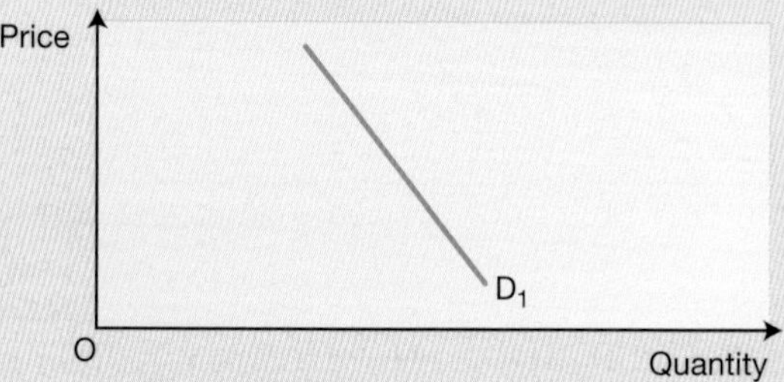

5 Explain how Apple benefits from specialisation and division of labour in the manufacturing and supply of iPads. *(10 marks)*

6 Evaluate the main factors that influence the total profit that Apple makes from the iPad. *(25 marks)*

Topic 4

Competitive & concentrated markets

Market structures

This chapter provides a brief introduction to the concept of market structure. The range of market structures and their features are described. The chapter concludes with a study of the factors that are used to distinguish between the different market structures.

The range of market structures

Figure 17.1 shows the range of market structures, from the most **competitive markets** (on the left) to the least competitive/most **concentrated markets** (on the right).

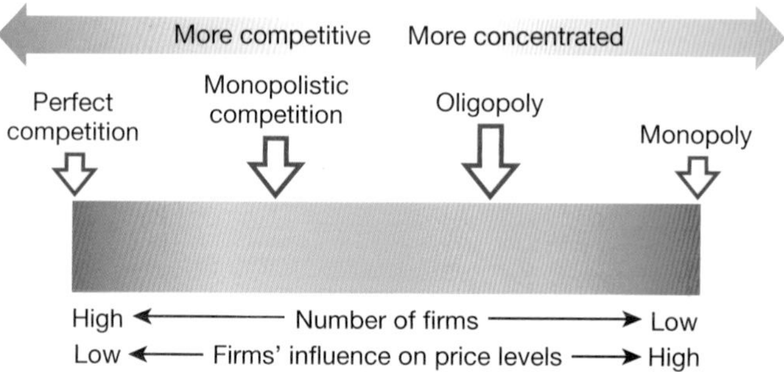

Figure 17.1 *The range of market structures*

Market structures are usually described in terms of the number of suppliers/producers, but other factors are also considered when classifying market structures.

Competitive markets are those that tend to feature the most firms. With so many firms competing, each individual firm has little or no influence on the market

Key terms

A **market structure** describes the characteristics of the market that affect the ways in which firms compete and also the welfare of consumers within that market.

Perfect competition describes a market structure in which there are many buyers and many sellers. There is freedom of entry into the market and freedom of exit out of the market. Buyers and sellers all possess perfect knowledge and all firms supply homogeneous (identical) goods.

Monopolistic competition describes a market structure in which there are many buyers and many sellers. Firms supply similar, but differentiated, goods. There is freedom of entry into the market and freedom of exit out of the market. Knowledge amongst buyers tends to be widespread but is not perfect.

An **oligopoly** is a market structure in which the supply of goods is dominated by a few firms. There are barriers to entry into the industry and may be barriers to restrict exit from the market by firms. Although some knowledge may be widespread, firms in oligopoly markets are likely to possess some knowledge that is not available to others.

A **monopoly** is a market structure in which there is only one firm supplying all the goods in an industry. There are barriers to entry into the industry that have prevented any competition from other firms. Perfect knowledge does not exist because a monopolist is likely to possess knowledge that other participants in the market do not have.

price. Topic 2 (Chapters 6 to 11) focused on price determination in a perfectly competitive market, and the forces of supply and demand determined the market price. Throughout the topic, the analysis of demand assumed that each single buyer has so little influence on the overall market demand that any one individual has no impact on the overall market price. The same assumption applied to supply. No single supplier has sufficient influence on the market supply to affect the overall market price. The logical conclusion to these assumptions is that both firms (as suppliers) and individuals (as buyers) are **price takers within perfect competition** (a perfectly competitive market). This means that all firms and individuals in a situation of perfect competition must accept the ruling market price as none of them has a large enough impact on the market to influence the market price in any way. In the case of **monopolistic competition,** there are many firms, each supplying similar but slightly differentiated goods. Consequently, individual firms have a minor impact on price in monopolistically competitive markets.

Concentrated markets are those markets that feature the fewest firms. **Monopoly** (where there is only one supplier in a market) is the extreme example of a concentrated market. In Chapter 20 we will look at the impact of monopoly on market price, but detailed analysis of price determination in concentrated markets, such as monopoly, will be studied in Year 2 of the A-level course. In the case of monopoly, the supplier has a significant impact on the market price, because all buyers must purchase goods from that supplier. In other concentrated markets, such as **oligopoly**, suppliers will have an influence on the market price, albeit a lesser influence than that of a monopoly supplier.

Factors used to distinguish between different market structures

Although the number of firms in a market provides a good approximation of a market structure, it is not the only factor to consider when classifying market structures. Two other major factors are **product differentiation** and **ease of entry.**

Product differentiation measures how distinct a good is from other goods. In perfect competition it is assumed that all goods are homogeneous (the same) and so there is *no* product differentiation. In monopoly, there is only one, unique product.

Ease of entry examines **barriers to entry.** These are factors that make it harder for firms that are new entrants into a market to compete with firms that are already established in the market.

The main factors that can be used to distinguish between different market structures are as follows:

1 Number of firms
2 Product differentiation
3 Ease of entry/barriers to entry
4 Extent to which information/knowledge is perfect
5 Influence of individual firms/suppliers on price

Key terms

Product differentiation is the degree to which buyers view a good as being distinct from the alternative goods being supplied by other firms within that particular market.

Ease of entry is the degree to which a new firm can enter/start supplying a market without experiencing factors that give it a competitive disadvantage against existing firms within that market.

1 Number of firms

Setting up a firm is a relatively straightforward process and so some markets have many firms competing for customers. However, the number of firms in some markets is restricted because existing firms can provide conditions that discourage new firms from entering the market. There is a high correlation between the number of firms and market structure, as shown below:

- perfect competition – many firms;
- monopolistic competition – many firms;
- oligopoly – few firms; this can vary from three firms upwards (a market with two firms is a duopoly);
- monopoly – one firm.

It should be noted that in the UK, a legal monopoly is defined as a firm with 25% or more of a market, but an economic monopoly is a single firm with 100% of the market.

2 Product differentiation

Firms like to differentiate their products because this may generate consumer brand loyalty. In extreme cases, product differentiation may be so significant that consumers insist on a particular brand because they perceive it to possess qualities that competitors' products lack. For example, the market for carbonated drinks contains many alternative versions of lemonade. However, there are relatively few cola-based carbonated drinks. In countries such as the UK and USA, Coca-Cola and PepsiCo have managed to differentiate their products so successfully that many consumers do not consider alternatives to be suitable. These two firms are therefore able to sell greater quantities *and* charge higher prices than other cola-based carbonated drinks. The strong brand loyalty also makes it very difficult for new competitors to enter this market.

- *Perfect competition* As indicated earlier, there is no product differentiation in a perfectly competitive market because all firms produce the same, homogeneous product.
- *Monopolistic competition* This market structure involves many small firms selling similar products. In order to gain a competitive advantage, individual firms try to differentiate their product from competitors. However, the high levels of competition tend to lead to low profit margins in the short run, and only normal profit in the long run. As a result, it is difficult for firms in monopolistic competition to achieve the funds and the market share required to support activities that might create barriers to entry. Therefore, although there is product differentiation, there is a tendency for products to be quite similar. As a result, the benefits from product differentiation are limited in this market structure.
- *Oligopoly* This market structure has a 'few' firms, each selling differentiated products. Oligopoly markets in the UK include cars, supermarkets, oil companies, soap powders and banking. In many of these industries there is a clear distinction between products and/or high brand loyalty.
- *Monopoly* There is no alternative source of supply and so a single unique product is provided in many monopoly markets. Variations may be provided to suit different customers, but pricing is based on the fact that there is no alternative available from another firm.

It should be noted that monopolists may find themselves in competition with different markets. For example, many train journeys in the UK are provided within a monopoly market structure. However, consumers can choose other forms of transport, such as cycling, cars, coaches, buses and aeroplanes.

3 Ease of entry/barriers to entry

Barriers to entry restrict the level of competition in many industries. These barriers can take many forms. Some of the main examples of barriers to entry are as follows:

- *Capital costs* In industries such as water supply, the initial cost of capital equipment needed to supply the good or service is very high. This means that it is not easy for new firms to enter the market and provide competition.
- *Internal economies of scale* In large industries, existing firms may operate on a very large scale and enjoy considerable internal economies of scale. This will enable them to charge a competitive price. New entrants are likely to operate on a much smaller scale and they are therefore unable to compete on price. The result is that they are discouraged from entering the market, as experience suggests that new entrants will not survive. In some cases, a firm may own particular assets, such as a gold mine with proven reserves of gold, that enable it to produce at a lower cost than potential competitors.
- *Sunk costs* These are costs that are not recoverable if a firm ceases to exist. A firm offering tailor-made ornaments online is unlikely to have many assets and so it is both easy to enter and leave this market without losing much money. However, firms such as mobile telephone networks will have spent a lot of money on assets that are worthless to other industries. These high 'sunk costs' discourage new firms from entering the market but also discourage existing firms from 'exiting'.
- *Legal barriers to entry* In order to encourage new products and innovation, governments award patents. These patents give firms a guaranteed monopoly of supply for goods that they have invented for a period of years. Once a patent has lapsed, the firm may still be able to prevent competition because of factors such as economies of scale. In some markets, such as broadcasting and public transport, the government awards a franchise giving exclusive rights for one firm to supply a particular service for a number of years, thus guaranteeing that firm a monopoly.
- *Marketing barriers* Successful product differentiation often requires considerable marketing expenditure in order to create a brand that customers perceive to be differentiated or even unique. For firms such as Apple, Google and Rolls-Royce, this can create a situation where new firms find it very difficult to enter the market. In some cases existing firms may operate a short-term strategy of setting low prices if they fear that a new firm may be considering entering the market. These low prices will reduce profits within the market and thus dissuade new entrants.

Perfect competition In this type of market structure it is assumed that there are no barriers to entry and so new competitors can freely enter the market. Similarly, there are no barriers to prevent existing firms leaving the market if their profit levels are unsatisfactory.

Monopolistic competition It is difficult for existing firms to create barriers to entry, as firms are free to create their own version of goods in monopolistically competitive markets. Ease of entry into this market structure is therefore high.

Oligopoly This market structure has considerable barriers to entry, mainly based on the economies of scale and marketing barriers created by existing competitors.

Monopoly Since there is only one firm within the market, the barriers to entry noted in oligopoly are magnified in the case of monopoly. Furthermore, many monopolies in the UK are based on legal barriers and therefore it is impossible for competitors to set up in that market.

The fourth and fifth factors noted below may also be used, alongside other factors, to distinguish between market structures.

4 Extent to which information knowledge is perfect

- *Perfect competition* It is assumed that both buyers and sellers have perfect knowledge and information. As a consequence, it is impossible for one firm to charge a different price from other firms.
- *Monopolistic competition* There are many firms, which means knowledge will not be perfect. However, firms and consumers will have a good understanding of alternative goods and their prices, so knowledge is widespread.
- *Oligopoly* Although some knowledge may be widespread, firms in oligopoly markets are likely to possess some knowledge and information that is not known by other firms or customers in the market.
- *Monopoly* Perfect knowledge does not exist as there is only one firm providing the goods in this market structure. Legal monopolies tend to be regulated by government and so the level of information and knowledge will vary according to the reasons for the existence of the monopoly.

5 Influence of individual firms/suppliers on price

- *Perfect competition* Firms have no influence on price.
- *Monopolistic competition* Firms' influence on price is low.
- *Oligopoly* Firms' influence on price is quite high.
- *Monopoly* Firms' influence on price is very high.

Table 17.1 provides a summary of the main distinguishing features of the four main market structures.

Table 17.1 *Factors used to distinguish market structures*

Factor	Perfect competition	Monopolistic competition	Oligopoly	Monopoly
Number of firms	Many	Many	Few	One
Product differentiation	None	Some	Relatively high	Unique product
Ease of entry/ barriers to entry	No barriers	Few barriers	Many barriers	Very many barriers
Information/ knowledge	Perfect knowledge	Widespread knowledge, but not perfect	Restricted knowledge	Restricted knowledge
Influence of firms on price	Zero	Low	Quite high	Very high

REALWORLD ECONOMICS 17.1

Lush Cosmetics and product differentiation

In the UK, the market for soaps and detergents is considered to be an oligopoly, dominated by two firms – Procter & Gamble and Unilever. In total there are 267 UK firms operating in this market, many of them providing differentiated soaps on a very small scale. The EU market has a similar structure, with the three largest firms accounting for 30% of the total market. In both markets there are few manufacturers of detergents in comparison to soaps.

In 2014 annual revenue in the UK market was £1 billion, though sales in the market have fallen over the last 10 years and declined by 4% per annum between 2010 and 2014. Barriers to entry are moderate on the whole, particularly with regard to soaps, which are easy to make on a small scale. However, a major barrier to entry is marketing and brand loyalty. In 2013 Procter & Gamble and Unilever were the UK's second and fourth largest spenders on advertising. This spending has helped to create significant product differentiation between branded products. The soap market also features high levels of innovation, and the need for new product development acts as another barrier to entry.

Lush stores are inspired by delicatessens, attracting customers with their highly scented, visually appealing and unpackaged products

Lush Cosmetics started trading in 1994. Having previously failed as a supplier to other firms, it decided to open its own retail outlets as an outlet for the products it manufactures. Lush achieves product differentiation through its wide range of products. Each product contains fresh ingredients, many of which are unusual. The company sees itself as operating in a niche rather than mass market, targeting consumers who want a varied and unusual selection of cosmetics.

Lush researches new products continuously and updates its product range every 3 months. Unlike its main competitors, it allows its customers to see and touch its products. Only 2% of UK consumers purchase soap bars priced above £3. However, Lush's approach means that it can target this market, competing with mainly small firms that find it especially difficult to secure shelf space in shops.

Exercises

Total: 20 marks

1 'In total there are 267 UK firms operating in this market, many of them providing differentiated soaps on a very small scale.'

(a) Identify the market structure that most closely meets this description. *(1 mark)*

(b) Explain your reasoning. *(4 marks)*

2 Explain how Lush uses product differentiation to compete in its market. *(6 marks)*

3 Explain the possible barriers to entry to the soap and cosmetics market. *(9 marks)*

Review questions

Total: 30 marks

1 Which one of these market structures is the most concentrated?

A Monopolistic competition
B Monopoly
C Oligopoly
D Perfect competition

(1 mark)

2 Which market structure has differentiated products and many suppliers?

A Monopolistic competition
B Monopoly
C Oligopoly
D Perfect competition

(1 mark)

3 'Price takers' exist in:

A Monopolistic competition
B Monopoly
C Oligopoly
D Perfect competition

(1 mark)

4 In which one of these market structures does knowledge and information *not* act as a barrier to entry?

A Monopolistic competition
B Monopoly
C Oligopoly
D Perfect competition *(1 mark)*

5 In which market structure is a firm likely to have most influence on price?

A Monopolistic competition
B Monopoly
C Oligopoly
D Perfect competition *(1 mark)*

6 Identify one factor that is common to both monopolistic competition and oligopoly, and one factor that differentiates them. *(2 marks)*

7 Explain the meaning of the term 'ease of entry'. *(3 marks)*

8 Explain the meaning of the term 'market structure'. *(4 marks)*

9 Explain how 'sunk costs' can act as a barrier to entry. *(5 marks)*

10 Explain how 'economies of scale' can act as a barrier to entry. *(5 marks)*

11 Explain the distinction between a competitive market and a concentrated market. *(6 marks)*

Chapter 18

The objectives of firms

In previous chapters we have introduced analysis that is based on the assumption that consumers aim to maximise their satisfaction (happiness) and firms aim to make or maximise their profits. In this chapter we examine the importance of profit as an objective of most firms. The chapter then studies alternative objectives and the reasons why profit is not the sole objective of most firms.

Profit objectives

Much of classical economic theory is based on the assumption that all individuals aim to maximise their satisfaction. Thus, in the same way that individuals will maximise their personal happiness, owners of firms will want to maximise the profits of their firms. However, there can be conflict between short-run profit maximisation (which tends to fit most closely with economic theory) and long-run profit maximisation.

Short-run profit maximisation

This objective assumes that firms will try to maximise profit from every action that they take. In theory, if every action maximises profit in the short run, then maximum profit will be achieved over any other time period. However, short-run profit maximisation is based on assumptions of rational behaviour by consumers and homogeneous products in competitive markets. In the real world, these assumptions may not apply. For example, a firm aiming to maximise short-run profit will not provide refunds to consumers who have purchased a product that is the wrong size because this is an error by the consumer and therefore there is no legal requirement for the firm to provide such a refund. Any refund will eliminate the profit from that transaction and so a firm aiming to maximise short-run profit will refuse to provide it. In theory, a rational consumer will accept their own error and return to that firm in the future, if it is providing a suitable good.

Behavioural economists challenge this conclusion. Such behaviour by a firm would upset the consumer, regardless of the legality of their approach. As a consequence, they would not perceive this firm so favourably as competitors, when deciding on future transactions. As a result, a decision that maximises profit in the short run might endanger long-run profit maximisation.

Long-run profit maximisation

This objective assumes that firms are prepared to make lower profits, and even possibly losses, in the short run in order to achieve the best possible level of long-run profit. In the example above, many firms would refund the customer in order to build up goodwill and brand loyalty. Although this might lead to a loss in the short run, in the long run higher profits would be achieved through repeat custom from the customer.

Similarly, many firms might incur losses by opening at times when few customers are likely to buy goods in order to build up loyalty from customers who may, on occasions, have to shop at unusual times.

It should be noted that, to some extent, economists assume short-run profit maximisation because it is easier to measure its achievement. It is much more difficult to prove long-run profit maximisation because it will be impossible to predict whether customer loyalty has been achieved and whether any extra purchases have led to greater profit overall. In contrast, short-run profit maximisation can be more easily proved because it focuses on single transactions.

Profit satisficing

Profit maximisation is based on the assumption that the aims of firms are governed solely by their owners – shareholders in the case of limited companies. For small firms, the entrepreneur owns and controls the firm. However, as firms grow, there tends to be a divorce between ownership and control – ownership rests with shareholders, but control is in the hands of senior managers, who may or may not own shares in the firm. Senior managers will have their own wishes, such as high personal rewards. They will also need to meet the needs of other people (stakeholders) who have an interest in the firm, such as customers, the local community, workers and suppliers. Decisions may therefore be taken to suit the needs of these other stakeholders, such as high wages for workers and high-quality goods for customers.

These pressures from other stakeholders in the firm are likely to lead to some compromise between profit and other objectives. This will lead to a situation where the main financial objective of the firm is to make a satisfactory profit, rather than maximising profit. This is known as profit satisficing. In practice, shareholders are unlikely to have sufficient understanding of the day-to-day activities of the firm to recognise whether the profit achieved is the maximum possible profit.

Other objectives of firms

Profit levels can be quite volatile and often depend on external factors, such as the level of competition within the market. Furthermore, during a recession it can be very difficult for a firm to achieve a high profit and so other objectives may come to the fore. These factors undermine the idea of profit as the sole objective of a firm.

Firms usually try to meet the different needs of their stakeholders. The shareholders are stakeholders, but their particular needs must be balanced with the requirements of other stakeholder groups. Consequently, the firm's objectives are often a compromise between the wishes of a range of interested individuals and groups. These objectives can vary according to circumstances. Some common objectives are as follows:

Key terms

Survival is the state of continuing to exist or avoid failure. A firm that fails to survive will go into liquidation (for limited companies) or bankruptcy if it is unincorporated, such as a sole trader or partnership.

Market share is the percentage of total sales in a market that is achieved by one particular firm (or good).

Growth means increasing the firm's sales volume or total revenue over a period of time, usually measured over a period of one year.

Survival

In certain situations this may be the most important objective of a firm. Start-up firms are particularly vulnerable, with many failing to survive the first few years. This occurs because new firms need to buy capital but are likely to receive less income than established firms. Once this challenging period is over, the firm can focus on more positive objectives, such as growth, profit and increasing market share.

All stakeholders have an interest in the firm's survival and so it is an objective that tends to unite stakeholders. It will help to maintain the value of owners' shares, give security to employees, and guarantee future products for customers and future business for suppliers.

Survival may also be an important objective when market conditions are challenging. During a recession, many firms will suffer losses, and so the firm will focus on surviving until the recession is over. When the economy starts to grow, profit can become the main objective again.

In some cases survival may be important because of changes affecting a specific market. Bookshops and record stores have suffered from changes in tastes and from growth of online sales, and so survival becomes the most important objective.

Inefficient use of resources or poor management may also lead to a need to prioritise survival. At present it could be argued that Morrisons, the supermarket, is prioritising survival, following some decisions that led to losses – notably its failure to recognise the importance of online selling and its takeover of Kiddicare.

Growth

A firm's success can be clearly demonstrated by its expansion and so this is a popular objective. Growth can be measured in a number of ways, such as sales revenue, sales volume and number of outlets.

Growth is a popular objective because it is easy to measure and monitor throughout the year. It can also be compared to the achievements of competitors or compared to overall growth of the market within which the firm is operating.

As with survival, growth tends to meet with approval from most stakeholders because it helps to secure jobs, profit and market share. However, it may impact negatively on the environment.

Growth is measured by the percentage change in sales over a period of time (usually a year). It can be calculated as follows:

$$\textbf{Annual growth} = \frac{\text{Sales in Year X} - \text{Sales in Year X}{-1}}{\text{Sales in Year X}{-1}} \times 100$$

For example, if sales grow from £65.2 million to £73.3 million in a year, annual growth is:

$$\frac{73.3 - 65.2}{65.2} \times 100 = \frac{8.1}{65.2} \times 100 = 12.4\%$$

Increasing market share

Market share describes the percentage of total sales in a market that have been achieved by one firm (or product). It is calculated as follows:

$$\textbf{Market share (\%)} = \frac{\text{Sales of Firm X}}{\text{Total sales in market}} \times 100$$

For example, if annual sales in the market are £289 million and Firm X has annual sales of £43 million, then its market share is:

$$\frac{43}{289} \times 100 = 14.9\%$$

Objectives such as profit and growth can be greatly influenced by external factors. For example, in the twenty-first century, mobile phone networks have all tended to achieve growth because this market has grown significantly. In contrast, printed newspapers have fallen in demand and so even the most successful newspaper companies have experienced falling sales. Over the last 20 years the *Sun* has remained as market leader, increasing its market share slightly from 28% to 29%. However, daily sales of the *Sun* have fallen from 4.3 million in 1994 to 2.2 million in 2014.

Market share is a good measure of success in comparison to competitors. The example above shows that the *Sun* is losing sales because newspapers are losing popularity. However, it is competing effectively with its competitor newspapers. Nevertheless, it could be argued that firms in declining markets should transfer their resources to other markets. In the case of the *Sun*, its parent company owns Sky, which is attracting a much higher level of investment.

Other objectives

There are many other objectives that are often pursued in order to please different stakeholders. However, this can lead to conflict because different stakeholders have different objectives. Other objectives that firms may pursue are noted below:

- *Social and ethical objectives* Some firms emphasise the importance of supporting the local community and ethical behaviour – 'doing the right thing' – such as ensuring that products are safe and that employees receive fair rewards and good working conditions. Many firms promote the idea of 'fair trade', which is based on giving suppliers and their workforces a fair deal.
- *Increasing shareholder value* Shareholders benefit from their shares in two ways: dividends (their share of the profit that is distributed to owners) and increases in share prices. Firms will take action, such as retaining profit to finance expansion, to help shareholders benefit from higher share prices and higher future profits.
- *Building brand loyalty* This objective will help firms to sell more goods and charge higher prices. It can lead to other benefits too. For example, customers will be more willing to try new products released by the firm and it will be easier to attract suppliers and employees.
- *Diversification* Firms try to protect themselves from risk, by diversifying into other activities. In this way, the failure of one part of the firm may be compensated by successes in other parts. Diversification can also be a growth strategy where a firm has limited scope for further expansion in its existing market.
- *Environmental objectives* As society has become more aware of the potentially negative impact of business activity on the environment, and the depletion of scarce, finite resources, many firms have prioritised environmental objectives for both ethical and commercial reasons. In the latter case, a firm's objectives and actions can attract consumers who have a desire to protect the environment.

Although economic analysis tends to focus on profit objectives, it is important for economists to recognise the need for firms to satisfy a wide range of stakeholders. These stakeholders will expect firms to have other objectives. The prioritisation of objectives will depend upon a variety of factors, such as the characters of the managers, the goods being produced, the attitudes of workers and suppliers, and external factors including competition and the economy. Consequently, objectives vary considerably between firms and over time.

REALWORLD ECONOMICS 18.1

Changing objectives at Jessops

A firm's objectives are not static because firms must adjust to changes in the market and also modify objectives in accordance with the firm's own internal capabilities.

In January 2013, Jessops, the camera retailer, collapsed with debts of £81 million. Six years earlier it had been achieving growth in profits, sales revenue and market share.

In the 1980s Jessops opened its second camera store. As personal cameras became more popular and prices became more accessible, the firm targeted and achieved rapid sales growth, mainly through the opening of new stores. By 2002 Jessops had more than 250 shops in the UK. By this time it had succeeded in achieving its objective of becoming the camera retailer with the highest market share. Jessops had been quick to recognise the growth of digital photography, but failed to recognise other changes in its market, such as mobile camera phones.

Closed for business: the Jessops store in Cambridge, January 2013

New entrants, including Tesco and internet competitors, were moving into the market, joining established competitors such as Currys and Argos. More significantly, camera phones were beginning to gain popularity.

The year 2006 saw Jessops at its peak. It had a 20% market share of retail photography, with a 37% share of the digital photography market. Sales revenue peaked in 2006, with 313 stores helping to achieve annual sales of £350 million and a profit of £13.2 million.

The combination of an economic downturn, growing competition and a declining market (as consumers switched to camera phones) led to a sudden switch in Jessops's objectives. Survival became the main objective.

In 2007 Jessops closed 80 stores and by 2008 sales revenue had fallen to £250 million. Losses of £50 million a year were recorded. By 2012, Jessops still had a market share of 18%, but the market was declining at a rate of 10% per annum. Losses had been cut to £5 million in 2012, but the continual losses meant that its suppliers, many of whom had lost money from the liquidation of Comet, the electrical retailer, demanded immediate payment for supplies. As a result, Jessops went into liquidation in January 2013.

Dragons' Den entrepreneur Peter Jones bought the brand name and some of the liquidated firm's assets in March 2013. His plan was to minimise costs by operating online, with only 40 stores operating in large centres. These stores would assist the online firm by providing access for 'click and collect' facilities for online customers. This streamlined model would cut central costs from £8 million per annum to £1.5 million. Peter Jones's objective for Jessops is to achieve sales revenue of £80 million in 2013/14, rising to £200 million within three to five years. If successful, this would represent a market share of more than 15%.

Sources: Evening Standard article, 'Jessops: history of the chain which transformed photography', 9.1.13. *Daily Telegraph* article, 'Dragons' Den star Peter Jones helps Jessops to return to high street with 40 new stores', 28.3.13.

Exercises

Total: 25 marks

1 State two examples of objectives from the article. *(2 marks)*

2 Explain why Jessops changed its main objectives between 2006 and 2007. *(8 marks)*

3 Evaluate whether Jessops's failure to achieve its objectives was caused by external factors outside the firm's control. *(15 marks)*

Review questions

Total: 40 marks

1 Classical economic theory suggests that firms aim to achieve:
   A Breakeven
   B Short-run profit maximisation
   C Long-run profit maximisation
   D Satisficing profit *(1 mark)*

2 Which one of the following stakeholders is least likely to agree with an objective of profit satisficing?
   A Consumers
   B Employees
   C Shareholders
   D Suppliers *(1 mark)*

3 Growth can be measured by all of the following except:
   A A change in sales revenue
   B A change in volume
   C A change in profit
   D A change in the number of outlets *(1 mark)*

4 State two examples of ethical objectives. *(2 marks)*

5 What is the formula for calculating market share? *(2 marks)*

6 A firm's sales are £840,000 in 2014 and £780,000 in 2015. What is the firm's rate of growth over this time period? *(3 marks)*

7 Explain the difference between short-run profit maximisation and long-run profit maximisation. *(4 marks)*

8 Give *one* reason why a firm's profit might not be related solely to how well it manages its resources. *(5 marks)*

9 What is meant by 'the divorce of ownership from control'? *(5 marks)*

10 Explain why new firms are likely to prioritise survival as an objective. *(6 marks)*

11 Explain why profit is likely to be more important than a firm's other objectives. *(10 marks)*

Competitive markets

This chapter extends the summary of the characteristics of a perfectly competitive market, first outlined in Chapter 17, by providing a more detailed examination of these characteristics. The determination of price in competitive markets through the interaction of demand and supply is then described. The chapter concludes by explaining why profits are likely to be lower in a competitive market than in a market that is dominated by a few large firms.

The main characteristics of a perfectly competitive market

In Chapter 17 we saw that perfectly competitive markets possess five key characteristics:

- Many firms
- No product differentiation
- No barriers to entry
- Perfect information and knowledge
- Firms have no influence on price

These characteristics will be developed further, alongside some other characteristics of a perfectly competitive market.

It is debatable whether a perfectly competitive market exists in real life because the above combination of characteristics is highly unlikely. However, it is a useful model with which to examine how lots of small firms operate in a very competitive market situation. This theoretical market can be used to explain certain aspects of behaviour in order to understand markets that possess many, but perhaps not all, of these characteristics.

The concept of a perfectly competitive market is based on a number of assumptions that form the key characteristics of the market. The main characteristics and their implications are described below.

1 Many buyers and many sellers

In a perfectly competitive market there are so many firms (sellers) that no single firm (seller) has any influence on the equilibrium price in the market. Although each seller contributes to the overall market supply, the sheer volume of firms within the market, and thus the small scale on which these firms operate, means that no single firm supplies sufficient goods to have a significant impact on the market supply. Consequently, no single firm has an influence on the equilibrium market price. In effect, each firm is a price taker.

Key term

A **price taker** is a firm that has to accept the equilibrium price set by the market in which it operates. Any quantity of goods that it supplies will be sold at the market price.

The same logic applies to buyers in a perfectly competitive market. No single buyer has any influence on the equilibrium price in the market. Each buyer contributes to the overall market demand, but the volume of buyers within the market means that no single buyer demands sufficient goods to have a significant impact on market demand. Consequently, no single buyer (consumer) has an influence on the equilibrium market price. As with the firms supplying the goods, each buyer is a price taker.

2 Rational behaviour

It is assumed that both firms and consumers act in a rational and logical manner. Firms aim to maximise profit and consumers aim to maximise their welfare/happiness. Any decisions taken by a participant in a perfectly competitive market will therefore be in pursuit of these particular objectives.

3 Homogeneous products (no product differentiation)

This means that all firms produce identical goods. There is no branding or loyalty to a particular firm's goods. Agriculture is often taken to be a close proximity to a perfectly competitive market but, since agricultural produce can vary in quality, product differentiation is often the reason why prices may vary from one supplier to another.

If there are identical products in a market, this means that each product is a perfect substitute for the other products in the market. This leads to the cross elasticity of demand between products having infinite cross elasticity. If a firm increases its price, it will lose all of its sales to its competitors.

4 No barriers to entry and exit

This is a critical characteristic/assumption of the perfectly competitive market. Rational behaviour would suggest that firms will wish to enter a market in which profit is being made by suppliers and will wish to exit a market in which losses are being made. This assumption leads to the logical conclusion that scarce resources within an economy will shift from unprofitable uses to profitable purposes. The profits (and losses) made by firms within a market act as a signal for other firms and indicate the financial viability of devoting resources to the production of goods in that market. Losses indicate that firms should exit that market, while profits indicate that firms should enter that market. In a perfectly competitive market there are none of the barriers to entry described in Chapter 17. For these signals to work, it must be possible for new firms to enter a market and be competitive; similarly, there should be no barriers, such as sunk costs, that might prevent a loss-making firm from leaving a market.

5 Perfect information and knowledge

The model of perfect competition assumes that buyers and sellers have perfect information and knowledge. As the products are homogeneous, the main significance of this assumption is that it means all buyers and sellers are aware of prices being charged. If a firm attempts to charge more than the market price, then all buyers will know that they can purchase the products more cheaply elsewhere and so this firm will not sell any. If the firm sets its price below the market price, then it will sell all the products that it supplies. However, as firms in a perfectly competitive market can sell all of their output at the market price, it is irrational for a firm to charge a lower price when the result of this action would be to lower revenue (selling the same quantity of goods but at a lower price).

The effect of perfect information means that a market has only one price at any particular moment in time – the market equilibrium price.

6 Firms have no influence on price

The characteristics described earlier lead to this particular characteristic. Individually, firms (and buyers) have no direct influence on price. Price is determined by the collective behaviour of all buyers and sellers in the market.

In effect, an individual firm faces a horizontal demand curve for *its* goods. Buyers will only be prepared to buy the goods of an individual firm at the market price. This is shown in Figure 19.1. If the market price changes, this horizontal line will shift upwards or downwards, but remain horizontal.

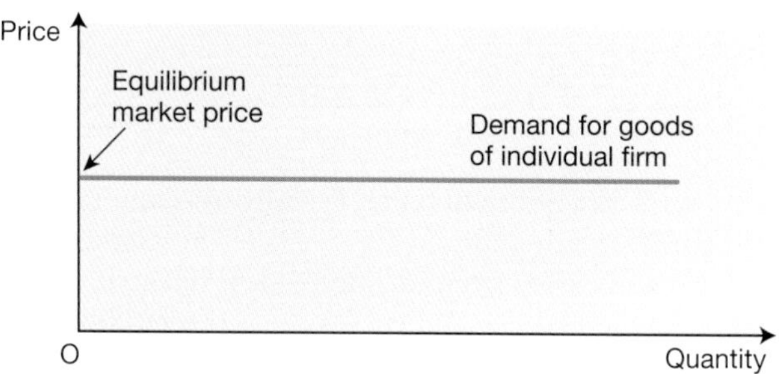

Figure 19.1 *The demand curve for an individual firm's goods in a perfectly competitive market*

7 Absence of transport or transaction costs

A characteristic of perfectly competitive markets is that there are no transport or transaction costs. Transport costs (such as fuel) and transaction costs (such as commission) might be incurred by consumers when comparing the goods offered by alternative suppliers. It is assumed that buyers will incur no extra costs in purchasing goods from one firm than from any other firm. This assumption is similar to the concept of barriers of entry. If one seller is some distance from the other sellers, buyers may be reluctant to incur the costs or time to visit that seller. In economies such as the UK, where time is valued highly by many buyers, this characteristic applies to very few, if any, markets. However, it is a necessary characteristic if a single price is to exist in a market. The increase in internet-based markets is making this assumption more realistic when considering real-life examples of perfectly competitive markets.

8 Perfect mobility of factors of production

In perfectly competitive markets, resources such as labour and capital are free to move from one occupation/use to another. This lack of restriction allows the market to adjust to changes in demand or supply. For example, if people switch demand from Good A to Good B, then the price of A will rise and the price of B will fall. Profit levels will increase in the market for Good A (and fall in the market for Good B). This will attract factors of production away from the production/supply of Good A towards the production of Good B.

Price determination in a perfectly competitive market

In a perfectly competitive market, price is determined by the market. Individual firms must accept the prevailing market price when selling their goods. In effect, **the market is the price maker** while **the individual firm is a price taker.**

Price is determined by the interaction of demand and supply in a market. Chapter 10 showed how demand and supply determine equilibrium price in a market economy. A market economy is an economy based on the characteristics of a perfectly competitive market. Figure 19.2 shows an example of price determination in a perfectly competitive market, based on the work covered in Chapter 6 (demand), Chapter 8 (supply) and Chapter 10 (price determination).

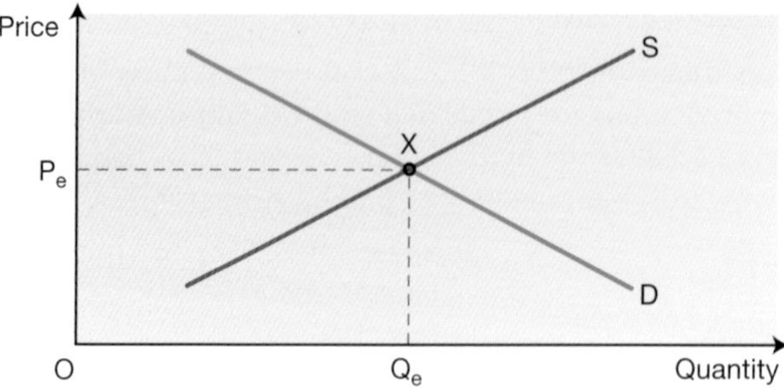

Figure 19.2 *Price determination in a perfectly competitive market*

In Figure 19.2, X shows the equilibrium point, P_e shows the equilibrium market price and Q_e shows the equilibrium quantity in the market. The market demand consists of many individual demand curves from each individual buyer. In comparison to the market demand, these individual demand curves are so insignificant that changes in demand by one individual will have no impact on the overall market demand curve shown in the diagram. The same logic applies to market supply and the individual firms that are supplying goods in this market. Thus no individual (buyer or seller) affects the market price.

Why profit levels tend to be lower in competitive markets

In any form of market, it is assumed that firms are aiming to make profit. Normal profit is the minimum level of profit that is required for a firm to continue to operate in a particular market. It represents the opportunity cost of the firm because if profits fall below this level, the firm will no longer choose to remain in business. Any profit above normal profit is known as abnormal (or supernormal) profit. If firms in a market are making abnormal profit, then new firms will wish to move into the market to take advantage of these high levels of profit. However, if profit levels are below normal profit, then new firms will not be tempted to enter that market.

What happens to profit levels in competitive markets?

In competitive markets, such as perfect competition, abnormal profits may occur through factors such as a sudden fall in costs or a change in consumer tastes that leads to an increase in demand. Figure 19.3 shows a situation in which demand has increased from D_1 to D_2. This moves the equilibrium point from X to Y and increases the market price from P_1 to P_2. At this new high price, existing firms will extend their supply from Q_1 to Q_2 and enjoy abnormal profits as a result of the increase in market price. Although one single firm cannot lead to greater supply, a large number of firms extending their output will lead to greater supply, as shown by the change from Q_1 to Q_2. However, these abnormal profits will only occur in the short run. If abnormal profits exist, then new firms will enter the market in order to obtain these high levels of profit. Since there are many new firms entering the market, there will be an impact on market supply that increases from S_1 towards S_2. As a result, the equilibrium point moves from Y towards Z. This leads to a fall in price. In this example, the price falls from P_2 back towards the original price of P_1. As the price falls from P_2, the level of abnormal profit falls. Eventually, price falls to P_1 (at which price there is no more abnormal profit being made). Once profit levels return to normal, new firms are no longer interested in entering the market and so there is no further increase in supply. This happens when the increase in supply reaches S_2. This process stops with the final equilibrium at Point Z and an overall increase in the quantity bought (from Q_2 to Q_3). At price P_1, profits have returned to normal profit levels.

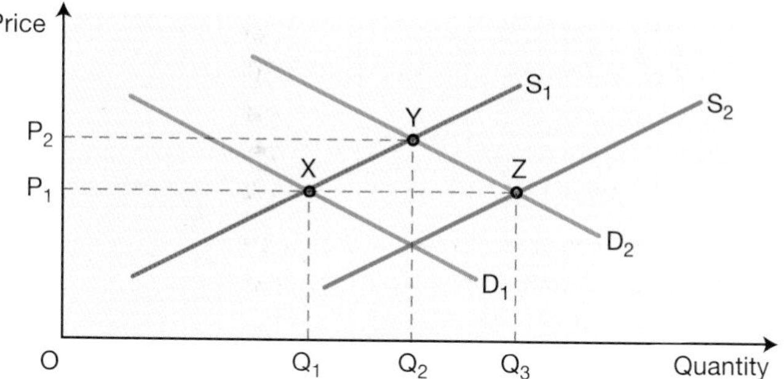

Figure 19.3 *The impact of profit on price determination in a perfectly competitive market*

It should be noted that if quantity increases so much that price falls below P_1, *then losses will be made. Existing firms will then leave the industry and so supply decreases, forcing the price back up to* P_1, *at which price the losses are eliminated and there is a return to normal profit.*

What happens to profit levels in markets dominated by a few firms?

In concentrated markets, such as monopoly and oligopoly, there are barriers to entry that prevent or limit new firms from entering the market. As a consequence, if there are abnormal/supernormal profits in a concentrated market, then existing firms in that market can continue to enjoy them because new firms will not enter the market.

If demand increases and higher levels of abnormal profits are made, it is difficult (but not impossible) for new firms to enter the market. With high barriers to entry, there is much greater scope for abnormal profits to be maintained and even increased, though such increases may be restricted by the possibility of sales being lost to existing competitors.

The lack of competition in these markets allows firms to maintain abnormal/supernormal profits. Goods are differentiated and brand loyalty allows firms to charge prices that exceed costs, without the fear that new firms will enter the market. Each firm supplies unique goods. However, because competitors provide goods that may be close substitutes, the demand for the firm's goods may fall if the price is increased.

Although firms in markets dominated by a few large firms will usually enjoy higher profits, this is not guaranteed. Competition may take other forms, such as non-price competition based on product quality, innovation or advertising. Very high profit levels may encourage new entrants. Although they may be at a competitive disadvantage because of the barriers to entry, they may feel that they can make more than normal profits because of the potential for profit in this industry. Growing demand in a market will also encourage new entrants, despite entry difficulties. For example, the growth of coffee shops has attracted many small firms, notwithstanding the market dominance of Costa, Starbucks and Caffè Nero.

Conclusion

Market conditions in concentrated markets with a few firms are more favourable for firms, allowing them to enjoy abnormal profits.

Barriers to entry in markets dominated by a few firms enable abnormal profits to be sustained in the long term.

In competitive markets, changes in the market may lead to short-term abnormal profits. However, the ease of entry into these markets will mean that any abnormal profit will be 'competed away' until profit levels return to the level of normal profit.

REALWORLD ECONOMICS 19.1

Does perfect competition exist in the UK?

Many economists treat perfect competition (perfectly competitive markets) as a purely theoretical model, arguing that the combination of characteristics required for a perfectly competitive market do not exist in real life. In subsistence economies, agricultural products are often cited as examples of perfect competition, but in the UK a few large buyers can dominate this market. There is also significant intervention by the government in order to influence both the supply and demand of agricultural products.

Three markets that have been suggested as possible examples of perfectly competitive markets in the UK are:

- The stock exchange
- Foreign exchange
- Goods purchased through eBay

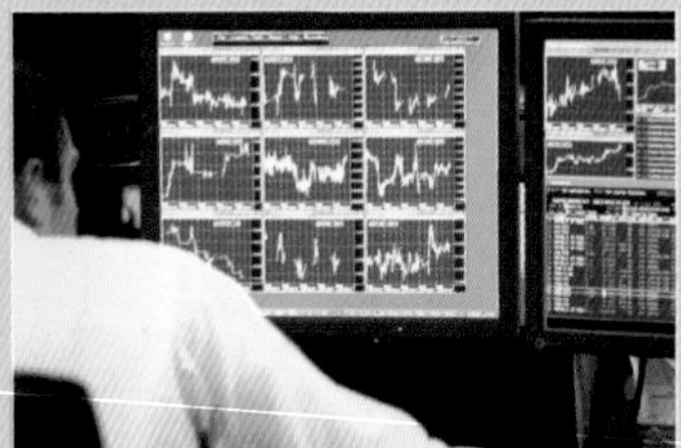

Does a trader at the London Stock Exchange operate in a perfectly competitive market?

Table 19.1 *Competitive market characteristics of certain markets*

Characteristic	Perfectly competitive market	Example markets		
		Stock market	Foreign exchange	eBay
Many buyers and sellers	Yes	Yes	Yes	Yes
Rational behaviour	Yes	Yes[a]	Yes	Yes
Homogeneous products	Yes	Yes	Yes	No[b]
Barriers to entry/exit	No	Yes	Yes	No
Perfect information	Yes	Quite high	High	Fairly high
No influence on price	Yes	Yes[c]	Yes	Not always
Transport/transaction costs	No	Yes	Yes	Yes
Perfect mobility[d]	Yes	No	No	No

Notes: (a) Can be speculative behaviour. (b) Exact details of product may be unclear. (c) Large buyers/sellers may have an influence on price. (d) No perfect mobility, but lack of mobility has limited impact on these markets.

The stock exchange

This provides a marketplace in which people can sell shares they own in a limited company. The shareowner contacts a broker (who must be registered), who then uses the stock exchange's facilities to make contact with potential buyers. Share price information is widely available and a particular share in a firm is, in effect, identical to any other share in that firm.

Foreign exchange

Registered providers of foreign exchange, such as commercial banks and travel agents, provide facilities for buyers to ascertain the exchange rate and decide on whether or not they wish to purchase a particular foreign currency from the provider.

Goods purchased through eBay

eBay itself has restricted competition. However, buyers and sellers using eBay have access to a wide range of sellers/buyers and prices are easy to monitor.

eBay is a marketplace in which people can trade any goods that they wish and make contact with a wide group of potential buyers.

Table 19.1 provides a summary of competitive market characteristics of certain markets.

Discussion points

Which one of these markets do you believe is the closest to a perfect market?

Are there better examples of perfectly competitive markets?

Review questions

Total: 35 marks

1 In the long run, firms in a competitive market that is experiencing a fall in demand will:

A Make losses

B Breakeven

C Make normal profit

D Make abnormal profit *(1 mark)*

2 Which one of the factors listed below is mostly likely to make a market more competitive?

A Better knowledge and information

B Some firms leaving the market

C Greater product differentiation

D More barriers to entry *(1 mark)*

3 The price elasticity of demand facing an individual firm for its goods in a perfectly competitive market is:

A $-\infty$ B -1 C 0 D $+1$ *(1 mark)*

4 State two examples of barriers to entry to a market. *(2 marks)*

5 What is meant by the term 'rational behaviour'? *(3 marks)*

6 What is meant by the term 'homogeneous products'? *(3 marks)*

7 Explain why an individual firm has no influence on price in a perfectly competitive market. *(5 marks)*

8 Explain why perfect mobility of factors of production is needed for a perfectly competitive market to operate. *(5 marks)*

9 Explain why firms in a market dominated by a few firms can continually achieve abnormal profits. *(5 marks)*

10 Explain, with the help of a diagram, how abnormal profits are 'competed away' in a perfectly competitive market. *(9 marks)*

Chapter 20

Monopoly & monopoly power

This chapter compares the concepts of pure monopoly and monopoly power, examining the main factors that influence monopoly power. The use of concentration ratios and their calculation is considered. The basic model of monopoly is explained and the implication that monopoly leads to higher prices, higher profits and inefficiency. The potential for monopoly to lead to a misallocation of resources, in comparison to a competitive market, is considered. The chapter concludes with an examination of the potential benefits from monopoly.

The difference between pure monopoly and monopoly power

Key terms

Pure monopoly exists when there is a single supplier in a market.

Monopoly power arises when firms exert considerable influence in a market because of their relatively large size.

Pure monopoly is very rare because there are few instances in which one firm supplies 100% of the goods in a market. In the UK the main rail network is owned 100% by Railtrack, which charges the train operators for its use. The Post Office currently has a pure monopoly on the delivery of letters (but not parcels). On an international scale, Japanese Steel is the only firm with the technical capability to make the large lead casings to contain the radioactivity in nuclear power stations.

Monopoly power is more common. Firms such as Google, which has an almost 90% market share of the search engine market, dominate their particular markets.

However, much smaller firms can exert influence on a market. In the UK, a **legal monopoly** *describes any firm with a market share in excess of 25% of the market.* Thus firms such as Tesco (supermarkets), First Group (train providers) and Lloyds Banking Group (banking) would be classified as legal monopolies because they have a market share in excess of 25%. Government considers these levels of market share to be sufficient to give them monopoly power because they are able to exert influence on the market in areas such as pricing.

In defining monopoly power, the government may take into consideration local situations. For example, the Stagecoach Group is a large bus and train operator but its market share in both markets is below 25%. However, it has local monopolies because it provides 100% of the bus services in some communities and is the only train provider for certain routes. Thus the Stagecoach Group has monopoly power in these areas, in the same way as the village store has monopoly power in a village.

Causes of monopoly

Monopoly can arise for a number of reasons:

- *natural monopoly*, where it is practical for there to be only one supplier of the product (such as water supply);
- *ownership of resources*, where access to a scarce resource is restricted by ownership of certain assets, such as mineral rights. For example, de Beers in South Africa controlled 90% of the world's diamond supply until the 1980s;

- *elimination of competition*, where successful firms have taken over competitors or forced them out of business;
- *legal monopolies*, such as patent laws guaranteeing monopoly status for a number of years, to encourage innovation and invention. Many legal monopolies are former public corporations (nationalised industries) that have been privatised so that they are now limited companies. There are regulatory bodies, such as Ofcom and Ofwat, to ensure that they do not abuse their monopoly power;
- *local monopolies*, where the size of the market is too small to support more than one firm, such as a village shop;
- *advertising*, where marketing gives monopoly power by creating high brand loyalty so that consumers are reluctant to buy alternative products.

The causes of monopoly can influence a monopolist's monopoly power.

Influences on monopoly power

The **degree of monopoly power** wielded by a monopolist is influenced by a variety of factors.

Barriers to entry

In Chapter 17 we saw that barriers to entry are factors that prevent competition from entering a market. These barriers can take many forms. Some of the main barriers, and their impact on monopoly power, are outlined below.

- *Legal monopolies* In the UK, firms providing public transport and those providing public utilities, such as water, enjoy considerable monopoly power. These firms were once government-owned monopolies and when they were transferred to private ownership (a process known as privatisation), many of the new businesses inherited high market shares. Since they provide basic necessities, this further increases monopoly power because there are few close substitutes. Monopoly power is reduced by the existence of regulatory bodies, such as Ofgem, which can influence factors such as market prices. However, in recent years high energy prices and high profits for energy firms have led to criticisms of Ofgem's control of monopoly power in the energy industry.
- *Natural monopolies* Natural monopolies exist in markets where it is difficult or uneconomic to provide competition. Water supply is a classic example, as it would be unnecessarily expensive to provide each house with alternative water supplies. Natural monopolies can exert considerable market influence because of the significant barriers to entry into this type of market. In the UK, the natural monopolies tend to be industries that were previously government owned.
- *Patent laws and intellectual property rights* These are specific types of legal monopoly. In order to encourage research and development and innovation, patents are awarded to firms that invent new products or processes. These patents guarantee a monopoly of that product for a period of 16 to 20 years. However, the monopoly power arising from patents depends on the uniqueness of the product. For some drug companies, where there have been no alternative treatments available, patents have given considerable monopoly power. Intellectual property rights apply to items such as books and music. The writer/creator has exclusive rights to the use of the material provided, although this can be very difficult to

enforce – especially for music. Again, the level of monopoly power depends on how much consumers value the good or service being produced.

- *Ownership of resources* The example of de Beers, mentioned earlier, shows how ownership of scarce resources can give considerable monopoly power. In the UK, BT's ownership of landline infrastructure gives it the ability to influence prices and the potential to make high profits, taking advantage of its monopoly power.
- *The need for expensive infrastructure/capital costs* In some industries, such as car manufacturing and mobile phone networks, some firms have undertaken significant capital costs to serve the needs of the market. Any new firm entering the market would need to match these high levels of expenditure, which for existing firms may have taken place over many years. This can be a major barrier to entry and allow existing firms to enjoy high levels of monopoly power.
- *Internal economies of scale* These economies allow existing firms to produce at a lower average cost than smaller firms, such as new entrants into the industry. Any new entrant is likely to be uncompetitive in terms of price and may therefore be forced out of the market. Existing firms will often enter a price war if they feel threatened by a new entrant, taking advantage of their economies of scale in order to set prices which are so low that the new entrant cannot make a profit. This can force the new entrant out of the market. This approach may also be used as a threat, to persuade firms not to try entering the market at all.

The number of competitors

The level of competition in a market can influence monopoly power. For example, Tesco has a market share of more than 25% of the supermarket trade. However, its share is below 30% and the market has become more competitive in recent years. This has occurred mainly because discount supermarkets, such as Aldi and Lidl, have invested more heavily in their UK supermarket chains. There has also been greater competition at the higher-price end of the market, with Waitrose and Marks & Spencer growing too. As a consequence, there has been a significant decline in Tesco's profit (although its market power is perhaps confirmed by the fact that its disappointing annual profit level is currently about £1.4 billion).

The oil industry is dominated by a limited number of large firms, both nationally and internationally. In the UK, BP and Shell enjoy high levels of monopoly power as a result of the lack of competitors in the oil industry. However, currently the world's most profitable firm in this industry is Russia's Gazprom, largely because of its dominance of gas supply to many countries.

In industries where there are many competitors, the market condition becomes closer to a perfectly competitive market, and so monopoly power is significantly reduced.

Later in this chapter we will examine market concentration. High concentration means that a few firms have a very high market share, making it harder for new firms to enter the market. High levels of market concentration mean that there are fewer competitors and so greater monopoly power for existing firms.

Advertising

In some industries, advertising helps firms to achieve monopoly power. By creating brand loyalty, firms can differentiate their product from competitors. For industries such as soap powder, advertising fulfils two different purposes:

Advertising changes consumers' tastes

Advertising leads to an increase in demand for the advertised good. However, it also creates a perception of uniqueness, so that consumers become more loyal to the product and they therefore become less likely to buy alternatives. In this way advertising not only increases the demand by shifting the demand curve to the right but also makes the demand become more price inelastic. As a consequence, if firms increase the price of these branded products, the loss in quantity demanded will be quite slight. This effect is shown in Figure 20.1.

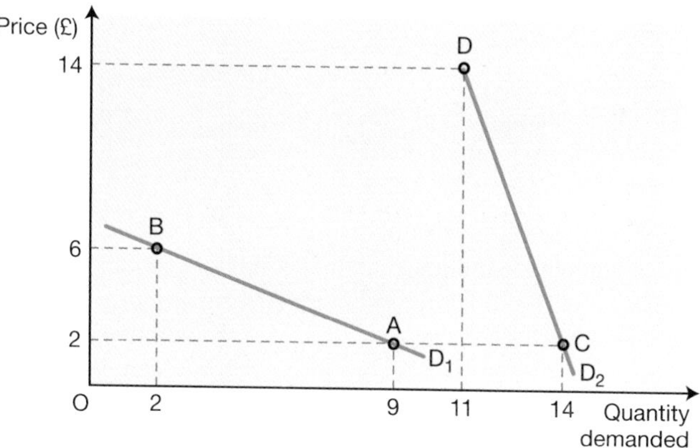

Figure 20.1 *The impact of advertising on demand*

Demand curve D_1 shows the level of demand before advertising. Point A shows that at a price of £2, quantity demanded is 9 units, giving a total revenue of £18 (9 x £2). An increase in price from £2 to £6 moves us along D_1 from Point A to Point B. At Point B, the quantity demanded is 2 units, giving total revenue of £12. Thus a price rise has led to lower total revenue.

Demand curve D_2 shows the result of successful advertising. This increases demand and makes demand more price inelastic. Point C shows that at a price of £2, the quantity demanded has now increased from 9 units to 14 units. Total revenue at a price of £2 has risen from £18 to £28. Since D_2 shows a demand curve that is price inelastic, the firm will increase its total revenue by increasing its price. Point D shows that a price of £14 will lead to demand of 11 units, resulting in total revenue of £154. Thus a price rise has led to higher total revenue.

Advertising acts as a barrier to entry

Heavy advertising expenditure can prevent smaller firms from entering a market. The market for bars of soap in the UK is quite competitive. However, the UK soap powder industry is dominated by two firms – Procter & Gamble and Unilever. For many years these two firms were the UK's largest advertisers in terms of spending. In 2013 they occupied second and fourth places in the UK advertising league table, with Procter & Gamble spending £177 million and Unilever spending £119 million, although not all of this was on soap powder. These huge sums of money make it very difficult for rival firms to get a foothold in this market and so advertising represents a major barrier to entry. The only serious competition arises from supermarket branded soap powders, which benefit from the large advertising budgets of the supermarkets. Tesco and Asda were the fifth and sixth largest advertisers in the UK respectively, with three other supermarkets and M&S being placed in the top 20.

The degree of product differentiation

In perfectly competitive markets, buyers can easily move between suppliers because there is no difference between the goods that they supply. With heterogeneous products, where products differ, it is more difficult for buyers to switch because the goods differ. The more significant the differences, the more difficult it will be for consumers to switch. In some markets there may be a high degree of product differentiation. An Apple Mac may provide similar outcomes to a PC, but to many consumers the two goods are highly differentiated and would not be considered as substitutes.

Product differentiation may arise from differences in the product or from perceptions created by advertising and marketing. Whatever the cause, if a product has a high degree of product differentiation its producer will enjoy greater monopoly power.

Conclusion

Each of the factors analysed above impacts on the price elasticity of demand of a product. High barriers of entry and fewer competitors both mean that there are fewer, if any, close substitutes for a good. Successful advertising and product differentiation also lead to consumers taking a view that there are no suitable alternatives to the product. Each of these factors leads to more price inelastic demand for the product, which makes it easier for the monopolist to increase profit by increasing price. Price inelastic demand increases the monopoly power of the supplier.

Concentration ratios

Concentration ratios provide a good indication of the potential monopoly power of the largest firms in a concentrated market. They tend to be used when looking at oligopoly markets, in which a few firms dominate, but can also be used to study monopolistic competition in which there are many firms with differentiated products.

There is no set number of firms used to calculate the concentration ratio for a market or industry, although four-firm and five-firm concentration ratios are probably the most commonly used measures. Ideally, the number of firms used should be the one that gives the clearest picture of the degree of dominance by large firms.

In the PC 'search engine' market (Table 20.1), the degree of dominance is best shown by a one-firm concentration ratio because Google's 88.4% market share means that it is quite close to being a pure monopoly. The three-firm concentration ratio adds together the market shares of Google, Bing and Yahoo to give 88.4% + 6.6% + 3.9% = 98.9%. This ratio also gives a clear indication of monopoly power in this market. However, a four-firm concentration ratio would add the market share of the fourth biggest search engine – Ask Jeeves. The four-firm concentration ratio would be 98.9% + 0.4% = 99.3%. This could be deemed to be a misleading measure because it is highly unlikely that Ask Jeeves's 0.4% market share gives it any degree of market power.

Key terms

A **concentration ratio** measures the combined market share of the largest firms in a particular market.

A **four-firm concentration ratio** measures the combined market share of the four largest firms in a particular market.

Table 20.1 *UK market shares of PC 'search engines'*

Google	88.4%
Bing	6.6%
Yahoo	3.9%
Ask Jeeves	0.4%
AOL	0.3%
Others	0.4%

Source: Forbes, December 2014

Calculating concentration ratios

In October 2014, the market shares of supermarkets in the UK were as shown in Figure 20.2. The pie chart shows that for UK supermarkets, the four-firm concentration ratio is 28.7 + 17.2 + 16.4 + 11.1 = 73.4%, and the five-firm concentration ratio is 28.7 + 17.2 + 16.4 + 11.1 + 6.2 = 79.6%.

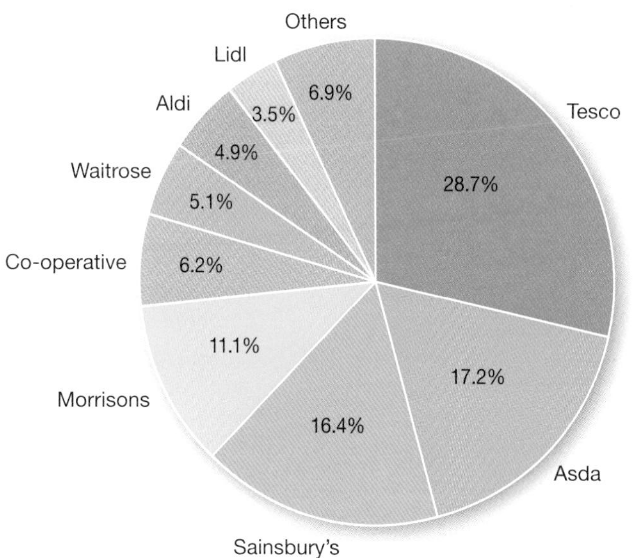

Figure 20.2 *Market share of UK supermarkets, October 2014*

In 2014, 42 car manufacturers accounted for all but 200 of the 2.3 million cars sold in the UK. This industry has become more competitive in recent decades, with Ford being the market leader with just over 13% of the market. For this reason, ten-firm and fifteen-firm concentration ratios are used. Concentration ratios for the car industry at the end of 2014 were as follows: a five-firm concentration ratio of 45.0%; a ten-firm concentration ratio of 67.1%; and a fifteen-firm concentration ratio of 82.1%.

Conclusion

Concentration ratios are a very good indicator of monopoly power because they provide a good indication of the number of competitors in a market, the strength of those competitors and an implied indication of whether there are barriers to entry. However, they do not give any indication of the level of product differentiation and price inelasticity of demand, and therefore they do not necessarily provide an overall indication of market power.

Monopoly and misallocation of resources

In Chapter 5 we saw that **allocative efficiency** means that resources are being used to produce the goods and services that consumers wish to buy. In comparison to a perfectly competitive market, a monopoly or market in which firms have monopoly power may lead to higher prices, higher profits and inefficiency. This will lead to a misallocation of resources in the monopoly market in comparison to resource allocation in a perfectly competitive market.

In Figure 20.3, Point X represents the market equilibrium point in a competitive market. The equilibrium price is P_1 and the equilibrium quantity is Q_1.

If a monopoly takes control of this market, it will increase price. Total revenue (TR) will change from OP_1XQ_1 to OP_2YQ_2. As demand is price inelastic, this is an increase in TR. Total costs (TC) will fall because fewer units are produced (quantity produced falls from OQ_1 to OQ_2). This increase in TR and fall in TC will mean that the

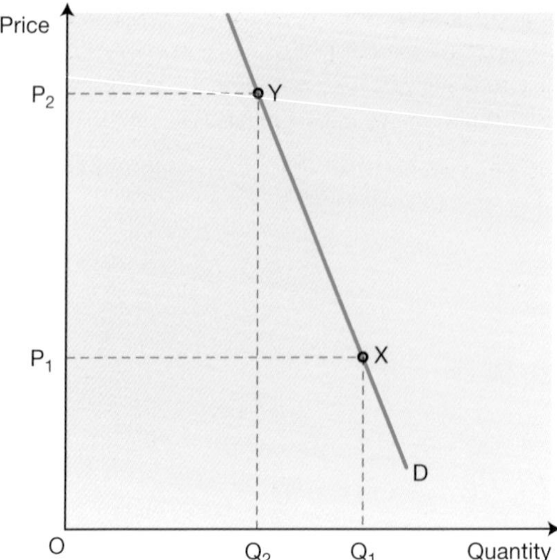

Figure 20.3 *Monopoly and misallocation of resources*

monopolist will make higher profit. The monopolist has benefited from this change, but at the expense of the consumers – fewer consumers now have the product *and* consumers are paying a higher price than when the market was perfectly competitive.

In a competitive market, firms will constantly strive to improve the efficiency with which they use the factors of production to produce goods. Since perfectly competitive firms only make normal profits in the long run, individual firms cannot afford to relax because if other firms discover lower-cost methods of production, those firms will cut their average costs. Any firm not using these new cost-saving methods will become uncompetitive and will be forced out of the market.

In contrast, a monopolist can make abnormal profit without necessarily losing sales because barriers to entry prevent competition. Thus in monopoly there is a possibility that a firm can become complacent because it can afford to become inefficient and yet still make more than normal profits.

Some large-scale monopolists, such as utility companies, will not necessarily produce at the lowest point of ATC because the firm needs a high capacity for peak-time supply. During off-peak periods it will be producing a lower output, not fully using its fixed capital resources. In these situations, ATC will be quite high and inefficiency results. However, this inefficiency is likely to occur in any market condition and so it results from the nature of the industry rather than the market structure.

Potential benefits from monopoly

Internal economies of scale leading to lower prices

A monopolist may benefit from economies of scale so much that, even when it adds on its profit margin, its price is less than the price in a perfectly competitive market.

Figure 20.4 shows two average total cost curves in a market. ATC (PC) is the average total cost curve of a firm in a perfectly competitive market. Since each firm in a perfectly competitive market is too small to influence market supply, there is little scope for internal economies of scale in the market. ATC (PC) is based on the assumption that the firm has a limited level of capital and therefore diseconomies of scale occur at low levels of output. The lowest point of ATC (PC) is shown by

Point X, giving an average total cost of C_P at the most efficient point on the ATC curve. Since firms in a perfectly competitive market only earn normal profit, which is included as a cost in ATC (PC), C_P will also be the long-run price at which the product is sold in a perfectly competitive market.

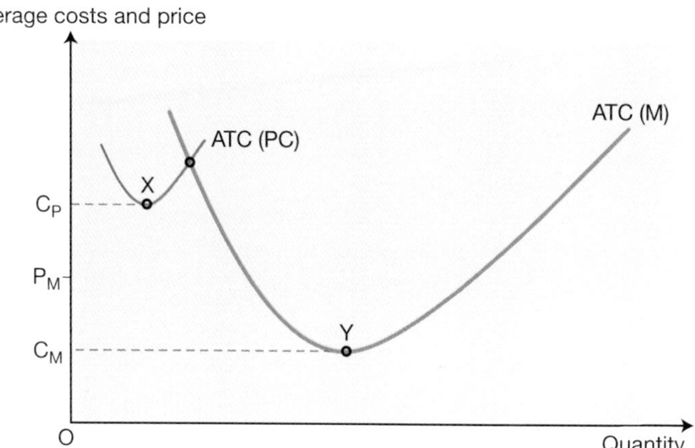

Figure 20.4 *Internal economies of scale and average costs*

ATC (M) is the average total cost curve of a monopolist. Since the monopolist supplies the whole market, there is considerable scope for internal economies of scale. ATC (M) is based on the assumption that the firm has a high level of capital that reduces average costs and allows the firm to produce a high quantity before diseconomies of scale occur. The lowest point of ATC (M) is shown by Point Y, giving an average total cost of C_M at the most efficient point on the ATC curve. Since monopolists earn abnormal/supernormal profit, the price will be set above this level. The extent to which the monopolist's price exceeds C_M will depend on factors such as price elasticity of demand and the degree to which other goods can be substituted for the good.

In Figure 20.4 there are considerable internal economies of scale achieved by the monopolist. Even if it therefore sets a price that is double its average total costs, as shown by price P_M, that price would still be below the perfectly competitive market price of C_P. Where there is considerable scope for internal economies of scale, it is quite possible that a monopolist will charge a lower price than that charged in a perfectly competitive market. In these situations, the fall in ATC outweighs the impact that the monopolist's abnormal profits have on the market price.

Greater innovation

Patent and copyright laws encourage firms to invent and innovate, as they give a monopoly to the inventor for a period of years. Society benefits from these new inventions in the form of newer and often more sophisticated goods. Some patents are for processes that may improve the quality of a good or lower the cost of production; both of these factors will benefit consumers.

In perfectly competitive markets, firms are driven by the desire to keep costs low, so that they can remain competitive. This tends to mean that firms are productively efficient as they produce at the lowest point of average total cost. However, it discourages innovation and new inventions. High research and development costs may force a firm out of the market before it can benefit from new inventions.

Typically, business activities, such as the research and development expenditure needed to create new inventions, are funded by a firm's retained profits. In a perfectly competitive market there is unlikely to be sufficient profit to finance this type of activity because all firms are just making normal profit. In contrast, firms with monopoly power will earn abnormal profits and therefore have the financial resources to finance activities such as research and development. Thus concentrated markets, particularly oligopoly – where there is scope to take market share from competitors – tend to be more fruitful in the creation of innovative products.

More choice

Usually, monopoly will restrict choice, as a pure monopoly will possess 100% of the market and so there is little to be gained by providing alternatives. In fact, these alternatives may lead to higher average costs because there will be less scope for internal economies of scale.

However, in certain circumstances monopoly may provide wider choice for consumers. For example, radio listeners who require a music channel tend to prefer popular music to classical music. At one time, all radio was controlled by a BBC monopoly. The BBC provided two main music stations: a popular music channel which attracted about 90% of music listeners; and a classical channel that catered for the other 10%. When commercial radio was launched nationally, all of the early channels focused on popular music because it was more profitable. The fifth channel to launch was faced with a choice: it could target a possible fifth of 90% (18% of music listeners) by offering popular music or it could gain a certain 10% by offering classical music. It chose to provide popular music, which meant that the first five commercial radio stations all played popular music. Eventually, when a tenth music channel was formed, the owners decided to focus on classical music. Economically, the monopoly situation meant that two channels catered for the whole population. In a competitive market it required 10 channels (and thus far more scarce resources) in order to meet the needs of all radio listeners.

REALWORLD ECONOMICS 20.1

The global pharmaceutical industry

The pharmaceutical industry is one market in which considerable monopoly power exists. On a global scale, research by *Forbes* in 2014 revealed this industry to be the most profitable large-scale industry in the world. *Forbes* measured profitability by measuring profit as a percentage of sales revenue. Table 20.2 shows the sales revenue, profits and market shares of the largest 10 global pharmaceutical companies.

There are over 600 competitors in this market. The five-firm concentration ratio is 40.62%, which is much lower than concentration ratios in many other global industries. Given that the concentration ratio is a very good measure of monopoly power, why is the global pharmaceutical industry so profitable? Pfizer, the world's second largest pharmaceutical company, made $22 billion profit from sales of $52.7 billion in 2013–14. For every dollar it earned, it made a profit of 42 cents – a phenomenal achievement.

The explanation lies in the characteristics of the industry. Developing new drugs is a very expensive undertaking, with much research and development proving to be unsuccessful. Furthermore, for safety reasons the testing process takes many years and can lead to the refusal of a drug that meets its main purpose but has potentially damaging side effects on patients. Successful research and development therefore tends to be highly rewarding for companies, with high prices for drugs that are eventually accepted as a suitable treatment. Patents lead to limited competition. If only one drug is patented for a particular treatment, the company has a worldwide monopoly in the provision of drugs to treat that illness.

High prices for drugs arise from a combination of factors. Consumers value these treatments because they can have dramatic effects on the quality of life and even prove to be life-saving goods. Of critical importance is the fact that in most countries, individual consumers are not expected to pay the selling price. In the UK, the National Health Service or private insurance companies actually pay the money. The NHS has agreed a maximum payment of £12 billion for branded drugs in 2014, with a further £2 billion for non-branded (generic) drugs. With a population of 64.5 million, this means that the NHS spends the equivalent of £2,170 per person each year on drugs alone. This figure excludes drug spending by private health providers.

Doctors in the UK are encouraged to prescribe generic rather than patented drugs, since these are much cheaper

Table 20.2 *Profitability of the world's largest pharmaceutical companies, 2013–14*

Company	Annual sales ($ billion)	Profit ($ billion)	Profit as a % of sales	Market share (%)
Novartis (Switzerland)	57.9	9.2	16	9.45
Pfizer (USA)	52.7	22	42	8.60
Roche (Switzerland)	50.5	12	24	8.24
Sanofi (France)	43.7	4.9	11	7.13
Merck & Co (USA)	44.1	4.4	10	7.20
GSK (UK)	41.4	8.5	21	6.76
AstraZeneca (UK)	25.7	2.6	10	4.19
Eli Lilly (USA)	23.1	4.7	20	3.77
Abbott Labs (USA)	21.8	2.6	12	3.56
Amgen (USA)	18.7	5.1	27	3.05
Average =			19%	
5-firm concentration ratio =				40.62%
10-firm concentration ratio =				61.95%

High drug prices last for the period of the patents, which is usually 20 years. Once a patent has expired, any company can produce a drug using the same formula. These 'generic' drugs are much cheaper. For example, the patent for Nurofen expired in 1985 and there are many companies producing the generic alternative – Ibuprofen (which uses the same ingredients). Until 1985, a pack of 16 caplets of Nurofen was priced at over £5. Since the expiry of the patent it still attracts brand loyal customers, who will pay £2 at Tesco. Ibuprofen – the generic equivalent – is available for 16 pence in Tesco.

One reason for Pfizer's profit is the number of unique patents it currently possesses. In time these patents will expire. At present, drug companies are making high profits because of the success of existing patents. However, this may be short term. In 2016, seven of the world's largest 10 prescription drugs will suffer from the end of their patents in key developed countries. As a consequence, spending on patented drugs is declining with an expected worldwide fall of $127 billion from 2012 to 2016, as patents expire and are replaced by cheaper, generic drugs. Countries such as Japan and the UK are also intensifying efforts to make doctors prescribe generic drugs, rather than branded goods on which patents have expired.

Sources: Forbes, 2014 and IMS Institute for Healthcare Informatics, 'The global use of medicines: outlook through 2016', published in July 2012.

Discussion point

Discuss the reasons why the global pharmaceutical industry is so profitable, despite its relatively low concentration ratio.

Review questions

Total: 60 marks

1 The legal definition of a monopoly in the UK is a firm with a market share of at least:

A 20% B 25% C 33% D 50% *(1 mark)*

2 Which one of these factors might be a barrier to entry to a market?

A Homogeneous products
B Many buyers and many sellers
C Patent laws
D Perfect knowledge *(1 mark)*

3 Abnormal profits would not result from:

A A high concentration ratio
B Monopoly power
C Perfect mobility of factors of production
D Product differentiation *(1 mark)*

The following data apply to questions 4 and 5.

Firm:	E	F	G	H	I	J
Market share (%) in 2015:	5	8	10	15	20	25

Firm J takes over Firm G

4 The four-firm concentration ratio *before* the takeover is:

A 70% B 78% C 87% D 95% *(1 mark)*

5 The four-firm concentration ratio *after* the takeover is:

A 70% B 78% C 87% D 95% *(1 mark)*

6 What is meant by the term 'pure monopoly'? *(3 marks)*

7 What is meant by the term 'monopoly power'? *(3 marks)*

8 Explain how 'natural monopoly' can occur. *(5 marks)*

9 Explain how concentration ratios provide an indication of the level of monopoly power in an industry. *(5 marks)*

10 Explain how internal economies of scale can act as a barrier to entry into a market. *(6 marks)*

11 Explain how advertising can increase the market power of a firm. *(6 marks)*

12 Explain two possible causes of monopoly. *(8 marks)*

13 Explain, using a diagram, how monopoly might lead to higher prices and profits. *(9 marks)*

14 Explain two possible benefits of monopoly to consumers. *(10 marks)*

The competitive market process

This chapter provides a brief introduction to the competitive market process. It examines how competition is based on price and then studies alternative non-price factors on which the competitive market process may be based.

The bases of competition

The Organisation for Economic Cooperation and Development (OECD) is an international body that was established in 1961 to encourage economic development through the sharing of information and ideas and the encouragement of trade between market economies. The OECD tries to improve the competitiveness of its member countries, and the firms from those countries, in the context of the world economy. It defines a **firm's competitiveness** as: 'the ability to produce better than other firms, the right goods or services of the right quality at the right price and the right time'. In effect, competitiveness is meeting customers' needs more effectively and more efficiently than other firms.

Although the OECD is a firm believer in the market economy, this definition recognises that, unlike perfect competition, price is not the only factor on which competition is based.

Price competition

The model of perfect competition assumes that all goods are homogeneous. Consequently, competition is based solely on price, as factors such as product quality and the quality of the service provided will be identical in every firm. However, some economists even refute this theoretical concept, arguing that there is only one possible price – the market price. Consequently all firms are reacting to the market price rather than competing on the basis of price.

In other market structures, product differentiation exists and so price is not the only factor to consider. However, price will be a significant influence in market structures such as monopolistic competition and oligopoly. In these markets, consumers will want value for money and therefore will not necessarily choose the 'best' product if it is priced excessively.

Price competition will be most significant in monopolistic competition, where there are very many firms, each with differentiated products. The sheer volume of suppliers (and thus products) will mean that the differentiation between products is likely to be small in most monopolistically competitive markets. As a result, price elasticity of demand will be highly elastic and so a small change in price can lead to a considerable change in the quantity demanded. This suggests that price competition will be a very important feature of this type of market structure.

In the case of an oligopoly market structure, there are a few firms, each with differentiated products. With fewer products, these levels of differentiation are likely to be much higher than in a market structure with very many firms. Furthermore, with less competition between firms there are likely to be significant barriers to entry, and so profits will probably be much higher. These profits provide funding for activities such as research and development, marketing and quality improvement, all of which can create brand loyalty and further product differentiation. As a result, consumers will perceive the products to be more differentiated, with few close substitutes. This will lead to price inelastic demand, and so changes in price will not have a large influence on the quantity demanded.

Conclusion

The greater the degree of product differentiation, the less influence price will have on the competitive market process.

Some of the main examples of non-price competition are introduced below. More detailed consideration of non-price competition will be provided in the second year of the course.

Non-price competition

Firms do not just compete on the basis of price. Three examples of non-price competition are improving products, reducing costs and improving the quality of the service provided.

- *Improving products* This can be achieved through research and development (R&D), which can lead to higher quality or more durable products. Product improvement might take the form of providing greater variety, to suit consumers' wants, or offering products that provide more functions (such as mobile phones). In some cases, effective marketing may improve the perception of the product in the eyes of consumers, rather than focusing on physical changes to the product. Nevertheless this does add value in the eyes of the consumer and is therefore meeting a want, even if the firm has partially created that want. Consequently, firms with improved products achieve product differentiation and charge higher prices. Where the higher price more than compensates for the costs of improving the product, the firm will generate greater profits.
- *Reducing costs* In some cases research and development is used to improve the process of manufacturing a good or providing a service. This will therefore lead to lower costs of production. Lower average costs can also be achieved by improving the method of production through changing the balance of factors of production, such as replacing labour with more efficient capital equipment, or by improving the productivity of the factors of production – for example, by training the workforce more efficiently. Lower average costs will enable the firm either to keep its price the same and earn more profit from each product that it sells, or to lower the price and benefit from an increase in the quantity sold. The ideal approach will depend on the price elasticity of demand for the product and the profit margin made from each product.
- *Improving the quality of the service provided* In the UK, expenditure on services is greater than expenditure on goods. In order to compete effectively, improvements to the quality of the service provided can be essential if a firm wishes to remain

competitive. Quality can be measured in terms of delivery, reliability, customer care and the extent to which the service matches the exact requirements of the consumer. The sale of goods can also depend on the quality of service provided, as an excellent good may lack value if it is not delivered promptly.

Other forms of non-price competition are factors such as branding, advertising, special offers and the quality of management. Each of these factors can enhance the reputation of a good (or firm) and thus improve popularity and demand.

Where markets are not perfect, there will always be scope for firms to take advantage of their monopoly power and thus exploit consumers. The lack of perfect knowledge means that consumers are unaware of the costs of making many products. Where firms compete using non-price methods, it is possible that competition may appear to be very vigorous, and yet all firms make considerable profits. Consumers are often dissatisfied with petrol prices but still purchase petrol as there are no close alternatives. If all suppliers maintain the same price, there may be an illusion of competition (because in perfect competition all firms will charge the same price), but these prices may be allowing high profits to be made. However, as firms' profits are not declared until the end of the financial year, consumers will be unaware of this exploitation until it is too late.

REALWORLD ECONOMICS 20.1

Supermarkets

In the UK, supermarkets use both price and non-price competition. Until recent years, Asda was noted for competing on the basis of price, whereas Sainsbury's aimed to create an image of quality but at reasonable prices – hence the slogan 'Good food costs less at Sainsbury's'. Tesco's market leadership arose from a combination of accessibility (it had more stores and was therefore closer to more customers) and product differentiation, with many branded goods and three own-label ranges aimed at customers wanting (a) quality, (b) mid-price/quality, and (c) low prices. In this way, Tesco believed it was able to appeal to a wider range of customers than its competitors.

In comparison to other countries, UK supermarkets tended to focus much more on non-price competition, a strategy that depended on product differentiation created by high-levels of loyalty towards certain brands, such as Heinz, Kellogg's, Whiskas and Persil, and loyalty to the supermarket brand too.

The recession began a change in attitudes, with consumers focusing much more on low price than other attributes. This shift was accentuated by the desire of many families for fresher products, requiring smaller, more regular shops rather than one large shop at the weekend. At the same time, Tesco's decision to reduce its range of economy products helped to create more of a gap for discount supermarkets, such as Aldi and Lidl. In 2010, Aldi and Lidl combined had a 3% market share; by the end of 2014 this had increased to 8.6%. This success has been built on providing a smaller range of alternative products, but bulk buying the items that are offered. Costs are also lowered by not selling many branded goods – 95% of Aldi's goods are own brands.

Table 21.1 *Supermarket profits, 2013–14*

Supermarket	Profit (loss) (£ million)	Profit as a % of sales
Tesco	2631	4.1
Sainsbury's	1009	4.2
Morrisons	(95)	-0.5
Asda	719	3.2
Aldi	271	5.1

The other supermarkets have intensified competition by focusing on price guarantee/price comparison tactics, whereby customers can be refunded if prices are more expensive than certain competitors. Has this vigorous competition affected supermarket profits?

Profits for 2013–14 suggest that consumers are still the victims of monopoly power wielded by supermarkets. As shown in Table 21.1, Tesco was able to record an operating profit of £2.6 billion and Sainsbury's profit exceeded £1 billion. Aldi, despite its reputation for low prices, recorded the highest profit as a percentage of sales at 5.1%. Its strategy of cutting costs and focusing on non-branded goods appeals to the shopping habits of supermarket customers.

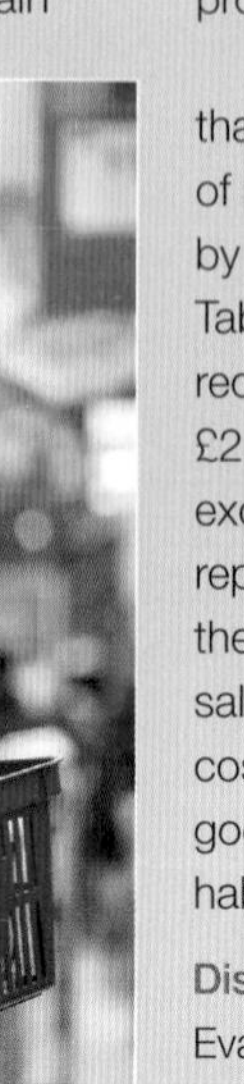

The rise of the discount supermarkets has intensified price competition

Discussion point

Evaluate whether price competition is now the most important factor in the competitive market process amongst UK supermarkets?

Review questions

Total: 15 marks

1 Which one of the following is *not* an example of a competitive market process used to improve a firm's competitiveness?

A Better quality of service
B Improving products
C Lowering costs
D Increasing price *(1 mark)*

2 In which situation is price competition most likely?

A High levels of product differentiation and price elastic demand
B High levels of product differentiation and price inelastic demand
C Low levels of product differentiation and price elastic demand
D Low levels of product differentiation and price inelastic demand *(1 mark)*

3 Copy out the text below and fill in the four gaps in the sentence.

According to the OECD, a firm will be competitive if it provides the right ______ at the right ______ at the right ______ and the right ______. *(4 marks)*

4 Explain why price competition is likely to be more significant in monopolistic competition than in an oligopoly market. *(4 marks)*

5 State one example of non-price competition and explain how it can improve a firm's competitiveness. *(5 marks)*

Topic 4 Exam-style questions

AS LEVEL PAPER 1

Total: 50 marks

Context – Whitbread

Extract A Data on ownership of public houses, 1989 and 2004

Owners of public houses	Number	(%)
National breweries		
Bass	7190	12.0
Allied	6678	11.1
Whitbread	6483	10.8
Grand Met	6419	10.7
Courage	5002	8.3
S&N	2287	3.8
Regional breweries	*9713*	*16.2*
Independently owned	*16,228*	*27.1*
	60,000	**100**

◂ **Table A** *Market share of UK public houses, 1989*

Owners of public houses	Number	(%)
National breweries	0	0
Regional breweries	8589	14.4
National chains of public houses	23,857	40.1
Other chains of public houses	10,268	17.2
Independently owned	16,850	28.3
	59,564	**100**

Sources: www.parliament.uk and House of Commons – DTI report

Table B *Market share of UK public houses, 2004*

Extract B The changing UK market for beer

In 1989 the market for beer was vertically integrated, with the breweries owning both the farms which grew the hops and most of the public houses in which beer was sold. Extract A, Table A, shows that in 1989, 72.9% of public houses were owned by breweries that ensured only their beer was sold in the 'tied' houses they owned. Breweries like Whitbread, which owned 10.8% of the pubs, knew that they could expect to achieve a market share of at least 10.8%, with additional sales from independently owned pubs, many of which had agreements to buy all of their beer from a single brewer in return for favours such as low-interest loans. For most beers, all of the profit made from a pint of beer went to the breweries. Furthermore, many breweries had considerable local monopoly power, with the vast majority of pubs in some towns being owned by one brewer and thus only selling their beer.

Government intervention in 1989 by the MMC – the predecessor of the CMA (the Competition and Markets Authority) – led to breweries having to sell most of their tied houses. This led to lower profit levels. Some breweries, faced with low offer prices for their pubs (because of the sudden availability of lots of pubs on the market), chose to sell their breweries and focus on being a chain of public houses.

Extract A, Table B shows the results of government intervention. By 2004, there were no public houses 'tied' to breweries. However, national chains of public houses now exert monopoly power to some extent, with the two largest chains having market shares of 15% and 14% respectively. On the other hand, the concentration ratio of brewers has increased. Large, multinational breweries were the only organisations in a position to buy the breweries made available. As a result, the six-firm concentration ratio for beer production changed from about 60% in 1989 to 84% in 2004, with many of the breweries now owned by overseas companies.

Whitbread chose to use the revenue earned from selling a combination of pubs and breweries to diversify into other markets, such as restaurants, coffees shops, leisure clubs and hotels.

Source: Whitbread plc

Extract C Whitbread's new markets

Since 2001 Whitbread has changed its focus. Having brewed beer since 1742, Whitbread moved out of brewing and pubs and focused on its newer interests, though it also sold its David Lloyd Leisure Clubs and TGI Friday's restaurants in 2007.

Since 2007 it has focused on coffee shops (Costa), budget hotels (Premier Inn) and restaurants (such as Brewers Fayre and Beefeater), which are mainly located close to its Premier Inn hotels.

Whitbread's focus has been on finding expanding markets in which it can achieve product differentiation from its competitors and gain monopoly power. It has also focused on the quality of service and competitive prices. Both Premier Inn and Costa achieve higher customer satisfaction ratings than their competitors.

Since 1997, the UK has moved towards a coffee culture, with coffee shops experiencing high growth rates. In January 2015, coffee shop sales were almost 11% higher than a year before. Costa (the market leader, with a market share of 46.5% of branded coffee shops) was a major beneficiary – its total revenue increased by 20% in 2014. Analysts expect the UK coffee market to keep growing for at least another 10 years. In 2014, Costa's profit was 13.6% of sales revenue.

Whitbread's hotels and restaurants also achieved growth, with total revenue increasing by 10% in 2014. The budget hotel market is about 20% of the total UK hotel market, but is expected to grow to between 25% and 33%. Premier Inn's market share is less than 10% of the hotel market, but almost 50% of the budget hotel market, which is the fastest growing sector of the hotel trade.

Questions

Total: 50 marks

1 Define the term 'monopoly power'. *(3 marks)*

2 Using Extract A, Table A, calculate the four-firm concentration ratio for ownership of UK public houses in 1989. *(4 marks)*

3 Using Extract A, Tables A and B, identify two significant points of comparison in the ownership of public houses in 1989 and in 2004. *(4 marks)*

4 The demand curve D_1 and supply curve S_1 in Figure A show the market for public houses in 1989.

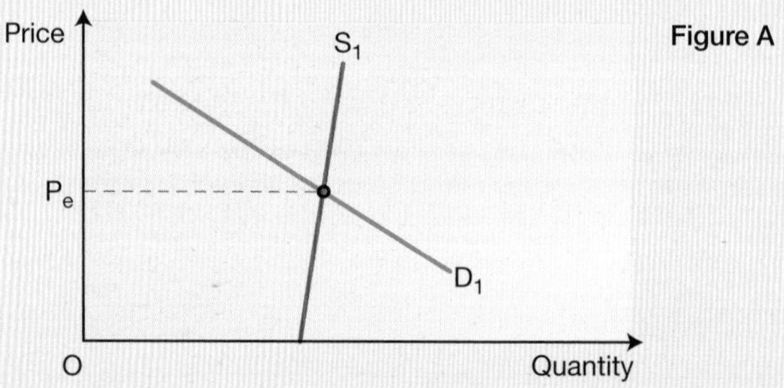

Figure A

In 1989, government intervention led to a number of breweries deciding to sell their public houses. Amend the diagram to show the result of this decision and its impact on the equilibrium price. *(4 marks)*

5 Explain why Whitbread moved from being a brewery to focusing on coffee shops and budget hotels. *(10 marks)*

6 Assess whether Whitbread's recent high profits have been achieved as a result of product differentiation and barriers to entry. *(25 marks)*

Topic 5

The market mechanism, market failure & government intervention in markets

How markets & prices allocate resources

This chapter studies how a market economy allocates resources. It examines the rationing, incentive and signalling functions of prices in coordinating the decisions of buyers and sellers. The chapter concludes by studying how the price mechanism resolves the basic economic problem of scarcity in a market economy.

The rationing, incentive and signalling functions of prices

Price carries out three main functions in allocating resources and coordinating the decisions of buyers and sellers.

1 The rationing function of prices

Price adjusts to ensure that scarce resources, which have alternative uses, are rationed so that they are allocated to the production of the most highly desired goods.

Economics is concerned with scarcity, based on consumers having unlimited wants but only access to limited resources with which to satisfy those wants. In a market economy, price acts as the way of rationing those scarce resources. If a good has high demand, relative to the resources available to provide it, this will lead to a high price in a market economy. In contrast, if a good is abundant but the demand for it is relatively low, then a market economy will set a low price for this good. For example, diamonds are a product with a reasonable level of demand, but most consumers do not purchase them regularly. This is to a large extent because diamonds are difficult to produce, as they depend on the discovery of a natural resource that is in limited supply. As there is a reasonable demand but very limited availability (supply), the interaction of demand and supply leads to a very high price. The price mechanism is, in effect, using a high price to ration the amount that buyers demand to a level that is

Key terms

The **rationing function of prices** arises because it is not possible to satisfy the unlimited wants of consumers with the scarce resources available. Price acts as a rationing device, as only consumers prepared to pay the market price are able to purchase. If a good becomes scarce, its price will rise, discouraging buyers and so preserving stocks.

The **signalling function of prices** refers to the importance of price in helping buyers and sellers make decisions about whether it is worthwhile to buy or sell a product.

The **incentive function of prices** refers to the way in which low prices act as an incentive for consumers to buy more of a product in order to increase their satisfaction, while high prices act as an incentive for suppliers to supply more in order to increase profit.

consistent with the low level of supply. Only those buyers who value diamonds very highly will pay the high market price.

The term 'ration' implies shortage. However, as economics studies 'scarcity', all economic goods experience scarcity to some extent. Thus the word 'ration' can be interchanged with 'allocation' in this context. The price is used to 'allocate' the appropriate number of goods to appropriate buyers. Thus the rationing (allocation) function also applies to goods with low demand and high supply. In the UK there is generally a high demand for water but also an abundant supply. The price per litre is quite low because this is consistent with the high level of supply. The low price rations/allocates water so that demand is encouraged by the low price and thus it matches the level of water available (the supply).

2 The incentive function of prices

Buyers aim to maximise their satisfaction by purchasing goods that give them high levels of welfare/happiness. If the price of a good is low, a buyer can increase their overall welfare by purchasing more of that particular good. The low price acts as an incentive to purchase more of that good. Similarly, if there is a high price, the buyer who wishes to maximise their welfare would buy less of that particular good. Instead, they would be given an incentive to look at other goods in order to maximise their welfare.

The incentive function also applies to sellers, who are aiming to maximise their profits. A high market price encourages sellers to supply more of a good, so that they can earn higher profit. However, a low price would give a firm the incentive to produce less of that particular good. In this case the supplier has an incentive to switch the resources that they possess to the production of a good that sells at a price that gives them a better chance of making profit.

The market economy gives firms and consumers the knowledge that they need in order to take decisions that will maximise their outcomes. High prices provide an incentive to firms to supply a greater quantity in order to maximise profit; low prices provide an incentive to consumers to adjust their spending patterns in favour of that good.

Price can also provide a disincentive – low prices provide firms with a disincentive to supply goods; high prices provide consumers with a disincentive to demand goods.

3 The signalling function of prices

Changes in prices provide a signal to buyers and sellers to show them whether to buy (or sell) more (or fewer) goods in a particular market.

The market economy encourages both firms and consumers to switch their preferences in order to maximise their profits or welfare, in response to changes in the conditions of supply and demand. These changing conditions lead to a change in price that gives a signal to the consumers and sellers, indicating the action they should take in order to maximise their welfare/profits.

If a market change leads to a higher price, this will give a signal to firms that they should supply more in order to make higher profit. However, this higher price will signal to consumers that they should reduce/contract their demand if they are to maximise their welfare.

Similarly, if the market price falls, this will give a signal to suppliers to supply less, or even leave the market if they can no longer cover their costs. A low price signals to consumers that they should purchase more of a particular good in order to maximise their welfare.

How the price mechanism resolves the basic economic problem in a market economy

In a pure market economy, the allocation of resources is determined by demand and supply. High demand shows a great want for a particular product while low demand shows a lack of consumer interest in a good. Supply depends on the cost of the scarce resources required to make that good. Low costs will make it easier to supply and therefore encourage greater supply, while high costs will make supply more difficult and therefore lead to a decrease in supply.

Prices are set by the interaction of demand by buyers and supply by sellers. A high price can result from a high demand by buyers, a low supply by sellers, or a combination of both. Similarly a low price can result from low demand by buyers and/or high supply by sellers. Through the price mechanism, the basic economic problem of scarcity will be resolved.

In theory, competitive markets help allocate resources effectively. If consumers want more of a product, there is an increase in demand and thus price, attracting suppliers to use scarce resources to make more of this product. Suppliers are also motivated to use resources efficiently, as suppliers with lower costs make more profit.

The market/price mechanism is a very effective way of allocating resources. Wants are indicated by demand, and so high demand is a sign that resources should be allocated to produce those goods. High prices that result from high demand encourage suppliers to supply more products, to earn high profits. As more suppliers enter the market, price falls. The mechanism has led to a shift of resources to the production of popular goods and away from unpopular (and hence unprofitable) goods.

This mechanism can be shown using supply and demand diagrams, which are based on the assumptions of a perfectly competitive market. Any change to a market must lead to one of four changes, as indicated below:

- an increase in demand, possibly caused by an increase in consumers' disposable incomes;
- a decrease in demand, possibly caused by a change in tastes away from a particular good;
- an increase in supply, possibly caused by more efficient production methods leading to higher productivity of factors of production;
- a decrease in supply, possibly caused by a shortage of raw materials.

In the example below, we will consider Change 2 – a decrease in demand caused by a change in tastes away from a particular good.

What change would you expect from a decrease in demand? Logically, if a good loses popularity, you would expect price and profit to fall. This would lead to scarce resources being moved away from its production and into the production of more popular/profitable goods.

Figure 22.1 shows how the price mechanism resolves the problem of scarcity when there is a fall in consumer demand for a particular good.

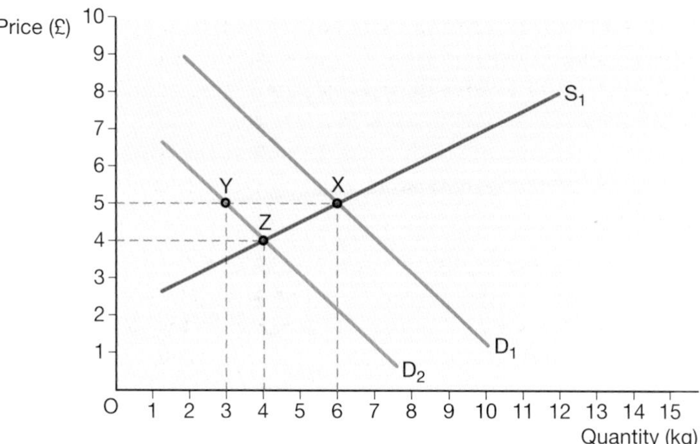

Figure 22.1 *How the price mechanism resolves the basic economic problem*

S_1 and D_1 are the original supply and demand curves. The equilibrium point is shown by Point X, giving an equilibrium price of £5 and an equilibrium quantity of 6 units. The decrease in demand is shown by the shift from D_1 to D_2. At the original equilibrium price of £5, there is now an excess supply of 3 units (shown by YX). In order to eliminate this excess supply, the price falls and reaches a new equilibrium point at Z. The market price has adjusted automatically to overcome the disequilibrium at £5. At £5, consumers want only 3 units (rather than the original 6), confirming the fact that consumers now place a lower value on this good.

The original supply curve S_1 slopes upwards from left to right because suppliers can make more profit at higher prices. However, this diagram shows that price has fallen and so supply has contracted along the supply curve from X to Z. At the lower price of £4, there is less scope for firms to make profit and so supply has fallen from 6 units to 4 units. This fall is likely to be a combination of two changes: (a) firms leaving the industry, and (b) existing firms cutting back on supply of this good in order to switch resources to more profitable goods.

In contrast, the lower price makes the good more attractive to consumers who believe that they will get better value for money at £4. The quantity demanded is therefore 4 units (rather than the 3 units shown at £5).

Overall, the short-run effect has been a price adjustment that switches resources away from the production of this good, as shown by the fall in production from 6 units to 4 units. The unemployed resources made available from this decline in demand will shift to goods experiencing an increase in demand.

The change in equilibrium price has acted as a **signal** to buyers (to buy more) and sellers (to supply less). The lower price has provided an **incentive** for buyers to buy more (shown by the move from Y to Z) but a **disincentive** for sellers (or an **incentive** to cut output from 6 units to 4 units). Since this good is less popular, the low price has **rationed** (or allocated) the resources made available for its production, diverting these resources to more profitable uses.

If firms believe that this decrease in demand is permanent, in the long run they will shift fixed capital away from the production of this good. In the long run this will move the supply curve to the left, giving the market as a whole less capacity to supply. This process of exit from the market is likely to lead to a rise in price, helping existing firms to restore their profits and thus remain in the market.

A decrease in supply arises because more scarce resources are needed to produce a given quantity of goods (thus increasing the costs of production of the good). Logically this should lead to a decrease in the production of that good – see Figure 22.2(a). In contrast, an increase in supply arises because fewer scarce resources are needed to produce a given quantity of goods (thus decreasing the costs of production of the good). This change should lead to an increase in the production of that good – see Figure 22.2(b).

Figure 22.2 *The working of the price mechanism for a change in supply*

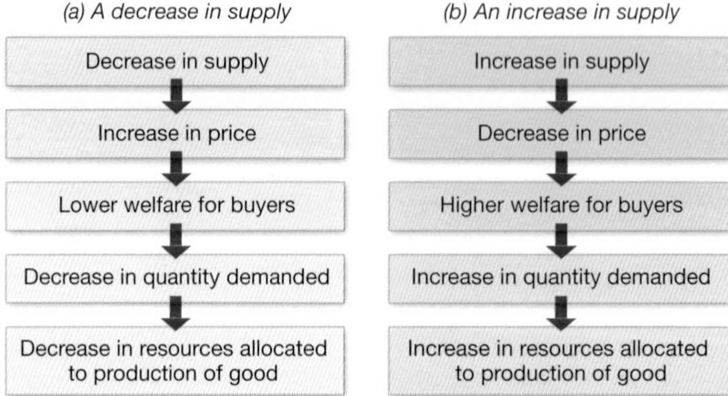

Does the price mechanism in a market economy solve scarcity in the best possible way? This is open to debate. In a market economy, an individual who is prepared to pay a high price will be able to purchase goods. However, this may reflect their wealth and income rather than their basic desire for a good. This issue will be examined further in Chapter 28.

REALWORLD **ECONOMICS** 22.1

The rise and fall of the UK coal industry

The working of the price mechanism can be illustrated through the UK coal industry. In the short run, prices fluctuated significantly in response to changes in demand or conditions of supply. However, in the long run the market tended to adjust, leading to relatively small changes in prices overall. Table 22.1 shows the peaks and troughs of UK prices for coal over the last 160 years.

In the nineteenth century the growth of UK manufacturing led to steady growth in the demand for coal. In 1854 UK coal mining employed just over 300,000 coal miners; by 1913 employment in the coal industry had risen to over 1 million workers. The increases in price in Table 22.1 tended to arise from short-term periods of growth, such as 1900 and 1961. The decreases in price tended to occur during recessions, such as 1880 and 1928. Overall, the industry grew steadily until its peak in 1913, when annual production reached 295 million tons. From 1854 to 1913 the increasing demand for coal led to higher prices and profits, which then attracted greater supply. Resources (such as labour) were attracted into the industry because of the profits available. The increase in supply in turn led to a steadying of prices within the range shown in Table 22.1.

Year	Price per ton (£)
1854	50
1880	33
1900	62
1928	30
1961	62
1973	25
1983	66
2000	30
2014	45

Table 22.1 *Price of UK coal per ton (at 1962 prices)*

UK coal had a reputation for high quality; this factor and the efficiency of production meant that the UK had a 59% market share of world coal in 1923. However, since then UK coal mining has declined for four main reasons:

Buffeted by market forces – a bleak outlook for UK miners

- Low demand, particularly between the two world wars, led to many mines becoming unviable, and lower demand for domestic heating.
- Cheaper coal has become available from other countries, particularly since 1945. The age of UK coal mining has meant that existing coal reserves are much less accessible and more costly to extract than coal in other countries.
- New forms of energy have emerged. In 1950 coal was the primary source of 90% of the UK's energy; by 2013 this had fallen to less than 25%. Petroleum and natural gas now dominate this market.
- Environmental considerations have led to cuts in the use of coal.

Although public ownership restricted the decline of the UK coal industry after 1947, market forces began to impact more noticeably after privatisation in the 1980s and 1990s. Since full exposure to market forces, UK coal mining has declined to less than 6000 workers. Demand factors account for much of this decline, but over 20% of UK electricity is generated by coal. However, that coal is largely imported.

Sources: ONS, World Bank, discussion paper by H. Benyon and A. Cox on 'The decline of King Coal', 1999, and other sources.

Discussion point

Analyse how changes in market forces have led to resources being shifted into and out of coal production in the UK.

Review questions

Total: 25 marks

1 In which one of these situations would the price mechanism allocate *more* resources to the production of a particular good?

A An increase in VAT
B A decrease in the price of a substitute
C A shortage of raw materials
D Introduction of more efficient production methods ***(1 mark)***

2 In which one of these situations would the price mechanism allocate *fewer* resources to the production of a particular good?

A A successful advertising campaign
B Increasing consumer wealth
C An increase in the price of a complement
D A government subsidy on the good ***(1 mark)***

3 Explain the 'rationing' function of price. ***(5 marks)***

4 Explain the 'incentive' function of price. ***(5 marks)***

5 Explain the 'signalling' function of price. ***(4 marks)***

6 With the help of a diagram, explain how the price mechanism resolves the basic economic problem. ***(9 marks)***

The meaning of market failure

This chapter explains the meanings of market failure and a misallocation of resources. The difference between complete market failure and partial market failure is explained. The possible causes of market failure are introduced and a brief summary of how they each lead to market failure is provided. The causes considered are public goods, externalities, merit goods and demerit goods, market imperfections such as monopoly, and inequalities of income and wealth. Each of these is studied in more detail in the next five chapters (Chapters 24 to 28).

Market failure

Key term

Market failure occurs when a market economy does not achieve an efficient allocation of resources.

An economy is efficient if it allocates resources effectively. An economy's efficiency is assessed in the following ways:

- *Productive efficiency* Are firms producing at the lowest possible average costs (i.e. at the minimum point of ATC)?
- *Allocative efficiency* Are the goods produced by an economy finding their way to the consumers who get the greatest welfare/happiness from those goods?

Market failure arises if one or both of the following situations exist:

- firms do not produce at the lowest point of average total cost;
- goods are not allocated to the people that receive the greatest welfare from those goods.

Economies can be organised in three main ways:

- a market economy, in which all goods and services are provided through the interaction of demand and supply;
- a planned or command economy, in which decisions on both production and allocation of resources are made by the government;
- a mixed economy, in which some goods and services are provided through a market economy and some are provided through government planning.

Although the term 'market failure' is applied to 'market economies', its principles can be applied to the two other types of economy too. In fact, it could be argued that the main factor causing the demise of many planned economies, such as Russia's, was their failure to achieve productive efficiency. In contrast, many interventions in market economies are made to try to overcome problems of allocative inefficiency.

Most countries' economies would be classified as mixed economies, though the balance of the mix varies considerably between countries. In the UK, most goods and services are provided through the market economy. However, where there is market failure, government might choose to intervene. This intervention can take the form of government provision of a good or service. However, it is more usual for government to try to influence the market in some way, such as taxation or legislation, in order to overcome the problem of market failure.

Misallocation of resources

In effect, market failure and a misallocation of resources are two ways of saying the same thing. In both cases, productive efficiency and/or allocative efficiency are not achieved and so the economy does not maximise the welfare of its consumers from the scarce resources available to it.

It is important to note that 'misallocation' is *not* just concerned with allocating the goods produced. If goods are not allocated to the right consumer, then clearly there is a misallocation of resources. However, if there are insufficient goods produced, because ATC is not minimised (and so there is productive inefficiency), then it becomes impossible to provide goods to the right consumers because there are not enough goods available. A misallocation of resources thus arises from allocative inefficiency or productive inefficiency or a combination of the two.

Types of market failure

There are two types of market failure: complete market failure and partial market failure.

Complete market failure occurs where a good or service is wanted but there is no firm supplying goods to satisfy that demand. An example is national defence. Although consumers will value defence, they are unlikely to see the benefit directly and be prepared to offer to pay for it. A service that would improve people's welfare is not therefore provided. There is a **missing market.** (A missing market means that there is complete market failure in the provision of a good or service.) Missing markets tend to occur where a good or service provides a collective benefit to a community, but where individuals are unlikely to understand and accurately value the benefit to themselves as individuals. Since this will lead to insufficient revenue for a profit-making firm, complete market failure is often overcome by government provision of the good or service. Individuals will be prepared to pay taxes to the government to provide defence, knowing that everyone else is paying taxes for this purpose too.

Partial market failure occurs more frequently. In this situation, the market economy does establish a market for the product. However, the quantity produced does not achieve a perfect allocation of resources. Often this partial market failure occurs because consumers have insufficient knowledge to appreciate the benefits of the good or service, or may lack the financial resources to pay for it. For example, education and health are both provided privately, but without the government providing free education and health, many people would not receive these services and so the market economy is *underproducing* them. In these two examples, government is more likely to be aware of the financial benefits to both individuals and society. Government is also able to afford the high costs more than individuals. A market economy may overproduce goods. For example, most people consider that too much tobacco is

Key terms

Misallocation of resources occurs when an economy fails to produce goods at the lowest average total cost and/or fails to achieve the goal of providing those goods to the consumers to whom they provide the greatest welfare.

Complete market failure occurs when a good or service is not supplied at all.

Partial market failure occurs when a market exists but where the level of production is too high or too low.

consumed in a free market economy. In this case, government uses measures such as taxation to discourage consumption in order to overcome market failure.

Discussion point

Both market failure and the misallocation of resources depend on value judgements rather than positive statements of fact. The lowest possible point of ATC may be hard to determine because costs are constantly changing. Furthermore, it may be possible to reduce ATC, but existing knowledge may make this impossible to achieve at present. More contentious are debates about to whom resources should be allocated. Supporters of market economies argue that those with greater access to resources (those with more money) have contributed more to the economy and therefore deserve access to more goods and services than people who have contributed less. Other people criticise market economies, arguing that wide discrepancies in income between people mean that it is impossible to achieve allocative efficiency if some people are living in luxury and others are starving.

Key note

When assessing market failure, value judgements are impossible to avoid. For example, people who support individual freedoms might argue that access to alcohol should be freely available. From this viewpoint, people would argue that currently there is underproduction of alcohol because some people who would choose to buy it are prevented by licensing laws. In contrast, other people might argue that people who drink alcohol are not fully aware of its negative effects and that there is therefore overproduction of alcohol. Both groups would see the current situation as market failure, but the first group would believe that the solution would be to produce more alcohol, while the second group would propose a cutback in production of alcohol.

Causes of market failure

This section introduces the main causes of market failure and provides illustrations of market failure that result from each cause. Chapters 24 to 28 provide a more detailed examination of each of these causes of market failure.

Public goods

Street lighting demonstrates the collective benefits of a public good

A public good is a good or service that does not fit well in a market economy, to the extent that it is unlikely to be provided in a market economy. This is because public goods are those where the people who are prepared to pay for them cannot prevent other people from benefiting from them. For example, if a person pays for street lighting, other people who refuse to pay for it can enjoy the benefits too. The street lighting can be used over and over again *and* it can be used by anyone using the street. Other examples of public goods are defence and lighthouses.

Public goods lead to market failure. The market mechanism is designed to deal with interaction between individual buyers (consumers) and individual suppliers (firms). For public goods, the benefits are collective. A group of people (for example, the residents of a country) may have a high desire for a public good, such as defence, because it may provide all of them with a high level of economic welfare. However, each individual is likely to decide not to pay in the hope that there is a sufficient number of other people willing to pay for it. As a rule, nearly everyone takes this view and so the public good is not provided by the market. In the case of street lighting, it may be possible for residents of some streets to organise street lighting, but even this is unlikely as the residents will resent the benefits received by non-residents and people may view it as poor value if they are possibly going to move to a different street in the near future.

In a mixed economy, such as the UK, this market failure can be overcome by government intervention. Government can use taxation to raise money to finance services such as street lighting and national defence.

Externalities

Externalities are the effects of a market decision to produce a good on someone who was not involved in the decision to produce or consume that good. These effects can be favourable to the person who was not involved in the transaction, such as a market gardener benefiting from a neighbour's decision to have beehives on his property. Externalities can also have adverse effects, such as the effect of aircraft noise on people living close to an airport.

Positive externalities

Positive externalities provide benefits to people who do not make a decision to buy a good but who receive beneficial effects from a decision to produce or consume a good. For example, a householder who creates an attractive garden that can be seen by passers-by will bring welfare/happiness to people walking past the garden.

A homeowner tending her front garden – an example of a positive externality

When a person decides to purchase a good in a market economy, the decision is based purely on the benefits received by that person. The person will not consider the positive externalities received by other individuals. For example, a person who pays for education and training should receive additional reward in the form of obtaining a job, which pays a higher income. However, that person's education may enable them to create greater wealth for their firm and thus provide benefits to other stakeholders of that firm, such as fellow workers and shareholders. Education may lead to new inventions that bring benefits to consumers. None of these 'third-party' benefits will be considered by the individual when making their decision on how much education to buy.

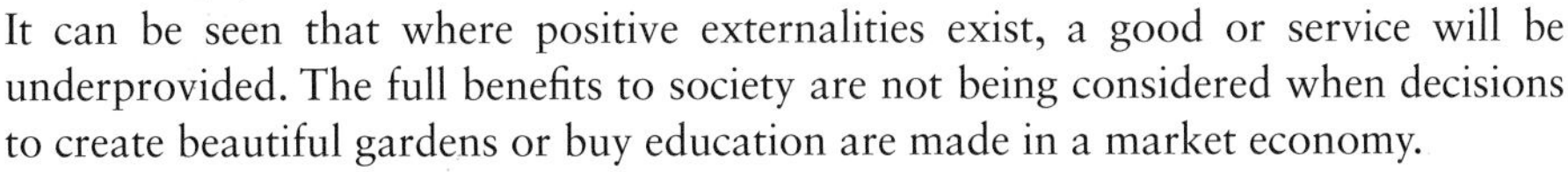

It can be seen that where positive externalities exist, a good or service will be underprovided. The full benefits to society are not being considered when decisions to create beautiful gardens or buy education are made in a market economy.

Key terms

Externalities are the effects of economic activity on third parties, who are not involved and have no say in the economic activity that has taken place.

A **positive externality** describes the benefits that accrue to third parties not involved in an economic activity. These benefits can be passed on due to either the consumption or production of a commodity by other members of society.

A **negative externality** describes the problems experienced by third parties not involved in an economic activity. These problems can be passed on due to either the consumption or production of a commodity by other members of society.

A **merit good** describes a good that is underproduced in a pure market economy.

A **demerit good** describes a good that is overproduced in a pure market economy.

Negative externalities

Negative externalities are the adverse effects on other people when a decision to produce or consume a good is made. A decision to buy a car will lead to pollution that will have a negative effect on passers-by. A decision to manufacture a product can also create the same negative externality.

Consumers in a market economy ignore externalities and so a product with negative externalities will reduce the economic welfare of third parties. For example, an individual's decision to smoke cigarettes will have an adverse effect on 'passive smokers' who inhale the smoke because they are nearby. The smoker will not consider this negative consequence when choosing to buy cigarettes.

It can be seen that where negative externalities exist, a good or service will be overprovided. The negative effects on society are not being considered when decisions to buy a car or smoke cigarettes are made in a market economy.

Summary

In a market economy:

- goods with positive externalities will be underproduced – society would benefit from greater levels of consumption;
- goods with negative externalities will be overproduced – society would benefit from lower levels of consumption.

Merit and demerit goods

Merit/demerit goods are goods that are underprovided/overprovided by the market mechanism.

Merit goods

Underproduction may result from positive externalities but can also be caused by imperfect information. For example, a decision not to undergo a training course may be made because the consumer is unaware of the true benefits of the training.

Regardless of the cause or causes, a market economy will produce too few merit goods because their benefits to society are not fully valued by individual consumers. Examples of merit goods are safety equipment, museums, healthcare and public parks.

Demerit goods

Overproduction may result from negative externalities but can also be caused by imperfect information. For example, a decision to drink alcohol may be made because the consumer is not fully aware of the damaging effects it can have on them.

A market economy will produce too many demerit goods because their negative consequences are not fully considered by individual consumers. Examples of demerit goods are tobacco, alcohol and drugs, such as legal highs.

Monopoly and other market imperfections

There are three main market imperfections that can cause market failure:

- *Monopoly* If there is only one supplier, market failure is likely to occur. The market mechanism operates through the profit motive and in a perfectly competitive market, firms must achieve the lowest possible costs in order to attract consumers. However, if there is only one supplier, then consumers have no alternative choice – other than to forego the product. Consequently, there is less incentive for the supplier to reduce costs and therefore product inefficiency will arise. A lack of productive efficiency is an example of market failure.

- *Imperfect information* Perfect competition relies on consumers and producers having perfect information. If consumers lack the necessary information to choose the best or cheapest product, the market will fail. If producers are not aware of the cheapest method of production, average costs will not be minimised and therefore market failure occurs.
- *Immobility of factors of production* In a market economy, changes in price act as signals to the market to adjust the allocation of resources. However, if resources (factors of production) are immobile, they may not shift easily between alternative uses. For example, immobile labour may stay in an occupation that offers a low income rather than shift to an occupation providing a higher income. Consequently, consumers may be unable to access the goods that they value most because there are insufficient workers producing those particular goods.

Inequalities in the distribution of income and wealth

The lack of factor immobility above can lead to market failure through inequality in the distribution of income and wealth. Labour is not a homogeneous factor of production and some people possess skills that are unique. As a consequence, they can earn much higher incomes than unskilled workers. Similarly, inherited wealth can enable a person to have much greater spending power than other members of the population.

The market economy is based on the principle that the willingness to spend is a reflection of the value of a good to a particular individual. However, in a world in which the richest 80 people possess the same amount of wealth as the poorest 50% of the world's population (over 3 billion people), the market mechanism fails to produce an equitable (fair) result. The lack of spending power for the poorest members of society means that their wishes are not granted because they lack *effective* demand (demand backed by the ability to pay). In contrast the richest 80 people have the ability to spend vast fortunes on luxury goods.

Most people would regard this situation, in which 80 people have the same purchasing power as over 3 billion people, as market failure.

REALWORLD
ECONOMICS 23.1

'Inactivity kills more than obesity'

Unhealthy diets have been blamed for ill health and heart failures arising from obesity. Health food markets and organisations such as Weight Watchers have advanced the view that diet is the key to good health. A recent survey showed that many doctors believe that treatment of some illnesses should be refused if patients are deemed to be culpable.

Smokers and obese people are already being denied operations such as IVF, breast reconstructions and a new hip or knee in some parts of England, with over a third of primary care trusts (PCTs) introducing bans or restrictions on treatment for those groups. Some doctors argue that unhealthy behaviour can make procedures less likely to work, and that the service is not obliged to devote scarce resources to them. However, senior doctors and patient groups have voiced alarm at what they call 'blackmailing' of the sick, and denial of their human rights.

A recent survey concluded that a lack of exercise could be killing twice as many people as obesity in Europe. University of Cambridge research concluded that 676,000 deaths each year were due to inactivity, compared with 337,000 from carrying too much weight.

Inactivity has become a serious health issue

Although inactivity and obesity can be interlinked, Norwegian-based scientist Professor Ulf Ekelund stated that inactivity gives the greatest risk of early death and that this conclusion applies to people regardless of their weight. He concluded that eliminating inactivity would cut mortality rates by nearly 7.5%, but eliminating obesity would only cut rates by 3.6%.

Organisations such as Saga argue that market failure is contributing. The sport and fitness market is primarily geared towards the active. Government intervention is needed to promote exercise amongst the elderly and less fit. The NHS should promote treatments that include activities such as dog walking, walking football, croquet and gyms geared for the unfit.

Sources: BBC article 'Inactivity kills more than obesity', by J. Gallagher, 15.1.15; 'Doctors back denial of treatment for smokers and the obese', *Observer* article by D. Campbell, 2. 9.12; Saga website.

Discussion point

Using the article and other sources of information, assess the degree to which opinions on market failure depend on value judgements and perfect information.

Review questions

Total: 35 marks

1 Economies can be organised in three main ways: (i) market economy; (ii) planned economy; and (iii) mixed economy. In which of the above types of economy can market failure exist?

A (i) only
B (ii) only
C (i) and (iii) only
D (i), (ii) and (iii) *(1 mark)*

2 Overproduction of a good occurs in a market economy when the good is:

A A demerit good
B A public good
C Produced by a monopolist
D The cause of positive externalities *(1 mark)*

3 Which one of the following statements is true? A missing market is evidence:

A Of partial market failure
B Of complete market failure
C That a good is not demanded
D That a good is impossible to manufacture *(1 mark)*

4 If a good experiences complete market failure, government is most likely to:

A Do nothing
B Tax that good
C Subsidise that good
D Produce that good *(1 mark)*

5 Which one of the following is a positive externality? Your neighbour's cat:
   A Eats your cat's food
   B Wails in the middle of the night
   C Catches the mice that steal your cheese
   D Eats your pet mouse *(1 mark)*

6 Underproduction of a good is certain to occur if the good:
   A Is a merit good which also creates positive externalities
   B Is a merit good which also creates negative externalities
   C Is a demerit good which also creates positive externalities
   D Is a demerit good which also creates negative externalities *(1 mark)*

7 Which one of the following is most likely to be a demerit good?
   A Defence
   B Museum
   C Sewer
   D Takeaway meal *(1 mark)*

8 For a merit good, government intervention is most likely to be in the form of an increase in:
   A Price
   B Subsidy
   C Licensing restrictions
   D Taxation *(1 mark)*

9 The owner of capital equipment is reluctant to transfer it to an alternative use. In this case, market failure is caused by:
   A Negative externalities
   B A demerit good
   C Immobility of factors of production
   D Imperfect information *(1 mark)*

10 Define the term 'market failure'. *(3 marks)*

11 Define the term 'externalities'. *(3 marks)*

12 Distinguish between complete market failure and partial market failure. *(5 marks)*

13 Briefly explain why public goods lead to market failure. *(5 marks)*

14 Briefly explain why monopoly leads to market failure. *(5 marks)*

15 Briefly explain how inequality of income leads to market failure. *(5 marks)*

Chapter 24

Public goods, private goods & quasi-public goods

This chapter considers the characteristics of private goods and public goods, in order to recognise their differences. We examine the free-rider problem and its effect on public goods. The chapter then analyses circumstances in which public goods take on some of the characteristics of a private good and become quasi-public goods. It concludes with an explanation of the impact of technological change on the characteristics of public goods.

Characteristics of private goods

The market economy works more effectively when dealing with private goods because the person buying the good can ensure that they receive all the benefits from that good. Hence if the good creates an improvement to their welfare that is equal to or greater than the price paid, the buyer knows that it was worthwhile. The characteristic of rivalry (or diminishability) means that less of the good is available for other people because it has been consumed. The buyer can also choose to prevent other people from enjoying the good's benefits (the characteristic of excludability). Examples of private goods include tea, bananas, haircuts and paper. For some private goods, such as cars, the owner may choose to allow other people to use it, but as the owner they can exclude others from its use if they so wish.

In all of these examples, the consumer also has the option of rejecting the good, and using alternative private goods instead.

Characteristics of public goods

The market mechanism does not work effectively for goods that possess non-rivalry. If the use of a good by one consumer does not affect the overall supply available, it is impossible to reach an equilibrium market price and output. If a good is non-excludable, as we saw with street lighting in the previous chapter, it is unlikely to be provided in a market economy. Each consumer would decide not to pay in the hope

Key terms

Rivalry (or **diminishability**) is a feature of a good or service whereby if a person consumes that good or service, the quantity available diminishes and so it is not available for others to consume.

Excludability is a feature of a good or service whereby if an individual pays for that good or service, it is possible to prevent others from having access to that good or service.

Rejectability is a feature of a good or service whereby any individual can choose not to consume that good.

Private goods are those that possess the three features described above (i.e. the good/service has rivalry, excludability and rejectability). It should be noted, however, that it is usual practice to define private goods in terms of the first two characteristics only (i.e. the good/service has rivalry and excludability).

that others will provide the good, allowing non-payers to reap the same benefits as the payers. Logically, nobody would be prepared to pay for that good. Examples of public goods are national defence, the judicial system, the police service, flood control provision, street lighting, television and radio broadcasting, and lighthouses.

The free-rider problem

Public goods possess the characteristic of non-excludability. This can mean that it is unlikely that the market will provide public goods. For example, an individual can operate a lighthouse for profit, charging boats that use the sea in the area of the lighthouse. Some boat owners may be prepared to pay for the services of the lighthouse, but others may choose to be 'free riders' – using the light provided but not paying the owner of the lighthouse. These 'free riders' reduce the revenue and so it is probable that it will be unprofitable to operate. The lighthouse provides a clear benefit to all boats, but it is impossible to exclude non-payers from those benefits.

Pendeen Lighthouse, Cornwall – an example of a public good

Since the lighthouse improves society's welfare, the solution is for the government to provide the service for all boats. Of course, the benefits must be weighed against the costs, and so lighthouses will only be provided if the government believes that the benefits to society will exceed the costs of building and operating the lighthouse. In the UK, commercial shipping using UK ports pay 'light dues' into the General Lighthouse Fund, which is under the stewardship of the Department of Transport.

The free-rider problem applies to all public goods, such as defence, because by definition they are non-excludable. For this reason public goods tend to be provided by government (the public sector).

If a public good is provided in a free market, it will be impossible to force 'free riders' to pay. This can lead to a **missing market** – a situation where there is a need for a product or service but the market mechanism does not provide it. It is usual for governments to intervene and provide public goods, using taxation to pay for their provision.

Pure public goods and quasi-public goods

It is not always possible to draw clear lines between public and private goods because some goods may have partial excludability and/or partial rivalry. For example, roads possess the key features of public goods because they are non-rivalry and non-excludable. However, it is possible to exclude users by erecting toll booths. For example, the M6 toll road allows drivers to avoid more congested (but free to use)

Key terms

Non-rivalry (or **non-diminishability**) is a feature of a good or service whereby if a person consumes that good or service, it does not reduce the quantity available for others to consume.

Non-excludability is a feature of a good or service whereby if that good or service is provided, it is impossible to prevent others from having access to the benefits (or demerits) of that good or service.

Non-rejectability is a feature of a good or service whereby if that good or service is provided, an individual must accept it, even if they would choose not to consume that good or service.

Public goods are goods that possess the first two features described above (i.e. the good/service has non-rivalry and non-excludability). It should be noted, however, that in practice some public goods are non-rejectable, but this is not a necessary characteristic for a good to be classified as a public good.

A **free rider** is someone who benefits from a good or service without paying for it.

Quasi-public goods are goods that are partly excludable or partly rivalrous (partly diminishable).

Overpriced and under-used? Another light traffic day for the M6 toll road

roads around Birmingham. Similarly, a road system within a private estate may have exclusive access for residents. In situations where it is possible to charge for a public good, such as roads, the goods can be described as **quasi-public goods** or **non-pure public goods**, as the good has taken on some of the characteristics of a private good. In this instance, the characteristic of excludability exists.

It could be argued that roads may also possess rivalry – a characteristic of a private good. Most road users would consider a road to be freely accessible, but if it is known that a road will be congested at a certain time (such as rush hour), other potential users may decide that there is insufficient accessibility for them. As a result, potential users may decide against using the road because there is rivalry for the limited amount of road available at that time.

A quasi-public good must have a mechanism to prevent 'free riders' accessing it. For roads, toll booths prevent 'free riders'. However, technological changes are providing opportunities to monitor activities and thus charge consumers who make use of a good or service. In this way many goods deemed to be public goods may become private goods in the future.

Public parks and beaches are generally considered to be public goods. However, it is possible to exclude members of the public from these areas and so they are not non-excludable. Very popular parks and beaches may become congested and this may act as a deterrent to potential users. Hence the characteristic of non-rivalry is also not applicable. It may be feasible for these quasi-public goods to be freely available at times when they are not popular, such as the winter, but for charges to be imposed during busy times. These charges may take the form of high prices for use of car parks.

Key note

It should be noted that government can choose to provide goods because of reasons such as the control of externalities or the encouragement of merit goods. Although public goods are invariably provided by the government (the public sector), it is *not* an acceptable way to define them. Similarly, private goods are not necessarily provided by the private sector.

Technological change and public goods

A market in which technological change is having a major impact on public goods is broadcasting. Subscription TV allows for the market mechanism to operate in broadcasting, by allowing consumers to choose whether to pay for a particular package of channels. Furthermore, developments in technology allow TV providers to charge customers to view individual programmes, on a pay-to-view basis. However, this market is likely to exclude certain genres of programme that attract smaller, more specialist audiences. Pay-to-view TV is also likely to exclude those on lower incomes. These changes allow excludability (a feature of private goods) to exist, but non-rivalry may still remain. For satellite customers, such as owners of pubs and clubs, additional payments are required for satellite TV broadcasting, in recognition that the benefits of the subscription are to be shared.

The most significant impact of technology on public goods is likely to remain in the areas of broadcasting and transport. However, technological developments may lead to further erosion of the distinct nature of some public goods. Clothing manufacturers have developed technology that enables wearers of clothing and shoes to be tracked, using radio signals and/or GPS technology. In the future it is feasible (although politically very unlikely) that this technology could be used to charge people for the use of public goods, such as pavements and public parks.

New technology can also have a significant influence on public goods in other ways:

- By enabling firms to exclude users, firms can overcome the free-rider problem. This can enable public goods to be provided by private firms.
- Technology can improve information so that goods, such as public goods, can be adapted to consumers' needs, thus reducing the chances of market failure.
- New technology can enable providers to lower average costs and make it easier to pay for goods and services. These factors allow more consumers to access both private and public goods.

REALWORLD ECONOMICS 24.1

Road pricing

Earlier we saw how the use of tolls may enable consumers to be excluded from public goods, such as roads. In general, toll booths are not seen as a suitable method for charging for road use because they can cause congestion and, if used widely, would create negative externalities, such as an excessive use of land.

Increases in road use in the UK are caused by three main factors:

London's solution to the negative externality of congestion

- *Population increases* The population of England is expected to rise by 20% by 2040.
- *Standard of living improvements* Economic growth is expected to be 66% between now and 2040.
- *Falling fuel costs* By 2040, fuel costs are expected to fall by 24% for cars and 7% for HGVs.

The use of new technology in the form of Automatic Number Plate Recognition (ANPR) allowed Durham City to introduce a congestion charge in 2002. London introduced the congestion charge in 2003. The main purpose is to overcome negative externalities caused by congestion and so the London charge only applies from 07.00 to 18.00 on weekdays. This scheme cost £200 million to set up. Annual costs for 2013 were estimated at £271 million with income of £295 million. Traffic levels have fallen by 20% since it was introduced, at a time when other cities have experienced traffic growth. However, road closures (often to support bus lanes) have meant that journeys are slower now than they were in 2000. AA President, Edmund King, believes that 'London drivers have paid a heavy price for slower journeys over the last decade. The congestion charge hasn't improved traffic speeds, but may have substituted some low-income drivers for those that can afford it or have no choice'. A proposal to introduce a congestion charge was rejected in Manchester, after a referendum showed that only 21% of inhabitants supported the scheme. Many residents believe that better public transport is the best solution to road congestion.

In the UK as a whole, car owners pay a vehicle licence tax, but this has little impact on road use. The government is currently reducing this tax for low or non-polluting vehicles. Taxes on fuel provide considerable tax revenue to help pay for the maintenance and improvement of roads. However, advances in technology, such as electric cars, mean that this source of tax revenue will fall in the future. Consequently, government is looking for a tax that can raise money and can also overcome the worst congestion. There is no guarantee that fuel tax will achieve this latter aim.

Vehicle tracking technology, using GPS, has made it possible to track the journeys that a vehicle takes, and government is currently investigating the feasibility of using this technology to charge vehicle users who contribute most to congestion. An AA survey indicated that only 29% of members supported the use of this technology, with 71% opposed. Support tended to be higher in areas in which it was least likely to be introduced, such as East Anglia and Wales.

Discussion point

Is road pricing inevitable in the UK in the twenty-first century?

Review questions

Total: 35 marks

1 'A feature of a good or service whereby if that good or service is paid for by an individual, it is not possible to prevent others from having access to that good or service.' The quotation is a definition of:

A Non-rivalry
B Non-diminishability
C Non-excludability
D Non-rejectability *(1 mark)*

2 'A feature of a good or service whereby any individual can choose not to consume that good.' The quotation is a definition of:

A Rivalry
B Diminishability
C Excludability
D Rejectability *(1 mark)*

3 A good that possesses rivalry, diminishability and rejectability is a:

A Free rider
B Private good
C Public good
D Quasi-public good *(1 mark)*

4 Which one of the following is a private good?

A Defence
B Lighthouse
C Satellite TV broadcast
D Street lighting *(1 mark)*

5 Technology can make public services *less* accessible by:

A Reducing average costs
B Providing better information
C Preventing free riders
D Making it easier to pay for goods *(1 mark)*

6 Define the term 'non-rivalry'. *(3 marks)*

7 Define the term 'missing market'. *(3 marks)*

8 Explain the meaning of the term 'public good'. *(4 marks)*

9 Explain the meaning of the term 'quasi-public good'. *(4 marks)*

10 Explain the meaning of the term 'free-rider problem'. *(6 marks)*

11 Explain how technology can lead to goods that have been classified as 'public goods' being provided by private firms. *(10 marks)*

Positive and negative externalities in consumption & production

The concept of externalities was introduced in Chapter 23. In this chapter we consider externalities more fully by examining the differences between private costs and benefits, and social costs and benefits. These concepts are used to demonstrate, through demand and supply diagrams, how negative externalities lead to overproduction of a good and how positive externalities lead to underproduction in a market economy.

Externalities

In Chapter 23 we saw that an **externality** is the effect of an economic decision, such as the manufacture or purchase of a good, on other people/organisations (known as third parties), whose interests were not taken into account.

A **positive externality** exists when the effect is beneficial to the outsiders. A **negative externality** occurs when the action has an adverse effect on the outsiders. There are four types of externalities:

- **Positive externalities in consumption** – for example, more people buying gym membership can lead to a fitter population. This can lead to lower government expenditure on health, saving tax payments for society as a whole. Similarly, more vaccinations by many consumers will lead to less chance of an epidemic affecting other people who have not been vaccinated. Both the factors may also lead to fewer absences from work and more productivity in UK industry. In some cases the positive externality might be quite limited, such as passers-by enjoying watching a casual game of football or tennis in a public park. However minor, all positive externalities increase the economic welfare of the population as a whole.
- **Negative externalities in consumption** – for example, cigarette smoke causing discomfort for non-smokers. In some cases passive smoking can even lead to lung cancer. Consumption of alcohol can have negative effects on third parties, who may suffer from abusive behaviour, violence or simply higher levels of noise.
- **Positive externalities in production** – for example, a company training its

Key terms

Positive externalities in consumption are benefits to outsiders/third parties arising from the purchase or use of a good or service.

Negative externalities in consumption are the adverse consequences to outsiders/third parties arising from the purchase or use of a good or service.

Positive externalities in production are benefits to outsiders/third parties arising from the manufacturing or provision of a good or service.

Negative externalities in production are the adverse consequences to outsiders/third parties arising from the manufacturing or provision of a good or service.

workforce and so leading to more wealth creation for society as a whole. Improved production processes can also have a positive effect on scarce resources. Processes, such as miniaturisation of components, have enabled firms to produce items such as televisions using far fewer materials. As a consequence, finite resources, such as metals, will last for many more years than originally expected.

- **Negative externalities in production** – for example, noise pollution created by road repairs that affect people who live in the vicinity of the road repairs. Other examples of pollution can include air pollution from factories, and water pollution, such as agricultural slurry finding its way into rivers or oil leaks affecting beaches. Factories and production plants may be viewed as an eyesore.

Private costs and benefits

Key terms

Private costs are the financial costs to an individual or firm of an economic transaction undertaken by that individual or firm.

Private benefits are the financial benefits to an individual or firm of an economic transaction undertaken by that individual or firm.

In a market economy, decisions to supply and demand are made by firms and individuals. Each party bases its decisions on the personal financial or economic benefits it can make as a result of a transaction.

In a market economy, supply will be based on the private costs of firms in that market. Each firm will be prepared to supply goods if it can cover its costs, including normal profit. Firms' individual supply curves are therefore based on their private/financial costs. At each price they will offer for supply the quantity of goods that enables them to achieve their normal profit. Consequently, the market supply is also based on the private costs facing suppliers in the market. In this way the supply curve represents the value of the resources involved in the production of that particular good.

In a market economy, demand will be based on the private benefits of individual buyers in the market. Each individual will be prepared to demand a good if the transaction means that the benefit they receive is equal to or greater than the price that they have paid. Individuals' demand curves are therefore based on the private/financial costs received by the buyers. Consequently, the market demand is also based on the private/financial benefits received by buyers in the market. The demand curve for a good or service represents the value of benefits received by buyers in the market.

In Figure 25.1 the demand curve is shown by line AXB. Above £9 there is no demand because no individual in the market believes that the level of private benefit they will receive from the goods is worth more than £9. Point A shows that one individual is willing to pay £9. This individual believes they will receive an extra private benefit worth £9 from buying one unit of this good. The demand curve shows that a second individual will demand the good if price falls just below £9; again, this will indicate that the second individual expects to receive an additional private benefit of just under £9. The line AXB shows that the 100th consumer expects to receive £5 additional private benefit from buying the good. Finally, Point B shows that the 200th consumer believes that the good will give them extra private benefit of £1.

The supply curve is shown by line LXM. Point L shows that one unit will be supplied at £1. This will occur because there is a firm that can produce this product for £1 and still cover their costs sufficiently to make normal profit. As price rises, more firms will enter the market because they will be able to cover their costs and make profit. Point X shows that when price reaches £5, the market can supply 100 units. In effect this means that producing the 100th unit will cost £5, including normal profit, to the supplier of that unit. At prices above £5, supply will extend. Point M shows that supply will be 200 units at £9.

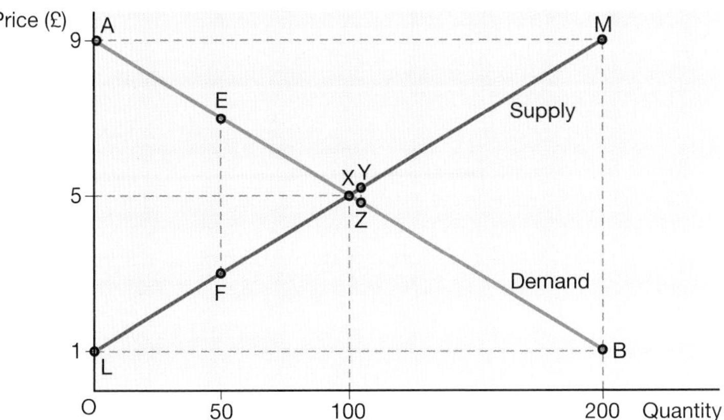

Figure 25.1 *Private costs and benefits in a market*

In a market economy, the equilibrium price of £5 results in a perfect allocation of resources. 100 units are produced in this market. The 100th unit adds £5 of private benefit to the buyer. It also adds £5 of private costs to the supplier. This is the signal for the market economy to stop producing more items. If an additional item is produced, the private cost is shown by Point Y and the private benefit is shown by Point Z. Since Z is below Y, this means that the benefit to society of producing that 101st good is less than the cost to society. Therefore the 101st good represents a misallocation of resources.

Producing less than 100 units is also a misallocation of resources. Society has benefited from the first unit, because it gives £9 of private benefit, but only incurs private costs of £1. Up to 100 units, each unit produced increases society's economic welfare. For example, it can be seen that producing the 50th unit has increased welfare by the difference between E and F, because the private benefit has exceeded the private cost by EF. Although the benefit per unit is falling, the total benefit is increasing by the vertical distance between the demand and supply lines for each product made. From society's viewpoint, production should keep increasing until private benefit (demand) no longer exceeds private cost (supply). This is at Point X because every unit of output up to this point is providing more benefit than cost.

Conclusion

The market economy provides the perfect allocation of resources because it is in equilibrium at the point at which the additional private benefit is exactly equal to the additional private cost of making the product.

The market mechanism is based solely on private benefits and private costs. If externalities exist in a market, the market economy will result in market failure because these externalities will not be taken into consideration.

Social costs and benefits

In order to overcome market failure in the market economy it is possible to take into consideration the value of externalities arising from a particular good. The external benefits can be added to the private benefits to show the overall benefits to society from that particular good. Similarly, the external costs can be added to the private costs of a good in order to show the true cost to society of making that good.

> **Key note**
> Private costs can be measured by the private financial costs of production. Private benefits can be measured by observing how much a consumer is prepared to pay for a good. However, external costs and external benefits require *value judgements* – estimates of the costs or benefits to society.

When assessing whether market failure has occurred, social costs and social benefits need to be considered.

Social costs = Private costs + External costs (the level of negative externalities)

Social benefits = Private benefits + External benefits (the level of positive externalities)

In the next two sections we will examine how knowledge of social costs and social benefits can be used to reduce or eliminate market failure.

In any situation in which externalities exist, there is likely to be market failure because the existence of externalities will mean that there is a discrepancy between social costs/benefits (which should be used to ensure that a perfect allocation of resources exists in a market) and private costs/benefits (which are used to decide the allocation of resources in a perfect market).

Negative externalities and overproduction

If there are negative externalities in a market, the market mechanism will overproduce that good. This is because the negative effects of production (or consumption), experienced by third parties, will be ignored by the market mechanism.

Figure 25.2 shows the demand curve (D) and the supply curve (S_1) for a good in a perfectly competitive market. These lines intersect at the equilibrium point (X), giving

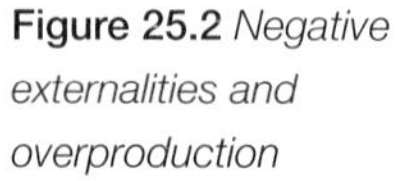
Figure 25.2 *Negative externalities and overproduction*

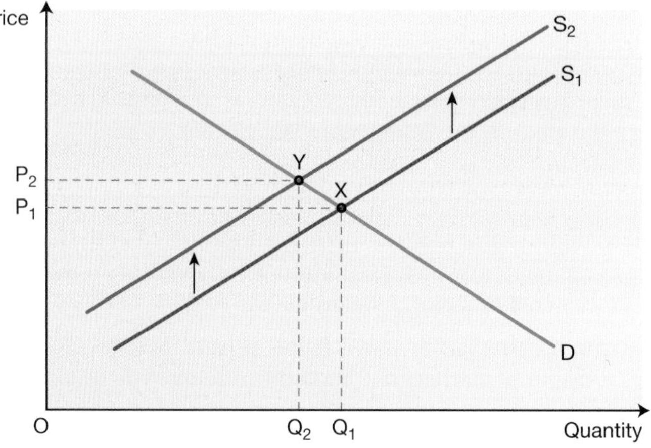

Key terms

External benefits are the value of positive externalities arising from the production and consumption of a particular good.

External costs are the value of negative externalities arising from the production and consumption of a particular good.

Social costs are the full costs to society of an economic activity, taking into consideration both private costs and external costs.

Social benefits are the full benefits to society of an economic activity, taking into consideration both private benefits and external benefits.

an equilibrium market price of P_1 and an equilibrium market quantity of Q_1. However, this good provides negative externalities to third parties (for example, pollution from the factory in which it is manufactured). Since buyers and sellers determine demand and supply, any impact on the third party is ignored by the market.

If the negative externalities are considered, there will be external costs to those third parties. These externalities are a **value judgement**, and so their impact can only be estimated. In Figure 25.2, the vertical distance between S_1 and S_2 (shown by the vertical arrows) represents the (estimated) external costs of the production of this good. This vertical difference between S_1 and S_2 is a measure of the costs imposed on third parties by this good. In effect, the line S_2 measures the social costs of providing the good, as it includes both the private costs (shown by S_1) and the negative externalities (shown by the vertical distance between S_1 and S_2).

Assuming that there are no positive externalities, the private benefits (shown by the demand curve) will represent the social benefits. The demand curve (D) therefore represents both private benefits and social benefits.

Market failure is overcome when social costs equal social benefits. In Figure 25.2, this is at Point Y, where D and S_2 intersect. This means that economic welfare is maximised when output is Q_2. Since the market mechanism has led to the production of Q_1 units, the difference between Q_1 and Q_2 is the level of overproduction caused by the market mechanism. Price P_2 shows the good's true cost to society, which is slightly higher than the market price of P_1.

In order to overcome market failure in the market for this good, government should take measures that will reduce the quantity sold from Q_1 to Q_2 and thus eliminate the overproduction of this good. (The measures that governments can take will be explained in Chapter 29.)

Positive externalities and underproduction

If there are positive externalities in a market, the market will underproduce that good. This is because the positive effects of the production (or consumption), experienced by third parties, will be ignored by the market mechanism.

Figure 25.3 shows the demand curve (D_1) and the supply curve (S) for a good in a perfectly competitive market. These lines intersect at the equilibrium point (X), giving an equilibrium market price of P_1 and an equilibrium market quantity of Q_1.

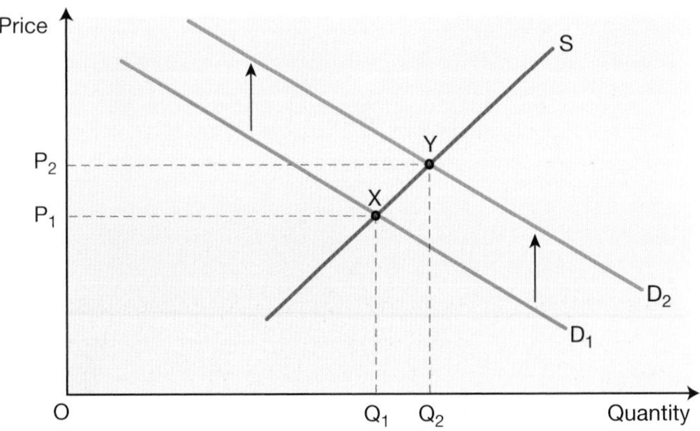

Figure 25.3 *Positive externalities and underproduction*

However, this good provides positive externalities to third parties. (For example, a passer-by might enjoy seeing a vintage car.) Since buyers and sellers determine demand and supply, the market ignores this impact on the third party.

If the positive externalities are considered, there will be external benefits to those third parties. These externalities are a **value judgement,** and so their impact can only be estimated. In Figure 25.3, the vertical distance between D_1 and D_2 (shown by the vertical arrows) represents the (estimated) external benefits of the production of this good. This vertical difference between D_1 and D_2 is a measure of the benefits received by third parties from this good. In effect, the line D_2 measures the social benefits received from the good, as it includes both the private benefits (shown by D_1) and the positive externalities (shown by the vertical distance between D_1 and D_2).

Assuming that there are no negative externalities, the private costs (shown by the supply curve) will represent the social costs. The supply curve (S) therefore represents both private costs and social costs.

Market failure is overcome when social costs equal social benefits. In Figure 25.3, this is at Point Y, where D_2 and S intersect. Thus economic welfare is maximised when output is Q_2. Since the market has provided Q_1 units, the difference between Q_1 and Q_2 is the level of underproduction caused by the market. Price P_2 shows the good's true cost to society, which is slightly higher than the market price of P_1.

In order to overcome market failure in the market for this good, government should take measures that will increase the quantity sold from Q_1 to Q_2 and thus eliminate the underproduction of this good.

REALWORLD ECONOMICS 25.1

Higher education's externalities

Higher education is often used as an example of a service that provides considerable positive externalities. However, this could be viewed as an oversimplification.

Graduation – a cause for celebration

In 1960, approximately 5% of the population went to university, with the majority of pupils leaving full-time education at the age of 15. By 1995, the percentage attending university had risen to 20%. From 1995 to 2008, this percentage doubled to 40% and has increased slightly since, reaching approximately 45%. However, this percentage is well below countries such as Finland, in which over three-quarters of the population experience university education. In terms of the percentage of students experiencing university education, the UK is placed below average amongst developed nations.

It is generally considered that education benefits the user, but does it benefit society as a whole?

Positive externalities include:

- Higher levels of specific job skills and generic skills, such as language and numeracy skills. These skills enable society to generate more wealth, thus increasing the profitability of firms and helping to improve the living standards of third parties. On average graduates earn 27% more money than A-level students during their working life. However, these benefits vary considerably between different subjects.
- Beneficial effects on government

finances. A 2011 government survey by BIS revealed that the average graduate provides a net benefit to the exchequer (the government) of £89,000 over their lifetime.

- Higher education leads to people gaining confidence and being more likely to take responsibility. It can thus improve independence and customer service, to the benefit of the economy as a whole.
- Students in university towns and cities contribute to the wealth and job prospects of residents in those communities.
- University education encourages creativity, imagination, critical thinking and enterprise, to the benefit of society as a whole.

However, there are negative externalities:

- Currently it is estimated that 47% of recent graduates are not employed in 'graduate jobs', although this may be a short-term, post-recession consequence.
- For many countries, graduates are more likely to emigrate to increase their living standards. However, although this is a negative externality relating to UK graduates, the UK benefits to a greater extent from graduates moving between countries.
- Higher education means that students are out of the labour market for more years. In 1960 most workers had careers that spanned about 50 years, from 15 to 65. With a degree, students will be 21 before they commence full-time work. This is likely to be a factor in the raising of the retirement age.
- If a country's growth is restricted by other factors, such as a lack of land or capital, additional graduates may not improve economic welfare.
- In recent years, HE has led to a widening of inequality. It also diverts income and wealth from small towns and rural areas to large cities with universities.

Discussion points

After considering the above article, discuss the following questions:

- What are the difficulties of quantifying externalities?
- Should the UK government seek to increase the number of graduates?
- Should government exert greater influence on subject choice? (Male medicine graduates earn a net return of over £400,000 (19%) in their lifetime, but linguistics degrees only provide male graduates with a 6% net return.)

Review questions

Total: 30 marks

1 Which *one* of the following is a negative externality in *consumption*?
  A Vaccinations leading to less illness in people who have not been vaccinated
  B Passive smoking
  C A drunk telling funny jokes
  D A factory built in a beauty spot *(1 mark)*

2 Which *one* of the following is a negative externality in *production*?
  A Vaccinations leading to less illness in people who have not been vaccinated
  B Passive smoking
  C A drunk telling funny jokes
  D A factory built in a beauty spot *(1 mark)*

3 A consumer is prepared to pay £5 for a good. This is a measure of:
  A External benefit
  B Social benefit
  C Positive externality
  D Private benefit *(1 mark)*

4 A private cost is:
A A cost that is not revealed
B The cost of making a product
C The external costs to a third party
D The social cost of a good *(1 mark)*

5 Many commuters have switched from using large laptops to small tablets (palmtops) during train journeys. Which one of the following is *not* a positive externality arising from this change?
A Relatively fewer resources being used to make the palmtops
B Other commuters having more space to read their newspapers during their journeys
C Palmtop owners finding them easier to carry than laptops
D A lower carbon footprint resulting from the switch to palmtops *(1 mark)*

Figure 25.4 applies to questions 6 and 7. S_1 and D_1 are the original supply and demand curves. S_2 and D_2 are curves that adjust the original supply and demand curves to take into consideration both positive externalities and negative externalities.

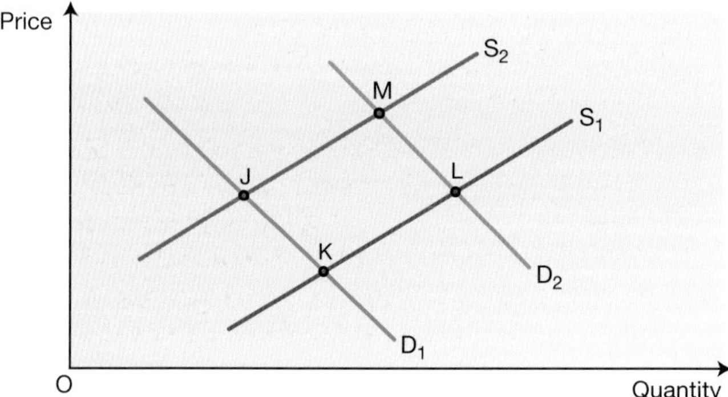

Figure 25.4

6 The market equilibrium point is shown by:
A J B K C L D M *(1 mark)*

7 Market failure is eliminated at point:
A J B K C L D M *(1 mark)*

8 What is meant by the term 'external benefit'? *(3 marks)*

9 How is social benefit calculated? *(3 marks)*

10 How is the level of 'underproduction' calculated? *(3 marks)*

11 What is the difference between a positive externality in consumption and a negative externality in production? *(5 marks)*

12 In the market for vehicles, market failure occurs because negative externalities such as pollution have not been considered. Explain, with the help of a diagram, how government can assess the level of overproduction or underproduction that has resulted from this market failure. *(9 marks)*

Merit & demerit goods

This chapter outlines the meaning of merit and demerit goods and explains why these concepts depend on value judgements. The connection between merit and demerit goods and externalities in consumption is examined. We analyse why merit goods are underprovided and why demerit goods are overprovided, using demand and supply diagrams. In conclusion, the link between imperfect information and merit/demerit goods is explained.

Merit and demerit goods and value judgements

Merit and demerit goods are a cause of market failure.

Merit goods are underprovided in a market economy for two main reasons:

- they provide positive externalities;
- consumers have imperfect information that leads them to underestimate the benefits they will receive from these goods.

The most well-known examples of merit goods are education and health. Other examples include recreation and leisure, safety equipment (such as seat belts and harnesses), pension provision, insurance (such as car, home and life assurance), public libraries and museums.

Demerit goods are overprovided in a market economy for opposite reasons:

- they provide negative externalities;
- consumers have imperfect information that leads them to overestimate the benefits they will receive from the demerit good.

Examples of demerit goods are tobacco, alcohol, offensive literature and broadcasts, and certain foodstuffs.

Although there is widespread agreement about the classification of most merit and demerit goods, the extent to which goods are one or the other is often arguable. For example, how valuable is an A-level education to a person's economic welfare? Financially, this value can only be gauged at the end of that person's career and even then the amount they could have earned without A-levels could only ever be an estimate. There is also the welfare of the individual to consider. Was the extra two years of study enjoyable or stressful? Did it lead to a career that gave satisfaction or disappointment? For these reasons, judgements on merit and demerit goods are always subject to personal opinion. 'Gap years' have become more popular in recent years. In terms of financial value, a gap year may take away a year from a person at a time when they have high earning potential. However, it is likely to be experienced at an age when it is most beneficial to the recipient in terms of 'happiness'.

Governments can try to overcome the market's failure to consider merit goods or demerit goods. However, the market mechanism is based on objective (positive) figures – the actual (private) costs of supply and the price that the consumers are willing to pay. Adjustments based on the external value placed on a merit or demerit good are likely to be subjective (normative) value judgements.

Merit and demerit goods and externalities in consumption

Many merit goods generate **positive externalities** that are not considered by the person who makes the decision to buy. In general, people are likely to take optimistic views of life, particularly when they are young. Value judgements on the worth of goods, such as a pension fund, life assurance and safety equipment, may therefore be underestimated (though pessimists may exaggerate the potential problems). *These merit goods are therefore underprovided in a market economy.* The lack of safety equipment may mean that workers suffer injury and so society loses the productive ability of those workers. It may also lead to hospital expenditure which society must pay, especially if the individual concerned has not taken out accident insurance. It is evident that safety equipment and insurance provide greater benefits to society than the level of benefit considered by the individual who makes the decision on its value. In these situations government can intervene to ensure that more of the good or service is provided.

Similarly, most consumers of demerit goods such as alcohol and violent films do not believe or recognise that these goods create **negative externalities**. Most individuals do not believe that alcohol will affect their behaviour in a negative way. In recent years there has been adverse publicity concerning the greater risk that four-wheel drive vehicles pose to pedestrians and other road users. This seems to have increased the popularity of these vehicles, since it reinforces the belief that these vehicles are safer for the *owner*. The true economic value to society of these demerit goods is exaggerated. *These demerit goods are therefore overprovided in a market economy.* Government can intervene to ensure that fewer demerit goods are provided.

With both merit and demerit goods it is a lack of regard for other people that can lead to a need for intervention.

Some merit and demerit goods are also affected by the **principal–agent problem,** where the person who gains or suffers loss from the decision is not the person who makes the decision. For example, decisions on paying for school education are made by parents rather than pupils. Similarly, third party car insurance is unlikely to be considered by many people because it benefits the owner of the other vehicle rather than the driver.

The impact of imperfect information

Key term
Imperfect information is when a buyer or seller lacks the information needed to make the best choice in a transaction.

Imperfect information is the other cause of market failure with regard to merit and demerit goods. In some cases this may arise because of the lack of understanding of the merits and demerits of a product. For example, free milk was provided for all schoolchildren until the 1970s because of its perceived health benefits. Over time a greater understanding of the impact of foods on health has led to a re-evaluation of the value of milk as a healthy product.

Imperfect information also causes misallocation of resources when consumers do not recognise the long-term consequences of decisions or make decisions based on short-term preferences. In terms of health, people may follow diets that suit short-term needs, such as consuming convenience foods when a person is experiencing time pressure. However, in the long term the negative consequences of these decisions are experienced by the consumer and possibly by society too.

This lack of knowledge and understanding may lead to an underprovision of merit goods because there is ignorance about their true value. Similarly it can lead to overprovision of demerit goods because their value is exaggerated.

Conclusion

Whether the cause is information failure or a lack of consideration of externalities, both merit and demerit goods cause market failure. This market failure takes the form of an underprovision of merit goods or an overprovision of demerit goods.

Figure 26.1 shows the demand curve (D_1) and the supply curve (S) for a good in a perfectly competitive market. These lines intersect at the equilibrium point (X), giving an equilibrium market price of P_1 and an equilibrium market quantity of Q_1. However, this good is a merit good. The buyer underestimates its true value because *either* it provides positive externalities to third parties, *or* information failure means that its true value is not recognised by the buyer.

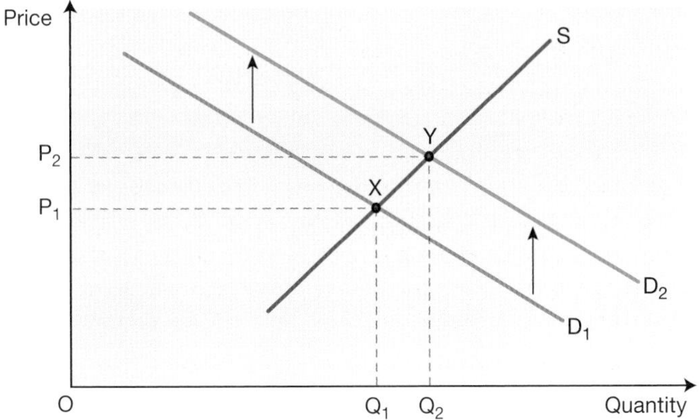

Figure 26.1 *The underprovision of merit goods in a market economy*

The true value of this good to society is shown by D_2. The vertical distance between D_1 and D_2 (shown by the vertical arrows) represents *either* the (estimated) positive externalities of this good *or* the additional value that has not been recognised because of information failure. In effect, the line D_2 measures the social benefits received from the good, since it includes both the private benefits (shown by D_1) and the external benefits (shown by the vertical distance between D_1 and D_2).

Assuming that there are no negative externalities, the private costs (shown by the supply curve) will represent the social costs. The supply curve (S) therefore represents both private costs and social costs.

Key note

Figure 26.1 is the same diagram as Figure 25.3 in the previous chapter, which showed how the existence of positive externalities led to underproduction. Similarly, a diagram to show how demerit goods lead to an overprovision of a good will be the same as Figure 25.2, which showed how the existence of negative externalities led to overproduction. Please refer back to Figure 25.2 for confirmation of how a demerit good leads to overprovision.

Market failure is overcome when social costs equal social benefits. In Figure 26.1, this is at Point Y, where D_2 and S intersect. This means that economic welfare is maximised when output is Q_2. Since the market mechanism has led to the production of Q_1 units, the difference between Q_1 and Q_2 is the level of underproduction caused by the market mechanism. Price P_2 shows the good's true cost to society; this is slightly lower than the market price of P_1.

In order to overcome market failure in the market for this good, government should take measures that will increase the quantity sold from Q_1 to Q_2, eliminating the underprovision of this good.

REALWORLD ECONOMICS 26.1

Wind farms – merit or demerit goods?

Wind farms illustrate the difficulties of classifying merit goods and demerit goods. There is clear evidence that their impact on society reaches beyond the people who make decisions on their construction and so they are responsible for certain externalities. There is also considerable debate about the merits and demerits of wind farms – as a relatively new form of energy, there is a lack of detailed information on the consequences of wind farming. The UK has a target of 15% of its energy from renewable resources, such as wind, by 2020. In 2014 there were over 4200 wind turbines in 531 wind farms, generating 7.5% of the UK's electricity.

Wind farms – a classification dilemma

Some key arguments, for and against wind farming, are summarised below.

Advantages of wind farming

- This is a very green form of energy, though there is a carbon footprint from the manufacturing and maintenance of wind turbines.
- It does not pollute the air or cause acid rain, unlike fossil fuels.
- The wind itself is a free form of energy and wind farming is one of the cheapest renewable energy technologies.
- It is flexible. A single house can have a small tower with an eight-foot blade, while a 20-storey tower with rotors spanning more than 100 yards can provide power to support 1400 houses.
- Over longer periods, such as a year, there is a consistent level of power generated by wind turbines. This means that the costs and thus the price of this form of energy are much more consistent than many other sources.
- Very little land is used as the space below the turbine can be used for agricultural purposes.

Disadvantages of wind farming

- The scale of the towers presents an eyesore (though this point is not universally agreed).
- The turbines emit noise that has a negative impact on neighbours.
- In the short term, output is inconsistent, as energy cannot be produced if there is a lack of wind or if wind speeds are too high.
- The blades are a danger to birds, but much less danger than power lines.
- To date, most of the construction of wind farms in the UK has been subsidised, and therefore its true costs are not being considered.
- Wind farms are most suited to offshore sites (which are very expensive to establish) and rural areas. In both cases, there are considerable storage and transmission costs to get the electricity to where it is needed.
- It is likely to be impractical in many areas. A city of 400,000 people needs over 1000 turbines.

One of the main objections to wind farms is their inefficiency. Original government planning assumed that turbines would have a lifetime of 25 years and would be producing less than 40% capacity after 19 years of operation. However, recent studies by Imperial College, London, have shown that the UK's earliest turbines, built in the 1990s, are still producing three-quarters of their original output. This means that they are comparable in performance to gas turbines used in power stations.

Sources: Various, including www3.imperial.ac.uk and http://homeguides.sfgate.com

Discussion points

1 Are wind farms an example of a merit or demerit good?

2 What additional information might you need in order to make this assessment?

Review questions

Total: 35 marks

1 Which one of the following is a merit good?
A Alcohol B Drugs C Insurance D Tobacco *(1 mark)*

2 Which one of the following is a demerit good?
A Leisure activities
B Loud music
C Museums
D Seatbelts *(1 mark)*

3 A wind farm might be classified as a demerit good because it:
A Is a green form of energy
B Is more expensive than some other forms of energy
C Does not pollute the air
D Can be unsightly *(1 mark)*

4 'A good is a demerit good if it produces ….(a)…. externalities and if imperfect information leads to an ….(b)…. of its benefits to society.' Which answer below provides the missing words at (a) and (b)?
A (a) positive (b) overestimation
B (a) positive (b) underestimation
C (a) negative (b) overestimation
D (a) negative (b) underestimation *(1 mark)*

5 Define the term 'merit good'. *(3 marks)*

6 Define the term 'imperfect information'. *(3 marks)*

7 Explain why the classification of a merit or demerit good might depend on value judgements. *(6 marks)*

8 In the market for education, market failure occurs because positive externalities have not been considered. Explain, with the help of a diagram, how government can assess the level of overproduction or underproduction that has resulted from this market failure. *(9 marks)*

9 Explain how imperfect information can lead to a product being classified as a demerit good. *(10 marks)*

Market imperfections

This chapter builds on imperfect information as a source of market failure and also considers how asymmetric information can lead to market failure. It then examines two other market imperfections that can cause market failure: monopoly and monopoly power, and the immobility of factors of production.

Why imperfect and asymmetric information can lead to market failure

Key terms

Symmetric information is when both the seller and the buyer are well informed about the goods and services and prices in the market.

Asymmetric information is when either the seller or the buyer has more information than the other party in a transaction.

The model of perfect competition assumes symmetric information. This requires both buyers and sellers to be equally well informed about the goods and services in the market. Consequently, both parties make rational decisions on whether to demand or supply the product at the market price.

In Chapter 26 we saw how imperfect information might lead to market failure. This might occur because positive or negative externalities are not recognised by participants in the decision-making process. A failure to recognise positive externalities leads to underprovision because the full social benefits of the good are not recognised. Similarly, a failure to recognise negative externalities leads to overprovision because the full social costs of the good are not recognised. Imperfect information might arise for a number of reasons:

- the complexity of the good or the marketplace in which it is bought and sold;
- irrational consumer behaviour, perhaps because of a preference or brand loyalty for a certain manufacturer or simply because the good is rarely purchased by the individual and so they know little about it;
- difficulties in keeping track of prices charged by the vast number of firms in a competitive market;
- insufficient knowledge about the actual (or 'claimed') differences between the various brands within the marketplace.

Where asymmetric information exists, there is also likely to be market failure because one party to the decision (usually, but not always, the seller) possesses more information on which to base the decision than the other party (usually, but not always, the buyer). For example, in healthcare a recommendation for treatment by a doctor is likely to be accepted by the patient, as the patient will not have the body of knowledge required to contest such a decision by a medical expert. Similarly, the seller of a good is likely to have a better understanding of the technical details of the product than a typical consumer. However, there are many consumers who have considerable knowledge in particular areas, and so it is feasible that certain consumers will have much more knowledge than the shop assistant who is selling them the good.

Where asymmetric information exists, the person with the greater knowledge will usually have greater bargaining power when it comes to deciding on the price. This will cause market failure because the quantity purchased will not relate purely to the value of the good being traded. If the seller has greater information, it is likely that the good will be overprovided or overpriced.

Why monopoly and monopoly power can lead to market failure

In Chapter 20 we saw how monopoly might result in a misallocation of resources. This example of market failure occurs because monopolists may restrict output in order to force up price. As there are barriers to entry into monopoly markets, the monopolist can enjoy abnormal profits by using this approach. Not only does this lead to higher prices but it also may lead to the monopolist producing at a level of output below the lowest point of ATC. Consequently, there is productive inefficiency too – a further cause of market failure. This inefficiency may be further compounded by a lack of incentive to strive continually to cut costs. In a market economy, constant competition provides the incentive for firms to reduce costs. A firm that does not reduce costs when its competitors do will be driven out of the market. However, monopolists set their own price and therefore there is less incentive to reduce costs, as barriers to entry will prevent inefficient monopolists from losing their market. Monopoly may also contribute to market failure by restricting the variety of products available to consumers. This can reduce the costs of the monopolists but have very little impact on sales revenue, as consumers are forced to purchase the product that the monopolist offers. For example, when BT had a monopoly of landlines, only one type of handset was available because BT was guaranteed 100% of the market. Furthermore, consumers were not given an option of purchasing their handset. Instead it was provided on a monthly rental basis, so that BT could earn money each month rather than receive a single payment.

Market failure is also likely to occur in concentrated markets, such as oligopoly. In these markets, each of the oligopolists enjoys a measure of monopoly power. The extent to which an individual oligopolist possesses market power depends on a number of factors:

- *The market share of a particular oligopolist and the concentration ratio for that industry* For example, Microsoft's 90% market share of the market for PC operating systems means that Microsoft has considerable market power and can force up the price.
- *The extent to which products in one market can be substituted by products from another market* For example, although over 70% of banana supplies are controlled by five oligopolists, many (but not all) consumers view other fruits as substitutes for bananas.
- *The extent of product differentiation between different oligopolists' products* For example, in the UK, consumers purchasing cars are moving from cheaper models towards higher quality, more expensive cars. Quality cars tend to have a greater range of product differentiation than cars that are sold mainly on the basis of their low price.
- *The level of brand loyalty for the products of a particular oligopolist* Although products such as soft drinks can be easily provided by small businesses, the high levels of brand loyalty experienced by companies such as Coca-Cola and PepsiCo act as a significant barrier to entry. Consequently, these companies have high levels of monopoly power that contribute to market failure.

- *The necessity of the product being provided* In markets such as pharmaceuticals, consumers may be totally dependent on a product that has a guaranteed monopoly because of patent laws. Some cancer treatments can cost over £60,000.
- *The extent to which there are barriers of entry to the market as a whole, or barriers which prevent direct competition with a particular product* Again, patent laws can give some oligopolists, such as Apple and Samsung, considerable monopoly power, enabling them to charge much higher prices than would exist in a competitive market.
- *The level of knowledge and information within the market* As goods and services become more complex, consumers' understanding of the market and its products tends to decline. Thus monopoly power can lead to asymmetric information and therefore market failure.

Wherever there is monopoly power, there is a likelihood of market failure. For this reason, most developed nations have a system of regulation to prevent the exploitation of consumers. Since April 2014, responsibility for this regulation in the UK rests with the Competition and Markets Authority (CMA), which replaced the Competition Commission.

Why the immobility of factors of production can lead to market failure

The market mechanism assumes that resources (factors of production) move automatically to where they are needed most. If peaches become more popular than apricots, then the higher price of peaches will attract resources away from apricot supply, which now offers lower rewards. This theory relies on *perfect mobility of factors of production*, meaning that factors of production can easily shift from one use to another.

If *immobility of factors of production* exists, then the factors of production do not easily transfer to different uses. This means that the market does not produce the desired market equilibrium and so *market failure* occurs.

Immobility takes two forms:

- **geographical immobility**, where the resources cannot easily move from one geographical area to another;
- **occupational immobility**, where the resources cannot easily move from a particular use or job to another.

Labour is often geographically immobile because workers are not happy to give up family and friends who live nearby. Regional variations in house prices and relocation costs can also cause geographical immobility, especially for workers on low incomes. Occupational mobility depends on the flexibility and skills of the worker. Ironically, those with the highest skills are often the most immobile, since workers are reluctant to waste the training and skills they have developed.

Enterprise tends to be much more mobile than labour, as entrepreneurs are risk takers and are likely to reap higher financial rewards than labour if they move to the right occupation or location. Nevertheless, entrepreneurs often operate from home when starting a business, and the most successful start-ups are often those that focus on the skills and knowledge of the entrepreneur. Consequently there can be both geographical and occupational immobility amongst entrepreneurs.

Land, in its traditional sense, is geographically immobile, but natural resources such as crops and gravel are very geographically mobile. In occupational terms, land can often be transferred easily to other uses and so it is occupationally mobile. However, 'brownfield' sites, on which an industry has already been established, are often more expensive to adapt than 'greenfield' sites, on which there has been no previous industry.

Capital tends to be much more mobile because it is often easy for equipment to be relocated and/or adapted to another use. However, some existing capital equipment, such as a coalmine, is very immobile, as it does not have an alternative use.

Perfect mobility and perfect information mean that any unemployed factors of production will find employment. If unemployment exists, it will drive down the price/cost of that factor of production. However, a perfectly mobile factor of production will be able and prepared to move from one occupation or geographical area to another in order to achieve the market rate paid to that factor of production. In this way, a perfectly competitive market achieves a perfect allocation of resources, with no market failure. However, the reasons for immobility, outlined earlier, lead to market failure. For example, property prices in London are an example of the consequences of an immobile factor of production (land). Since new land cannot move into the area in which demand is high, its price is forced upwards.

The European Union operates on the principle of the free movement of labour in order to reap the benefits of perfectly competitive markets. Workers from Eastern European countries such as Poland have migrated to countries such as the UK and Germany in order to seek greater rewards and greater prospects of employment. This migration has led to the elimination of labour shortages and a lowering of labour costs in certain occupations in the UK and Germany, while reducing unemployment in Poland as there are fewer workers seeking employment there. This process is illustrated in Figure 27.1.

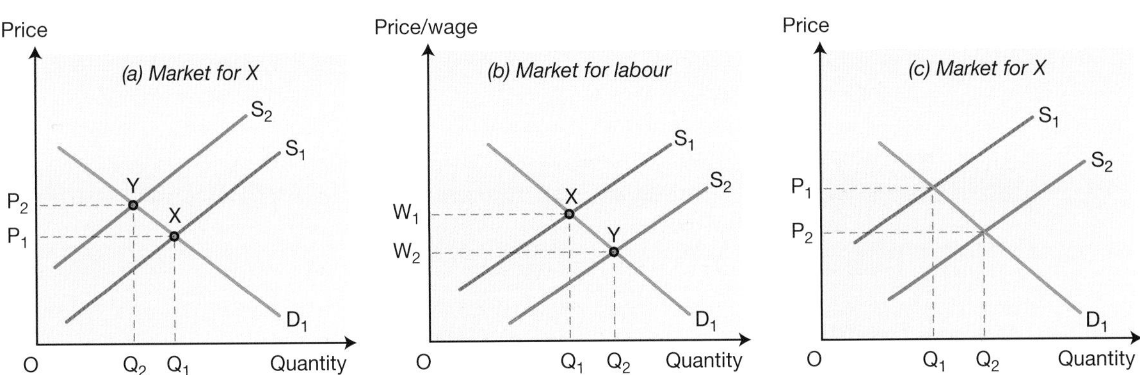

Figure 27.1 *The market for goods and the market for factors of production*

Figure 27.1(a) shows the market for Good X. Producers of Good X in this market experience a shortage of labour, due to immobility. This leads to a cutback in supply from S_1 to S_2, forcing price up from P_1 to P_2. This higher price leads to higher rewards for factors of production, particularly labour, as it is in short supply.

Figure 27.1(b) shows the market for labour. Attracted by the prospect of higher wages, workers from other countries migrate to this country to take advantage of the higher wages in this particular market. This leads to an increase in labour supply from S_1 to S_2, forcing down the price of labour (the wage level) but increasing the number of people employed. Although the wage in the UK has fallen from W_1 to W_2, W_2 is likely to be a higher wage than that available in the country from which people have emigrated, as migration would stop if the UK wage fell below wages in the migrants' country of origin.

Figure 27.1(c) shows the impact of this change on the market for Good X. The additional labour force enables supply to increase from S_1 to S_2, increasing the quantity produced from Q_1 to Q_2 but lowering the price from P_1 to P_2. In a perfectly competitive market, price P_2 would be the one that provides normal profit and so at this price there will be no further incentive for firms to produce more, and for more employees to seek work in this industry.

REALWORLD ECONOMICS 27.1

Footballers' wages – an example of market failure?

In theory, perfect mobility of labour should lead to an equalling out of wages. However, in practice, labour is not homogeneous because different workers have widely varying levels of skill.

A study by the *Daily Mail* in 2014 indicated that the average annual wage paid to a Premier League player in England was £2.27 million. This compared to £1.46 million in Germany, £1.31 million in Italy and £1.21 million in Spain. The differentials are largely due to differences in income received, with the English Premiership having slightly higher gate revenues but much higher earnings from television rights. Furthermore, there are significant differences between individual clubs within those leagues.

The English Premiership acts as a cartel when it sells TV rights to matches

Geographical mobility of labour in world football is much higher than in most occupations. The English Premier League provided 112 of the 700 players at the 2014 World Cup, but there are limitations on transfers between some countries. Occupational mobility is very restricted at this level, as few people have the natural ability to perform at the highest level. This is the key reason for the permanence of the very high wage levels earned by top footballers.

Monopoly power is considerable because a few clubs, such as Real Madrid, attract global support. Consequently, TV audiences in many countries are willing to pay more for games featuring top clubs. The high revenue received by top clubs enables them to keep buying the better players, thus restricting the advancement of clubs in lower league positions.

The bidding process for TV rights is an example of imperfect information. Bidders such as Sky and BT are reluctant to reveal their bids to competitors and will tend to make a high bid to ensure that they gain exclusive rights. This can lead to very high prices paid for TV rights. The Premiership acts as a cartel, selling rights collectively. Some clubs, such as Manchester United, have considered selling the rights to their games individually, but at present they are prevented by Premiership rules.

Many have argued that football is an example of market failure because television companies (rather than fans) seem to be able to dictate factors such as kick-off times and dates. However, as TV provides more income for these clubs than ticket sales to fans, this could be seen to be a market that is working to serve its customers' needs, namely the TV viewers. Nevertheless, it does illustrate the fact that the market economy favours those consumers with high levels of money (such as Sky TV viewers) in comparison to the individual fans who attend matches.

Source: Daily Mail, 15.11.14

Discussion points

1 Is professional football an example of market failure?

2 Can high wages for footballers be justified?

Review questions

Total: 35 marks

1 In comparison to perfect competition, monopoly power is most likely to result in:

A A higher price and higher output
B A higher price and lower output
C A lower price and higher output
D A lower price and lower output *(1 mark)*

2 Which one of the following is *not* a possible cause of imperfect information?

A Rational consumers
B The complexity of a good
C Insufficient knowledge of competing products
D Monopoly power *(1 mark)*

3 A local council insists that a particular shop must remain as a restaurant. This is an example of:

A Occupational immobility and geographical immobility
B Occupational immobility and geographical mobility
C Occupational mobility and geographical immobility
D Occupational mobility and geographical mobility *(1 mark)*

4 Define the term 'asymmetric information'. *(3 marks)*

5 What do the initials CMA stand for? *(3 marks)*

6 What is meant by the term 'occupational immobility of capital'? *(3 marks)*

7 Explain why a lack of competition might lead to higher costs for a monopolist. *(4 marks)*

8 Explain why a perfectly competitive market relies on perfect information to prevent market failure. *(5 marks)*

9 Explain how immobility of a factor of production might cause market failure. *(6 marks)*

10 Explain two factors that might increase monopoly power in an oligopoly market. *(8 marks)*

An inequitable distribution of income & wealth

This chapter explains how the market mechanism leads to an unequal and inequitable distribution of income and wealth. We consider the impact of inequality on the market, with a particular focus on how inequality leads to market failure. The chapter concludes with an examination of how taxation and government spending influence the distribution of income, showing how progressive taxes and government spending are used to reduce inequality.

The market mechanism and inequality of income and wealth

When considering inequality, it is important to distinguish between income and wealth. Income measures the earnings received over a period of time, such as a monthly wage or annual salary. Although there can be large differences between people's incomes, the total value of these differences is constrained by the fact that income is usually measured annually. Wealth measures the value of assets owned by a person or organisation. This ownership may have been developed throughout a person's working life, and so differences in wealth tend to be greater than differences in annual income. Furthermore, wealth is often inherited from family members and so can represent the accumulation of wealth over hundreds of years. Since wealth can be accumulated over many years, there tends to be much greater inequality of wealth than income. Despite the growth of self-made entrepreneurs, inheritance is the main source of wealth in the UK.

In Chapter 27 we saw how some professional footballers could earn very high wages. In a market economy this can happen if there is not complete mobility of factors of production. High earnings by a factor of production, whether it is labour, capital, land or enterprise, can remain if competing factors cannot take away the factor of production's market advantage. In the case of professional footballers it is the high level of skill in a market in which there is a very high level of demand. This shortage of skilled labour means that competing firms (football clubs) will offer a high wage to those footballers with the highest skills because those skills may guarantee financial success for the firm (football club).

Skilled workers are major beneficiaries from the market mechanism because their scarcity leads to a high price/wage. However, these high wages are dependent on high demand too. For example, acting can be a very lucrative career, but most actors have careers that are not financially rewarding because there is a high supply of willing actors. Consequently, wages are often low.

In the UK, there is a very unequal and inequitable distribution of income and wealth. Although wages and salaries paid to labour are a significant cause of inequality, the greatest variations in income and wealth can often be attributed to ownership of the three other factors of production. The wealthiest person born and living in the UK is the Duke of Westminster, whose income and wealth has been largely gained through inheritance of land in places such as Mayfair and Belgravia. The top 10 rich list is dominated by entrepreneurs, with owners of capital and land also featuring. The market mechanism offers high rewards to assets and skills that are not easy to replicate and so entrepreneurs with bright ideas can earn substantial sums, particularly if there are barriers to entry to restrict competition.

Key note

Be cautious when interpreting data on inequality. Inequality of wealth tends to give much more impressive 'headline' figures and so it is often used to illustrate inequality. In some countries it is also easier to measure a person's assets than their annual income. However, many assets cannot be turned into usable money quickly, and so high wealth is not necessarily an accurate measure of the goods and services that a person could buy in the short term. In contrast, although high income is likely to be a better representation of spending power, a person with large debts, such as a recent graduate with a good job but a sizeable mortgage, might not have as much spending power as their income would suggest.

Inequality and market failure

The market economy operates on the principle that goods flow to the people that value them most. In effect, demand is a vote for a product. Those consumers that are prepared to pay the highest price for a good, because they value it the most, will be the consumers who are able to purchase the good. Consumers who place less value on that good will be happy to settle for other goods, for which they have offered a higher price because they valued the second good more highly than the first.

One of the many homeless people living rough in London – an example of market failure

However, this principle works most effectively when everyone has the same access to goods and services. Unfortunately, inequality undermines this principle and thus causes market failure. A person with considerable wealth or high income can afford to pay high prices for most goods and services – even those that they do not need so much or value so highly. In contrast, a person with low income and wealth may not even be able to pay the price required for basic necessities such as food and shelter, as can be seen by the large numbers of homeless people, particularly in places such as London, where property prices are very high. Similarly, in parts of the country such as Cornwall there are many homeowners who live elsewhere but have a second property, because they can afford to pay a higher price for a second home than the price that many Cornish residents could offer for a first home.

Market failure and the misallocation of resources are value judgements. However, there is a general consensus that the market is failing if there are many people homeless at a time when other people can afford to retain additional properties that they only use occasionally.

There is also a general consensus amongst economists that government should intervene to shape a fairer society when the market economy creates these types of unfair situations. However, it is widely accepted that the market economy rewards enterprise, encourages firms to seek efficiency and rewards workers for developing unique skills. Consequently, this is the ideal model for ensuring that the economy's scarce resources are used as effectively as possible in order to produce the maximum amount of goods and services.

As a result, mixed economies are most common. This approach bases economic decisions on the market economy but encourages government intervention to overcome market failure in situations such as inequality.

Inequality, market failure and government intervention

Key terms

Progressive tax is a tax that takes a higher proportion of taxpayers' incomes as their incomes increase.

Regressive tax is a tax that takes a lower proportion of taxpayers' incomes as their incomes increase.

Proportional tax is a tax that takes the same proportion of taxpayers' incomes, regardless of their income level.

Governments intervene in order to try to overcome market failure caused by inequality. In general, the government's aim is to use its budget to try to redistribute income and wealth from the rich to the poor.

The extent to which an economy should create a more even distribution of income and wealth is a value judgement. Governments take actions to improve social welfare through taxation, but also through government spending.

Using taxation to redistribute income and wealth requires progressive taxes. For example, income tax has a higher percentage rate for higher incomes and so the rich pay a higher proportion of their income in tax. It should be noted that 'progressive' taxation also applies to wealth, and so inheritance tax is seen to be a progressive tax that focuses on wealth rather than income. Regressive taxes take a higher proportion of income from those on lower incomes; these taxes worsen inequality. Proportional taxes leave relative levels of inequality unchanged.

In the UK, redistribution of income is also achieved through government spending. Examples include welfare benefits, such as the Jobseeker's Allowance and the state pension. Redistribution is helped in many cases by providing goods and services at low or zero cost, such as health and education.

Real World Economics 28.1 examines the extent to which the current tax system in the UK does redistribute income. A more detailed examination of taxation policy is provided in Chapter 44 and a more detailed study of inequality will be provided in our companion textbook, *AQA A-Level Year 2 Economics.*

REALWORLD ECONOMICS 28.1

Is the UK tax system progressive?

Discussions on whether the UK tax system is progressive tend to focus on income tax. However, income tax only accounts for 27% of tax revenue. Table 28.1 shows the impact of UK taxes on three groups of taxpayers: the bottom 10%; the middle 10%; and the top 10%.

The table shows the UK tax system is regressive rather than progressive. Rather than reducing inequalities of income, the UK tax system increases those inequalities by taking almost 43% of the income of the bottom 10% of income earners. The top 10% of earners pay 35% of their income in

Table 28.1 *Tax as a percentage of income, 2013*

	Percentage of income taken from:			
Tax	**Bottom 10%**	**Middle 10%**	**Top 10%**	**Progressive or regressive?**
Income tax	4.61	13.24	19.67	Progressive
National insurance	1.64	5.47	5.18	Progressive[a]
Council tax	5.59	2.47	1.39	Regressive
VAT	11.62	6.11	4.39	Regressive
Fuel duty	2.20	1.33	0.74	Regressive
Tobacco duty	3.59	0.92	0.22	Regressive
Other taxes/duties	13.67	5.85	3.84	Regressive
Overall taxation	**42.92**	**35.39**	**35.43**	**Regressive[b]**

Notes: (a) Slightly regressive between middle 10% and top 10%. (b) Slightly progressive between middle 10% and top 10%.

Sources: Equality Trust: article entitled 'Unfair and unclear' by Madeleine Power and Tim Stacey, June 2014; and ONS: 'Effects of tax and benefits on household income, 2013', June 2014.

tax – the same percentage as the middle 10%.

Although these figures conflict with stated government policy, overall the government's budget does redistribute income from rich to poor. This is achieved through government spending. Table 28.2 shows the overall impact of government spending and taxation on different households in 2012–13.

Table 28.2 shows that, in absolute terms, lower income families receive the highest cash benefits and benefits in kind, so that overall government taxation and spending does help to redistribute income. The following bullet points summarise this impact:

- *Before* taxes and benefits, the richest fifth of households had an income of £81,300 per year; the poorest fifth had an average income of £5500.
- *After* taxes and benefits, the richest fifth of households had an income of £59,900 per year; the poorest fifth had an average income of £15,600.

Discussion points

1 Is it right for the UK tax system to be regressive?

2 Is the overall impact of government spending and taxation doing enough to reduce inequality?

Table 28.2 *Overall impact of government spending and taxes on UK households, 2012–13*

	Average income per household (£ per year), based on quintile groups					
	Bottom 20%	**2nd quintile**	**3rd quintile**	**4th quintile**	**Top 20%**	**Overall**
Cash benefits	7154	8817	6622	4691	2666	5990
Benefits in kind [a]	7646	7617	7026	6193	5403	6777
Taxation	–4744	–6243	–9649	–15,109	–29,462	–13,041
Net effect	**10,056**	**10,191**	**3999**	**–4225**	**–21,393**	**–274**

Note: (a) Benefits in kind = free education, health and other government services.

Review questions

Total: 25 marks

1 The level of inequality is greater if inequality is measured using:

A Gross income
B Income after tax
C Income after tax and benefits
D Wealth

(1 mark)

2 Table 28.3 below shows gross income (before income tax) and net income (after income tax).

Table 28.3

Gross income (£)	Net income (£)	Net income as a % of gross income
100	80	80
200	160	80
300	200	67
400	280	70
500	350	70

Income tax is regressive for incomes between:

A £100 to £200
B £200 to £300
C £300 to £400
D £400 to £500

(1 mark)

3 Based on the 10 wealthiest people in the UK, which factor of production is responsible for creating most inequality?

A Capital
B Enterprise
C Labour
D Land *(1 mark)*

4 Based on Tables 28.1 and 28.2, which one of the following was most responsible for the redistribution of income from rich to poor in the UK in 2013?

A VAT
B Tobacco duty
C Cash benefits
D Benefits in kind *(1 mark)*

5 Define the term 'progressive tax'. *(3 marks)*

6 What is the difference between income and wealth? *(4 marks)*

7 Explain how inequality causes market failure. *(6 marks)*

8 Explain how the market mechanism can cause inequality. *(8 marks)*

Government intervention in markets

This chapter shows how market failure leads to government intervention in markets. The different methods of government intervention are introduced and these methods are linked to the specific and overall objectives of government intervention. We conclude with an examination of how certain methods, such as indirect taxation, subsidies and price controls, are used to adjust the market in order to overcome a misallocation of resources.

Market failure and government intervention in markets

Governments choose to take actions to affect economic activity and the ways in which resources are allocated in an economy. These actions are invariably geared towards intervening in the market economy to overcome or prevent market failure. Examples of government intervention include taxation, subsidies, price controls and regulations.

Key term

Government intervention describes government actions that are designed to affect economic activity and the allocation of resources.

In a laissez-faire economy the market economy will be allowed to operate freely because, in theory, it creates both productive efficiency and allocative efficiency. However, we have seen that the free market may fail to achieve a perfect allocation of resources. This failure takes many forms and each of these forms provides a reason for government intervention. The extent of market failure, and the form that it takes, can both influence the type of intervention used by government. In most cases, this intervention still allows the market mechanism to operate, but government influence can modify the eventual outcome of the market mechanism, whereby the good or service is not provided at all by the market mechanism.

Reasons for government intervention

Public goods

Public goods are non-excludable and non-rivalrous. This leads to the free-rider problem because it is not possible to exclude someone who does not pay for the good or service from enjoying its benefits. Without government intervention, there may well be underproduction and possibly even a missing market.

Positive and negative externalities

Externalities occur when the price mechanism fails to reflect the true benefit or true cost to society of the production and/or consumption of a good. For example, when negative externalities such as pollution exist, there will be overproduction of the good. Government intervention will therefore aim to reduce the level of consumption of the good. When positive externalities exist, the good will be underprovided and so government must take action to increase the level of consumption.

Merit and demerit goods

Merit goods provide greater benefits than the level of benefit recognised by the purchaser. Consequently, they tend to be underprovided and so government intervention will take the form of ensuring that a greater quantity of merit goods is consumed. Demerit goods are overprovided by the market mechanism and so government action will be taken to reduce the consumption of these goods.

Imperfect or asymmetric information

Imperfect information can lead to a misallocation of resources because a person making an economic decision will be unable to act rationally if they are not in full possession of the facts. For example, an individual may pay a high price for a good because they are unaware that it is on sale for a lower price elsewhere. Similarly, asymmetric information means that one of the parties to the decision has more information than the other and is therefore likely to be in a stronger bargaining position. This may lead to an unfair allocation of resources. Governments can take action to try to ensure that information is evenly shared among all parties to economic decisions, though this can be a difficult challenge.

Monopoly or monopoly power

Monopolists can set the price of a good, knowing that there is no alternative supplier. Consequently, consumers are likely to be exploited by the monopolist in the form of higher prices. Furthermore, the monopolist may have little incentive to improve efficiency and so productive inefficiency may result. Monopoly power, such as that possessed by oligopolists, can also lead to market failure, though the existence of some competition will reduce the extent to which monopoly power distorts the working of the free market. Government can intervene either to prevent monopoly power occurring or, where monopoly power already exists, to restrict the behaviour of the person or organisation with monopoly power.

Immobility of factors of production

Perfect competition is based on the assumption that factors of production can flow freely between alternative uses. All four factors of production experience immobility, to varying degrees. Land for construction is completely immobile, and the economic success of London has led to a breakdown in the market mechanism. In theory, less profitable firms should be forced into other areas by the high land prices and rents in London. However, to some extent, firms have been able to afford these rents much more than labour. This has led to upward pressure on wages because of the relatively scarce supply of labour in London and the high transport costs for London's workforce. As seen earlier, labour is both geographically and occupationally immobile and this leads to situations where there is unemployment in some geographical and occupational areas and yet shortages of jobs in other areas. Arguably, this is the area of market failure that the government has found hardest to resolve through government intervention.

Inequality of income and wealth

In Chapter 28 we saw how government tackled inequalities in income and wealth through government spending and taxation, in order to allow the market mechanism to work in accordance with people's needs rather than their access to money. Inequalities from discrimination, such as disability and race discrimination, have been dealt with by government intervention through legislation. However, it has not proved possible to use legislation to accommodate the disadvantages experienced by people on low incomes.

Ways in which governments intervene

Governments influence the allocation of resources in a variety of ways, notably through public expenditure, taxation and regulations. The main methods of government intervention are: (1) public expenditure; (2) improving the quality of information; (3) direct taxation; (4) indirect taxation; (5) subsidies; (6) price controls; (7) state provision of a good or service; (8) regulations and legislation. *(Methods 1 to 3 are described below. Methods 4 to 8 will be explained in detail in the final section of this chapter.)*

1 Public expenditure

In Chapter 28 we saw how public (government) expenditure and taxation can be used in order to redistribute income and wealth and thus overcome market failure. UK taxation is regressive overall, though some taxes, such as income tax, are progressive. This is because most taxes, such as VAT and excise duties, are regressive. Redistribution of income and wealth is therefore primarily conducted through public expenditure. Benefits in kind are largely used to finance the provision of public goods and encourage the production of merit goods, such as healthcare and education. These goods are provided freely to people, usually regardless of their financial circumstances. Cash-in-hand payments are used to overcome problems of inequality by providing financial support to those families whose incomes are deemed to be too low. These payments are usually means tested and based on the income of the recipient.

Key term

Public expenditure describes spending by government on the provision of goods and services and spending on cash benefits. It is often referred to as government spending.

Economists who support the market economy believe that public expenditure on welfare benefits undermines the operation of the market by taking away the incentive to earn money from people who receive benefits. Economists who support intervention argue that the necessity for benefits arises because the market mechanism has failed and so government intervention is necessary to ensure that economic welfare is maximised. Since views of market failure and its extent are based on value judgements, it is impossible to provide a completely objective view on the desirability of this public expenditure. Intervention means that taxpayers are paying to overcome perceived failure in the achievement of economic welfare.

Public expenditure is also required to support specific methods of overcoming market failure, such as:

- providing information to overcome information failure;
- paying subsidies to producers of merit goods;
- monitoring and regulating price controls;
- spending on goods and services that are provided by the state, such as the rail network;
- enforcing regulations.

These items of public expenditure will be dealt with in the relevant sections of this chapter, when examining other methods of government intervention.

2 Improving the quality of information

Government can take action in order to improve the quality of information flowing to consumers where, as participants in economic decisions, they suffer from a lack of information. By improving their quality of information, market failure arising from asymmetric information can be reduced. This also allows the market mechanism to work more smoothly because the operation of the market is not being impaired by a lack of information for some participants.

In effect, government is trying to influence the demand for products where that demand may be influenced by incorrect information. Information may also be provided to make consumers aware of the externalities arising from some of their decisions, so that they may be aware of them in future purchasing decisions. Examples of government intervention to improve the quality of information include:

- legislation on how interest rates are calculated and defined, so that consumers can compare different loans;
- public information broadcasts, to educate people on factors such as the effects of speed on the safety of pedestrians;
- labelling of food products, to help people overcome the dangers of food allergies;
- promotion and advertising of health screening programmes, to help people avoid addiction and/or certain illnesses;
- warnings on cigarette packets, advising potential consumers on the risks of smoking.

In general, government information is used most widely to discourage consumption of demerit goods, by educating people about the damaging effects of these products that might not otherwise be known to consumers. In some cases, the information is geared towards encouraging the use of merit goods, particularly healthy foods. Financed by the taxpayers (who meet the cost of advertising and enforcement) and producers (who may need to modify and relabel their products), comparatively little money is spent on these activities.

3 Direct taxation

Key term
Direct taxes are those levied on income or wealth such as income tax.

In the context of government intervention, taxation is vital because it is needed to finance the costs of government intervention. Specifically, direct taxation is used to overcome market failure arising from inequality. In Chapter 28 we saw that only two of the UK's major taxes are progressive – income tax and national insurance contributions. Inheritance tax is also progressive, though the revenue received from it is quite small in comparison to many other taxes. These progressive taxes enable the government to redistribute income and, to a lesser extent, wealth from the rich to the poor in order to increase economic welfare.

The burden of direct taxation falls on the taxpayer. Progressive taxes take a larger percentage of income from the rich than the poor. However, whether the UK tax system is most beneficial to the rich or the poor is a value judgement. There is widespread agreement that, in terms of financial burden, the rich should pay not just more tax but a larger percentage of their income than the poor. However, the extent to which taxation should be progressive is again a value judgement. In 1976 the basic rate of income tax was 36%, increasing to 83% for incomes above a certain level. In 2015 the rates are 20% and 45% respectively – much less progressive.

(Methods 4 to 8 will be explained in detail in the final section of this chapter.)

Government objectives and their impact on government intervention

Government intervention in the marketplace is intended to overcome market failure. We saw in the first section of this chapter that there are many possible causes of market failure. Consequently, different examples of government intervention may have different objectives to achieve, such as ensuring the production of public goods, restricting the negative externalities of a good or service, or overcoming information failure. Some forms of government intervention are better suited to overcoming certain forms of market failure. Table 29.1 summarises the different causes of market failure and the possible methods that could be used to overcome the consequences.

A list of the main methods/ways of overcoming market failure was provided on p. 253. The first three methods on this list – public expenditure, improving the quality of information and direct taxation – have been explained on pp. 253–254. The remaining five methods are explained in the next section.)

The use of indirect taxation, subsidies, price controls, state provision and regulation to correct market failure

4 Indirect taxation to correct market failure

Indirect taxes are taxes on a good or a service. This method of government intervention is most suited to overcome market failure caused by demerit goods or goods with negative externalities.

Key term

Indirect taxes are paid on spending by firms, households and other organisations. The major indirect tax in the UK is value added tax (VAT).

Indirect taxes can be ad valorem (percentage) or specific.

- An ad valorem tax adds a certain percentage to the cost of the good. VAT is the most well-known ad valorem tax in the UK. For most products, VAT is charged at a rate of 20%. Thus a product costing £1 will be subject to VAT of 20p; a product costing £50 will have VAT of £10 added. Other examples of ad valorem taxes are betting tax (15%) and bingo tax (10%).
- A specific tax is one that adds a certain amount regardless of the price of the good. For example, petrol duty is currently (2015) 57.95p per litre while a pint of 4%-proof alcohol has a tax of 42.58 pence.

Some goods have both specific and ad valorem taxes. For example, petrol, alcohol and tobacco all have specific taxes and VAT added to their cost.

Ad valorem (%) taxes

In Figure 29.1, the market equilibrium point is X, with the equilibrium quantity being OQ_E. The government imposes a percentage, or ad valorem, tax (e.g. VAT). Consequently, the amount offered for supply moves from line S to line S + T, with the vertical difference between them (shown by the arrows) being the amount of tax. The imposition of the tax has shifted the supply curve to the left, indicating a decrease in supply. The tax acts in the same way as a rise in the costs of production. Note how the vertical distance between the two lines increases as the selling price increases. At higher prices an ad valorem tax is a higher sum than it is at lower prices.

Figure 29.1 shows the effect of the tax on both producers and consumers. Before the tax was imposed the equilibrium point was X, giving an equilibrium price of P_E and an equilibrium quantity of Q_E. The amount spent by consumers (and the total revenue for the firms) *before* the tax was therefore OP_EXQ_E. After the tax is imposed, Y is the new equilibrium point, with a new equilibrium price of P_2 and

Cause of market failure	Possible methods of government intervention	Effects of intervention
Public goods	■ State provision/public expenditure ■ Regulations and legislation ■ Subsidies	Since public goods are underprovided by the market mechanism, and may even be missing markets, state provision can be used to ensure they are provided. If there is some provision, subsidies and legislation can be used to increase the level of output in order to overcome market failure.
Positive externalities	■ Subsidies ■ Regulations and legislation ■ Price controls	Subsidies and price controls tend to be used to encourage producers to provide more goods where positive externalities exist. Regulations may be used to ensure producers provide better information in order to encourage more consumption of these products.
Negative externalities	■ Indirect taxes ■ Regulations and legislation ■ Price controls	Indirect taxes and price controls are used to increase prices and discourage consumers from buying products with negative externalities. Regulations are mainly used to limit output where the negative externalities arise from production; however, better information for consumers may be used to discourage consumption of these products.
Merit goods	■ State provision ■ Subsidies ■ Regulations and legislation ■ Price controls	State provision can be used if the merits are significant but not fully recognised by consumers, such as in health and education. Subsidies and price controls tend to be used to encourage producers to provide more merit goods, such as agricultural products and private health and education, as private provision reduces the government's financial expenditure. Government might also provide better information to encourage more consumption of these products.
Demerit goods	■ Indirect taxes ■ Regulations and legislation ■ Price controls	Indirect taxes and price controls are used to increase prices and discourage consumers from buying demerit goods. Regulations are mainly used to limit output, and possibly even ban products; for example, there are bans on certain drugs or age limits on products, such as tobacco and alcohol. Better information for consumers may be used to discourage consumption of these products.
Information failure	■ Legislation, such as consumer protection laws ■ Education, including state education ■ Public expenditure to promote the virtues of merit goods and educate people on the negative effects of demerit goods	Consumer protection laws and health and safety legislation are used to overcome information failure. A better-educated population should assist this process. Firms with monopoly power experience greater government scrutiny as these markets tend to have the most asymmetric information.
Monopoly and monopoly power	■ Regulations and legislation ■ State provision/public expenditure ■ Direct taxation ■ Price controls	The MCA regulates monopoly and monopoly power. Certain industries are supervised by regulatory bodies such as Ofgem and Ofcom, with possible price controls enforced if approved by government. Occasionally increases in direct taxes on profits can be used to discourage the use of monopoly power.
Immobility of factors of production	■ State provision of housing, to ease house moving ■ Education, to encourage the development of workforce skills and flexibility ■ Regulations and legislation, such as rent control	In general, education is seen to be the key factor to encourage greater occupational mobility, while a more flexible housing market can encourage greater geographical mobility of labour.
Inequality of income and wealth	■ Public expenditure ■ Direct taxes ■ Subsidies	Progressive direct taxes can help to redistribute income and wealth, and many subsidised products are those purchased predominantly by people on lower incomes. However, public expenditure, particularly on welfare benefits, is the most usual way of achieving greater equality.

Table 29.1 *The possible methods and effects of government intervention in response to market failure*

a new equilibrium quantity of Q_2. The amount spent by consumers *after* the tax is therefore OP_2YQ_2. The vertical distance between S and S + T is the level of tax. At the new output of Q_2, the tax per unit is the distance ZY. This means the government's tax revenue is BP_2YZ. Although the tax per unit is the distance ZY, the price increase is equivalent to AY – slightly less than the tax increase. This means that the suppliers receive a total revenue shown by the area $OBZQ_2$.

Indirect taxes are popular with governments because they can improve economic welfare *and* also bring in extra government revenue. The equilibrium output has fallen (from Q_E to Q_2) and so fewer negative externalities are experienced *or* fewer demerit goods are produced. Consequently, economic welfare has been improved at no cost to the government. In fact the government has gained extra tax revenue of BP_2YZ.

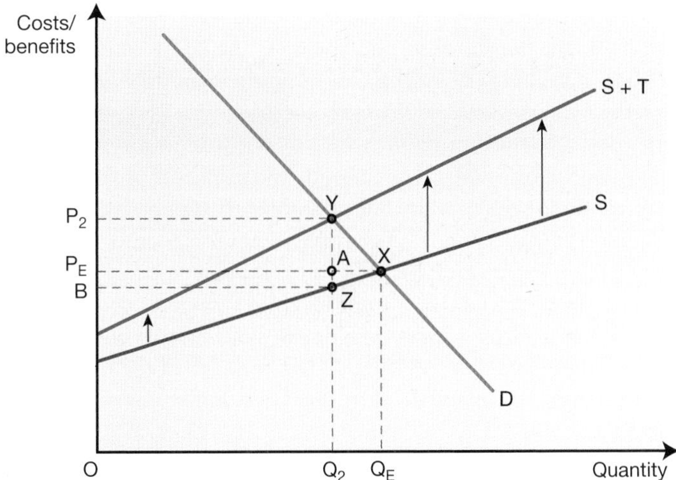

Figure 29.1 *Effect of an ad valorem tax on a good*

Key note

The **incidence of a tax** shows who has suffered the financial burden. In this case the tax is ZY per unit (or the vertical distance BP_2). The price has increased from P_E to P_2. The consumers pay for this price rise. The *incidence* of the tax has fallen mostly on the consumers, but a small percentage of it has fallen on the suppliers because they receive OB per item rather than OP_E.

Specific taxes

Value added tax (VAT) is the main indirect tax in the UK, but specific taxes (X pence per item) are used for many demerit goods. A specific tax moves supply parallel to the original line: there is no increase in gradient as there is with VAT. In this way the government can plan its intervention with some precision. If the government believes that the external cost of the negative externalities that a good imposes is valued at £2, then it can impose a specific tax of £2 per unit. With this £2 tax, the market mechanism is now taking into consideration the cost of the negative externalities. (For demerit goods, the negative consequences can also be measured in order to set the level of tax.) This can be seen in taxes on alcohol, where the tax increases as the level of alcohol in a drink increases.

The exact effect of an indirect tax on price and quantity bought depends on both the price elasticity of demand and the price elasticity of supply. Figures 29.2 and 29.3 show the effects of a specific tax (a fixed sum per unit) on the equilibrium price and quantity. However, in Figure 29.2 demand is price inelastic, whereas in Figure 29.3 demand is price elastic.

Note how the supply lines (S and S + T) are parallel. A specific tax of £4 per unit means that it is £4 more expensive to supply each unit of the good, regardless of its selling price.

In Figure 29.2, the market equilibrium point is X. The government imposes a specific tax of £4 per unit, decreasing supply from line S to line S + T, with the vertical difference between them (shown by the arrows) being the amount of tax. The tax acts in the same way as a rise in the costs of production of £4.

Figure 29.2 shows the effect of the tax on both producers and consumers. Before the tax was imposed, the equilibrium point was X, giving an equilibrium price of £7 and an equilibrium quantity of 7 units. The amount spent by consumers (and the total revenue for the firms) *before* the tax was therefore £7 × 7 = £49. After the tax is imposed, Y is the new equilibrium point, with a new equilibrium price of £10 and a new equilibrium quantity of 6 units. The amount spent by consumers *after* the tax is therefore £10 × 6 = £60. At the new output of 6 units, the tax per unit is the distance ZY (£4). This means the government's tax revenue is £4 × 6 units = £24. Although the tax per unit is the distance ZY (£4), the price increase is equivalent to AY (£3). This means that the suppliers receive a total revenue shown by the area OBZC: £6 × 6 units = £36. For each of the 6 units bought, the consumer is paying an extra £3, giving £18 in total. The supplier is receiving £1 less for each of the 6 units sold (£6 in total). Thus three-quarters of the incidence of the tax is falling on the consumer, with the supplier paying one-quarter of the tax.

Figure 29.2 *Effect of a specific tax on a good with price inelastic demand*

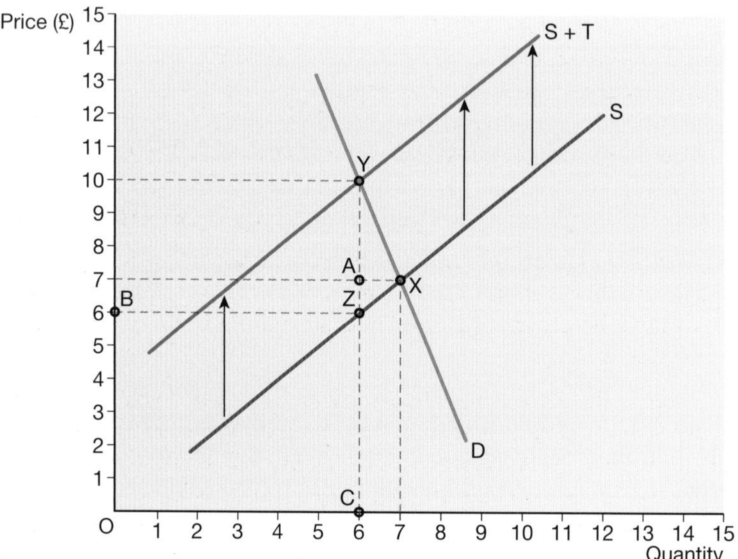

Conclusion: Where price elasticity of demand is inelastic, the incidence of the tax falls mainly on the consumer. The price rises significantly, but the quantity purchased only falls slightly. As there is just a slight decline in the quantity purchased, government tax revenue is quite high. In this scenario the consumer is bearing the brunt of efforts to improve economic welfare.

In Figure 29.3, the market equilibrium point is X. The government imposes a specific tax of £4 per unit, decreasing supply from line S to line S + T.

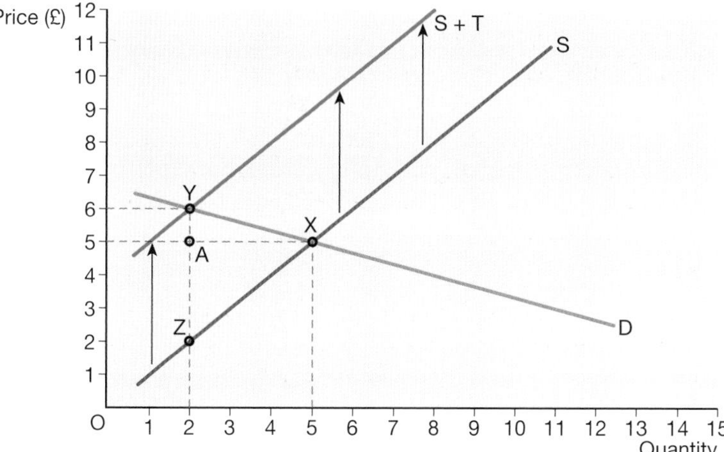

Figure 29.3 *Effect of a specific tax on a good with price elastic demand*

Figure 29.3 shows the effect of the tax on both producers and consumers. Before the tax was imposed the equilibrium point was X, giving an equilibrium price of £5 and an equilibrium quantity of 5 units. The amount spent by consumers (and the total revenue for the firms) *before* the tax was therefore £5 × 5 = £25. After the tax is imposed, Y is the new equilibrium point, with a new equilibrium price of £6 and a new equilibrium quantity of 2 units. The amount spent by consumers *after* the tax is therefore £6 × 2 = £12. At the new output of 2 units, the tax per unit is the distance ZY (£4). This means that the government's tax revenue is £4 × 2 units = £8. Although the tax per unit is the distance ZY (£4), the price increase is equivalent to AY (£1). This means that the suppliers receive total revenue of £2 × 2 units = £4. For each of the 2 units bought, the consumer is paying an extra £1, giving £2 in total. The supplier is receiving £3 less for each of the 2 units sold (£6 in total). Thus one-quarter of the incidence of the tax is falling on the consumer, with the supplier paying three-quarters of the tax.

Conclusion: Where price elasticity of demand is elastic, the incidence of the tax falls mainly on the supplier. The price rises slightly, but the quantity purchased falls significantly. As there is a major decline in the quantity purchased, government tax revenue is low. In this scenario the supplier is bearing the brunt of efforts to improve economic welfare.

Overall summary: Where demand is price inelastic, indirect taxation is likely to be ineffective in overcoming market failure because it has relatively little impact on the quantity purchased. However, it is a very useful strategy for raising tax revenue. Where demand is price elastic, indirect taxation is likely to be very effective in overcoming market failure because it has a significant impact on the quantity purchased. However, it is very damaging to the firms affected by the tax and it raises very little revenue. Consequently, governments are reluctant to tax goods with very price elastic demand unless they have serious negative repercussions on economic welfare.

Author tip

Draw diagrams based on different price elasticities of supply so that you can demonstrate the impact of an indirect tax on price and quantity.

Key note

The impact of an indirect tax on price and quantity is also influenced by the price elasticity of supply.

If the price elasticity of supply is elastic, an indirect tax tends to cause a large increase in price and also a significant fall in the quantity purchased. If the price elasticity of supply is inelastic, an indirect tax tends to cause a smaller increase in price and also a more limited fall in the quantity purchased.

For extreme values of price elasticity of demand and price elasticity of supply, the whole of the incidence of the tax may fall on either the supplier (producer) or the consumer. Table 29.2 summarises where the incidence falls in these situations.

Table 29.2 *Price elasticity of demand and the impact on price, incidence of tax and quantity purchased*

Price elasticity for good	Effect on price	Incidence of tax	Effect on quantity
Perfectly price elastic demand (PED = – ∞)	No change in price	All on supplier	Significant fall
Perfectly price inelastic demand (PED = 0)	Price increases by the full amount of the tax	All on consumer	No change in quantity
Perfectly price elastic supply (PES = + ∞)	Price increases by the full amount of the tax	All on consumer	Significant fall
Perfectly price inelastic supply (PES = 0)	No change in price	All on supplier	No change in quantity

5 Subsidies to correct market failure

Key term

A **subsidy** is a payment to a producer in order to encourage greater production of a good.

A subsidy involves government giving producers a sum of money for each unit produced, thus lowering the costs of supply. Subsidies are ideal for merit goods or goods that provide positive externalities in their consumption or production.

In Figure 29.4, the vertical distance between the original supply line (S) and the new supply line (S with subsidy) is the amount of the subsidy. This can be adjusted to take into consideration the level of positive externalities provided by the good, or the value of the unrecognised merits of the merit good. If a good provides considerable external benefits, then a larger subsidy should be provided.

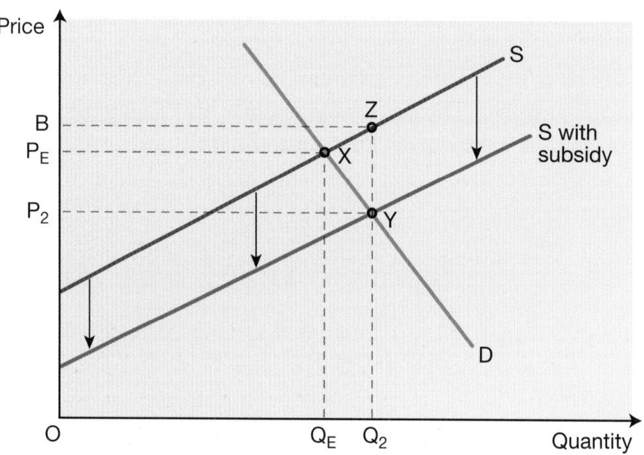

Figure 29.4 *Effect of a subsidy*

The original equilibrium is shown by Point X. After the subsidy, the equilibrium point moves from X to Y, so price falls from P_E to P_2 and quantity rises from Q_E to Q_2. The total expenditure by consumers is OP_2YQ_2, but the government subsidy is the vertical distance YZ. Subsidies reduce prices but cost governments money (the area P_2BZY). The total revenue received by suppliers has thus increased from OP_EXQ_E to $OBZQ_2$.

If demand is price inelastic, subsidies are very effective at reducing price. If demand is price elastic, subsidies are very effective at increasing consumption.

For supply elasticity, a highly price elastic supply will lead to a more significant cut in price and a more significant increase in the quantity purchased. For a more price inelastic supply, the effect on both price and quantity will be less.

Summary: Subsidies benefit consumers because they lead to a fall in the equilibrium price of the goods. They also benefit producers/suppliers because, as Figure 29.4 illustrates, the total revenue received by suppliers increases. However, subsidies are an example of government expenditure and so the taxpayers must meet the cost.

6 Price controls to correct market failure

Price controls take two main forms: minimum prices and maximum prices.

Key term

Price controls exist when government takes action to affect directly the price paid for a good.

Minimum prices

This method of government intervention usually takes the form of a guaranteed minimum price. Government will pay this price if the market price is too low in order to encourage suppliers to produce vital products. For example, it is used in agriculture to ensure that farmers produce certain products.

In Figure 29.5, P_{MIN} is the guaranteed minimum price and so suppliers supply Q_S items. This increases production, as only Q_E items would be produced in the free market. At P_{MIN} the consumers will only buy Q_D items and so government purchases the excess supply (AB). The area Q_DABQ_S shows the money spent by government to achieve its aim of higher production of this item.

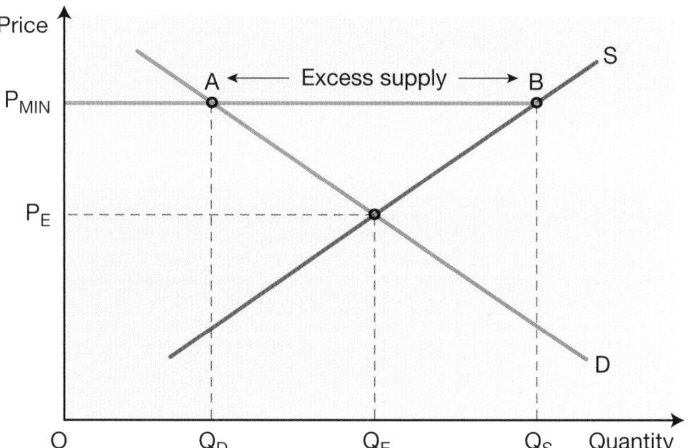

Figure 29.5 *Effects of a minimum price*

Where minimum prices are used, government might accumulate stocks of agricultural products (AB items in the case above). If the product can be preserved, government can use these **buffer stocks** to increase supply when a poor harvest occurs. This can prevent shortages and high prices that occur when supply is scarce. In times of shortage, government uses up buffer stock so that prices do not rise excessively. In times of good harvests, government builds up its buffer stock levels so that producers are guaranteed a price that encourages them to stay in the industry.

The most notable example of minimum pricing in the UK is the national minimum wage (NMW). This guarantees a minimum hourly wage rate for workers in the UK. For a minimum price to have an effect on a market, it must be set above the equilibrium price (wage).

Summary: Minimum prices tend to benefit suppliers, who will find it easier to earn profit. However, they lead to higher prices, which penalise consumers. If government buys the surplus, this will be a burden to taxpayers, though consumers may then receive benefits if buffer stocks are used to achieve greater price stability in future years.

Maximum prices

Maximum prices are usually used to ensure that everyone can afford a basic product. In times of shortage there is a danger that people with high incomes can buy all the supplies of a necessity in short supply, and so a maximum price may be introduced so that the product is more affordable.

In Figure 29.6, Point X shows the original equilibrium point. This leads to an equilibrium price of P_E and an equilibrium quantity of Q_E. Price P_E may be deemed to be excessive or beyond the means of some consumers. Thus government sets a maximum price of P_{MAX}. With a maximum price of P_{MAX}, which is below the equilibrium price, the supply falls to Q_S items but demand rises to Q_D. This leads to an excess demand of YZ. Consequently, there will be a shortage of the good. Goods may be sold on a first-come, first-serve basis, but this can lead to unfairness. Government may introduce rationing so that demand is restricted to the level available (Q_S).

Usually this situation will lead to a secondary market (often known as a black market) forming. Some people who receive the good through the first-come, first-serve method or through rationing may sell it in the secondary market. Due to the limited availability of goods in the secondary market, prices in the secondary market are likely to be much higher than the previous equilibrium price.

Figure 29.6 *Effects of a maximum price*

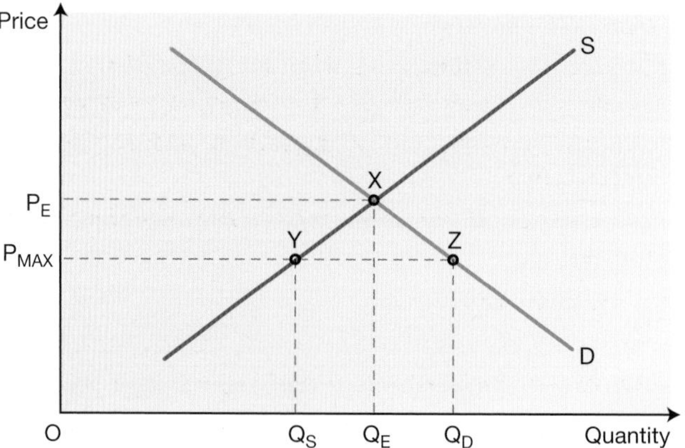

For a maximum price to have an effect on a market, it must be set below the equilibrium price.

Summary: Maximum prices tend to benefit consumers who are now able to buy products because the price is set below the original equilibrium price. However, it can mean that other consumers do not manage to access products or have to pay high prices through secondary (black) markets. Rationing can lead to fairness of allocation, but organising any system of rationing is a cost to the government and thus taxpayers. Suppliers suffer because they receive lower prices for their goods. Maximum pricing is not used very often because it is difficult to manage the eventual outcomes. Consequently it can lead to government failure (see Chapter 30).

7 State provision of a good or service to correct market failure

If there is complete market failure (a missing market), government may decide to provide that good or service. For example, street lighting and defence are provided because complete market failure is likely if supply is left to the market mechanism. Where partial market failure is likely to occur, government may offer state provision as an alternative to goods and services provided through the market mechanism.

For merit goods or in markets that have significant positive externalities, government may choose state provision as the best means to guarantee the right level of production (such as education for all children).

Views on the best level of state provision have varied over time. In the twentieth century it increased, most notably in the period just after the Second World War. Since 1979, there has been a steady reduction in the level of state provision. This has occurred because of changes in value judgements on market failure and the best ways to overcome it. Many goods and services that are funded by government are now provided through subcontracting the work to private firms. In this way, government hopes to retain control but improve productive efficiency.

8 Regulations to correct market failure

Regulation is where government intervenes through:

- consumer protection legislation;
- health and safety legislation;
- legislation to control specific causes of market failure, such as pollution legislation;
- banning products, such as drugs;
- placing restrictions on consumption, such as age restrictions for alcohol and restrictions on where products such as tobacco can be consumed;
- labelling to dissuade consumption or provide important information, such as ingredients and contents;
- advertising and persuasion to try to influence people's decisions, such as education on global warming.

Other examples of regulation are:

- pollution permits;
- giving property rights to firms, such as fishing rights;
- control of monopoly power through organisations such as the Competition and Markets Authority (CMA) and regulatory bodies, such as Ofcom and Ofgem.

There is no guarantee that government regulations will succeed. For example, banning products will often lead to unofficial markets arising. In some countries, such as the Netherlands, some drugs have been legalised, partly because legal transactions can be more easily taxed. When deciding on the use of regulation, government will consider carefully the likely outcome of the strategy.

REALWORLD ECONOMICS 29.1

Market failure and alcohol

Government intervention to limit market failure in the market for alcohol relies on regulations and indirect taxation. In Chapter 7 we saw how government used elasticity of demand data to influence its tax policy. Such data can also be used to overcome market failure in this market.

The use of taxation to control market failure depends on price elasticity of demand. If demand is price elastic, a small percentage change in price will lead to a larger percentage change in demand. The data in Table 29.4 show us that a 10% tax on spirits (on-trade) will lead to an 11.5% fall in demand. If demand is price inelastic, a large percentage change in price will lead to a smaller percentage change in demand. The data in Table 29.4 show us that a 10% tax on wine (on-trade) will lead to a 4.6% fall in demand.

If the government wishes to cut consumption of alcohol by 23%, it will need to levy different taxes. For spirits (on-trade), a 20% tax will lead to a 23% fall in demand. For wine (on-trade), a 50% tax will be needed to achieve a 23% fall in demand.

Table 29.4 *Price elasticity of demand for certain types of alcohol*

	Price elasticity of demand
Beer (on-trade)	−0.77
Beer (off-trade)	−1.11
Wine (on-trade)	−0.46
Wine (off-trade)	−0.54
Spirits (on-trade)	−1.15
Spirits (off-trade)	−0.90

Note: On-trade = public houses; off-trade = shops and off-licences

Table 29.3 *Key features of the market for alcohol and their implications for overcoming market failure*

Feature	Implication
40% of 15–16 year olds have consumed alcohol within the last 30 days.	Better education of families is required coupled with enforcement of age-restriction legislation.
The legal age for drinking is significant.	Research shows that a rise in the legal age reduces alcohol dependency in a population for people of all ages, as its effects can last for a lifetime.
The demand for alcohol tends to be price inelastic.	Indirect taxes need to be high if they are to reduce consumption significantly.
The demand for wine is more price inelastic than the demand for beer and spirits.	Taxes on wine need to be relatively high if the government's aim is to overcome market failure.
Price elasticity of demand is more price elastic for shop purchases than pub purchases.	Tax rises have a greater impact on supermarket sales than pub sales.

How should government tax different types of alcohol?

The government also calculates cross elasticities of demand between different types of alcohol. For example, the cross elasticity of demand between on-trade beer and on-trade wine is +0.54. This means that government will be under pressure to treat different types of alcohol in the same way. A 10% tax on beer will lead to a 5.4% increase in the demand for wine. This will be unfair on beer suppliers and will mean that there is more market failure caused by wine (instead of beer). For this reason, government tries to treat each type of alcohol in a similar way if possible.

Government policy on alcohol must also recognise the private benefits to consumers. People pay high prices for alcohol because they enjoy its consumption. This factor (and the political consequences of policies such as a ban) must be taken into account when government considers policies to overcome market failure.

Sources: European Commission, Eyes on Ages report, 2013; HMRC, 2010 and 2011

Exercises

Total: 40 marks

1 Calculate the effect on the quantity demanded of beer of a 20% tax on beer (on-trade). *(3 marks)*

2 In order to overcome market failure, government wants to

reduce demand for on-trade beer by 25%. What percentage tax would achieve this aim? *(4 marks)*

3 Give two reasons why on-trade/pub alcohol is more price inelastic than off-trade/shop alcohol. *(8 marks)*

4 Assess how the information here would help government decide on how to intervene in this market. *(25 marks)*

Review questions

Total: 70 marks

1 The government provides education because:
- A It would be a missing market in a free market economy
- B It wishes to limit free education to those within a certain age range
- C The social benefit from education exceeds the private benefit
- D Its negative externalities exceed its positive externalities *(1 mark)*

2 Public expenditure on welfare benefits is most likely to be used to overcome market failure caused by:
- A Inequality of income
- B Demerit goods
- C Monopoly power
- D Public goods *(1 mark)*

3 A subsidy is most likely to be used to overcome market failure in the case of:
- A Immobility of factors of production
- B Negative externalities
- C Asymmetric information
- D A merit good *(1 mark)*

4 The government might place an indirect tax on a particular good because it:
- A Reduces inequality
- B Is a merit good
- C Would be underproduced in a free market
- D Imposes costs on third parties *(1 mark)*

5 State *three* examples of regulations used to overcome market failure. *(3 marks)*

6 Define the term 'government intervention'. *(3 marks)*

7 Define the term 'subsidy'. *(3 marks)*

8 Explain how government might use legislation to overcome market failure. *(6 marks)*

9 Explain how the price elasticity of demand of a good influences the extent to which a specific tax changes the price and quantity bought of that good. *(8 marks)*

10 Explain, with the help of a diagram, how a government might use indirect taxation to overcome market failure. *(9 marks)*

11 Explain, with the help of a diagram, how a government might use minimum pricing to overcome market failure. *(9 marks)*

12 Evaluate the view that the most effective ways of overcoming market failure depend on the specific causes of market failure. *(25 marks)*

Government failure

This chapter introduces the concept of government failure and examines the possible sources of government failure. The ways in which governments may create rather than remove market distortions are considered. We conclude with a study of the law of unintended consequences.

Meaning of government failure

Key term

Government failure occurs when government intervention in the economy leads to a net loss in economic welfare and a misallocation of resources.

Government intervention attempts to improve the allocation of resources. However, there is no guarantee that intervention will lead to a perfect allocation of resources or maximisation of economic welfare. In fact, it is possible that government intervention worsens economic welfare. Such a situation is known as government failure. Government failure tends to arise when the eventual outcome of intervention is not the outcome that the government expected. It can be caused by many different factors, as described below.

Sources of government failure

Inadequate information

Government failure may arise because government lacks the necessary information to assess the level of intervention needed. For example, in the past, government encouraged high consumption of dairy products, such as milk, because medical information suggested it was healthy. This advice has been amended as new information has been acquired.

Control of energy companies tends to focus on the energy suppliers, such as EDF, which sell energy to customers. However, the finances of these companies are very complex because the suppliers tend to be owned by the companies that generate the energy, often from sources in other countries. Government attempts to regulate prices, by limiting the profit margins of the suppliers, has simply led to the firms that generate the energy charging much more to the suppliers. These are divisions of the same company, but the division being regulated does not make high profits. This failure is caused by asymmetric information because the energy companies have more knowledge than the regulatory body.

Author tip

Do not confuse market failure and government failure. The former term relates to failure of the market mechanism; the latter relates to the government trying to overcome market failure but failing to improve matters.

Conflicting objectives

The market mechanism is considered by some people to be the best means of maximising output because it rewards factors of production with unique qualities. However, it is also recognised as a contributor to inequality. Government therefore faces conflict in achieving higher output and greater equality, since the two objectives may not be mutually compatible.

There may also be other conflicts. For example, in agricultural intervention, government may offer guaranteed higher prices to encourage farmers to produce more. These higher prices will lead to more expensive food or higher taxation to enable final prices to be kept down. The benefits of intervention in terms of food production will therefore lead to negative consequences for other economic participants.

Administrative costs

Where government intervenes, administration of the process is needed. In the market economy, there is no need to pay anyone to organise the process because the market economy operates through the 'invisible hand'. The costs of government bureaucracy can seriously undermine any benefits gained from government intervention.

If government intervention produces welfare benefits, but the value of these benefits is less than the administrative costs of organising the policy, then the intervention has not been worthwhile. This means government failure has occurred.

Other sources of government failure

Disincentives

The market mechanism works through incentives. Each factor of production can earn a higher income through greater efficiency and the identification of new opportunities. However, intervention, such as government ownership, has a tendency to reduce incentives because the profit motive is lost. This can lead to productive inefficiency and therefore government failure.

Political decisions

Decisions may be based on politics rather than economics. For example, constant changes in education policy tend to be based on the political beliefs of the party in power. Expenditure is often geared towards areas of large population, particularly London. In 2014, public infrastructure projects, such as transport improvements, varied between regions. The total value of these projects in London was equivalent to £4952 for each resident. The next most generously funded region was the Northwest, with £1226 per person. In the Northeast, expenditure was £221 per person, and spending in the West Midlands was £380 per person.

Powerful interest groups, such as tobacco companies, can exert considerable influence on government. Decisions on major projects, such as airports, are often influenced by MPs whose constituencies will be affected. Politically popular policies are often announced just prior to general elections.

Short termism

There is a tendency for government to prefer short-term solutions. Long-term projects tend to drain government finances in the short run but provide benefits in the future. These benefits might take place when a different government is in power, receiving the popularity that the project brings. Consequently, government failure will often occur because the most effective policy is rejected due to short-term costs.

Regulatory capture

An important element of UK government control of monopoly power is in the form of regulatory bodies, such as Ofwat and ORR (railway companies). Due to the close links between the regulatory body and the companies, there is sometimes a perception that the regulator acts in the interests of the companies rather than consumers. Similarly, agricultural controls, originally intended to meet the needs of consumers, are often criticised for promoting the needs of farmers.

Government intervention and market distortions

The intention of government intervention is often to overcome distortions in the market. For example, externalities are not considered by the market mechanism, and information failure and monopoly power can distort the market so that it does not allocate resources in order to maximise economic welfare.

However, government intervention causes market distortions by not allowing the market to reach its equilibrium price. Intervention, such as subsidies, will reduce the price below the equilibrium and may therefore encourage greater use of resources by the subsidised industry at the expense of other industries.

Government intervention relies on distortion of the market in order for market failure to be overcome. However, these distortions may not eliminate the original problem or may create other problems.

In order to assess whether government intervention has led to an improvement in economic welfare or led to government failure by reducing net economic welfare, certain factors should be taken into consideration:

- *The efficiency of the specific government intervention* For example, intervention to negate monopoly power should lead to lower prices for consumers. If intervention leads to small firms with higher costs and higher prices, then government failure has occurred. Similarly, government intervention to overcome inequality is intended to lead to greater allocative efficiency. If intervention has achieved this aim, then government intervention has succeeded.
- *Fairness* Government intervention is intended to improve economic welfare for society as a whole. In the case of negative externalities, the beneficiaries of government intervention should be the people who have experienced the negative effects of those externalities. If government intervention leads to a reallocation of resources from the person or firm causing the negative externalities to groups that were not affected by the negative externalities, then the outcome is not equitable for those people still suffering from the negative externalities. For example, government may fine a polluting firm but spend the money elsewhere in the economy rather than compensating the people suffering from the pollution.
- *Sustainability* This principle of fairness should also apply to future generations. For example, when considering the use of non-renewable resources, government intervention should take into consideration the needs of the country in the future.

The law of unintended consequences

Key term

The **law of unintended consequences** occurs when the actions of participants in economic decisions, such as government, producers and consumers, are not the actions that were expected.

When government intervention leads to unintended consequences, then it is likely that the government has failed to eliminate market failure. For example, the UK's minimum wage is intended to ensure reasonable living standards for people who are at a disadvantage in the labour market, because they lack the skills to earn higher wages. However, for a minimum wage to be effective it must be above the market rate in certain occupations. In Chapter 29 we saw that a minimum price leads to lower demand for a good or service. In this case the service is the worker's job and so, in theory, a minimum wage should lead to lower levels of employment. In conclusion, a minimum wage will help people in low-paid occupations but may lead to some workers losing their jobs. Another possible consequence of minimum wage legislation is that it may take away the incentive to undertake some training. A person in a job that would pay a very low wage in a competitive market might consider training in order to move into a better-paid job. However, if both jobs are on the minimum wage, the incentive for the worker to improve their skills has been reduced.

The law of unintended consequences does not just apply to government intervention. An academic paper by Edmans, Fang and Lewellen (2013) entitled 'Equity vesting and managerial myopia' links share options to actions of CEOs (chief executive officers) of large businesses. In the 1970s many CEOs operated takeover and growth strategies that could be used to justify their large salaries, even though this growth often had negative effects on profit and thus shareholders' incomes. In order to overcome this problem, many firms introduced 'share options' where CEOs could buy company shares at a fixed price but were only allowed to sell them after a fixed period of time. This was intended to ensure that CEOs acted in the interests of shareholders rather than in the pursuit of personal 'power'.

The paper by Edmans et al. suggests that this has unintended consequences. Long-term strategies such as R&D and large-scale investment lead to lower short-term profits, due to the high initial costs, but greater profits in the long term. Edmans et al. have discovered that CEOs tend to cut back on these long-term strategies just prior to the dates on which they can cash in their shares, so that short-term profits (and share prices) rise. Consequently, CEOs are not serving the interests of shareholders who intend to keep their shareholdings for long periods.

Source: Edmans, Fang and Lewellen, 'Equity vesting and managerial myopia', September 2013, National Bureau of Economic Research, Working Paper No. 19407.

REALWORLD ECONOMICS 30.1

The Common Agricultural Policy (CAP) – an example of government failure?

The Common Agricultural Policy (CAP) was introduced in 1958 with five main aims. It seeks to:

- increase agricultural productivity;
- improve incomes for farmers;
- stabilise agricultural prices;
- ensure continuity of supply of agricultural products;
- ensure reasonable prices for consumers.

The CAP mainly uses price controls to achieve these aims. Primarily there is a guaranteed minimum price at which the European Union will buy surplus products and take them off the market. In order to restrict foreign competition, there is a threshold price: when world prices are lower than EU prices, the prices of imports from non-EU countries are increased to the EU price level. In recent years there have been policies to encourage environmentally friendly farming and 'set-aside', where farmers are paid to ensure that land is not used (thus ensuring continuity of long-term supply but avoiding short-term excesses that would lead to lower prices and the need for CAP intervention).

The CAP accounts for over 40% of the EU expenditure budget, though agriculture only represents 2% of the EU's gross domestic product (output) and 5% of its employment. This is equivalent to €100 per year for each resident of the EU.

The CAP is often cited as an example of government failure, for a number of reasons:

- It distorts markets. Europe does not have a natural advantage in most agricultural products and yet it is the second largest exporter of these products. This arises because of the surpluses bought by the EU, which are then disposed of outside the EU at low prices. These low prices distort the market, particularly for developing countries whose exports are reduced. Furthermore, this means that these countries have less national income with which to buy secondary and tertiary products from the EU.

- Productive efficiency is hindered by policies such as set-aside, where land is deliberately not used. The basic principle of CAP is to overproduce agricultural products – a clear example of allocative inefficiency in the market. Furthermore, the policy means that land is kept for agricultural use when it would be better suited for other purposes.
- The policy is considered to be inequitable as it has tended to lead to increases in farm incomes, mainly benefiting the large farms. It also leads to higher prices and, as foodstuffs take up a larger percentage of the budgets of people on low incomes, it is argued that the CAP redistributes income away from the poor.
- For most of its existence, the CAP encouraged the use of pesticides and other strategies that have caused damage to the environment, though more recent approaches are trying to redress this failure.
- Within the EU, the CAP redistributes income between countries in a random fashion that is not linked to living standards, though since the expansion of the EU to include Eastern European countries there has been greater equity in the policy.

However, the CAP has succeeded in achieving most of its aims. Continuity of supply and self-sufficiency in most products have been achieved, though people question whether this is a sensible objective. European agriculture has also benefited from modernisation, which has improved productive efficiency. Prices have generally been more stable than prior to the CAP, but price levels have tended to be higher in countries such as the UK, which previously used subsidies as a means of controlling agricultural prices. Farm incomes have kept pace with other incomes within the EU.

Discussion point

The CAP has succeeded in achieving most of its original aims. Does this mean that it is not an example of government failure?

Review questions

Total: 30 marks

1 If Ofgem is reluctant to cut energy prices because it needs the continual cooperation of the energy suppliers, this is an example of government failure through:

A Disincentives
B Political decisions
C Regulatory capture
D Short termism

(1 mark)

2 If government is reluctant to undertake large-scale projects, such as the HS2 high-speed rail link, because they worsen the current budget, this is an example of government failure through:

A Disincentives
B Conflicting objectives
C Regulatory capture
D Short termism

(1 mark)

3 State two examples of conflicting government objectives that might lead to government failure. ***(2 marks)***

4 Define 'government failure'. ***(3 marks)***

5 Explain how inadequate information can lead to government failure. ***(5 marks)***

6 Why does government intervention require more administrative costs than the market mechanism? ***(5 marks)***

7 Explain 'the law of unintended consequences'. ***(5 marks)***

8 Explain two ways in which government intervention can lead to market distortion. ***(8 marks)***

Topic 5 Exam-style questions

AS LEVEL PAPER 1

Context – The BBC and TV broadcasting

Extract A **TV industry revenues, by share, 2008–13**

UK television industry	2008	2009	2010	2011	2012	2013
Total TV industry revenue (£ billion)	11.2	11.0	11.8	12.3	12.4	12.9
Revenue from public funds (%)	23	23	22	21	21	20
Revenue from advertising (%)	31	28	30	29	28	29
Revenue from subscriptions (%)	39	42	43	44	44	46
Revenue from other sources (%)[a]	7	7	5	6	7	5
TOTAL	**100**	**100**	**100**	**100**	**100**	**100**
Viewing per head – hours per day	*3.74*	*3.75*	*4.04*	*4.03*	*4.01*	*3.9*
Market share of five main channels (%)	*61*	*58*	*56*	*54*	*52*	*51*
Number of channels broadcasting	*495*	*490*	*510*	*515*	*529*	*527*

Note: (a) Other sources include sponsorship, TV shopping and interactive revenue. *Source:* Ofcom Annual Report on Telecommunications, August 2014

Extract B **Regulating the pay-TV market**

The subscription TV market is dominated by Sky, which had a 70% share of this market in 2014. Satellite/subscription broadcasting commenced in the late-1980s with two suppliers (BSB and Sky), but high start-up costs confirmed the view of many people that satellite broadcasting was a natural monopoly. Early competition in this market was eliminated when Sky took over the other main provider (BSB) in 1990, with both companies suffering from heavy debts from high start-up costs. These costs proved to be a very effective barrier to entry in this industry, allowing Sky to maintain its dominance.

Sky's financial success derived from its successful bid for exclusive rights to live TV broadcasting of Premiership football. Sports programmes account for 43% of all revenue for commercial broadcasters and Sky's dominance of this market has enabled it to create barriers to entry. Furthermore, from 1990 to 2008 subscription TV's market share of TV viewing rose to 38%, though it has fallen back slightly in recent years.

In 2010 Ofcom, the regulatory body for TV, ruled that Sky was exploiting its monopoly power and so Sky had to offer its sports channels to other broadcasters on 'fair terms'. In May 2013, BT sparked a price war with Sky when it entered this market by offering free access to live football matches for its broadband subscribers. Sky offered access to its football matches to TalkTalk, a small competitor. However, it refused to allow BT to access its channels in the same way. BT complained to Ofcom that Sky was abusing its monopoly power. Currently (March 2015) Ofcom has not ruled on this dispute.

Sources: Various, including *Independent*, 19.6.13

Extract C **The BBC – from public good to merit good?**

The BBC was formed in 1922 to provide radio (and subsequently) TV broadcasting. At the time the technology and high start-up costs led to the view that it was a natural monopoly. It also possessed the characteristics of a public good and so it was funded by government, through a licensing system. Initially only the rich had radios and so the licence fee was considered to be a progressive 'tax'. However, currently the fixed annual fee paid by all TV/radio owners is seen to be a regressive tax.

In the 1950s, ITV was introduced, funded by TV advertising, and in 1990 satellite broadcasting was introduced, funded by customers paying a subscription to providers such as Sky.

Is the £4 billion licence fee paid annually to the BBC now justifiable? Supporters of the BBC argue that the Corporation can prevent market failure in different ways:

- Commercial TV providers focus on populist programmes, such as soaps and football. Thus a free market would limit breadth of choice.
- The BBC provides quality broadcasting, aided by its guaranteed source of income and its charter that requires it to provide some programmes for minority tastes.
- The BBC's focus on news brings positive externalities to the UK's population as a whole. Its duty to 'inform' also helps to educate people to select their programme choices more knowledgeably.
- Negative externalities, such as commercial programmes including violence and offensive language, can be limited.
- It is a progressive service because it is more affordable than subscription TV and is not the cause of firms increasing prices to fund TV advertising.
- Large-scale broadcasting involves many barriers to entry – high entry costs and high costs to obtain certain licences – leading to a few large firms having monopoly power.

Thus the BBC acts as a merit good because it:

- acts as a counterweight to the private concentration of market power;
- provides a guarantee of quality and minority programming;
- widens choice.

Sources: Various, including Review of the Future Funding of the BBC

Questions

Total: 50 marks

1 Define the term 'public good'. *(3 marks)*

2 Using Extract A, calculate the revenue received by TV broadcasters from subscriptions in 2013. *(4 marks)*

3 Using Extract A, identify two significant points of comparison relating to changes in the TV broadcasting market between 2008 and 2013. *(4 marks)*

4 The government considers violence on TV to be a demerit good. Using a suitable diagram, show how the government can influence the TV market to try to ensure that people are less likely to view programmes depicting violence. *(4 marks)*

5 Explain why it is difficult to avoid market failure in the market for subscription TV broadcasting. *(10 marks)*

6 Assess whether the government should continue to fund the BBC. *(25 marks)*

Section 2

The national economy in a global context

Topic 6

The measure of macroeconomic performance

Chapter 31

The objectives of government economic policy

This chapter introduces you to the concept of macroeconomics and the major issues that comprise this branch of economics. It focuses on the main macroeconomic objectives that governments pursue when making policy decisions and considers other, possibly less common, objectives that might influence macroeconomic policy decisions. The chapter also explores the possibility of conflict arising in that a decision to achieve one macroeconomic policy objective may make another objective less attainable.

What is macroeconomics?

Key term

Macroeconomics is that part of economics that is concerned with data, decisions, performance, policies and objectives that relate to the whole economy.

The term 'macro' comes from the Greek word 'Makro', which means large. Thus any study of policies, behaviour, decisions and objectives that relate to the whole economy form a part of this branch of economics.

Issues related to macroeconomics are covered extensively in the media, including the following:

- the rate at which the output or production of the economy is growing. This may be fast, as in China and Nigeria in recent years, or slow (or perhaps even negative), which has been the case in several European Union countries since 2014.
- what is happening to the general price level in an economy. Prices may be rising quickly, causing problems for businesses and households. More unusually, prices may be falling.
- the value of the country's currency falling or rising against other countries' currencies. This will have implications for consumers who are considering a holiday overseas and for businesses that trade overseas.
- changes in the number of people looking for work but unable to find it. The inability to find employment can lead to considerable hardship for those concerned and may have significant implications for government expenditure on unemployment benefit as well as the amount of revenue received from income tax.

Key macroeconomic objectives

A good starting point for the study of macroeconomics is to consider the goals or objectives that a government may set to guide its economic decision making. This means that decisions taken by government officials on a wide range of matters such as government spending, taxation, setting interest rates and negotiating trade agreements with other countries will be influenced by the need to achieve these objectives.

Successive UK governments have pursued four main macroeconomic objectives when implementing their economic policies. These macroeconomic objectives are:

- price stability, i.e. a low rate of inflation;
- sustainable rates of economic growth;
- low unemployment;
- a balanced balance of payments.

REALWORLD ECONOMICS 31.1

UK unemployment at its lowest since 2008

The percentage of the UK's workforce that is unemployed fell to 5.7% in the three months to January 2015. This is the lowest rate of unemployment since 2008. A report by the Office for National Statistics (ONS) revealed that the number of people seeking work fell by 102,000 to 1.86 million.

At the same time the number claiming Jobseeker's Allowance (a benefit paid to those who are out of work and actively seeking employment) fell to 700,000 in February 2015. During the year to February 2015 the number of unemployed people in the UK fell by 381,000. Simultaneously the number of people in the UK in employment rose by 617,000 in the year from March 2014 to February 2015.

Exercise

1 Explain why the UK government might be very pleased with this report from the Office for National Statistics. *(10 marks)*

Price stability

If prices are stable, then they are changing little and the rate of inflation is low and relatively predictable. Inflation measures the rate at which the general level of prices is increasing and the associated fall in the value of money, as a given sum of money buys fewer products after a period of inflation. If the general price level falls over a period of time, this is termed 'deflation' and will result in a rise in the value of money. High inflation rates or deflation can be very damaging to an economy and so price stability is judged to be a key government macroeconomic objective.

Key term

Inflation is the rate of increase of the general price level and the corresponding fall in the value of money.

The UK government has targeted inflation through its economic policies since 1992, and in 1997 it gave the Bank of England an inflation target along with responsibility for setting interest rates. The UK government expects the Bank of England to take decisions (such as changing the bank – or base – rate of interest) with the aim of achieving price stability. The bank is allowed some flexibility in achieving this objective: although the official target rate for inflation is currently 2%, any figure within the range 1% to 3% is acceptable. If the rate moves outside this 1–3% range, the Bank of England is expected to take appropriate actions. We will consider the role of the Bank of England more fully in Chapter 45.

Figure 31.1 shows that for much of the period from 2008 to 2014, UK inflation has been within 1% of its target, though it reached 5% briefly in 2008 and again in 2011.

Why is price stability a macroeconomic objective?

High rates of inflation are undesirable for a number of reasons:

- If UK inflation is high in comparison to other countries, it reduces the competitiveness of UK products and so exports fall and imports increase.
- High inflation can distort spending patterns, with people spending more on goods such as housing, which tends to increase in value. If prices are expected to increase, people may be prompted to replace durable goods, such as cars and furniture.

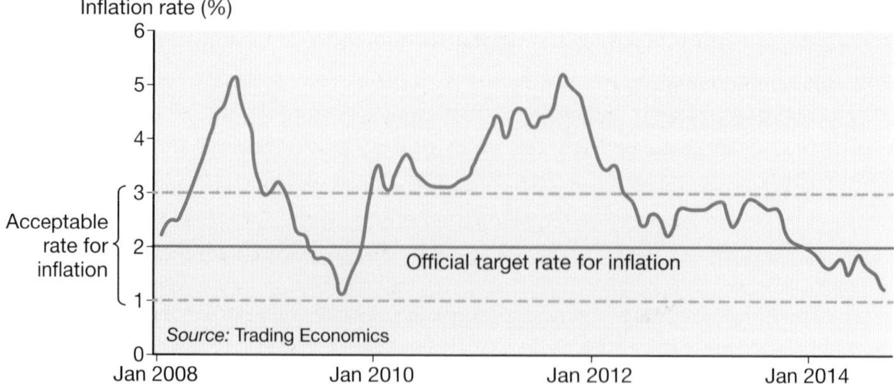

Figure 31.1 *UK rate of inflation, as measured by the Consumer Prices Index, 2008–14*

- Consumers spend more time researching constantly changing prices, and businesses devote increasing amounts of time and money to updating prices and catalogues.
- Inflation can redistribute income and wealth in a random manner. In general, inflation hits the poor more than the rich, as the poor are often in a weaker position to gain income increases to match price rises.

Deflation is frequently considered to be a greater problem than inflation. When prices fall, people postpone spending, and businesses may invest less in new factories, offices, shops and other resources used to produce goods and services. This may lead to an economy producing fewer goods and services and it may also result in fewer jobs. These are severe consequences and this is why price stability is the most important macroeconomic objective. Fortunately, deflation in the UK is rare, especially when using the government's favoured measure, the Consumer Prices Index (CPI), to measure the rate of UK inflation.

If price stability is achieved, and low and predictable rates of inflation are the norm, businesses will have greater confidence in the future stability of the economy. This will encourage them to invest in factories, machinery and other resources, leading to the economy growing and more jobs becoming available. As a result, people's incomes and standards of living should rise.

Sustainable rates of economic growth

You will see in Chapter 38 that economic growth occurs when, over time, an economy expands its capacity to produce goods and services. The UK government does not simply pursue the highest rate of economic growth possible. This would lead to a range of other problems including damage to the environment, the depletion of non-renewable resources and the possibility of fuelling high rates of inflation. Instead it aims to achieve a 'sustainable' rate of economic growth. This is a rate of growth that has the potential to increase levels of production in the economy and people's

Key terms

Economic growth occurs when, over time, an economy expands its capacity to produce goods and services.

Gross domestic product or **GDP** is the value of all goods and services produced within an economy over a given period of time.

A **recession** is a decline in the level of economic activity (as measured by a fall in GDP) that occurs over a six-month period or longer.

incomes, and to do so with minimal adverse side effects. In this way the growth rate of the economy should be able to continue into the future and thus be sustainable.

It is difficult to measure the productive capacity of an economy and particularly tricky to measure changes in it. As a result, the percentage change in gross domestic product (or GDP) per annum is used to measure economic growth. Historically, the UK economy has experienced economic growth rates of 2–3% per annum.

Economic growth has been an important objective for the UK government in recent years. Following the financial crisis of 2008, the UK entered a recession in which growth rates were negative for a period of more than six months, or two quarters. Since that time, rates have slowly recovered, reaching 3.2% in 2014. However, it was only in 2014 that the economy regained the level of GDP that it had achieved in 2008 before the recession.

REALWORLD ECONOMICS 31.2

The size of the UK economy is back to 2008 levels

The UK's economy has bounced back and is now bigger than it was before the financial crisis struck, according to official figures. David Cameron said the news was a 'credit' to the hard work of the British people. Gross domestic product (GDP) – the UK's national output – kept up the same strong pace it had set in the first three months of 2014 and expanded 0.8% between April and June 2014.

The figures from the Office for National Statistics (ONS) mark the UK's recovery from the deepest recession since the 1930s, with the first official confirmation that the economy is now larger than the first three months of 2008 – when the big contraction began. The UK's economy had grown little after the recession began in 2008 but sprang back to life last year.

However, for individuals the depression is not yet past. GDP per head is still below its previous peak, as the population has grown quickly in the intervening six years. In a vindication of the government's economic plan, the economy is now set to grow 3.2% in 2014, making it the fastest growing of all the major developed economies.

The key cause of recovery has been rapid growth in the services sector of the economy, which represents more than 75% of UK output. Manufacturing and construction are taking longer to recover.

Source: Adapted from *Daily Telegraph*, 25.7.14

Exercise

1 How might the sudden increase in rates of economic growth in the economy affect the ability of the UK government to reduce levels of unemployment and control the rate of inflation? *(10 marks)*

Why is economic growth a macroeconomic objective?

Economic growth is a government target because higher real GDP means more wants are satisfied and the population can benefit from higher living standards. The UK has benefited from rates of growth that average out at between 2% and 3% since 1945. This means that the size of the UK economy (and potentially people's incomes) has doubled every 30 years or so, resulting in steady increases in the standard of living of most people in the UK.

Key term

Real GDP is GDP data adjusted to remove the effects of inflation.

However, there have been increasing concerns about the damage that decades of economic growth have inflicted on the environment. Some economists have argued that continued growth may not increase people's welfare and that other ways of measuring changes in the standard of living of a country's inhabitants should be used.

A low level of unemployment

Key term
Unemployment exists when people are seeking work but are unable to find it.

Employment describes people actively involved in work; in contrast, unemployment occurs when people are unable to find employment. Many governments, including that of the UK, have low levels of unemployment as a macroeconomic objective. This objective can take the form of full employment, which really means very low levels of unemployment. A level of unemployment will always exist, not least because some people are changing jobs and are therefore unemployed temporarily. For reasons such as this, many economists believe that having 3% of the workforce unemployed is as close to full employment as is possible.

Why is a low level of unemployment a macroeconomic objective?

Unemployment is undesirable for a number of social and economic reasons.

- It represents a waste of human resources and so prevents an economy from reaching its capacity to produce goods and services.
- If unemployment lasts for an extended period, it can mean workers losing their job skills and thus their future employability.
- It reduces income and spending by consumers and so it leads to lower rates of economic growth. Unused human resources means that the UK economy will be at a point within its **production possibility boundary.**
- It increases government spending on welfare benefits, diverting resources from more productive investment such as in roads and universities.
- It is a major cause of poverty and the human suffering that results.

All of these factors mean that an economy is less likely to maximise economic welfare if it suffers from high levels of unemployment.

REALWORLD ECONOMICS 31.3

The number of people in the UK claiming Jobseeker's Allowance

	No. of claimants		No. of claimants
2007	741,100	2011	1,478,430
2008	1,036,480	2012	1,443,540
2009	1,469,920	2013	1,132,780
2010	1,328,910		

Table 31.1 *The number of UK claimants of Jobseeker's Allowance (JSA), 2007–13*

Note: Weekly rates of JSA range between £57.35 and £72.40.

Source: Office for National Statistics

Exercise

1 Why might unemployment cause difficulties for governments as well as those who claim JSA? *(10 marks)*

Key term
The **balance of payments** records transactions between UK residents and the rest of the world.

A balanced balance of payments on current account

The UK's balance of payments is a set of accounts that records the transactions that take place between UK residents and the rest of the world. It records the financial flows that accompany transactions such as:

- buying a Volkswagen car from Germany (a financial outflow from the UK);
- selling a case of Scotch whisky overseas (a financial inflow to the UK).

The balance of payments comprises three major sections, of which the current account receives most attention. This element of the balance of payments comprises:

- transactions (or the import and export) of goods and services – this is international trade;
- the earnings of UK nationals from employment overseas along with earnings paid by the UK to those living overseas;
- transfers of income, which are mainly transactions between governments.

Key term

The **current account of the balance of payments** records transactions in goods and services between UK residents and the rest of the world.

The UK government has a macroeconomic objective of achieving a stable balance of payments on current account. This means that over a specific time period the inflows from the sale of goods and services overseas will be roughly equal to expenditure on imported goods and services and not subject to sudden and large changes. A balance of payments on current account that is near to equilibrium is necessary if the UK is to pay its way in the world. The UK earns foreign currency from the sale of exports and needs this to pay for its imports of goods and services. Over time it has to ensure that it earns sufficient foreign currency, and a stable and balanced balance of payments is necessary in order to do this.

Why is a balanced balance of payments a macroeconomic objective?

A stable and balanced balance of payments over time is a sign of a healthy economy that is competitive and able to sell sufficient goods and services overseas to pay for its imports. Continued deficits on the current account of the balance of payments mean that the UK earns less foreign currency than it needs to finance its imports. This shortfall may be covered by the UK selling assets overseas, but this will reduce future earnings of foreign currencies from these assets and will thus reduce income from abroad in the future.

Continual surpluses on the current account of the balance of payments are also undesirable because they indicate that the country is not using its reserves of foreign currency to enjoy fully the imports it can afford. Consequently, welfare is unlikely to be maximised. Furthermore, if one country has a surplus on its balance of payments, others must have a deficit. They are likely to take action to remove this deficit, which could reduce the volume of international trade. This could damage the economic welfare of citizens in all countries concerned. In the third quarter of 2014 the UK's current account recorded a deficit of £27,010 million. Over the same period, Germany achieved a surplus of £18,550 million. In part, Germany's surplus explains the UK's deficit, and vice versa.

Other macroeconomic objectives

Many governments, including that of the UK, implement their economic policies in pursuit of objectives other than those outlined above. As with the four we have already discussed, these vary in importance over time.

Balancing the budget

This macroeconomic objective refers to balancing the government's budget, i.e. achieving a position in which the revenue the government receives (for example from taxation) is equal to its expenditure over a time period. This has received a great deal of attention in the UK since the financial crisis of 2007–09 and the subsequent recession. At this time the government's expenditure rose significantly. It had to spend heavily on rescuing some of the UK's major banks, and its revenues from taxation fell sharply as more people became unemployed and spending declined, reducing income from VAT.

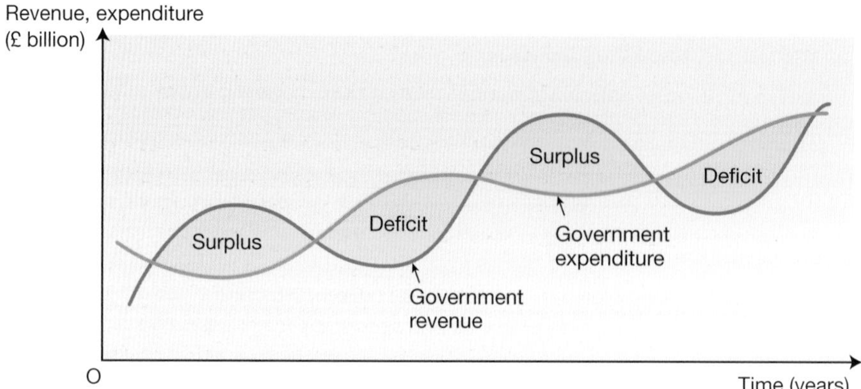

Figure 31.2 *Balancing the government's budget over time*

Many economists believe that the government's budget should balance over time. Thus a deficit may be incurred when the economy is weak and possibly in recession. This might occur naturally as receipts from taxes fall and government spending, for example on unemployment benefit, rises. In fact a rise in government spending can be a positive factor in helping the economy to recover because government expenditure can result in businesses enjoying increased orders for goods and services. In turn, this can lead to rises in employment and in the incomes of consumers. At other times, when the economy is performing well, government revenue should exceed its expenditure and a surplus will occur. If a budget is to balance over time, the amounts of the surpluses and deficits (shown by the shaded areas in Figure 31.2) should be roughly equal.

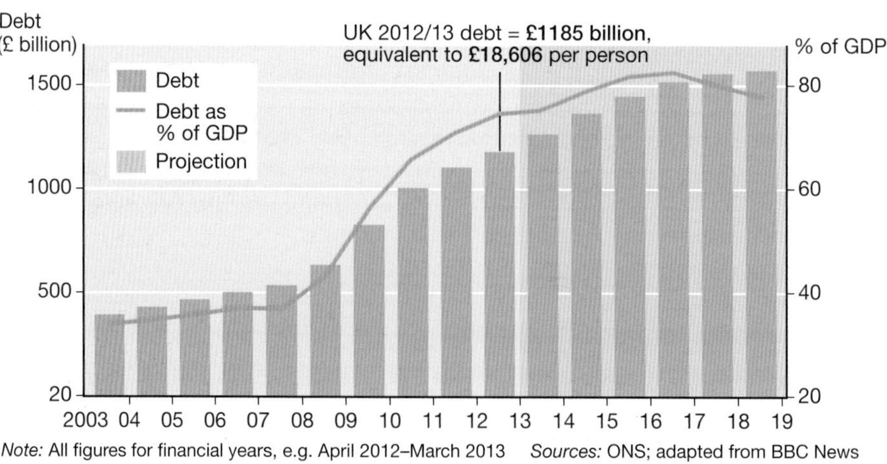

Note: All figures for financial years, e.g. April 2012–March 2013 *Sources:* ONS; adapted from BBC News

Figure 31.3 *UK government's debt*

The benefit of a balanced budget for the government is that it reduces the interest payments it has to make on its borrowing. Since the UK government has had a deficit on its budget in most years recently, this has added to the total debt that is owed by the UK government. This is the national debt. In 2014–15 the national debt is forecast to be approximately £1400 billion, as shown in Figure 31.3. Interest payments on this debt are forecast to be approximately £50 billion in the financial year 2014–15. This is a good example of opportunity cost, as this money could have alternatively been spent on health and education.

Increasing productivity rates

A productive economy will use a minimum quantity possible of its factors of production to produce each unit of output. This offers the economy significant benefits. First, it means that it can produce a greater volume of goods and services from a given amount of factors of production. This has the effect of moving its production possibility boundary to the right. In addition, it has the potential to make the economy highly competitive if other nations are less productive. The use of relatively few resources to produce a unit of output means that this unit can be sold at a lower price, making it attractive to consumers.

If an economy enjoys increasing levels of productivity, this can help it to achieve other macroeconomic objectives. For example, rising productivity can promote high rates of economic growth as the economy produces a greater number of goods and services from given resources. It may also help to improve a country's balance of payments on current account if its products are priced competitively.

Over recent years the UK economy has performed poorly in terms of productivity rates.

REALWORLD ECONOMICS 31.4

UK productivity gap widest for 20 years

The UK's productivity gap with its main developed country rivals is at its widest for 20 years, following the deep recession of 2008–09. International comparisons released by the Office for National Statistics (ONS) show that output per hour worked in the UK is 21% lower than the average for six other major economies – the USA, Germany, France, Italy, Japan and Canada.

The ONS said that this was the biggest productivity shortfall since 1992, and that on an alternative measure – output per worker – the gap was 25%.

Source: Adapted from *Guardian*, 20.2.14

Exercise

1 Why might the UK government be very concerned by the implications of these data from the ONS? *(10 marks)*

Achieving an equitable distribution of income

Incomes in the UK are not distributed equally among the country's inhabitants, as Figure 31.4 shows. Some people have very high incomes while others have incomes that, in comparison, are very low. The top 10% of earners in the UK have incomes that are equal to more than the bottom 40% of earners combined, according to figures released by the Treasury. The highest-earning 10% of single adults earn a median income of £60,500, compared to just £8,600 for those in the bottom 10%.

Income inequality in the UK rose sharply between 1977 and 1990. However, it has changed relatively little since 1990. Despite this, large differences continue to exist between the poorest and richest households in the UK.

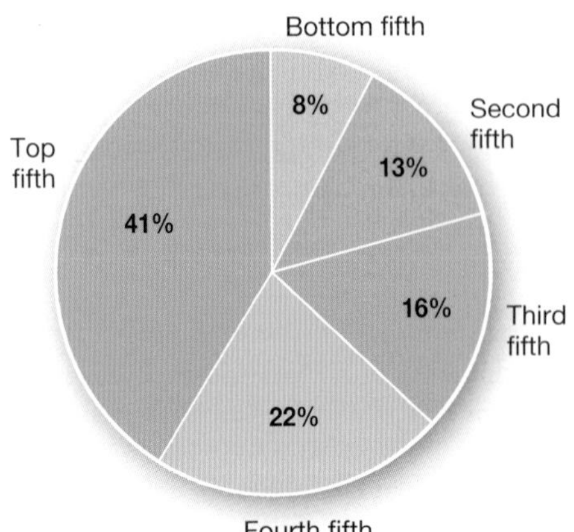

Figure 31.4 *How income is shared amongst the UK's households, 2012*

Key term

The **distribution of income** measures how a nation's total income is spread between that country's inhabitants.

Given the extent of these differences, it is not surprising that many governments have implemented economic policies with an objective of ensuring that incomes are distributed relatively equitably between the country's citizens. This does not mean that everyone will receive the same income; rather, it entails the use of taxation and benefit systems, among other measures, to control the gap between the income actually received by the highest- and lowest-earning households. Governments have income equality as a macroeconomic objective because high levels of inequality are considered to have a number of adverse consequences for households on relatively low incomes. People living in these households are thought to suffer poorer health, making it more difficult for them to contribute to the economy and to enjoy a good standard of living and a happy lifestyle. Furthermore, income inequality is seen as a barrier to social mobility. Many talented people from disadvantaged backgrounds cannot achieve their full potential, possibly because they are unable to take advantage of educational and other opportunities. The economy is, to some extent, denied the benefits of their skills and abilities.

The changing importance of macroeconomic objectives

At the time of writing, price stability remains a major macroeconomic objective for the UK government and this has been the case for the last 20 years or so. However, the financial crisis of 2007–09 and the subsequent deep recession have made balancing the government's budget an economic (and political) necessity. The current coalition government operates with a commitment to balance the budget by 2019. This objective has underpinned many of its decisions, including limiting pay increases for public sector employees such as nurses and teachers and reducing the amount it spends on social security benefits.

However, in the past, other macroeconomic objectives have been given greater importance. In the 1960s the UK government targeted a balanced current account on the country's balance of payments. In part this was because the exchange rate was fixed against other currencies, and imbalances on the balance of payments had more severe consequences. Additionally, some government officials believed that the prestige of a nation was measured to some extent by its trading performance and thus economic decisions were taken with this macroeconomic objective firmly in mind.

In contrast, a low level of unemployment has been a vital macroeconomic objective for some governments. The Labour government that was elected in 1945 considered achieving full employment to be a priority partly because memories of the very high levels of unemployment in the 1930s were still fresh.

Possible conflict between a government's macroeconomic objectives

It is nearly impossible for any government to achieve all of its macroeconomic objectives simultaneously. Attempts to achieve one macroeconomic objective are likely to make it more difficult to achieve others, at least in the short run. It is therefore important to consider the implications of attempting to achieve each of the four major macroeconomic objectives.

The possible implications of focusing on price stability

In recent years price stability (interpreted as a targeted inflation rate of 2%) has been the major macroeconomic objective of successive governments, but the effects on other macroeconomic variables can be problematic.

- AW Philips, a New Zealand economist, analysed the rates of unemployment and inflation for the British economy over nearly 100 years. His most significant finding was that there was an inverse relationship between unemployment and inflation. Although there is evidence that this relationship has weakened over recent years (Figure 31.5), the Bank of England is well aware that an increase in interest rates to try to control inflation is likely to have an adverse effect on unemployment.

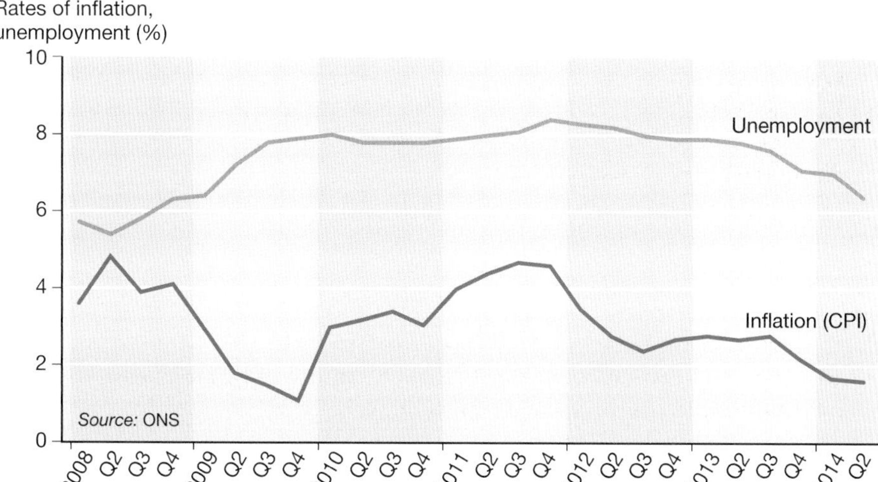

Figure 31.5 *UK inflation and unemployment, 2008–14*

- Attempts to control inflation may also have adverse negative effects on economic growth in the short run. However, it is likely that low rates of inflation will boost an economy's competitiveness and growth rates in the longer term, especially if inflation is lower than the rates experienced in other rival economies.

The possible implications of focusing on promoting economic growth

The potential for conflict between pursuing economic growth as a macroeconomic objective and other macroeconomic objectives depends on the timescale and the policies a government adopts to achieve its growth rate objective.

If a government seeks to achieve higher rates of economic growth in the short term by boosting its own spending and cutting taxes, this might increase the rate of inflation where it results in a relative scarcity of resources. Some economists would argue that it could also result in higher rates of inflation in the longer term as well. However, if a government opts for a longer-term strategy of increasing economic growth rates by adopting policies to increase economic efficiency, such as increasing productivity, then in the longer term the objective of higher rates of economic growth may be attained with relatively little conflict.

On the other hand, high rates of economic growth bring with them the potential for increasing inflation. As an economy grows and nears its maximum production levels, it requires further resources and these can become scarce, especially in the case of skilled labour. As a consequence, the cost of these resources can be expected to rise, increasing businesses' costs and ultimately their prices. At the same time, increased rates of growth may draw more imports into the country. As businesses grow and increase production, they will require more raw materials and components, many of which may be imported. Simultaneously, employees may be enjoying higher incomes (perhaps from working overtime) and this could lead to them spending more heavily on a range of products, including imports – UK consumers have a particular fondness for imported products. The result could be a worsening of the current account of the balance of payments.

The possible implications of focusing on achieving low levels of unemployment

The effects here are likely to be similar to those experienced when attempting to increase rates of economic growth. In both cases the government could be expected to introduce policies designed to expand economic activity. If the economy is producing more (and growing relatively quickly), there should be more jobs and reduced levels of unemployment. The potential for conflict between macroeconomic objectives is the same. Inflation may rise (and AW Phillips would have predicted this) and the economy may increase its consumption of imports with adverse consequences for the balance of payments.

The possible implications of focusing on achieving a balanced current account

In order to achieve an improvement on the current account of the balance of payments, a government may need to increase exports and/or reduce imports. Policies designed to increase exports can, if successful, boost growth and raise employment levels, though they carry the risk of increasing the rate of inflation as resources become scarcer.

In contrast, attempts to reduce imports have much greater potential for conflict with other macroeconomic objectives. Policies designed to achieve this may reduce consumers' incomes and spending power, with adverse consequences for rates of economic growth and unemployment.

Review questions

Total: 28 marks

1 Which of the following topics is *not* part of the study of macroeconomics?
A Unemployment
B Perfect competition
C The balance of payments
D Inflation *(1 mark)*

2 Which of the following three factors can be considered to be the result of inflation?
(i) A rise in the value of money
(ii) A fall in the value of money
(iii) A rise in the general price level
A (i) only B (iii) only C (i) and (iii) D (ii) and (iii) *(1 mark)*

3 Which of the following might be a consequence of an economy experiencing high rates of economic growth?
A A rapid fall in consumers' incomes
B More depletion of non-renewable resources
C The rate of unemployment increases
D The economy suffers a recession *(1 mark)*

4 Which of the following macroeconomic objectives is considered very important by the UK government currently?
A Low levels of unemployment
B Balanced balance of payments on current account
C Achieving a more equitable distribution of income
D Achieving a balanced government budget *(1 mark)*

5 Which of the following would *not* be a likely consequence of a country achieving a significant improvement in its levels of productivity?
A Its production possibility boundary moves inwards
B The economy becomes more competitive in comparison to other similar economies
C Many businesses are able to sell products at lower prices
D The volume of goods and services produced increases *(1 mark)*

6 What is meant by the term 'distribution of income'? *(3 marks)*

7 Explain two possible advantages to the UK economy that might result from policies to achieve a more equitable distribution of income. *(10 marks)*

8 Explain why the UK government may not be able to pursue policies to achieve high rates of economic growth without causing conflict with other macroeconomic objectives.

(10 marks)

Macroeconomic indicators

This chapter focuses on macroeconomic data of various types. These data can be used to measure the performance of an economy against the objectives we identified in Chapter 31. The data are of great value to governments in judging the success of their economic policies and in making decisions about future policies. The interpretation of all types of data, including macroeconomic data, is an important part of the work of an economist. This chapter examines what the data reveal as well as considering their limitations.

Ways of presenting economic data

In this book and in your wider reading on economics you will encounter economic data that are presented in a variety of ways. It is important to understand the implications of a particular method of presentation and to be aware of any issues arising.

Tables of data

This is a common way of presenting a wide variety of economic data and an example is shown in Table 32.1. This table provides a range of data for the UK economy over the period 2010–14.

Table 32.1 *Selected GDP data for the UK, 2010–14*

Year	Column 1 GDP at constant prices (£ million)	Column 2 Nominal GDP (£ million)	Column 3 GDP annual percentage growth	Column 4 GDP per capita (£)
2010	1,591,494	1,458,452	1.7	22,410.33
2011	1,617,677	1,508,836	1.1	22,607.28
2012	1,628,338	1,529,921	0.3	22,579.19
2013	1,656,498	1,583,892	1.7	22,796.24
2014	1,275,445[a]	–	*3.0*[b]	–

Notes: (a) First three quarters of the year only (b) Forecast *Sources:* ONS; Measuring Worth; World Bank

Data presented in tables can be quite complex and it is important to understand the basis on which they are presented. In Table 32.1 there are four columns of data relating to the UK's gross domestic product (or GDP) over the period 2010–14. The first column presents the value of the UK's GDP at constant prices. This approach (which is also known as GDP in real terms) removes the effects of inflation by fixing the prices of goods and services in one period (the base year), so that only the volumes change. This removes the possibility of rises in GDP being caused by increases in prices rather than increased production of goods and services.

The second column presents GDP data using nominal prices. This method shows the actual prices paid or charged at the time the goods and services were produced or consumed. In this case, rises in GDP may be due to rising prices as well as, or instead of, increases in the volume of production. This method is also referred to as using current prices.

The third column presents the UK's GDP data by showing the percentage increase annually in GDP at constant prices. We can show the calculation that underlies this percentage figure.

The increase in GDP in 2013 compared with 2012 was £28,160 million (£1,656,498 million – £1,628,338 million). In order to convert this into a percentage, we compare the change with the original figure (the one for 2012) and multiply it by 100: £28,160 million × 100/£1,628,338 million = 1.729%. This is rounded to 1.7% for convenience and ease of comparison.

Number crunching

Use relevant information from Table 32.1 to calculate the percentage annual change in the UK's nominal GDP between 2011 and 2012 and between 2012 and 2013.

Annual percentage change data are sometimes referred to as year-on-year (YOY) data because they compare one year with the position one year before. This approach can be used at any time in the year and makes the data easier to interpret – the numbers are much smaller, which means that it is easier to identify changes and trends.

It is important to look at footnotes because these can be important. In Table 32.1, for example, the final entry of the first column relates only to the first three quarters of 2014 as the data were collected before the end of the relevant year. This means it is more difficult to make direct comparisons. The third column (showing percentage change in GDP) has a forecast for the UK's GDP for 2014 for the same reason. This may not prove to be accurate.

Data presented in tables can also tell you other things. The final column in Table 32.1 shows the UK's GDP per capita, i.e. the UK's GDP divided by the number of people. This calculation is based on GDP at constant prices. We can see that although the UK's GDP increased (by 0.3%) in 2012, the figure for GDP per capita fell compared with the year before. This tells us that the UK's population grew more quickly than its GDP.

When looking at data such as these, it is important to identify trends. Is the value shown by the data rising or falling? However, it is also important to consider the rate of change. Thus the percentage growth rate for the UK's GDP is increasing significantly over the last two years covered by Table 32.1. This could represent good news for the UK government and other stakeholders, such as businesses and employees.

The data in tables (and graphs) are often based on index numbers. Index numbers are used to present complex data in a relatively straightforward manner. Changes in the data are measured from a base time period that is given the value of 100. This makes it simpler to judge subsequent or previous changes. We will consider index numbers fully in the next chapter.

Graphs and charts

You will encounter a wide variety of charts and graphs presenting economic data. Line graphs and bars charts are frequently used and can enable you to identify trends

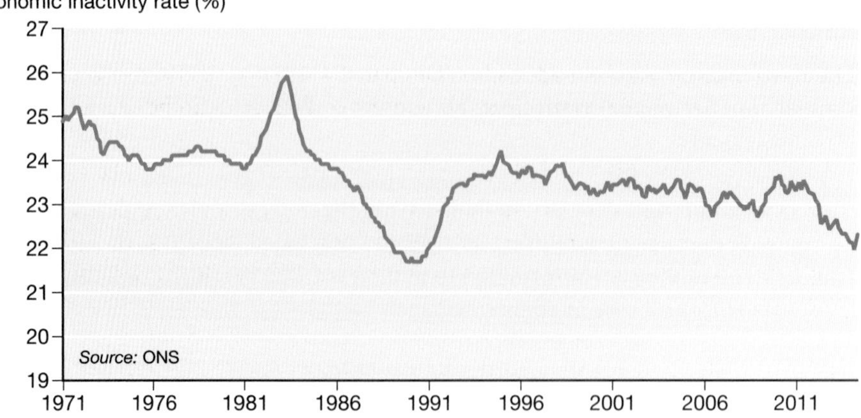

Figure 32.1 *Economic inactivity rate as a percentage of the UK population (aged 16–64), 1971–2014*

in the data as well as absolute figures.

Key term

Economic inactivity refers to people who are not in employment and who are not actively looking for work.

Figure 32.1 is a line graph illustrating the percentage of the UK population that was economically inactive between 1971 and 2014. The trend of these data is that the percentage has generally fallen, although peaks and troughs have occurred (most pronounced around 1983 and 1990). When analysing data presented in this way, it is often possible to identify rates of change and periods when data rose or fell at relatively high rates. In the case of Figure 32.1 the rate of economic inactivity rose and fell quickly in the mid-1980s; it also fell at a comparatively high rate in 2012.

Figure 32.2 shows a bar chart illustrating the change between 2013 and 2014 in the number of people in the UK who were unemployed. The format of this graph allows for a number of different categories to be displayed and compared. Thus it is apparent that there has been a much larger fall in male unemployment and that this has been most notable in men who have been unemployed for a relatively short period of time – under six months. In contrast, women who have been unemployed for more than a year have had most success in finding employment.

The data in Figure 32.2 have been seasonally adjusted. This means that regular and expected patterns in the data associated with the time of the year are removed to allow comparison with the underlying changes in the data. To take another example, consumer expenditure can be expected to rise each year in December as a result of Christmas shopping. The removal of this element from consumer expenditure

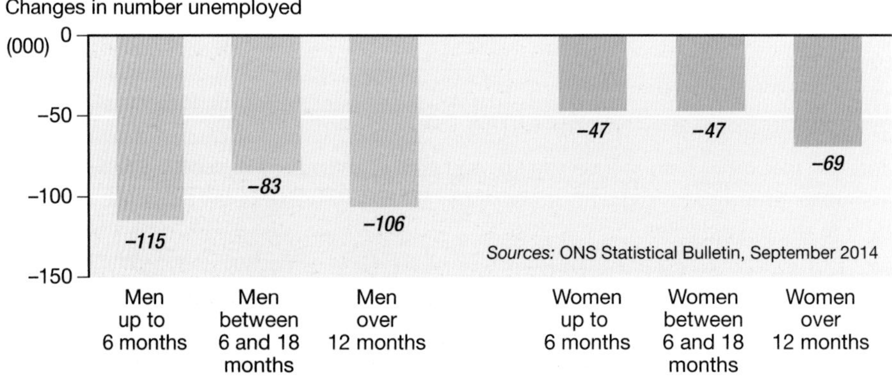

Figure 32.2 *Changes in the number of unemployed people in the UK between May–July 2013 and May–July 2014, seasonally adjusted*

data over a time period will permit an analysis of the underlying trend in consumer expenditure.

Other graphs may also be used, such as pie charts. These can be effective when making comparisons between a relatively small number of data and can be easy to assess.

Macroeconomic indicators

Macroeconomic indicators are statistics that indicate the current performance of an economy and are frequently used as the basis for forecasts. They are published at regular intervals by government, international agencies and private organisations.

1 Gross domestic product (GDP)

Gross domestic product or GDP is the value of all goods and services produced within an economy over a given period of time. If measured in a particular year's prices, the value is referred to as nominal GDP. Nominal GDP can be adjusted to remove the effect of inflation in order to provide a clearer indication of the change in the volume of goods and services that has been produced over a given time period. This is termed real GDP or GDP at constant prices. As an example, if nominal GDP

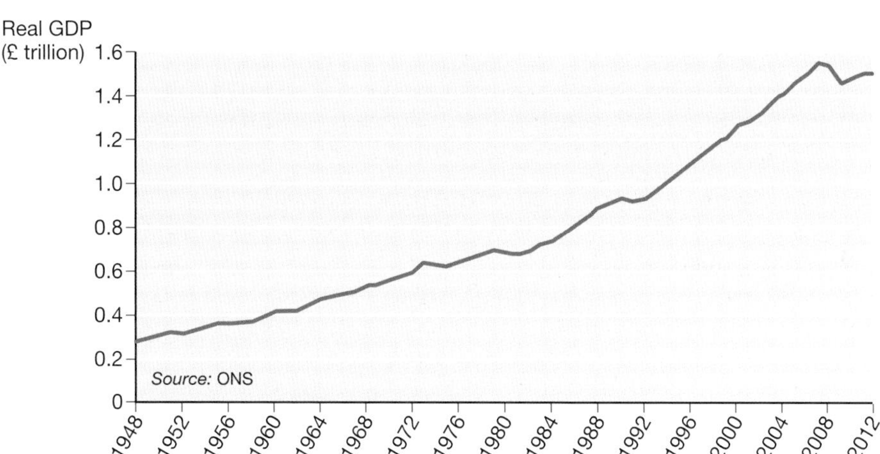

Figure 32.3 *UK real GDP, 1948–2012 (£ trillion)*

is 5% higher than in the previous year, but prices have also risen by 5%, the increase in real GDP is zero – the output of goods and services is unchanged.

The real GDP of the UK has risen substantially since the end of the Second World War (See Figure 32.3). This large rise in production is the result of a number of factors including:

- investment in more efficient methods of production including technology;
- an increase in the size of the working population;
- increased labour productivity (perhaps as a result of training).

Key terms

Real GDP per capita measures the average income per person in a country after allowing for the effects of inflation.

Nominal GDP measures the value of all goods and services that are produced in an economy over a given period of time, using their price at the time of production. Thus it does not exclude the effects of inflation on the value of output.

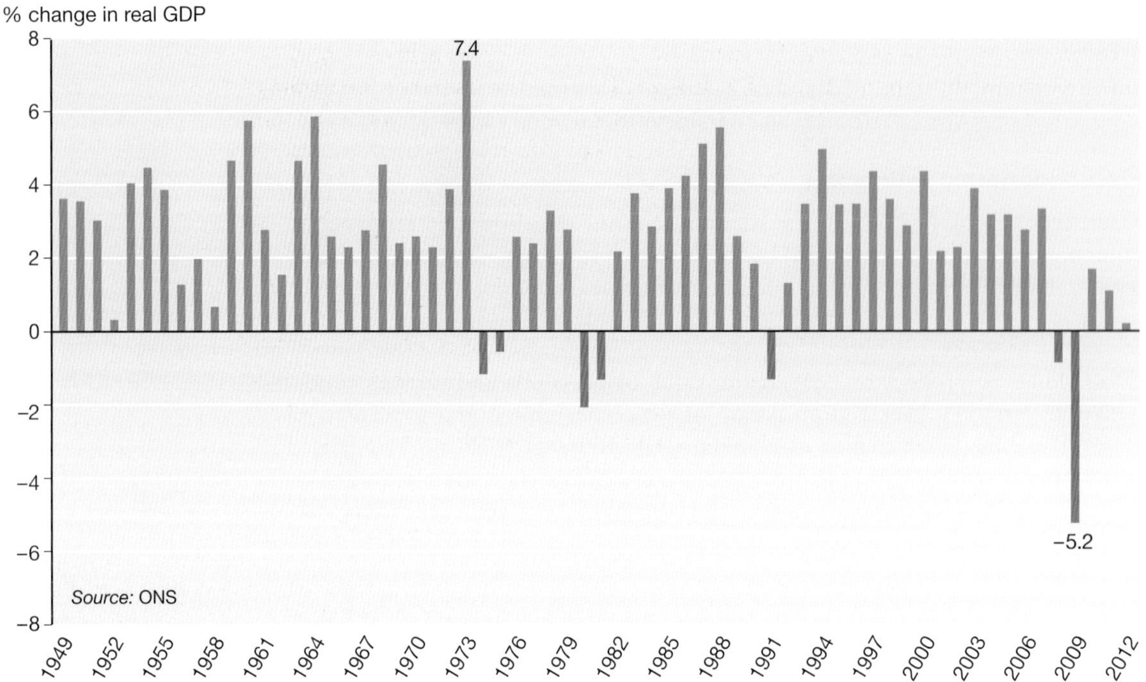

Figure 32.4 *Annual percentage change in UK real GDP, 1949–2012*

The Office for National Statistics has calculated that the UK's economy grew by 2.6% each year on average between 1949 (the first year for which comparable data are available) and 2012. However, average figures can disguise wide variations in the performance of an economy. The highest annual rate of GDP growth in the UK was 7.4% in 1973, while the sharpest decline was –5.2% in 2009, which can be seen clearly in Figure 32.4. Thus data are available showing annual percentage changes that provide governments, economists and other interested parties with more information. In the UK these data are available quarterly.

Figure 32.4 highlights those periods during which the UK's economy has been in recession as the value of output has been in decline. The depth of the recession following the financial crisis of 2008 is very apparent when the data are presented in this format.

It is also possible to present GDP data that relate the value of an economy's output to the size of its population. This gives GDP per capita or per head of the population. The use of GDP per capita data means that the measure of value of output is adjusted to allow for changes in the population of the country concerned. Table 32.2 considers real GDP data, which means the data are adjusted to allow for inflation.

Table 32.2 *Real GDP per capita data (in euros) for a selection of countries, 2005–13*

Country	2005	2006	2007	2008	2009	2010	2011	2012	2013
UK	31,000	31,700	32,500	32,100	30,200	30,500	30,600	30,200	30,600
USA	35,600	36,200	36,500	36,000	34,700	35,300	35,600	36,200	36,700
Japan	28,800	29,300	29,900	29,700	28,100	29,200	29,200	n/a	n/a
Germany	27,000	28,000	29,000	29,300	27,900	29,100	30,000	30,200	30,200
France	27,300	27,800	28,200	28,100	27,000	27,400	27,800	27,600	27,600

Source: Eurostat

The value of GDP as a macroeconomic indicator

GDP is commonly used as an indicator of a country's performance because it offers some insight into the standard of living enjoyed by the country's inhabitants. A government needs to assess the effectiveness of its economic policies on the wellbeing of those who live in the country. When GDP data are presented as a rate of percentage increase (as in Figure 32.4) or in terms of per capita, it is relatively simple to understand and to identify changes and trends. Thus, for example, the effects of the financial crisis and subsequent recession of 2008–09 are easy to observe. This method of measuring the performance of economies also facilitates comparisons. Table 32.2 allows a simple and direct comparison between five of the world's major economies. On the basis of these data, none of the selected economies has recovered to any significant extent from the effects of the recession. Income per head in the UK was lower in 2013 than before the financial crisis in 2007 – the decline amounted to 5.85%, which represents a substantial fall in the standard of living for those affected.

REALWORLD
ECONOMICS 32.1

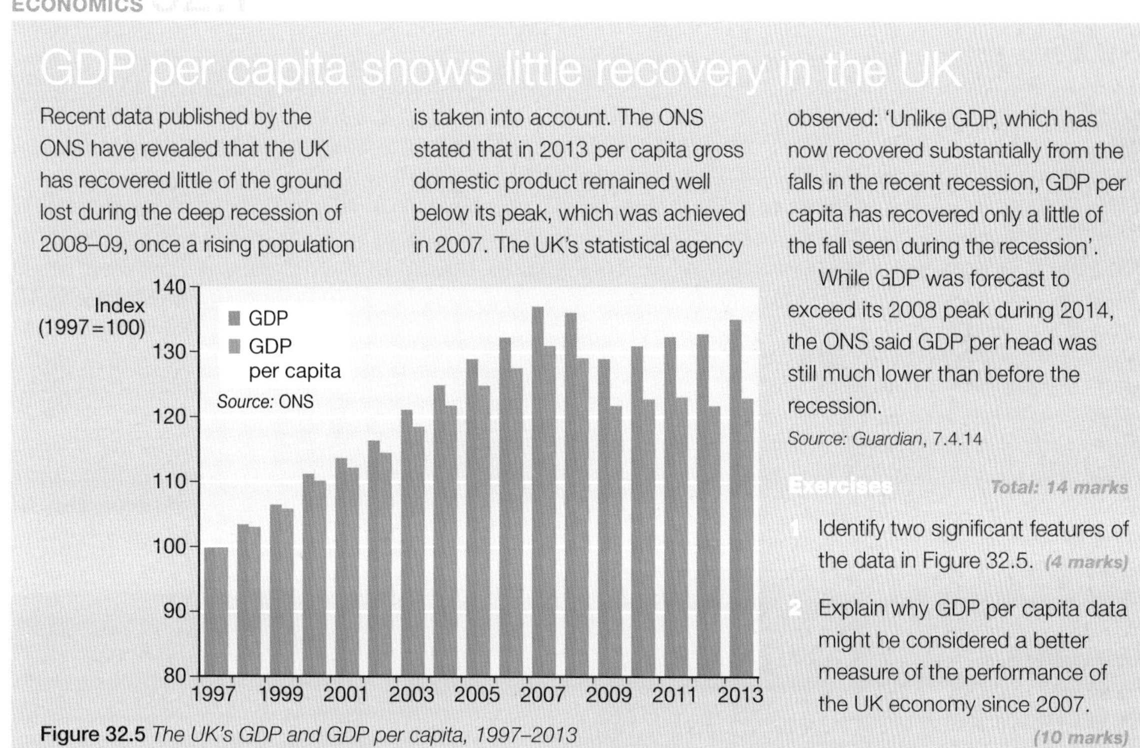

GDP per capita shows little recovery in the UK

Recent data published by the ONS have revealed that the UK has recovered little of the ground lost during the deep recession of 2008–09, once a rising population is taken into account. The ONS stated that in 2013 per capita gross domestic product remained well below its peak, which was achieved in 2007. The UK's statistical agency observed: 'Unlike GDP, which has now recovered substantially from the falls in the recent recession, GDP per capita has recovered only a little of the fall seen during the recession'.

While GDP was forecast to exceed its 2008 peak during 2014, the ONS said GDP per head was still much lower than before the recession.

Source: Guardian, 7.4.14

Figure 32.5 *The UK's GDP and GDP per capita, 1997–2013*

Exercises *Total: 14 marks*

1. Identify two significant features of the data in Figure 32.5. *(4 marks)*
2. Explain why GDP per capita data might be considered a better measure of the performance of the UK economy since 2007. *(10 marks)*

However, measuring GDP is a tricky task, as we shall see in Chapter 34. Hence data may not be entirely accurate, especially when first published. The Office for National Statistics (ONS) publishes UK GDP data about four weeks after the end of the three months (or quarter) to which they relate. At this time, relatively few sources of information are available. This first estimate is based on estimates of industrial output collected from monthly business surveys run by the ONS. The second and third estimates follow between one and two months afterwards. These are reckoned to be more accurate because they draw on new expenditure and income sources as well as on indicators of output. The full annual national accounts, which set out the UK's GDP data in detail, are published in July, and estimates of GDP from the previous year may then be further revised. In recent years the UK has seen relatively large revisions to its GDP data. Hence any judgements about the performance of the UK economy may need to be delayed until more reliable data are available.

A common method of measuring economic performance is to compare GDP data, as in Table 32.2. However, such comparisons can be affected by changes in the exchange rate. In this case the figures for GDP in the UK, USA and Japan have been converted into euros to allow for effective comparison. Changes in the exchange rate between the pound, the US dollar, the yen and the euro will affect the data and any judgements based on them. GDP per capita data are based on averages – not everyone's incomes will have risen at the same rate. Inevitably there will be winners and losers. There is evidence to suggest that income inequality has become more pronounced in the UK in recent years and that GDP per capita data could mask a substantial fall in living standards for some groups.

2 Consumer prices and retail prices

We saw in the previous chapter that the rate of change of prices, or inflation, is the primary macroeconomic objective of the UK government. The government has empowered the Bank of England to target a 2% rate of changes in prices. There are two major measures of inflation that are used within the UK:

- **Consumer Prices Index (CPI)** This is the government's favoured measure, and the inflation target pursued by the Bank of England is measured using this approach. The CPI is an important measure of inflation throughout the European Union and its use allows comparisons between inflation rates in different member states.
- **Retail Prices Index (RPI)** This measure of inflation has been in operation over a longer period in the UK, though the government has used the CPI as its principal official measure of inflation since 2003. The government still uses the RPI for a number of purposes, including the amount of interest it pays on some of its borrowing.

The CPI and the RPI are both calculated in similar ways by measuring the changes in the prices of a collection (or basket) of goods and services over time. The CPI excludes some housing costs from its chosen basket of goods and services and tends to give a lower inflation rate than the RPI. We will look in more detail at how inflation is measured in the next chapter.

Figure 32.6 shows the UK's rate of inflation for a 10-year period. The measure used here is the CPI and in each month throughout the 10-year period the prices of the basket of goods and services are compared with the prices a year earlier. The change in prices gives the rate of inflation over the relevant 12 months.

The work by the ONS showed that inflation in the UK, as measured by the CPI, was 1.5% between August 2013 and August 2014. This does not mean that all prices rose by 1.5%; rather it is an average figure taking into account the relative importance of goods in the budget of a typical household. Over the 12 months to August 2014, rising prices of alcohol, tobacco, clothing and footwear made a major contribution to inflation. This was offset to some extent by falls in the prices of food, furniture and household goods such as washing machines. This may explain why inflation for the year was relatively low and below the 2% target.

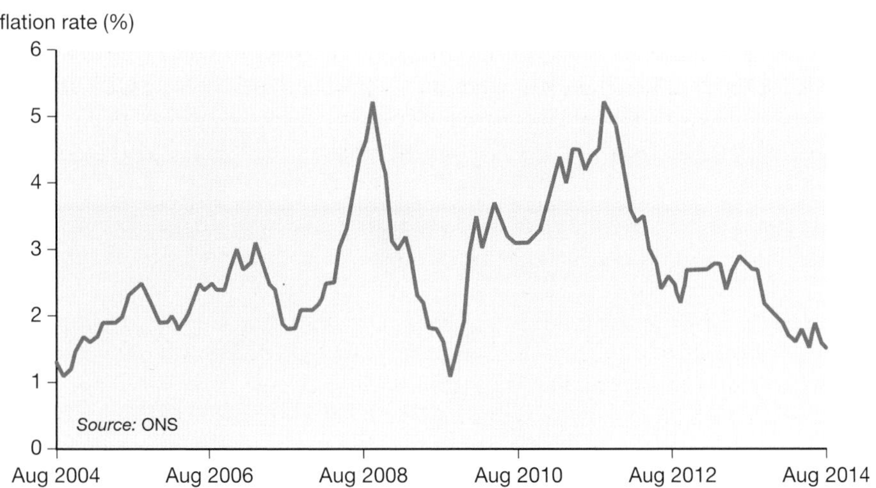

Figure 32.6 *The UK's CPI 12-month inflation rate, August 2004–August 2014*

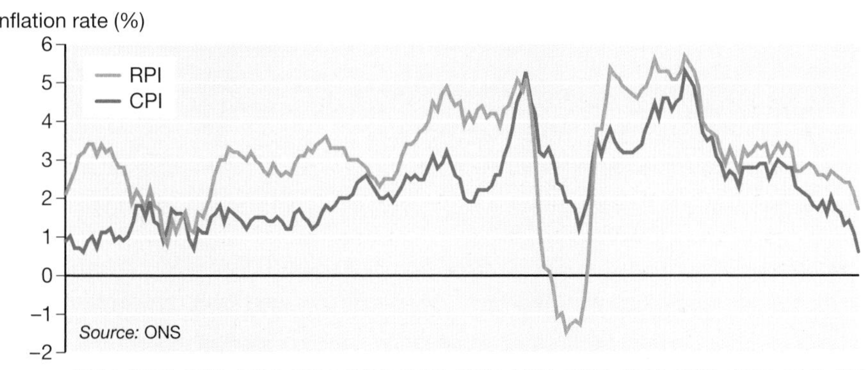

Figure 32.7 *CPI and RPI inflation rates in the UK (percentage change over 12 months), 2000–14*

Inflation, as measured by the RPI, is generally higher than that shown by the CPI, as illustrated in Figure 32.7. Studies suggest that, on average, the RPI measure gives an inflation rate that is 0.7% higher. This difference occurs because different items are used in the calculation of the two measures and the methods of calculation also differ.

The value of inflation as a macroeconomic indicator

Inflation is a key indictor of the performance of an economy. It is important for a number of reasons. First, it can be an indicator of the competitiveness of an economy when judged against others. An economy that is suffering higher rates of inflation in comparison to its rivals may struggle to compete in terms of prices with products supplied by other, lower-inflation economies. Its export sales may decline, especially if demand is price elastic, and its domestic businesses could become more vulnerable to lower-priced imports. In turn this may adversely affect its rate of GDP growth and its employment levels.

Rising rates of inflation can indicate that an economy is growing too quickly. The rising rate of price increase could be the result of resources (such as skilled labour and raw materials) becoming increasingly scarce. In such a situation prices will rise to allocate the scarce resources. Such a scenario can herald an economic downturn as businesses become less profitable and competitive.

The Bank of England believes that price stability (by which it means inflation around the target rate of 2%) is essential to create a stable economic environment in which businesses can flourish. It believes that price stability provides the right conditions for 'sustainable growth in output and employment'.

REALWORLD ECONOMICS 32.2

Comparative inflation data

The data in Table 32.3 show the actual inflation rates for seven major economies based on the Consumer Prices Index. Some notable features of these data are that Russia has experienced higher rates of inflation over this period and a sharp rise in 2014. Japan's inflation rate was negative in 2012 – this means that consumer prices fell, albeit only by 0.1% over the year.

Table 32.3 *Comparative percentage rates of inflation for a selection of countries, 2012–14*

	2012	2013	2014
UK	2.7	1.9	0.5
USA	1.6	1.6	0.8
Japan	–0.1	1.4	2.4
Germany	1.8	1.4	0.2
France	1.3	0.7	0.1
Russia	6.9	6.3	11.4
China	2.1	2.5	1.5

Sources: Economist; Trading Economics

Exercise

1 To what extent is it possible to assess the performance of the UK economy on the basis of these data? *(15 marks)*

3 Unemployment

Unemployment exists when people are actively looking for work but are unable to find it. There are various ways of measuring the level of unemployment experienced by an economy and these will be considered in detail in Chapter 42. In this section we will focus on unemployment as measured through the Labour Force Survey. This is used to define the rate of unemployment as defined by the International Labour Organisation (ILO), which makes international comparisons easier.

Figure 32.8 *UK unemployment rate (aged 16 and over), seasonally adjusted, 2009–14*

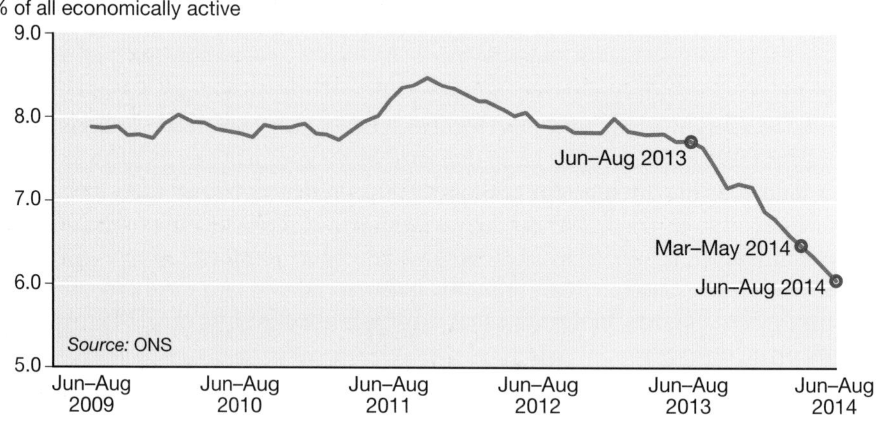

Figure 32.8 was taken from a statistical survey conducted by the Office for National Statistics in October 2014. The report revealed that the unemployment rate for those aged 16 and over in the third quarter of 2014 was 6.0%. This was:

- down from 6.5% for March to May 2014;
- down from 7.7% for a year earlier; but
- higher than the pre-downturn trough of 5.2% for late 2007/early 2008.

In this quarter there were 1.97 million unemployed people, which was 538,000 fewer than a year earlier. This was the largest annual fall since comparable records began in 1972, suggesting that, in terms of employment at least, the UK economy is showing strong signs of recovering from the recession of 2008–09.

The value of unemployment as a macroeconomic indicator

Unemployment has the potential to be politically sensitive for governments because it can result in considerable hardship for those who are without work and it can be difficult for those who have been unemployed for long periods to get back into work. Becoming unemployed obviously has an immediate and significant impact on a person's standard of living.

Unemployment can be an important measure of macroeconomic performance. A falling rate of unemployment, as experienced by the UK between 2012 and 2014, normally shows that the economy is growing and that GDP is rising. This was the case for the UK, where economic growth for 2014 was 2.6%. However, significant falls in unemployment can indicate that labour is becoming relatively scarce and may result in higher rates of inflation. Thus unemployment alone is not necessarily a good indicator of macroeconomic performance.

If unemployment is rising, this normally indicates an economy in which growth is slowing, with incomes rising less quickly and inflationary pressures lessening. Rapid and increasing rates of unemployment can be associated with a recession in which output and average living standards fall. This was the case in the UK during 2008–09.

4 Productivity

We saw in Chapter 31 that productivity measures the efficiency with which an economy uses its resources, or factors of production, to produce goods and services. This can relate to all factors of production used within an economy – this is referred to as 'total factor productivity'. Changes in total factor productivity indicate changes in output or production that are not explained by alterations in the quantity of factors of production used as inputs, and reflect the efficiency with which these inputs are utilised.

However, it is common for economists to analyse productivity data that relate output to a single factor of production. There is much data available on labour productivity, for example. This measures the amount of output that is produced by a unit of labour as an input.

Figure 32.9 shows information relating to the UK's labour productivity performance and includes productivity data from 1973 onwards. It can be seen that labour productivity has declined since the recession of 2008–09. In part this explains why unemployment fell substantially between 2011 and 2014. During this time the output of the UK economy increased, especially in 2014. If labour productivity is falling, it will require a significant rise in the numbers employed to increase output; as a consequence more people are employed, and unemployment falls.

WHAT IS LABOUR PRODUCTIVITY?

Labour productivity measures the amount of economic output that is produced by a unit of **labour input**.

How is labour productivity calculated?

Labour productivity is calculated by dividing a measure of economic output by **workers**, **jobs** or **hours worked**.

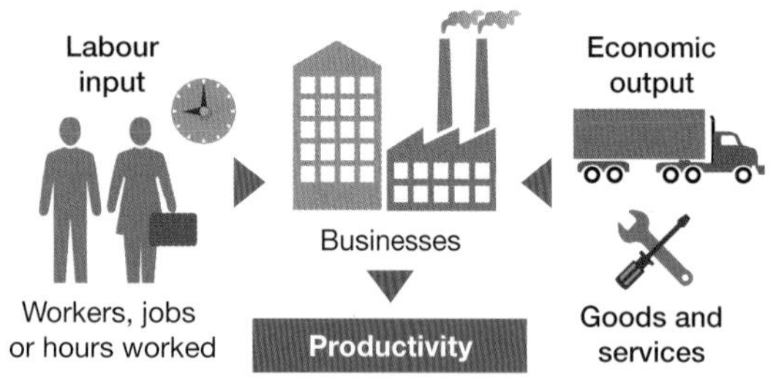

How has labour productivity changed over time?

Labour productivity has shown an increasing trend from the 1970s up to the economic downturn in 2008.

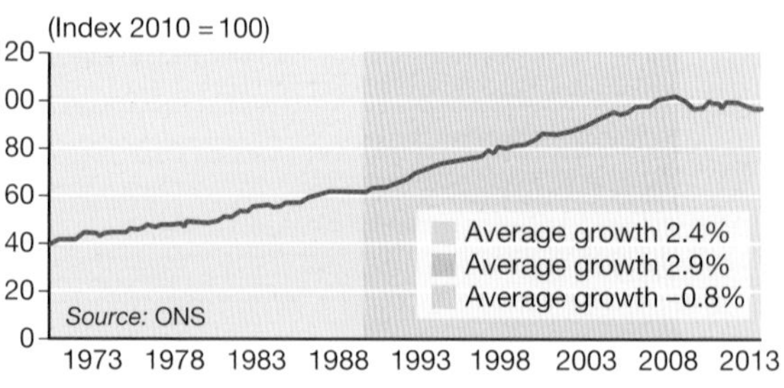

What are the statistics used for?

Productivity estimates are used both within and outside the government. In combination with other economic indicators, these help us build a comprehensive picture of the UK economy.

Source: ONS

Why does labour productivity matter?

Labour productivity is the main determinant of national living standards. Increasing labour productivity means a greater output of goods and services can be produced from a given set of labour inputs.

Figure 32.9 *Information about UK labour productivity*

Labour productivity figures may be low because employees are not highly skilled, perhaps due to a lack of training and/or education. Alternatively they may be low because there is relatively little technology used in production, or the technology that is used is not sophisticated and highly productive. This can limit the efficiency of labour.

The value of labour productivity as a macroeconomic indicator

Labour productivity can be seen as an important determinant of the competitiveness of an economy. An economy that has levels of labour productivity that are comparatively high and increasing will enjoy significant benefits – products can be sold on international markets at competitive prices, and multinational businesses will be attracted to the location. High labour productivity will enable businesses to produce goods and services relatively cheaply, assuming they use their other resources efficiently. Governments rightly give considerable importance to improving productivity, and the UK's recent poor performance in this area is a matter of concern.

Labour productivity is also an important determinant of living standards in an economy. An increase in labour productivity allows for a given quantity of labour to produce an increased quantity of goods and services. This can generate higher incomes for those who live and work in the economy, enhancing their standard of living.

However, labour productivity as an indicator can be deceptive to some degree. First, it only considers the efficiency of a single type of input or factor of production. It may be the case that other resources are utilised efficiently, offsetting the poor performance of labour inputs. Secondly, in a recession, businesses may choose to retain labour despite underutilisation. Managers may consider this to be a sensible decision in order to avoid the costs of recruiting and retraining new employees once sales and output recover. While this will result in a decline in labour productivity, it protects employment.

REALWORLD
ECONOMICS 32.3

How important are labour productivity data?

Table 32.4 *Annual percentage changes in labour productivity for a selection of countries, 2006–13*

Country	2006	2007	2008	2009	2010	2011	2012	2013
France	2.9	0.1	-1.0	-0.6	1.2	1.2	0.2	0.4
Germany	3.6	1.7	-0.1	-2.5	1.8	1.8	0.4	0.3
Japan	0.7	1.7	0.2	-0.9	3.9	0.0	0.4	1.5
UK	2.2	2.6	-0.2	-3.2	1.2	0.6	-1.8	-0.2
USA	0.8	1.0	0.8	2.9	2.8	0.4	0.8	0.9

Source: OECD

Exercise

1 Explain the limitations of these data in measuring the macroeconomic performance of the UK economy since 2006. (9 marks)

5 The balance of payments on current account

The UK has recorded a deficit on its current account for decades (see Figure 32.10). The UK trade in goods and services (which makes up a significant proportion of the current account balance) was last in surplus in 1997. The patterns of trade in goods and in services are very different. In every year from 1993 until 2013 the UK recorded a surplus in its trade in services (i.e. it earned more from exporting services such as banking and insurance than it paid in importing them). In contrast the UK spent more on imports of goods every year from 1993 until 2013 than it received from exports of goods. In part, this is due to the decline in the UK manufacturing industry. However, the surplus earned on services has been smaller than the deficit on goods every year since 1998, and by 2013 the net deficit for goods and services had increased to a little under £40 billion.

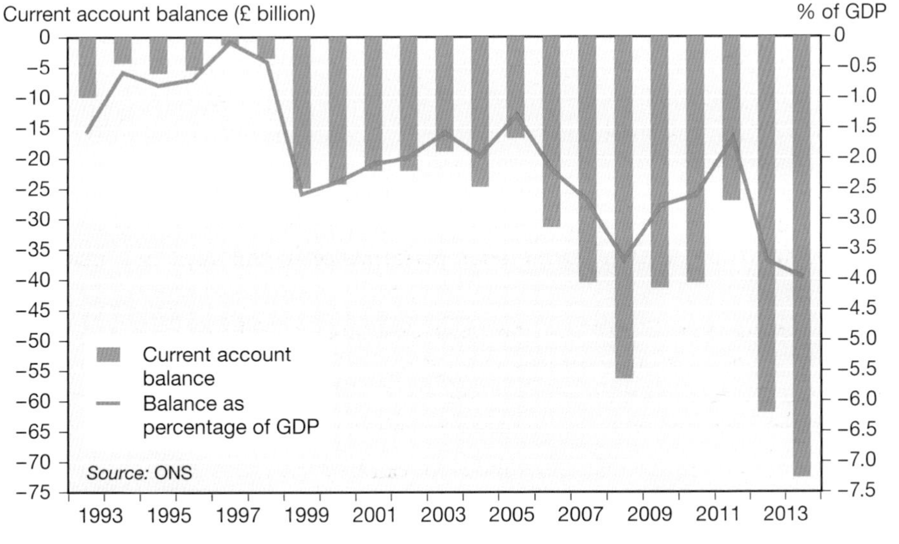

Figure 32.10 *The UK's current account balance and balance as percentage of GDP, 1993–2013*

Discussion point

Can the performance of an economy be judged from a single macroeconomic indicator or is an accurate assessment only possible by considering all the major macroeconomic indicators?

Yet the weakness of the UK's balance of payments position on current account is not due primarily to its imbalance in trade of goods and services. Increasingly it is due to overseas residents earning more on their investments in the UK than UK citizens earn from investments overseas. Hence more income is flowing out of the UK than is entering.

The value of the current account of the balance of payments as a macroeconomic indicator

The current account of the balance of payments is not necessarily a good indicator of the health of an economy. A deficit on the current account of the balance of payments means that the economy is a net debtor with the rest of the world. The economy is using resources from other economies to meet its domestic consumption and investment requirements.

Such a deficit could occur because of an imbalance in earnings (or credits) from exports of goods and services when measured against expenditure on imports (debits). This may be regarded as unfavourable because the economy may be judged to be uncompetitive, which could result in lower growth rates for GDP and lower levels of future employment.

However, a deficit could also arise due to increased investments from abroad and the consequent requirement for the economy to pay investment income (a debit under income in the current account). These investments from overseas often have a favourable effect on an economy because they can increase productive capacity, GDP, employment and the standard of living. In the longer term this may assist an economy in increasing its exports, which may improve the future balance of payments on current account.

An overview of the UK's macroeconomic performance

Table 32.5 summarises the performance of the UK economy since 2005 using a range of macroeconomic indicators. In many ways the UK is recovering strongly from the depths of the recession it experienced in 2008–09. As the economy has recovered, unemployment has started to fall and GDP is growing at an increasing rate. However, economic growth in some of the UK's major markets (the EU and the United States, for example) remains slow, which is depressing export sales. In addition, real incomes in the UK have fallen since 2007, which has depressed the level of sales achieved by UK businesses, though there are signs that they are now rising.

Table 32.5 *The performance of the UK economy, 2005–14*

Year	Economic growth (% change)	CPI inflation (% change)	RPI inflation (% change)	Unemployment, ILO (%)	Balance of payments (current account, £ billion)
2005	2.0	2.2	2.8	4.8	–26.6
2006	2.6	2.5	3.2	5.4	–44.6
2007	3.5	2.4	4.3	5.3	–44.6
2008	–1.1	3.8	4.0	5.7	–23.8
2009	–4.4	3.4	–0.5	7.7	–15.5
2010	1.8	1.7	4.6	7.8	–36.7
2011	0.7	3.0	5.2	7.9	–29.0
2012	–0.1	2.2	2.6	8.1	–52.3
2013	1.9	2.0	2.7	7.8	–71.1
2014	2.6	0.5	1.6	5.7	n/a

Source: ONS

Discussion point

Do you think that the UK economy has performed well over the past five years given the macroeconomic objectives set out in Chapter 31?

Author tip

Make sure you have the latest macroeconomic data for the UK.

Review questions

Total: 43 marks

1 Explain the difference between nominal and real GDP data. *(5 marks)*

2 What is meant by the term 'seasonally adjusted'? *(2 marks)*

3 Which of the following best describes the difference between nominal GDP data and real GDP per capita data?
- A The GDP data are adjusted to allow for the effects of inflation.
- B The GDP data are manipulated to allow for the size of the country's population.
- C The GDP data are manipulated to allow for the size of the country's population and for the effects of inflation.
- D The GDP data are revised to reflect further information that has become available. *(1 mark)*

4 Explain why a rise in real GDP per capita may not result in a rise in living standards for all of a country's inhabitants. *(5 marks)*

5 Explain two reasons why it may be difficult to judge an economy's performance by analysing its GDP data. *(8 marks)*

6 Which of the following is *not* a reason why inflation is generally considered to be an important indicator of the performance of an economy?
- A Relatively high rates of inflation can affect the competitiveness of an economy.
- B Rising rates of inflation may indicate that an economy is growing too quickly.
- C Price stability can provide suitable conditions for sustainable growth in output.
- D High rates of inflation create greater differences between nominal and real GDP data. *(1 mark)*

7 Explain one reason why a significant fall in unemployment might not be a good indicator of the future performance of an economy. *(5 marks)*

8 Explain the difference between labour productivity and total factor productivity. *(5 marks)*

9 Which of the following best describes why labour productivity may be a good indicator of the performance of an economy?
- A It considers the efficiency of the human input into production.
- B Labour productivity is an important determinant of an economy's competitiveness.
- C Businesses may deliberately hoard and underutilise labour during a recession.
- D Labour productivity data exclude the effect of several factors of production. *(1 mark)*

10 Explain why the current account of the balance of payments may not necessarily be a good indicator of the performance of an economy. *(10 marks)*

Uses of index numbers

We mentioned index numbers in the previous chapter. This chapter looks at them in some detail and considers how they are calculated and interpreted. It also covers the use of index numbers to measure changes in the price level (or inflation) as well as their use in measuring other important macroeconomic variables.

The calculation and interpretation of index numbers

Economists use index numbers to make comparisons on the performance of economic variables over time. They are used to measure changes in a range of economic data including inflation, wages, GDP, production levels, share prices and other key prices such as those for oil or houses. They can be presented in the form of tables or as graphs, as shown in Figure 33.1.

Figure 33.1 *Manufacturing production in the UK shown on a graph using index numbers, 2003–14*

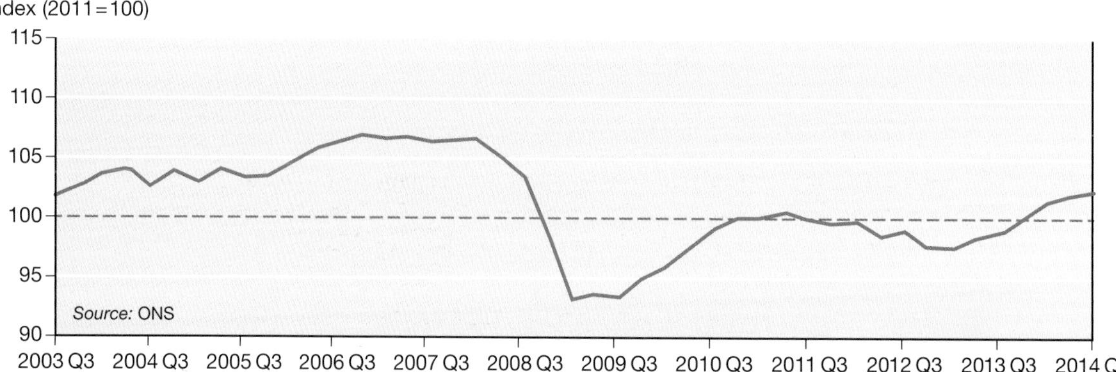

Why do economists use index numbers?

Key term
An **index number** is a means of measuring changes in data over time by relating changes to a base year that is given the value of 100.

Economists use index numbers extensively because they help simplify data. An index starts in a selected year, which is called the base year. The data for that year are given the index number of 100. In the years after the base year, percentage increases in the data that are being measured will move the index number above 100. For example, if oil prices rise by 2.5% in the year after the base year, the index number of that second year will be 102.5. However, if there is a percentage decline in the data, then the index will fall below 100. Thus, if oil prices fell by 3% in the year following the base year, the index number for that year would be 97.

Furthermore, using a system that is based on the number 100 makes it easier to spot trends and to assess their magnitude. This is especially valuable when the data are complex or involve large numbers. Figure 33.1 shows manufacturing production for the UK from Quarter 3 in 2003 until Quarter 3 in 2014. The base year for these data is 2011. The data tell us that the level of manufacturing in volume terms (as the effects of price changes are removed) fell dramatically during the recession. It is apparent that even by 2014, some five years after the recession, manufacturing production in the UK was about 5% below its 2007 level.

It is also possible to present these data in numerical form, as shown in Table 33.1 for the period 2009–14. This form of presentation enables the reader to view precise data, and to make more accurate comparisons between time periods and different economies. However, it may make the trend more difficult to see, especially over a longer time period.

Table 33.1 *The UK's index of manufacturing, 2009–14*

Year	2009	2010	2011	2012	2013	2014
Index of manufacturing	93.8	98.2	100.0	98.7	98.9	101.4

Source: Adapted from ONS

Whether presented numerically or graphically, the use of index numbers to measure and illustrate changes in manufacturing production over time avoids the need to interpret what can be very large numbers. Despite representing only about 10% of the GDP of the UK, the value of manufacturing output is large, making it suitable for presenting in the form of index numbers. For example, in 2012 manufacturing output was valued at £139.3 billion.

We will see in the next section on calculating index numbers that they allow for different elements of the data that make up a calculation to be weighted to reflect their relative importance in the overall calculation. This is important to provide accurate data for comparisons.

Calculating index numbers

Simple index numbers

It is possible to calculate index numbers for simple data. For example, we could present the UK's level of unemployment as an index number. Table 33.2 shows the number of unemployed and the associated index numbers for the period 2007–14. The base year for these calculations is 2008.

Table 33.2 *UK unemployment data, 2007–14*

Year	Unemployment figure (millions)	Index number
2007	1.62	78.6
2008 (Base year)	2.06	100.0
2009	2.43	118.0
2010	2.51	121.8
2011	2.65	128.6
2012	2.52	122.3
2013	2.34	113.6
2014	1.86	90.3

Source: ONS

The calculation of the index number for years other than 2008 is a straightforward process. For example, we calculate the index number for 2009 by dividing the unemployment figure for the year in which we are interested by the figure for the base year and multiplying by 100. Thus for 2009:

$$\frac{2.43 \text{ million}}{2.06 \text{ million}} \times 100 = 117.96, \text{ rounded up to } 118.0$$

This result tells us that unemployment in the UK in 2009 was 18% higher than in 2008, reflecting the impact of the recession on the number of jobs available.

In contrast, we can calculate the index number of 2014:

$$\frac{1.86 \text{ million}}{2.06 \text{ million}} \times 100 = 90.29, \text{ rounded up to } 90.3$$

This result shows the improvement in employment prospects that had taken place by 2014. Unemployment had fallen by a little under 10% in comparison with the base year of 2008.

Remember, we can only talk about changes in index numbers in percentage terms if we are comparing a specific year with the base year. If we wanted the percentage change in unemployment in the UK between, say, 2007 and 2012, we would need to conduct a different calculation. This would require the following formula: change in unemployment between 2007 and 2012 × 100/unemployment in 2007. Thus:

$$\frac{2.52 \text{ million} - 1.62 \text{ million}}{1.62 \text{ million}} \times 100 = \frac{0.9 \text{ million}}{1.62 \text{ million}} \times 100 = 55.6\%$$

Hence unemployment in the UK rose by 55.6% between 2007 and 2012.

Number crunching

In 2005 the level of unemployment in the UK was 1.56 million. In contrast, in 1992 it was much higher at 2.98 million. Using 2008 as the base year, calculate the index number for unemployment for these two years. Calculate the percentage change in unemployment between 1992 and 2005.

Weighted index numbers

Key term

Weighted index numbers show the average change in a large number of variables and this average reflects the importance or weight of its various components.

Index numbers are arguably more effective when illustrating trends over time in more complex data. One of the most well-known uses of index numbers is to calculate the rate of inflation. We saw in the previous chapter that the UK has two measures of inflation – the Consumer Prices Index (CPI) and the Retail Prices Index (RPI). Although these two are different, they are calculated using the same method.

The key difference in calculating a weighted index is that a number of different items contribute to the overall figure, and the relative importance of these has to be allowed for when calculating a weighted index. Thus a price index measures the rate of increase of prices for a range of products which consumers buy. However, these are not all equally important in terms of the amount of money that consumers spend on them. As a simple example, imagine that consumers spend all their income on just two items – food and housing – but also assume that they spend three times as much on housing as they do on food (see Table 33.3). We need to reflect this in our calculation. If we fail to do this, we arrive at an incorrect figure for inflation.

Product	Weight	Price index number	Price x weight
Housing	3	115	345
Food	1	105	105
Total	**4**		**450**

Table 33.3 *A simplified calculation of a weighted price index*

Suppose inflation is 5% for food and 15% for housing between the base year and the following year. If we simply take an average, without any weighting to reflect the importance of these items to consumers, we arrive at an inflation rate of 10%. However, this underestimates the rate of inflation experienced by consumers because they spend much more on housing, which has increased by 15%. Table 33.3 shows one way in which we can weight the data to give a more accurate figure for inflation.

In order to arrive at a weighted price index for the year following the base year for our simple scenario, we divide the total of the price x weight calculation by the total of the weights: 450/4 = 112.5. Thus the true rate of inflation experienced by consumers between the base year and the following year is 12.5%. This is higher than our average of 10% because consumers spend three times as much on housing, which is increasing in price more rapidly.

Calculating a weighted price index

The government's statisticians at the Office for National Statistics (ONS) take several steps in calculating a price index.

1 First, they need to establish how consumers spend their incomes to allow weights for the range of products to be developed. They seek to identify the 'basket' of goods and services that an average household would purchase. The quantities included reflect the amount that would be spent on each item in the basket. This is a complex

REALWORLD ECONOMICS 33.1

The weights used in calculating the CPI in the UK

Item	CPI weight (%)
Food & non-alcoholic beverages	11.2
Alcohol & tobacco	4.5
Clothing & footwear	7.2
Housing & household services	12.9
Furniture & household goods	6.0
Health	2.4
Transport	15.2
Communication	3.2
Recreation & culture	14.4
Education	2.2
Restaurants & hotels	12.0
Miscellaneous goods & services	8.8

Source: ONS

Table 33.4 *The major divisions of weights used in calculating the CPI in 2014*

Table 33.4 shows the weights used by the ONS to calculate the Consumer Prices Index in 2014. Each of these items is further subdivided and each of these elements is given a weight. Thus food includes a range of products such as bread, milk and cheese. The amount spent on alcohol and tobacco has fallen since the 1980s as a percentage of total consumer expenditure. This has resulted in it being given a lower weight.

Exercise

1 Explain the possible reasons why the amount spent on alcohol and tobacco as a percentage of total consumer expenditure has fallen over recent years? (6 marks)

task and one that needs to be repeated at regular intervals to reflect changes in consumers' spending habits. The contents of the CPI basket of goods and services and its associated expenditure weights are updated annually. This is important to reflect changes in expenditure patterns because new goods and services emerge, and consumers' tastes and fashions change. For example, in 2014 wild bird food was added to the basket of goods (with a very low weighting) to reflect the increasing popularity of feeding birds and the greater amounts of money being spent on bird food. At the same time, wallpaper paste was removed from the index because DIY activities (including hanging wallpaper) have become less popular.

The total of the weights allocated to the goods and services in the calculation is 1000. This means that, for example, the various products that make up the food and non-alcoholic beverages division of the index will be given weights totalling 112.

The ONS faces numerous difficulties in constructing a basket of goods and services for an average or typical family. Most families or households spend their money in slightly different ways and so an average is unlikely to match many precisely. Figure 33.2 shows how consumers' expenditure varies according to the relative wealth of the household. Other factors can affect the spending patterns of UK households, such as the age of the people in the household and where they live.

REALWORLD **ECONOMICS** 33.2

Is there an 'average family'?

In December 2013 the average household in the UK spent £489 a week according to data from the Office for National Statistics – £7.70 less a week than in 2012. These data were based on a survey of over 5000 households.

Weekly expenditure varies considerably, making it difficult to identify an average family in terms of spending patterns. The wealthiest 10% of the UK's population spend £1397 each week, compared with just £170 by the poorest 20%. Unsurprisingly, wealth also affects spending patterns. Out of every £1 they spend, the poorest spend 25p on housing, while the richest 10% spend just 9p on this. There's a similar difference with food: this is an item on which the poorest 10% spend 15p in each £1, while the richest spend 8p in each £1.

Age also influences households' spending decisions. Those aged under 30 are likely to spend the least amount of money on food each week, while households headed by people aged 50–64 spend more on alcohol and tobacco. Finally, spending varies between the UK's regions. Spending per person per week is highest in the Southeast at £236.90 per week and lowest in Wales at £174.10 pence per person per week.

Source: Guardian, 11.12.13

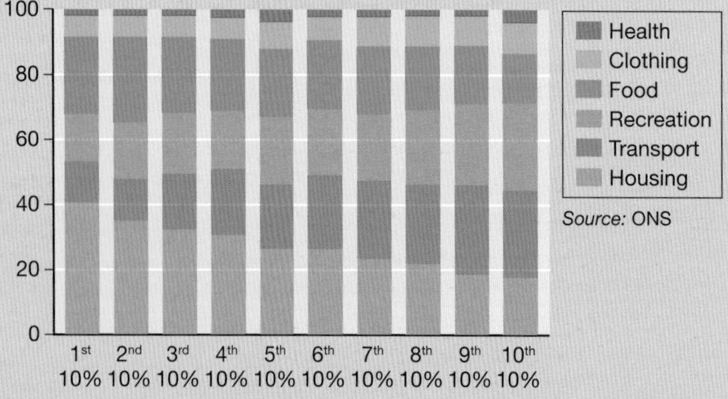

Figure 33.2 *Wealth and consumer spending*

Exercise

1 Explain why the rate of inflation in the UK, as measured by the CPI, may not represent the rate actually faced by most households. *(10 marks)*

2 Next, it is necessary to research what has happened to prices over the latest month. The ONS collects a sample of prices for its chosen 'basket' in a range of UK retail locations. Currently, around 180,000 separate price quotations are used every month in compiling the price indices, covering around 700 different goods and services bought by consumers. These prices are collected in approximately 150 locations across the UK. For the purpose of this calculation, each of these changes is converted into a simple index number reflecting the change from the previous time period.

3 Finally, it is necessary to carry through the calculation. The price increase for each item is multiplied by its weight to calculate the overall rate of inflation. The total of the price x weight calculations is divided by the total of weights to give the Retail Prices Index and the rate of inflation. Table 33.5 shows a simplified version of calculating a price index such as the CPI. It has just four items and the total weights add to 1000, as in the case of the CPI. However, the simplification means that the weights attached to individual items are not realistic.

Table 33.5 *An example of calculating a weighted price index*

Product	Weight	Price index number	Price x weight
Housing	350	103	36,050
Clothing	150	97	14,550
Food	200	107	21,400
Other items	300	102	30,600
Total	**1000**		**102,600**

Note: The new price index is 102,600/1000 = **102.6**. Thus inflation between this period and the base period was 2.6%.

It can be seen from the calculation in Table 33.5 that 'Other items' and 'Housing' have the strongest influence on the rate of inflation (as they have the highest weights), and the more extreme price changes of 'Clothing' and 'Food' have a smaller impact and offset one another.

Number crunching

Recalculate the price index in Table 33.5 assuming the weights are evenly distributed, i.e. each product has a weight of 250.

Interpreting index numbers

Index numbers provide a simple but valuable means of assessing and understanding changes in economic data over a period of time. Making comparisons between the base year and any other year is straightforward, and comparing any two years only requires a percentage calculation, as we saw earlier. The use of index numbers makes it easy to identify trends:

- Figures below 100 indicate that the value of the data is lower than in the base year.
- Figures above 100 show that the value of the data has risen in comparison to the base year.
- The size of the difference between a given year's figure and 100 reveals the extent of the change in percentage terms.

However, complications in interpretation can arise. It is not unusual for a new base year to be adopted after a period of time. For example, the ONS changes the base years used in its production indexes about every five years. This updating of base years can make it more difficult to compare changes in data over longer time periods.

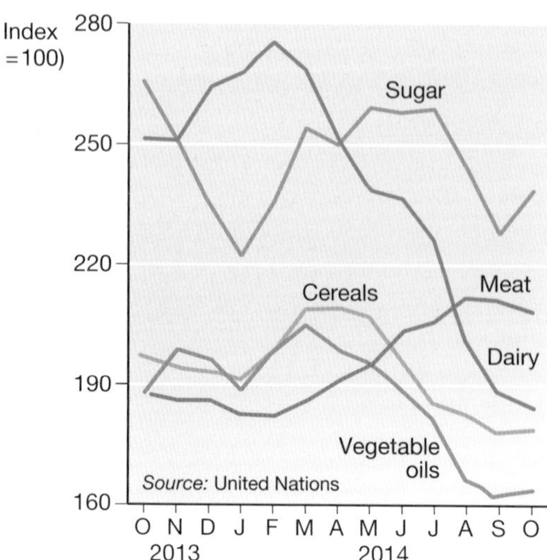

Figure 33.3 *Price indices for a selection of food products, 2013 and 2014*

Index numbers can be used to compare price changes in different products and they allow economists to assess relative changes in prices for different products, even when those products have very different prices. Figure 33.3 shows changes in the global prices of a number of basic groups of food. Food prices have risen globally over recent years for a number of reasons – a phenomenon that has attracted much attention. The graph indicates that some of the pressure on global food prices lessened in 2013 and 2014, though meat prices continued to rise. This method of presenting data for comparison is very user friendly.

Index numbers and other economic data

The UK and other governments, as well as international bodies, use index numbers to illustrate changes in many economic variables and not just prices.

Table 33.6 *An extract from the UK's Index of Production, September 2014*

	Production industries	Mining and quarrying	Manufacturing	Electricity, gas etc...	Water supply, sewerage and waste
Section	**B + C + D + E**	**B**	**C**	**D**	**E**
Latest weight	1000	156.8	693.6	71.0	78.6
2009	97.8	121.1	93.8	102.5	95.2
2010	100.8	116.5	98.2	106.6	95.0
2011	100.0	100.0	100.0	100.0	100.0
2012	97.3	89.2	98.7	99.2	99.1
2013	97.2	87.0	98.6	99.4	102.4

Source: ONS

Discussion point

Which of the four sections (B, C, D or E) performed best over the period between 2009 and 2013?

Indices of production

Earlier in this chapter we looked at an index of manufacturing for the UK. Index numbers are used to illustrate changes in production across the entire economy and not just for manufacturing. In the UK the ONS produces its Index of Production each month. This indicates growth in the output of production industries. The index is based on constant prices to eliminate the impact of inflation. It is a key economic indicator and a good short-term measure of economic activity.

Table 33.6 shows that the Index of Production is constructed in a similar way to a price index, with the use of weights to reflect the relative importance of the industries that comprise the index. You will see that manufacturing is by far the most important element of the Index of Production, having over 693 of the 1000 weights available for the index.

Trade indices

Index numbers are used in a variety of ways in measuring data relating to international trade. In the UK the ONS produces indices of export and import prices, while the World Bank supplies indices of the value of exports and imports and of the penetration of export markets by industries based in specific countries.

Earnings

Many countries produce data on the earnings of employees within their labour markets. These may be presented in terms of actual average earnings or as index numbers that assist long-term analysis of the data.

REALWORLD ECONOMICS 33.3

Earnings in the UK 2008–14

Table 33.7 *UK index of average earnings 2008–14*

Year	Whole economy	Private sector	Public sector
2008	139.2	139.4	140.3
2009	139.8	138.1	145.5
2010	143.0	141.2	149.3
2011	145.6	143.9	152.3
2012	148.2	146.4	155.6
2013	149.4	148.0	155.5
2014	151.5	150.4	157.0

Source: ONS

The data in Table 33.7 separate the public and private sectors of the economy. The base year was 2000.

Exercise

1 Identify one period during which wages in the private sector increased more rapidly than those in the public sector and explain your reasoning. You may wish to use calculations to support your argument. *(7 marks)*

These are just some examples of where index numbers may be used to good effect. Index numbers are of considerable value to governments and other decision makers within the economy, helping them to understand the trends in economic activity and accordingly adopt suitable tax and spending policies, foreign trade policies and general economic policies.

Review questions

Total: 42 marks

1 Define the term 'index number'. *(3 marks)*

2 Explain why economists use index numbers to illustrate economic data. *(5 marks)*

3 In 2012 the production of an economy totalled £3500 billion; in 2014 it was £3850 billion. Assuming 2012 was the base year, calculate the index number of 2014. *(4 marks)*

4 The data below relate to a price index in which 2012 is the base year.

2011	102.5
2012	100.0
2013	98.8
2014	100.4

Which of the following statements relating to the above data is true?

A Prices rose by 4% between 2012 and 2014
B Prices fell by 1.2% between 2011 and 2013
C Prices fell by 1.2% between 2012 and 2013
D Prices rose by 2.5% between 2011 and 2012 *(1 mark)*

5 Explain why it is difficult for the UK government to identify the spending patterns of an average family. *(7 marks)*

6 Explain why the Office for National Statistics has to change the 'basket' of goods and services on which it bases its CPI calculations regularly. *(5 marks)*

7 The data in Table 33.8 are a simplification of a consumer prices index.

Table 33.8

Product	Weight	Price index number	Price x weight
Food, clothing, alcohol and tobacco	250	104	?
Housing and household products	180	97	17,460
Health, transport and communication	?	106	21,200
Other items	370	?	37,740
Total	**1000**		**?**

Calculate the four values that are missing from this table. *(4 marks)*

8 With reference to the data in Table 33.8, what was the rate of inflation between the base year and the year shown by the data?

A 2.4% B 1.2% C 4.2% D 2.0%

9 Explain why a weighted price index, such as that used in the previous question, is likely to give a more accurate figure for the rate of price inflation experienced by an average family than an unweighted one. *(8 marks)*

10 Explain why the Index of Production produced monthly by the ONS is of value to economists and the UK government. *(5 marks)*

Topic 6 Exam-style questions

AS LEVEL PAPER 2

Context – Measuring the performance of the UK economy

Extract A **The Consumer Prices Index**

The contents of the Consumer Prices Index (CPI) basket of goods and services and their associated expenditure weights are updated every year as part of the calculation of this index number. This is important in helping to avoid potential biases that might otherwise develop over time. It would be both difficult as well as unnecessary to measure price changes of every item bought by every household in compiling the UK's CPI, but there are some goods and services where spending by the 'average' household is so large that they are included in the basket of products in their own right. Examples include petrol and the supply of electricity and gas.

The vast majority of the 700 or so representative items used to calculate CPI were unchanged in 2014. In total, 14 items have been added to the CPI basket, 9 items have been removed and 25 items have been modified out of a total of 699 items.

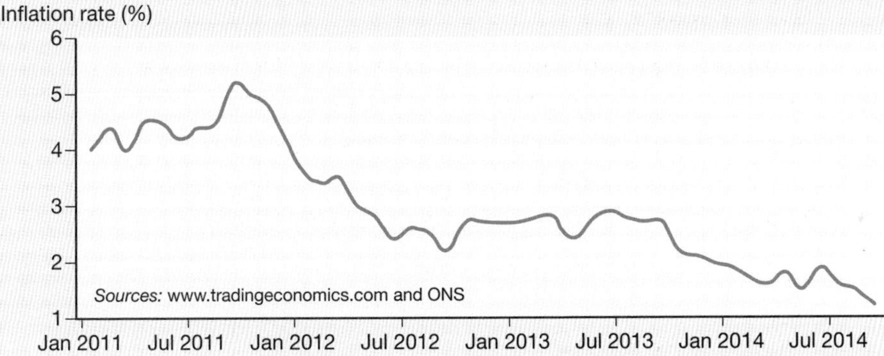

Figure A *UK inflation rate, as measured by the CPI, 2011–14*

Extract B **Labour productivity in the UK**

Since the onset of the 2007–08 financial crisis, labour productivity in the UK has been exceptionally weak. Despite some modest improvements in 2013, whole-economy output per hour remains around 16% below the level implied by its pre-crisis trend. Even taking into account possible measurement issues, this shortfall is large.

As a result, the UK's labour productivity is significantly below that of its major international rivals. International comparisons provided by the Office for National Statistics (ONS) show that output per hour worked in the UK is 21% lower than the average for the other six members of the group of seven major economies (G7) – the USA, Germany, France, Italy, Japan and Canada. This is the widest negative productivity gap for over 20 years and a cause of concern for the UK government.

Measures of productivity can be used to inform estimates of an economy's ability to grow without generating excessive inflationary pressure, which makes understanding recent movements important for the conduct of monetary policy. The level of labour productivity is a key macroeconomic indicator, as it measures the quantity of output that an economy is capable of producing with its existing resources. In the long run, technological progress, which leads to advances in measured productivity, is one of the main determinants of economic growth and improvements in standards of living.

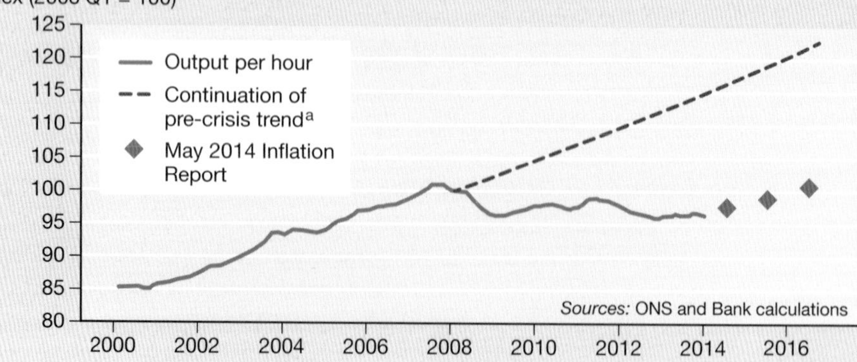

Figure B *Whole-economy labour productivity per hour, 2000–14*

Note: (a) Pre-crisis trend growth is calculated between 1997 and 2008 Q1, and is projected forward from 2008 Q1.

Extract C **The balance of payments on current account**

The ONS has announced that the UK's current account deficit reached £72.4 billion in 2013, the highest ever figure in monetary terms. The deficit amounts to 4.2% of the UK's GDP and is the biggest current account deficit of any major developed economy.

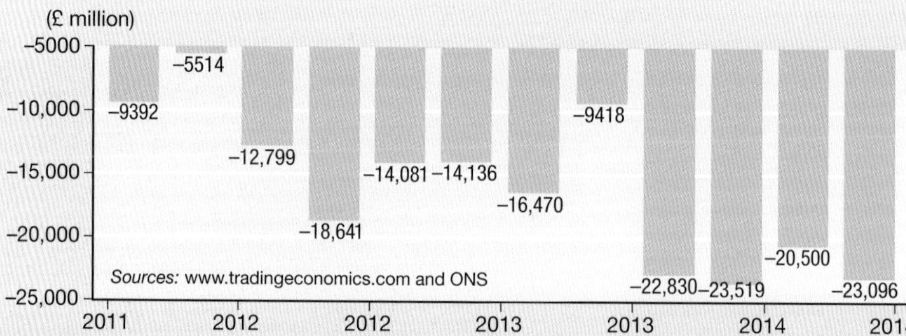

Figure C *UK current account balance, 2011–14*

George Osborne, the Chancellor of the Exchequer, has hoped that rising levels of exports would play a significant part in the UK's continuing recovery from the recession of 2008–09.

Questions

Total: 50 marks

1 Define the term 'unemployment'. *(3 marks)*

2 With reference to Figure A in Extract A, state the year in which prices in the UK were at their highest. Explain your answer. *(4 marks)*

3 Explain the purpose of the 'basket of goods and services' that is used to calculate the Consumer Prices Index (CPI). *(4 marks)*

4 Use the data in Extract C to calculate the UK's level of GDP for 2013. *(4 marks)*

5 Explain why the UK government is concerned by the UK's recent poor performance in terms of labour productivity. *(10 marks)*

6 To what extent does having price stability as its most important macroeconomic objective prevent the UK government from achieving all of its macroeconomic objectives? *(25 marks)*

Topic 7

How the macroeconomy works

Chapter 34

The circular flow of income

In Topic 6 we looked at the macroeconomic objectives that governments pursue and the indicators they use to measure the performance of their economies. Gross domestic product (or GDP) is one such measure and many governments seek to achieve steady growth here. In this chapter we look at how economists measure GDP and other indicators of a country's national income. We also look at some different measures of national income and the notion of full employment national income. The chapter then introduces you to the circular flow of income as well as the impacts of injections and withdrawals on the circular flow.

What national income measures

National income is a fundamental measure of the level of activity in an economy. Since production takes place continuously within an economy, national income represents a flow. There are many millions of transactions occurring in the UK economy each day that add to the country's national income. The scale of the UK's economic activity, the risk of counting some transactions twice and the existence of non-monetary transactions or production (housework, for example) make it difficult to measure national income accurately.

National income measures the total production of goods and services produced within an economy over a time period. When measuring national income it is important to be careful only to add the final value of new goods and services produced during the relevant time period. To do otherwise would result in an inaccurate, and probably overstated, figure.

Final output and value added to production

Economists only include value added during production when measuring national income. For example, many manufactured goods pass through several stages of production before reaching the final consumer. If we added the total value of the product at each stage of production, we would be including value from the early stages of production more than once. This is known as double counting.

Figure 34.1 illustrates the dangers of double counting in relation to the manufacture

Key terms

National income is the monetary value of the total output of an economy over a specific time period.

Value added is the amount by which the worth of a good or service increases at each stage of its production.

Nominal national income is an economy's total income expressed in money terms, valued in current prices.

Real national income is a measure of national income that removes the effects of rising prices in order to show changes in the volume of production between time periods.

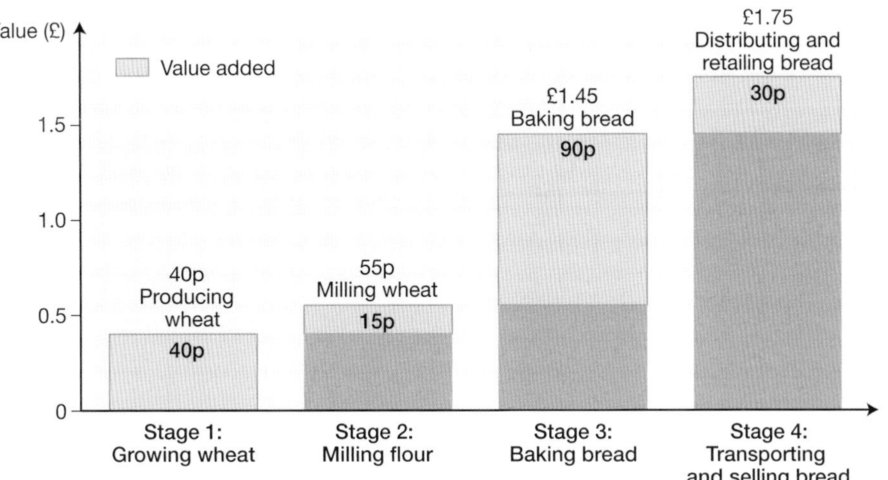

Figure 34.1 *Value added and the avoidance of double counting*

of a loaf of bread. If the full value of the transaction at each stage of the production of this single loaf is included, the total value of production is (£0.40 + £0.55 + £1.45 + £1.75) = £4.15. This exceeds the value of a loaf of bread because several elements, or stages of production, have been counted more than once. For example, the cost of growing and harvesting the wheat used in the bread is counted four times. In order to avoid this, economists only include the value added. In this example, this is £0.40 + £0.15 + £0.90 + £0.30 = £1.75. This, of course, is the same as the final value of the bread once it is sold to the consumer and it is the value of final output that is recorded in national income accounts.

The value of the production of new goods and services

Transactions that involve second-hand goods and services are common, and the popularity of websites such as eBay and Gumtree reflects this. However, to include the value of these transactions when measuring national income would result in an exaggerated figure. The value of the production of these goods and services was accounted for when they were new. Therefore national income measurement only includes the value of the new goods and services.

The difference between nominal and real income

We have seen that it is necessary to use the final value of goods and services to measure national income. The simplest approach is to use the prices for the year in question to measure the value of the goods and services produced. This is known as using current prices and results in a figure known as nominal national income. This approach requires different prices to be used in each time period that national income is measured, assuming that prices are changing (i.e. that there is inflation or, less likely, deflation).

Economists can remove the effects of inflation by using constant prices. This gives a measure of national income known as real national income. The volume of production is valued using price indices from a particular year – the base year. (We discussed the use of base years and index numbers to measure the rate of inflation in Chapter 33.) The effect of using constant prices is that any change in national income figures is the result of producing an increased quantity of goods and services and not as a consequence of rising prices. This allows more effective comparisons of national income data between economies and for a single economy over time.

Different measures of national income

In reading about national income you will encounter a number of measures that have similar meanings, but there are subtle differences. Figure 34.2 illustrates the distinctions between these terms. GDP is the most common measure of a country's national income mainly because it is the simplest.

However, gross national product (GNP) provides more information because foreigners own some of the UK economy, and income from their property and businesses will be paid overseas. Equally UK firms and households receive earnings from assets that they own overseas. GNP takes account of these two flows of income.

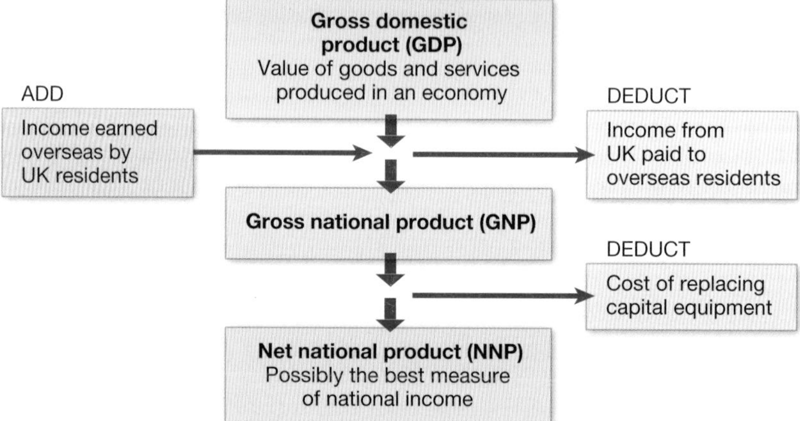

Figure 34.2 *GDP and national income*

Some income in the UK is diverted into replacing worn out or obsolete capital that is used in production. This is termed 'depreciation' or 'capital consumption', and when GNP is adjusted for this we have net national product (NNP), which is arguably the best measure of national income. However, GDP continues to be the most widely used measure because of its relative simplicity.

Real national income as an indicator of economic performance

Data for nominal national income can be misleading. The prime cause of rises in nominal national income may be periods of inflation, which may come about because of increases in the prices of inputs such as materials and labour. In such circumstances the effect on the standard of living of the citizens of a country is unlikely to be positive. Indeed, if wages and salaries rise less quickly than prices, the outcome will be a fall in average living standards.

Growth in the real national income of an economy is thought to increase the welfare of individuals within that economy because average incomes can rise, supporting a higher level of consumption. In contrast a period of negative real growth in national income is associated with lower incomes, lower consumption and consequently a lower standard of living. Thus measuring national income using real data, adjusted for the effects of inflation, provides greater insight into the performance of one or more economies.

REALWORLD ECONOMICS 34.1

Economic performance and the G7 group of economies

Representatives from the G7 (Canada, France, Germany, Italy, Japan, the UK and USA) meet regularly to discuss economic policies and matters relating to the world economy. The seven countries are represented by their finance ministers and the governors of the central banks – the Governor of the Bank of England (currently Mark Carney) in the case of the UK. At the meeting in June 2014 the group discussed the global economic outlook and climate change.

Exercise

1 Explain how the members of the G7 might compare the performance of their economies. *(10 marks)*

Increases in a country's population will diminish the impact of rising GDP on the standard of living because the income has to be shared more widely. The data also exclude a number of factors such as income earned overseas and that paid abroad, as well as certain economic activities.

Number crunching

Year	Nominal GDP (£ million)	Population (millions)	Price index
2012	550,000	25.0	100.0
2013	575,000	26.0	101.0
2014	640,000	28.6	105.0

Table 34.1 *Economic data for an economy, 2012–14*

Use the data in Table 34.1 to calculate the real income per head for the three years. Has the standard of living risen on average for the people who live in this economy?

Full employment income

Higher levels of national income are associated with higher levels of economic activity and employment. If the level of income rises to a sufficient level, this can result in full employment – known as full employment (national) income. This does not mean, however, that an economy will have removed all unemployment. Rather it means that employment is at a level when there is enough overall demand in the economy for everyone who wants a job to have one.

Three ways of measuring national income

Measuring national income requires economists to measure the size of the flow of income that is passing through the economy over a period of time. The size of this flow reflects the level of activity that is occurring in an economy and therefore its national income.

It is possible to measure this flow in three different ways. This may be best understood by considering any transaction involving the production of new goods or services.

Our example of a loaf of bread is such a transaction.

- **Output** The production of the loaf of bread adds to the value of goods and services produced within the economy and this effect can be measured. The output approach to measuring national income can be extended to include the value of final output of all new goods and services produced in the economy over the time period. This is further adjusted for taxes and subsidies on products to create a measure of national income.
- **Income** Those responsible for supplying the factors of production necessary to produce the loaf of bread (land, labour, capital and enterprise) receive income payments in return for supplying these factors. The value of these income payments (rent, wages, interest and profits) represents another way of measuring the value of the loaf of bread. This income approach applies to the whole economy by measuring the incomes earned by individuals (for example, wages) and corporations (for example, profits) directly from the production of goods and services. The main data for this approach to measuring national income come from quarterly operating profits, average weekly earnings and from HM Revenue & Customs.
- **Expenditure** A further way of measuring the value of this loaf of bread is to record the amount spent by consumers in purchasing the product. This would be £1.75 and provides an accurate valuation of its contribution to national income. Once again this approach can be used for the entire economy. The expenditure approach measures the value of spending by corporations, consumers, overseas purchasers and government on goods and services. The primary data for this measure come from expenditure surveys of households and businesses, as well as from data on government expenditure.

Households, firms and the flow of income

Key term

The **circular flow of income** is a model that shows how money flows within a simplified economy, with households and firms as key components.

The model of the circular flow of income can help us to understand how it is possible to measure national income in three different ways and to arrive at the same figure.

In a relatively simple market economy, producers and consumers of goods and services are separate groups and are represented in Figure 34.3 as households (consumers) and firms (producers). Households are assumed to own all of the economy's factors of production such as land, labour and capital. These factors are sold to firms, which use them to supply goods and services. The firms then sell these products to households and receive payment in return. This is the two-sector model of the circular flow of income as it just comprises households and firms.

This two-sector model (households and firms) is based on three assumptions that simplify its operation:

- There is no government sector – hence no taxes are paid and there is no government spending.
- Households spend all the income they receive – there is no saving; firms spend all the money they receive from households on factor services.
- The economy does not trade with the rest of the world – there are no exports or imports.

It is possible to measure the size of this flow at various points on the circular flow of income. Figure 34.3 identifies three such points. At Point A the size of the flow represents the income received by households. Similarly, Point B measures expenditure by households and Point C measures the value of output of goods and services. These should all give the same value because they are measuring the same flow at different points.

In this model, income = expenditure = output or, using symbols, Y = E = O. This means that it is possible to measure a country's national income using three methods that provide the same answer because they are three ways of measuring the same flow: income method; expenditure method; and output method.

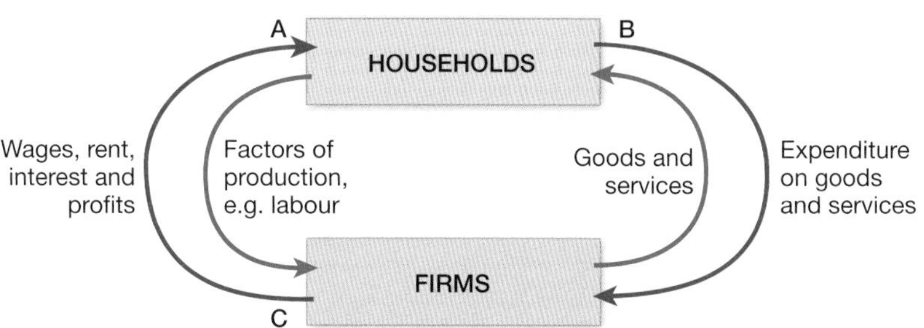

Figure 34.3 *A two-sector model of the circular flow of income*

Injections, withdrawals and the circular flow of income

The economy in our two-sector model is in equilibrium because the flow of money around the economy is stable – there are no factors within it likely to promote any change. We can now relax some of the assumptions we made above and introduce savings and investment, a government sector and foreign trade to the circular flow model.

The three-sector model: savings and investment

It is unreasonable to assume that all households will spend all of the income that they receive. Many will opt to save a proportion of their income, possibly as a form of insurance against less prosperous times in the future. Savings represent a withdrawal (or a leakage) from the circular flow because income received by households is not passed on in the circular flow. Instead, it is withdrawn and deposited in a financial institution such as a bank; at this stage the model includes a financial sector (see Figure 34.4). This financial sector comprises banks and other financial institutions that accept deposits of funds and lend money.

It is also unreasonable to assume that firms will only spend money on purchasing factor services and never invest in new capital. Investment in new capital, possibly in the form of machinery or stocks of raw materials, represents an injection into the circular flow because it arises from outside the flow, borrowed from the financial sector.

Key terms

Withdrawals (or **leakages**) are factors that lead to income not being passed on within the circular flow – these comprise savings, taxation and imports.

Injections are additions to the circular flow of income from outside it – these comprise investment, government spending and exports.

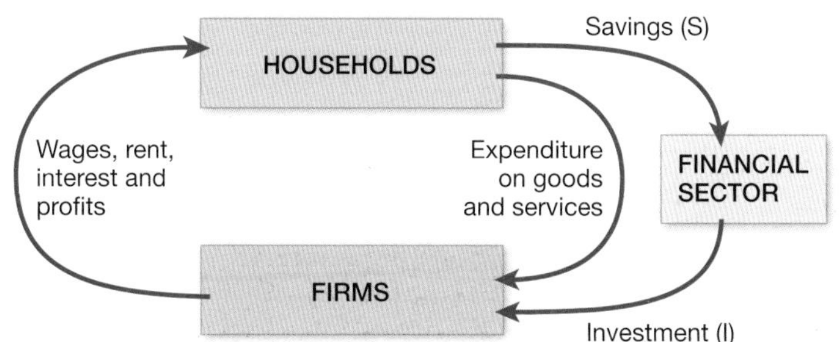

Figure 34.4 *The three-sector model – adding savings and investment*

The four-sector model: government expenditure and taxation

Every country and economy has a government that influences the level and type of economic activity in a variety of ways. Two key actions by governments that can affect the level of economic activity are the levying of taxes (on households and firms) and spending by the government. Government spending on pensions and welfare benefits can affect households, while its spending on training and research and development may benefit firms.

Taxation represents a withdrawal from the circular flow because it is money received by firms and households that is not passed on within the circular flow. Instead it is withdrawn to the government sector. This money is likely to be used to finance government spending, which is an injection as it enters the circular flow from an external source (see Figure 34.5).

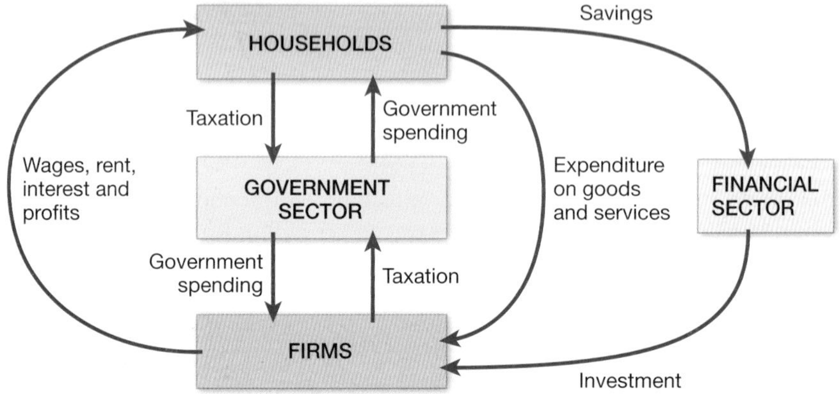

Figure 34.5 *The four-sector model – adding the government sector*

The five-sector model: international trade

All countries engage in international trade to some extent and the importance of trade is increasing as economies become more interdependent as a consequence of markets becoming more global. According to the World Trade Organisation (WTO), the growth in the volume of international trade between 1950 and 2011 averaged 6% each year.

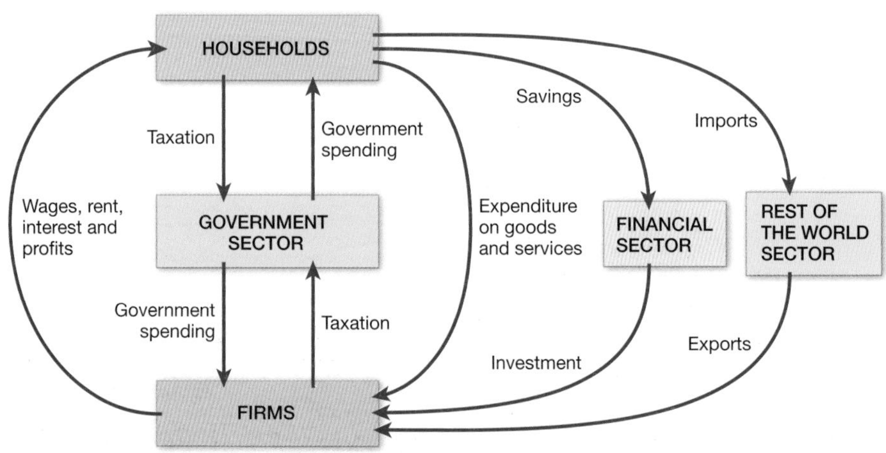

Figure 34.6 *The five-sector model – adding the rest of the world*

By introducing international trade and a fifth sector – the rest of the world – we create a new withdrawal and a new injection. Imports represent a withdrawal because money spent on imports leaves the domestic economy to be received by the rest of the world (remember, it is the flow of money that we are analysing, not that of goods and services). In contrast, exports are an injection. Sales of exports provide an additional and external source of income for the domestic economy from the rest of the world.

Figure 34.6 summarises the flows of injections and withdrawals within a five-sector model of the circular flow. Once again the fact that income equals expenditure means that total actual withdrawals must equal total actual injections: $Y = C + S + T + M$ and $E = C + I + G + X$. As $Y = E$, if we cancel consumption on either side, we get $S + M + T = I + G + X$.

The effects of changes in injections and withdrawals

The level of injections and withdrawals can change. For example, a new government, with different priorities, may choose to reduce government spending. The factors leading to change in the level of injections are generally external and are assumed to be independent of the country's level of national income.

Changes in withdrawals are caused by changes in the level of national income. Withdrawals are assumed to have a direct relationship with the level of national income. Thus they will increase or decrease together. This means that the levels of savings, imports and taxation are dependent on, or a function of, the level of national income. The level of savings, however, is slightly different in this respect from the other two withdrawals. At very low levels of national income, taxation and imports will be very low as well. If households have very low incomes, they will spend little on imports and be liable for few taxes. Savings are different. At low levels of income people are likely to reduce their savings (a process known as 'dissaving') in an attempt to maintain their living standards. This means that savings and therefore withdrawals become negative at very low levels of national income.

REALWORLD ECONOMICS 34.1

The UK's changing savings ratio

Disposable income is the money available to households to spend and save once personal taxes and pension contributions have been deducted from gross income. The savings ratio in the UK is the percentage of disposable income that is saved. As shown in Figure 34.7, since the financial crisis of 2008–09 the savings ratio has risen as households have sought to strengthen their financial positions by reducing borrowing and increasing savings.

Source: Trading Economics

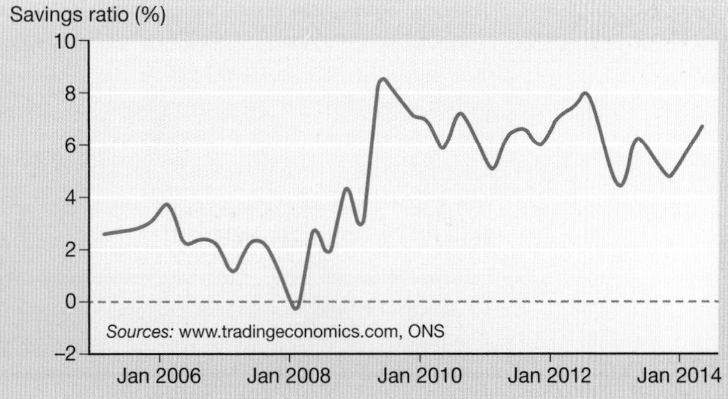

Savings ratio (%)

Sources: www.tradingeconomics.com, ONS

Figure 34.7 *UK household savings ratio, January 2006–January 2014*

Exercises *Total: 16 marks*

1 The UK's savings ratio rose significantly between 2008 and 2010. Explain the likely consequences of this for the level of national income in the UK. *(7 marks)*

2 The savings ratio in the UK fell from 8% to approximately 5% during the second half of 2012. Explain why this might not inevitably result in an increase in the UK's level of national income. *(9 marks)*

Dissaving is illustrated in the position of the withdrawals line or function shown in Figure 34.8. It moves below the 'x' axis at very low levels of national income because households draw on their savings. At a zero income, households would not buy imports and would pay no taxes, but would use their savings to finance purchases of goods and services.

Injections in Figure 34.8 are assumed to be independent of national income because they are determined by a range of different factors. Thus the injections line or function is parallel to the 'x' axis in order to indicate that there is no relationship.

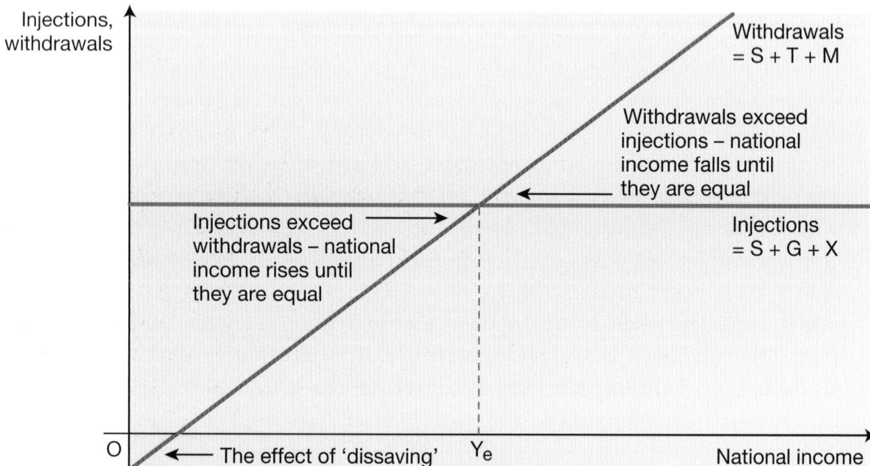

Figure 34.8 *Injections, withdrawals and equilibrium national income*

The levels of injections and withdrawals determine the equilibrium level of national income. When these two are equal, the level of national income (or the size of the circular flow of income) will be stable and unchanging. If injections are higher than withdrawals, national income will increase. As national income rises, so will withdrawals because they are dependent upon it. This process will continue until withdrawals have risen to match the level of injections and equilibrium is restored. Alternatively, if withdrawals are greater than injections, the level of national income will fall and withdrawals will fall along with it. Once again this process will continue until the two are equal and national income is at equilibrium.

Figures 34.9 and 34.10 illustrate the effects of changes in injections and withdrawals. These can be summarised as follows.

- **Changes in injections** A rise in injections will result in an increase in national income. For example, investment by UK firms in 2013 was £56 billion – 8.5% higher than the equivalent figure for 2012. This change in isolation would increase the equilibrium level of national income. This is shown in Figure 34.9 by the shift to Injections 3 and national income increasing from Ye_1 to Ye_3. Conversely, a fall in injections will reduce national income to Ye_2. The UK government is committed to reducing government expenditure and if it achieves this, this would, in isolation, reduce national income.

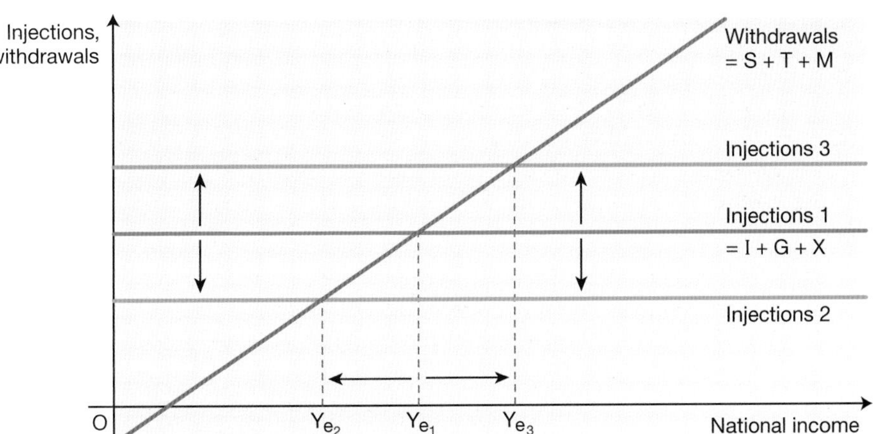

Figure 34.9 *The effects of changes in injections*

- **Changes in withdrawals** A fall in the proportion of income that is withdrawn will result in a rise in national income. As national income rises, the amount of withdrawals will increase, resulting in a new equilibrium at a higher level of national income. For example, a cut in the rate of income tax in the UK could lead to national income increasing. The amount of tax paid will rise with income, and withdrawals and injections will once again be equal and national income will be in equilibrium. This is illustrated by the shift from Withdrawals 1 to Withdrawals 2 in Figure 34.10 and the rise in national income from Ye_1 to Ye_2. The reverse is a rise in withdrawals to Withdrawals 3, resulting in a fall in national income to Ye_3. Such a change might be caused if consumers spend a higher proportion of their incomes on imports.

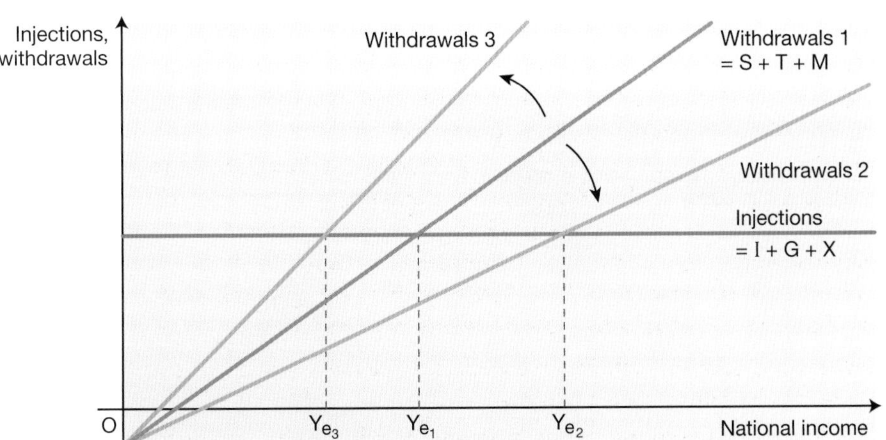

Figure 34.10 *The effects of changes in withdrawals*

It is possible to show the effects of changes in injections and withdrawals using aggregate demand and aggregate supply analysis. Chapter 35 introduces this topic.

Review questions

Total: 45 marks

1 Define the term 'national income'. *(3 marks)*

2 The production of a product involves three stages. The value of the product at the end of the first stage is £12.50, at the end of the second stage, £42.00, and at the end of the final stage, £86.75. Which of the following values should be included for this product in calculating national income?

A £141.25 B £86.75 C £42.00 D £12.50 *(1 mark)*

3 Explain why a nominal figure for the UK's GDP will normally be higher than a real value for the same year. *(6 marks)*

4 Explain why the output, expenditure and income methods of measuring national income should give the same result. *(7 marks)*

5 Explain why a government may have an increase in real national income per head as an indicator of economic performance. *(6 marks)*

6 Which of the following best describes full employment income?

A A household's income when all its adult members are in full-time employment

B A country's level of national income when every person is in employment

C A country's level of national income when all who want employment are in work

D The average wage or salary received by employees when unemployment reaches zero *(1 mark)*

7 Which of the following is an injection into the circular flow?

A Investment

B Consumption

C Expenditure

D Imports *(1 mark)*

8 Explain, with the aid of examples, the distinction between withdrawals and injections. *(5 marks)*

9 In a model of a five-sector economy, explain why injections will equal withdrawals when national income is in equilibrium. *(7 marks)*

10 Use a diagram to explain the effect on a country's national income of a significant rise in its export sales. *(8 marks)*

Chapter 35

The determinants of aggregate demand & the multiplier effect

This chapter introduces you to the concept of aggregate demand as the first stage in developing the widely used model of aggregate demand and supply. It considers components of aggregate demand and the factors that influence its level including consumption, investment, government spending and exports and imports. Later chapters will examine the consequences of changes in the level of aggregate demand.

The meaning of aggregate demand

In the previous chapter we encountered the model of the circular flow of income that demonstrated income flows between households and governments as well as the concepts of injections and withdrawals. This model helps us to understand the meaning of aggregate demand. It illustrates that demand for an economy's goods and services can arise from a number of potential sources:

- spending on consumption of goods and services by households;
- government expenditure;
- investment expenditure by firms on new assets for use in production;
- expenditure by foreigners on exported goods and services.

However, some of this expenditure by households, governments and firms will be on goods and services produced overseas and imported. Thus, we need to deduct imports from these forms of spending to arrive at the total or aggregate demand for an economy. This means that aggregate demand is the total demand by domestic and overseas economic agents for an economy's goods and services minus domestic demand for goods and services produced overseas.

This can be expressed more simply as a formula:

Aggregate demand (AD) = C + I + G + (X – M)

where C = consumption, I = investment, G = government spending, X = exports and M = imports.

Key terms

Aggregate demand is the total planned demand for an economy's goods and services at a given price level over a specific time period.

Investment is the planned spending by firms that adds to an economy's capital stock (property, machinery, vehicles and other items used in production).

Government spending is expenditure by central and local governments on goods and services.

Net exports is spending by foreigners on exported goods and services minus expenditure by households, firms and government on imported products.

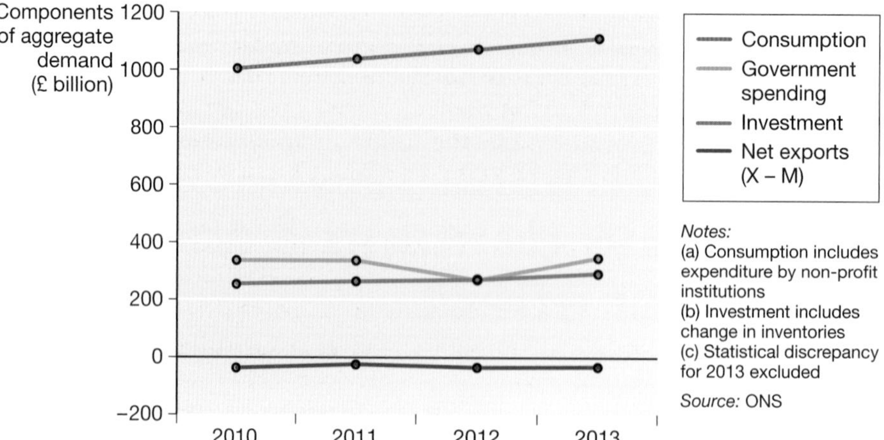

Figure 35.1 *The components of the UK's aggregate demand 2010–13 in current prices*

'Exports minus imports' is normally referred to as 'net exports'.

Planned and actual values

In the previous chapter we saw that the circular flow model could be used to measure national income and we showed that total output would equal total income, which would equal total expenditure, if they were calculated accurately. It is true to say that expenditure, income and output will be the same at the end of a particular period of time. However, it may not be the case that the plans of households, government and firms have been fulfilled. Thus it may be that planned expenditure and output are not equal and that the economy is not at a point of equilibrium. When considering whether or not an economy is in a macroeconomic equilibrium, it is essential to consider the factors that influence planned aggregate demand.

The determinants of aggregate demand

1 Consumption and saving

It is apparent from Figure 35.1 that consumption is by far the largest component of aggregate demand. There are a number of factors that determine the level of consumption by households, including decisions about saving. Decisions about saving and consumption are closely related because a decision to consume more (or less) results in a household saving less (or more).

Economists have identified various factors that influence the level of consumption and saving undertaken by households.

(a) Actual income

John Maynard Keynes (writing in *The General Theory of Employment, Interest and*

Key terms

Consumption is planned spending by households on goods and services.

Ceteris paribus is a Latin term that means 'everything else remaining constant'.

Saving is income that is received but which is not spent and is not a component of aggregate demand.

Disposable income is the amount of income received by households after taking into account taxes on income and benefits received.

Money, 1936) argued that the most important influence on the level of consumption is the amount of disposable income actually received by the household at a point in time. He believed that households would spend the majority of any increase in income that they received, but that they would also save some of this additional income. Keynes's view of the relationship between real income (i.e. adjusted for the effects of inflation) and consumption is shown by the consumption function in Figure 35.2.

Figure 35.2 shows that real income is an important determinant of consumption and that consumption will rise as income rises, but less quickly as a proportion of any additional income is saved. There are a number of important elements:

- **Autonomous consumption** is the level of consumption expenditure by households that is independent of the level of income received. This is financed by the use of savings – a process known as 'dissaving' (a term that we encountered in Chapter 34).
- **Marginal propensity to consume (MPC)** is the proportion of any additional income that is spent on consumption. We can see that a rise in income from Y_1 to Y_2 increases consumption from C_1 to C_2. The MPC measures the change in consumption divided by the change in income. This can be expressed by $\Delta C/\Delta Y$, where Δ represents the amount of change. The MPC is represented by the slope of the consumption function and by the value 'b' in the formula in Figure 35.2.
- **Marginal propensity to save (MPS)** is the proportion of any increase in income that is saved. The MPS measures the size of a change in saving in relation to the size of the change in real income that caused it. This can be expressed by $\Delta S/\Delta Y$, where Δ represents the amount of change.
- **Average propensity to consume (APC)** is the proportion of income that is consumed. This is measured by dividing consumption by income: C/Y. In Figure 35.2 at an income level of Y_1, the average propensity to consume will be C_1/Y_1.

It should be noted that MPC + MPS = 1 because any increase in income will either be consumed or saved.

The consumption function in Figure 35.2 illustrates the relationship between consumption and real income, assuming any other factors that might influence income

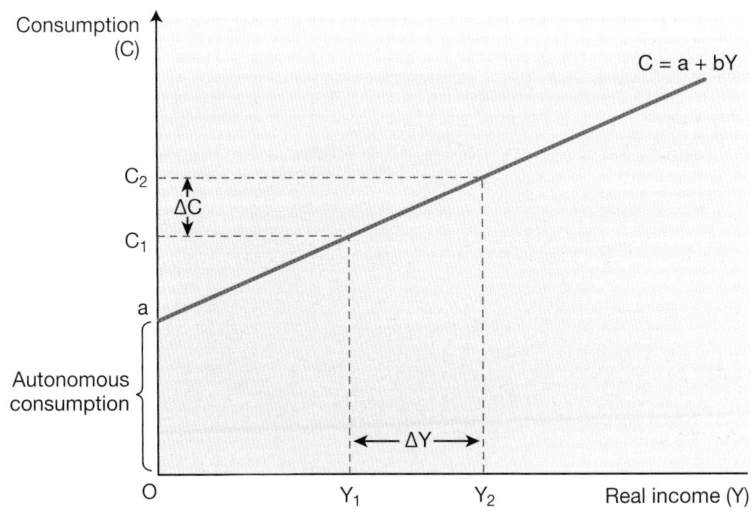

Figure 35.2
A consumption function showing the relationship between consumption and real income

(which we explore below) are constant. In other words, the consumption function is based on the assumption of 'ceteris paribus'. However, other factors with the potential to influence consumption may change. A change in factors other than real income would *shift* the consumption function rather than cause a *movement along* it. We shall now consider some factors that would affect the level of consumption and cause a shift in the consumption function.

(b) Expected income

Other economists have developed different theories about the way in which income levels can influence households' decisions on consumption and therefore saving:

- Milton Friedman, who won the Nobel Prize for Economics, developed the **permanent income hypothesis.** This theory states that households will consume at a level that reflects their expected long-term average income. This view of their long-term income gives a 'permanent' income that becomes a key determinant of consumption. Saving will take place when a household's actual income is higher than its permanent income. One important dimension of this theory is that changes in consumption cannot be predicted easily because they are dependent upon the expectations of individual households. This implies that governments may have difficulties in forecasting future patterns of consumption.
- Franco Modigliani and his student Richard Brumberg developed the **life-cycle hypothesis**, which takes a similar stance. The life-cycle hypothesis implies that individuals plan their consumption and savings behaviour over their whole lives, spending more in relation to income when young and again later in life. The life-cycle hypothesis states that the average propensity to consume is greater in households comprising younger or older individuals, because they consume relatively heavily on the expectation of future income or the use of savings – another example of dissaving. Middle-aged households have a higher propensity to save and a lower propensity to consume, reflecting their generally higher levels of income.

(c) Wealth

The amount of wealth held by households can be an important determinant of consumption decisions. Households can store wealth in a number of ways, such as in the form of property, savings accounts or a portfolio of company shares. Figure 35.3 shows the main forms of wealth in the UK in 2012.

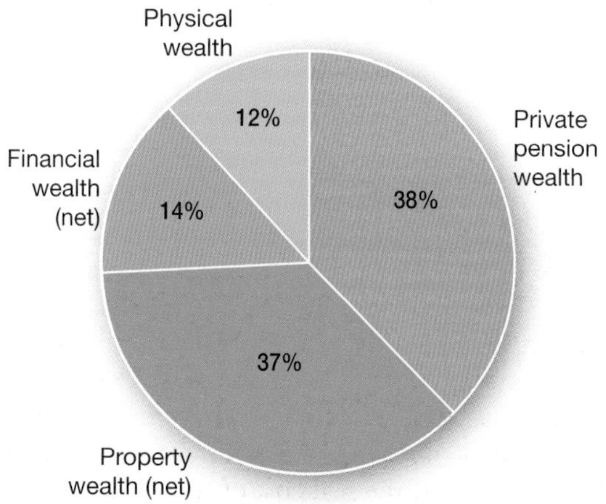

Figure 35.3 *Components of wealth in Great Britain, 2012*

An increase in wealth is likely to increase consumer confidence and lead to increased consumption. Some decisions by the UK government have the side effect of increasing wealth – for example, the Help to Buy scheme, which assists people in buying their homes, has boosted the housing market and increased the value of property. This could be expected to have a positive effect on consumption, helping the UK economy to continue its recovery from the recession of 2008–09.

(d) The distribution of income and wealth

The distribution of income and wealth is an issue that has attracted much attention recently. Recent trends in income inequality have seen a substantial rise in incomes received by the richest, especially the top 1% who earn the highest incomes, while incomes for the poorest have declined and those of middle earners have stagnated.

Key term
A **mortgage** is a long-term loan (frequently up to 25 years) used to purchase property.

Rising income inequality may reduce the level of consumption in an economy. This can occur because households enjoying higher incomes tend to have a lower marginal propensity to consume (i.e. they spend a lower proportion of any additional income earned). In contrast, households receiving lower incomes frequently have a high marginal propensity to consume. Thus any transfer of income from poorer to richer households is likely to reduce consumption within an economy. Government measures to transfer income from richer to poorer households can result in higher levels of consumption.

Wealth in the UK shows a more unequal distribution than income. Research in 2014 by the Office for National Statistics revealed that the richest 1% have accumulated as much wealth as the poorest 55% of the population put together. The top 10% of households owned 44% of wealth, while the poorest half of the country owned only 9%.

(e) The rate of interest

Changes in the rate of interest can influence the level of consumption by households for three main reasons:

- A fall in the rate of interest may increase consumption because it makes it cheaper for households to borrow money to finance consumption.
- At the same time, it is likely to reduce saving (as the return is lower).
- Perhaps even more important is a 'mortgage effect', which links changes in interest rates to levels of consumption. A fall in interest rates reduces the payments many households make on their mortgages (often by significant amounts), releasing more income to fund consumption of goods and services.

(f) Expected rates of future inflation

It may seem surprising that households' expectations of future rates of price increase can influence their current decisions on consumption. However, they can be a significant influence. At the time of writing, numerous economies in the world are experiencing or anticipate very low rates of inflation, or even negative rates of inflation (called deflation) where average prices fall over time. Prices in Japan have fallen for much of the past 15 years and prices are falling in Greece, Israel, Poland and Spain. Deflation can reduce consumption because households postpone consumption decisions in the expectation of being able to buy products more cheaply in the future. Households can also be dissuaded from borrowing to finance consumption – if incomes decline in line with prices, the real cost of repaying loans increases.

At times of rising inflation, consumption can be boosted as consumers spend early in order to take advantage of currently lower prices. Furthermore, borrowing to finance consumption is more attractive because the real cost of repaying loans will decline over time.

Saving

Saving is not a component of aggregate demand, but it is appropriate to discuss it here because it has a very direct influence on the level of consumption. A range of factors influence saving:

- **Levels of real income** The Keynesian consumption function set out in Figure 35.2 suggests that saving and real income have a direct relationship. Of each additional element of income, a proportion will be saved. At higher levels of real income, households may increase the proportion of additional income that is saved.

REALWORLD ECONOMICS 35.1

Saving in the UK

The typical proportion of income saved by households has halved over the last 40 years, according to research by Lloyds Bank. The bank found that households saved around 9.9% of their income between 1974 to 1984, when interest rates were rising: rates exceeded 10% for the first time in 1979. However, following five years in which the Bank of England base rate has sat at its historic low of 0.5%, households are saving around 4.8% of their incomes.

In 1980, households were saving 12.3% of their income, but the savings ratio declined rapidly during the noughties decade (Figure 35.4), fuelled by rising levels of consumer spending and borrowing. The UK's average savings ratio fell to a low point of 4.6% in 2008, before heading back on an upward path.

The savings ratio is based on the total income that is not spent by households, which can be saved in the bank or put into pensions and shares.

Source: Daily Telegraph, 21.8.14

Exercises **Total: 13 marks**

1 Identify and explain two significant features of the data shown in Figure 35.4. *(6 marks)*

2 Explain how the factors that have changed the savings ratio might have affected the level of consumption in the UK. *(7 marks)*

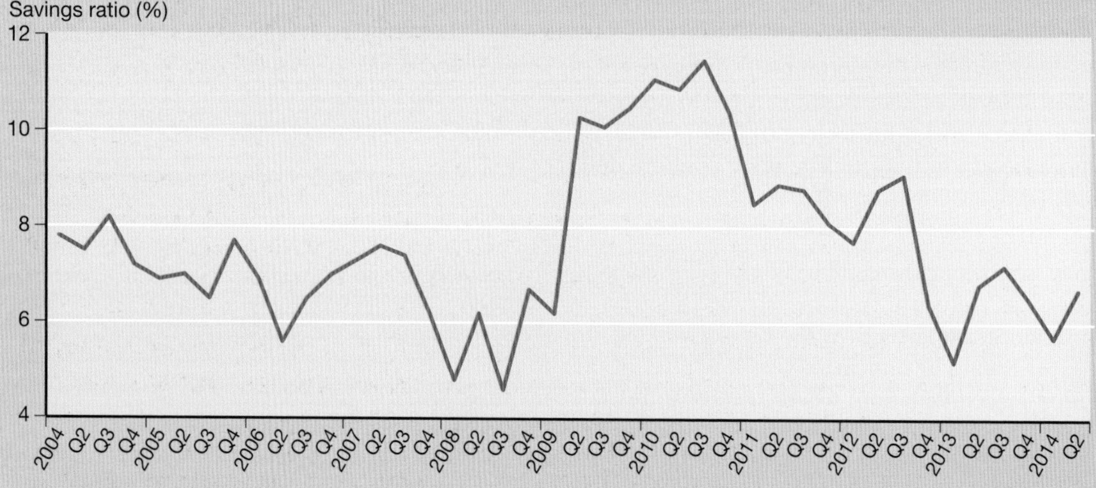

Figure 35.4 *UK's savings ratio 2004–14*

- **Government policies on taxation and welfare** Increases in taxation may reduce the level of saving by households as they experience reductions in disposable income and consequently lower the amount of income that is not spent (saving) in order to maintain their living standards. Increases in welfare payments have the potential to increase saving because they increase the level of disposable income received by households. However, this may have a limited effect because welfare payments are targeted mainly at lower income households that are likely to spend a higher proportion of disposable income and save relatively little.
- **The rate of interest** Falls in the rate of interest tend to reduce savings because the reward for using income in this way is lowered. The effect may be particularly pronounced if the rate of interest received on savings is lower than the current rate of inflation, meaning that the value of savings declines in real terms (i.e. in terms of what these savings would buy), even after interest has been paid on the savings.
- **Savings schemes available** Economies with efficient and trustworthy banking systems are likely to result in higher levels of savings than would otherwise be the case. Similarly, government policies to offer low taxes (or even zero taxes) on interest paid on savings can be an encouragement.

Construction of a new factory is a form of investment, representing an injection into the circular flow of income; cash deposited at a building society is a form of savings, representing a withdrawal from the circular flow of income.

2 Investment

Investment and savings are different concepts when used by economists, though non-specialists often use these terms interchangeably. Investment is the planned spending by firms that adds to an economy's capital stock. Capital stock includes property, machinery, vehicles and other items used in production. Investment also includes the purchase by firms of raw materials and components used in production. We saw in Chapter 34 that investment represents an injection into the circular flow of income.

In contrast, savings can be defined as income that is not passed on in the circular flow by households (i.e. they are a withdrawal) and may be placed in bank accounts, pensions or other savings schemes. 'Investing' money in buying a company's newly issued shares is not really investment – it is saving. However, if the company uses the funds raised from selling shares to build a new factory, then this is an example of investment because it adds to the economy's capital stock.

Households' savings may be channelled to firms as loans by banks and other financial institutions, and they may then be used for investment. However, the two are very different concepts.

Capital is a *stock*: it is the physical assets used in production and its total value in an economy is referred to as capital stock. Over time, some part of an economy's capital stock will become unusable because it is worn out, damaged or obsolete. This is termed *depreciation* or *capital consumption*.

Investment is a *flow*: it adds to the capital stock of an economy. Investment can take two forms. Gross investment is the value of the total spending by firms on physical assets used in production. However, some of this investment will have been necessary to replace the capital consumption that has taken place. Net investment is that part of investment that results in the purchase of new capital items and therefore increases the size of the economy's capital stock.

Key terms

Capital stock is the value of all physical assets used in production in the economy that are still in use, such as machinery, property and vehicles.

Capital consumption (or **depreciation**) is the decline in value of an economy's physical assets used in production due to wear and tear or obsolescence.

In summary:

Gross investment – Capital consumption = Net investment

The level of investment that occurs in an economy is influenced by a range of factors.

(a) The rate of interest

Firms invest with the objective of making a positive financial return, and the higher the better. For example, a retailer investing in a new store in a rapidly growing town may expect to make a return of 12% on its investment each year.

However, much investment may be financed by borrowing from banks and other financial institutions that recycle savings from households. A firm will only invest if the expected return from the investment exceeds the costs of the borrowed funds. Thus the retailer in our example will not undertake the investment in the new store unless the rate of interest is lower then 12%. Even if the firm planning the investment does not have to borrow the money needed, perhaps instead using profits retained from previous trading, the rate of interest plays a vital role in the decision. If the firm does not use its retained profits to fund the proposed investment, it will possibly save the profits. This will mean that it is again using the current rate of interest as a yardstick on whether or not to invest – in this case the rate of interest represents the opportunity cost of investment.

One final factor will be at work here. Investment will fall as the rate of interest rises because firms will be aware of the likely impact of rising interest rates on consumption. They will recognise that consumers will be less inclined to borrow money, and more prepared to save, at higher rates of interest. Both these factors will reduce consumption and the likely returns from investing in capital with the aim of producing goods and services.

Figure 35.5 illustrates the relationship between the rate of interest and planned investment. For this economy, a rate of interest of 16% will result in investment totalling £50 billion per time period. In this case there are investments totalling

Figure 35.5 *The marginal efficiency of capital*

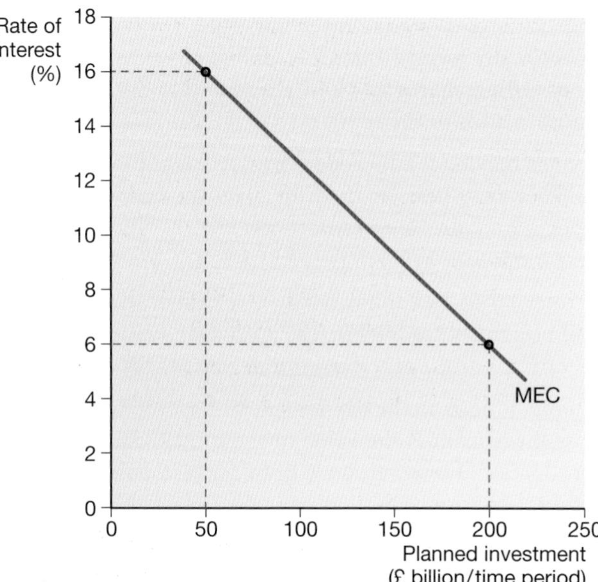

Key term

The **marginal efficiency of capital (MEC)** is the net rate of return that is expected from an investment.

£50 billion in which the return is higher than the prevailing rate of interest and therefore worthwhile from the perspective of firms. However, if the rate of interest is much lower, at 6% for example, many more investments become profitable where the return is higher than the rate of interest. In Figure 35.5 an interest rate of 6% would result in investment totalling £200 billion.

When we looked at the consumption function earlier in this chapter we saw that a change in real income would provoke a movement up or down an existing function. A change in any other determinant of consumption such as wealth or the expected rate of inflation will lead to a shift in the function. The same principle applies to investment: a change in the rate of interest will change the level of investment and cause a movement up or down the MEC curve. However, there are a number of other factors that can cause the curve to shift to the left or right and we shall consider these below.

(b) Technological advances

Advances in technology have increased the productive potential of new capital equipment and or reduced the cost of their use. For example, mining companies in Western Australia are using driverless trucks in their mining operations, avoiding the need to pay drivers and allowing the trucks to be operational for a greater number of hours. As a result, the productivity of the trucks increases and the return from investing in them is higher.

Technology can reduce costs and increase returns, which results in a shift in the MEC curve to the right, leading to a higher level of investment at any given rate of interest.

(c) The price of capital equipment

If the price of new productive assets rises, this reduces the profit or return that can be expected from any given investment. As a result, the MEC curve shifts to the left.

Alternatively, if the cost of capital equipment declines, returns from an investment rise, correspondingly increasing the expected return. A fall in the cost of capital shifts the MEC curve to the right, increasing the level of investment at any given rate of interest. For example, the price of microprocessors has fallen steadily in recent years, reducing the cost of a wide range of technology used in production.

(d) Government policies

A number of government policies can influence the cost and likely returns from investing and therefore the amount of investment that takes place. Research and development financed by the government may result in new technological developments or in lower costs for using existing technology. Such government activities are likely to increase the level of investment.

Other decisions could reduce the level of investment. For example, an increase in corporation tax, which is paid on company profits, will reduce the expected return and the amount that is invested.

The accelerator theory of investment

The accelerator theory links changes in the planned level of investment to changes in the level of national income. Firms invest to replace obsolete or worn out capital

Key terms

The **accelerator theory of investment** states that the level of planned investment depends on the rate of change of national income.

The **capital–output ratio** expresses the relationship between the cost of capital and the value of output produced annually by that capital.

stock and to increase their productive capacity. If the level of national income is falling, as in a recession, then the demand for goods and services is likely to be falling and firms may not invest at all. There may be no need to replace capital equipment as it becomes unproductive. In contrast, at a time when national income is rising quickly, firms may need to increase their capital quickly to be able to respond to rising demand for their products.

The following example illustrates the workings of the accelerator model. A firm manufacturing radios uses machines as an important part of its production process. We make a number of assumptions.

- No machines need replacing during the period of time covered by our example (i.e. there is no capital consumption to simplify the model).
- The firm is operating with a capital–output ratio of 2:1. This means that it needs £1 million of capital equipment (its machines) to be able to produce £500,000 of radios annually.
- The firm in question always responds to increases in sales by increasing production and it has no spare capacity in its factory.

In years 1 and 2 there is no need for any investment because the firm has sufficient capital to produce the desired number of radios and its output is not changing, since national income is not changing. However, in years 3 and 4, spending on the firm's products rises at a steady rate, increasing by £20 million in each year as incomes rise. As a result, investment increases from zero to £40 million because the firm has to invest £2 to produce each extra £1 of output every year. So, a relatively small rise in income and spending on radios (of 10%) provokes a very large rise in investment.

Table 35.1 *An example of the accelerator in operation (£ million)*

Year	Annual production	Actual capital stock	Desired capital stock	Investment in capital
1	200	400	400	0
2	200	400	400	0
3	220	400	440	40
4	240	440	480	40
5	280	480	560	80
6	290	560	580	20
7	270	580	540	0

The accelerator effect is emphasised by the events of Year 5. In this year, spending on the firm's radios rises from £240 million to £280 million – an increase of 16.7%. However, the firm requires a capital stock valued at £560 million in order to meet demand for its products, but it only has £480 million at the start of the year. Thus it has to invest £80 million to acquire the necessary increase in capital. In Year 5, rising incomes lead to an increase in expenditure on its products of 16.7%, which calls for an increase in investment of 100% (from 40 to 80). In Year 6, when the rate of growth of income and spending on radios slows, the level of investment falls back dramatically, even though income is still rising.

This example illustrates the key element of the accelerator theory, namely that the level of investment depends on the rate of change of national income (and spending) and not simply its level.

- When income is not rising, investment is zero (as in years 1 and 2).

- When income is rising at a constant rate (as in years 3 and 4), investment is positive but stable.
- When income is rising at an increasing rate (in years 4 and 5), investment increases very rapidly.
- When income is rising but at a declining rate (in years 5 and 6), investment is positive but falling.

Number crunching

Assume that in Year 7 in Table 35.1, the level of spending on radios rises to £320 million (rather than the existing figure of £270 million). What would be the percentage increase in (a) income (or spending) and (b) investment?

We can express the accelerator relationship as a formula:

$$I_t = a(Y_t - Y_{t-1})$$

where I_t is investment in the current time period, a is the capital–output ratio, Y_t is income in the current year and Y_{t-1} is income in the previous year. Therefore $(Y_t - Y_{t-1})$ measures the change in income. This formula highlights the importance of the capital output ratio in the accelerator model. It determines the magnitude of the changes in investment following a change in income. In our example, we assumed a ratio of 2; if we had assumed a higher capital output ratio of, say, 4 or 5, the changes in investment would have been considerably greater.

While the accelerator model has value in explaining changes in investment, it is a simplification. The assumptions we had to make, about the firm always responding to increased income and demand by increasing output (and not prices) and not having any spare capacity, reduce its explanatory power.

3 Government expenditure

Government spending in 2014–15 in the UK amounted to more than £350 billion. This expenditure covers a wide range of categories including welfare payments such as pensions and disability benefits, the provision of social and merit goods including health and education, and expenditure on defence, local government services and interest payments on the national debt.

REALWORLD ECONOMICS 35.1

UK government plans to cut spending

At the time of writing, the Chancellor of the Exchequer, George Osborne, announced plans to reduce government spending as a percentage of GDP to its lowest level since the 1930s. This major reduction in spending, totalling £60 billion by 2019–20, will affect a range of government departments, including local government and justice.

The plans, according to the Office for Budget Responsibility, are based on cutting one million jobs in the public sector by 2020, tight controls on pay rises for public sector workers, and further reductions in welfare spending.

Exercise

1. Explain why the government's planned spending cuts might not reduce aggregate demand by £60 billion by 2019–20. *(6 marks)*

The level of government expenditure depends on a number of factors, only some of which are economic. It can be difficult to relate government expenditure to economic performance. A growing economy may generate higher receipts from taxes such as income and corporation tax, offering governments the chance to boost spending. However, a period of poor economic performance may result in higher welfare payments such as unemployment benefit.

The level of government spending can also be determined by political factors. Some governments believe in a smaller public sector and seek to reduce the role of the state in the operation of the economy. One highly visible outcome of this philosophy is privatisation – the sale and transfer of publicly owned enterprises into the private sector. For example, the Royal Mail was privatised in 2013.

In terms of aggregate demand, the level of government expenditure is best viewed as autonomous or independent of the macroeconomic variables that have been discussed above.

4 Net exports

Net exports are receipts from the sale of exports minus expenditure on imported goods and services. In recent years this figure has been negative for the UK, reflecting the fact that the country has spent more on imports than it has received from the sale of exports.

Exchange rates

Key term

The **exchange rate** is the price of one currency expressed in terms of another – for example, £1 = $1.60 or €1.20.

The exchange rate of a currency can be a major influence on an economy's purchases of imports as well as its sales of exports (Figure 35.6). A change in a country's exchange rate will affect the prices paid for its exports and its imports and, since most currencies are traded freely on world markets, their values are altering constantly.

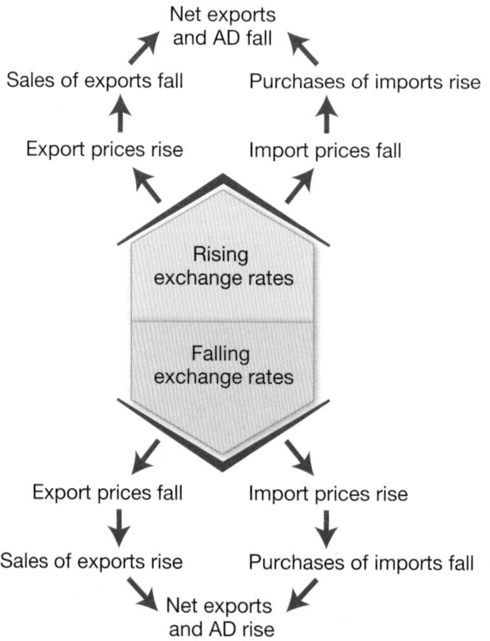

Figure 35.6 *Exchange rates, net exports and aggregate demand*

- **A rise in the value of a currency** If, for example, the value of the pound increases, then it means that a greater amount of a foreign currency will be needed to buy each pound. As a consequence, exports will become more expensive overseas as a greater amount of the foreign currency will be required to purchase them. Depending on the price elasticity of demand for exports, their sales will fall and this will reduce aggregate demand. Simultaneously, the price of imported products in the UK will fall. Since the pound has risen in value, a smaller amount of the currency will be needed to buy each unit of foreign currency. Imports will rise, although the extent of the impact will depend on price elasticity of demand. A rise in imports will also have the effect of reducing aggregate demand. Remember that AD = C + I + G + (X – M), so a rise in imports reduces net exports and aggregate demand.
- **A fall in the value of the currency** This has broadly the opposite effects to those outlined above. Exports become cheaper and sales can be expected to rise. At the same time, imports decline as they become more expensive. The combined effect should increase aggregate demand, though again the extent of the change depends on factors such as the price elasticity of demand for imports and exports.

Domestic and overseas income levels

Demand for imports in the UK will be determined to some extent by the level of national income. If UK residents are enjoying rising incomes, they are likely to increase expenditure on imported products. This is a relatively pronounced feature of expenditure by UK households. In contrast, sales of UK exports depend upon income levels overseas. One reason why UK export sales have been unimpressive over recent years is slow economic growth in the EU, one of the UK's major export markets. The growth of incomes in EU countries has been slow, and at the time of writing some countries such as Italy are in recession, depressing demand for UK exports.

Aggregate demand curves

In Chapter 6 you encountered demand curves, which illustrated how the level of demand for a particular product changes as its price changes. Aggregate demand (AD) curves perform the same function at a macroeconomic level. In other words, they show how the total demand for goods and services in an economy changes as the general level of prices changes. Figure 35.7 shows an aggregate demand curve.

In microeconomics, a demand curve relates demand for a single good or service to the price of that good. An aggregate demand curve shows total demand (or planned expenditure) in relation to the general price level in the economy.

Key term

An **aggregate demand curve** shows the relationship between the total level of demand in an economy and the general level of prices.

Why does an aggregate demand curve slope downwards from left to right?

Aggregate demand curves have this shape principally because when the general price level falls, aggregate demand is likely to rise. We can relate this to various components of aggregate demand.

Consumption Consumption is likely to rise when the general level of prices falls because the purchasing power of money (the amount that a unit of money will buy) will be greater. If the price level is lower, it follows that the rate of interest will frequently be lower too. This will boost consumption as the opportunity cost of saving is reduced, as is the cost of borrowing to finance a rise in consumption. If consumption increases when prices fall, so will aggregate demand.

Investment The level of investment could be expected to rise when the price level falls for two reasons. First, the cost of capital goods may fall, making more investments profitable. Secondly, firms may expect consumption to rise and therefore invest in anticipation of this.

Net exports If prices are reduced in an economy, this should be reflected in the price of its exports. Assuming the country's exchange rate does not change, this should make its products more competitive on global markets, boosting export sales. At the same time, imports will appear relatively expensive in comparison to domestically produced goods and services. As a result, purchases of imports may fall. The combined effect of rising export sales and falling import purchases will increase aggregate demand when the general price level falls.

Figure 35.7 *An aggregate demand curve*

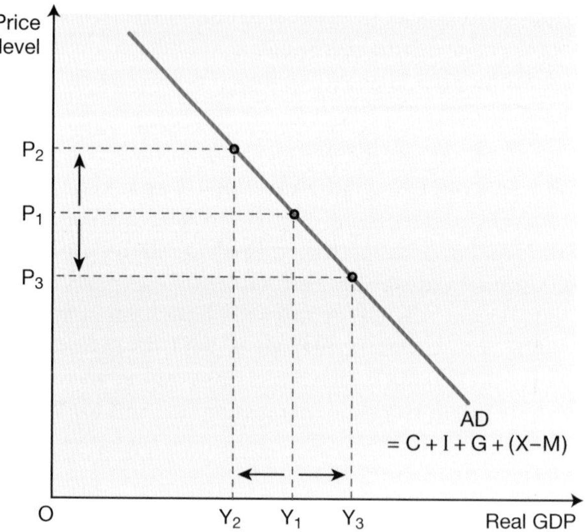

Figure 35.7 illustrates that a change in the general price level will affect aggregate demand by causing a movement up or down the curve. Thus a rise in the general price level from P_1 to P_2 causes a reduction in the level of aggregate demand and a fall in national income or output as measured by real GDP (from Y_1 to Y_2); a fall in the general price level from P_1 to P_3 causes an increase in the level of aggregate demand and a rise in national income or output as measured by real GDP (from Y_1 to Y_3).

The causes of shifts in the aggregate demand curve

It is only a change in the general price level that will cause a movement up or down an aggregate demand curve. However, there are numerous factors that will lead to a shift in the aggregate demand curve, as illustrated in Figure 35.8.

In general, a rise in consumption, investment, government spending or exports will increase aggregate demand. A fall in these factors or a rise in imports will reduce aggregate demand.

Table 35.2 summarises some of the factors that will cause aggregate demand curves to shift to the right (an increase in AD) or to the left (a fall in AD).

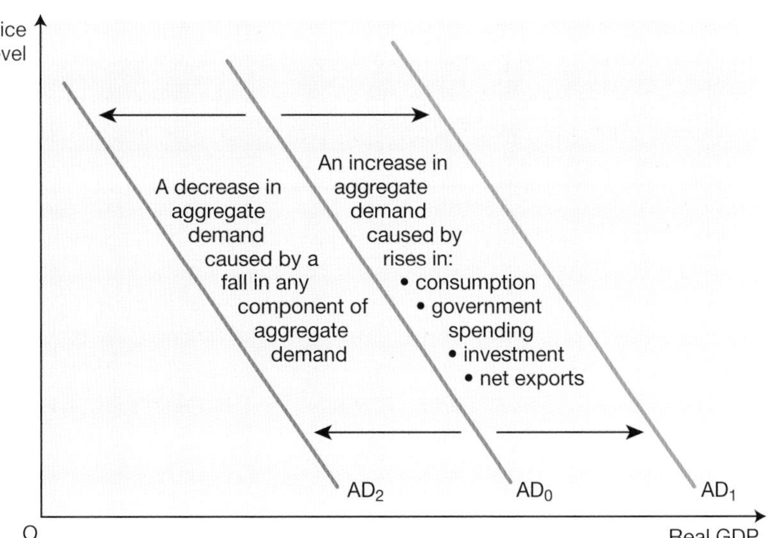

Figure 35.8 *Shifts in aggregate demand curves*

We can see from Table 35.2 that some factors, such as a change in interest rates, can influence the level of aggregate demand in a number of ways. These factors will be considered when we look at the government's use of monetary policy in Chapter 43.

Table 35.2 *Factors that cause a shift in the aggregate demand curve*

Factors causing a fall in AD	Component of AD	Factors causing a rise in AD
▪ A fall in disposable income or expected disposable income ▪ An increase in interest rates ▪ A fall in wealth ▪ Greater inequality of income and wealth	**Consumption**	▪ A rise in disposable income or expected disposable income ▪ An decrease in interest rates ▪ An increase in wealth ▪ Rising rates of inflation ▪ Reduced inequality of income and wealth
▪ An increase in interest rates ▪ Increases in the price of capital equipment ▪ Government policies such as increasing company taxes	**Investment**	▪ A reduction in interest rates ▪ Decreases in the price of capital equipment ▪ Advances increasing technological productivity
▪ Government decisions to reduce the size of the public sector	**Government expenditure**	▪ Government decisions to increase the size of the public sector
▪ A rise in interest rates ▪ Falling incomes overseas	**Net exports**	▪ A fall in interest rates ▪ Rising incomes overseas

Aggregate demand and the multiplier effect

In Chapter 34 we studied the circular flow of income and saw that a rise in injections will result in an increase in national income, or real GDP. The reverse is also true: a fall in injections will lead to a decrease in national income or real GDP.

The effect of a change in the level of injections is a little more complex than might be expected. This is because it ultimately leads to a magnified or multiplied effect on national income. Known as the **multiplier effect**, this process can operate on an entire economy or within a local economy.

Key term

The **multiplier** is a process through which any change in a component of aggregate demand results in a magnified change in real GDP or national income.

Figure 35.9 illustrates the effect of the multiplier and what determines the size of its effect. In the diagram we assume that a rise in investment leads to an increase in injections. This is a realistic reflection of what is happening in the UK economy where investment has risen steadily from £254 billion in 2010 to over £300 billion in 2014. However, a change in the level of government spending or export sales can also create the multiplier effect.

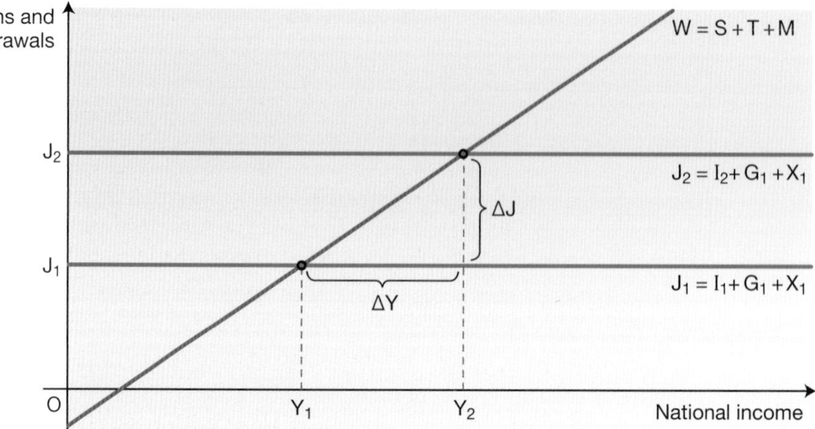

Figure 35.9 *An increase in injections and the multiplier effect*

Figure 35.9 shows that a rise in injections from J_1 to J_2 (ΔJ) leads to a larger rise in national income, as shown by the rise from Y_1 to Y_2 (ΔY).

What causes the multiplier effect?

The multiplier effect arises because income that is injected into the economy joins the circular flow and a declining amount of it is spent repeatedly. Thus if an economy receives a rise in injections amounting to £200 billion, initially the economy will experience of rise in income of £200 billion. However, this money, once spent, will be received by households and firms in the form of income as it flows through the economy. Not all of this income will be spent in the domestic economy: some will be saved, some will be paid to the government as taxes, and some will flow overseas as a result of the purchase of imports. However, a proportion will be spent on consumption and will be passed around the circular flow. The proportion that is spent will be received again by households and firms so that the process is repeated, with the same proportion of the second instalment of income being spent. This process of spending a set proportion of a declining additional amount of income continues until the sums involved are tiny.

Table 35.3 *The multiplier effect of a £200 billion injection into an economy (£ billion)*

Stage	Increase in income (= change in consumption from previous stage)	Change in withdrawals (assuming 40% of income is saved, paid in taxes or spent on imports)	Change in consumption
1	200	80	120
2	120	48	72
3	72	28.8	43.2
4	43.2	17.3	25.9
Final effect	**500**	**200**	**300**

Table 35.3 provides a more detailed version of the example of the multiplier explained in the previous paragraph. It only shows the first few stages of the operation of the multiplier effect, but you can see that income that is not withdrawn as savings, taxes or imports passes round the economy and is, in effect, spent again. However, the amount that is spent at each stage of the multiplier process declines because a proportion (we have assumed 40% or 0.4) is withdrawn at each stage, with only the balance of 60% or 0.6 being passed on within the circular flow.

How to measure the size of the multiplier effect

We can use the following formula to measure the size of the multiplier effect:

Multiplier (K) = $\Delta Y / \Delta J$

In the example, this would give a multiplier value of 2.5 (= £500 billion/£200 billion). This means that an increase in injections will result in a final rise in national income that is two-and-a-half times larger. The multiplier also works in reverse. This means that a fall in injections will provoke a larger fall in national income.

Author tip

This is how the AQA AS specification expects you to be able to measure the multiplier effect.

The size of the multiplier is determined by the proportion of income that is not passed on at each stage of the operation of the multiplier. If a higher proportion were withdrawn as savings, taxes and imports at each stage, a smaller amount would be spent on consumption and passed on in the circular flow. The final effect on national income would be smaller and the size of the multiplier would be lower.

This means that the size of the multiplier can be determined by an alternative formula:

K = 1/MPW

where MPW is the marginal propensity to withdraw or the proportion of any income that is not passed on within the circular flow. The size of the MPW is expressed as a decimal. In our earlier example we assumed that 40% of income was withdrawn at each stage. This means that the MPW = 0.4. Hence K = 1/0.4 = 2.5, which confirms our earlier result.

Key term

The **marginal propensity to withdraw (MPW)** is the proportion of any income that is not passed on within the circular flow.

Review questions

Total: 46 marks

1 Define the term 'aggregate demand'. *(3 marks)*

2 Which of the following is not a component of aggregate demand?

A Net exports
B Savings
C Investment
D Government spending *(1 mark)*

3 Explain why a rise in imports, ceteris paribus, will lead to a reduction in aggregate demand. *(4 marks)*

4 An economy experiences a rise in income of £2500 million and, as a result, its withdrawals rise by £625 million. Which of the following is the economy's marginal propensity to consume?

A 0.75 B 0.625 C 0.25 D £1875 million *(1 mark)*

5 Explain why rising income inequality may reduce the level of consumption in an economy. *(6 marks)*

6 Explain, with the aid of examples, the difference between investment and saving. *(5 marks)*

7 According to the accelerator theory, the level of investment in an economy depends upon which of the following?

A The level of national income
B The rate of interest
C The cost of capital equipment
D The rate of change of national income *(1 mark)*

8 Explain why a rise in the value of a country's currency can be expected, ceteris paribus, to reduce its aggregate demand. *(7 marks)*

9 Explain why an aggregate demand curve slopes downward from left to right. *(9 marks)*

10 Which of the following would be most likely to cause an aggregate demand curve to shift to the left?

A An increase in wealth
B Falling incomes overseas
C Reduced inequality of income and wealth
D A fall in the price of capital equipment

11 Explain why an increase in injections leads to a magnified or multiplied increase in national income. *(8 marks)*

12 A rise in government spending resulted in an increase in income of £240 million. The multiplier is estimated to have a value of 4. By how much did government spending increase?

A £960 million
B £60 million
C £240 million
D 25% *(1 mark)*

The determinants of aggregate supply

This chapter introduces you to the concept of aggregate supply, the partner of aggregate demand that was the focus of Chapter 35. It considers the factors that will determine the level of aggregate supply in both the short term and long term, and analyses how the shape of a typical aggregate supply curve may vary according to the timescale under consideration. In Chapter 37 we will combine aggregate supply and aggregate demand to enable us to study the concept of a macroeconomic equilibrium and to analyse a range of macroeconomic issues and problems.

Short-run aggregate supply

In Chapter 8 you studied the concept of supply in a microeconomic context. You discovered the relationship that exists between the amount of a specific product that producers are willing to supply and the price of that individual product. The concept of aggregate supply looks at the relationship between the quantity of all products (both goods and services) that producers are willing to supply in an economy and the general level of prices that exist within that economy.

Key term

Aggregate supply is the total quantity of output that producers in an economy are willing to supply at specific price levels over a specific time period.

Price and the short-run aggregate supply curve

The short-run aggregate supply (SRAS) curve is upward sloping from left to right. Why is this the case? Essentially this is because firms face higher costs in increasing short-run supply and will only do so in response to rising prices to avoid a reduction in profits. Thus firms will only increase output from, for example, Y_1 to Y_2 in Figure 36.1, in response to a price rise from P_1 to P_2.

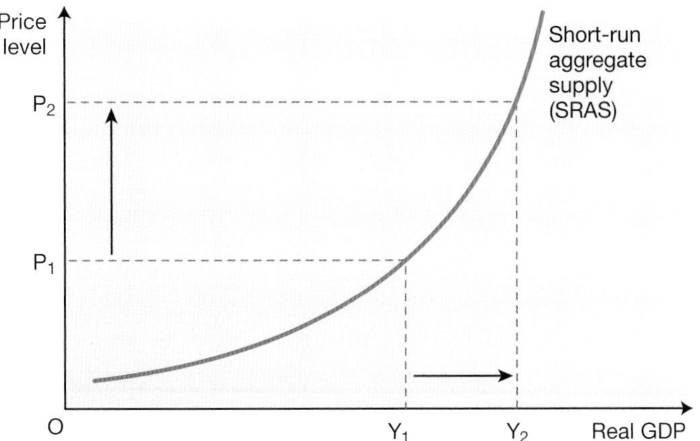

Figure 36.1 *A short-run aggregate supply (SRAS) curve*

It is assumed that to produce more in the short run, a firm is likely to incur higher operating costs principally because it is difficult for firms to acquire additional resources without paying more. It may not be desirable or feasible for firms to hire additional workers in the short term because the increase in production might only be temporary and, even if not, the recruitment process may take time. Increasing production may therefore mean that it is necessary for the firm to pay existing employees overtime rates in the short term, forcing up costs. In order to maintain profits, firms will only be willing to increase production in return for receiving higher prices.

A similar argument may equally apply to the price of other resources used in production. Additional supplies of raw materials and components may only be available at higher prices as rising demand in the markets for these resources pushes up prices. In the longer term, it may be that additional sources of supply for these raw materials and components become available and the price falls, but in the short term this is unlikely to occur.

Some resources used in production cannot be varied in the short term: over this time period the quantity available for productive use is fixed. This includes resources such as machinery and buildings. Thus any increase in short-run supply must use factors such as labour that are variable in the short term.

Hence the shape of the SRAS curve indicates that, ceteris paribus, firms will increase aggregate supply in response to an increase in the general price level.

The other determinants of short-run aggregate supply

As you will have seen in Chapter 8 when studying the law of supply in microeconomic markets, a change in price causes a movement up or down a supply curve while changes in other factors, such as indirect taxes or subsidies, result in a shift in the supply curve. The same principle applies to aggregate supply curves. Figure 36.1 illustrates that a change in the general price level will provoke a change in short-run aggregate supply. We shall now consider how changes in a variety of costs as well as increases in productivity can cause shifts in the SRAS curve.

Money wage rates

A rise in money wages (i.e. wages not adjusted for the effect of inflation), ceteris paribus, is likely to result in firms facing higher production costs, especially in economies when many firms use labour-intensive methods of production. Assuming firms are profit maximising, they will respond to higher money wage costs by reducing production. Some may cease production entirely. The result is that the SRAS curve will shift upwards and to the left, leading to a reduction in short-run aggregate supply. This is illustrated by the move from $SRAS_1$ to $SRAS_2$ in Figure 36.2.

Raw material and component prices

The prices of raw materials and components can be an important part of the total costs of many businesses, particularly manufacturers. A rise in prices will increase costs of firms, leading to a leftward shift of the SRAS curve as discussed above. In contrast, a fall in the prices of raw materials and components can lead to an increase in SRAS as this, in effect, reduces the costs of production incurred by firms, boosting profits. This encourages existing firms to increase output because they seek to maximise profits. This is illustrated in Figure 36.2 by the shift from $SRAS_1$ to $SRAS_3$.

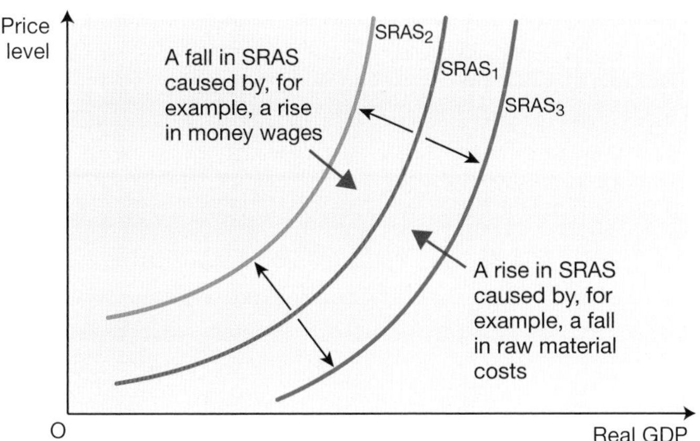

Figure 36.2 *Shifts in the SRAS curve*

The UK is susceptible to changes in SRAS brought about by changes in the price of imported components and raw materials. In part this can be because the prices of these products in the economies that produce them have changed, but also because of exchange rate changes. The change in the price of oil between June and December 2014 illustrates this. Over this six-month period the price of oil fell from \$115 a barrel to \$68 a barrel. The price change alone represents a 41% fall. However, oil is priced in dollars, not pounds, and this change could be magnified if the value of the pound rose against the dollar, meaning that fewer pounds were required to buy the dollars needed to purchase oil. In fact, the value of the pound reduced against the dollar over the same period from £1 = \$1.72 to £1 = \$1.56. This would have reduced the effect of the fall in the price of oil on the UK's SRAS.

Taxation on firms

Firms in the UK pay a variety of business taxes. They pay corporation tax on profits, and value added tax (VAT) on a range of inputs used in production. An increase in the rates of these taxes will have the same effect as an increase in costs, causing a shift in the economy's SRAS to the left ($SRAS_1$ to $SRAS_2$). In 2011 the UK government increased the rate of VAT from 17.5% to 20%. This alone would have had the potential to cause a significant reduction in SRAS in the following periods, though other factors would have affected SRAS at the same time.

Productivity

The productivity of inputs to production such as labour, land and capital can change, even in the short run. A rise in productivity is similar in effect to a fall in costs. For example, if the productivity of an economy's workforce increases by 5%, ceteris paribus, firms will enjoy a reduction in their costs. This takes place because firms are able to produce the same amount of production using 5% less labour, reducing labour costs. This creates the opportunity for firms to generate higher profits and leads to an increase in SRAS. However, as shown in Real World Economics 36.1, labour productivity in the UK fell between 2009 and 2013. The impact of this would effectively have been to raise the costs of firms in the UK and thus shift the SRAS to the left. This is shown by the move from $SRAS_1$ to $SRAS_2$ in Figure 36.2. The outcome would be a reduction in real GDP and upward pressure on the price level.

REALWORLD ECONOMICS 36.1

UK labour productivity falls

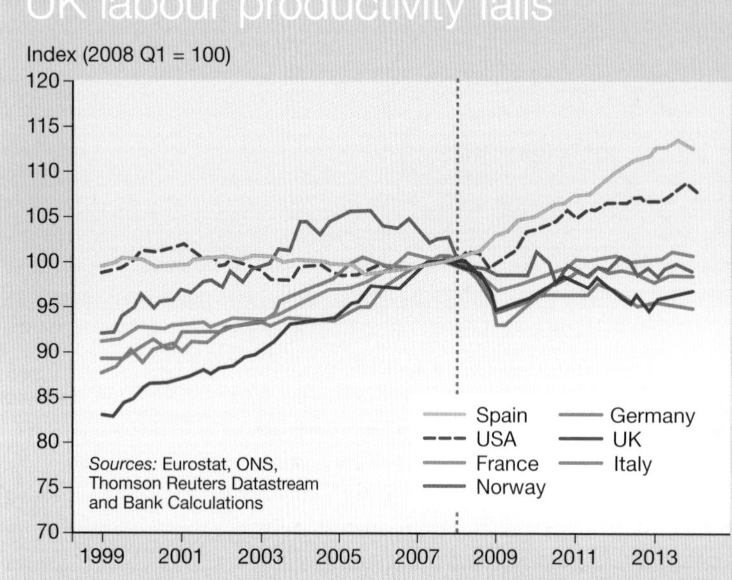

Figure 36.3 *Labour productivity per person for a selection of major economies, 1999–2013*

The UK economy grew by 2.6% in 2014 (as measured by real GDP) and is forecast to grow by over 2.5% in 2015. This represents faster growth than many of the UK's major rivals such as Spain and France.

At the same time, labour productivity in the UK has performed particularly poorly, especially when compared to other major economies (see Figure 36.3).

Source: Bank of England Quarterly Bulletin Q2 2014

Exercise

1 Explain the possible reasons why the UK's real GDP is rising strongly at a time when its labour productivity is performing poorly. *(9 marks)*

Long-run aggregate supply

Long-run aggregate supply (LRAS) is the total quantity of output that producers in an economy are willing to supply over a longer time period in which the prices of all factors of production can vary. Many economists believe that in the long run the aggregate supply (LRAS) curve is independent of the general price level in an economy.

Long-run aggregate supply is dependent upon other factors such as advances in technology as well as the quantity and productivity of all of an economy's factors of production. For example, the level of foreign investment in the UK was high in 2013–14, boosting LRAS.

As no relationship is assumed to exist between price and LRAS, the LRAS curve is a straight vertical line, as illustrated in Figure 36.4. However, it is important to note that not all economists agree with this view, an issue to which we will return, briefly, later in this chapter and more fully in our companion volume, *AQA A-Level Year 2 Economics*.

Key note

The AQA AS specification states that 'it is assumed that the long-run AS curve is vertical'. This reflects the belief of a group of economists (known as classical or new classical economists) that LRAS is independent of the price level.

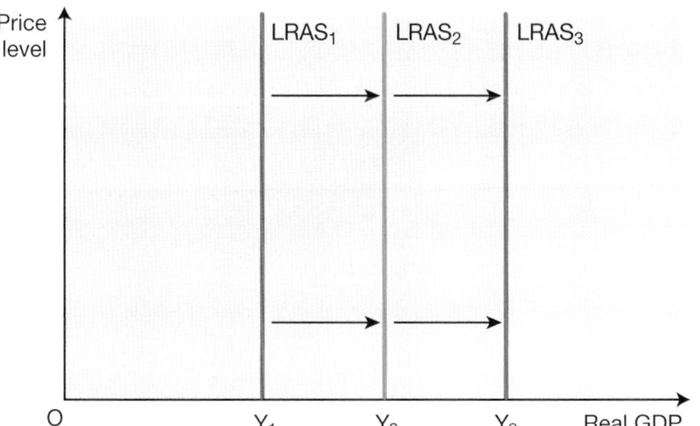

Figure 36.4 *Shifts in an economy's LRAS curve showing increases in productive potential*

The position of an economy's LRAS curve

The position of the LRAS curve shows the economy's potential level of output – the level of output that an economy could achieve if it operated at full employment level. This means that everyone who is seeking employment at the current wage is employed and that the economy is producing its maximum output. A shift to the right in the LRAS curve (such as $LRAS_1$ to $LRAS_2$ in Figure 36.4) indicates that the economy is experiencing economic growth. This can also be shown by an outward shift in the production possibility boundary that you studied in Chapter 5. LRAS shows, in effect, the amount that can be produced by an economy assuming that all of its resources are utilised.

The determinants of long-run aggregate supply

So, assuming that the LRAS curve is vertical, we will examine the factors that can cause the curve to shift. The major determinants of LRAS are the quantity and quality of factors of production available to the economy.

Key term

Factors of production are the scarce resources (land, labour, capital and enterprise) used in production.

The quality of factors of production

By using factors of production that are of higher quality and more productive, it is possible to increase the amount produced by a given stock of factors and thus shift the LRAS curve to the right. In this way, an economy can increase its productive potential without increasing the amount of resources at its disposal.

- *Capital* Developments in technology are a significant factor, increasing the potential of economies throughout the world to produce more. One example is the use of robotic manufacturing technology, which allows factories to operate for longer hours and to produce vast quantities of standard quality products. Foxconn, the manufacturer responsible for producing a wide range of technology products, including Apple's iPhone, anticipates installing one million robots in its factories in 2014–15. This development alone could have a considerable impact on the productive potential of the Asian countries in which it is based.
- *Labour* The quality (and hence productivity) of labour used in production can be improved in a number of ways. Better education and training are likely to improve the skills and attitudes of employees and, as a result, their performance in the workplace. The outcome should be increased productivity. Firms in many

economies are implementing policies to improve not only employees' skills through training but also their engagement (or involvement) in firms' activities by, for example, giving them a greater say in decision making.

- *Enterprise* Governments seek to increase the quality of entrepreneurs who operate within their countries. By providing training, they aim to reduce the failure rate of new firms and to help promote growth in this category of business. Such actions can boost output from these firms and increase LRAS. In the UK, despite significant cuts in government expenditure since 2010, the government is investing in enterprise education in primary and secondary schools.

The quantity of factors of production

An alternative approach to increasing LRAS is to increase the amount of factors of production available to firms. This can entail acquiring additional factors of production, or using existing ones more intensively.

- *Capital* Increasing the quantity of capital available to firms within an economy will increase its productive potential. This will be the result of net investment, i.e. levels of investment greater than that required to replace worn out or obsolete capital equipment. We saw in Chapter 35 that this will also impact on aggregate demand and will depend on factors such as the rate of interest and the price of capital equipment.
- *Labour – birth rate* This is an important topic in the UK currently. The size of the UK's population has been increasing by around 400,000 people each year, as shown in Figure 36.5. In part this is the result of an increase in the number of births. However, an increasing number of births will not affect the productive capacity of the UK economy until these people enter the labour force, which will not happen for at least 18 years.
- *Labour – net migration* Another more immediate factor affecting the quantity of labour available to firms is migration, i.e. the number of people entering and leaving the country. The key statistic here is net migration. Figure 36.5 shows that net migration into the UK has risen significantly since the early 1990s. Migration has the potential to have a significant impact on the productive potential of the UK. Many people emigrating from the UK are older, possibly retired with less potential to affect long-run aggregate supply. In contrast, many immigrants are younger and become an active part of the UK's working population.
- *Labour – population structure and economic incentives* The existence of a larger population does not necessarily lead to a larger working population and a greater productive potential. A large percentage of the population may be too young or too old to be part of the labour force; the UK's population is ageing, resulting in a larger number of older people who are not working or seeking work. The age

Key terms

Net migration is the difference between immigration (i.e. people moving to the UK for more than one year) and emigration (i.e. people leaving the UK for more than one year).

The **participation rate** is the percentage of working age people within an economy who are either employed or are actively looking for work.

Factor mobility measures the ease with which factors of production (land, labour, capital and enterprise) move from one use to another.

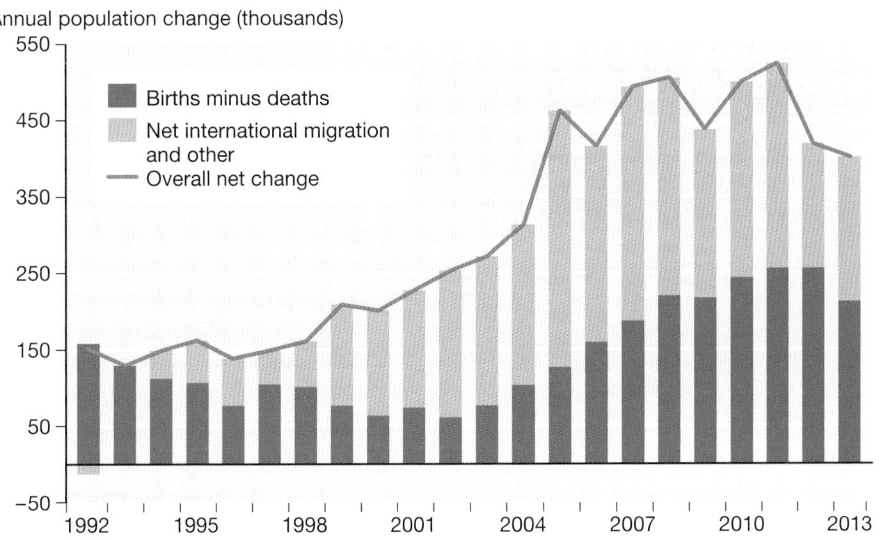

Figure 36.5 *The causes of change in the UK's population, 1992–2013*

structure of a population affects the size of the economy's working population – those who are in the working age groups, normally 16–65, though these limits are blurring over time. Not all of those people in the working age group may opt to be an active part of the workforce; some may be studying or caring for dependants, but others may be voluntarily unemployed and thus not seeking employment. In some economies a relatively small proportion of females are employed. Some economists believe that voluntary unemployment is a significant factor, reducing LRAS and the result of a lack of suitable incentives. In part this could be the consequence of benefit payments, which are relatively similar to the potential earnings of this group of people. This is one factor behind the UK government's move to reduce them.

REALWORLD ECONOMICS 36.2

International differences in labour force participation rates

	2000	2007	2012
France	68.8	69.9	70.4
Germany	71.1	75.6	77.2
Iceland	86.6	87.8	85.2
Turkey	52.4	49.8	53.8
UK	76.4	76.5	76.5

Source: OECD, Employment Outlook, 2013

Table 36.1 *Labour force participation rates for a selection of countries, 2000–12 (%)*

Exercises **Total (16 marks)**

1 Explain the possible benefits to the Icelandic economy of having a very high labour force participation rate. **(7 marks)**

2 Explain the possible reasons why a relatively low labour force participation rate, such as in France, may not result in an adverse impact on LRAS. **(9 marks)**

- ***Enterprise*** We saw earlier that the UK government seeks to improve the quality of enterprise activities through education and training. It also seeks to increase the number of start-up businesses through its policies. It has created 24 Enterprise Zones across the UK and provides financial incentives to increase the number of business creations. This may be having some effect on the UK's LRAS, since in 2014 95.5% of UK businesses employed fewer than 10 people.

It is also possible to increase LRAS by having factors of production that are mobile and responsive to incentives in the form of higher prices. This reduces the possibility of factors of production remaining idle, which detracts from a country's productive potential.

The Keynesian view of the LRAS curve

It is important to understand the assumptions that lie behind various theories and models to enable us to assess their value and explanatory power. As mentioned earlier, the assumption within the AQA AS specification that the LRAS curve is vertical would not receive the support of all economists.

Economists whose views are based on the writings and thoughts of John Maynard Keynes, one of the UK's foremost economists, are known as Keynesian economists. Many of them would argue that the LRAS curve is not vertical. They would dispute the belief that maximum potential output will be supplied in the long term and contend that demand-deficient unemployment can exist in the long term. Keynesian economists argue that LRAS has three distinct stages.

- First, there is a stage in which LRAS is highly price elastic, which allows output to be increased without the price level rising. This may occur in a recession. This produces a much more horizontal curve and reflects the existence of unused or spare productive capacity.
- There is a second stage in which increases in output can only be achieved at the expense of rises in the general price level as resources become relatively scarce and spare productive capacity diminishes.
- In the final stage, full employment has been reached and attempts to increase aggregate supply will only result in a rise in the general price level.

The Keynesian view of the LRAS curve is shown in Figure 36.6.

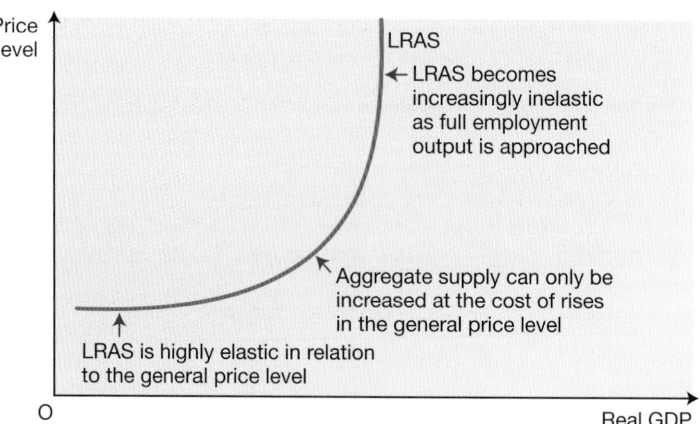

Figure 36.6 *The Keynesian view of the LRAS curve*

It is true to say that a large number of economists support the idea of a vertical LRAS curve and many argue that the Keynesian notion of an aggregate supply curve with varying price elasticity represents the relationship between aggregate supply and the general price level in the short term.

Author tip

This is a debate that is explored fully in the second year of the AQA specification.

Review questions

Total: 42 marks

1 Define the term 'aggregate supply'. *(3 marks)*

2 Explain why the short-run aggregate supply curve is upward sloping from left to right. *(6 marks)*

3 Which of the following might be expected to shift a short-run aggregate supply curve to the right?
 A An increase in money wages
 B An increase in commodity prices
 C An increase in labour productivity
 D An increase in corporation tax *(1 mark)*

4 Explain why an increase in business taxation might shift the SRAS to the left. *(4 marks)*

5 Explain why some economists assume that the LRAS curve is vertical. *(5 marks)*

6 Explain the relationship between the LRAS curve and the production possibility boundary. *(4 marks)*

7 Which of the following might be most likely to shift a long-run aggregate supply curve to the left?
 A An increase in net migration
 B An increase in voluntary unemployment
 C An increase in government expenditure on enterprise schemes
 D An increase in the productivity of capital equipment *(1 mark)*

8 Explain why the recent positive levels of net migration into the UK could be expected to have a positive impact on the economy's LRAS. *(9 marks)*

9 Which of the following might be least likely to have a positive impact on the UK's LRAS?
 A An increase in rates of unemployment benefit
 B An increase in labour force participation rates
 C An increase in factor mobility
 D An improvement in employees' attitudes to work *(1 mark)*

10 Explain how the Keynesian view of LRAS differs from the vertical LRAS. *(8 marks)*

Chapter 37

Aggregate demand & aggregate supply analysis

This chapter builds upon the previous three in Topic 7 to explain how aggregate demand and aggregate supply can be combined to illustrate the macroeconomic equilibrium. It explores how the model of aggregate demand and aggregate supply can be used to analyse the effects of changes in the price level, aggregate demand and aggregate supply as well as demand-side and supply-side shocks on the economy. The model is extremely useful in explaining a range of macroeconomic issues and problems.

The model of aggregate demand and aggregate supply

In the previous two chapters we considered the nature and determinants of aggregate demand and short- and long-run aggregate supply. It is now possible to bring these two together and to examine how the aggregate demand and aggregate supply (AD–AS) model can be used to analyse the effect of a wide range of factors including:

- changes in spending decisions by consumers, governments, firms and overseas residents;
- changes in key variables such as the rate of interest or the exchange rate;
- the implementation of government policies to affect its spending, taxation and production within the economy.

The AD–AS model is intended to provide a simplification of what might occur within a real economy. The use of models enables economists to analyse the likely effects of changes in the decision making of important groups such as households or possible policy decisions by governments. In particular the AD–AS model can be used to analyse the effect on the general price level, the level of real GDP or output, and therefore on related factors such as the level of employment.

The macroeconomic equilibrium

Key term
A **macroeconomic equilibrium** is a level of economic activity that occurs when aggregate demand and aggregate supply are equal.

A macroeconomic equilibrium can occur in the short run when aggregate demand (AD) is equal to short-run aggregate supply (SRAS) and in the long-run where AD equals long-run aggregate supply (LRAS). At a macroeconomic equilibrium, the level of planned aggregate demand within an economy (arising from consumption, investment, government expenditure and net exports) equates precisely to the amount of real output (or GDP) that firms are willing to produce over some period of time. Figure 37.1 illustrates a short-run macroeconomic equilibrium.

This equilibrium continues until something occurs to disturb it such as an increase in AD, possibly as a result of a fall in the rate of interest or a rise in export sales. A new equilibrium will be reached as a result of a change in AS or AD. If AD and AS are not equal, because the general price level is too high or too low, then the equilibrium level of real GDP, at which AD = AS, will be achieved automatically.

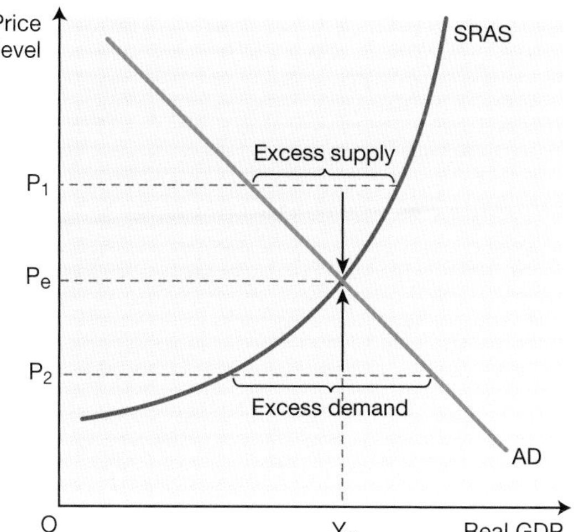

Figure 37.1 *A short-run macroeconomic equilibrium*

Consider Figure 37.1. If the general price level is at P_1, above that required for a macroeconomic equilibrium at Y_e, a quantity of goods and services will be supplied that is in excess of the level of demand. As a result, firms will have increasing quantities of unsold products. A logical reaction to this situation would be to reduce prices or cut back on production. Both actions will help to bring SRAS and AD into equality. Similarly, if the general price level is at P_2, AD will exceed SRAS and shortages will occur, offering profit-maximising firms the opportunity to increase prices. This may encourage them to increase production (so long as no bottlenecks in supply emerge) and SRAS will rise to meet AD.

Changes in aggregate demand

Aggregate demand is the sum of expenditure on consumption, investment by firms, government expenditure and expenditure on net exports – that is, spending by foreigners on exports minus expenditure domestically on imported products. A change in any one of these components will, ceteris paribus, affect the overall level of aggregate demand. This, in turn, will influence the position of the AD curve. Any change in the position of the AD curve will depend upon the balance of the components of AD: it is unlikely that the components will change in the same direction. For example, in 2012 expenditure on consumption, investment and net exports increased by small percentages, while government spending fell sharply.

Changes in aggregate demand and the short-run aggregate supply curve

Figure 37.2 illustrates the effects of increases and decreases in aggregate demand with a short-run aggregate supply curve.

Rising aggregate demand

A shift to the right of the AD curve represents an increase in aggregate demand and will result in an expansion of real GDP or output and a rise in the general price level. You will see that the shift of AD_1 to AD_2 results in a movement up the SRAS curve – this mirrors the effect of an increase in demand that you will have studied as part of microeconomics. The result of a rise in aggregate demand from AD_1 to AD_2

Figure 37.2 *The effects of shifts in the AD curve with a short-run aggregate supply*

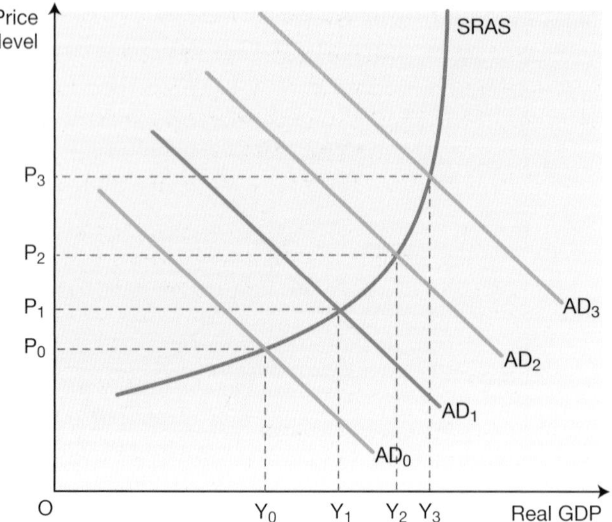

is an increase in real GDP from Y_1 to Y_2 and a higher price level (P_2). This reflects the fact that the economy is operating at a higher level of economic activity. The rise in economic activity will in turn lead to a higher level of employment and can be expected to reduce unemployment unless the size of the available workforce is increasing rapidly.

The extent of the impact on real GDP and the general price level will depend upon the slope of the SRAS curve. The shift of the AD curve from AD_1 to AD_2 occurs along a relatively shallow section of the SRAS curve. This produces a comparatively large rise in real GDP (Y_1 to Y_2) and a smaller rise in the general price level (P_1 to P_2). A further shift in the AD curve to AD_3 again increases real GDP and the price level, but the effects are slightly different here. The increase in real GDP is relatively small (Y_2 to Y_3) and the effect on the price level is greater.

Why do the effects of an increase in AD vary in this way? The simple reason is that the SRAS curve becomes steeper as real GDP increases. We saw in the previous chapter that a firm may increase output in the short term at the expense of higher costs of production. The greater the rise in short-term output that is called for, the more significant is the effect on costs of production. Production costs will increasingly rise more quickly than production, so that the SRAS curve moves from being relatively flat to relatively steep. Aggregate supply becomes more inelastic (i.e. less responsive to changes in the price level) as real GDP increases.

The increase in AD illustrated in Figure 37.2 results in an expansionary movement along the SRAS curve. The increase in aggregate demand could be caused by a number of factors including the following:

- consumers' decisions to save less and to increase consumption;
- decisions by firms to increase investment, possibly due to a fall in the cost of capital equipment;
- a decision by a government to increase its spending, possibly to meet its social goals;
- increased demand for a country's exports, for example following a fall in its exchange rate.

The shift of the AD curve from AD_1 to AD_0

Of course, aggregate demand can also fall. A number of economies are suffering from falling aggregate demand at the time of writing including Japan and Italy. A fall in aggregate demand leads to a fall in the general price level in the short term and also to a fall in real GDP. In Figure 37.2 this is shown by the shift in the aggregate demand curve from AD_1 to AD_0 and the consequent fall in the general price level to P_0.

Once again the relative effects on the general price level and real GDP of a shift to the left depends upon the slope (and hence the degree of elasticity in relation to the general price level) of the SRAS curve. If it is relatively price inelastic, the impact on the general price level will be comparatively large.

Changes in aggregate demand and the long-run aggregate supply curve

In Chapter 36 we saw that classical economists assume that the long-run aggregate supply (LRAS) curve is vertical. They believe that an increase in aggregate demand will cause a rise in the general price level and real GDP in the short run, as we saw above. However, in the long run they believe that the only effect will be to increase the price level.

Now consider Figure 37.3. Prior to the increase in aggregate demand, the economy is in long-term equilibrium with real GDP equalling Y_e and the price level at P_1. The increase in aggregate demand is shown by the shift from AD_1 to AD_2. This shift could be caused by an increase in one or more of the components of aggregate demand (consumption, investment, government expenditure and net exports). The rise in aggregate demand initially leads to a higher level of real GDP at Y_2 as firms respond to the increased demand and as additional workers are attracted into the workforce because they believe real wages are rising. This is shown by a movement along the relevant short-run aggregate supply curve ($SRAS_1$). However, this move forces up production costs in the longer term as resources become scarcer, and this is reflected in higher prices for these resources. The effect of this rise in the cost of resources is to shift the short-run aggregate supply curve upwards and to the left to $SRAS_2$. The firms that increased output in response to higher prices realise that, as costs have also increased, their real incomes have not increased and output is reduced once more to Y_e. Those employees who were attracted by rising real wages realise that these wages

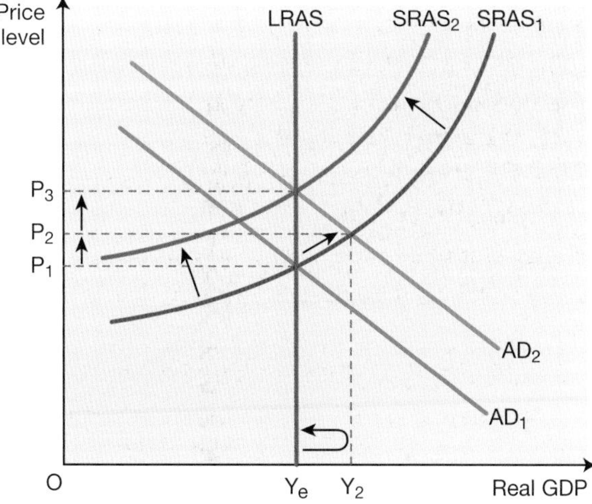

Figure 37.3 *The effect of an increase in aggregate demand in the long run*

are not increasing and they leave the workforce. Thus the economy is still in long-run equilibrium on the LRAS curve and the only long-run consequence of the rise in aggregate demand is an increase in the price level.

The analysis in the previous paragraph is based on the assumption of a vertical LRAS and full employment output. It is this assumption that underlies our conclusion that an increase in aggregate demand will result only in a rise in the general price level in the long run. This assumption has significant implications for the management of the economy, as we shall see in later chapters.

It is important to remember that there is another view of the shape of the LRAS curve as put forward by Keynesian economists. We saw in the previous chapter that this LRAS curve has varying price elasticity of supply along its length and is drawn on the assumption that long-run aggregate supply can co-exist with spare capacity. This means that the effects of a change in aggregate demand depend upon the initial level of real GDP and the extent to which the economy's existing capacity is being used.

Changes in aggregate supply

Changes in short-run aggregate supply

In Chapter 36 we saw that changes in the price of certain factors of production, including money wages and components and raw materials, will shift the short-run supply curve. Thus a rise in the cost of components could cause a decrease in short-run aggregate supply. This is shown by a shift in the SRAS curve upwards and to the left, as illustrated in Figure 37.4, and a movement up the aggregate demand curve (known as a contraction).

The effect of this decrease in SRAS is to reduce the level of real GDP from Y_1 to Y_2 and an increase in the price level to P_2.

In contrast, a reduction in the cost of factors of production that can be varied in the short term will encourage firms to increase production of goods and services in the short term and cause a shift to the right of the SRAS curve. This would cause a movement down the aggregate demand curve (an expansion). The effect would be to increase real GDP and lower the price level. This is the reverse of the situation illustrated in Figure 37.4 and would normally be a more desirable outcome.

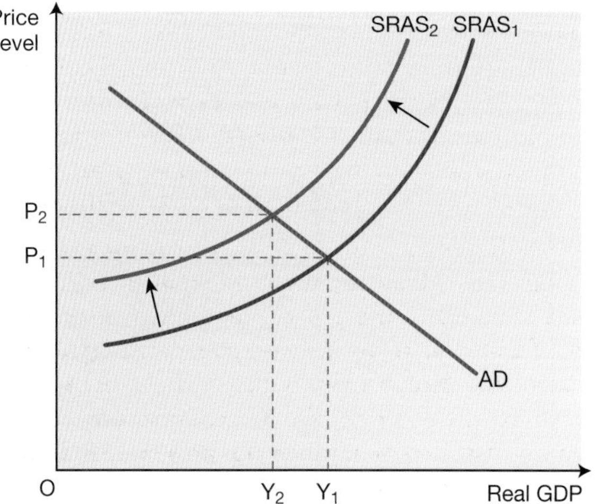

Figure 37.4 *A decrease in short-run aggregate supply*

Changes in long-run aggregate supply

An increase in an economy's productive capacity will cause its long-run aggregate supply (LRAS) curve to shift to the right. This is the equivalent of an outward shift in the economy's production possibility boundary as the vertical LRAS represents full employment level of output or real GDP. Figure 37.5 shows an increase in LRAS with the assumption that the curve is vertical.

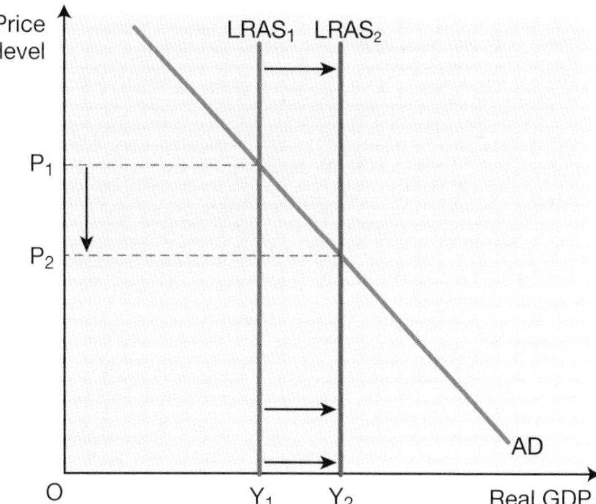

Figure 37.5 *An increase in long-run aggregate supply*

A rise in long-run aggregate supply offers significant benefits to an economy and could be expected to assist a government in achieving its macroeconomic objectives. Figure 37.5 shows that an increase in long-run aggregate supply from $LRAS_1$ to $LRAS_2$ increases the real GDP of the economy from Y_1 to Y_2. This rise in real GDP represents economic growth because the quantity of goods and services that are produced by the economy has increased. This can result in a higher standard of living for the country's inhabitants or permit a higher level of investment that will assist in promoting further growth in the economy in the future. There is another feature of an increase in long-run aggregate supply. On the assumption of a vertical LRAS curve, a rightward shift results in a fall in the price level – from P_1 to P_2 in Figure 37.5. This can enhance the competitiveness of an economy because its products will become relatively cheaper on world markets.

We saw in Chapter 36 that an increase in long-run aggregate supply can be caused by an increase in the quantity and/or quality of factors of production. The UK has experienced high levels of net migration since 2000 and this will have increased aggregate supply and produced a rightward shift in the LRAS curve. The increased provision of training could enhance the job-related skills of an economy's workforce and the levels of productivity from a given workforce. A similar effect might be achieved through investment in more productive capital equipment.

Once again a traditional Keynesian view of an increase in long-run aggregate supply can have different outcomes. Many Keynesian economists believe that a long-run equilibrium can exist alongside spare capacity and unemployment. Increasing the productive potential of the economy by increasing long-run aggregate supply in such circumstances will have little effect because it merely increases the amount of unused capacity that exists within the economy. We will consider the contrast between the views of Keynesian and Classical economists in this area more fully in our companion book, *AQA A-Level Year 2 Economics*.

REALWORLD ECONOMICS 37.1

UK's economy set to be Europe's largest

According to new projections by the European Commission, the UK will be Europe's biggest economy by some degree within 45 years, with France in second position and Germany pushed back into third place. However, this position of European primacy for the UK will have been largely won on the back of population growth (Figure 37.6).

The rapid economic growth for the UK is likely to be in part because of the country's higher fertility rate – the UK has more babies per head of population than much of the rest of Europe. In terms of demography, the UK is already a younger country than Germany. The report by the commission assumes that net immigration into the UK will continue at current elevated levels for much of the period, adding a further 9 million people to the population by 2060.

Source: Adapted from *Daily Telegraph*, 9.12.14

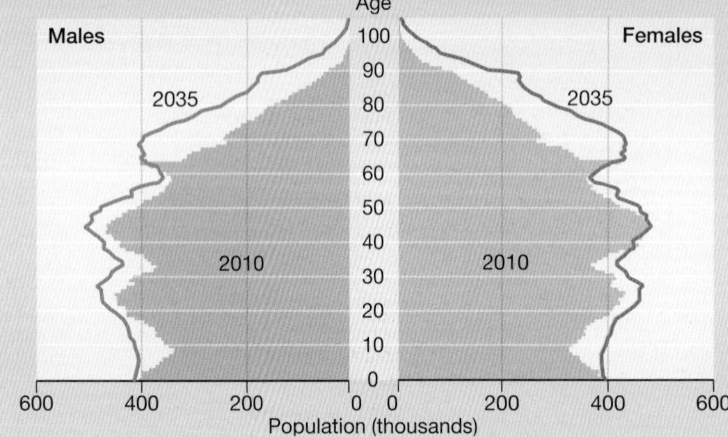

Figure 37.6 *Age pyramid of the actual and projected UK population, 2010 and 2035*

Exercises *Total: 14 marks*

1. Explain the likely effects of rapid growth in population on the price level and the level of real GDP in the UK in the future. *(7 marks)*
2. Explain why this economic growth may not result in major improvements in the standard of living for people living in the UK in the future. *(7 marks)*

Demand-side and supply-side shocks and the macroeconomy

In this context a shock is simply an unexpected event that affects the entire economy. It is a significant factor which impacts on macroeconomic variables, such as real GDP and the price level.

We differentiate between demand-side and supply-side shocks because these different types of shock affect the economy through either aggregate demand or aggregate supply.

Key terms

Demand-side shocks are unexpected factors that affect aggregate demand negatively or positively, such as a significant reduction in income tax rates.

Supply-side shocks are unexpected factors that affect aggregate supply negatively or positively, such as a major fall in the price of oil.

Demand-side shocks

A demand-side shock can take a variety of forms, but all are caused by factors that ultimately affect one or more components of aggregate demand (see Table 37.1). An unexpected and significant fall in the rate of interest, for example, could result in a substantial rise in aggregate demand. This might occur because:

- households increase consumption and reduce savings, as the return on saving is lowered and the opportunity cost of consumption is reduced;
- households increase borrowing to finance higher consumption, as the cost of borrowed money is lowered;
- firms increase investment, as the return on more investment projects exceeds the cost of borrowing money.

Table 37.1 *Examples of possible causes and effects of positive and negative demand-side shocks*

Positive	Negative
Possible causes	**Possible causes**
■ A construction boom, such as that occurring in China. ■ A large unexpected cut in income tax rates. ■ A fall in the rate of interest, boosting consumption and investment. ■ A major trading nation seeking to expand its economy, as in the case of Japan in 2015. ■ A sustained rise in company share prices, improving consumers' perceptions of their wealth.	■ Difficulties in consumers and firms acquiring loans from banks. ■ A significant decline in business confidence, reducing investment. ■ Substantial reductions in government spending, as in the UK in 2015. ■ A major economy going into recession, reducing purchases of exports. ■ A sudden rise in the country's exchange rate, increasing export prices and reducing those of imports.
Likely effects	**Likely effects**
■ The general price level is likely to rise – the impact will be greater if the economy is operating near to full capacity. ■ The level of output (or national income) will increase, though the effect will be relatively small as full employment output is approached.	■ The general price level is likely to fall, with falls being more significant if the economy is initially operating near to maximum capacity. ■ The level of output (or national income) will decline, though possibly by comparatively small amounts, if the economy is operating near to full employment.

This would represent a positive demand-side shock in that it would increase aggregate demand, shifting the aggregate demand curve to the right as shown by the shift of AD_1 to AD_2 in Figure 37.7. This diagram illustrates that the effect of such a demand-side shock is to increase the general price level from P_1 to P_2, while simultaneously increasing the level of real GDP from Y_1 to Y_2. If such a demand-side shock occurred at a high level of output, then the effect is likely to be greater on the price level and the rise in real GDP may be relatively small. These effects will occur as the rise in aggregate demand will take place on a relatively inelastic (or steep) section of the short-run aggregate supply curve, resulting in rising aggregate demand having a greater effect on price than output.

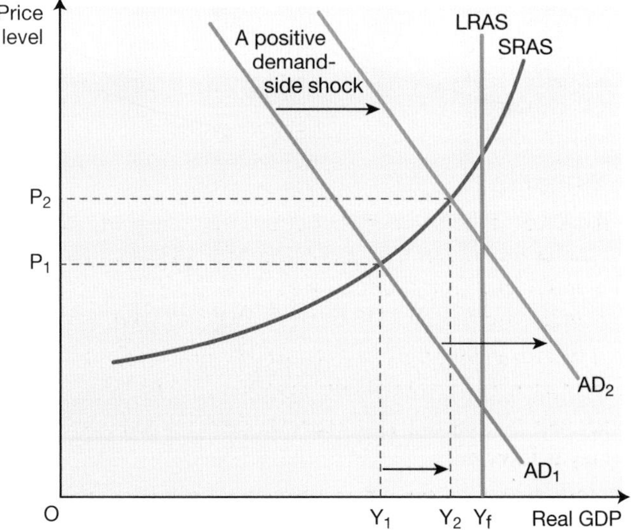

Figure 37.7 *The impact of a positive demand-side shock*

Negative demand-side shocks can also occur. The financial crisis of 2008 provides an example of a massive demand-side shock that affected most of the world's economies. Banks in many countries made risky loans that could not be repaid, leaving some of these financial institutions in a very weak position. This resulted in the collapse of one of the USA's largest investment banks – Lehman Brothers. Governments and consumers in many countries, including the UK, suddenly realised that many major banks were at risk from extensive loans that were unlikely ever to be repaid. Flows of lending to the private sector were choked off at the same time as consumer and business confidence collapsed. Aggregate demand fell sharply, reducing the real GDP of many countries and placing downward pressure on the general price level.

Supply-side shocks

Supply-side shocks are very similar to those occurring on the demand side, except that the effect on the economy occurs through the supply side of the economy and causes a shift in the aggregate supply curve.

As with demand-side changes, supply-side shocks can be positive or negative (see Table 37.2). A positive supply-side shock will result in the aggregate supply curve shifting to the right, as illustrated in Figure 37.8. This may be caused by a range of factors that impact on the costs of production of producers or their willingness to supply products.

A major advance in production technology could lead to a positive supply-side shock, as illustrated in Figure 37.8. Technological advances can reduce the costs of production for businesses, perhaps by allowing them to substitute cheaper technology for relatively expensive labour. This reduction in costs encourages existing producers to increase output and may attract new producers who believe they can make a profit using the new technology.

Figure 37.8 shows a positive supply-side shock that has affected the short-run aggregate supply curve of an economy. This may be the result of factors such as a fall in the price of key commodities like wheat. Commodities such as wheat are used in a range of manufacturing industries, but their prices on global markets can be volatile and are likely to fluctuate in the long term.

Table 37.2 *Examples of possible causes and effects of positive and negative supply-side shocks*

Positive	Negative
Possible causes	**Possible causes**
▪ A sudden increase in net migration, as occurred in the UK after 2004. ▪ Significant advances in technology, with positive implications for production techniques. ▪ A rise in productivity for any factors of production.	▪ A substantial rise in the general wage level in an economy. ▪ An increase in business taxes. ▪ A fall in the price of key products sold, such as oil. ▪ The occurrence of natural disasters, such as earthquakes, hurricanes and tsunamis.
Likely effects	**Likely effects**
▪ The general price level is likely to fall. ▪ The level of output (or national income) will increase, the extent of which will depend on a range of factors, particularly the cause of the shock.	▪ A rise in the general price level. ▪ A decline in the level of output, which could be long term in the case of some causes, such as natural disasters.

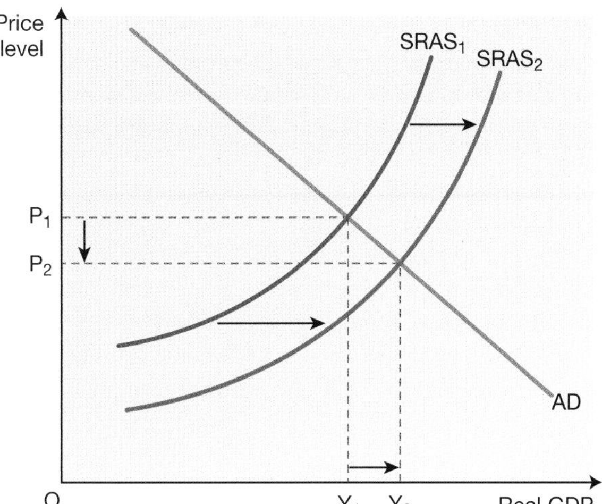

Figure 37.8 *A positive supply-side shock*

However, there are some supply-side shocks that can impact on an economy's long-run aggregate supply because they have a significant and lasting impact on an economy's productive potential. A number of natural disasters can provoke an enduring fall in an economy's ability to supply goods and services. This is shown by a leftward shift in the long-run aggregate supply curve, as shown in Figure 37.9.

In January 2010, Haiti (located on the West Indian island of Hispaniola) suffered a major earthquake that occurred close to the country's capital, Port-au-Prince, and killed an estimated 300,000 people. The country's GDP fell by more than 5% in 2011 alone, and the effect on the Haitian economy was huge and long lasting.

The devastating impact on Port-au-Prince of the 2010 Haiti earthquake – a dramatic, long-term negative supply-side shock

Sometimes factors can provoke demand-side and supply-side shocks at the same time. In the latter part of 2014, the price of oil on world markets fell substantially from $115 a barrel in June to $59 a barrel in December. This has a positive impact on demand in many countries such as the UK because consumers have more income to spend on other products. However, a negative supply-side shock could occur simultaneously in the UK because oil production from the North Sea is forecast to decline, as fewer fields are economic. At the time of writing the UK oil industry is cutting investment and making employees redundant because of the falling price of oil.

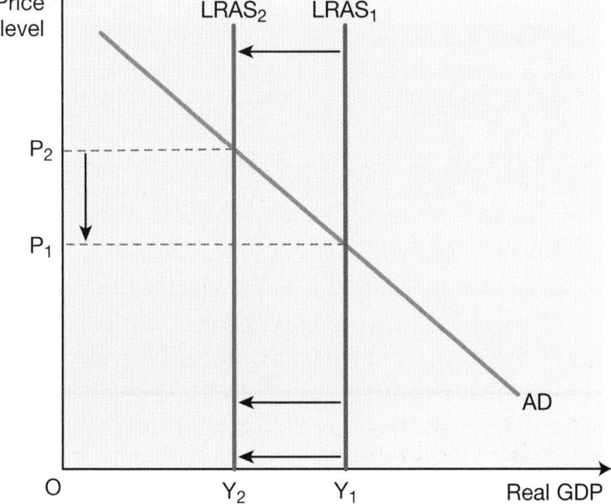

Figure 37.9 *The effect of a long-term negative supply-side shock*

Using aggregate demand and aggregate supply analysis

Aggregate demand and aggregate supply analysis can be used effectively to explain a range of macroeconomic problems and issues. We will also use the theory in Topic 9 to explain the effects of government policies on key macroeconomic variables.

Changes in the price level

Changes in aggregate demand

Any change in aggregate demand or supply has implications for the price level within an economy. Increases in aggregate demand will shift the curve to the right. This will increase the price level as resources become scarcer and costs of production increase. In the short run, firms increase supply only in response to increased profits that are possible with higher prices. We saw in Figure 37.2 that if aggregate demand is rising from a relatively low level, the major impact will be on the level of real GDP with a comparatively small effect on the price level. However, at higher levels of output, where resources are relatively scarce, the major effect of a rise in aggregate demand is felt in terms of a rising price level. If the economy is operating at full employment and on its long-run aggregate supply curve, the sole effect of an increase in aggregate demand will be to increase prices, assuming that the LRAS is vertical. This will occur because there are no additional resources available for production and therefore increased demand simply pushes up prices.

A fall in the level of aggregate demand has the opposite effect. In general, falls in aggregate demand have the potential to reduce the price level existing within an economy.

Changes in aggregate supply

A rise in aggregate supply in the short term or the long term will result in a reduction in the price level. In the short term, rising aggregate supply occurs for reasons including increases in productivity and falling costs of resources; both factors contribute to driving down prices. Similarly in the long term the rise in output is achieved in part through more productive factors of production allowing firms to sell at lower prices without damaging profitability.

Unemployment

The long-run aggregate supply curve shows a position in which an economy is operating at its maximum level of production – in effect, it is on its production possibility boundary. This means that the economy's labour force is fully employed in the sense that everyone who wants a job at the current wage rate will have one. However, a lack of aggregate demand can lead to unemployment – this is termed 'demand-deficient unemployment' – and is associated with the trade cycle. Many economies experience this type of unemployment, which is at its worst during a recession and can be expected to diminish steadily thereafter.

Figure 37.10 illustrates an economy suffering from demand-deficient unemployment. The long-run aggregate supply (LRAS) curve indicates the position at which the economy is achieving full employment (Y_f). The rise in aggregate demand shown by the move from AD_1 to AD_2 increases real GDP from Y_1 to Y_2. This will increase output and the level of employment. As a result, demand-deficient unemployment will decline but will not be eliminated entirely. If we assume a vertical LRAS curve, full employment will occur when the economy reaches a long-run macroeconomic equilibrium.

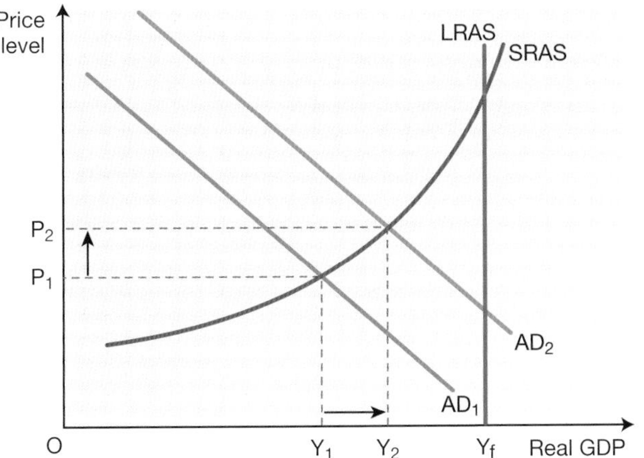

Figure 37.10
An economy suffering from demand-deficient unemployment

Economic growth

We saw in Chapter 36 that the position of the LRAS curve shows the economy's potential level of output – the level of output that an economy could achieve if it operated at the full employment level. Figure 36.4 shows a shift to the right in the LRAS curve (such as $LRAS_1$ to $LRAS_2$), indicating that the economy is experiencing economic growth. The AD–AS model can be used to illustrate economic growth or the opposite effect when a recession occurs.

The analysis in Figure 36.4 is based on a vertical LRAS. We shall see in the companion volume to this book, *AQA A-Level Year 2 Economics*, that for Keynesian economists a rightward shift in the LRAS curve does not necessarily result in economic growth.

REALWORLD **ECONOMICS** 37.2

Brazil's economy slips into recession

In 2014 Brazil's economy slipped into recession for the first time in more than five years as GDP fell by 0.6% in the April–June period compared to the previous three months. The country's economy had shrunk by 0.2% in the first quarter of 2014, the Brazilian statistics agency announced, meaning that economic growth had been negative for a six-month period. Households and firms both suffered declining confidence about the future of the economy.

Dilma Rousseff, President of Brazil, cut taxes and boosted spending in 2014 in an attempt to revive growth

Investment fell by 5.3% in the second quarter of 2014 from the previous three months. This accounted for the majority of the decline in gross domestic product, the Brazilian national statistics agency revealed. Household consumption, still sustained by increases in wages, rose 0.3%.

Dilma Rousseff, the President of Brazil, has attempted to revive economic growth with tax cuts and higher government spending, especially on welfare benefits. It is the first time that the Brazilian economy has contracted for two consecutive quarters since the aftermath of the global financial crisis in 2008.

Source: Adapted from Bloomberg.com

Exercises **Total: 18 marks**

1 Explain, with the aid of an aggregate demand and supply diagram, why a fall in investment of 5.3% could result in a fall in Brazil's GDP. (9 marks)

2 Explain why consumption in Brazil grew slightly in the second quarter of 2014 despite a loss of confidence by households. (9 marks)

Review questions

Total: 49 marks

1 Define the term 'macroeconomic equilibrium'. *(3 marks)*

2 A rise in aggregate demand is most likely to have which of the following effects in the short term?

A A rise in the price level and a rise in real GDP
B A rise in the price level and a fall in real GDP
C A rise in the price level and no change in real GDP
D A fall in the price level and a rise in real GDP *(1 mark)*

3 Use a diagram to explain why a rise in aggregate demand might have differing effects on the level of real GDP, depending on its original level. *(8 marks)*

4 Given an assumption of a vertical LRAS curve, explain why increases in aggregate demand only affect the price level in the long term. *(9 marks)*

5 A rise in long-run aggregate supply is most likely to result in which of the following?

A A rise in the price level and a rise in real GDP
B A fall in the price level and a rise in real GDP
C A rise in the price level and no change in real GDP
D A fall in the price level and no change in real GDP *(1 mark)*

6 Explain why Keynesian economists do not agree that the LRAS curve is vertical. *(6 marks)*

7 Use a diagram to explain the effect of a positive demand-side shock on an economy in the short term. *(7 marks)*

8 Which of the following is most likely to cause a positive supply-side shock?

A A large and unexpected rise in income tax rates
B A sustained rise in share prices
C A rise in the productivity of factors of production
D A large rise in the general wage level in an economy *(1 mark)*

9 Use a diagram to explain the effect of a negative supply-side shock on an economy in the short term. *(7 marks)*

10 Use an aggregate demand and supply diagram to illustrate the existence of demand-deficient short-run unemployment. *(6 marks)*

Topic 7 **Exam-style questions**

AS LEVEL PAPER 2

Context – How the macroeconomy works

Extract A **Rebalancing the UK economy**

The UK needs to increase business investment and net exports by adopting a new approach to its industrial policy. The Confederation of British Industry (CBI), an organisation representing UK businesses, has written a *Vision for Rebalancing the Economy* that makes it clear that the economic stability between 1993 and 2007 masked growing imbalances. The UK economy has become dominated by household consumption financed by debt and by government expenditure. Together, these two components of aggregate demand accounted for 89% of GDP in 2009 – more than in France, Germany or the USA. The CBI is now working on developing a new industrial strategy for the UK.

A focus on increasing investment and net exports is required as a means of creating sustainable economic growth in order to rebalance the UK economy. This is essential because real wages have been falling for some time and, even now, are only rising slowly, and because the government is committed to substantial decreases in its expenditure.

Source: CBI's *Vision for Rebalancing the Economy*

Extract B **The UK returns to growth**

The UK's economic recovery remains on track, with economic growth continuing. However, growth has been dependent on household spending (consumption) and the services sector at a time when the national ambition is to rebalance towards more exports and business investment. Table A shows the UK's national income over the period 2011–13, in terms of nominal income.

Table A *Expenditure components and UK GDP at current prices, 2011–13*

Component/year	2011		2012		2013	
	£ million	%	£ million	%	£ million	%
Consumption	1,039,102	64.23	1,072,545	64.79	1,110,807	64.83
Government expenditure	337,294	20.85	343,878	20.77	346,774	20.24
Investment	265,106	16.39	273,430	16.52	291,717	17.03
Net exports	−23,825	−1.47	−34,469	−2.08	−32,100	−1.87
Statistical adjustment	0	0	0	0	−3,896	−0.23
National income	**1,617,677**	**100.0**	**1,655,384**	**100.0**	**1,713,302**	**100.0**

Source: ONS, Blue Book, 2014

The level of investment in the UK has risen steadily since 2011, but the decline in investment by businesses in 2014 has led to further concerns about the balance of the UK's economic recovery, given its reliance on consumption and the continued weakness of UK exports.

Extract C **UK migration**

Most migrants entering the UK are seeking work. Those entering from the EU account for more than 50% of workers in the UK who are not British citizens. Some studies suggest that EU migrants may be more productive than UK citizens. National insurance numbers issued to EU citizens increased 6% to 421,000 between June 2013 and June 2014. According to the ONS, there was a statistically significant increase in immigration for work. Estimated employment of

EU nationals resident in the UK was 16% higher in July to September 2014 compared to the same quarter in 2013.

Figure A *UK migration, 1995–2014*

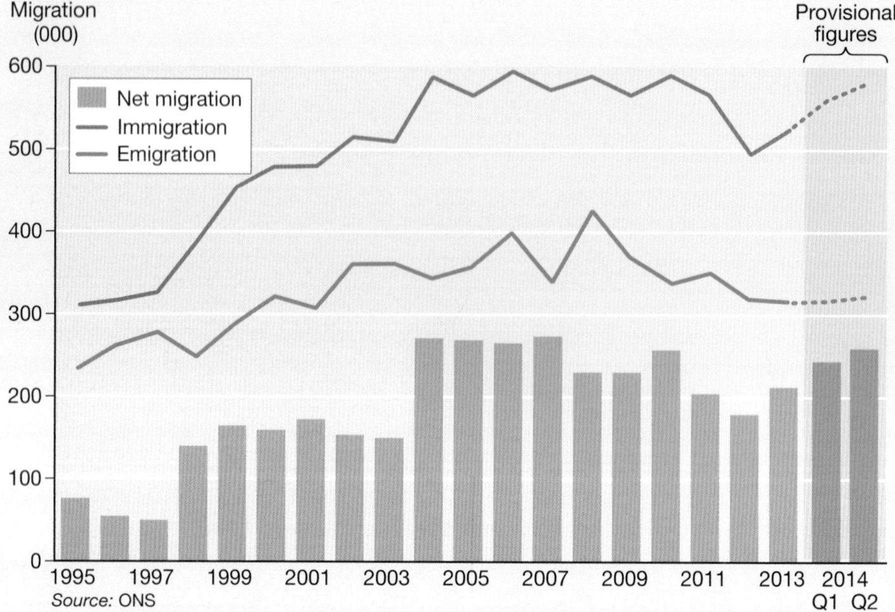

Research at Oxford University has indicated that high levels of migration into the UK (see Figure A) have had relatively little effect on wage rates. However, the greater impact has been seen in occupations where wages are low. A 1% rise in the proportion of migrants in this type of workforce reduced average wages by 0.5%.

Questions

Total: 50 marks

1 Define the term 'nominal income' (Extract B). *(3 marks)*

2 Identify and explain one significant point of comparison in the data in Figure A in Extract C. *(4 marks)*

3 Draw an aggregate demand and supply diagram to illustrate how a rise in investment results in a higher level of national income. *(4 marks)*

4 Explain one reason why UK investment might have increased between 2011 and 2013. *(4 marks)*

5 Analyse the possible effects on household consumption of real wages 'falling for some time' (Extract A). *(10 marks)*

6 To what extent do you agree that the best way of increasing the UK's GDP in a sustainable way is to achieve higher levels of investment and net exports at the expense of government expenditure and consumption? *(25 marks)*

Topic 8

Economic performance

Economic growth & the economic cycle

This chapter takes an in-depth look at ways in which the economic performance of an economy can be judged through the analysis of data on economic growth. It contrasts short-run and long-run economic growth, and examines the difference between positive and negative output gaps. It also studies the various demand-side and supply-side factors that determine short-run and long-run economic growth, building on material covered in Topic 7. We introduce the concept of the economic cycle and the economic indicators that can be used to identify the various stages of the cycle. Finally, we look at the ways in which demand-side and supply-side shocks can affect the level of activity in an economy.

Short-run and long-run economic growth

Economic growth is normally measured by an increase in an economy's GDP over a specific time period, usually one year. Figure 38.1 shows the rate of growth of the UK's economy over an eight-year period as measured by growth in real GDP.

It can be seen that over this period the value of goods and services produced by the

Figure 38.1 *Economic growth in the UK 2007–14, measured by growth of real GDP*

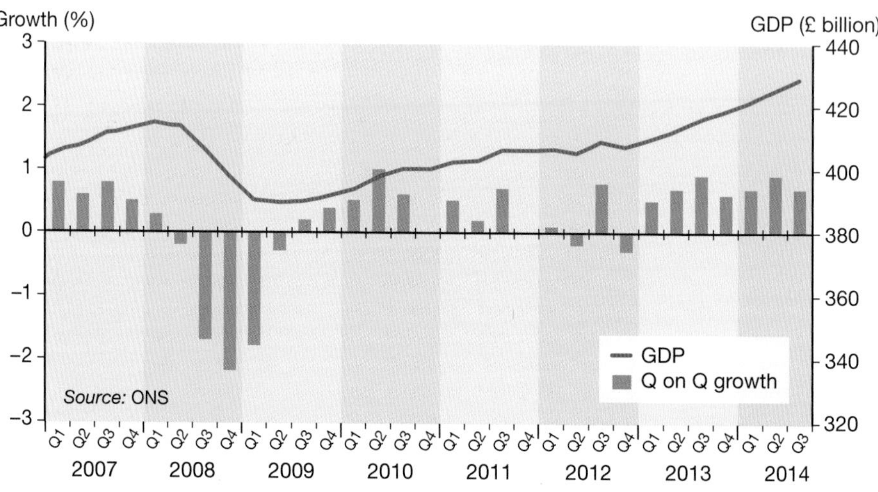

Key terms

Short-run economic growth is an increase in production of goods and services that occurs without an economy acquiring additional factors of production. This is because the available resources within the economy are used more intensively.

Long-run economic growth refers to an increase in an economy's productive potential and is what is usually meant by the term 'economic growth'.

UK economy grew, but the level of GDP fluctuated widely. The UK's rate of economic growth over this period was relatively slow. The cause of this relatively slow growth was the major recession in 2008–09 during which economic growth was negative, dragging down the average growth figure. The UK's trend rate of economic growth is that rate which is achieved over a long period of time without fuelling increases in the rate of inflation. In other words it is a long-term, sustainable rate of economic growth for an economy. We will return to the notion of the trend rate of economic growth later in this chapter.

The economic growth shown by the overall rise in GDP in Figure 38.1 was a mixture of short-run and long-run economic growth as well as a period of negative economic growth in 2008–09.

Short-run economic growth

This type of economic growth does not involve an expansion of the productive potential of an economy; rather it entails using the resources that are already available to an economy more fully. For example, output as measured by GDP may rise because previously idle factories or other types of unused capital equipment are brought back into production or because firms hire people who were unable to find employment. Utilising these resources, which are already available, allows an economy to increase its production of goods and services without the need to acquire additional resources.

The production possibility boundary in Figure 38.2(a) illustrates the process of short-run economic growth. Initially the economy may be operating at Point X and producing OC of capital goods (those that can be used to produce other goods) and OA of consumer goods. However, since this economy is operating at a point within its production possibility boundary, it is not utilising all the resources available to it. The economy can increase its output by merely using the resources available to it more fully. This is illustrated by the move from Point X to Point Y. As a consequence, the output of consumer and capital goods rises – from OA to OB and from OC to OD respectively. This leads to an increase in the economy's GDP.

Figure 38.2 *Different ways of presenting short-run economic growth*

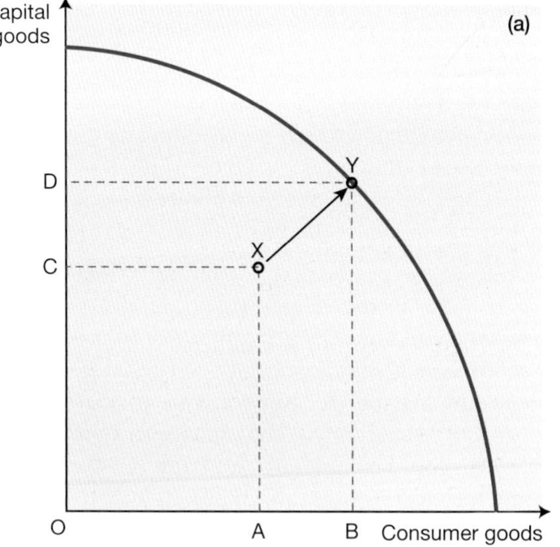

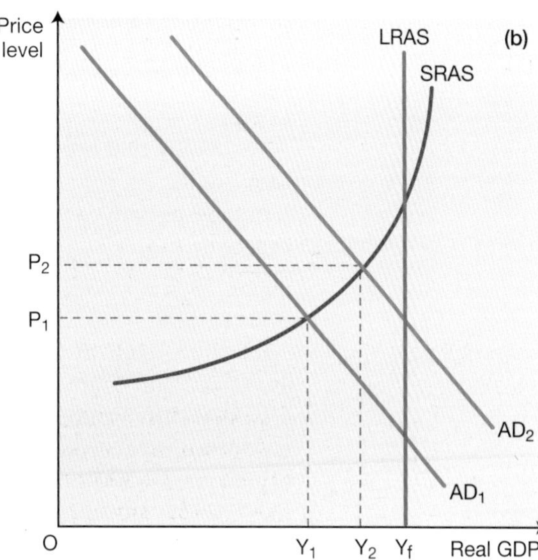

We can also illustrate short-run economic growth by using the AD–AS model that we developed in Topic 7. Since short-run growth does not involve an expansion in the economy's productive capacity, it is shown by increases in aggregate demand below full employment output. Meeting such increases in aggregate demand requires an economy to use more of its available resources. This type of growth is characterised by an economy recovering from recession. In Figure 38.2(b) a rise in aggregate demand from AD_1 to AD_2 stimulates an increase in output, increasing real GDP from Y_1 to Y_2. However, this economy is still operating below its full employment level of real GDP (Y_f) and is therefore within its production possibility boundary. Note that one consequence of this short-run economic growth is a rise in the price level.

It is likely that the economic growth experienced by the UK economy during 2010 and 2011 was short-run economic growth as it slowly began to recover from the financial crisis and subsequent deep recession. At this point unemployment in the UK was relatively high and some firms were engaged in short-term working (i.e. not using their resources to their full extent). For example, in 2009 Honda, the Japanese car manufacturer, closed its factory in Swindon for four months but retained the services of its 4200 employees by paying them reduced wages. When the factory reopened, production increased as demand for new cars slowly increased. The restarting of production at Honda would have contributed to short-run economic growth in the UK as the economy moved out of recession and as existing productive capacity was used more intensively.

Causes of short-run economic growth

Short-run economic growth is caused by an increase in one or more of the components of aggregate demand – consumption, investment, government spending or net exports. Thus a rise in consumption by households or investment by businesses would result in an increase in aggregate demand and, via the multiplier process, an increase in GDP. This is shown in Figure 38.2(b) by the shift from AD_1 to AD_2. If an economy is increasing its productive capacity, it is important that aggregate demand matches the potential of the economy to supply products. In Figure 38.2(b), despite the rise of aggregate demand to AD_2, the economy is still not in long-run equilibrium and some demand-deficient unemployment will result.

Long-run economic growth

Long-run economic growth is what we describe when we define economic growth. An economy that is enjoying long-run economic growth is expanding its productive capacity or its potential to supply goods and services. Once again this type of economic growth can be presented using both production possibility boundaries and aggregate supply and demand analysis, as in Figure 38.3.

Figure 38.3(a) shows an outward shift of the production possibility boundary from PPB_1 to PPB_2, which indicates an increase in the economy's productive potential. Prior to the shift in the boundary, the economy was utilising all of its productive assets at Point Y to supply OB of consumer goods and OD of capital goods. As a consequence of the shift in the boundary, the economy is able to increase the production of consumer goods from OB to OE and, at the same time, supply more capital goods – OF rather than OD. This move from Point Y to Point Z assumes that the economy moves from a point at which its resources are employed fully to another with no intermediate stage. This is perhaps unlikely.

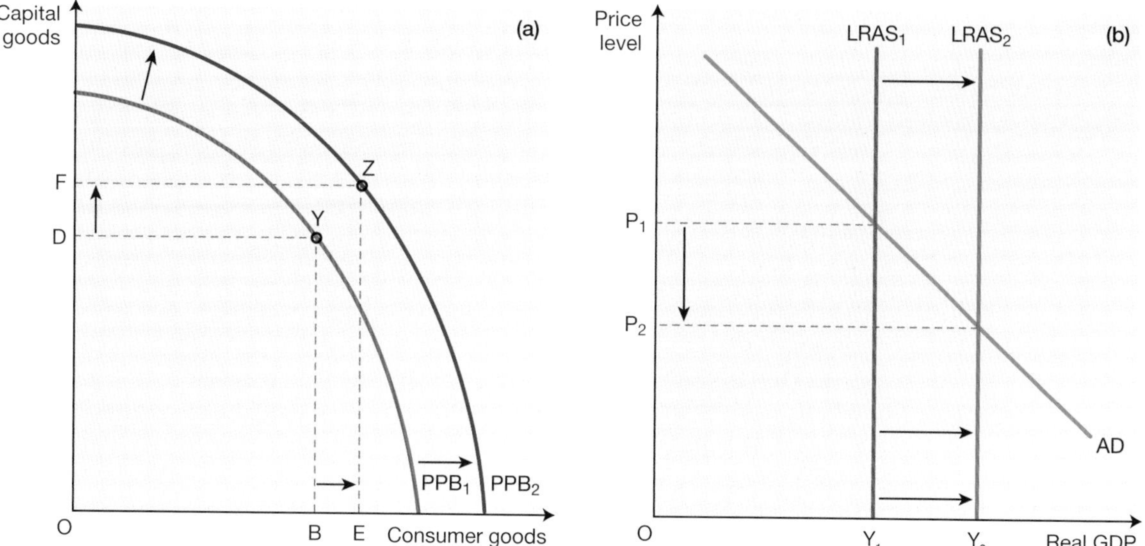

Figure 38.3 *Different ways of presenting long-run economic growth*

Long-run economic growth can also be shown using the AD–AS model. It is shown in Figure 38.3(b) by a shift to the right in the long-run aggregate supply curve from $LRAS_1$ to $LRAS_2$. This increases the level of real GDP (or national output) from Y_1 to Y_2 and, at the same time, results in a reduction in the price level from P_1 to P_2. This type of economic growth offers a range of benefits to an economy. It has the potential to increase living standards so long as the rate of population increase does not exceed the rate of growth. The reduction in the price level that accompanies long-run economic growth can increase the global competitiveness of an economy. It may result in higher sales of exports and reduced purchases of imports, depending on price elasticities. This can improve the economy's balance of payments on current account.

Causes of long-run economic growth

The long-run trend rate of economic growth is determined by the quantity and quality of resources available to an economy. This type of economic growth arises because an economy has a greater quantity of resources available to it to produce goods and services. This might occur, for example, because the economy benefits from an inflow of skilled migrants of working age or because firms invest in productive capacity such as factories, production machinery or vehicles.

Alternatively, improvements in the quality of resources may occur. Thus an economy may make more effective use of the resources available to it. This may be the result of technological advances that bring about more efficient methods of production or the result of investing in the skills of the workforce (known as investing in human capital). Both these factors should increase the productivity of the resources used within the economy, creating a greater output from a given stock of resources.

It is likely that the economic growth experienced by the UK economy prior to the financial crisis in 2008 was of the long-term variety. The number of jobs available and vacant in the UK had been rising steadily to nearly 700,000, despite high rates of immigration, and wages had risen sharply, suggesting an economy producing at or near to capacity. Thus the rise in GDP in that period could reflect a rise in productive capacity. Further evidence of this is provided by the steady rise in net investment.

The trend rate of economic growth

Key term

The **long-run trend rate of economic growth** is a rate of economic growth that is sustainable over long periods of time.

Long-run economic growth also refers to the average or trend rate of growth of an economy. We saw earlier that this is the rate of economic growth that can be achieved over time without fuelling inflation. It is a rate of economic growth at which significant differences do not emerge between levels of aggregate demand and aggregate supply. If economic growth is too rapid, aggregate supply is unable to match the growth in aggregate demand, shortages begin to occur and prices are forced up to allocate relatively scarce products. In contrast if growth is slow, or negative, then unemployment will begin to rise because there is insufficient aggregate demand. The trend rate of economic growth is a happy medium that avoids either of these scenarios.

For the UK the trend rate of economic growth has been between 2.25% and 2.5% over a long period of time. Figure 38.4 shows the rates of economic growth recorded for the UK economy since 1949. This identifies periods in which growth has been negative (when the economy has been in recession) and shows the depth of the recession in 2008 when the economy shrank by more than 4%. It also provides evidence that the average rate of growth in the UK economy was a little over 2% over this period.

The economic cycle

Figure 38.4 reveals enormous fluctuations in the rate of economic growth in the UK (compared year on year). Since 1949 the economy has shown annual growth rates ranging from 6.3% to –4.2%. Economists have long believed that there are regular patterns in the level of economic activity for an economy. Some have identified a very long-term fluctuation in global economic activity, occurring over a period of between 40 and 60 years. This is called the **Kondratieff cycle** or wave and is named after the Russian economist who first wrote about it. Other regular patterns in economic activity have been observed and there is general agreement amongst economists that economies are subject to the **economic cycle**. This is a regular pattern of economic activity that occurs over a period of between five and 11 years. It is also called

Figure 38.4 *Annual growth of UK GDP, 1949–2012*

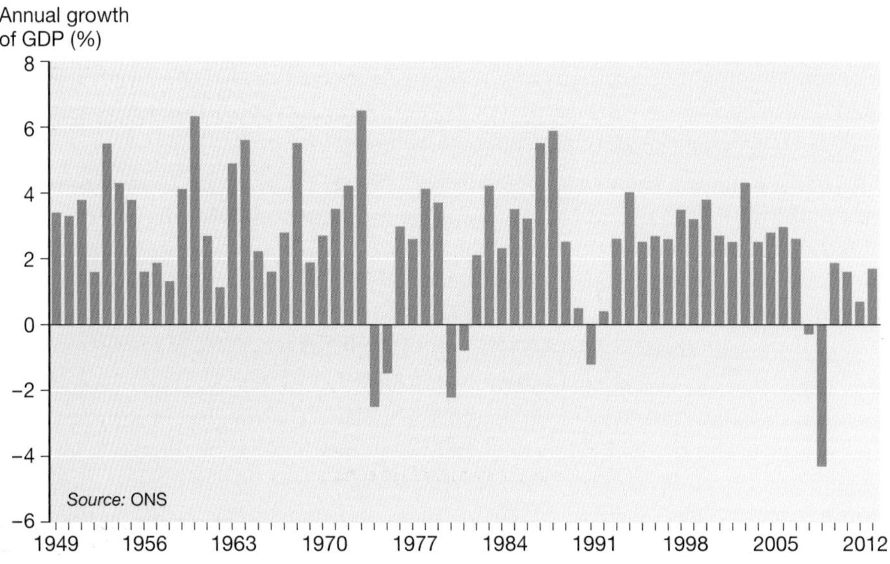

REALWORLD
ECONOMICS 38.1

Economic growth in Vietnam

Vietnam is one of the fastest growing economies in Asia (see Figure 38.5). It relies heavily on its productive agricultural sector but is also expanding its manufacturing sector. The country has become a highly successful exporter, with sales of exports rising by 20% in 2012 and 16% in 2013. It is a very popular destination for international investors: foreign investment in Vietnam exceeded £9.4 billion in 2013. Overseas investors are attracted by the country's large pool of low-cost labour. Vietnam's population is over 90 million, young and growing at 1% per annum. Wage levels are lower than elsewhere in Asia. According to a report, monthly pay for general workers in Vietnam is roughly 32% of levels in China, 43% in Malaysia and Thailand, and 62% in Indonesia. Vietnam has a large domestic market in which consumption is growing by about 5% annually.

Source: Adapted from *International Business Times*, 3.1.14

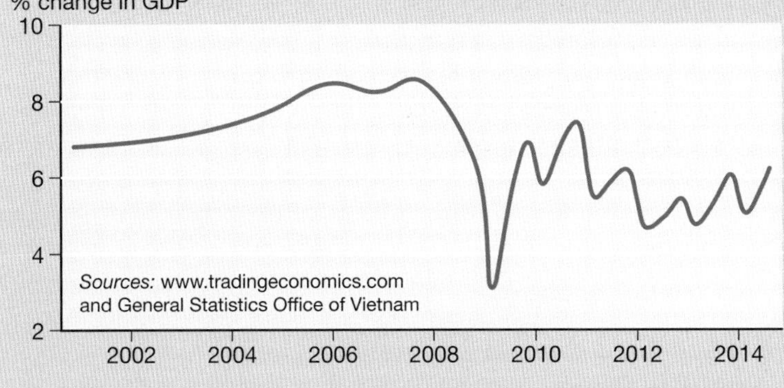

Figure 38.5 *GDP growth rates for Vietnam, 2000–14*

Exercise

Total: 11 marks

1 What do you estimate to be Vietnam's trend rate of economic growth since 2000? **(2 marks)**

2 Explain the possible reasons why Vietnam's trend rate of economic growth is higher than that of the UK. **(9 marks)**

the business cycle or trade cycle. The general pattern of the economic cycle and its relationship to the long-term trend of GDP is shown in Figure 38.6.

It is apparent from Figure 38.4 that the pattern of economic activity and the changing rate of growth of GDP over time are not as smooth or regular as Figure 38.6 might

Key term

The **economic cycle** occurs when an economy's actual level of GDP shows a regular pattern of variation compared with its long-term trend.

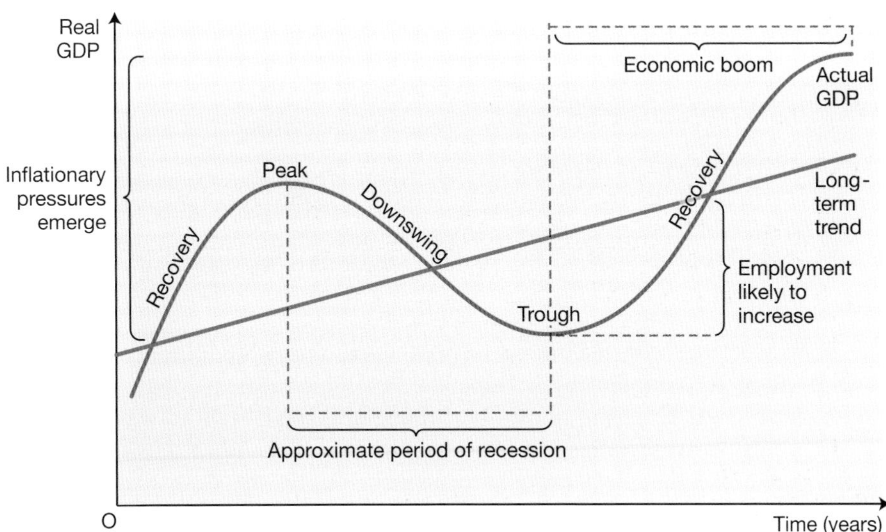

Figure 38.6 *The pattern of the economic cycle*

suggest. However, over time all economies have experienced fluctuations in the growth of GDP similar to those illustrated. Globalisation has led to the economies of the world becoming increasingly interdependent and experiencing similar patterns in growth of GDP. This was seen in 2008–09 as the impact of the financial crisis turned into a recession in many countries and a slowing of rates of economic growth in most others.

The phases of the economic cycle

Economic cycles have four distinct phases, as identified in Figure 38.6: recovery, peak, downswing and trough. The movement of an economy from one phase to the next has implications for key economic indicators such as the rate of inflation, the level of unemployment, the level of investment and, of course, the level of real GDP.

1 Recovery

As the economy recovers from the trough phase of the economic cycle, output and employment both begin to increase. Households will generally spend more on consumption because they are more confident in the security of their employment. Initially businesses may respond cautiously to signs of increasing consumer confidence. No major decisions are required to meet rising demand while spare capacity exists: firms simply begin to utilise idle factories, production machinery and other capital equipment more fully, leading to short-term economic growth. As business confidence increases, firms may take the decision to increase investment, further stimulating aggregate demand. Employees experience less difficulty in finding jobs, and wages may begin to rise. As a consequence, inflationary pressures may begin to build (see Figure 38.7).

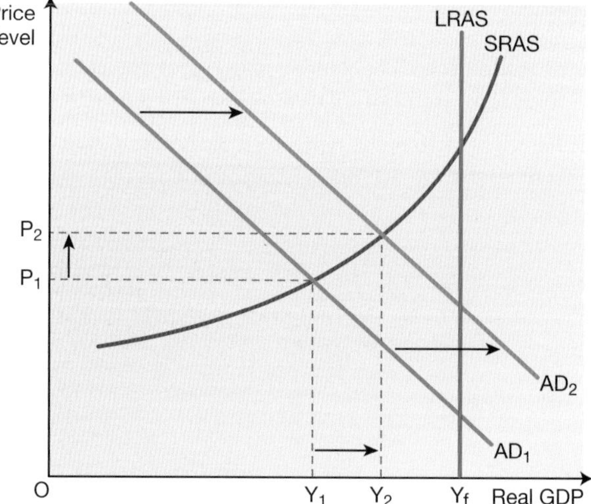

Figure 38.7 *Rising aggregate demand in the recovery phase of the economic cycle can lead to increased inflationary pressure*

2 Peak

A peak is associated with high levels of production and expenditure by firms, and rising levels of consumption by households. Peaks are normally characterised by confidence amongst firms and households, though this may begin to wane towards the end of this phase. Investment is likely to increase at such times. However, many sectors of the economy will experience pressure during the peak phase. Skilled workers may become scarce, and firms competing for workers may offer higher wages. Simultaneously, as the economy approaches maximum production, shortages and bottlenecks will occur as insufficient raw materials and components exist to meet demand. In effect, aggregate supply becomes highly price inelastic, which will inevitably result in the price level rising. It is the existence of inflation that usually leads to the end of a peak phase of the economic cycle.

REALWORLD
ECONOMICS 38.2

The Spanish economy 2008–11

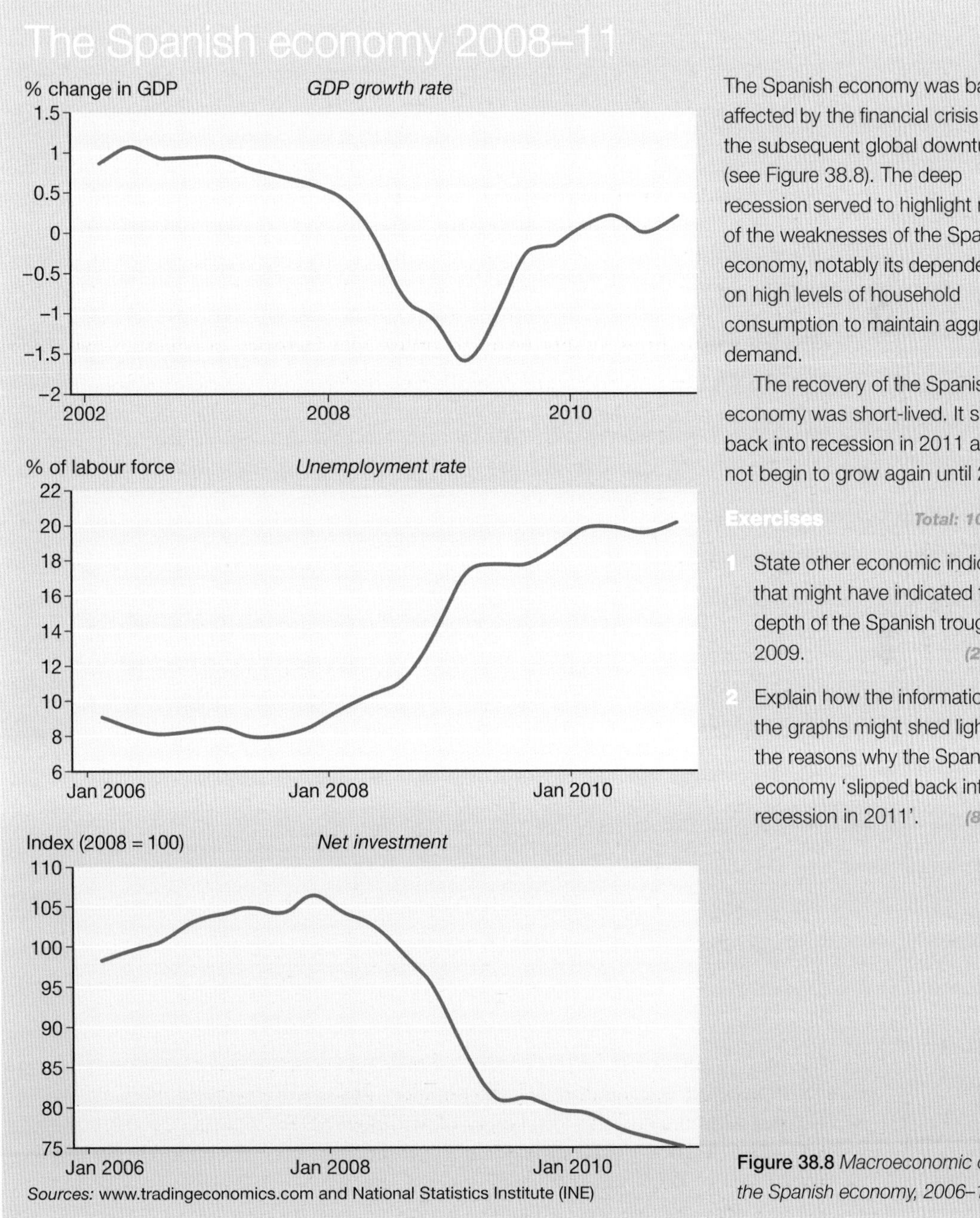

The Spanish economy was badly affected by the financial crisis and the subsequent global downturn (see Figure 38.8). The deep recession served to highlight many of the weaknesses of the Spanish economy, notably its dependence on high levels of household consumption to maintain aggregate demand.

The recovery of the Spanish economy was short-lived. It slipped back into recession in 2011 and did not begin to grow again until 2013.

Exercises *Total: 10 marks*

1. State other economic indicators that might have indicated the depth of the Spanish trough in 2009. *(2 marks)*
2. Explain how the information in the graphs might shed light on the reasons why the Spanish economy 'slipped back into recession in 2011'. *(8 marks)*

Figure 38.8 *Macroeconomic data for the Spanish economy, 2006–10*

3 Downswing

This phase occurs when incomes and output start to fall. Rising prices of labour and materials mean that firms face increased costs of production. These will begin to eat into their profits. Falling profits are likely to reduce the level of investment. The level of production in the economy is likely to fall, which, if it lasts for more than six months, creates a recession. The amount of spare capacity within the economy will rise. Inflationary pressure will decline throughout this phase of the economic cycle as aggregate demand is reduced.

4 Trough

A trough sees production (and real GDP) at its lowest, with unemployment high and increasing numbers of firms failing. Inflation will be low and, in a deep trough, prices may be falling – this is termed **deflation**. In Spain in 2009, during the trough phase, prices were falling by about 1.4% annually. Investment in a trough will be low, but reduced demand for capital equipment may drive the price of capital down, increasing the potential return from investment. This may slowly lead to increases in investment and herald the start of the recovery phase of the economic cycle.

Output gaps

Figure 38.6 illustrated that the operation of the economic cycle causes actual GDP to fluctuate around the long-term trend of GDP growth for the economy. When an economy's actual GDP differs from its long-term trend level of GDP, an output gap exists. Output gaps can be positive or negative, as shown in Figure 38.9.

Figure 38.9 *Positive and negative output gaps*

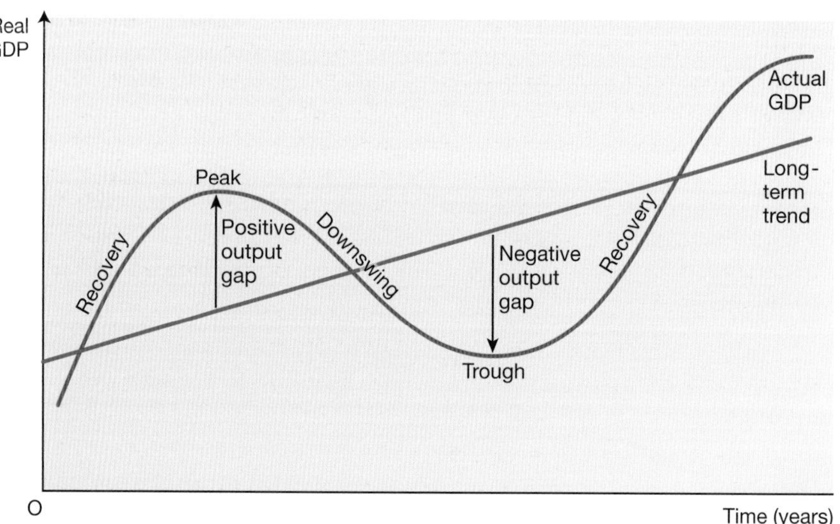

Key terms

An **output gap** measures the difference between an economy's actual level of real GDP and its long-term trend level of real GDP.

A **positive output gap** exists when the actual level of real GDP is above the long-term trend level.

A **negative output gap** exists when the actual level of real GDP is below the long-term trend level.

Positive output gaps

At times, in Figure 38.9, actual GDP exceeds the long-term trend, for example during the peak stage of the economic cycle. This is an example of a positive gap because the level of actual GDP exceeds the long-term trend of GDP for that economy.

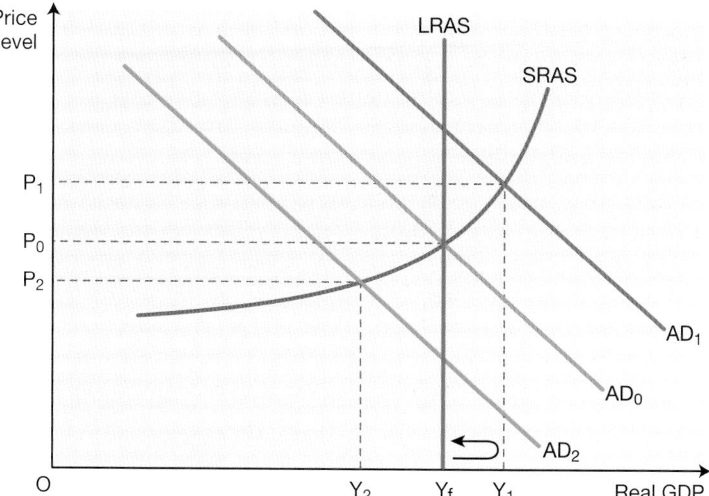

Figure 38.10 *Using AD and AS analysis to illustrate output gaps*

This situation can also be shown on an aggregate demand and supply diagram. In Figure 38.10, the level of aggregate demand shown by AD_1 results in an economy producing a level of output, or real GDP, of Y_1, which exceeds the full employment level of output, Y_f. This equilibrium exists between aggregate demand and a short-run aggregate supply curve because a positive output gap is only a short-term phenomenon. Output exceeds the full employment level of output temporarily following a rise in aggregate demand from, say, AD_0 to AD_1. The rise in aggregate demand pushes up wages, and more employees enter the workforce attracted by the apparent increase in earnings. Profits also appear to rise, temporarily attracting additional output from firms. However, a consequence of rising profits is higher prices, which means that wages and profits have not increased in real terms. The higher level of employment and output is a short-term phenomenon and real GDP falls back once more.

Positive output gaps have a number of important characteristics:

- they are only temporary, as output in excess of full employment output is not sustainable;
- high levels of aggregate demand exist;
- they are associated with high levels of production and levels of employment and the peak stage of the economic cycle;
- they are accompanied by an increase in inflationary pressure – in Figure 38.10, the rise in aggregate demand to AD_1 increases the price level to P_1, and possibly higher.

A small number of economies currently exhibit characteristics associated with positive output gaps. The Mongolian economy grew by more than 7% in 2014 (having reached 11.5% in the last quarter of 2014) on the basis of a boom in mining, fuelled by demand for natural resources from China. Mongolia's rate of unemployment fell sharply from 9.4% to 6.4% over the year. Unsurprisingly, the Mongolian economy is experiencing inflationary pressures: prices were rising by an annual rate of 11.5% at the end of 2014. However, recent falls in the price of key minerals such as coal may slow growth in this economy.

Negative output gaps

Negative output gaps are more common in economies across the world at the time of writing, as the effects of the deep recession that started in 2008 continue to be felt, particularly in Europe. A negative output gap exists when the actual level of real GDP is lower than the long-term trend. In Figure 38.9 this type of output gap can be seen to exist in the trough phase of the economic cycle.

Negative output gaps can also be shown using aggregate demand and supply analysis, as in Figure 38.10. If aggregate demand is at a level shown by AD_2, then output is below the full employment level of output (Y_f). This type of output gap is associated with lower levels of production, higher levels of unemployment and reduced levels of inflationary pressure. The price level is at P_2 in Figure 38.10 with a negative output gap.

Despite GDP rising at about 3% annually during 2014, and falling levels of unemployment, it is likely that the UK continues to suffer the effects of a negative output gap. Many analysts believe that a high level of spare capacity exists within the economy and there is little evidence of a rising price level: the inflation figure was just 0% in March 2015.

Shocks and economic growth

In Chapter 37 we analysed the effects of demand-side and supply-side shocks using aggregate demand and aggregate supply analysis. Such shocks have the potential to have a major impact on the economic performance of economies, not least the rate of economic growth. Negative demand-side shocks have the potential to create negative output gaps by slowing or reversing rates of economic growth. In contrast, positive demand-side shocks can contribute to an economy experiencing high rates of economic growth and possibly positive output gaps by providing a substantial boost to aggregate demand. This can result in the economy's level of aggregate demand exceeding its ability to supply goods and services. Cambodia, in SE Asia, has enjoyed positive demand-side shocks because it has become an increasingly popular destination for tourists at the same time as demand for its exports of textiles and shoes have risen. The country's growth rate was over 7% in 2014.

The streets of Galle, Sri Lanka – one of the areas most affected by the devastating Boxing Day 2004 tsunami

Supply-side shocks can also create output gaps. On Boxing Day 2004 the island of Sri Lanka was devastated by a tsunami following an earthquake beneath the Indian Ocean. This was a major negative supply-side shock. Before and after 2004 the Sri Lankan economy was experiencing growth rates of real GDP of around 7%. However, in 2005 the Sri Lankan economy grew at 4%. This was a fine achievement in view of the enormous impact of the tsunami, but clearly below the economy's long-term trend.

Supply-side shocks can be positive and have the potential to contribute to positive output gaps, though such shocks can increase the long-term trend of growth in GDP. Cambodia has the good fortune to have discovered substantial deposits of oil as well as other minerals including bauxite and gold. This will have made a contribution to the country's high rates of economic growth.

REALWORLD ECONOMICS 38.3

Problems for the Russian economy

The Russian economy moved into recession in 2015 – a much gloomier economic scenario than forecast. It is anticipated that the economy will shrink by 0.8% by the end of 2015, compared with a previous forecast of 1.2% growth in real GDP.

Russia's economy has been affected by economic sanctions, imposed by many Western countries following its annexation of Crimea. In particular this has reduced investment in the country. The economy was also damaged by heavy falls in global oil prices in the second half of 2014. Furthermore, household disposable incomes are forecast to decline by 2.8%, compared with a prior forecast of 0.4% growth.

Exercise

1 Explain the impact of the shocks that the Russian economy experienced in 2014 on its GDP growth. *(9 marks)*

Review questions

Total: 40 marks

1 Define the term 'economic growth'. *(3 marks)*

2 Explain, with the aid of a production possibility boundary, the difference between short-run and long-run economic growth. *(8 marks)*

3 Which of the following is usually associated with short-run economic growth?
- A A rightward shift in the long-run aggregate supply curve
- B A shift to the right in the aggregate demand curve
- C A fall in the price level
- D A contraction along the short-run aggregate supply curve *(1 mark)*

4 Explain the possible benefits to an economy arising from long-run economic growth. *(6 marks)*

5 Explain the term 'the long-run trend rate of economic growth'. *(4 marks)*

6 What is meant by the term 'the economic cycle'? *(3 marks)*

7 Which stage of the economic cycle is most associated with high levels of unemployment and minimal inflationary pressures?
- A Recovery
- B Peak
- C Downswing
- D Trough *(1 mark)*

8 Explain, with the aid of a diagram, the difference between a positive and a negative output gap. *(8 marks)*

9 Which of the following is normally associated with a negative output gap?
- A High and rising levels of real GDP
- B Rising price level
- C High and rising level of investment
- D Rising level of unemployment *(1 mark)*

10 Explain why a negative demand-side shock might result in an economy suffering an output gap. *(5 marks)*

Employment & unemployment

This chapter looks at the ways in which governments can measure the level of unemployment and the different types of unemployment that commonly occur. We consider the ways in which demand-side and supply-side factors can determine the levels of employment and unemployment, and how changes in the rest of the world affect the employment situation in the UK.

Employment and unemployment classification

The distinction between employed and unemployed within an economy is more complex than might at first appear. The International Labour Organisation (ILO), which is part of the United Nations, has developed a classification that is used in many countries throughout the world (see Figure 39.1). It classifies all of a country's inhabitants aged over 16 in one of three ways:

In employment The ILO definition considers anyone who works for at least an hour a week as being in employment. Thus it includes people who are working part- or full-time and those on temporary contracts, as well as people on government training schemes.

Unemployed Under ILO criteria, a person who is not working but who is available for work and seeking work is unemployed. The UK authorities interpret the ILO guidelines to mean that anyone who has actively sought work in the last four weeks and is available to start work in the next two weeks is unemployed.

Economically inactive The ILO guidelines state that a person who is not employed or unemployed must be classified as economically inactive. People in the UK may be economically inactive for a number of reasons. A major category of economically

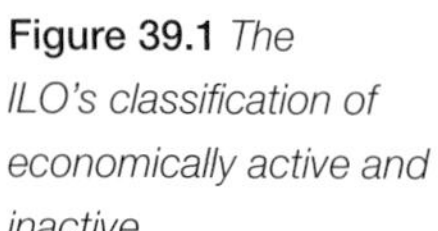

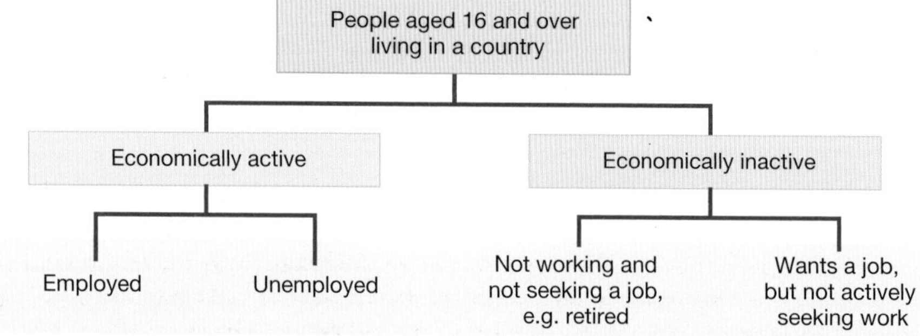

Figure 39.1 *The ILO's classification of economically active and inactive*

Key terms

Employment is a measure of the number of people who are in work at a particular time.

Economically active refers to a person who is either in employment (including self-employed) or who is unemployed and therefore seeking work.

The **employment rate** is the percentage of the population aged 16 to 64 who are in work.

inactive people is pensioners who have retired from the workforce. The economically inactive group also includes students, those who are unable to work due to poor health or disability, and people who are caring for family members.

Measuring employment

In the three months between October and December 2014, 30.90 million people were employed in the UK; this represented an increase of 608,000 people in work in comparison with the same period in 2013. This is a simple measure of the number of people in work. However, we can also measure the rate of employment: this is the percentage of people aged between 16 and 64 who are working.

Over the period October to December 2014, the UK's employment rate was calculated as follows:

Employment rate = 30.9 million × 100/42.19 million = 73.2%.

This is the second highest rate of employment in the UK since comparable records began in 1971. The steady improvement in the rate of employment in the UK since 2011 is shown in Figure 39.2.

Number crunching
What level of employment would have been required in October to December 2014 to achieve an employment rate of 75%?

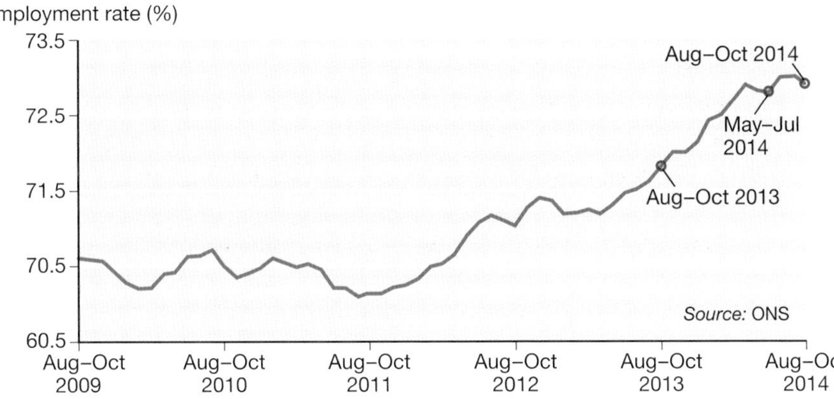

Figure 39.2 *The UK's employment rate, 2009–14*

An improvement in the employment rate has the potential to offer a range of benefits to an economy. Most obviously it can increase the real GDP of the country and consequently its living standards. It can also bring increased tax revenue as people's incomes (and possibly firms' profits) rise, leading to a higher tax yield for the government. This gives the government more revenue to provide important services such as health and education and can reduce expenditure on welfare, allowing the government to divert this spending elsewhere.

However, the employment rate can be misleading. In order to be classified as employed, an employee only has to work one hour each week. Thus a high employment rate (as in the UK in 2014) can disguise a degree of underemployment, where workers are in part-time employment but would prefer to have a full-time job. If a high percentage of employees in an economy are employed part-time when seeking full-time employment, output will not be at its maximum and the economy will be operating within its production possibility boundary.

Furthermore, the employment rate does not offer any information about wage rates or productivity levels. These will impact on the level of consumers' expenditure and the level of real GDP attained by the economy.

Methods of measuring unemployment

The authorities in the UK use two main methods to measure unemployment: the Labour Force Survey (LFS) and the claimant count. The Office for National Statistics (ONS) is part of the UK Statistics Authority that, in turn, is part of the government. The ONS is responsible for the collection and publication of economic statistics in the UK including unemployment data.

The Labour Force Survey

The ONS uses the LFS to measure the rate of unemployment in the UK – all EU member states are legally required to do this. The LFS is based on the internationally agreed definition of unemployment that is recommended by the International Labour Organisation (ILO). This approach is also used by numerous other countries as well as by the European Union.

The survey requires the collection of information from households in the UK about their activities in the labour market. The ONS designs its survey so that each quarter (or three months) it interviews 80,000 people aged over 16 in approximately 41,000 households in the UK. This approach to measuring unemployment is not entirely accurate because it is based on asking a sample of people in the UK about their employment. However, the size of the survey means that it is 95% accurate (i.e. correct in 95 cases out of 100). The results of the LFS are used to produce regional and national data on unemployment.

The claimant count

This method of measuring unemployment counts the number of people in the UK who are receiving benefits mainly for reasons of unemployment. People included in the claimant count will be receiving unemployment benefit (known as Job Seeker's Allowance) or National Insurance credits. Introduced experimentally from April 2013, those who receive Universal Credit principally because they are unemployed are becoming part of the claimant count measure of unemployment. Universal Credit is a wide-ranging welfare payment that will replace many of those paid to people who are unemployed or on low incomes.

The claimant count measure of unemployment is collected from records held by the Department for Work and Pensions (DWP). The DWP is the government department responsible for administering benefits relating to unemployment. The DWP's records show the number of people in the UK who are claiming relevant benefits on a particular day each month as well as the number who have been added to, and left, the claimant count.

Comparing the results of the two methods of measurement

The claimant count measure provides a lower figure for unemployment because a number of people who might be judged to be unemployed by the ILO, and therefore by the Labour Force Survey, are not entitled to claim relevant benefits such as Universal Credit or Job Seeker's Allowance.

There are several reasons why unemployed people in the UK may not be able to claim benefits:

- they are above the age at which state pensions are paid;

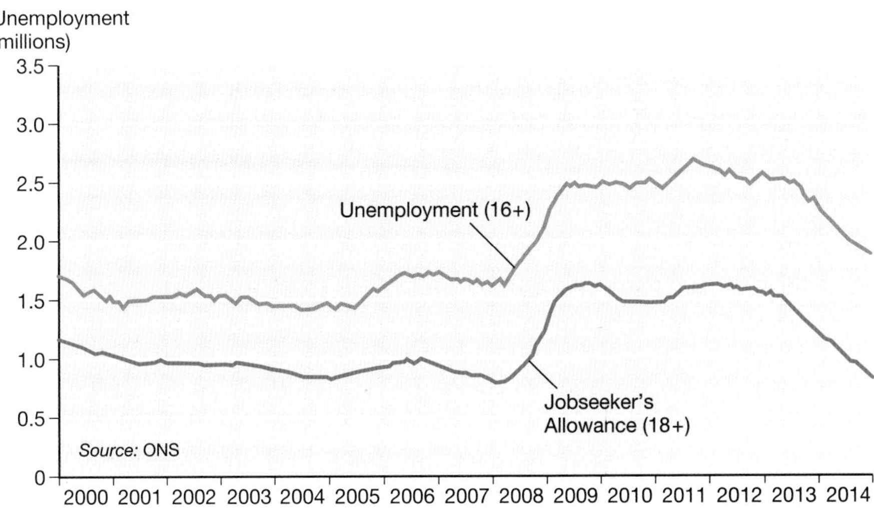

Figure 39.3
Unemployment and claimant count data for the UK, 2000–14

- their partners earn incomes above a certain level;
- they are full-time students;
- they are from overseas and not eligible to claim benefits in the UK.

Figure 39.3 shows the number of unemployed people in the UK as measured by the two methods since 2000. The difference between the two methods has become larger as the government has tightened access to benefits and as more people over the state retirement age actively seek employment. The diagram also shows clearly that the recession in the UK which started in 2008 led to a sharp rise in unemployment, however it is measured.

Types of unemployment data

Whichever method of measurement is used, it is possible to present unemployment data in two major ways: the actual number unemployed or the rate of unemployment. Unemployment data supplied by the ONS is seasonally adjusted to remove fluctuations in employment and unemployment figures associated with the time of the year. For example, school leavers enter the workforce each July and the process of seasonal adjustment removes the effects of occurrences such as this and allows us to identify underlying changes.

Key term
The **rate of unemployment** is the proportion or percentage of economically active people within a country who are unemployed.

The actual number of unemployed

Measurement of the actual number unemployed provides relatively little information. The data in Figure 39.3 reveal that the LFS recorded unemployment as approximately 1.96 million in November 2014 and that approximately 900,000 were shown as unemployed by the claimant count.

Such a measurement of the actual number unemployed at any time has shortcomings. It reveals nothing about the size of the workforce (i.e. the number of people who are working or actively seeking employment). The number of people unemployed may grow, but the number of economically active people may be growing more quickly. This means that more people in the economy have jobs, which should boost real GDP, despite the rise in the number unemployed.

The rate of unemployment

It is possible to overcome some of the weaknesses of simply showing the number of people unemployed by measuring the rate of unemployment. The unemployment rate is the proportion of the number of economically active people in a country who are unemployed. This rate can be measured by use of the following formula:

$$\textbf{Rate of unemployment} = \frac{\text{Number unemployed} \times 100}{\text{Number employed} + \text{Number unemployed}}$$

From Table 39.1 it is possible to calculate the UK's rate of unemployment for the three-month period of October to December 2014.

$$\text{Rate of unemployment (October–December 2014)} = \frac{1{,}862{,}000 \times 100}{30{,}896{,}000 + 1{,}862{,}000} = \frac{186{,}200{,}000}{32{,}758{,}000} = 5.68\%$$

Number crunching

Use the data in Table 39.1 to calculate the rate of unemployment in the UK for October to December 2013.

	Oct–Dec 2014	Oct–Dec 2013
Employed	**30,896**	**30,288**
Aged 16–65	29,769	29,213
Aged 65+	1127	1075
Unemployed	**1862**	**2348**
Aged 16–65	1844	2318
Aged 65+	18	30

Table 39.1 *Employment data for the UK, 2014 and 2013 (thousands)*

Why is it important to measure unemployment accurately?

In the UK, the government and other organisations such as the Bank of England take important policy decisions using the level of unemployment as one piece of evidence.

- We will see in Topic 9 that judgements regarding the bank rate of interest to be set by the Bank of England and changes in rates of taxation by the Treasury (the government department responsible for financial matters) require accurate economic data to inform their decision making.
- If the Bank of England believes unemployment to be lower than it actually is, it may take a decision to raise interest rates at a time when they need to remain relatively low to encourage investment and consumption and to discourage saving.
- The UK government would not be sure whether its policy decisions on the economy were resulting in it reaching its macroeconomic objective in terms of the level of unemployment.
- Different types of unemployment exist (see below). Accurate data can help the authorities to identify the different types and to propose suitable remedies.

Types of unemployment

It may seem strange to differentiate between different types of unemployment, but it is important for governments and others making decisions on matters relating to employment and unemployment. If decision makers understand the type of unemployment with which they are dealing, it is possible to identify its likely causes and to take appropriate action to reduce its level and impact. The fact that unemployment takes different forms and has different causes emphasises that there is no single 'cure' for the problem. We shall see in Topic 9 that governments use a range of policies to reduce unemployment.

Seasonal unemployment

Shut up for winter – seasonal unemployment affects many of the UK's seaside resorts

Seasonal unemployment occurs when people lose their jobs at a particular time of the year in a way that is predictable because it has happened previously. Thus workers in agriculture and the building trade may lose their jobs in the winter months due to poor weather and firms requiring fewer employees as workloads diminish. A further cause of seasonal unemployment is a pattern of demand for a product or service that only, or mainly, exists at certain times of the year. Tourism in the UK is an example in that much demand for hotels, restaurants and tourist activities such as theme parks occurs between April and October.

It is not surprising, given the association with tourism, that seasonal unemployment can occur in particular locations and regions within the UK. For example, the UK government is concerned by the high level of unemployment associated with seasonal factors in many of the UK's seaside resorts such as Southwold, Clacton and Blackpool. Much of this seasonal unemployment is the result of temporary employment contracts in the tourism industry coming to an end in the autumn and because few other opportunities for employment exist in these areas.

Many UK unemployment statistics, including those provided by the ONS, are seasonally adjusted to remove the effect of predictable seasonal unemployment.

Frictional unemployment

Frictional unemployment is always present in an economy. It is unemployment that exists because people are moving between jobs. It is also called 'search unemployment' because it occurs while unemployed workers are searching for new employment. A low level of frictional unemployment is not necessarily a problem, since in a healthy economy people are moving to new, and often better-paid or more rewarding, employment.

Frictional unemployment is often associated with a lack of information about what is happening in the labour market. Thus an employee who has lost his or her job may be frictionally unemployed because they do not have sufficient information about jobs that are available. Another cause is that a firm may decide not to hire employees because it believes that no suitable applicants are available, when in reality they are available and seeking employment. Some evidence of the existence of frictional unemployment is provided by the level of job vacancies that are available at the same time as unemployment. However, imperfect information is just one cause of the coexistence of unemployment and job vacancies.

Frictional unemployment can also be caused by the reluctance or inability of workers to retrain for employment in new occupations. A worker who has been made redundant may be unwilling to retrain, especially if the training required is extensive or if there are barriers to entry to a new occupation, such as qualifications that are difficult to obtain.

Key terms

Seasonal unemployment is unemployment that exhibits regular and predictable fluctuations throughout the year.

Frictional unemployment exists when workers are in the process of moving to a new job.

Structural unemployment is job losses from the long-term decline of specific industries.

Cyclical unemployment is unemployment arising from a fall in aggregate demand.

Voluntary unemployment occurs when workers take a decision not to enter the labour market at the current wage rate.

Structural unemployment

In the UK a number of industries have become smaller, or even disappeared, as they have become subject to factors promoting long-term change. Changes such as the three outlined below can lead to structural unemployment. People who are structurally unemployed may have skills that are obsolete or may live in a region of the UK where few suitable jobs exist.

1 Increased competition from overseas

The process of globalisation means that many markets are becoming more global in nature. As a consequence, UK firms have become subject to intense competition from overseas. Some have struggled to survive in the face of this fierce rivalry and have reduced production or even ceased production entirely. An obvious outcome of this process is structural unemployment.

2 Technological change

Some structural unemployment is the result of advances in technology. Capital equipment may replace labour in the production process. For example, many firms have replaced switchboard operators with automated telephone systems that can take messages and direct callers to appropriate people within the organisation. In manufacturing, robots may be used on production lines.

3 Permanent decline in demand for goods and services

Some products have experienced heavy falls in demand over time as consumers' tastes and fashions change. Today most houses in the UK are heated using gas, oil or electricity. This has resulted in a huge fall in demand for coal because consumers have opted for cleaner and more convenient sources of energy. This long-term decline in demand has caused some of the unemployment experienced in the UK coal industry. It has led to job losses for coal miners and others in the industry, such as those who deliver coal to homes and businesses.

The impact of structural unemployment

Structural unemployment can create major problems for governments. It can result in large and sudden rises in unemployment, and it is frequently concentrated in particular areas or regions within the UK. Sometimes people who are structurally unemployed are unable or unwilling to use their skills to find employment in different parts of the country due to housing costs or a reluctance to leave friends and family. This is termed **geographic immobility of labour**.

Cyclical unemployment

Cyclical unemployment is associated with changes in aggregate demand at various stages of the economic cycle. It rises as an economy moves into a downswing and its trough, and then declines as the economic cycle moves into its upswing. Cyclical unemployment has an inverse relationship with aggregate demand: it rises when aggregate demand declines and falls when aggregate demand increases.

If aggregate demand falls, output declines in response, and firms require fewer employees to meet their production targets. Demand for employees by firms depends upon the level of demand for goods and services in the economy. The demand for labour is an example of derived demand – this is a type of demand that occurs not for the item itself but for what it can produce. When demand for goods and services declines, this reduces the demand for employees and creates structural unemployment. Structural unemployment is also called **demand-deficient unemployment**.

Voluntary unemployment

The previous types of unemployment we have discussed have all been involuntary – workers lose their jobs and leave the labour market against their wishes. However, some employees choose not to enter the labour market and remain unemployed, believing that the current wage rate is not sufficient compensation for giving up leisure time. Classical economists believe that, in the long term, unemployment will solely comprise voluntary unemployment because all those people in an economy who want a job at the current wage rate in the labour market will be able to find one.

Voluntary unemployment can occur because welfare benefits available to unemployed workers are too high in relation to the wage rates currently on offer. Some economists argue that governments should reduce the level of voluntary unemployment by lowering the benefits paid to unemployed workers in order to reduce the disincentive to entering employment. Alternatively, it may be caused by high rates of income tax, especially if paid by those on relatively low wages.

Frictional unemployment can be voluntary to some extent because initially unemployed workers may not accept positions that do not meet their expectations. For example, a worker may seek a relatively high wage and flexible working hours. During the early stages of seeking a new job, positions that do not offer these benefits might be turned down. However, at some point the unemployed worker may adjust expectations and take a job that offers fewer benefits.

Table 39.2 *Possible causes of different types of unemployment*

Type of unemployment	Supply-side causes	Demand-side causes
Seasonal	■ Climatic factors may mean that production can only occur in specific seasons, as in agriculture.	■ Demand only exists at certain times of the year, e.g. for tourism in UK seaside resorts.
Frictional	■ Imperfect information exists in the labour market regarding vacancies and unemployed people. ■ A growing economy develops new industries, creating new roles to attract already employed workers.	
Structural	■ Geographic immobility of labour occurs as workers are unwilling or unable to move to areas where suitable jobs remain. ■ Overseas firms become significantly more competitive.	■ Changes in consumers' tastes or fashions lead to a change in demand for an industry's products, e.g. products associated with home baking or sewing. ■ Technological change makes certain skills obsolete in the labour market.
Cyclical		■ Aggregate demand may fall due to declining consumption, investment or export sales. ■ Demand for labour falls (it is a derived demand) as firms' sales are reduced.
Voluntary	■ Unemployment benefit rates are relatively high in relation to current market wage rates, acting as a disincentive. ■ Income tax rates take a high proportion of wages, discouraging employment.	■ Demand for labour declines, forcing wages down relative to unemployment benefits.

Determinants of employment and unemployment

We saw earlier that it is important to understand the different types of unemployment so as to be able to identify their likely causes. This enables decision makers to implement suitable policies to reduce the level of unemployment.

We can separate the possible causes into demand-side and supply-side factors, as outlined in Table 39.2. Unemployment in the UK comprises most of the types listed in the table. Over time, however, their relative importance may change. For example, demand-side factors were a primary cause of the rise in unemployment that took place after 2008, as cyclical unemployment grew.

Demand-side influences on employment and unemployment

A change in aggregate demand can have a direct and immediate impact on the level of employment. As shown in Figure 39.4, a fall in aggregate demand will reduce the level of production and hence real GDP, with negative consequences for employment. The impact on employment will depend upon the size of the decline in aggregate demand and also upon the slope of the short-run aggregate supply curve – the price elasticity of supply. Thus the impact of the fall from AD_1 to AD_2 has a lesser effect on real GDP (and on the level of employment or unemployment) than the similarly sized fall from AD_3 to AD_4. At lower levels of income, output is more sensitive to changes in demand and the price level, possibly because firms do not opt to hoard labour when aggregate demand is so low.

Figure 39.4 *Changing aggregate demand and unemployment*

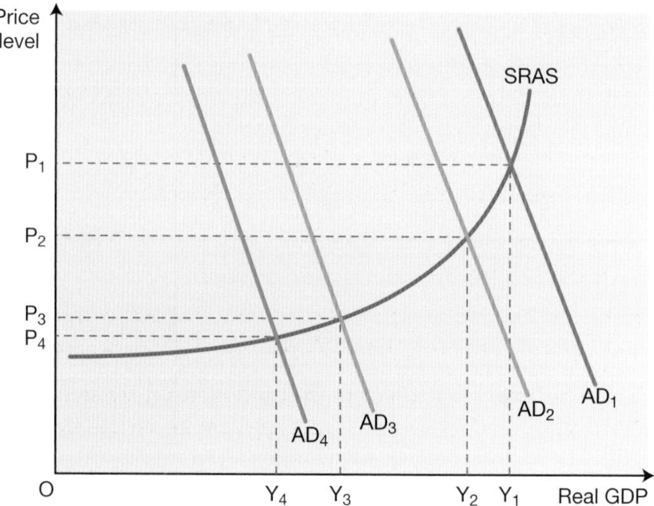

Aggregate demand comprises consumption, investment, government expenditure and net exports, as we saw in Chapter 35. The effects of changes in the level of each of these components may not always be the same. Since 2010 the UK government has reduced its expenditure from 47.7% of GDP in 2009–10 to 43.3% in 2014–15 and it is forecast to fall to 39.5% by 2017–18. Between 2009 and 2015, just under 1 million jobs have been lost in the public sector. The UK government is a major employer in a number of labour-intensive industries such as local government, the police force and education. Hence any changes in its level of expenditure can have a disproportionately large impact on employment and unemployment.

Investment has the potential to create employment and to reduce it. Investment in technology can create jobs, not only in producing the technology itself but also in maintaining it. For example, while the investment in internet retailing by firms may have led to the closure of some shops (bookshops, for example), it has created jobs directly in developing websites and managing e-tailing systems. Further employment has been created in delivering products to consumers. In contrast, other types of investment, for example in production-line technology in the form of robots, may replace jobs.

Supply-side influences on employment and unemployment

There are a range of supply-side influences on the level of employment and unemployment in the UK.

Migration

In Chapter 36 we saw that the UK has been subject to high levels of positive net migration over recent years. This trend has received extensive coverage in the media, partly because it has the potential to affect employment and unemployment in the UK. Migration, particularly from other EU states, has been cited as the cause of some unemployment in the UK, as migrants are prepared to work for lower wages. However, research by the Home Office (a government department) suggests that any impact on the level of unemployment is actually very small. It is more certain that migration has contributed to the unprecedented level of employment in the UK. It has risen from 29 million at the start of 2010 to 30.9 million in December 2014 – over the same period the UK has experienced positive net migration of around 200,000 annually.

Government policies

The government has sought to reduce the level of unemployment through a series of measures to support the operation of the UK labour market.

Enterprise allowance This scheme offers financial support to unemployed people seeking to start their own businesses.

Work programmes These are designed to provide support, work experience and training for up to two years to help unemployed people find and keep jobs.

Work experience Unemployed people can receive financial assistance and practical support to find suitable work placements to help them into employment.

The government has focused policies on reducing the number of long-term unemployed (those out of work for over 12 months) and the number of young people who are unemployed. Measures targeting the long-term unemployed include a requirement to meet an adviser every day, or doing community work for up to six months. Youth unemployment (those aged 16–24) reached 740,000 in December 2014. This has prompted the UK government to implement a number of policies, including the payment of financial incentives to firms who employ young people, improved careers advice and the removal of some benefits previously paid to out-of-work youngsters.

The UK government also offers financial support to parents and carers to help them to enter the workforce. This policy boosts employment and the employment rate by encouraging more people, especially women, into the workforce.

REALWORLD ECONOMICS 39.1

Foreign investment in the UK

The UK's foreign direct investment (FDI) was greater than that of any other European country in 2013–14, according to a government report. More than 1773 new projects were established using funding from overseas (see Figure 39.5), setting a record for the UK. Over half of the investment was in energy or infrastructure schemes.

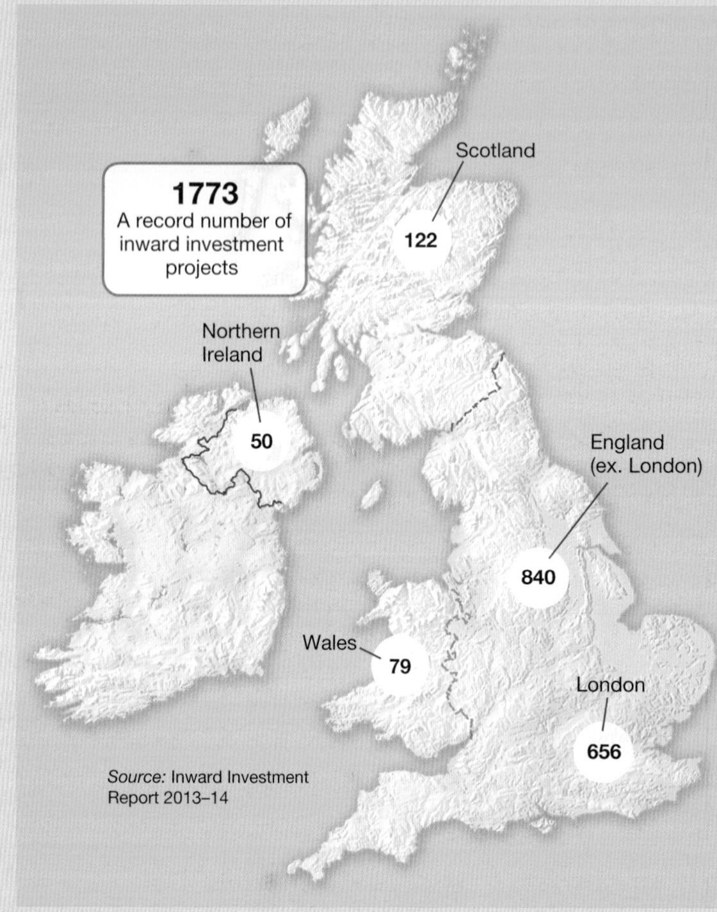

Figure 39.5 *Distribution of inward investment projects in the UK, 2013–14*

According to the guide released by UK Trade and Industry, there have been five key areas for foreign investment in 2013–14. These are:

- Hinkley Point power station, Somerset – France's EDF energy
- Royal Albert Docks, London – China's Advanced Business Parks
- London Array wind farm, Kent – Canadian pension fund La Caisse
- Nine Elms hotel, office and housing, London – China's Wanda conglomerate
- Airport City Manchester – China's Beijing Construction Engineering Group

Source: Adapted from City AM, 20.7.14

Exercises *Total: 14 marks*

1 Explain the effect of foreign investment in the UK on the level of employment in the economy. *(6 marks)*

2 Explain why foreign investment in the UK might not reduce all types of unemployment. *(8 marks)*

The impact of globalisation on employment and unemployment in the UK

Key term
Globalisation is the trend for many markets to become worldwide in scope.

Globalisation has increased the interconnectedness of the world's economies. The UK is no exception to this trend: it operates a very open economy with relatively few regulations and a highly flexible labour market, making it attractive to foreign firms. One consequence of this is that the UK economy is sensitive to changes in the global economy and this has implications for the level of employment (and unemployment) within the economy.

Positive effects on employment

Globalisation has had a positive impact on the level of employment in the UK, operating through demand-side and supply-side factors. Globalisation has encouraged inward investment into the UK economy, boosting aggregate demand while simultaneously increasing the economy's productive potential. The extent and impact of foreign direct investment (FDI) on the UK is illustrated in Real World Economics 39.1.

Globalisation has also opened up new foreign markets to UK exports, increasing the level of aggregate demand. Between 2008 and 2013, sales of UK exports to China increased 120%, albeit from a low base. Some economists predict that growth in UK output and employment will be fuelled through trade with Latin America and Asia over the coming decade.

Negative effects on employment

On the negative side, globalisation has made UK industries more vulnerable to competition from overseas and has undoubtedly contributed to structural unemployment. It has resulted in increased imports of manufactured goods and the loss of jobs as many manufacturers have moved operations to countries with lower wage costs, such as Poland and Vietnam. Globalisation has played a significant part in the deindustrialisation of the UK and other developed economies. Some service industries have relocated certain operations, such as call centres, overseas, notably to India. This has impacted particularly on those carrying out relatively unskilled work and has resulted in increased unemployment, often in specific areas or regions.

The interconnectedness of the UK economy with the rest of the world has created cyclical unemployment. In 2008 the financial crisis originated in the USA. Close links exist within financial industries throughout the world and the effects were soon felt in the UK and most other major economies. Unemployment rose from 0.8 million in 2008 to 1.6 million just two years later as aggregate demand slumped in most developed economies.

Key term

Deindustrialisation describes the process of removing manufacturing industries from an economy and the economic and social consequences, such as unemployment, which follow.

Review questions

Total marks: 49 marks

1 Define the terms 'employment' and 'unemployment'. *(6 marks)*

2 Which of the following, according to the International Labour Organisation, is considered to be employed?
(i) An employee who works two hours each week
(ii) An employee on a temporary contract
(iii) Someone on a government training scheme
A (i) and (ii)
B (ii) only
C (i) and (iii)
D (i), (ii) and (iii) *(1 mark)*

3 Explain the major differences between the Labour Force Survey and the claimant count methods of measuring unemployment in the UK. *(8 marks)*

4 Which of the following, ceteris paribus, would *not* increase a country's employment rate?

A An increase in the number of people aged 16–64
B An increase in the number of people who are self-employed
C An increase in the number of people on temporary employment contracts
D A reduction in the number of people aged 16–64 due to emigration *(1 mark)*

5 Explain why the claimant count measure of unemployment normally gives a lower figure than the Labour Force Survey. *(7 marks)*

6 Using examples, explain the difference between the level of unemployment and the rate of unemployment. *(6 marks)*

7 At the end of last year, an economy had the following figures relating to employment and unemployment:

- 25.5 million aged 16–65 employed
- 2.5 million aged over 65 employed
- 0.25 million aged over 65 unemployed
- 2 million aged 16–65 unemployed

What is the unemployment rate?

A 8.93%
B 2.25 million
C 7.84%
D 7.44% *(1 mark)*

8 Explain the difference between frictional and structural unemployment. *(5 marks)*

9 Explain the effect of net migration on employment in the UK in recent years. *(6 marks)*

10 Explain how changes in the international economy may have had a negative effect on the level of employment in the UK. *(8 marks)*

Inflation & deflation

This chapter builds on some of the material covered in Chapter 33 when we explored the use of index numbers to measure the rate of inflation. It looks at the ways in which the general level of prices in an economy can change, and the factors such as changes in aggregate demand and changes in costs that cause prices to rise or fall. It also examines how changes in the prices of important commodities and events in other economies can affect the general price level in the UK.

How prices can change in an economy

When economists talk about the price level, they are usually referring to the general level of prices in an economy. In other words, they discuss the change in the price of a 'basket' of goods and services that is constructed to reflect the spending of the 'average' family. The change in price measures the average of changes of the goods and services in the basket using index numbers. The calculation allows for the differing importance of each item in the basket through a process known as weighting. We looked at the process of calculating changes in the general price level in detail in Chapter 33 as part of our study of index numbers and it may be worth you revisiting those pages before continuing with this chapter.

Inflation and disinflation

Over time the general level of prices in an economy may rise or fall, though rising prices are more common. A rise in the general level of prices means that money will purchase fewer goods or services, which means its value is falling. This is inflation. The rate of inflation in the UK is measured in several ways, but the major measure is the Consumer Prices Index (or CPI). This common measure is used throughout the European Union, allowing effective comparisons between price changes in member states and improved policy decisions.

Figure 40.1 shows the rate of inflation in the UK as measured by the CPI between 2000 and 2014. The first point to note is that prices in the UK, as measured by the CPI, were rising throughout this period, though at different rates. For example, in 2008 the rate of inflation was 2.2% in January. This means that the total price of the basket of goods purchased by the 'average' household was 2.2% higher than in January 2007. However, by September 2008 the rate of inflation had risen to 5.2% (when compared to prices in September 2007). Thus over the first nine months of 2008, prices in the UK were rising and doing so at an increasing rate.

Key terms

Deflation is the rate of decrease of the general price level and the corresponding rise in the value of money. It has become more common recently as a number of countries have experienced falls in their general price levels.

Disinflation occurs when prices are rising, but at a decreasing rate.

There is a somewhat different story of price changes in late 2011 and early 2012. Once again prices rose, but they were increasing at a slower rate. In September 2011 the rate of inflation, as measured by the CPI, was again 5.2% when compared with a year earlier. However, over the next nine months, though prices continued to increase, they did so at a declining rate. In June 2012 the rate of inflation was 2.4%. When prices rise at a falling rate, this is termed disinflation, and two recent periods of disinflation in the UK are illustrated in Figure 40.1.

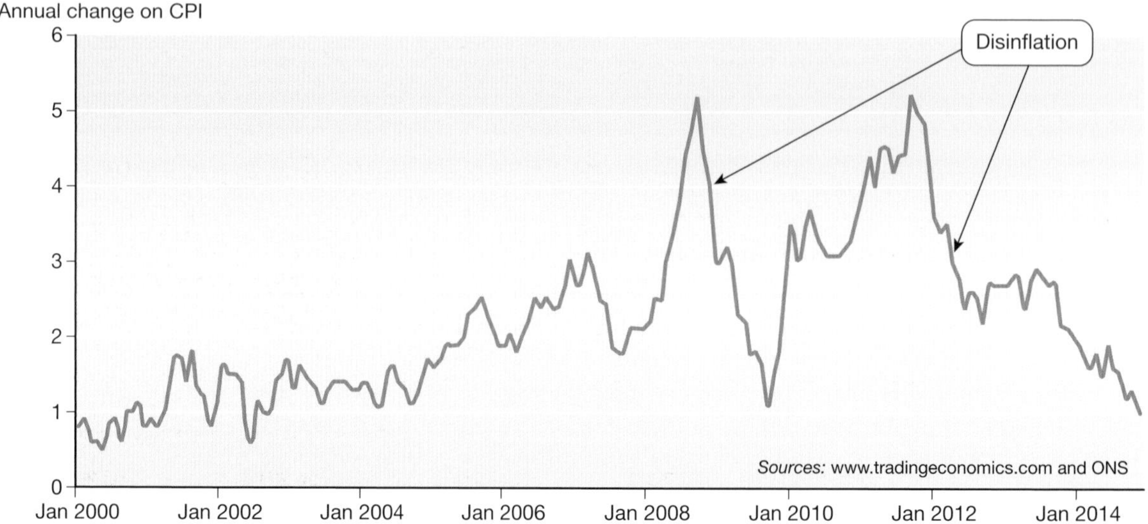

Figure 40.1 *UK inflation as measured by the CPI, 2000–14*

The key distinction between inflation and disinflation is the rate of change of prices. In both cases prices are rising, but with disinflation they are rising less quickly over time.

The core inflation rate

This is another measure of inflation, which is based on the CPI but excludes certain products whose prices are volatile. There are several ways of calculating the core inflation rate. Basically it is the CPI rate of inflation less prices that are subject to wide short-term fluctuations. For example:

- food prices are volatile due to fluctuations in supply and the activities of speculators;
- oil prices are volatile for reasons relating to both supply and demand.

The purpose of calculating the core inflation rate is to measure the underlying rate of inflation in the economy by excluding items subject to short-term fluctuations. However, it is not calculated by the ONS, and the Bank of England does not set targets for it.

Deflation and deflationary policies

Deflation is the opposite of inflation: it is a situation in which the general level of prices is falling and consequently the value of money is rising. The rate of inflation is negative and thus households and firms find that they are able to buy an increased quantity of goods and services with a given sum of money.

Deflation is less common than inflation but does occur and has become more frequent over recent years as the global economy has experienced a period in which rates of inflation have been relatively low. At the start of 2015 the 19 EU member states that use the euro as their national currency entered a period of falling prices. Figure 40.2 shows the rate of inflation for these countries (collectively called the 'eurozone') from 2004 to 2014.

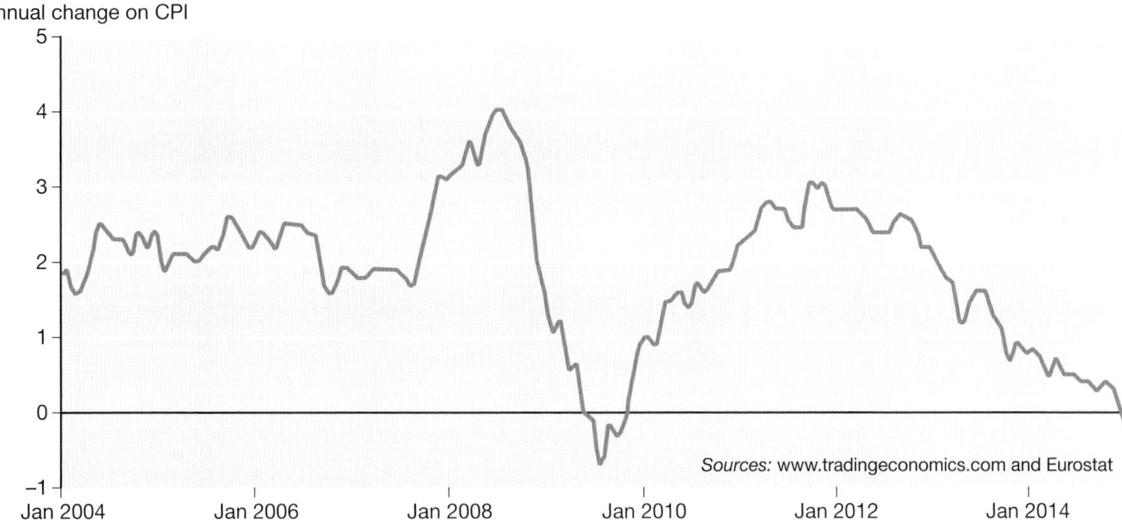

Figure 40.2 *Eurozone inflation rate as measured by the CPI, 2004–14*

Figure 40.2 shows that the eurozone countries have already experienced a period of deflation in 2009, reaching a low of –0.7% in July. This deflation followed a prolonged period of disinflation associated with the recession. Since 2012 the general price level in the eurozone countries has risen increasingly slowly and became negative at –0.3% in February 2015. This overall figure disguises the fact that some of the eurozone's member states are suffering more serious deflation: the inflation rate in Greece was –2% and in Hungary it was –1.0%. The European Central Bank has set a target for inflation in the eurozone of just below 2%.

The dangers of deflation

It may appear that a period of deflation could be a positive experience for an economy because firms and consumers possess money which is increasing in value. However, this increase in value is likely to stop them spending as they wait for prices to fall further. A sudden fall in consumption and hence aggregate demand is likely to result in firms reducing production and making employees redundant. The outcome can be a dramatic reduction in real GDP.

Aggregate demand in an economy that is suffering from deflation will fall for a second reason. The burden of debts will increase. Thus households that have mortgages and firms that have loans will find that the real value of these debts increases. This will make households and firms less willing to spend money and extremely reluctant to finance consumption or investment by borrowing, as the value of these debts will increase too. In addition, almost all governments have debts and some have very large debts. Deflation increases their value, so this may lead them to reduce expenditure.

Finally, real interest rates (that is actual interest rates minus the rate of inflation) will become positive. If deflation is occurring at –2%, this means that the value of savings will rise at 2% annually. This is likely to encourage saving at the expense of consumption and investment.

It is for such reasons that central banks such as the Bank of England set a low but positive figure as a target for the rate of inflation. The target rate of the Bank of England is 2%, which encourages spending in the short term and slowly erodes the real value of debts.

Deflationary policies and the price level

In managing their economies, governments throughout the world have implemented deflationary policies at times. These are policies designed to lower the level of economic activity and would include raising interest rates or cutting government expenditure. (We will look in detail at government economic policies in Topic 9.) Deflationary policies are often implemented with the intention of lowering inflationary pressure in an economy, but the normal outcome is disinflation rather than deflation.

Factors causing changes in the price level

The causes of inflation and deflation are normally divided into two categories: demand-pull factors and cost-push factors. As a result, economists often refer to demand-pull and cost-push inflation.

Demand-pull factors

This cause of inflation has its origins in increases in the level of aggregate demand in an economy that pushes up prices. Increases in aggregate demand have the potential

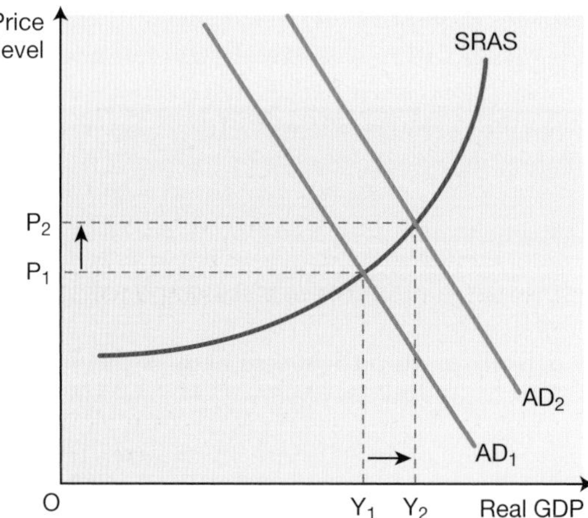

Figure 40.3 *The creation of demand-pull inflation*

Key terms

A **deflationary policy** is an action by governments or other authorities implemented with the intention of reducing aggregate demand.

Demand-pull inflation is a rise in the general price level that results from an increase in aggregate demand.

Cost-push inflation arises from firms facing increased costs of production and originates in the supply side of the economy.

Depreciation is a fall in the value of a country's currency against other currencies.

to place considerable upward pressure on prices, especially if an economy is operating at, or near to, full capacity and is unable to increase production significantly to match the rise in aggregate demand. Figure 40.3 illustrates such as situation in which the short-run aggregate supply curve is relatively steep or inelastic as the economy is near to full capacity. In such circumstances, prices will need to rise significantly from P_1 to P_2 to act as an incentive for firms to increase output further. This price rise does attract additional output (from Y_1 to Y_2) and increases employment.

Demand-pull inflation is associated with a positive output gap in which actual GDP exceeds potential GDP. We studied output gaps in Chapter 38. A number of factors may cause aggregate demand to rise and to create a situation where aggregate demand outstrips the ability of the economy to supply goods and services.

1 Increases in the supply of money

As long ago as 1911 Irving Fisher, an American economist, argued in 'the equation of exchange' that the price level in an economy had a direct relationship with the amount of money in circulation. Fisher's work led later economists to argue that, in the short run at least, real output in an economy is not responsive to increases in the money supply and demand. Thus in the short run an increase in the amount of money in an economy (termed the 'money supply') may only result in an increase in the price level.

Many governments and monetary authorities have recognised the importance of this relationship and have sought to control the amount of money in the economy. This is a challenging objective in a modern economy with diverse forms of money. However, the belief remains that too much money in circulation has the potential to fuel aggregate demand beyond the economy's ability to supply goods and services.

2 Consumer and business confidence

If consumers are confident about the security and levels of income they expect to receive in the future, this can encourage borrowing and spending, boosting aggregate demand to levels that the economy cannot match in terms of production of goods and services. If this is accompanied by high levels of lending by banks and other financial organisations (effectively increasing the supply of money), the impact can be considerable. Remember that consumption is by far the largest element of aggregate demand in the UK and so large increases in this component can quickly affect the price level in the economy.

In the short run, spending by firms may have a similar effect. However, if firms are investing, this can be expected to increase the productive capacity of the economy in the longer term, reducing the pressure on the price level arising from increases in aggregate demand.

3 A depreciation in the exchange rate

If a country's exchange rate falls against other currencies, it means that more of that currency is needed to buy a unit of another currency. For example, in July 2014 an American dollar could be bought for 58 pence; by January 2015 the value of the pound had fallen so that a dollar was worth 66 pence. This process is termed depreciation and has two important consequences: the price of UK exports overseas declines, and the price of imports in the UK rises.

Both of these factors can contribute to a rise in aggregate demand (see Figure 40.4). Demand for exports may rise, and that for imports fall, and these effects will be greater if demand for exports and for imports is price elastic. Rising exports and falling imports will boost aggregate demand by increasing the value of the net exports component of aggregate demand. Some of the demand for imports may be switched to domestically produced goods and services, increasing consumption and boosting aggregate demand further.

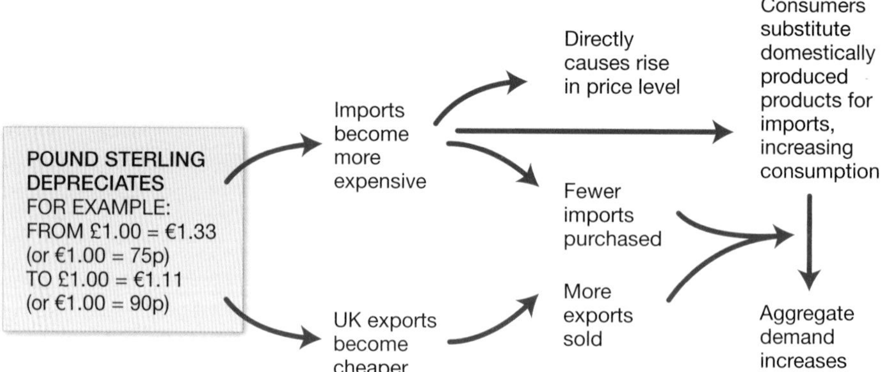

Figure 40.4 *Depreciation and demand-pull inflation*

4 Decisions by government

A decision by a government to increase the level of its expenditure can have a direct impact on the price level because government expenditure is a component of aggregate demand. In addition, decisions to cut levels of taxation may add to aggregate demand by increasing consumer confidence, resulting in higher levels of consumption.

Cost-push factors

This form of inflation is caused by the rising cost of inputs to the production process. In part this may be caused by rising domestic costs, such as wages. If wages increase faster than the level of productivity achieved by the workforce, the result is rising unit labour costs. This means that the cost of the labour input to a unit of output rises. This puts firms under pressure to raise prices to maintain their profits, especially if wages are a high proportion of total costs, and this increases inflationary pressures.

One of the factors contributing to the low and declining rate of inflation in the UK since the start of 2012 is real wages. We look at this in more detail in Real World Economics 40.1.

However, events in the global economy can also contribute to cost-push inflation in the UK. If major trading partners are suffering from relatively high rates of inflation, this can be 'imported' in the form of higher priced imports. As an 'open' economy, which imports and exports a large proportion of its production, the UK is vulnerable to this source of inflation. At the time of writing (March 2015), inflation rates in the UK's major trading partner, the European Union, are very low, which partly explains the recent period of disinflation in this country.

Changes in the prices of important commodities (such as wheat, oil and steel) on global markets can also have significant effects on cost-push inflation in the UK. We shall explore the impact of changes in commodity prices and in other economies in the following sections.

REALWORLD
ECONOMICS 40.1

Falling real wages in the UK

British workers have suffered an 'unprecedented' decline in real wages over the past six years, with the average employee £2000 worse off since the financial crisis hit, according to new research by the National Institute of Economic and Social Research (NIESR).

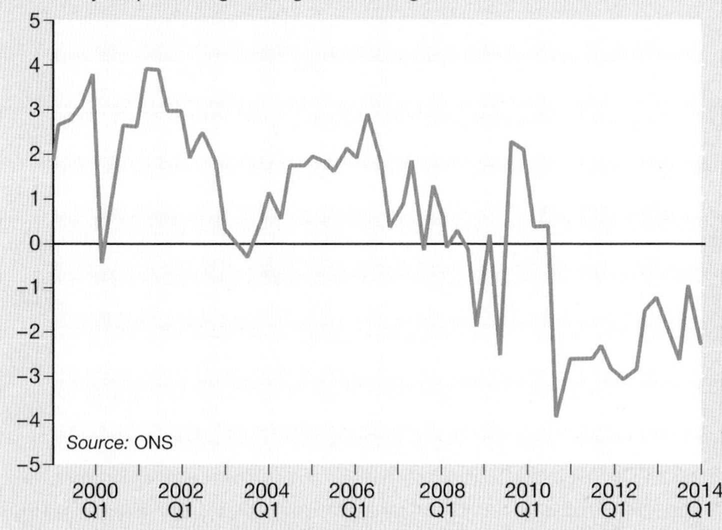

Figure 40.5 *Real wages in the UK, 2000–14*

The average worker saw an 8% decline in real wages between 2008 and 2013. 'The scale of the real wage falls is historically unprecedented, certainly in the past 50 years where broadly comparable records exist,' said the authors of the report.

Official data this month showed that workers experienced a 7.6% fall in real wages over the past six years. However, the research published by NIESR revealed that young workers, among the hardest hit by the downturn, also saw the biggest decline over the period, with pay falling by 14% between 2008 and 2013.

Source: Daily Telegraph, 1.5.14

Exercise

1 Explain the ways in which falling real wages in an economy might reduce inflationary pressures. *(9 marks)*

How changes in world commodity prices affect UK inflation

The UK imports many of the commodities it requires including metals, minerals, food and textiles. In 2011, commodities made up a substantial proportion of UK imports and these included the following items:

- *Minerals such as oil* Imports were valued at £69.23 billion, representing 12.55% of total UK imports.
- *Foodstuffs* Expenditure on this category of imports totalled £57.77 billion or 10.48% of the value of imported goods and services.

Number crunching
Use the information here to calculate the total value of UK imports in 2011.

As a result, changes in the prices of commodities such as wheat, rice and oil on world markets can have a significant effect on the rate of inflation in the UK via the cost-push mechanism. In the UK the long-term price movements in food and motor fuels have been two of the main causes of price changes. Both these product groups have a significant impact on inflation for two reasons:

- they are part of the basket of goods and services that is used to calculate the CPI;
- they are used in other products and so can affect prices indirectly. For example, oil is the basis of fuel that is used to transport many goods nationally and internationally as well as being used as a raw material in the production of products, including plastics. Thus oil has a significant effect on inflation.

Figure 40.6 shows the UK's rate of inflation as measured by the CPI alongside the rate of inflation for these two product groups. It is apparent that the prices of these two product groups show some correlation to CPI and that they are major contributors to the rate of inflation. For example, in February 2011 they contributed 1.2% to the UK's rate of inflation. If the prices of these two product groups had not changed, the UK's rate of inflation would have been 3.2% rather than the actual figure of 4.4%.

Figure 40.6 *The contribution of food and fuel to UK inflation, 2009–14*

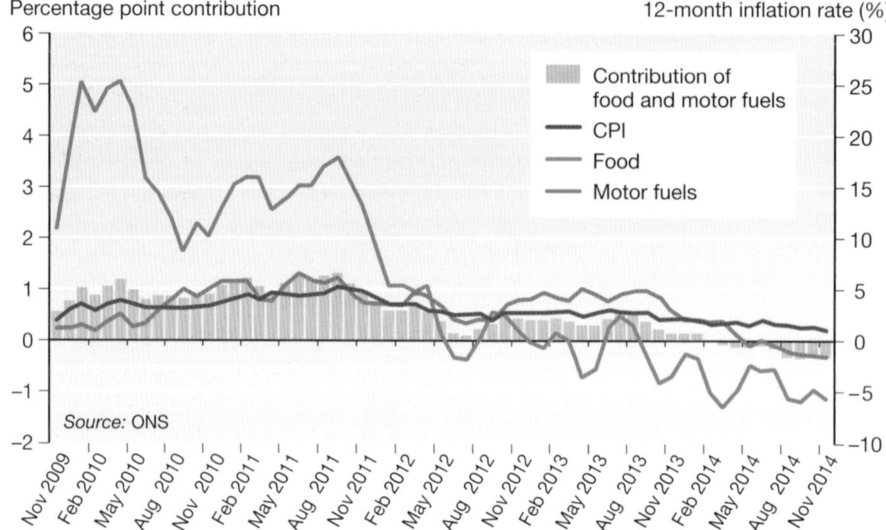

Recently, however, the prices of these two product groups have been falling. Weak global demand for oil alongside increased production by oil-exporting economies such as Saudi Arabia and rising output of shale oil in the USA have all contributed to falling prices. Wheat prices fell in 2014 following a good harvest: this has reduced the price of basic products such as pasta and bread and has made animal feed cheaper, potentially lowering the price of meat. Thus in November 2014 the prices of motor fuels and food had a negative impact on the rate of CPI inflation in the UK. The actual rate was 1.0%. Without the deflationary effects of these products it would have been 1.37%.

How changes in other economies affect UK inflation

The UK economy is becoming more integrated with other economies as a consequence of the process of globalisation whereby many markets are becoming international (or global) in nature. This means that the potential for events in other economies to have an impact on the UK economy is growing. Changes in other countries can have an effect on a range of UK macroeconomic indicators, including the rate of inflation.

The effect of emerging markets

Key term

An **emerging market** describes an economy that has a low income per capita but is enjoying high rates of economic growth.

Emerging markets are an essential part of the process of globalisation. Globalisation has made international trade more possible by reducing barriers to trade while improving international transport and communication links. Political change in countries such as China has also encouraged this process.

The UK has benefited in some ways from the high rates of economic growth in emerging economies such as China, India, Brazil and Russia. The rapid growth of the

Chinese economy has been based on its enormous supply of low-cost labour, enabling it to manufacture goods cheaply. This has contributed to falls in the real prices of many consumer products such as televisions over the last 20 years, helping to keep inflation low. Research by the Bank of England suggested that cheap imports from China reduced UK inflation by about 0.2% per annum over the period 2000–04.

However, activities in emerging markets also have the potential to add to UK inflation. Rising demand for some globally traded commodities in huge economies such as Brazil and China can lead to price rises as supply of the products becomes relatively low. This can be seen in the rising demand for minerals such as oil, copper and iron ore that has taken place at times since the mid-1990s, but also in the rising demand for some food products as consumers' incomes increase in these countries. Consumption of beef in emerging markets such as China, India, Vietnam and Mexico is forecast to rise strongly by 2030. This has the potential to increase global prices and to impact on the rate of inflation in the UK.

Rates of inflation overseas

The UK can import inflation from abroad if its major trading partners are suffering from relatively high rates of inflation and if exchange rate changes do not eliminate the effects. As we saw earlier in this chapter, the rate of inflation in the eurozone, the UK's major trading partner, was –0.3% in February 2015. This reduces the potential of cost-push inflation occurring as import prices rise. However, policy decisions by monetary authorities can change the situation. The European Central Bank (ECB) has taken the decision to inject €60 billion each month into the eurozone economy through a programme known as quantitative easing. This could lead to an increasing rate of inflation in the eurozone economy that may affect the UK rate of inflation.

The economic performance of major economies

It is not simply the rates of inflation overseas that have the potential to impact on inflation in the UK. The broader macroeconomic performance of major economies such as the USA can be a determinant of the rate of inflation in the UK. The American economy is performing relatively strongly at the time of writing, with its growth in GDP reaching 5% in the third quarter of 2014. This increase in demand in a very large economy is helping to boost demand for exports of commodities and goods and services from other countries. By helping to hold aggregate demand up, it may prevent inflation rates from falling to very low levels in some countries. This includes the UK, which is a major trading partner of the USA.

The US economy can impact on UK inflation in another way. Many commodities are priced in dollars, including oil. If the dollar rises in value, then more pounds are required to buy a barrel of oil, which has the potential to add to UK inflation. As an example of this factor, the dollar price of zinc rose by only 1.5% between the end of July and November 2014. However a rise in the value of the dollar against the euro meant that German car parts manufacturers had to pay 15% more in euros for zinc.

Changes in exchange rates in any country with which the UK trades can affect the rate of inflation. For example, if economic policy decisions taken by the Japanese government result in the value of the Japanese yen falling against the pound, this will result in imports from Japan becoming cheaper in the UK and will help to restrict the rate of inflation.

Improvements in technology and productivity

Advances in technology allow industries overseas to supply products more cost effectively. This reduces inflationary pressures in the UK because it has the potential to reduce the price of imported goods and services. As the UK is an open economy and dependent on international trade, such advances can have a considerable impact on price stability.

Similarly, improvements in productivity in foreign economies offer the possibility for UK firms and households to purchase goods and services more cheaply, again helping to reduce cost-push pressures.

Review questions

Total: 48 marks

1 Define the term 'inflation'. *(3 marks)*

2 In which of the following situations is an economy suffering from disinflation?
A The annual rate of inflation changes from 4% to 2.5%
B The annual rate of inflation has changed from –2% to –1%
C The annual rate of inflation is zero
D The annual rate of inflation is constant at 2% *(1 mark)*

3 Explain why economists might be interested in the UK's core inflation rate. *(4 marks)*

4 In which of the following situations is an economy suffering from deflation?
A The annual rate of inflation is falling from 4% to 2.5%
B The annual rate of inflation has risen from 2% to 5%
C The annual rate of inflation is zero
D The annual rate of inflation is constant at –2% *(1 mark)*

5 Explain why governments try to avoid periods of deflation. *(8 marks)*

6 Which of the following is an example of demand-pull inflation?
A A rise in consumer confidence and the level of consumption
B A rise in the price of wheat
C A rise in average real wages
D A rise in the rate of inflation in a major trading partner

7 Explain how a depreciation in the value of the pound might result in demand-pull inflation. *(7 marks)*

8 Explain the effects of a sustained fall in real wages, such as that experienced in the UK recently, on the rate of inflation. *(9 marks)*

9 Explain why changes in the prices of commodities such as wheat and oil can have a significant impact on the rate of inflation in the UK. *(6 marks)*

10 Explain the possible effects of the growth of emerging economies such as China and Brazil on the rate of inflation in the UK. *(9 marks)*

The balance of payments on current account

This chapter looks in some detail at the current account of the balance of payments. It outlines the overall structure of the UK's balance of payments and examines the items that make up the current account. We consider the distinction between a deficit and a surplus on the current account of the balance of payments as well as the factors that determine the balance recorded on the current account.

The importance of international trade

In the nineteenth century the British economist David Ricardo developed the most fundamental argument in support of international trade. His theory of comparative advantage states that countries benefit from international trade even if they are inefficient at producing goods and services relative to their competitors. Ricardo's theory shows that output in an economy is greater if the economy concentrates on producing products at which it is most efficient (i.e. in which it has the least disadvantage, or comparative advantage). Such concentration on a few products is known as **specialisation** and was covered in detail in Chapter 13. Ricardo's theory sets out the benefits of international trade in terms of higher levels of GDP. Some economists do not believe that all economies gain from trade and they frequently cite the disadvantages of international trade to underdeveloped countries. Despite this, there is a widespread view that it brings many benefits.

David Ricardo – the British political economist who developed the theory of comparative advantage

The principle of **comparative advantage** says that countries achieve the highest possible levels of GDP by using the resources available to them to produce goods and services in which they are least disadvantaged and then by engaging in international trade.

There is evidence that there is a statistical link between international trade and economic growth. Periods of rapid economic growth are associated with times in which trade has grown quickly. The HSBC Bank has forecasted that up to 2030 international trade will grow by around 8% a year, while GDP growth is expected to be around 4% annually. Economies that can engage as fully as possible in international trade will stand to benefit from engaging in markets that are expected to grow quickly.

Key terms

International trade is the sale of goods and services across national frontiers.

The **theory of comparative advantage** states that even relatively inefficient economies can benefit from international trade.

Economies of scale are the advantages that a firm gains due to an increase in its size or in the size of the industry in which it operates.

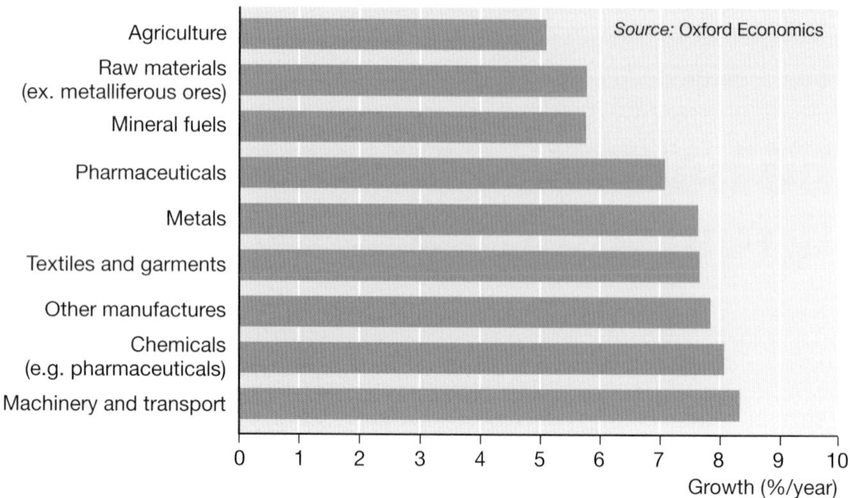

Figure 41.1 *Forecast growth in global trade by sector, 2014–30*

Figure 41.1 shows high growth rates forecast for a range of industries, from the primary sector (agriculture and minerals) to highly specialised manufactured products such as pharmaceuticals.

International trade brings other benefits to economies, though these relate to the principle of comparative advantage.

1 More competitive industries

Industries that are open to the full force of global competition as a consequence of international trade have to be highly efficient to survive. A fiercely competitive environment demands the most effective use of resources and assists economies in maximising output and GDP from a given stock of resources. This can promote high levels of labour and total or multi-factor productivity, which can spill over into industries that may not be engaged directly in international trade.

2 Innovation

The need to sell products in a global market encourages firms to adopt innovative and efficient approaches to production and to develop new products that have an international appeal. The American technology industry led by companies such as Google, Apple and Microsoft is a good example of how trade can act as an impetus to innovative processes and products.

3 Benefits of scale

The size of even the largest single economy is dwarfed by the global economy. International trade provides the basis for firms and industries to benefit from economies of scale by selling internationally rather than just nationally. In Chapter 15 we saw that economies of scale allow firms to produce goods and services more cheaply because their costs are reduced. This can help firms to achieve higher profits, which then means they can invest in more productive techniques, or lower prices, and to benefit from higher sales, promoting employment and growth in GDP. The latter approach is more likely in international markets in which demand is price elastic.

REALWORLD
ECONOMICS 41.1

The UK's geographical pattern of trade

The European Union (EU) accounted for 45% of UK exports and 52% of imports into the UK in 2013. The EU's share of UK trade has declined in recent years. The EU's share of UK exports fell from 53% to 45% between 2003 and 2013. The EU's share of UK imports fell from 58% to 52% over the same period. The economic growth expectations for the EU are low, with the Economist Intelligence Unit forecasting rates of around 1.8% per annum for 2016–18.

The share accounted for by four major emerging economies, known as the BRICs (Brazil, Russia, India and China), has increased rapidly. In absolute terms, however, trade with these countries is still much lower than with the EU. In 2013, the BRICs made up 7% of UK exports (up from 4% in 2003) and 10% of UK imports (up from 5% in 2003). China is by some way the most significant UK trading partner among the BRICs.

Source: Adapted from Economic Indicators, November 2014 (Research Paper 14/58), House of Commons Library

Table 41.1 *The UK's largest trading partners, 2013*

Exports				Imports			
Rank	**Country/ area**	**£ billion**	**(%)**	**Rank**	**Country/ area**	**£ billion**	**(%)**
1	USA	90.1	17.6	1	Germany	66.6	12.3
2	Germany	42.7	8.3	2	USA	48.7	9.0
3	Netherlands	35.6	7.0	3	Netherlands	41.4	7.6
4	France	32.2	6.3	4	France	36.6	6.7
5	Ireland	26.7	5.2	5	China	35.3	6.5
–	EU	228.0	44.5	–	EU	284.0	52.2
–	Non-EU	284.0	55.5	–	Non-EU	260.0	47.8

Source: ONS, Pink Book, 2014

Exercises *Total: 14 marks*

1 Why might slow rates of economic growth in the euro-zone countries be bad news for the UK economy? *(6 marks)*

2 Explain why increasing trade with the BRIC countries might be important for the UK economy in the future. *(8 marks)*

The UK and international trade

The UK is an open economy. This means that international trade is important to it and that exports and imports represent a high proportion of the country's GDP. It is possible to judge the trade openness of the UK economy (or any other) by using a simple ratio:

$$\text{Trade openness ratio} = \frac{\text{Imports + Exports (of goods and services) in £ billion}}{\text{GDP in £ billion}}$$

The UK's trade openness ratio has risen steadily from 53% in 2003 to 66% in 2012, reflecting that the UK has become a more open trading economy over time. In 2012 the UK was the second-ranked economy in the G8 major economies behind Germany in terms of trade openness.

Key terms

An **open economy** is one in which international trade represents a high proportion of its GDP. The UK is an increasingly open economy.

Imports are products bought by households, firms and the government in one country that are produced in other countries.

Exports are products produced in the 'home' economy and sold to customers overseas.

The UK's balance of payments

The structure of the balance of payments

The balance of payments records the financial and trading transactions of the UK with the rest of the world. These transactions are recorded in three main accounts in the balance of payments: the current account; the capital account; and the financial account.

1 The current account

The current account comprises the trade in goods and services as well as flows of primary income and secondary income. The difference in the monetary value of inflows and outflows on these accounts is known as the current account balance.

2 The capital account

The capital account comprises two components: capital transfers between countries; and the sale and purchase of certain assets such as franchises, leases and copyrights.

3 The financial account

The financial account records transactions that result in a change of ownership of financial assets between UK residents and non-residents. Examples include the sale and purchase of shares in foreign businesses by people who live in the UK.

Author tip

Although you need to be aware that the UK's balance of payments has three accounts, the AQA AS specification only requires you to have knowledge of the current account and we shall examine this in detail.

The current account of the balance of payments

There are four components of the current account of the balance of payments that include imports and exports of goods and services as well as certain financial flows.

(a) Trade in goods This component records, for example, the financial effects of a UK resident buying a car imported from Volkswagen in Germany that would result in an outflow of currency from the UK. It also includes the sale of Scotch whisky to retailers in Japan (an export), which would lead to an inflow of currency. This component of the current account is called 'visible' trade.

(b) Trade in services This component of the current account includes the financial effects of imports, such as a UK resident buying insurance from a French company which would cause an outflow of currency. It also records inflows of currency

Key terms

A **current account surplus** exists when inflows of currency recorded on the current account exceed outflows over some period of time.

A **current account deficit** exists when inflows of currency recorded on the current account are smaller than outflows over some period of time.

resulting from the exports of services, such as a bank in the UK providing financial services to a customer in Sweden. Trade in services is termed 'invisible' trade.

(c) Investment income In Chapter 39 we saw that the UK attracts more investment from overseas than any other European country. This inward investment is recorded on the capital account, but any income resulting from it – interest payments, profits or dividends, for example – is investment income and recorded on this section of the current account. For example, in 2014 the French energy company, EDF, agreed to invest £25 billion in a new nuclear power station at Hinkley Point in Somerset. The £25 billion investment will be recorded on the capital account of the balance of payments. However, any profit from the investment that flows back to EDF in France is investment income and would represent an outflow on this component of the current account. Similarly, UK residents and firms receive income from investments overseas, which is recorded as an inflow here. The current account records the balance from investment income received and paid – this is known as primary income.

(d) Total current transfers These are flows of money between countries, such as international aid (e.g. disaster relief) and gifts sent overseas or received from abroad. This is sometimes referred to as secondary income.

Surpluses and deficits on the current account

The current account of the balance of payments receives a lot of attention from the media in the UK. When a newspaper or television programme refers to the UK's balance of payments, it is usually the current account. This indicates the importance of the current account, as it measures the extent to which a country is able to pay for the resources it requires from overseas. The UK government has a macroeconomic objective of achieving a stable balance of payments on current account. This means that over a period of time the inflows from the sales of goods and services overseas will be roughly equal to expenditure on imported goods and services (see Figure 41.2).

If the outflows of currency on a country's current account exceed the inflows over some period of time, it is said to have a current account deficit. In contrast, if the inflows of currency are greater than the outflows for an economy over a period of time, it is said to have a current account surplus.

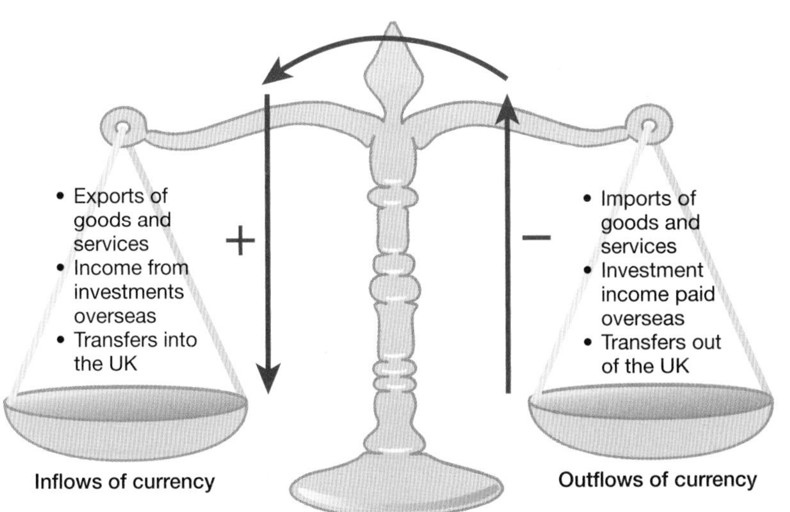

Figure 41.2 *The components of the current account of the balance of payments*

Recent trends in the current account of the UK's balance of payments

Since the 1990s the current account position of the UK has deteriorated, as can be seen from Figure 41.3. Since 2000 the UK's current account has continually been in deficit and this deficit worsened significantly after 2011, amounting to £72.4 billion in 2013, which represented 4.2% of the economy's GDP. This included a £32.1 billion deficit in the UK's trade with the rest of the world in goods and services.

Figure 41.3 *The UK's current account balance 1990–2014*

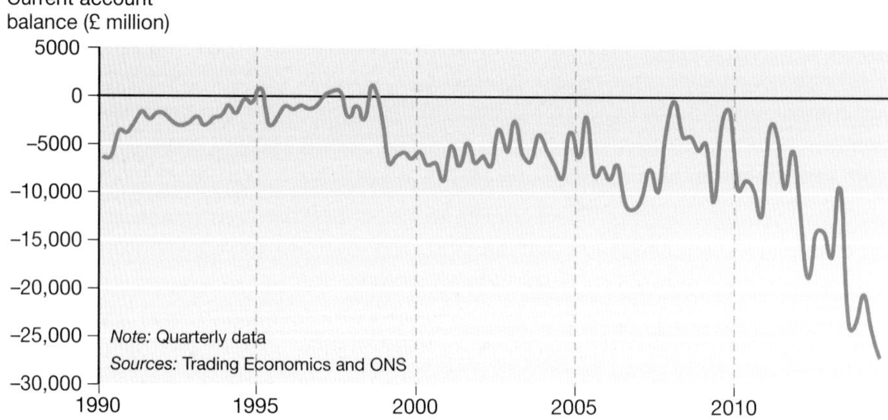

Figure 41.4 shows the more recent performance of the UK's current account balance expressed as quarterly data and as a percentage of the economy's GDP. This reinforces the view that, despite some improvement in 2011, the UK's current account position weakened in 2013 and 2014.

Figure 41.4 *The UK's balance of trade in goods and services 2007–14 (quarterly data)*

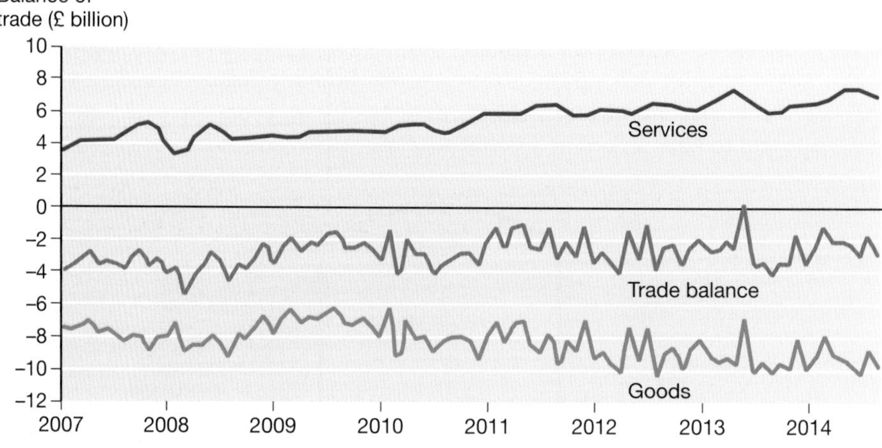

We can see from the data that the UK's balance of trade (i.e. trade in goods and services) is only part of the problem, though the UK's performance in global markets for goods (as opposed to services) remains poor, reflecting a lack of competitiveness of the country's manufacturing sector. The UK traditionally performs better in terms of trade in services than in trade in goods. Figure 41.4 shows that the UK achieved a positive balance in its trade in services over the period 2007–14, while recording a deficit on its trade in goods over the same period. The deficit on goods has generally been larger than the surplus earned on services, resulting in an overall deficit on trade in goods and services.

Despite the UK's poor performance in global markets for manufactured goods, the deficit on the current account is principally caused by patterns of currency flows associated with investment income and transfers. Table 42.2 shows that in 2014, net investment income and transfers recorded a figure of –£64.1 billion. This figure represents the difference between the overall current account balance (–£97.9 billion) and the balance of trade in goods and services (–£33.8 billion).

Table 41.2 *The components of the UK's current account balance, 2012–14*

	Goods & services (£ billion)			Current account	
Year (quarter)	Exports	Imports	Balance	£ billion	% GDP
2012	500.7	535.2	–34.5	–61.9	–3.7
2013	511.3	543.4	–32.1	–72.4	–4.2
2014	507.7	541.5	–33.8	–97.9	–5.5

Source: ONS

A major cause of the deficit on the UK's current account is a dramatic decline in net investment or primary income, which is broadly the balance between the income received by the UK on investments abroad and income paid to foreign owners of investments in the UK.

For many years the UK recorded a surplus on primary income. However, from 2012 onwards the UK's primary income balance went into deficit – a deficit that has grown. Between 2012 and 2014 the UK has experienced a sudden movement from surplus to deficit on its primary income component of its current account.

What has caused the decline in the UK's primary income position? A major factor has been a decline in earnings from investments overseas. This has been particularly the case with regard to the UK's investments in the 19 eurozone countries where returns have been low, as these economies have performed very poorly over the last few years.

Influences on the current account of the balance of payments

The UK's current account of the balance of payments (as for any other country) is determined by a number of factors that can be classified as internal or external factors (see Figure 41.5).

Internal factors

Productivity

A productive economy will use a minimal quantity of its factors of production to produce each unit of output. This means that it can produce a greater volume of goods and services from a given amount of factors of production. This might affect its trade in goods and services in two ways.

- *Sales of exports* A productive economy is likely to be competitive in export markets because it uses relatively few resources to produce goods and services in comparison to rival economies. This enables it to be price competitive, which could result in high export sales in international markets and thus boost the trade balance within its current account.

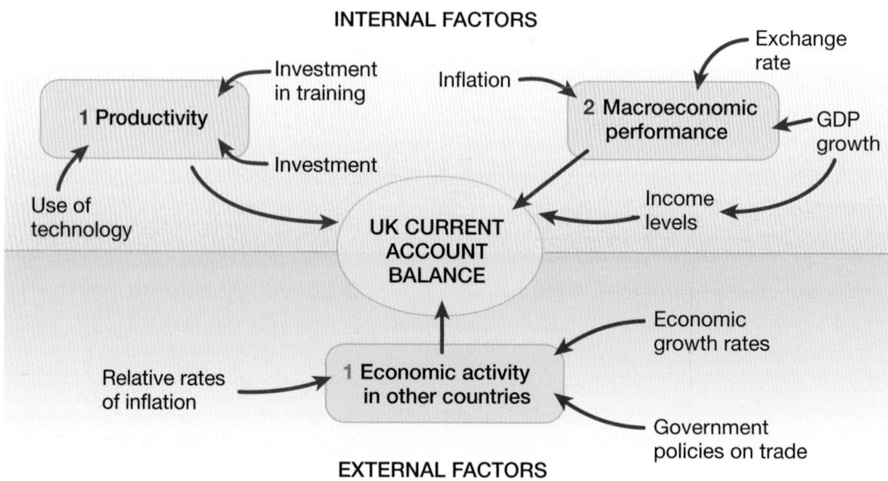

Figure 41.5 *Influences on the UK's current account balance*

- *Purchases of imports* A productive economy will have the potential to produce cost-effective goods and services that may reduce the degree of import penetration, as consumers prefer domestically produced products to imports.

Firms operating in productive economies may also benefit from higher levels of profitability, allowing them to invest in acquiring the latest technology and in training employees to improve labour performance and future productivity. Higher levels of profits also allow firms to invest in new and innovative methods of production that could increase productivity rates further.

Since 2009, Germany has consistently recorded a current account surplus in excess of 6% of its GDP. At the same time the German economy has achieved high rates of productivity, with its rate of multifactor productivity (productivity based on all inputs, not just labour) rising annually at 2% over the same period.

Macroeconomic performance

The relationship between a country's macroeconomic performance and the balance on the current account of its balance of payments is complex.

GDP levels and growth Many economists accept that a positive relationship exists between the level of a country's GDP and the volume of imports. Keynesian economists believe a direct relationship exists, since consumers spend a significant proportion of rising incomes on imported products. Figure 41.6 provides some evidence in support of this view. It shows a relationship, with the change in import purchases showing a slight time delay.

Thus, an economy that is performing strongly and exhibiting high rates of economic growth may experience a deteriorating trade balance on its current account. However, this may be offset to some extent by inward investment. Economies that experience high rates of growth are likely to be attractive to international investors. This may lead to a high level of inward investment that creates or expands businesses, leading to higher exports and reducing import penetration. Thus the current account balance is improved.

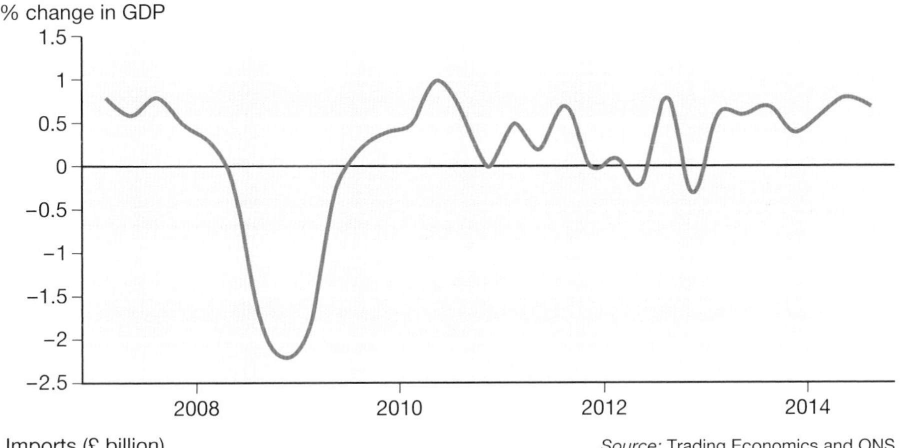

Source: Trading Economics and ONS

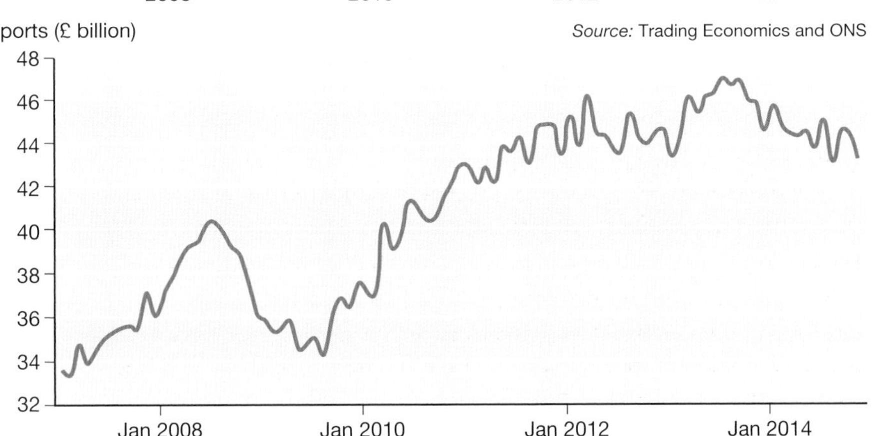

Figure 41.6 *A comparison between GDP growth and the level of imports in the UK, 2007–14*

The exchange rate Exchange rates have the potential to influence all elements of a country's current account balance. Changes in the exchange rate affect the prices paid by foreigners for a country's exports as well as those paid for imports by the country's residents. A rise (or an appreciation) in the exchange rate of the pound sterling means that buyers of UK exports overseas need more of their domestic currency to purchase UK exports. Unless demand is very price inelastic, sales are likely to fall, adversely affecting the current account balance. Simultaneously, such a rise in the exchange rate will make imports cheaper because fewer pounds are required to buy foreign currencies required to purchase imports. Thus a rise in the value of the pound (or any currency) can, after a delay, be expected to weaken a country's current account balance, ceteris paribus. Conversely, a fall (or a depreciation) in the value of the pound will strengthen the current account balance. This relationship is summarised in Table 41.3. A time lag (of possibly 12–18 months) will occur between the change in the exchange rate and the effects on the current account balance.

Table 41.3 *The effects of exchange rate changes on the current account balance*

The exchange rate of pounds	Prices of UK exports overseas (in £s)	Prices of imported products in the UK (in £s)	Possible impact on the current account of the balance of payments
Appreciates (rises)	Increase	Fall	Weakens
Depreciates (falls)	Fall	Increase	Strengthens

Changes in the exchange rate also impact upon inward and outward investment levels and, in the longer term, the level of primary or investment income. As a currency weakens, overseas investors require smaller amounts of their domestic currencies to invest in the UK. This could encourage inward investment, improving the current account position in the longer term. An appreciating currency might discourage investment. However, international investors take decisions based on likely returns as well as the immediate costs of the investment decision.

Inflation A country's relative rate of inflation can have a significant influence on purchases of imports and sales of exports and therefore its current account balance. If a country benefits from comparatively low rates of inflation, it is likely to increase its competitiveness. Its exports may sell well in price competitive markets, and domestic producers will be able to compete effectively (in price terms at least) with imported products. Both these factors can impact positively on the current account balance. In contrast, an economy suffering from relatively high inflation rates may be less internationally competitive, to the detriment of its current account balance.

REALWORLD ECONOMICS 41.2

UK whisky exports

Austerity measures in Southeast Asia helped slow Scotch whisky exports in 2013, leaving flat figures in one of the UK's most valuable industries.

Volumes of the spirit shipped climbed by 2.5% to the equivalent of 1.23 billion 70cl bottles during the 12 months to the end of December 2013, but the value of exports only rose by 0.33% to £4.26 billion in the face of global price pressures.

These figures reveal a stagnation in the global market, with a slowdown in the second half of 2013 following an encouraging start during the first six months. Volumes had previously fallen by around 5% during 2012.

The Scotch Whisky Association (SWA) stated that 'star performers' included the USA, Mexico and India, while the growing popularity of single malt had also contributed to the result. 'Scotch Whisky exports remain strong and the industry's impressive performance makes a major contribution to the UK's trade performance,' said SWA Chief Executive, David Frost. He continued: 'The unprecedented investment programmes in Scotch whisky by producers show that in the long term they are confident that demand will continue to grow'.

Exports to India, Brazil, Mexico and Eastern Europe also grew, with a 38% rise in Poland making it a £60 million market, having grown tenfold since the country joined the EU a decade ago.

However, direct exports to Taiwan, South Korea and Japan all fell in value by between 13% and 15%. China fell out of the top 20 markets, with direct exports declining nearly 30% to £51 million amid a crackdown on conspicuous consumption.

Source: Adapted from *The Courier* (James Williamson), 11.4.14

Exercise

1 To what extent is the level of economic activity in foreign countries the major determinant of exports of luxury goods such as Scotch whisky? *(15 marks)*

External factors

Key term
Import penetration measures the value of imports as a percentage of consumption.

A country's current account on its balance of payments is equally subject to influences from outside the country – primarily the level of economic activity in other countries. If other economies are generally experiencing lower rates of inflation, then the country's current account is likely to weaken because the country loses export sales and import penetration increases.

High rates of economic growth overseas can stimulate a country's export sales. This may occur because consumers have increased incomes and will spend a proportion of their disposable incomes on imports (i.e. another country's exports). This can be a particularly important factor if the exporting country sells products that are at the luxury end of the spectrum and are income elastic.

Finally, the policies of foreign governments with regard to trade can influence the current account balance of other countries. By taking policy decisions that encourage free trade, governments can create an environment in which exporters find it easier to make sales to the benefit of the country's balance of trade.

Review questions

Total: 48 marks

1 Define the term 'balance of payments'. *(3 marks)*

2 Explain two benefits to an economy from engaging in international trade. *(8 marks)*

3 The currency flows associated with which of the following would *not* be recorded on the current account of the balance of payments?
A The sale of clothing manufactured in the UK to buyers in Italy
B The purchase of South African wine by a UK supermarket chain
C An investment in building a retail park in the UK by a Chinese bank
D Interest payments to a company in Dubai on an investment it has made in the UK *(1 mark)*

4 Explain the difference between a surplus and a deficit on a country's current account of its balance of payments. *(5 marks)*

5 Which of the following is an example of invisible trade?
A Chinese parents buying education for a son at Warwick University
B The sale of beef produced in the UK to food processors in Slovakia
C The purchase of tablet computers manufactured in Taiwan by UK retailers
D An investment by a Japanese investor in a Scottish insurance company *(1 mark)*

6 Explain one possible reason why the UK's current account position deteriorated after 2012. *(6 marks)*

7 Explain why an improvement in a country's productivity rates is likely to improve the current account position of a country's balance of payments. *(7 marks)*

8 Which of the following is *most likely* to weaken a country's current account position, ceteris paribus?
A A fall in the value of the country's currency
B A rise in the disposable incomes available to a country's consumers
C A fall in a country's relative rate of inflation
D Increased investment in training by firms in the economy *(1 mark)*

9 Explain how a change in the value of a country's currency might affect its current account balance. *(8 marks)*

10 Explain how the level of economic activity overseas might influence the balance on a country's current account of its balance of payments. *(8 marks)*

Chapter 42

Possible conflicts between macroeconomic policy objectives

This chapter examines how negative and positive output gaps relate to unemployment and inflationary pressures. It analyses the possible causes of policy conflicts in both the short run and in the long run and considers how economic policies might be used to try to reconcile such conflicts.

Output gaps, unemployment and inflation

In Chapter 38 we encountered output gaps and explored their characteristics and their relationship to actual and long-term trend rates of economic growth. We saw that an output gap measures the difference between an economy's actual level of real GDP and its long-term trend level of real GDP. Output gaps can be positive or negative.

- A **positive output gap** occurs when actual GDP exceeds the long-term trend of GDP, for example during the peak stage of the economic cycle. This is associated with high levels of employment and inflationary pressures.
- A **negative output gap** exists when the actual level of real GDP is lower than the long-term trend. In Figure 42.1 this type of output gap can be seen to exist in the trough phase of the economic cycle and is normally accompanied by rising levels of unemployment but a reduction in inflationary pressures. The UK economy experienced a substantial negative output gap for several years following the severe recession of 2008–09.

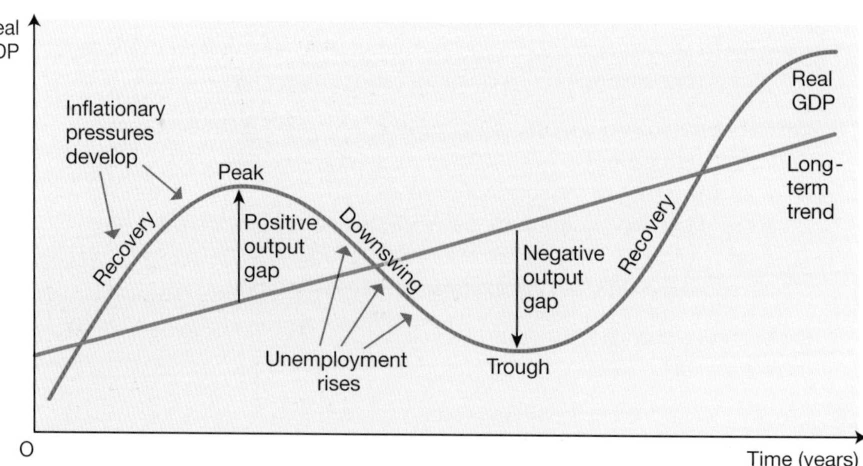

Figure 42.1 *Output gaps, unemployment and inflation*

Positive output gaps and inflationary pressures

As shown in Figure 42.1, inflationary pressures are associated with positive output gaps. As an economy's rate of growth of GDP increases, it exerts upward pressure on prices because resources become increasingly scarce due to rising aggregate demand.

However, these pressures will become more acute as the rate of growth in the economy's GDP exceeds the long-term trend. Once this occurs, the rate of growth becomes unsustainable: the economy is, in effect, operating outside its production possibility boundary.

Positive output gaps occur temporarily and prices play an important part in their existence. Short-term production can exceed the economy's productive capacity in the short term for a number of reasons:

- firms may increase output in response to rising prices, believing that this offers the opportunity to earn higher profits than using resources in some alternative way;
- employees who have been voluntarily unemployed may enter the labour market as wages increase in the belief that real wages are rising;
- some firms may accept that the level of demand for their products is only short term and opt to use temporary techniques, such as paying employees overtime rates, to increase output.

The increase in aggregate demand from AD_1 to AD_2 in Figure 42.2 results in a movement along the short-run aggregate supply curve, increasing real GDP from Y_1 (the full employment level of output) to Y_2. This very high level of output, in excess of the economy's level of productive capacity, is achieved in the short run due to the factors listed above and at the cost of the price level rising to P_2.

However, output at Y_2 is not sustainable in the long term. Firms recognise that profits have not increased in real terms as costs of production have risen and so they reduce output to a level that is sustainable. Employees return to voluntary unemployment once they realise that although money wages have risen, real wages have not. The level of output falls back to Y_1 (the full employment level) and the price level rises to P_3, causing a contraction in aggregate demand. The positive output gap has resulted in a significant increase in the price level from P_1 to P_3.

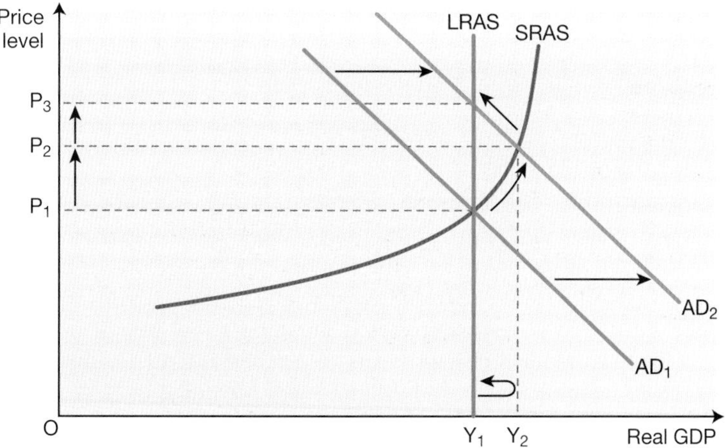

Figure 42.2 *Inflation and positive output gaps*

Negative output gaps and rising unemployment

Negative output gaps are associated with much lower rates of growth in GDP or even with falling growth rates that constitute a recession if they persist for more than six months. The unemployment created by low or negative rates of growth is cyclical unemployment because firms reduce production and less labour is required. Unemployment rises as a consequence, since the supply of labour at current wage rates exceeds the demand for labour.

Wider negative output gaps are likely to result in higher levels of cyclical unemployment. However, unemployment in the UK was not as high as might have been feared following the recession of 2008–09. In the aftermath of the financial crisis and recession, unemployment in the UK reached 2.49 million as measured by the Labour Force Survey. This amounted to an unemployment rate of 7.9%. At the same time France and the USA were experiencing unemployment rates in excess of 9%.

Conflicts between macroeconomic objectives

In Chapter 31 we saw that the UK government pursues four main macroeconomic objectives:

- price stability (i.e. a low rate of inflation);
- sustainable rates of economic growth;
- low unemployment;
- a balanced balance of payments.

We also saw that UK governments have pursued other macroeconomic policy objectives, such as achieving a balance between government income and expenditure (balancing the budget), improving the UK's comparatively low rates of productivity, and promoting greater equality in the distribution of income.

Governments in the UK and elsewhere are unlikely to be able to achieve all of these policies simultaneously. A number of major tradeoffs exist, which means a potentially significant cost for governments pursuing a particular macroeconomic objective.

Author tip

The government and the Bank of England use a range of policies to achieve their macroeconomic policy objectives. These include changing interest rates, altering taxation rates, adjusting the level of government spending and implementing policies to improve the operation of the UK economy. We look at these policies in detail in Topic 9.

The tradeoff between unemployment and inflation

This is arguably the fundamental dilemma facing officials responsible for macroeconomic policy decisions. Any policy designed to increase the level of economic activity in an economy with the aim of reducing the rate of unemployment is likely to increase inflationary pressures, especially as the economy approaches full employment. Equally, a government that is pursuing a low rate of inflation single-mindedly is likely to incur a cost in terms of a rising rate of unemployment. This tradeoff between unemployment and inflation was identified by A W Phillips in the 1950s. We will consider Phillips's work in this area more fully in our companion book, *AQA A-Level Year 2 Economics*.

REALWORLD
ECONOMICS 42.1

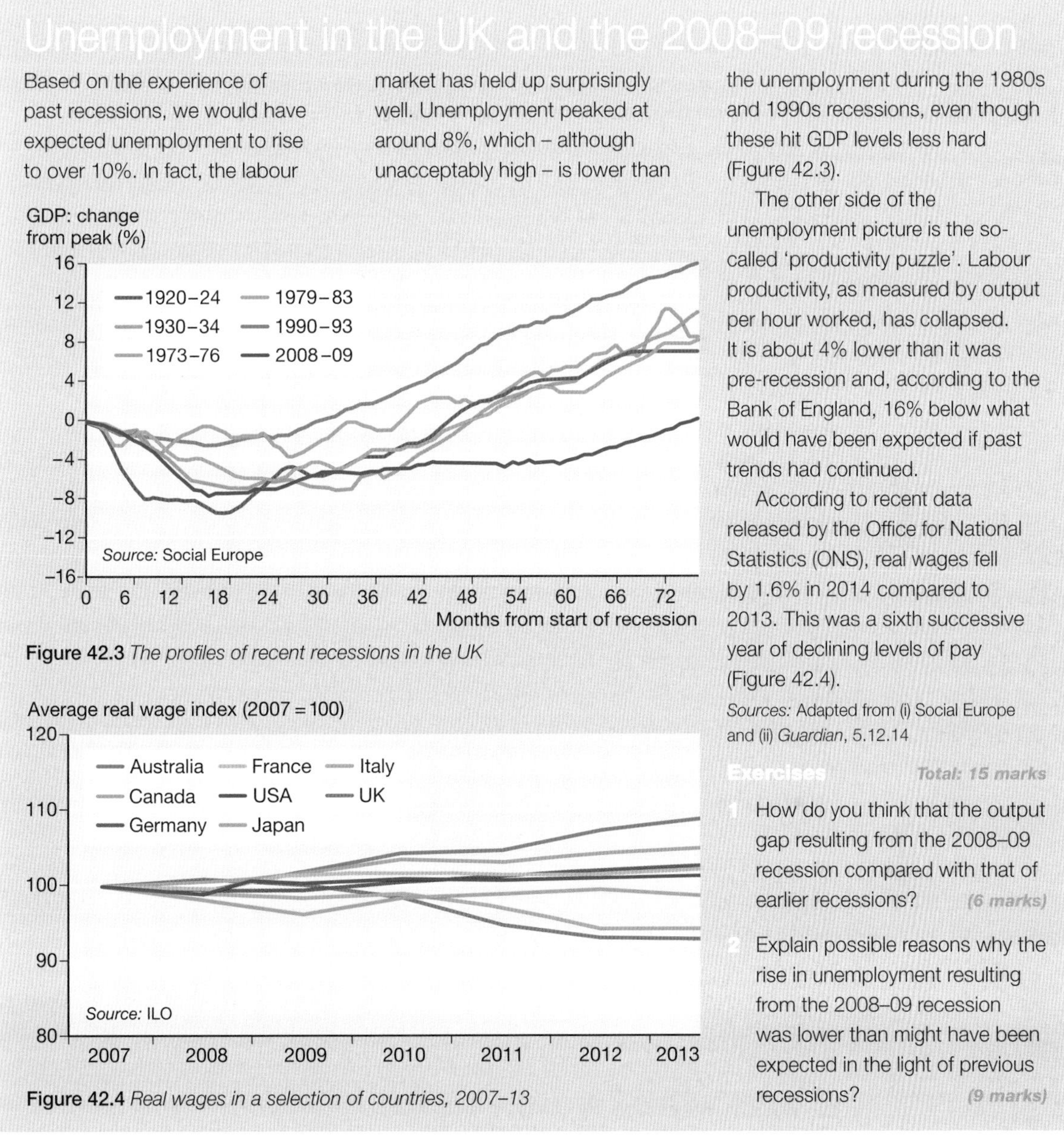

Unemployment in the UK and the 2008–09 recession

Based on the experience of past recessions, we would have expected unemployment to rise to over 10%. In fact, the labour market has held up surprisingly well. Unemployment peaked at around 8%, which – although unacceptably high – is lower than the unemployment during the 1980s and 1990s recessions, even though these hit GDP levels less hard (Figure 42.3).

Figure 42.3 *The profiles of recent recessions in the UK*

Figure 42.4 *Real wages in a selection of countries, 2007–13*

The other side of the unemployment picture is the so-called 'productivity puzzle'. Labour productivity, as measured by output per hour worked, has collapsed. It is about 4% lower than it was pre-recession and, according to the Bank of England, 16% below what would have been expected if past trends had continued.

According to recent data released by the Office for National Statistics (ONS), real wages fell by 1.6% in 2014 compared to 2013. This was a sixth successive year of declining levels of pay (Figure 42.4).

Sources: Adapted from (i) Social Europe and (ii) *Guardian*, 5.12.14

Exercises **Total: 15 marks**

1. How do you think that the output gap resulting from the 2008–09 recession compared with that of earlier recessions? *(6 marks)*
2. Explain possible reasons why the rise in unemployment resulting from the 2008–09 recession was lower than might have been expected in the light of previous recessions? *(9 marks)*

Figure 42.5 illustrates the nature of this tradeoff in the short term. If the government increases aggregate demand by, for example, increasing the level of its own spending, this will shift the aggregate demand curve to AD_2. As a consequence, real GDP rises from Y_1 to Y_2, taking the level of output closer to Y_f, at which full employment is reached. At Y_f, all those who want work at the current wage rate have found employment. Unemployment will be reduced as a result of this action on the part of the government as firms increase employment levels to achieve the higher level of output necessary to generate a real GDP equivalent to Y_2.

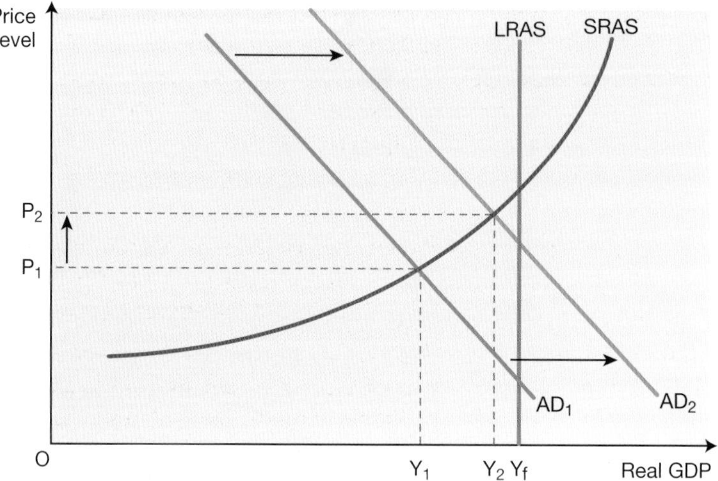

Figure 42.5 *An illustration of the unemployment–inflation tradeoff using an AD–AS diagram*

However, there is a price to be paid for this reduction in the level of unemployment. The increased output can only be achieved at a higher price level. This increase in price is necessary to persuade firms to increase production, offering the prospect of higher profits. The higher prices will cover any additional costs of production (such as overtime rates) and ensure sufficient profits are generated.

If the long-run aggregate supply curve is assumed to be vertical and there is an attempt to reduce unemployment below its long-term level by implementing policies to increase aggregate demand, the only long-term outcome will be an increase in the price level. This process was illustrated in Figure 42.2.

It is possible to argue that this tradeoff has been weaker over recent years in the UK. The UK's rate of inflation has barely been above 5% since the mid-1990s. For much of this period, unemployment has been relatively low, only rising to a little over 8% even during and following the 2008–09 recession.

The tradeoff between economic growth and the current account of the balance of payments

Key term

The **balance of trade** is a part of the current account of the balance of payments and measures the earnings from exports minus the expenditure on imports.

In Chapter 34 we studied injections, withdrawals and the circular flow of income. The analysis showed that injections are assumed to be independent of the level of national income, while a direct relationship exists between withdrawals and the level of national income. This distinction has important implications for decisions by governments on policies to achieve macroeconomic objectives.

If the UK government implements policies to achieve higher levels of GDP by, for example, investing in infrastructure, it will have implications for a country's exports and imports.

Imports

The model of injections and withdrawals assumes that there is a direct relationship between a country's GDP and its level of imports. This occurs because, when an economy is growing strongly, consumption and investment are also likely to be rising quickly as wages and profits will be growing. A proportion of this expenditure will be on consumer and investment products from overseas.

In the case of the UK, imports also have a tendency to increase as a proportion of GDP when GDP itself is rising. This occurs, in part, because the UK manufactures relatively few income elastic consumer products such as computers and televisions. Expenditure on such items increases substantially when GDP and incomes are rising, leading to the UK 'sucking in' more imports.

Exports

Exports are not dependent upon the level of GDP in the domestic (or exporting) nation. Instead they are determined by a range of factors, such as the level of income in other economies as well as the competitiveness of the exporting economy.

The implications of these relationships are that if the UK government takes policy decisions intended to increase the level of GDP to reduce the rate of unemployment, for example, it is likely to worsen the country's balance of trade and its current account balance. This will occur because more imports will be drawn in, while exports may remain relatively unchanged as income levels rise.

Conversely, deflationary policies intended to reduce the rate of inflation by lowering the level of economic activity may improve the balance of trade and hence, ceteris paribus, the current account of the balance of payments by reducing the deficit, or possibly increasing a surplus.

However, in the longer term the relationship between economic growth and the current account may not be so clear. Increased government expenditure could draw in imports and weaken the current account of the balance of payments in the short or medium term. However, if this additional expenditure is focused on increasing the country's productive capacity and competitiveness, it may enable it to sell greater quantities of exports in the longer term and to reduce import penetration. This could lead to an improvement in the current account balance in the long term.

The tradeoff between economic growth and inflation

This is a tradeoff relating to the trend rate of economic growth that exists in an economy. If growth rates are generally below this long-run trend rate of growth, it is not likely to create inflationary pressures. However, periods in which growth rates exceed the trend, when a positive output gap exists, have the potential to create or increase inflationary pressures. Thus, government policy decisions that seek to increase the rate of economic growth can be inflationary if they provoke excessive rates of growth associated with the peak or boom stage of the economic cycle. In such situations the rate of increase of aggregate demand exceeds the rate of increase of aggregate supply in an economy, especially one with little unused productive capacity.

However, economic growth may not always be inflationary, especially if it is short-term growth when the economy is operating below full capacity and within its production possibility boundary. In such circumstances, a scarcity of resources is less likely to bid up prices because firms can increase output by using existing facilities more intensively. Low and stable rates of economic growth, and especially periods of recession, exert little, if any, upward pressure on prices.

At the time of writing (March 2015), the UK economy is growing at a respectable 2.8% annually, slightly above its long-run trend of 2.25%–2.5%. At the same time the UK's rate of inflation has fallen to 0%, a level at which economists are discussing the possibility of deflation occurring in the near future. The downward pressure on prices, though, is an international phenomenon caused in part by falling global prices for important products including food and oil. Furthermore, some of the UK's major trading partners, such as the eurozone countries, are experiencing low rates of inflation or even deflation. The UK is, in effect, importing lower prices. Thus, although a tradeoff can exist between economic growth and inflation, relatively high rates of growth do not always fuel inflation.

Long-term growth is the result of an economy increasing the quantity and quality of available productive resources. This results in a shift of the long-run supply curve to the right. Such a movement, even at a time of rising aggregate demand, can reduce or even eliminate inflationary pressures.

Figure 42.6 illustrates how a rightward shift in the long-run aggregate supply curve can result in a lower price level even when aggregate demand increases from AD_1 to AD_2. In such circumstances an increased quantity of productive resources, or the use of resources with higher productivity rates, allows the economy to meet the increased demand for goods and services without inflationary pressures emerging. In fact, this combination of circumstances may reduce the price level, as occurs in Figure 42.6, from P_1 to P_2.

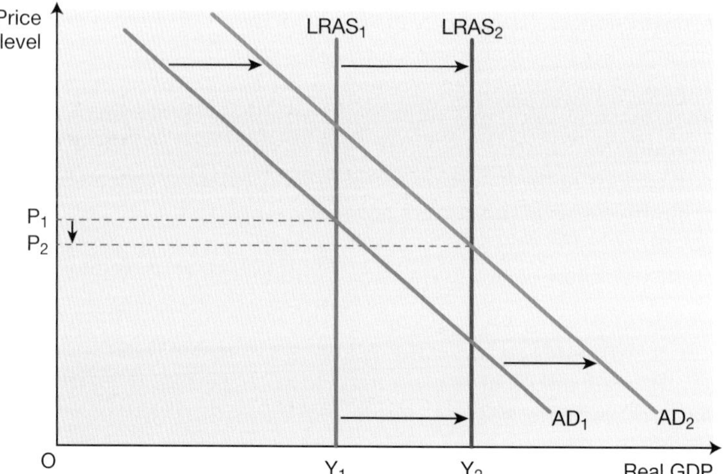

Figure 42.6 *Long-run economic growth shifts the LRAS curve, reducing inflationary pressures*

Other potential conflicts in objectives

Economic growth and protecting the environment

The achievement of acceptable rates of economic growth may have implications for other aspects of economic management. Economic growth can easily have an adverse impact on the environment, and the negative externalities that may accompany growth can reduce its positive effects on economic welfare. Take the UK government's plans to build a high-speed railway (HS2) from London to Birmingham and, in a later stage of construction, to the cities of Manchester and Leeds. The government forecasts that the construction of the first stage of HS2 to Birmingham will increase economic activity in the West Midlands by £4 billion per annum (KPMG's estimate is more conservative, at £2.3 billion – see p. 41), thereby adding significantly to the UK's real GDP.

Construction of HS2 is due to commence in 2017 and to be complete by 2032. Although this may boost economic growth in the UK, the negative impact on the environment of its construction and operation, such as the damage to rural areas in Buckinghamshire, may offset the benefits.

HS2 may boost economic growth, but at the expense of the environment – one of the many policy conflicts faced by the UK government

Economic growth and income equality

In Chapter 31 it was shown that incomes in the UK are not distributed equally amongst the country's inhabitants. The top 10% of earners in the UK have salaries that are equal to more than the bottom 40% of earners combined, according to figures released by the Treasury. The UK government has created flexible labour markets to attract foreign companies to invest and produce in the UK as well as to improve the competitiveness of the UK economy. Flexible labour markets are those that adjust easily and quickly to changes in the demand for labour. This may require a higher proportion of part-time workers, workers on zero hour contracts (with no guaranteed work) and less legal protection for employees at work.

The operation of flexible labour markets can boost the UK's real GDP and contribute to high rates of growth. However, many economists believe that flexible labour markets contribute to a greater inequality of incomes because those working part-time and on zero hour contracts earn lower incomes in relation to employees in full-time permanent jobs.

Reconciling policy conflicts

This chapter has identified a number of conflicts or tradeoffs between the government's macroeconomic objectives. In Topic 9 we study three macroeconomic policies available to the UK government and consider how these may be used to reconcile possible policy conflicts in the short and long run.

Review questions

Total: 52 marks

1 Distinguish between a negative and a positive output gap. *(6 marks)*

2 Explain why a positive output gap might contribute to inflationary pressures in an economy. *(9 marks)*

3 Which type of unemployment is most associated with negative output gaps?
- A Seasonal unemployment
- B Frictional unemployment
- C Structural unemployment
- D Cyclical unemployment *(1 mark)*

4 List four macroeconomic objectives pursued by the UK government. *(4 marks)*

5 Explain, with the aid of an aggregate demand and supply diagram, why an attempt to reduce the level of unemployment in an economy may lead to increased inflationary pressures. *(8 marks)*

6 Explain why a period of rapid economic growth might adversely affect an economy's current account of its balance of payments. *(7 marks)*

7 Which of the following terms describes the earnings from exports minus the expenditure on imports?

A Balance of invisible trade

B Balance of visible trade

C Balance of trade

D Balance of payments *(1 mark)*

8 Why might short-run economic growth not result in inflationary pressures? *(5 marks)*

9 Explain why a high rate of economic growth could damage the physical environment of an economy. *(5 marks)*

10 Explain why the operation of flexible labour markets in the UK might have contributed to increased income inequality. *(6 marks)*

Topic 8 **Exam-style questions**

AS LEVEL PAPER 2

Context – Economic performance

Extract A **Inflation**

The UK economy continues to experience disinflation, and fears of imminent deflation are beginning to appear. The Consumer Prices Index (CPI) grew by 0.5% in the year to December 2014, down from 1.0% in November (see Figure A). In the year to December 2014, food prices fell by 1.9% and prices of motor fuels fell by 10.5%.

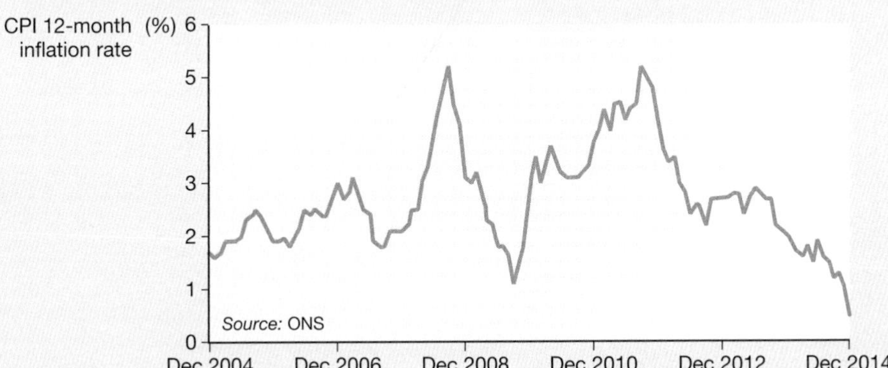

Figure A *The Consumer Prices Index, 2004–14*

The global rate of inflation was 3.8% in 2014, down from 6.4% in 2008 and 5.2% in 2011. The global figure hides significantly different patterns of inflation internationally. Inflation rates in Europe are generally very low: few economies recorded rates in excess of 2% in 2014, and several suffered deflation including Poland, Spain, Greece and Switzerland. Rates in Asia vary but are generally higher, with key economies such as China, India and Malaysia reporting rates of between 1.5% and 5%. Inflation in the USA in 2014 was 1.3%.

Extract B **The current account of the balance of payments**

The UK's current account deficit widened faster than expected in the third quarter of 2014 to reach a record high of £27 billion. The Office for National Statistics (ONS) reported that the deficit in the third quarter of 2014 was £27 billion, up from £24.3 billion in the second quarter and significantly worse than economists' expectations of £23 billion. The current account deficit of £27 billion is equal to 6% of the UK's GDP in the third quarter of 2014.

The widening was due to an increase in the deficit on the primary income account from £8.2 billion in the second quarter to £12.6 billion in the third quarter. A fall in foreign direct investment and an increase in payments to foreign investors were the two main causes of this drop in the primary or investment income element of the current account, according to the ONS.

In a sign of ongoing worries that a further widening of the current account deficit could lead to the value of the pound sterling falling significantly against the dollar, the pound weakened following publication of the data.

There was better news on the trade deficit, however, which narrowed to £9 billion from £9.2 billion in the previous quarter due to a larger surplus on trade in services overseas. The surplus on trade in services for the third quarter equates to 5.1% of GDP for that quarter.

Source: Adapted from *Investment Week*, 23.12.14

Extract C **Economic growth**

The UK's economy performed better than that of any other member of the group of 7 developed economies (G7) in the first three quarters of 2014 (see Figure B). The UK's performance in terms of economic growth is expected to be 3.2% in 2014, and the IMF forecasts that the economy will grow by 2.7% in 2015. The UK economy expanded at its fastest rate in the first three quarters of 2014 than at any time since 2007.

Figure B *UK economic growth for 2014 expected to lead the G7*

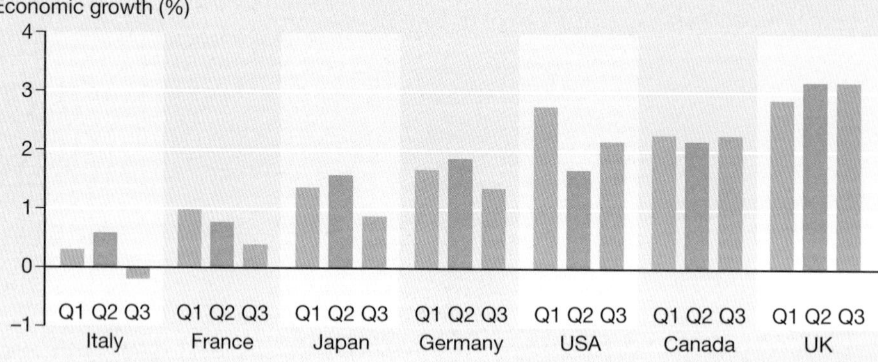

The IMF estimates that the economic growth rate in the USA in 2015 will be 3.1%. Olivier Blanchard, the IMF's Chief Economist, said that Britain and the USA were 'leaving the financial crisis behind and achieving decent growth'. The IMF added, in its World Economic Outlook: 'The United Kingdom's economy is expected to continue to grow strongly. Demand is becoming more balanced, with stronger business investment'.

A comparison of the UK in August–October 2014 with August–October 2013 shows that the number of people:

- in employment increased by 588,000, to 30.8 million;
- unemployed fell by 455,000, to 1.96 million;
- aged from 16 to 64 who were out of work but not seeking or available to work (economically inactive) was unchanged, at 9.06 million.

Source: Adapted from *Daily Telegraph*, 7.10.14

Questions

Total: 50 marks

1 Define the term 'economic growth rate' (Extract C). *(3 marks)*

2 Extract A refers to 'deflation' and 'disinflation'. Explain the difference between these two terms. *(4 marks)*

3 Extract C says that 'stronger business investment' is taking place in the UK. Draw an aggregate demand and aggregate supply diagram to illustrate the likely effects of this. *(4 marks)*

4 Use the data in Extract C to calculate the UK's employment rate for August–October 2014. *(4 marks)*

5 Extract B states that the UK's current account deficit widened to a record deficit of £27 billion in the third quarter of 2014. Explain how economic activity in other countries might have influenced this outcome. *(10 marks)*

6 Using the data in the extracts and your economic knowledge, assess the possible effects on UK macroeconomic performance if the UK's GDP continues to grow at a rate in excess of 2.5% annually. *(25 marks)*

Topic 9

Macroeconomic policy

Chapter

43

Monetary policy

Topic 9 considers three different types of macroeconomic policy available to the UK government: monetary policy, fiscal policy and supply-side policies. The latter two are covered in Chapters 44 and 45. This chapter concentrates on monetary policy, investigating the forms that monetary policy may take in the UK, the objectives of monetary policy and the range of actions that the Bank of England may take to achieve these objectives. We examine the role of the Monetary Policy Committee and the part it plays in the operation of monetary policy in the UK. We consider the factors the Committee takes into account when making decisions on bank rate. Finally, we study the role that the exchange rate can play in monetary policy and how changes in the exchange rate can affect aggregate demand and the UK government's success in achieving its macroeconomic policy objectives.

What is monetary policy?

The UK authorities implement monetary policy with the aim of price stability (i.e. inflation around the target figure of 2%) and confidence in the currency. Monetary policy has three main elements:

- changing the bank rate of interest, which influences the level of interest rates throughout the economy;
- controlling the supply of money within the economy;
- influencing the value of the pound sterling in terms of other currencies.

We will see later in this chapter that the government and the Bank of England are developing new tools or instruments of monetary policy to meet changing economic circumstances.

Recent developments in monetary policy in the UK

In recent years monetary policy has become more important as a means of controlling the UK economy, with a major shift in responsibility for its management.

Key terms

Monetary policy refers to actions taken by the government (or the central bank acting on its behalf) to manipulate interest rates, the supply of money and credit, and the exchange rate to achieve its macroeconomic objectives.

A **central bank** is responsible for managing the monetary system in an economy.

The **bank rate** is the rate of interest at which the Bank of England is willing to lend money short term to other financial institutions such as commercial banks.

Monetary policy instruments are the tools available to a central bank to influence money market and credit conditions in the economy, such as changing interest rates.

Credit is a general term for borrowing. It is money that a bank or other organisation allows a person or organisation to use and to repay at a later date.

> **Author tip**
> The AQA AS specification focuses mainly on the use of interest rates as the key instrument of monetary policy as well as the consequences of changes in the exchange rate.

More powers granted to the Bank of England

In May 1997 the newly elected Labour government gave the UK's central bank, the Bank of England, control over the setting of the bank rate. The bank rate is an important rate of interest that influences rates charged throughout the UK economy and, for reasons we shall see later, the level of macroeconomic activity. Previously the bank rate had been set by the government. Gordon Brown, who was the Chancellor of the Exchequer (the member of the UK government responsible for financial matters) at the time, hoped that it would allow more long-term decision making and a pattern of economic growth that avoided the worst troughs and peaks. However, the government retained powers to give instructions to the Bank of England on interest rates for a limited period if it were in the national interest.

The Bank of England was given responsibility for setting interest rates with the objective of achieving the government's stated inflation target. In 2004 this inflation objective was altered to 2% using the Consumer Prices Index (CPI).

The increasing importance of monetary policy

Monetary policy is arguably the most important of the government's economic policy weapons at the current time. In part this has occurred because the UK government faces a large budget deficit (a topic we will explore in the next chapter), reducing its ability to use changes in taxes and spending (known as fiscal policy) to help to achieve its macroeconomic objectives.

The authorities in the UK have used new tools of monetary policy (monetary policy instruments) alongside interest rates. The Bank of England has created money (thereby increasing its supply) by buying government bonds, from banks and other financial institutions, with electronic cash that did not exist before. This is a process called **quantitative easing** (QE) and its aim is to increase bank lending and the levels of consumption and investment. Since August 2013 the Bank of England has been instructed by the government to issue 'forward guidance' on its monetary policy to influence business and consumer confidence and decision making. The expectation is that guidance from the Bank on the length of time over which the bank rate will remain low will help to hold down longer-term interest rates in the economy, boosting levels of consumption and investment. It will also help households and firms to plan spending and investment with greater levels of confidence. These instruments are considered in detail in *AQA A-Level Year 2 Economics*.

The objectives of monetary policy

The prime objective or goal of UK monetary policy is price stability. As we have seen, that is translated into a target rate for inflation, measured in terms of the CPI. The Chancellor of the Exchequer announces the target each spring as part of a statement of the government's spending and taxation plans for the coming year. The current target is a rate of inflation of 2% as measured by the 12-month increase in the CPI. The use of inflation targets reflects the short-term and long-term objectives of monetary policy.

Short-term objectives

In the long term the inflation objective of monetary policy is to create an environment in which prices are stable, thereby encouraging steady rates of economic growth and the avoidance of excessive peaks and troughs in the economic cycle. However, in the short term, decisions on monetary policy take into account tradeoffs that exist between controlling inflation and achieving satisfactory rates of economic growth and levels of employment. Monetary policy can be an effective means of achieving a balance between competing macroeconomic objectives and, in the short term, a move away from the inflation target may be acceptable if it helps attain other macroeconomic objectives.

Furthermore, the actual inflation rate may differ from its target because of supply-side or demand-side shocks. The Bank of England may permit this in the short term to avoid undesirable volatility in levels of output.

Long-term objectives

The intention of using inflation targets to guide monetary policy decisions is to achieve long-term economic growth. The Bank of England recognises that medium-term price stability (as measured by its inflation target) complements the most efficient allocation of resources within the economy. This in turn helps to achieve high and sustainable rates of economic growth as well as the government's other macroeconomic objectives.

REALWORLD **ECONOMICS** 43.1

Threat of UK experiencing deflation

Mark Carney, the Governor of the Bank of England, has warned that the UK economy is in danger of falling into deflation following a fall in the UK's Consumer Prices Index (CPI) rate of inflation to 0.5%. This is a 14-year low and is below what many economists expected. By reaching 0.5%, inflation has now hit a level only once before recorded by the Office for National Statistics – in May 2000. Much of the falling rate is the result of a sharp decline in the price of oil and lower food prices. George Osborne, the Chancellor of the Exchequer, said that the data were 'welcome news' with 'inflation at its lowest level in modern times'.

The Governor of the Bank of England told BBC News: 'We will expect it to fall further, and inflation to continue to drift down in the coming months'. In a separate interview, Mr Carney told ITV News that deflation was now 'possible'.

'These figures are good news in the short term for British households,' Mr Carney told the BBC. Danny Alexander, the Chief Secretary to the Treasury, said that the low inflation levels had acted like a 'giant tax cut'. He continued: 'These figures show that the falling price of oil is working its way into lower prices... putting more money in the pockets of hard-pressed consumers'.

However, economists have warned that, while low inflation might serve as a short-term tonic, deflation could damage the economy if it were to become entrenched. The Centre for Economics and Business Research has predicted that inflation will become negative during 2015. It expects inflation of –0.2% to be recorded in March 2015. The rate of economic growth in the UK is 2.6%, though the future growth rate is uncertain and many economists have forecast that it will fall over the months ahead.

Source: Adapted from *Daily Telegraph*, 13.1.15

Exercises *Total: 17 marks*

1 Explain the possible implications for the economy's rate of economic growth if the UK were to experience a period of deflation. *(8 marks)*

2 Explain the possible reasons why the Chancellor of the Exchequer said an inflation rate of 0.5% was 'welcome news' when the official target is 2%. *(9 marks)*

The Monetary Policy Committee and interest rates

An important method by which the Bank of England seeks to meet its inflation target is by setting the bank rate – a key interest rate for the entire economy. Although the Bank of England has responsibility for setting the bank rate of interest each month, it is actually its Monetary Policy Committee that takes the decision.

The Monetary Policy Committee

The Monetary Policy Committee (MPC) of the Bank of England meets each month to set a bank rate of interest that will meet the government's 2% inflation target (see Figure 43.1). However, the Bank of England estimates that it takes up to two years for a change in the bank rate to have its full effect on the rate of inflation in the UK. This means that the MPC is setting interest rates based on its forecast for inflation two years or more in the future. Thus, decisions on the bank rate taken in late 2015 will be based on forecasts for inflation in 2017–18.

The MPC has nine members: five from the Bank of England including the Governor (currently Mark Carney) and four independent experts in economics or monetary policy. The government appoints the four independent members to provide specialised knowledge and to broaden expertise beyond that available within the Bank.

Key terms

The **Monetary Policy Committee (MPC)** is a group of nine experts in monetary issues who meet monthly to make a decision on the UK's bank rate.

Liquidity measures the proportion of a business's assets that are held in a form that can be easily converted into cash.

The **real interest rate** is the rate of interest adjusted for inflation to show the true cost of borrowing money.

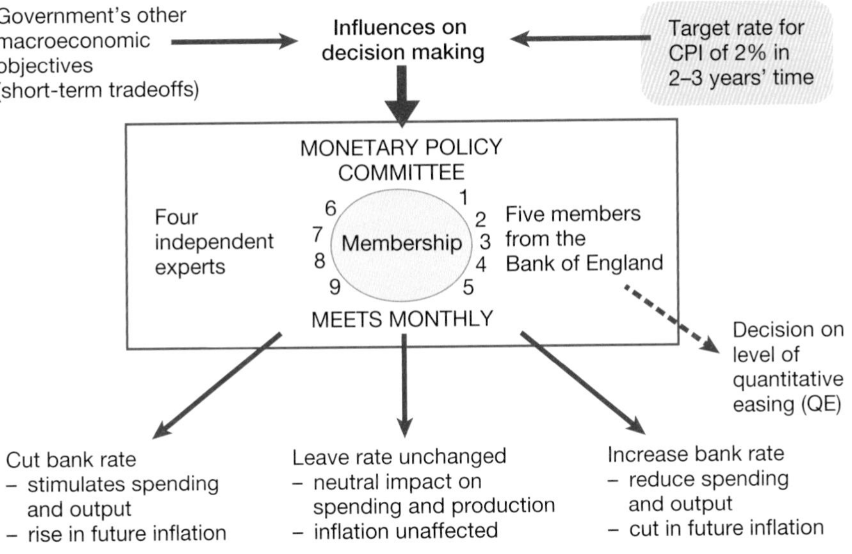

Figure 43.1 *The MPC and its decisions*

MPC meetings

These meetings are held in the first week of every month and last two days.

The MPC decides on a level for the bank rate that is designed to influence the level of economic activity in an economy in such a way as to control aggregate demand within the UK economy at a level which can be broadly matched by aggregate supply and therefore maintain the rate of inflation at around 2%. A reduction in interest rates to the extent that aggregate demand rises quickly, as households and firms save less and spend more, will fuel future inflation and may harm the economy. Similarly, if the MPC sets a bank rate that is too high, it will depress the level of economic activity and reduce inflation below 2%. This may damage future economic growth rates.

Factors influencing the MPC's decisions

The key factor influencing the decisions taken by the MPC is the forecast for the CPI rate of inflation in the UK approximately two years in the future. Evidence on this is provided to the Committee each month by Bank of England staff. The Committee will also be influenced, as we have seen, by short-term macroeconomic considerations. For example, the MPC may take the decision to allow the rate of inflation to move away from its target temporarily in order to avoid sharp slowdowns in economic growth and excessive rates of unemployment.

The composition of the Monetary Policy Committee also influences its decision making. The media is keen to categorise the nine individual committee members as either 'hawks' or 'doves'. Hawks generally favour higher interest rates that will keep the potentially damaging effects of inflation under control. In contrast, doves seek to keep interest rates lower for a longer period to promote economic growth.

In 2014 the composition of the MPC changed due to retirements and changes in personnel at the Bank of England. The balance of the Committee has altered as a consequence, with a majority of members considered by the media to be towards the dove end of the spectrum on interest rate decisions. Since the government appoints the four independent members of the MPC, it has the potential to influence its decision making to some extent.

Finally, the decisions taken by the MPC will be subject to influence from other economic policies implemented by the government. Recently, the government has sought to impose substantial cuts on its own expenditure in order to reduce (and eventually eliminate) the deficit on its budget. This could be expected to have a deflationary impact on the economy because government expenditure represents an injection into the circular flow and reductions can generate a negative multiplier effect. This is likely to encourage the MPC to keep the bank rate at its historic low.

The effects of the MPC's interest rate decisions

The bank rate is a very influential rate of interest in the economy because it is able to affect the level of interest charged on borrowing of all types across the economy. How does it do this?

How the bank rate influences other rates of interest in the economy

One role that the Bank of England performs is to act as 'lender of last resort'. In this role, the Bank will lend money to commercial or high street banks such as Barclays and Lloyds Banking Group if they suffer a shortage of liquidity, and the rate of interest at which it lends is the bank rate.

Key term

Commercial banks provide a wide range of financial services to individuals, firms and other organisations with the intention of making a profit. Examples include the Lloyds Banking Group and HSBC.

The commercial banks are protected from the effects of liquidity crises by the Bank of England acting as lender of last resort. This means that it agrees to lend money, if necessary, to maintain consumer confidence in the banking system. It is quite normal for commercial banks to borrow from the Bank of England on a regular basis and the rate at which they borrow is the bank rate. This means that a change in the bank rate can directly affect the rates at which commercial banks lend money because if they have to pay the Bank of England a higher rate for loans, they are likely to pass these on to their customers in order to maintain their profits. As a consequence, most rates of interest in the economy move up. If the bank rate falls, commercial banks are likely to reduce their rates as well for fear of losing customers if considered uncompetitive.

> **Author tip**
> The AQA AS specification does not require you to know how interest rates or exchange rates are determined.

In March 2009 the bank rate was lowered to 0.5% and, up until the time of writing in March 2015, it has remained at the same rate (see Figure 43.2). This does not mean that all rates of interest are set at this level. Many other factors influence the rate of interest that is charged for a loan, but the bank rate influences other rates and they tend to move in unison.

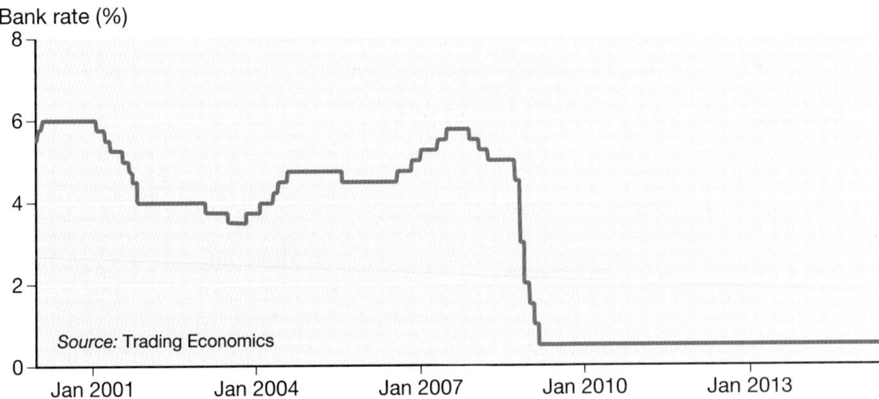

Figure 43.2 *The UK's bank rate 2000–15*

Interest rates changes and aggregate demand

The MPC takes decisions on the bank rate with the intention of influencing the level of demand for money in the UK economy and therefore the level of aggregate demand (see Table 43.1). By increasing interest rates, the MPC can affect the level of aggregate demand in three ways:

Type of monetary policy	A RISE in the bank rate – this is a contractionary monetary policy	A FALL in the bank rate – this is an expansionary monetary policy
Effect on aggregate demand	▪ Consumption falls because many households have reduced discretionary income as mortgage costs rise. ▪ Higher rates attract increased savings. ▪ Cost of borrowing (or credit) increases, reducing consumption of expensive items such as fitted kitchens. ▪ Demand for net exports falls because import purchases rise while export sales decline. ▪ Aggregate demand falls.	▪ Consumption rises because many households have increased discretionary income due to falling mortgage costs. ▪ Lower rates reduce savings and increase consumption. ▪ Cost of borrowing (or credit) reduces, increasing consumption of expensive items such as digital TVs. ▪ Demand for net exports rises because import purchases fall while export sales rise. ▪ Aggregate demand increases.
Consequences for macroeconomic objectives	▪ Inflationary pressures are reduced in the economy. ▪ Real GDP decreases. ▪ The rate of unemployment rises.	▪ Inflationary pressures increase, especially for an economy near full employment. ▪ Real GDP rises. ▪ The rate of unemployment falls.

Table 43.1 *How changes in the bank rate are likely to affect aggregate demand and macroeconomic objectives*

Key term

Discretionary income is equal to a household's disposable income minus expenditure on essential items including housing costs (mortgages or rent) and food.

- *The impact on consumption* Households will reduce consumption when interest rates are raised. This can occur for a number of reasons. First, it may be more attractive for them to save a higher proportion of their disposable incomes because the return from saving is likely to be higher. In other words, the opportunity cost of spending has risen. Secondly, it is likely that many households will be paying higher repayments each month on their mortgages, which can have a big impact on discretionary income and consumption expenditure. Finally, consumption that is financed by borrowing (the purchase of cars, for example) is likely to fall when interest rates rise. Reductions in the rate of interest will have the opposite effects.
- *The impact on investment* Borrowing finances a great deal of investment and we saw in Chapter 35 that a firm will only invest if the expected return from the investment exceeds the costs of the borrowed funds. A rise in the cost of borrowing following an increase in the rate of interest will therefore reduce investment. Conversely, a fall in the rate of interest will increase investment. In the long term, increased investment may also increase aggregate supply, which may help to reduce inflationary pressure.
- *The impact on net exports* A rise in the rate of interest will tend to lead to a rise in demand for a currency, increasing its value or exchange rate. A rise in the value of a currency increases the price of UK exports while making imports less expensive. This is likely to reduce sales of exports and increase purchases of imports. The overall effect will be to reduce net exports. Once again, a fall in the rate of interest will have the opposite effect, increasing net exports. We will consider this in more detail in the next section.

Figure 43.3 illustrates the consequences of a contractionary monetary policy that reduces aggregate demand. The fall in aggregate demand shifts the AD curve to the left, reducing the price level and the level of real GDP. This lower level of economic activity will reduce employment opportunities and would be expected to increase the rate of unemployment.

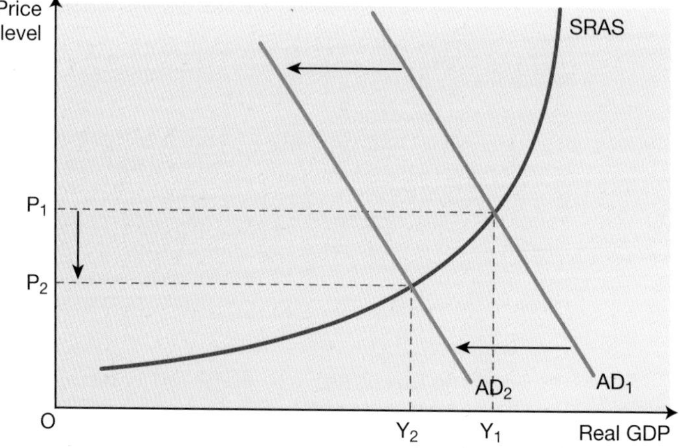

Figure 43.3 *The macroeconomic consequences of a contractionary monetary policy*

Monetary policy and the exchange rate

The relationship between interest rates and the exchange rate

The UK does not operate a monetary policy directly with regard to its exchange rate because the free market forces of demand and supply broadly determine the value of the pound sterling. However, changes in interest rates resulting from the decisions of the Monetary Policy Committee do affect the exchange rate and consequently the level of aggregate demand in the UK economy. This can in turn have an effect on the extent to which the performance of the UK economy meets its macroeconomic objectives.

There is a positive relationship between the rate of interest in the UK and the exchange rate of the pound. A rise in the rate of interest will result in an increase in the exchange rate of the pound, and a fall in interest rates in the UK will reduce or depreciate the pound's value against other currencies, ceteris paribus.

If the MPC votes to increase interest rates, the effect is to make the UK a more attractive and rewarding place in which to invest. Money that flows regularly between financial markets as investors attempt to earn the highest short-term interest rates possible is known as 'hot money'. Hot money will flow from low interest rate yielding countries into higher interest rate countries as investors look to make the highest return. Thus an increase in interest rates in the UK is likely to lead to an inflow of funds into the UK. This requires international investors to purchase pounds and will result in an increase in demand for pounds. As with any commodity, a rise in demand for a product tends to increase its price – hence the exchange rate of the pound will rise. In the same way, a fall in interest rates will increase the supply of pounds as hot money leaves the UK to seek relatively higher returns elsewhere. As a consequence, the exchange rate will fall.

Key term

Hot money refers to funds that flow between financial markets as investors attempt to earn the highest short-term interest rates possible.

The consequences of changes in the exchange rate for aggregate demand

A fall in the exchange rate can be expected to increase aggregate demand, and a rise in the exchange rate will reduce it.

- *A fall in the exchange rate* An example of such a fall would be from £1 = $1.50 to £1 = $1.25. This will make exports cheaper and imports more expensive. This could be expected to increase the quantity of exports sold and earnings from them. At the same time, purchases of imports will decline as they have become more expensive in comparison to domestically produced goods and services. Given that net exports = X – M, a rise in exports and a fall in imports will increase the value of net exports and thus also increase aggregate demand.

Number crunching

Assume the pound sterling increases in value from £1 = €1.10 to £1 = €1.25. What effect would this have on the price of a bottle of wine imported from France priced at €10?

- *A rise in the exchange rate* In this case a pound is worth more units of a foreign currency, say $1.50 rather than $1.40. The consequence of this is that exports become more expensive and imports cheaper. As quantities adjust to the change in prices, net exports decline, reducing aggregate demand.

There are a number of factors to take into account when considering the effect on the level of aggregate demand in the UK of a change in the exchange rate of the pound.

- *The size and extent of the change in the exchange rate* A larger fall in an exchange rate will, unsurprisingly, have the potential to have a greater impact on aggregate demand. However, a currency may not fall in value against all other currencies.

It may fall against some and rise against others. The impact may depend upon the extent to which it falls against the currencies of the country's major trading partners.

- *Price elasticity of demand for exports and imports* If demand for a country's exports and imports are both price elastic, then the effect of the change in the exchange rate on exports and imports, and consequently aggregate demand, will be greater because buyers are more responsive to price changes. For some internationally traded products, quality, design or brand name may be more important than price. In contrast, the effects of an exchange rate change will be dampened by inelastic demand.
- *The time lag* The impact on aggregate demand of a change in the exchange rate can take time to have an effect. Orders for exports and imports may be placed in advance and therefore the quantities bought and sold may take a while to adjust to the new prices.

The effects of changes in the exchange rate on macroeconomic policy objectives

A fall in the exchange rate of a currency will have a range of effects on the government's macroeconomic objectives as aggregate demand rises. (A rise in the exchange rate will generally have the opposite effects to those outlined below.)

- Unemployment is likely to fall as sales of exports rise and domestically produced goods become more competitive against imports. The extent of this fall will depend on factors such as the importance of labour in the industries that are affected and whether the exchange rate change is seen as short term.
- The rate of GDP growth will receive a boost from the increased production and sale of exports and from the reduced level of imports. The impact will be greater in an open trading economy such as the UK.
- Inflationary pressure will increase as aggregate demand rises, especially if the economy is operating near to its full employment position. In 2012 the Chinese currency (the yuan) fell against the dollar. The USA is a major trading partner for China. In November 2012, China's exports rose sharply, fuelling an increase in the country's rate of inflation.
- The balance of payments on current account will benefit from an improved trade performance. After some delay, the rise in exports and fall in imports will improve the trade balance. However, if the exchange rate rise occurred due to increased overseas investment in a country, this could have longer-term adverse consequences on the current account balance as profits and dividends associated with the investment flow overseas. These outflows will weaken the investment income element of the current account.

Has monetary policy worked for the UK?

A general assessment of monetary policy might offer the following conclusions.

- Monetary policy operates with a significant time lag. It is estimated that up to 18 months may elapse between a change in a monetary policy instrument and the full impact being seen in terms of aggregate demand. This means that monetary policy cannot be used to respond immediately to short-term shocks to the economy.

- Monetary policy decisions tend to impact on the entire economy, even when this is not desirable. Thus a rise in the bank rate in response to rising inflationary expectations brought about primarily by increasing economic activity in certain regions (perhaps London and the Southeast) may have undesirable deflationary effects in less prosperous regions of the UK.
- The effects of monetary policy tend to be felt more in certain areas of the economy. For example, a fall in the bank rate would reduce the costs of borrowing for all firms and households in the economy. However, the impact would be mixed for businesses that import significant quantities of resources used in production, since their costs would rise as a consequence of a falling exchange rate increasing the costs of imported products.
- Monetary policy decisions do not always lead to the expected outcomes. Consumers may decide not to increase consumption, even when interest rates are very low, perhaps because they fear for their future financial security if unemployment rates are rising.

Monetary policy has had some notable successes in the UK economy since the recession of 2008–09. It has offset the contractionary effects of the deep cuts in the level of government expenditure. Low interest rates have helped to stimulate consumption through keeping mortgages cheap and bolstering discretionary income at a time when real wages have risen only towards the end of 2014. Low interest rates have also helped to stimulate business investment in the UK by reducing its cost and by improving business confidence. In 2014 investment in the UK was growing at an annual rate of 11% and this was its fastest growth rate since 2007. Rising investment and strong consumption have helped to keep unemployment rates below the level expected by many economists during and following the recession.

However, the experience of the UK economy since the recession has demonstrated some of the limitations of monetary policy. The prime one is that inflation has undershot its 2% target since late 2013 and a threat of deflation has emerged as inflation reached 0% in February 2015.

Monetary policy cannot operate in isolation from the rest of the world. Much of the downward pressure on prices has been imported as commodity prices (oil, for example) have fallen sharply. Furthermore, the pound has been strong against some key currencies, notably the euro, reducing import prices. This has occurred despite the historically low rates of interest in the UK, because foreign economies have also reduced interest rates to low levels. The relatively encouraging performance of the UK economy has attracted increasing levels of investment from overseas, increasing the demand for pounds on foreign exchange markets, and increasing the exchange rate of the currency.

REALWORLD ECONOMICS 43.1

A change of mind on the MPC

Two Monetary Policy Committee 'hawks' have ditched their long-standing calls for an end to record-low interest rates in the face of disinflation, prompting economists to push back again their forecasts of when the Bank of England will start to tighten monetary policy. A slump in oil prices caused British inflation to drop far more than expected to a 14-year low of 0.5% in December 2014, far below the Bank's 2% target.

Minutes of the January 2015 MPC meeting published afterwards revealed that Martin Weale and Ian McCafferty voted to maintain the bank rate at 0.5%, saying that raising rates now might cause below-target inflation to become entrenched.

The UK's central bank faces a dilemma over the extent to which it should look beyond falls in inflation driven by lower oil prices (which it expects to be temporary) towards longer-term drivers of price rises such as higher wages.

In the medium term, the MPC saw potential upward pressures on prices from signs of a pick-up in wages and falling mortgage interest rates, both of which would increase households' disposable income.

Exercise

1 Explain how holding the b
rate down might benefit
economy in the short ter
(7 ma

Review questions

Total: 50 marks

1 Define the term 'monetary policy'. *(3 marks)*

2 Who is responsible for setting the bank rate in the UK each month?
A The Treasury
B The government
C The Monetary Policy Committee
D The Chancellor of the Exchequer *(1 mark)*

3 Explain why monetary policy has become a more important policy for the government to achieve its macroeconomic objectives since 2009. *(7 marks)*

4 Explain how the role of the Bank of England as 'lender of last resort' allows it to influence interest rates throughout the UK. *(8 marks)*

5 Which of the following is most likely to be a consequence of a rise in the bank rate in the UK?
A A rise in the level of investment
B A rise in net exports
C A rise in consumption
D A rise in the exchange rate *(1 mark)*

6 Explain two ways in which a fall in the bank rate might affect the level of consumption in the UK. *(6 marks)*

7 Explain how aggregate demand in the UK might be affected by a fall in the exchange rate of the pound. *(7 marks)*

8 The value of the pound sterling against the euro rises from £1 = €1.05 to £1 = €1.25. Which of the following statements is true?
A The price of an imported Italian car valued at €20,000 will fall to £16,000
B The price of a £25 bottle of Scotch whisky will rise in Germany to £26.25
C The price of imported Italian pasta will rise by 19%
D All of the above are true *(1 mark)*

9 Explain how a rise in the exchange rate of the pound might affect the ability of the UK government to meet its macroeconomic objectives. *(7 marks)*

10 Explain why monetary policy in the UK might be considered to have been successful since 2009. *(9 marks)*

Fiscal policy

This chapter introduces you to fiscal policy, explaining its components and how it can be used to attain macroeconomic and microeconomic policy objectives. We explore how fiscal policy can be used to manage aggregate demand, influence aggregate supply and adjust the pattern of activity within the economy. The chapter also explains the distinction between direct and indirect taxes, and how taxes can be classified as progressive, proportional or regressive. It considers the relationship between the budget balance and the national debt – a highly topical issue – and concludes by assessing the strengths and weaknesses of fiscal policy.

What is fiscal policy?

Fiscal policy has three major elements. In its broadest sense it describes the use of changes in government spending and taxation as well as the budget balance to achieve the government's macroeconomic objectives. The work of John Maynard Keynes influenced economic policies in the 30 years after 1945, which meant that fiscal policy was used widely by UK governments to manage the level of aggregate demand. Its use was severely curtailed in the period after 1979 because the government relied principally on the use of monetary policy to achieve its macroeconomic objectives, particularly the control of inflation. The government's stated aim is to operate a balanced budget over the period of the economic cycle.

Keynesian economics made a dramatic comeback in 2008 as many governments, including that of the UK, used fiscal policy to combat the effects of the recession that followed the financial crisis. However, this resulted in governments having huge budget deficits as spending soared while tax revenues were depressed. In 2010 the coalition government in the UK abandoned fiscal policies designed to increase aggregate demand in the face of unsustainable rises in the cost of borrowing on world markets.

The role of fiscal policy in a modern economy is wider and more complex than a simple definition might suggest. Fiscal policy currently has a number of functions within the UK economy:

- to manage the level of aggregate demand;
- to influence the level of aggregate supply within the economy;

Key terms

Fiscal policy refers to the government's manipulation of its expenditure, taxation and the budget balance to manage the economy.

The **budget balance** is the difference between government spending and revenue over the financial year.

The **Treasury** is the UK government's economic and finance ministry responsible for public spending and for setting the direction of the UK's economic policy.

- to achieve a range of microeconomic goals, including providing support to a particular industry;
- to redistribute income and wealth from the rich to the poor.

Unlike monetary policy, fiscal policy is the responsibility of the government, with decisions taken by the Chancellor of the Exchequer, other ministers and officials at the Treasury.

The components of fiscal policy

Governments can manipulate the level of their spending as well as its composition as part of their fiscal policy. In addition, they can change the overall receipts from taxation as well as the types of taxes that are used. Chart 1 in Figure 44.1 shows forecast government spending and revenue from taxation for 2014–15.

Chart 2 in Figure 44.1 shows the main sources of revenue for the UK government for its 2014–15 financial year. The UK government's financial year runs from 6 April to 5 April in the following year.

> **Number crunching**
> Use the information in Figure 44.1 to calculate the government's budget balance for the 2014–15 financial year.

The balance between government spending and taxation is an important one for the economy. The budget balance is calculated by deducting tax revenues from government expenditure. This can provide three possible outcomes:

- a **budget surplus** when government expenditure is less than revenue from taxation;
- a **budget deficit** when government expenditure is greater than revenue from taxation;

Figure 44.1 *UK government spending and revenue, 2014–15*

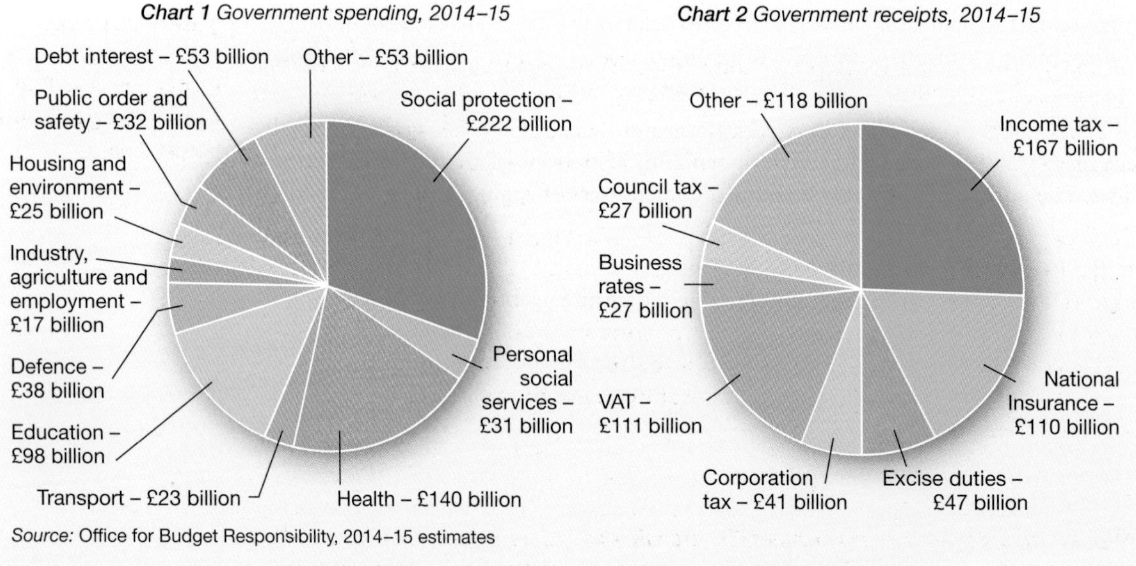

Source: Office for Budget Responsibility, 2014–15 estimates

- a **balanced budget** in the unlikely circumstances that government spending and revenue from taxation are equal.

Government expenditure

Chart 1 in Figure 44.1 provides information about the breakdown of government spending. It is apparent that government spending is dominated by two major categories of expenditure: social protection and health.

Social protection

This is government expenditure targeted at preventing, managing and overcoming situations that adversely affect people's wellbeing. It is the largest single category of government expenditure in the UK and covers the following elements:

- welfare payments to those who may be unable to work due to incapacity, disability or injury;
- payments in the form of income support, tax credits or family benefits intended to boost the incomes of low earners or those responsible for children;
- payments to older people either in the form of pensions or to provide personal social services;
- unemployment benefits paid to those who are out of work and actively seeking employment.

Health

This expenditure is primarily on the National Health Service (NHS) to cover the operation of hospitals and surgeries as well as the wages and salaries of healthcare workers such as nurses. It does, however, also include the costs of research into issues relating to health. The demand for healthcare in the UK is growing rapidly due to the country's growing and ageing population. This has led to calls for greater expenditure on the NHS, despite the current programme of austerity in the UK.

Key term

Austerity describes government policies to reduce expenditure and increase revenues from taxation during periods of budget deficits.

The current debate on government spending

Although spending on social protection and health amounted to nearly half of total government expenditure in the UK in 2014–15, there are other significant areas of government spending such as education and defence. The UK government also engages in capital expenditure, such as building schools, hospitals, roads and railway lines. This can have positive implications for the level of aggregate supply.

The level of government spending in the UK is a matter of considerable debate at the time of writing (March 2015). The government is under pressure to reduce its spending to close the gap between its expenditure and its revenue. The current coalition government has pledged to 'protect' spending in some areas, such as health and education, while social protection and defence have suffered substantial cuts. Further reductions in the level of government expenditure will occur over the period up until at least 2018.

Taxation in the UK

Almost every consumer and business in the UK pays taxes in one form or another. Taxes are financial levies or payments imposed on a variety of economic activities.

REALWORLD
ECONOMICS 44.1

UK warned by OECD over austerity measures

The Organisation for Economic Cooperation and Development (OECD) has warned the UK government that capping benefit levels could 'entrench poverty for families who depend on income support'.

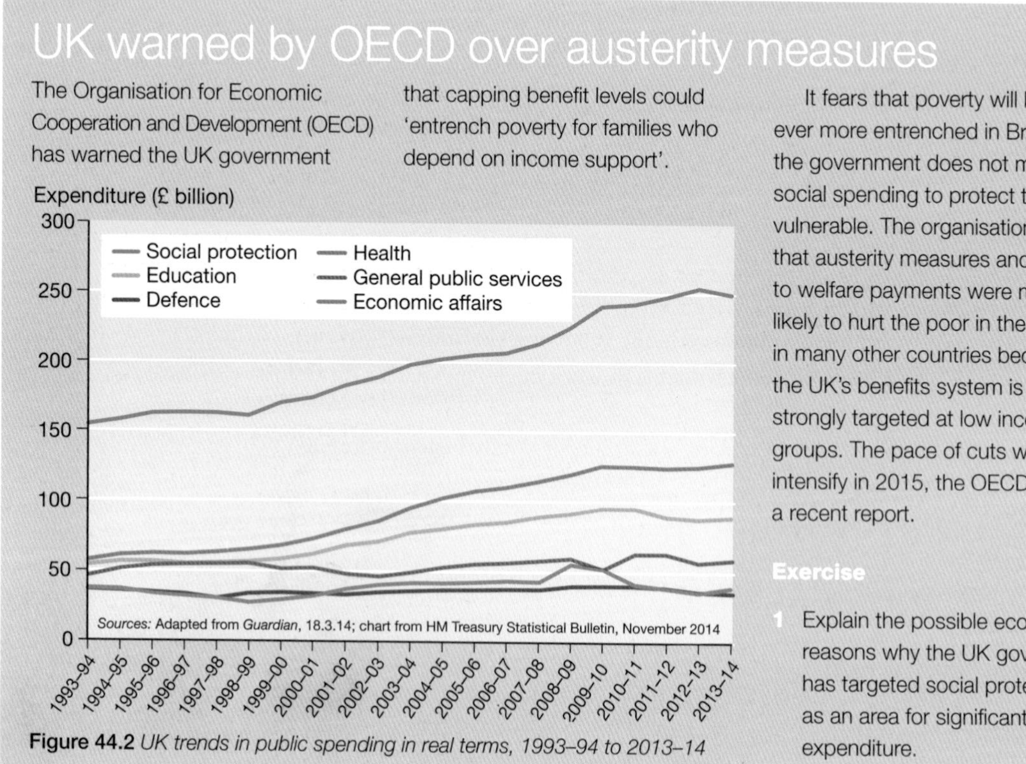

Figure 44.2 *UK trends in public spending in real terms, 1993–94 to 2013–14*

It fears that poverty will become ever more entrenched in Britain if the government does not maintain social spending to protect the most vulnerable. The organisation stated that austerity measures and cuts to welfare payments were more likely to hurt the poor in the UK than in many other countries because the UK's benefits system is more strongly targeted at low income groups. The pace of cuts will intensify in 2015, the OECD noted in a recent report.

Exercise

1 Explain the possible economic reasons why the UK government has targeted social protection as an area for significant cuts in expenditure. *(7 marks)*

Table 44.1 *Direct and indirect taxes in the UK*

Category of tax	Direct taxes	Indirect taxes
Description	Direct taxes are imposed on the income or wealth of individuals and on the profits or other aspects of the operations of firms. The liability to pay direct taxes cannot be passed onto other persons or organisations. Direct taxes offer advantages to the UK government in that it can predict with reasonable accuracy the amount it can expect to receive over the next financial year. However, the UK government does encounter problems with households and firms taking steps to avoid paying direct taxes.	Indirect taxes are levied on spending. It is possible for firms to pass these taxes onto consumers in the prices of products. Indirect taxes are often levied on goods and services for which demand is price inelastic. This is essential to ensure that the government receives a reasonable level of revenue from the tax. However, the government imposes indirect taxes for reasons other than raising revenue. High rates of indirect taxes can be a burden on those on lower incomes.
Examples	▪ Income tax including Pay As You Earn (PAYE) ▪ Corporation tax ▪ Capital gains tax ▪ National insurance contributions ▪ Inheritance tax	▪ Value added tax (VAT) ▪ Customs duties on imported products ▪ Excise duties on petrol and alcohol ▪ Insurance premium tax ▪ Air passenger duty

Direct and indirect taxes

Taxes can be categorised in a number of ways, including distinguishing between direct and indirect taxes (see Table 44.1).

Progressive, regressive and proportional taxes

Taxes in the UK can be classified as progressive, regressive or proportional according to how the proportion of income that is taken as tax changes as consumers' incomes change. A progressive tax takes a higher proportion of income as tax. This means that taxpayers earning higher incomes do not just pay more tax – they pay a higher percentage of their incomes as tax. A regressive tax takes a lower proportion of consumers' incomes as tax as their incomes rise. With regressive taxes, those on higher incomes can pay greater amounts of tax. However, the amount of tax paid will be a smaller percentage of the taxpayer's income for a person with a higher income. This situation is illustrated in Table 44.2 along with examples of progressive and proportional taxes. Finally, a proportional tax takes the same proportion or percentage of all taxpayers' incomes irrespective of how much, or how little, they earn. Taxes can also be classified as progressive, proportional or regressive in relation to wealth in precisely the same way as to income.

Key term

Taxation is a payment that has to be made to the government or other authority by households, firms or other organisations.

Category of tax	*Taxpayer A's income:* £100,000 per annum		*Taxpayer B's income:* £50,000 per annum		*Taxpayer C's income:* £10,000 per annum	
	Tax paid (£)	(%)	Tax paid (£)	(%)	Tax paid (£)	(%)
Progressive	35,000	35.0	12,500	25.0	750	7.5
Regressive	2500	2.5	1500	3.0	400	4
Proportional	5000	5.0	2500	5.0	500	5.0

Table 44.2 *Numerical examples of progressive, regressive and proportional taxes*

Progressive taxes are commonly used as the basis for redistributing income from those earning high incomes to those earning smaller amounts. Progressive taxes normally operate alongside welfare or benefit systems designed to provide additional income to those in society in most need. The income that is taken in the form of a progressive tax is paid to those on low incomes as a benefit, providing greater equality of final income.

The UK's main taxes

Income tax This is the most important tax to the UK government in terms of tax yield and it is paid by all UK taxpayers earning over a certain amount annually. In 2014–15 it is forecast to yield £167 billion – over 25% of government receipts from taxation. Income tax in the UK is progressive (as shown in Table 44.3), with different rates of tax paid on different bands of taxpayers' incomes. This means that taxpayers on higher incomes do not just pay more tax – they pay a higher proportion of their earnings as income tax. Progressive taxes such as income tax can lead to a phenomenon known as **fiscal drag.** This occurs during a period of inflation when taxpayers' incomes rise and they move into higher income tax bands, which means they pay more tax. This can result in the government receiving an increased tax yield without having to increase tax rates. However, fiscal drag tends to have a deflationary impact because it reduces consumption and aggregate demand.

Key term

Fiscal drag occurs when inflation results in taxpayers receiving higher incomes and moving into higher income tax bands – hence paying a higher percentage of income as tax.

Table 44.3 *Income levels and tax rates for a UK taxpayer aged under 67, 2015–16*

Income tax band (£)	Tax rate (%)
0–10,600	0
10,601–42,385	20
42,386–150,000	40
Over 150,000	45

Example:
A taxpayer earning £45,000 during the 2015–16 financial year would pay:

- 0% on the first £10,600 — £0
- 20% tax on the next £31,785 — £6357
- 40% on the remaining £7615 — £3046
- **Total tax paid** — **£9403** – a tax rate of 18.81% overall

Number crunching

Use the information in Table 44.3 to calculate the amount of income tax paid and the percentage of income taken as income tax for the following two taxpayers in 2014–15:
(a) a gardener earning £16,200 from employment over the financial year;
(b) a manager earning £95,000 from employment during the financial year.

Value added tax (VAT) This is an indirect tax levied on spending. Most goods and services sold in the UK have VAT at a rate of 20% added to their price. Some, such as car seats for children, have a 5% rate while other products, including most foods, are zero rated – purchasers do not have to pay VAT on these products. VAT is a tax that is imposed in all member states of the European Union, though rates vary. In January 2011 the UK government increased the rate of VAT from 17.5% to 20%. The Institute for Fiscal Studies stated that this change would take a significantly higher proportion of the incomes of low earners because VAT is a regressive tax.

Inheritance tax Inheritance tax is levied on the value of a person's estate at the time of their death and is therefore a tax on wealth. In the UK the tax is charged at 40%

Figure 44.3 *Corporation tax rates for the G20 group of economies, 2015*

G20	Rank	Rate
UK	1	20%
Russia	1	20%
Saudi Arabia	1	20%
Turkey	1	20%
Korea	5	24%
China	6	25%
Indonesia	6	25%
Canada	8	26%
South Africa	9	28%
Mexico	9	28%
Germany	11	29%
Australia	12	30%
Italy	13	31%
India	14	32%
France	15	33%
Brazil	16	34%
Argentina	17	35%
Japan	18	38%
USA	19	40%

Note: Based on announced plans *Source:* KPMG Global Tax Rates Online above a tax-free allowance of £325,000. In 2013 the government announced that the tax-free threshold would remain frozen at this level until April 2018.

National insurance payments National insurance payments are contributions made towards the cost of certain state benefits such as pensions. In the 2015–16 financial year, both employers and employees pay national insurance contributions on earnings over £155 per week. Employees pay 12% of their salary up to earnings of £815 a week and employers pay 13.8% of the employee's salary over the same range of income.

Corporation tax This tax is paid by companies in the UK on their profits. The UK government is committed to creating a very competitive tax regime for corporation tax in the expectation of attracting international businesses to the UK. The rate of corporation tax in the UK has been cut substantially from 28% in 2010 to 20% in 2015 – this is the joint lowest in the G20 group of major economies, as shown in Figure 44.3.

The budget balance

The budget balance is the difference between government spending and revenue over the financial year. Whether the government operates a budget deficit or a budget surplus has implications for the performance of the economy.

- *Budget deficits* These exist when government spending during the year exceeds the revenue received from taxation. This has been the situation in the UK for most years since 2000 and is likely to continue for the next few financial years. A budget deficit can act as a stimulus to the economy because it is likely to stimulate aggregate demand. Furthermore, increases in government spending will initiate the multiplier effect.
- *Budget surpluses* These result when receipts from taxation exceed government expenditure and they are less common in the UK. The UK last had a budget surplus in the 2001–02 financial year. Budget surpluses can have a deflationary effect on an economy, as they reduce the level of aggregate demand.

The budget balance and the national debt

The UK's national debt is the total amount of borrowing by all past governments that has not been repaid. The UK's national debt was £1457.2 billion (equal to 79.5% of GDP) at the end of November 2014 – an increase of £89.7 billion compared with November 2013. A budget deficit adds to the national debt in most cases, while a budget surplus reduces it, assuming debt is repaid.

Key term

The **national debt** is the total of all past government borrowing that has never been repaid.

Figure 44.4 confirms this relationship between the budget balance and the level of national debt. Since 1979 the UK has recorded four budget surpluses and 29 budget deficits. The more recent imbalance between government spending and revenue is shown in Figure 44.4, where the effects of the financial crisis and subsequent recession on both the budget balance and the UK's national debt are very evident.

The national debt has been built up over many years, but the total figure does exclude any liquid assets held by the government. It is apparent that the series of very large budget deficits after 2008 have added significantly to the size of the UK's national debt. The UK is forecast to record budget surpluses from 2017–18 and this will have the potential to lead to a reduction in the size of the country's national debt.

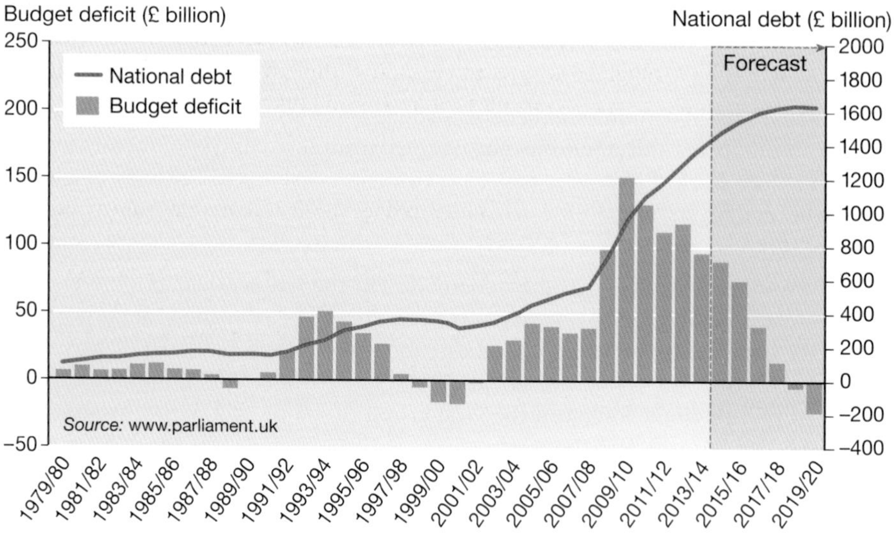

Figure 44.4 *UK budget balance and national debt, 1979–80 to 2019–20*

How fiscal policy operates

There are two aspects of fiscal policy that may operate within an economy. One element, known as discretionary fiscal policy, occurs as the result of government decisions relating to spending or taxation that are implemented with the intention of achieving macroeconomic aims. A decision by the government to increase its spending in the expectation of reducing unemployment is an example of discretionary fiscal policy.

In contrast, automatic stabilisers operate through fiscal policy as the economy moves through its economic cycle. As the economy moves through its upswing and into the boom stage of the economic cycle, the government receives more tax, and incomes and profits rise. Simultaneously, government expenditure may fall as fewer people are unemployed or on low incomes and receiving welfare payments.

Given that AD = C + I + G + (X − M), a rise in taxation and a fall in government spending will reduce aggregate demand and dampen the effects of the economic cycle at the peak stage of the economic cycle. As the economy moves through its downswing and towards a trough, the automatic stabilisers operate in reverse. Government spending rises as more people become unemployed and the taxation yield declines, thus helping to sustain consumption. These changes mitigate some of the effects of the economic cycle.

Influencing aggregate demand

Before Keynesian economics became influential in the 1940s, governments merely

Key terms

Discretionary fiscal policy is the deliberate manipulation of the budget to achieve macroeconomic aims.

Automatic stabilisers are elements of fiscal policy that occur independently as the economy moves through its economic cycle.

Demand management is the use of macroeconomic policies to manipulate an economy's level of aggregate demand.

aimed to balance their budgets, with revenue from taxation equalling government spending. Keynesian economists believe that an economy's macroeconomic objectives can be achieved by managing the level of demand within an economy. They advocate the use of fiscal policy as an important tool in demand management.

Expansionary fiscal policy

An expansionary fiscal policy entails increasing government expenditure and/or reducing the level of taxation. This may result in a budget deficit, or possibly a larger budget deficit. An expansionary fiscal policy will increase the level of aggregate demand and this will shift the aggregate demand curve to the right. This is shown by the shift from AD to AD_2 in Figure 44.5. An expansionary fiscal policy may be expected to have the following effects, at least in the short term:

- an increase in real GDP and a higher rate of economic growth;
- a fall in the rate of unemployment;
- an increase in the price level, depending on the shape of the AS curve (i.e. the price elasticity of aggregate supply);
- a weakening of the balance of payments on current account as higher incomes lead to increased consumption of imports and as rising prices make exports less competitive.

This highlights a problem in the use of fiscal policy for demand management: tradeoffs exist between macroeconomic objectives. An expansionary fiscal policy may assist a government in reducing unemployment and increasing economic growth, but only at the expense of higher inflation and a weaker balance of payments on current account.

The tradeoff entailed in the increase in aggregate demand from AD to AD_2 is probably acceptable for a government. It generates a substantial increase in real GDP (from Y to Y_2), which should reduce unemployment and at a relatively small cost in terms of inflation (as prices rise from P to P_2).

Contractionary fiscal policy

A contractionary fiscal policy requires a government to decrease its expenditure and/or increase its level of taxation. This may result in a budget surplus, or possibly a smaller budget deficit. A contractionary fiscal policy will decrease the level of

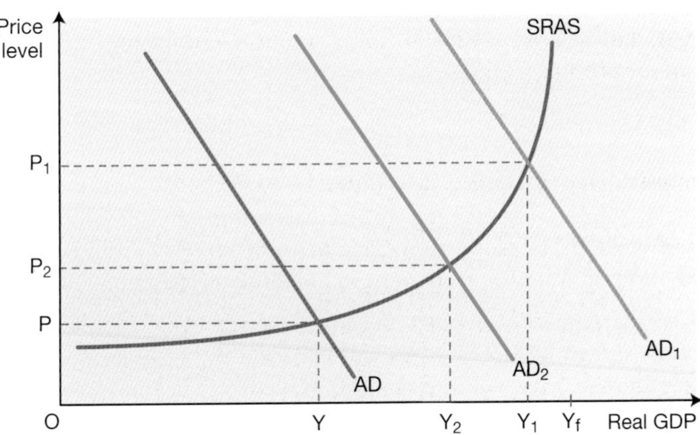

Figure 44.5 *The effects of expansionary and contractionary fiscal policies*

aggregate demand and this will shift the aggregate demand curve to the left. This is shown by the shift from AD_1 to AD_2 in Figure 44.5.

A contractionary fiscal policy manages the level of aggregate demand in such a way as to reduce inflationary pressures and improve the current account position on the balance of payments. The shift of the AD curve from AD_1 to AD_2 in Figure 44.5 achieves a significant drop in the price level from P_1 to P_2, while only reducing real GDP by a comparatively small amount – from Y_1 to Y_2. The rate of unemployment is likely to increase.

Neutral fiscal policies

Governments may pursue neutral fiscal policies, not intended to increase or reduce the level of aggregate demand within the economy. This has happened in the UK when the government has relied primarily upon monetary policy and supply-side policies to achieve its macroeconomic objectives.

The UK government aims to operate a fiscal policy that is neutral over the duration of an economic cycle. It operates its fiscal policy according to the Golden Rule. This states that over an economic cycle the government will borrow only for investment purposes, which will benefit future generations. Its day-to-day spending on pensions, benefits and other services should be funded from taxation.

Influencing aggregate supply

Key terms

Supply-side policies are intended to increase aggregate supply by improving the effectiveness of markets.

Infrastructure refers to the basic facilities available to a society that support economic activity, such as transport and communication links as well as supplies of power and water.

In recent years, the aim of fiscal policy in the UK has been to encourage the more efficient working of markets and thereby to result in an increase in long-run aggregate supply. These supply-side policies have taken a number of forms.

One prominent element of supply-side fiscal policy is capital spending. This is the government's finance of projects intended to improve the UK's infrastructure, such as the construction of improved transport and communication links. The government also uses supply-side policies to intervene in the UK labour market with the aim of improving its operation. This intervention has included reducing income tax, especially for low earners, to improve incentives for those who might otherwise remain voluntarily unemployed. Moves to improve incentives have included reducing benefits for those out of work.

Author tip

We shall consider supply-side policies, including those implemented as part of the UK government's fiscal policy, in detail in Chapter 45. Here we shall only include a very brief summary.

The government has encouraged new business start-ups in the economy and also offers financial support for training and research into, and development of, new products and methods of production. This financial support from the government can take the form of grants or reductions in liabilities to pay tax.

Fiscal supply-side policies can cause the long-run aggregate supply curve to shift to the right, as shown in Figure 44.6. This can help the government to achieve its macroeconomic objectives without painful tradeoffs. The move from $LRAS_1$ to $LRAS_2$ increases real GDP, along with employment, while the price level falls.

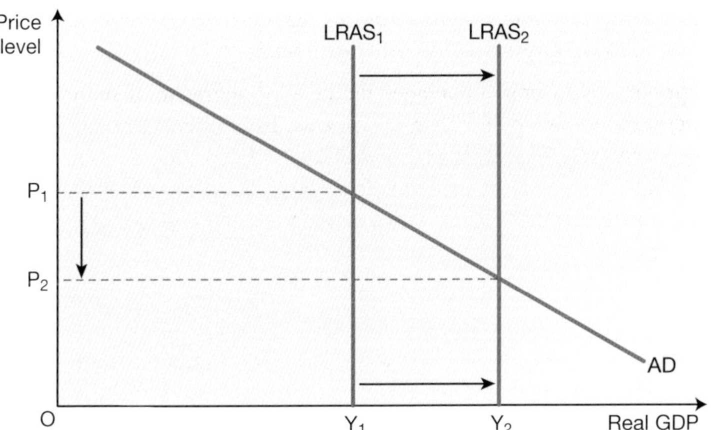

Figure 44.6 *The effects of supply-side fiscal policies*

Fiscal policy and microeconomic goals

Government spending and taxation can be used to achieve three main aspects of microeconomic policy:

- to overcome market failure;
- to support specific regions or industries that are judged to be in need of financial support;
- to redistribute income and wealth from the rich to the poor.

> **Author tip**
> We looked at the causes of market failure and the responses that governments make in Topic 5. It may be worth revisiting this topic to refresh your memory.

Fiscal policy and market failure

A market can fail because it supplies too little or too much of a product. This results in resources being misallocated. Market failure may be due to the existence of externalities or because the products in question are merit or demerit goods.

A government may respond to the existence of merit goods such as healthcare or education by subsidising the supply of the product (i.e. by paying part of its costs of production) to ensure that sufficient quantities are produced and consumed. Alternatively, it may supply the product itself. This has been the major approach taken in the UK to the supply of healthcare and education. We saw earlier in this chapter that these are significant categories of UK government expenditure.

Demerit goods are likely to be overconsumed in a free market economy due to lack of information about the potentially harmful effects of the products. The response of the UK government to the existence of demerit goods such as alcohol and tobacco is to enhance the level of information available to consumers to improve their decision making and to support this by the imposition of indirect taxes on these products.

Externalities may be positive or negative. Negative externalities are the adverse effects on other people resulting from a decision to produce or consume a good. The existence of negative externalities results in oversupply of a particular good or service. The government may respond to negative externalities such as pollution by imposing fines on the firms that cause pollution or by imposing indirect taxes to discourage the production and consumption of the products in question.

REALWORLD ECONOMICS 44.2

UK government set to enforce plain cigarette packaging

The government intends to pass legislation enforcing the plain packaging of cigarettes sold in England in the spring of 2015.

Smoking-related disease remains the main cause of preventable deaths in the UK, killing more than 100,000 people a year. The government also announced that a ban on smoking in private cars would come into force on 1 October. Cancer Research UK welcomed the move, which will make brightly coloured and slickly designed packs illegal, with all packs becoming uniform in size, shape and design as well as including large picture health warnings.

Source: Adapted from *Guardian*, 22.1.15

Exercise

1 Explain why the government does not simply raise the price of cigarettes in England. *(5 marks)*

Discussion point

Do you think that the UK government imposes indirect taxes on demerit goods such as alcohol, tobacco and gambling because they contribute to market failure or because demand for them is price inelastic and therefore they offer a comparatively reliable source of revenue?

Fiscal policy and support to regions or industries

The government may direct some of its spending towards (or offer some relief from taxes for) industries or regions of the country that it considers to be significantly disadvantaged. Some parts of the UK have been granted assisted area status, prompting financial support known as regional aid. The aim is to help drive growth and innovation in less advantaged local economies, thereby increasing long-run aggregate supply. Parts of north and west Wales as well as Cornwall are designated assisted areas, benefiting from government expenditure as part of its regional policy.

Fiscal policy and redistribution

In the past an important aim of UK government spending was to redistribute income and wealth from the rich to the poor. Government spending on welfare benefits, pensions, the NHS and education are primary examples of ways in which it has supported those on lower incomes. This has been used in combination with progressive taxation. Progressive taxation, such as income tax, helps this redistribution by ensuring that those on higher incomes do not just pay more tax but pay a higher proportion of their income as tax. This provides the government with the funds necessary to subsidise consumption of merit goods such as healthcare and education as well as to provide welfare benefits.

However, some economists and some governments fear that policies intended to redistribute income and wealth can act as disincentives to work and stifle entrepreneurship. Thus a conflict may exist between fiscal policies intended to redistribute income and wealth and fiscal supply-side policies designed to increase aggregate supply. The coalition government elected in the UK in 2010 has sought to use fiscal policy to increase incentives at the expense of redistribution. The result has been increased inequality of income and wealth in the UK.

An assessment of fiscal policy

Fiscal policy offers a number of benefits to governments when seeking to attain macroeconomic and other economic policy objectives.

- Fiscal policy incorporates automatic stabilisers, which adjust the level of government spending and revenue from taxation to dampen the worst elements of the economic cycle. This helps to avoid the creation of large negative and positive output gaps.
- Fiscal policy can assist a government in attaining microeconomic as well as macroeconomic objectives. Thus changes in taxation or government spending can target particular industries or regions of the UK or can be used for particular issues such as protecting the environment. Alternatively, policy can be directed at the entire economy.
- Fiscal policy can be used to operate through the supply side of the economy as well as the demand side. This offers a significant benefit in that it avoids significant tradeoffs in macroeconomic objectives when implementing policies.
- Changing government spending and taxes can be time consuming and their effects are likely to have a time lag, with the exception of changes in indirect taxes that can be implemented quickly.
- The impact of fiscal policy is not always easy to predict. The effect of a change in indirect taxes on consumption will be determined to a great extent by the price elasticity of demand for the products concerned. This is not always easy to predict and may mean that the desired level of aggregate demand is not achieved.
- Some economists argue that the use of fiscal policy to manage the level of aggregate demand may only affect real GDP in the short term and that the long-run effect, given a vertical LRAS curve, is only to increase or decrease the price level. Keynesian economists would oppose this view and this debate will be explored more fully in our companion book, *AQA A-Level Year 2 Economics*.
- Some economists believe that 'crowding out' can reduce the impact of fiscal policy. An example of this might be if a government increases its expenditure and this leads to reduced expenditure by firms and households. This may occur because increased government borrowing could drive up interest rates in the economy, reducing both consumption and investment and thus offsetting to some degree the positive impact on aggregate demand resulting from the increase in government spending and its consequent multiplier effect.

Review questions

Total: 48 marks

1 Define the term 'fiscal policy'. ***(3 marks)***

2 Explain how the UK government's substantial reductions in its expenditure (known as austerity) might impact on its ability to meet its macroeconomic objectives. ***(8 marks)***

3 Which of the following situations will result in a budget surplus?

A The government increases its expenditure to £675 billion while revenue from taxation falls 5% from £700 billion

B Revenue from taxation rises to £695 billion, precisely the same as government expenditure

C Government expenditure falls 10% to £685 billion while taxation revenue rises to £690 billion

D The government reduces its expenditure to £702 billion and taxation receipts remain constant at £690 billion *(1 mark)*

4 Which of the following taxes is regressive?

A Tax A takes 20% of income from all taxpayers, meaning richer taxpayers pay a larger amount of tax

B Tax B results in a taxpayer earning £10,000 paying £100 in tax and a taxpayer earning £75,000 paying £1500

C Tax C is based on bands varying from 10% of income for those earning below £20,000 and rising to 50% of income for people earning over £125,000

D Tax D requires all taxpayers to pay £250 per year, irrespective of their income *(1 mark)*

5 Explain, with the aid of examples, the difference between direct and indirect taxes. *(6 marks)*

6 Use an aggregate demand and supply diagram to explain the difference between an expansionary and a contractionary fiscal policy. *(9 marks)*

7 Explain how fiscal supply-side policies can help the government to achieve its macroeconomic objectives without tradeoffs occurring. *(8 marks)*

8 Which of the following examples of fiscal policy might be most appropriate in overcoming the problems associated with a demerit good?

A A subsidy to encourage production and consumption of the product

B An increase in the indirect tax levied on the product

C A reduction in the rate of VAT

D The government increasing spending to produce the product itself *(1 mark)*

9 Explain how fiscal policy in the UK might be used to redistribute income from those on high incomes to those earning lower incomes. *(5 marks)*

10 Explain one advantage and one disadvantage to governments of the use of fiscal policy. *(6 marks)*

Chapter 45

Supply-side policies

This chapter explains the difference between supply-side policies and supply-side improvements and the relationship that exists between the two. We examine how supply-side policies may increase the economy's potential output and its underlying trend rate of economic growth, and how they may affect macroeconomic objectives such as unemployment, inflation and the balance of payments. We conclude by assessing the strengths and weaknesses of supply-side policies.

Supply-side policies and supply-side improvements

Supply-side policies focus on factors that influence aggregate supply and aim to increase the economy's productive potential. If successful, they can move an economy's production possibility boundary to the right or shift its long-run aggregate supply curve to the right. Governments in the UK gave greater emphasis to supply-side policies from the 1980s onwards in contrast to the dominance of Keynesian policies of demand management that were favoured in the period after 1945.

The UK's coalition government, elected in 2010, believes strongly in the power of supply-side reform to deliver sustainable economic growth. The Chancellor of the Exchequer, George Osborne, has argued that economic growth will come from productivity improvements, which in turn come from supply-side reforms. These reforms at the time of writing are wide ranging but include new international agreements promoting trade, the innovation of new products and manufacturing processes, and making the UK's tax system more competitive in global terms.

Supply-side policies aim to improve the efficiency with which markets operate and are mainly microeconomic in nature as they focus on the workings of markets. The UK government's supply-side policies can be separated into two distinct categories:

- Labour market policies designed to improve the working of the labour market and therefore the productivity of employees.
- Policies targeted at product markets (i.e. markets supplying goods and services) intended to improve efficiency, for example by increasing the degree of competition between firms.

Supply-side improvements are the actions taken to increase the efficiency with which goods and services are produced and therefore the overall productive potential of

Key terms

Supply-side improvements are actions taken, primarily by firms, to increase the efficiency of their operations and thereby raise output.

Occupational immobility of labour exists when workers cannot transfer easily to employment in a different type of job.

Geographic immobility of labour occurs when workers cannot move freely to take employment in a new location.

the economy. Some supply-side improvements may originate with the government, such as building new roads that assist firms in transporting products cheaply and efficiently throughout the production process. This may help to attract businesses to an area (possibly from overseas) or support existing businesses in expanding production; both actions will increase output.

However, many supply-side improvements originate in the private sector, possibly because the government has created the right business environment or provided the right incentives. Thus firms may invest in training employees or in buying capital equipment, perhaps because the government has reduced laws and regulations affecting business activity or because it provides financial support for such activities, though the initiative for the improvement in the firm's ability to supply products will come from within the business itself.

Other supply-side improvements initiated by the private sector may include the development of new and more efficient production processes or the recruitment of low-cost and productive workers directly from other countries within the European Union.

Supply-side policies are sometimes described as reducing the level of government intervention in an economy. We shall see that this can be the case, but sometimes, as in Real World Economics 45.1, supply-side policies are based on government intervention. The aim of this intervention is to promote economic growth in rural areas as well as to increase aggregate supply.

REALWORLD ECONOMICS 45.1

DEFRA supports rural initiatives

More than 2500 rural businesses in the UK are benefiting from a share of £19 million of government funding. This funding has been specifically designed to boost the competitiveness of rural farming and forestry businesses and it is believed that this extra funding will support around 5000 jobs across England.

The Department for the Environment, Food and Rural Affairs (DEFRA) invested nearly £6900 to help a farmer in Norfolk to buy a GPS system to be fitted to his tractor to improve its operation. This has allowed him to expand his business, using the equipment to target fertiliser application on both his own land and on other farms where he is contracted to help.

The result is supply-side improvements, as accurate application of nutrients will not only save him money but also increase potential yield of the crops while limiting any possible environmental damage.

Source: Adapted from government website

Exercise

1 Explain why this government policy should result in an increase in the UK's aggregate supply. *(5 marks)*

Types of supply-side policies

Supply-side policies can be classified into those that operate through the labour market and those that affect one or more markets for products.

Author tip

The material in this section overlaps to some extent with that covered in Chapter 36 when we considered factors affecting aggregate supply in the short and long run.

Labour market supply-side policies

The government's labour market supply-side policies aim to improve the effectiveness of the operation of this market by improving the quality of the workforce to increase productivity levels. These policies also have the aim of making employees more mobile in response to market signals. Labour market immobility may exist because employees do not have the skills to transfer into new and different jobs or are unable to move to take up employment in a different location, possibly due to high housing costs. Supply-side policies are implemented to provide incentives to encourage people into the labour market, including the voluntarily unemployed.

1 Education and training

Expenditure on education and training by the government can provide a workforce that is more skilled and flexible in the face of changing demands from employers. This expenditure should improve the performance of the workforce in terms of labour productivity. Higher levels of productivity will increase the productive capacity of the economy directly and may attract multinational businesses, further increasing the potential output of the economy.

Investment in education and training is increasingly important, as many expanding industries require employees to have skills associated with mental rather than physical activities. It also plays a vital role in combating occupational immobility by assisting employees to transfer to new roles in different industries.

Supply-side policies based on education and training can be expensive and are likely to be effective only in the long term. Despite this, such policies have been popular with recent UK governments.

2 Changes to the taxation and benefits systems

Economists who support the use of supply-side measures regard tax systems as a means of offering incentives to people and firms to increase output, rather than a technique of managing aggregate demand. High rates of direct tax (such as income tax and corporation tax) can act as disincentives to households and firms and discourage them from engaging in productive activity. Firms may choose not to invest in extending productive capacity if potential profits are subject to high rates of tax because fewer investment projects will provide a worthwhile return. Similarly, employees may opt to leave (or not enter) the labour force if their earnings are subject to high income tax rates.

Making adjustments to the welfare system – one of the government's labour market supply-side policies

The UK government has reduced the rate of corporation tax, as we saw in Chapter 44. In 2015 it is levied at a very internationally competitive rate of 20%. At the same time the level of income that can be earned before most employees pay income tax has been increased from £7475 in 2011–12 to £10,600 in 2015–16.

These tax changes have been supported by adjustments to the welfare system to encourage employees to enter the workforce and support them once they are working. The UK government began to introduce Universal Credit in 2013. The Department for Work and Pensions, which is responsible for administering the benefits system, states that Universal Credit will:

- encourage people on welfare benefits to start paid work or increase their hours by making sure work pays;

- make it easier for people to manage the move into work.

At the same time, other benefits paid to those not in work have been cut, helping to reduce government expenditure by £22 billion between 2010 and 2015 and lowering the level of benefits available in comparison to the average wage that might be expected. The government hopes that a combination of increasing financial incentives for work and a reduction in benefits for those not in work will create sufficient incentives to increase the participation rate and therefore the labour supply in the UK.

3 The passing of laws to control the power of trade unions

Trade unions impact on the free working of the labour market, and their activities usually keep wages higher than the free market equilibrium level. They may also limit the supply of labour into certain occupations and impose working practices intended to benefit employees. These actions are known as restrictive practices.

> **Key note**
> The term 'restrictive practices' has two uses in economics, though the meaning is similar in both cases. It can refer to the activities of trade unions as outlined in the paragraph above. However, it can also relate to firms taking action to prevent the free and competitive working of markets.

Trade unions support the use of national bargaining for pay in many occupations in the public sector such as nursing and teaching. This results in similar rates of pay and working conditions across the country. This may prevent labour being geographically mobile as it may prevent pay being increased in areas with high housing and other costs, meaning many workers cannot afford to move to these areas.

Between 1980 and 1993, Conservative governments passed six acts of Parliament to limit the power of trade unions. Secondary action, better known as 'sympathy strikes', was outlawed. Picketing (protesting outside a business where strikes are taking place to influence the actions of other workers as well as to gain attention from the public) was restricted. Ballots were needed for official industrial action from 1984, and these had to be postal from 1993 in order to reduce the possibility of employees being influenced in their voting behaviour. These laws were designed to reduce the power of trade unions to influence decisions by businesses relating to the workforce, enabling labour markets to operate more freely.

> **Key terms**
> A **trade union** is an organisation formed with the objective of enhancing and protecting the working conditions and economic position of its members.
>
> **Restrictive practices** are actions taken by trade unions to limit the freedom of businesses to take decisions regarding the use of labour in production.

4 Migration policies

The attraction of skilled workers to an economy can be an effective way of increasing the quantity and quality of the labour force available to firms. It enables businesses to avoid considerable training costs as well as providing a relatively quick solution to skills shortages.

However, large-scale migration can result in a range of social issues, and governments can be under pressure to control it. This is currently the case in the UK where the coalition government is under political pressure to implement migration policies that most economists do not believe will assist it in reaching its macroeconomic objectives.

REALWORLD ECONOMICS 45.2

Government policy on migration criticised

Migration will benefit the UK and so government policy towards non-EU citizens is failing the economy, according to a survey by the Centre for Macroeconomics (CFM). It stated that 84% of academics and economists agree that migration will increase average UK incomes in the next decade. Asked about the coalition government's migration policies, 70% declared that they will not maximise economic benefits.

While the UK government has said its migration policy should not stop companies attracting skilled workers, the number of highly educated migrant workers entering the UK decreased from 338,000 in 2007 to 242,000 in 2013. With net migration rising to 212,000 people in 2014, the UK government is on track to miss its target of cutting it to below 100,000 a year by 2015.

Respondents to the survey highlighted the benefits of migration. Oxford University Professor Martin Ellison said it increases the overall number of jobs rather than taking them from native workers. Richard Portes of the London Business School said that properly regulated immigration can increase labour market flexibility and alleviate specific skills shortages.

Source: Adapted from Bloomberg

Exercise

1 Explain why most economists believe that migration will increase average incomes in the UK. *(6 marks)*

Product market supply-side policies

Governments can implement other supply-side policies that are designed to impact upon one or more markets for products.

1 Industrial policy

The UK government separates its industrial policy (which is also called 'industrial strategy') into two elements.

- **Horizontal policies** address issues in many, if not all, product markets. They provide the resources and help to create an economic environment that make it easier for businesses and individuals to be productive. Examples of this type of policy include establishing tax regimes that favour business (e.g. lowering rates of corporation tax), taking actions to encourage innovation, and the development of a more skilled workforce.
- **Sectoral policies** (or 'selective' policies) include any policies directed towards one specific sector in the economy. Examples include subsidies to support the production of low carbon technology, funding for high-tech industries or groups of firms, and support for research and development in particular industries.

The coalition government's industrial policy is arranged around five key themes:

- Boosting the development of 11 key sectors or industries including aerospace, construction, oil and gas, nuclear and the information economy.

Key terms

Industrial policy refers to government intervention that seeks to support or develop some industries to enhance economic growth.

Privatisation is the transfer of state-owned organisations to the private sector, where they are owned by individuals and private firms.

Deregulation is the reduction of the extent of state or government control over a business activity.

- Supporting the development of eight key technologies such as energy storage, agricultural science, satellites and robotics.
- Increasing access to finance for businesses to support investment plans. This involves the government offering financial support directly to qualifying businesses in a variety of ways. It also encompasses the 'Funding for Lending' scheme under which the Bank of England provides loans at cheap rates to banks and building societies to encourage them to provide loans to firms.
- Developing the skills of employees in key sectors. For example, the UK government supported over half a million people on apprenticeships in 2013–14.
- Using public procurement to create opportunities for UK firms. The public sector purchased (or procured) goods and services totalling £280 billion in 2013–14. Government spending of this magnitude offers the government significant opportunities to support the development of various industries and sectors within the UK economy.

2 Privatisation and deregulation

The UK experienced a major programme of privatisation in the 1980s when a number of state-owned organisations were sold to the private sector. The rate of privatisation has slowed since then as the government has had fewer assets to sell. However, in 2014 Royal Mail was privatised and the government sold its holdings in Eurostar. To some extent more recent privatisation decisions have been driven by the government's need to raise funds to reduce its budget deficit.

Privatisation is a supply-side policy, as its supporters argue that the removal of state control from an organisation and the introduction of the profit motive increase efficiency and competitiveness in a firm or industry. This can in turn increase aggregate supply. While this argument may be valid when privatisation creates genuine competition within a market, it is much less so when it simply turns a state monopoly into a privately owned monopoly.

Deregulation is similar to privatisation but entails a reduction in control over some business activity rather than its sale to private owners. Deregulation of markets can encourage new producers, increase competition and improve cost effectiveness, making the market operate more efficiently. Examples of markets that have been deregulated in the UK include bus and legal services, and plans are in place to deregulate the taxi and minicab industry.

3 International trade

The UK government is a supporter of international trade and advocates the reduction of barriers that prevent free trade. Trade can be an engine for economic growth because the removal of tariffs and other barriers to trade can increase output and living standards. Thus increasing the volume of trade can be an effective supply-side policy.

The UK is a member of the World Trade Organisation (WTO), which is a global organisation (with 160 countries as members) that negotiates agreements to reduce barriers to trade. The UK government is currently party to negotiations on trade between the USA and the EU. The Transatlantic Trade and Investment Partnership (TTIP) is a possible agreement designed to reduce tariffs and other barriers to trade between the USA and EU countries. If implemented, this will make it easier for companies in Europe and America to sell products in each other's markets. It has the potential to have a substantial impact on a range of industries including pharmaceuticals, vehicle manufacture, energy, chemicals, and banking and finance.

Supply-side policies and macroeconomic objectives

As was the case with monetary and fiscal policies, the UK government implements supply-side policies to help it achieve its macroeconomic objectives. The effects of successful supply-side policies can be shown using production possibility boundaries. Figure 45.1 illustrates the effects of using existing resources more effectively as well as increasing the resources available to the economy.

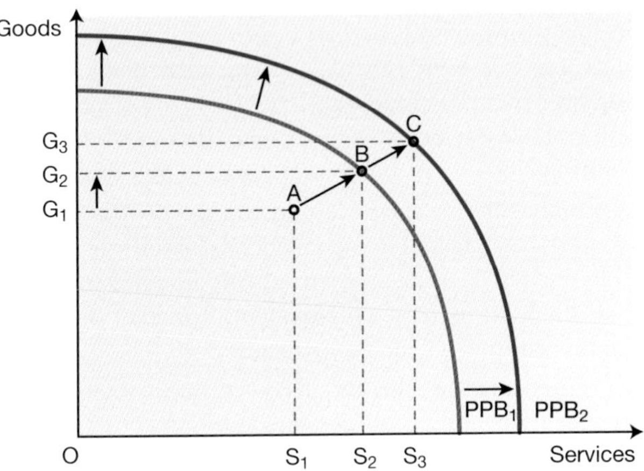

Figure 45.1 *Supply-side measures and production possibility boundaries*

The movement from Point A to Point B within the initial production possibility boundary (PPB_1) represents a more intensive use of existing resources, possibly due to the use of spare productive capacity such as unemployed workers.

The shift of the production possibility boundary to PPB_2 (and the move from B to C) illustrates the effect of expanding the productive capacity of the economy by increasing the quantity of resources available to it. This might be the result of significant levels of net migration of working age people, increasing the country's workforce.

The impact of supply-side policies can be shown on an aggregate demand and aggregate supply diagram, as in Figure 45.2. The primary effect is to shift the

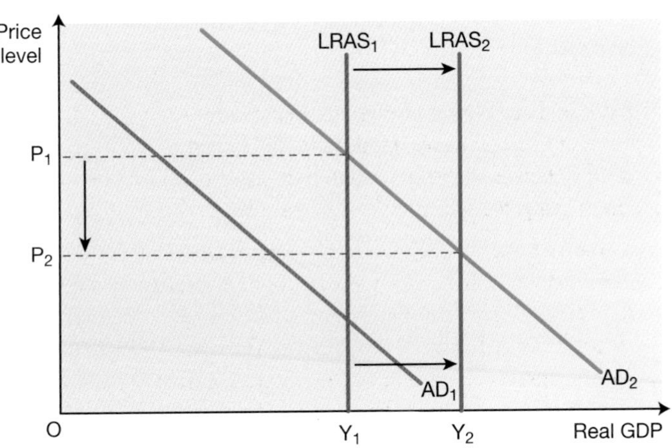

Figure 45.2 *The effects of supply-side policies*

aggregate supply curve to the right, as shown by the shift to $LRAS_2$. Assuming aggregate demand in the economy is at the level shown by AD_2, the increase in aggregate supply can have a number of positive consequences.

- *Inflation* Supply-side policies can lessen inflationary pressures because of improvements in production efficiency. For example, improvements in labour or capital productivity can reduce unit costs, helping to enhance firms' price competitiveness. This explains the lower price level shown in Figure 45.2 where the price level falls to P_2.
- *Economic growth* Increased productive capacity allows an economy to increase its output of goods and services, thereby raising its GDP. It can increase the rate at which it can grow sustainably (i.e. without creating inflationary pressures). This increase in its long-run trend rate of economic growth allows real incomes to rise more quickly over time. Furthermore, other elements of supply-side measures (such as reducing welfare payments to those who are out of work) may assist an economy in operating closer to its maximum capacity and thus also raise GDP.
- *Unemployment* Supply-side measures can encourage people into work directly. Reductions in welfare benefits and in income tax rates for low earners, improving the mobility of labour, and creating an environment designed to stimulate business investment are all likely to increase employment. Provided the workforce is not growing quickly, this will reduce unemployment.
- *The balance of payments on current account* Improvements in productive efficiency will reduce costs and encourage the development of new and attractive products as well as more efficient methods of production. These developments should promote sales of UK exports overseas as the competitiveness of domestic industries increases.

REALWORLD ECONOMICS 45.3

Enterprise Zones

Established in 2012, Enterprise Zones are at the heart of the UK government's long-term economic plan, supporting businesses to grow. Since their start in April 2012 they have attracted over 430 businesses, securing more than £2 billion pounds of private sector investment, building world class business facilities and transport links, and creating over 12,500 jobs.

Businesses basing themselves on Enterprise Zones can access a number of benefits:

- up to a 100% business rate (a form of business tax) discount worth up to £275,000 per business over a five-year period;
- simplified local authority planning – for example, granting automatic planning permission for certain developments such as new industrial buildings within the Zones;
- government support to ensure that superfast broadband is rolled out throughout the Zones and, if necessary, public funding;
- 100% capital allowances (reducing tax payable) to businesses making large investments in plant and machinery on eight of the Zones.

The Chancellor of the Exchequer announced in his 2014 Budget that the deadlines for accessing business rate discounts and enhanced capital allowances on Enterprise Zones would be extended by three years. This means that businesses have until March 2018 to locate on an Enterprise Zone in order to be able to access business rate discounts.

Source: Adapted from government website

Exercise

1 How might the creation of 24 Enterprise Zones across England assist the government in meeting its macroeconomic objectives? (8 marks)

An assessment of supply-side policies

There are differing views amongst economists regarding the effectiveness of supply-side policies. Keynesian economists would argue that they are unlikely to be effective unless supported by the use of demand management policies to ensure sufficient aggregate demand exists. In Figure 45.2, if the level of aggregate demand is at AD_1, there will be little or no impact from increasing the productive potential of the economy to $LRAS_2$. Key macroeconomic performance indicators, such as the rates of inflation and unemployment and the level of real GDP, will be unchanged. Keynesian economists would also argue that unemployment exists because people are unable to find work and not because welfare benefits are too high.

Other groups, such as neo-classical economists, would strongly advocate the use of supply-side policies. They would argue that their potential to improve macroeconomic performance is considerable and does not entail any conflict. In other words, improvements of one macroeconomic indicator are not gained at the expense of another: a higher long-term rate of economic growth without inflationary pressures is one consequence of supply-side policies. This group of economists also believes that a number of supply-side policies do boost aggregate demand. For example, supply-side policies that increase the level of investment by businesses and the government can also raise the level of government spending (for example, on education and training) and increase the value of net exports.

There are a number of other aspects of supply-side policies that should be considered when assessing their effectiveness.

- *Their impact on the distribution of income* Policies relating to reforming income tax bands have reduced the rates payable by those on high incomes as well as increasing the amount of income that is tax free. As recently as 1980 the top rate of income tax in the UK was 83%. The increased reliance on regressive taxes such as VAT (which was increased from 17.5% to 20% in January 2011) also means that those on low incomes bear a greater tax burden. Alongside this, welfare reforms have reduced payments to those receiving benefits since 2010, and the decline in trade union power has weakened the bargaining position of many workers receiving low pay. These effects have combined to make the distribution of income in the UK less equal. A similar pattern has been observed in other countries that have employed supply-side policies.
- *The ability to target the policies* Unlike monetary policy, supply-side policies can be focused on particular industries or regions of the economy that are either in need or have the potential to achieve high rates of growth in the future. The UK government's support for aerospace and the information economy is an example of using government resources in the area where they are most likely to be effective.
- *The impact on government expenditure* Some supply-side policies are very costly to implement and this poses considerable difficulties for the UK government at a time when it is seeking to achieve a large reduction in its budget deficit through its policy of austerity. Education and training are important but expensive elements of a supply-side strategy: the UK government spent nearly £100 billion on education in 2014–15. Policies in these areas also take effect only after a time lag, which can be considerable in the case of education.
- *The difficulties of implementing a long-term supply-side strategy* Some supply-side policies are controversial, especially those that relate to the labour market. They

may be reversed when a different political party forms a government. The reforms to welfare that have been implemented since 2010 have been heavily criticised and may be altered or reversed in the medium term. Similarly, tax reforms may be abandoned. This lack of a long-term strategy reduces the likelihood of a consistent approach and a successful outcome.

Review questions

Total: 58 marks

1 Define the term 'supply-side policy'. ***(3 marks)***

2 Explain, using examples, the difference between supply-side policies and supply-side improvements. ***(6 marks)***

3 Which of the following would *not* be classified as a supply-side policy?

A A reduction in income tax rates with the aim of increasing consumption

B Government investment in training and education

C A reduction in benefits paid to unemployed workers in order to improve employment incentives

D Deregulation of an industry to stimulate competition ***(1 mark)***

4 Explain why the UK government's industrial policy might improve productivity within the economy. ***(7 marks)***

5 Explain why passing laws to limit the power of trade unions might result in a more effective operation of the UK labour market. ***(6 marks)***

6 Explain the difference between privatisation and deregulation. ***(5 marks)***

7 Explain why a policy of privatisation might increase the long-run aggregate supply in an economy. ***(6 marks)***

8 Explain the impact of a substantial increase in long-run aggregate supply on the UK government's macroeconomic objectives. Use a diagram to support your answer. ***(9 marks)***

9 Give two reasons why Keynesian economists doubt the effectiveness of supply-side policies. ***(8 marks)***

10 Explain why supply-side policies might lead to a more unequal distribution of income. ***(7 marks)***

Topic 9 **Exam-style questions**

AS LEVEL PAPER 2

Context – Macroeconomic policy

Extract A **Aspects of monetary policy**

The UK government's economic strategy consists of four elements or pillars:

- Using monetary policy actively and positively to stimulate demand, to maintain price stability and to support the flow of credit throughout the economy.
- Reducing the government's substantial budget deficit, returning the public finances to a sustainable position. This will assist in ensuring low long-term interest rates.
- Reforming the regulation of the financial system to reduce the risk of future financial crises.
- Strengthening the UK economy for the future by, for example, implementing a £5 billion programme of investment in infrastructure by 2015.

The UK bank rate (or base rate) has remained at 0.5% since 2009 for two major reasons. First, a sustained expansionary monetary policy has been necessary to offset various aspects of its fiscal policy that are contractionary. Secondly, the difference between commercial bank interest rates and the Bank of England's bank rate has been much wider than was the case previously. This has required the Monetary Policy Committee to set the bank rate much lower in order to achieve an expansionary monetary policy.

Extract B **UK productivity**

UK productivity performance has been poor recently and many economists argue that productivity is a key driver of sustainable economic growth. In 2013, based on levels of GDP per hour, the UK was sixth out of the G7 group of major economies. UK productivity was 17 percentage points lower than the average for the rest of the G7 – the widest gap since 1992.

Productivity across the whole UK economy, measured by output per hour, is estimated to have decreased by 0.3% during 2013. In the third quarter of 2014, manufacturing productivity grew by 5.2%, while services productivity increased by 0.8%. Productivity across the whole economy increased by 0.6% over the same period.

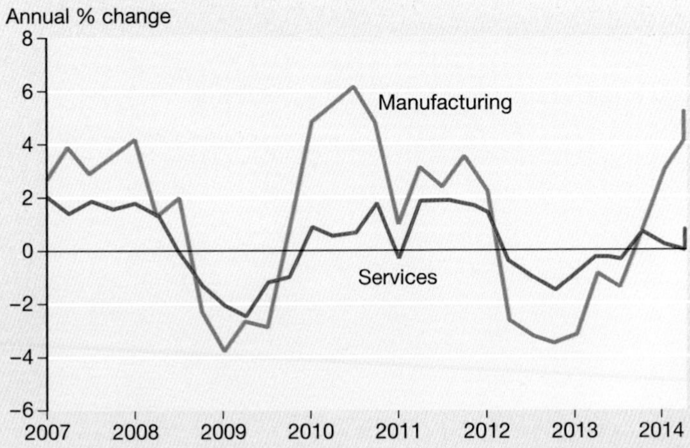

Figure A *UK productivity data, 2007–14*

Extract C Supply-side policies in the 2014 Budget

In his Budget Speech in 2014 the Chancellor of the Exchequer, George Osborne, announced a limit of welfare spending of £100 billion per year. The Budget Speech also included many supply-side reforms designed to increase manufacturing output, UK exports, regional development and employees' skills.

The Chancellor revealed new official forecasts showing that while economic growth in the UK is accelerating, its budget deficit remains worryingly large and more big cuts in government spending will be needed in the future.

While sticking to his plan to reduce the UK's budget deficit, Mr Osborne is also expected to find some money to fund an increase in the amount individuals can earn before they pay income tax from £10,000 to at least £10,600. Money for this policy, thought to be the most expensive budget measure, will come from a further £1 billion squeeze on public spending in education, health and administration and a new crackdown on tax avoidance.

Source: Adapted from *Financial Times*, 18.3.14

Questions

Total: 50 marks

1 Define the term 'expansionary monetary policy' (Extract A). *(3 marks)*

2 Use the information in Extract A to identify one element of the government's fiscal policy that is contractionary and explain your reasoning. *(4 marks)*

3 Explain, using an aggregate supply and demand diagram, the likely effect of 'big cuts in government spending' (Extract C) on the macroeconomic performance of the UK economy. *(4 marks)*

4 Use the data in Extract C to explain how increasing the amount UK taxpayers can earn before paying income tax might help the government to achieve a higher rate of economic growth. *(4 marks)*

5 Explain how the government's macroeconomic policies might be used to improve productivity rates in the UK. *(10 marks)*

6 Using the data in the extracts and your economic knowledge, assess the extent to which the UK government should rely on monetary policy alone to achieve its macroeconomic objectives. *(25 marks)*

Index

Definitions of key terms have been highlighted in **bold red** type.

D

E

Q

R

S